CONVERGENCES
Inventories of the Present

EDWARD W. SAID, General Editor

REFLECTIONS ON EXILE

and Other Essays

EDWARD W. SAID

HARVARD UNIVERSITY PRESS
Cambridge, Massachusetts
2000

Library of Congress Cataloging-in-Publication Data

Said, Edward W.
    Reflections on exile and other essays / Edward W. Said
        p. cm. — (Convergences : inventories of the present)
    Includes bibliographical references and index.
    ISBN 0-674-00302-0 (alk. paper)
        1. Politics and literature.   2. Literature, Modern—20th century—History and
criticism—Theory, etc.   3. Politics and culture.   4. Criticism—Political aspects.
    5. Literature, Modern—20th century—History and criticism.   I. Title.   II. Convergences
(Cambridge, Mass.)

PN98.P64 S35 2000
  814'.54--dc21   00-044996

ACKNOWLEDGMENTS

Several of the essays in this book appeared in *Raritan Review, The London Review of Books,* and *Critical Inquiry.* I am particularly grateful to their respective editors, and to my good friends, Richard Poirier, Mary-Kay Wilmers, and Tom Mitchell, for their support and care. As always, I am indebted to my assistant, Dr. Zaineb Istrabadi, for her help in producing this book as well as many of its essays as they originally appeared.

E. W. S.
New York City
June 2000

To the memory of
F. W. Dupee

CONTENTS

Contents

Contents

INTRODUCTION:
CRITICISM AND EXILE

Written over a period of roughly thirty-five years, these essays constitute some of the intellectual results of teaching and studying in one
academic institution, Columbia University in New York. I arrived there
fresh from graduate school in the fall of 1963 and, as of this writing, I
am still there as a professor in the Department of English and
Comparative Literature. Aside from this abbreviated testimonial to my
deep satisfaction for such a long time in the place—the American university generally being for its academic staff and many of its students
the last remaining utopia—it is the fact of New York that plays an important role in the kind of criticism and interpretation which I have
done, and of which this book is a kind of record. Restless, turbulent,
unceasingly various, energetic, unsettling, resistant, and absorptive,
New York today is what Paris was a hundred years ago, the capital of
our time. It may seem paradoxical and even willful to add that the
city's centrality is due to its eccentricity and the peculiar mix of its attributes, but I think that that is so. This is not always a positive or
comforting thing, and for a resident who is connected to neither the
corporate nor the real estate nor the media world, New York's strange
status as a city unlike all others is often a troubling aspect of daily life,
since marginality, and the solitude of the outsider, can frequently overcome one's sense of habitually being in it.

For a good part of the twentieth century New York's cultural life seemed to take a number of fairly well recognized paths, most of them deriving from the city's geographical feature as the major American port of entry. Ellis Island, as the immigrant location par excellence, processed the waves of mostly poor arrivals into American society with New York as their first, if not always their subsequent, place of residence: these were the Irish, Italian, East European Jewish and non-Jewish, African, Caribbean, Middle and Far Eastern peoples. From these immigrant communities came a great deal of the city's identity as a center of radical political and artistic life as embodied in the socialist and anarchist movements, the Harlem renaissance (so well documented recently by Ann Douglas in *Terrible Honesty*), and various pioneers and innovators in painting, photography, music, drama, dance, and sculpture. That set of urban expatriate narratives has over time acquired an almost canonical status, as have the various museums, schools, universities, concert halls, opera houses, theaters, galleries, and dance companies that have earned New York its considerable status as a sort of permanent theatrical showplace—with, over time, less and less real contact with its earlier immigrant roots. As a publishing center, for example, New York is no longer the place where experimental presses and writers had once ventured into new territory, and has instead become a prime location of large-scale conglomerate and media empires. Moreover, Greenwich Village has also passed away as America's Bohemia, as have most of the little magazines and the artistic communities that nourished them. What remains is an immigrants' and exiles' city that exists in tension with the symbolic (and at times actual) center of the world's globalized late capitalist economy whose raw power, projected economically, militarily, and politically everywhere, demonstrates how America is the only superpower today.

When I arrived in New York there was still some vitality left in its most celebrated group of intellectuals, those clustered around *Partisan Review*, City College and Columbia University, where Lionel Trilling and F. W. Dupee were good friends and solicitous senior colleagues of mine in the Columbia College English Department (as it was then known to distinguish it from the more professional Graduate English program). Very early on, however, I discovered that the battles the New

York intellectuals were still engaged in over Stalinism and Soviet Communism simply did not have much interest for me or for most of my generation, for whom the civil rights movement and the resistance against the U.S. war in Vietnam were much more important and formative. And even though I shall always retain a great affection for Trilling as an older colleague and friend, it was the altogether more radical and open spirit of Fred Dupee that counted for me as I began to write and teach: his untimely death in 1979 was an event of immense personal loss and regret, which I still feel to this day. Dupee was principally an essayist (as was Trilling to a great degree), and in the intellectual as well as political sense he was also a real subversive, a man of incomparable charm whose amazing literary gifts were, I felt, much less caught up than those of his colleagues in the Anglophilia so endemic to New York intellectual style, among whose worst features were also a tiresome narcissism and a fatal propensity to self-important, rightward-tending shifts. Fred was never like that. It was he who encouraged my interest in the new styles of French theorizing, in experimental fiction and poetry, and above all, in the art of the essay as a way of exploring what was new and original in our time regardless of professional hobbles. And it was Fred Dupee who after 1967, when the great Arab debacle occurred, supported me in my lonely fight on behalf of the Palestinian cause, just as he remained faithful to the radical, anti-authoritarian politics of his early Trotskyist years. It is important to note parenthetically that Dupee and his wife Andy were the only friends from my academic New York life ever actually to pay me a visit in Beirut, at that time (fall 1972) the center of revolutionary politics in the Middle East. I spent my first full year there (since leaving as a student for the United States in 1951) on sabbatical, reacquainting myself with the Arab-Islamic tradition through daily tutorials in Arabic philology and literature.

The experience of 1967, the re-emergence of the Palestinian people as a political force, and my own engagement with that movement was what New York in a sense made it possible for me to live, despite the frequent death threats, acts of vandalism, and abusive behavior directed at me and my family. In that rather more agitated and urgent environment than the one fussed over tiresomely by the New York intellectuals (discredited forever, I believe, by their shoddy involvement in the cultural Cold War as managed by the CIA and so well exposed by Frances Stonor Saunders in her book *The CIA and the Cultural Cold War*), a wholly different set of concerns from those of the *Partisan Review*—for whom I wrote one of the early essays in this book—gradually surfaced in my work, coming to an explicit statement first in my book *Beginnings: Intention and Method,* then in *Orientalism,* then still more insistently in my various writings on Palestine. These concerns, I believe, were magnified and made clear by the other New York, that of the diasporic communities from the Third World, expatriate politics, and the cultural debates, the so-called canon wars, that were to dominate academic life in the 1980s and after. In the elucidation of this other New York, either unknown or despised by its Establishment counterpart, it was also Fred Dupee who indirectly opened the way for me, not so much in what he said specifically about it but rather in the attitude of interest and encouragement that, as a deracinated, adventurous, and hospitable native-born American, he gave me, an outsider and recent arrival.

The greatest single fact of the past three decades has been, I believe, the vast human migration attendant upon war, colonialism and decolonization, economic and political revolution, and such devastating occurrences as famine, ethnic cleansing, and great power machinations. In a place like New York, but surely also in other Western metropoles like London, Paris, Stockholm, and Berlin, all these things are reflected immediately in the changes that transform neighborhoods, professions, cultural production, and topography on an almost hour-by-hour basis. Exiles, émigrés, refugees, and expatriates uprooted from their lands must make do in new surroundings, and the creativity as well as the sadness that can be seen in what they do is one of the experiences that has still to find its chroniclers, even though a splendid cohort of writers that includes such different figures as Salman Rushdie and V. S. Naipaul has already opened further the door first tried by Conrad.

Nevertheless, and despite the all-pervading power and scope of these large historical movements, there has been great resistance to them, whether in the strident choruses of "let's go back to the great books of OUR culture," or in the appalling racism that gives tiresome evidence of itself in attacks on non-European cultures, traditions, and peoples as somehow unworthy of serious attention or consideration.

Despite all this, a great revision has taken place in cultural discussion which in my own way I feel I have contributed to, namely, the critique of Eurocentrism, which has enabled readers and critics to see the relative poverty of identity politics, the silliness of affirming the "purity" of an essential essence, and the utter falseness of ascribing to one tradition a kind of priority, which in reality cannot be truthfully asserted, over all the others. In short, it comes down to the realization that cultures are always made up of mixed, heterogeneous, and even contradictory discourses, never more themselves in a sense than when they are not just being themselves, in other words not being in that state of unattractive and aggressive affirmativeness into which they are twisted by authoritarian figures who, like so many pharisees or mullahs, pretend to speak for the whole culture. In fact no such statement is really possible, despite the many efforts and reams of paper expended fruitlessly for that purpose.

To value literature at all is fundamentally to value it as the individual work of an individual writer tangled up in circumstances taken for granted by everyone, such things as residence, nationality, a familiar locale, language, friends, and so on. The problem for the interpreter, therefore, is how to align these circumstances with the work, how to separate as well as incorporate them, how to read the work *and* its worldly situation. The novelty of our time, to which New York gives special emphasis, is that so many individuals have experienced the uprooting and dislocations that have made them expatriates and exiles. Out of such travail there comes an urgency, not to say a precariousness of vision and a tentativeness of statement, that renders the use of language something much more interesting and provisional than it would otherwise be. This is not at all to say, however, that only an exile can feel the pain of recollection as well as the often desperate search for adequate (and usually unfamiliar) expression so characteristic of a Conrad, but it is to say that Conrad, Nabokov, Joyce, Ishiguro in their use of language provoke their readers into an awareness of how language is about experience and not just about itself. For if you feel you cannot take for granted the luxury of long residence, habitual environment, native idiom, and you must somehow compensate for these things, what you write necessarily bears a unique freight of anxiety, elaborateness, perhaps even overstatement—exactly those things that a comfortably settled tradition of modern (and now postmodern) reading and criticism has either scanted or avoided.

There is a moment in Samuel Butler's *The Way of All Flesh* that has always had for me the startling and completely pleasurable force of a benign epiphany, despite the fact that the novel itself is as much an artifact of late Victorianism as the characters and attitudes it mocks. Butler asks rhetorically about the appalling life of a clergyman's children: "How was it possible that a child only a little past five years old, trained in such an atmosphere of prayers and hymns and sums and happy Sunday evenings—to say nothing of daily repeated beatings over the said prayers and hymns, etc., ...—how was it possible that a lad so trained should grow up in any healthy or vigorous development?" As the plot goes on to show, young Ernest Pontifex would have a dreadful time because of this strenuously virtuous upbringing, but the problem goes back to the way Rev. Theobald, Ernest's father, was himself brought up to behave. "The clergyman," Butler says, "is expected to be a kind of human Sunday."

This brilliant reversal, by which a person suddenly becomes a day, scarcely needs the preachy explanation given a moment later by Butler. Priests, he goes on, are supposed to live stricter lives than anyone else; as vicars their "vicarious goodness" is meant to substitute for the goodness of others; the children of such professionally righteous individuals end up as the ones most damaged by the pretense. Yet for anyone who (perhaps more frequently in an earlier age) was required to dress up, go to religious services, attend a solemn family dinner, and otherwise face the rigors of a day from which many of the sins and pleasures of life had been forcibly swept, to be a human Sunday is an immediately horrible thing. And although the phrase "human Sunday" is compressed in the extreme, it has the effect of releasing a whole storehouse of experiences refracted in as well as pointed to directly by the two words.

Butler's novel is not very much in fashion these days. He stands at the threshold of modernism, but really belongs to an age in which questions of religion, upbringing and family pressures still represented *the* important questions, as they did for Newman, Arnold, and

Dickens. Moreover, *The Way of All Flesh* is hardly a novel at all but rather a semi-fictionalized autobiographical account of Butler's own unhappy youth, full of scarcely veiled attacks on his own father, his own early religious inclinations, and the pre-Darwinian age in which he grew up, when how to deal with faith, and not science or ideas, was the preeminent concern. It would not, I think, be doing *The Way of All Flesh* an injustice to say that it provides readers with principally a historical, rather than an aesthetic, experience. Literary art, rhetoric, figurative language, and structure are there to be looked for, to be occasionally encountered and admired, but only minimally and momentarily, as a way of leading readers directly back to particular experiences of life at a particular time and place. One neither could nor would want to compare Butler with Henry James or Thomas Hardy, two of his immediate contemporaries: they represent a far more complete encoding of historical experience by aesthetic or literary form.

It would be more appropriate somehow to read *The Way of All Flesh* along with Newman's *Apologia*, Mill's *Autobiography*, and even so eccentric and rousing a work as Swift's *Tale of a Tub*, than it would to compare Butler's novel with *The Golden Bowl* or *The Ambassadors*, works that have been far more influential in setting the standard for interpretation and critical theory in our time than the story of Ernest Pontifex. The point I am trying to make in all this, however, is related to the recent trends in the criticism and study of literature that have shied away from the unsettling contentiousness of experiences like this one, or from exiled or silenced voices. Most of what has been exciting and contentious about the vogue of formalist and deconstructive theory has been its focus on purely linguistic and textual matters. A phrase like "the clergyman is expected to be a kind of human Sunday" is too transparent on one level, too inchoate in its recollection and summonings on another, for the theorists of simile, metaphor, topology, or phallologocentrism.

Looking back from the present, one can discern a trend in much of the great Western criticism of the early twentieth century that draws readers away from experience and pushes them instead toward form and formalism. What seems guarded against in this trend is *immediacy*, that untreated bolus of direct experience, experience that can only be reflected whole or as replicable, dogmatically insistent items called facts. "If those are the facts," said Lukács contemptuously of immediate reality, "then so much the worse for the facts." This line is really the motto of *History and Class Consciousness,* which perhaps more than any other early twentieth century work is the founding text of an astonishing range of later criticism. Out of the great essay on reification and the antinomies of bourgeois thought in that book there derived most of what is still significant about the work of Adorno, Benjamin, Bloch, Horkheimer, and Habermas, all of whom are paradoxically steeped in the experience of fascism in Germany and yet who erected immense theoretical and formal bulwarks against it in their writing. In France, Lukács stimulated not only the brilliant discipleship of Lucien Goldmann but also the relentless enmity of Louis Althusser, much of whose work, I believe, can be read as a lifelong project to counteract and finally defeat Lukács and his Hegelian antecedents in the young, so-called humanistic Karl Marx; Althusser does this not by bringing Lukács back to immediacy but by moving theory and theorists *further away* from immediacy. In the United States the work of Fredric Jameson owes a huge debt to Lukács, particularly in *Marxism and Form,* the very influential *The Prison House of Language,* and *The Political Unconscious.*

When we leave the realm of Marxist critical discourse and look at the criticism fostered by some of the modernists, the wish to escape from experience perceived as futile panorama is central. T. S. Eliot is unintelligible without this emphasis on art opposed in some way to life, to the historical experience of the middle class, and to the disorder and dislocation of urban existence. Eliot's extraordinary powers of codification and influence produced the almost too familiar canon of critical practices and touchstones associated with the New Criticism, along with its rejection of biography, history, and pathos in the form of various fallacies. Northrop Frye's giant system took the art of formal combinations as far as anyone would (or could) have, as in his own way did Kenneth Burke. By the time "theory" advanced intellectually into departments of English, French, and German in the United States, the notion of "text" had been transformed into something almost metaphysically isolated from experience. The sway of semiology, deconstruction, and even the archaeological descriptions of Foucault, as they have commonly been received, reduced and in many instances eliminated the messier precincts of "life" and historical experience.

Perhaps the most convenient symbol of what I have in mind here is Hayden White's celebrated book *Metahistory: The Historical Imagination in Nineteenth-Century Europe,* published in 1973. The paradox of White's book is, I think, that it really is a remarkably brilliant and ingenious Foucauldian, and even in some ways a Vichian, work and one from which I have derived a great deal of instruction. I have no argument with White's description of what he calls the deep poetical structure of the historical consciousness of Marx, Michelet, and Croce, nor even with the classifications of metaphor, metonymy, synecdoche, and irony. Yet White treats the categories as somehow necessary and even inevitable, arranged in a closed cyclical form rather like Frye's. No attention is paid to other alternatives, or to institutions, or to the constitutive role of power which in Nietzsche and Marx (but also in the others) is crucial, but in White is added retrospectively (very much like the early Foucault). These are difficulties of a relatively minor kind, however. White is totally silent about the force, the passion, the drive to write and invest texts *with* history and not the other way around. Texts are, after all, physical things as well, not just the rarefied emanation of a theory. The result in White's work is that the lived experience, and the geography or setting of that experience, is alchemically transmuted into an unrecognizably slender form, and a totally European one at that.

Critical practice is far from a unified thing, of course, but one can read back into a whole generation of critics and criticism something very much like a Eurocentric consensus only because dramatic changes in that consensus did and do occur. What is most impressive in the general consensus *against* historical experience that I have been describing in the dominant style of twentieth-century criticism that produced Frye, White, and Burke, and the readings of literature they enabled, is first evident when we begin to look closely at the bristling and pretty constant hostility to historical experience as found in work after work, writer after writer. What had linked such unlikely allies as Lukács and T. S. Eliot was a refusal of the capitalist and middle-class order produced by the revolution in capital itself. Lukács's "standpoint of the proletariat," he was at great pains to show, was manifestly *not* the actual empirical experience of grimy-faced workers, any more than Eliot's notion of literature was equivalent to the lives of writers depicted so memorably in Gissing's *New Grub Street*. Both Lukács and Eliot defined their efforts as establishing a distance between the creative powers of mind functioning primarily through language and immediate history, the former producing a new and daring structure, a "putative totality" Lukács called it, that would stand against the debilitations and darkness of the latter. Both men were very close in rejecting the pain of experience in favor of poetry in Eliot's case, insurrectionary theory in Lukács's.

Yet to be able to see Lukács and Eliot, or for that matter Cleanth Brooks and Paul de Man, as belonging to roughly the same consensus there would have to be, as I said earlier, a strikingly different approach emerging in the study of literature. Signs of this are strongly evident, I believe, in the new voice of feminist writers for whom the world of literature and literary criticism hitherto constituted was premised on the absence, silence, and exclusion of women. One senses the power of this new sensibility in the title of one of the most celebrated of modern feminist works, Sandra Gilbert and Susan Gubar's *The Madwoman in the Attic*. For all the complexity and richness of available literary discourse, their book argues, there is a female presence banished to the attic, by an act of deliberate, programmatic exclusion. Not to take note of that presence, or to take note of it as Charlotte Brontë does in her novel only in passing and by resolutely confining it far away, is to deny the validity of an experience fully entitled to equal representation. And this sense of entitlement has the effect of breaking open the formal constructions of literary genres, as the phrase "human Sunday" is shattered by the experience of pressure and force it alludes to.

With such force in mind then, Joyce emerges as a far more threatening and insurgent a figure than he has usually been taken to be. As a high modernist, he appears to share traits with Eliot and Proust, for example, which everything he actually said about himself and his work contradicts. It was, he said, "the reality of experience" that as an Irish writer he wished to render, not its absence or avoidance. *Dubliners* was to be the first chapter in "the spiritual liberation of my people" and, as no one needs reminding, Stephen Dedalus sought to escape church, family, and nation in order to create freedom and have experience. But we owe *this* reading of Joyce to a new generation of Irish critics— Seamus Deane, Emer Nolan, Declan Kiberd, David Lloyd, Tom Paulin,

Luke Gibbons, among others—for whom the direct, humiliating, impoverishing experience of colonialism, not that of high modernism, was the one that counted. This readjustment of perspective parallels the feminist one in which consensus and centrality are directly and immediately challenged by experiences that may seem peripheral but carry their own freight of urgency that can no longer be denied, either because it isn't male or because it isn't European high art situated at several removes from the perceived debasements of ordinary life.

In my own case I found myself drawn quite early on to writers like Conrad, Merleau-Ponty, Cioran, and Vico who were verbal technicians of the highest order and yet eccentric in that they stood apart from, and were untimely, anxious witnesses to, the dominant currents of their own time. Except for Merleau-Ponty, they were outsiders whose insights were achieved at great expense as they struggled with the impingements of sometimes overwhelming and even threatening circumstances which they could neither ignore nor elude. Nor could they escape to some promontory outside the troubling element of what I call worldliness. So it was Merleau-Ponty who struck me as best understanding the predicament of a reality without absolutes, of language as a synthesis of constantly experienced moments, and of mind as incarnated irremediably in things where, despite all our efforts, "we never see our ideas or freedom face to face." Moreover, for me Vico's greatness was not just his astonishing insights into the relationship of reciprocity between a history made by human beings and the knowledge they have of it *because* they made it, but his stubborn habit as a philologist of forcing words back into the messy physical reality from which, because of their human uses, words necessarily emanate. "Monuments of unaging intellect" were for him misleading facades to be traced back into the copulating bodies of heroic men and women.

Reading historiographers like Hayden White or the philosopher Richard Rorty, one finds oneself remarking that only minds so untroubled by and free of the immediate experience of the turbulence of war, ethnic cleansing, forced migration, and unhappy dislocation can formulate such theories as theirs. No, you want to say, what a language user registers is not just the pressure of other language users or, as in Rorty's particular case, the goal of having a conversation with other philosophers in which the verification of a sentence is only another sentence, but also the sometimes horrific pressures that render even the most humdrum and ordinary of sentences both threatening and full of dislocating force. Conrad's writing, for instance, wears its author's existential unsettlement on its surface and in the conditions it always seems to describe: for example, in the story "Amy Foster," the notion of a "death illuminated by unresponsive eyes." Or in Adorno's instance, the thesis that for the displaced person, "homes are always provisional."

Another breach in the formalist construct of language and literature has come from ethnic and minority historical experience, which in work done by African-American, Asian-American, and native American writers opens literature to the claims of raw testimonials that cannot easily be dismissed as irrelevant. It is very important to remember that before the claims of testimonial became the kind of thing parodied and attacked by Robert Hughes as "the culture of complaint," it was and in many cases still is very far from being a laundry list of imprecations attributed to "high" (that is, European) culture. Nor was it at bottom a prescription for separatist enterprises like the Afrocentric dogmas criticized so robustly by Hughes. When you look at the history recounted in Richard Slotkin's *Regeneration Through Violence* or at the line of writing that is carried from Frederick Douglass to W. E. B. Du Bois and Zora Neale Hurston and then into the critical work of Toni Morrison, Houston Baker, and Henry Louis Gates, you see very persuasive and eloquent arguments made for *including* and *remembering*, rather than for merely giving focus to or encoding crucial historical experiences.

It would be wrong to pretend, however, that both feminist and what has been called ethnic criticism did not in fact since lend themselves either to formalism or to an esoteric and jargon-ridden exclusivism. They have and do, but what gathered readers and practitioners to them in the first place was the prospect of integrating experiences into literary discussions that had for a long time left those experiences unacknowledged. This integrative impulse in its finest and truest form is plainly evident in Toni Morrison's *Playing in the Dark: Whiteness and the Literary Imagination*. Morrison's book is moved not by anger but by delight, as well as from what she knows "about the ways writers transform aspects of their social grounding into aspects of language" (4).

The accent throughout her book is less on aspects of language than on the social grounding that gives rise to inflections and distortions in language; this social principle assumes preeminence and priority for her in the creation of literature. In American literature "what did happen frequently was an effort to talk about [the presence of Africans] . . . with a vocabulary designed to disguise the subject. It did not always succeed, and in the work of many writers disguise was never intended. But the consequence was a master narrative that spoke *for* Africans and their descendants, or *of* them. The legislator's narrative could not coexist with a response from the Africanist persona" (50).

The drama of Morrison's charge is best caught in her account of images of punishing whiteness in American literature—Poe's Arthur Gordon Pym and Melville's Moby Dick, for example—which, she says, "seem to function as both antidote for and meditation on the shadow that is companion to this whiteness—a dark and abiding presence that moves the hearts and texts of American literature with fear and longing" (33). For Paul de Man, one recalls, allegory is haunted by the absence and priority of an experience that is excluded from literature, and this, he goes on to argue, leads to a critical aporia for interpreters without apparent means to rectify or treat the exclusion. For Morrison the exclusion is ultimately unsuccessful, and derives from a social and historical experience which, as critic and reader, it is her role to re-include, re-inscribe, re-define. That this role need not, and in fact does not, include an attack on the literature *as literature* itself is part of its extraordinary merit. Morrison makes no sentimental appeal to another, perhaps more accurately representative literature, and no appeal either to a folk, or popular, or sub-literary nativist genre. What she discusses are instances of the master narrative, works by Poe, Mark Twain, Hemingway, Cather, whose significance on aesthetic and historical grounds is granted in a manner that is neither hectoring nor vengeful.

Many readers and professional students of literature in England and America have become so used to the impoverishing terms of an almost purely ideological, and even caricatural, debate about the canon that they have forgotten that readings such as those Toni Morrison offers are, in fact, the historical norm. The Battle of the Books, the debate over the Higher Criticism, over the meaning of philology (as fought out between Wilamovitz and Nietzsche)—these and many more canonical disputes have always been the antecedents and have set the standard for energetic, unacademic, real-life discussion about the canon, and about how great books should, or can be, read for actual use in actual life. It has been most unfortunate, I think, that the almost total absence of a historical sense allowed the nearsighted, media- and mammon-controlled spirit of the Reagan and Thatcher administrations to control for so long discussions whose true import was never really about how to manage reading lists and codify course requirements but about how the real experience of large groups of people might be grasped, clarified, reinterpreted, and rediscovered in the great works of literature and philosophy. As if such misleading and trivialized phrases as political correctness, or multiculturalism, or William Bennett's grandiose "to reclaim a heritage" really had anything to do with the kind of thing Toni Morrison was talking about! Of course not.

This brings me to the third important approach whose impulse and effect have been to lessen the formalist hold on the study of literature in favor of approaches based on reinstating historical experiences both misrepresented and largely excluded from the mainstream canon as well as its criticism. What gives a special intelligibility and status to the concept of a "mainstream canon" is, of course, the kind of social authority that is crucial to the life of a nation. This has been perfectly clear during the debates about ethnic identity in the United States and abroad as well, during the past few years when it seemed to perspicacious observers that what was at stake could not be comprehended by so unimportant a thing as a school reading list; rather it was the image of America itself, and the coherence of its society, that seemed to be threatened. This fear stands at the center of Arthur Schlesinger's book *The Disuniting of America:* that to press the claims of minorities and other nationalities on the main core of American history (even if it is, after all, an immigrants', diasporic history) is to dislodge traditional authority in favor of a new and possibly fractious one.

Yet never was this sense of a compelling, enduringly stable identity stronger than in the time since the nineteenth century, whose legacy in the contemporary cultural and political discourses I have been discussing is the heightened, and indeed embattled, sense of *national* identity which really appears for the first time on a world scale because of imperialism which pits one race, society, culture against (or on top of) another. As Eric Hobsbawm puts it, "The major fact about the nineteenth century is the creation of a simple global economy, progressively reaching into the most remote corners of the world, an increasingly dense web of economic transactions, communications and movement of goods, money and people linking the developed countries with each other and with the undeveloped" (*Age of Empire*, 62). Throughout the age of empire a rigid division obtained between the European colonizers and their non-European colonized peoples—a division which, although millions of transactions were permitted across it, was given a cultural correlative of extraordinary proportions, since in essence it maintained a strict social and cultural hierarchy between whites and non-whites, between members of the dominant and members of the subject race. It was this asymmetry in power that Fanon was to characterize as the Manicheanism of colonial rule and whose profound cultural effects I have examined in *Orientalism* and *Culture and Imperialism*.

It is not too simple a formulation to say that the whole concept of national identity, in America as elsewhere, was brought to a new pitch of contested fraughtness by imperialism. Not only did a new discourse of national greatness take hold inside the culture of the colonizing powers, but a discourse of national resistance developed within the culture of the colonized people. To think of the French rhetoric of *mission civilisatrice* and opposing it, the rhetoric of *négritude* and Pan-Africanism, is to gauge how profoundly experienced and how deadly serious cultural identities had become by the mid-twentieth century. Or there was *manifest destiny*, and the many Latin American doctrines of native authenticity. And after the post–World War II dismantling of the classical empires, after the colonial wars and the mass insurrections of decolonization, the exigencies of national and cultural identity did not lessen; they increased. National identity (and very often little else) became the program of many newly independent countries in the Third World, who required an airline, a diplomatic service, and (of course) an army to maintain themselves in the face of poverty, illness, and hunger. In the United States, the postwar period brought the Cold War and, as frequently *not* noted, the taking on by the U.S. and its superpower opposite, the Soviet Union, of the roles once played by Britain and France.

The twentieth century was supposed to have been the American century, and perhaps indeed it was, although it's still too early to prophesy about *this* century. Certainly the great overseas ventures like the war in Vietnam or Operation Desert Storm have made a difference to the more and more heightened, as well as problematic, sense of American cultural identity. But there is also no doubt that the emergence of opposition to the earlier empires has had consequences for the battles around identity all over the world, even if now a weary globalized consciousness has overtaken intellectuals at "the end of history." But their lack of energy is not the only story.

When during the 1980s students and faculty at Stanford, for example, proposed Fanon as an item on the humanities reading list, it was felt that Fanon's engagement in the 1950s on behalf of the Algerian FLN against French colonialism was of some particular relevance to American students in the 1980s. Why? Because his work signified opposition to empire, and empire was a title to which the United States had so unmistakably succeeded. Moreover—and this, I believe, is a more interesting reason for concern with Fanon—writers like him, C. L. R. James, W. E. B. Du Bois, Walter Rodney, Aimé Césaire, and José Marti represented an unusual intellectual trajectory: they were writers and activists whose intellectual pedigree was often entirely metropolitan but whose work could be characterized as providing an alternative consciousness to that of the mainstream, orthodox, or establishment consciousness prevailing in Europe and the United States. Cities like New York, full of immigrants and unaccommodated "aliens," hold a place of honor in this history as housing precisely that alternative intellectual at odds with the city's almost overpowering status as a center of global capital.

The opposition to empire is so important a feature of my work after *Orientalism* that it requires a little more elaboration and historical precision. I think it can be said that the appearance of nationalist and independence parties all across the Third World, and within the already independent countries of North and South America, from the end of the nineteenth century until the period between the two world wars was a massive response to the cultural and political domination of the West. This was the world in which, as a young Arab, I grew up. Many of the Pan-African, Pan-Asian, and Pan-Arab parties took as their mandate not only political independence but also the need for a new, and often renewed and reinvigorated, sense of independent cultural identity. I believe that many (if not all) of these efforts were seen as making a place in the world's culture for these new cultural identities that were formerly suppressed and excluded. To Césaire and Du Bois, for instance, racial thought and the persecution of the black individual were the responsibility of aspects of white or European mainstream culture, but they did not at all mean that *all* whites and Europeans, or *all* white and European culture, were to be thrown out and rejected. There had to be careful discriminations made between liberation on the one hand, and a sort of reverse racism, by which pernicious theories of racial discrimination were now replicated in a reversed form (blacks hating and discriminating against whites) in the new and emergent black nationalism. Tagore in India nobly undertook a critique of nationalism as containing too much negative force and resentment.

Certainly there was a great deal of nativism and violently separatist thought in the anti-imperialist nationalism of the mid-twentieth century. What is even more sadly ironic is that some intellectuals who were once critical of the separatist nationalism in their liberation movements were later to be transformed into the most energetic and insistent of nativists, those who uncritically reiterated the importance of belonging to the "right" group, and therefore were neither alien nor united. Thus the celebrated Nigerian writer Wole Soyinka attacks Senghor's *négritude* in the early 1960s—attacks it brilliantly and resourcefully for its defeatism, its implicit concessions to European ethnocentrism and supremacist thought—and then thirty years later in his own journal *Transition* attacks the well-known Kenyan political theorist Ali Mazrui for not being enough of a "pure" African. Such divagations as this are all too frequent, particularly in the continued denigration of native and non-Western cultures in the late twentieth century. But what distinguished the great liberationist cultural movements that stood against Western imperialism was that they wanted liberation within the same universe of discourse inhabited by Western culture. As Césaire put it in his greatest poem (in a phrase echoed and re-echoed by C. L. R. James), "no race has a monopoly on beauty, or intelligence, or strength, and there is room for everyone at the convocation of conquest."

The historical experience of imperialism for the imperialized entailed subservience and exclusion; therefore the historical experience of nationalist resistance and decolonization was designed for liberation and inclusion. Much of what went wrong in the subsequent development of nationalism was the direct result of either forgetting or rejecting this edifying equation—but that is another story that I have tried to pursue in the later essays of this book on the politics of knowledge. It is necessary, however, to add one further thing to the narrative of liberation that concerns me here: that so far as liberation was concerned, the very notion of historical experience itself involved an acknowledgment that both the dominant and the subaltern peoples in imperialism actually shared the same irreducibly secular world. And if so, there was only one worldly cultural space, the common possession of all humankind, and also a universal language of rights and ideals, in which to wage the struggle for liberation and inclusion. To some extent this acknowledgment reflected the national reality, that is, if as a Senegalese or an Indian you were educated under imperialism, English or French culture would perforce be a part of your world. Césaire's language, conceptual vocabulary, and values in his *Discourse on Colonialism* were those of Voltaire and Marx; the object of his polemic was to rescue their liberating ideas from the corruptions forced on poor West Indian natives by empire. To read and interpret meant to read in French (and other languages) for liberation and inclusion. It did not mean throwing out the masterpieces of "Western" culture along with the language of the colonial bureaucrat who claimed to be representing them, and who in the end was forced to leave. Nor did it mean inventing a special jargon to be used only by "natives." If Western humanism was discredited by its practices and hypocrisy, these needed to be exposed, and a more universal humanism enacted and taught.

I have taken so much time to sketch this enormously rich history because it serves as the general background for many of the essays in this book, which have derived both from my own travel and from work being done in England, Ireland, Africa, India, the Caribbean and the Middle East. The noisy debates that now rage around post-colonial and African-American studies, as well as the radical feminism that focuses principally on non-white women, sometimes obscure the well-spring of hope, generosity, and courage from which those approaches originally derived. Reading Du Bois, for instance, one could hear in his accents, first of all, the sound of an interpreter partly shaped in language and sensitivity by the great European and American poets and novelists, some of whose modern ideological followers unfortunately affirmed only their preferred authors' relatively official and perhaps even authoritarian selves, and scanted what else in the poetry and prose was, or could be interpreted as being, heterodox, subversive, and contradictory. But second, and no less important, one could learn from interpretations such as his, Toni Morrison's, and C. L. R. James's to see in the canon *other* structures of feeling, attitude, and reference, structures that testified to a much more worldly, active, and political involvement by major writers with topics of great importance to non-Europeans—topics such as the limits of colonial penal rehabilitation in *Great Expectations*, the quandaries of imperialism in Tennyson, slavery and racialist thought in Carlyle, and outright colonialism in Ruskin. The challenge therefore was to re-read and re-examine, not simply to distort or reject.

Far from rejecting or disqualifying canonical writers because of crudely political considerations, my approach has tried to re-situate writers in their own history, with a particular emphasis on those apparently marginal aspects of their work which because of the historical experience of non-European readers have acquired a new prominence. A prototype for this method exists, of course, in the magnificent historical and cultural studies of E. P. Thompson and Raymond Williams, which have been especially important to me. Williams's *The Country and the City*, for instance, is such a compelling work because it restores to individual works of literature and art the lived experiences of losers in the social contest, losers whose absence Williams was the first to point to as having an essential part in the aesthetic work's structure and meaning. He shows, for example, that the absence of dispossessed peasants in a picture of opulent country-house elegance is implicitly memorialized by the seventeenth-century arranged landscapes represented by Ben Jonson at Penshurst estate: "a rural landscape emptied of rural labour and of labourers; a sylvan and watery prospect with a hundred analogies in neo-pastoral painting and poetry, from which the facts of production had been banished: the roads and approaches artfully concealed by trees, so that the very fact of communication could be visually suppressed; inconvenient barns and mills cleared away out of sight (the bourgeois Sterling, in Coleman and Garrick's *Clandestine Marriage* had 'made a greenhouse out of the old laundry and turned the brewhouse into a pinery'); avenues opening to the distant hills, where no details disturbed the distant view; and this landscape seen from above, from the new elevated sites; the large windows, the terraces, the lawns; the cleared lines of vision; the expression of control and of command" (125).

This is not *ressentiment*, nor is it anger at "high culture." Williams is a great critic to the precise extent that his scholarship and criticism are based on the immediacy of connection he can discern between the great literary work and the historical experience—all the relevant sides of it— that gave rise to the work. To read Jonson's *Penshurst* is therefore to appreciate its figures, its structures and fluent accents, but also to grasp the way in which these were earned, achieved, constructed by individual genius *and* by social contest. What one ends up feeling in Williams's work is not so much a sense of his cleverness, or his sophisticated way with a lot of sources and scholarship, but his ability to project himself back into the past, and thereby to comprehend its felt structures and its laboriously wrought works as a sort of inventory or genealogy of the present, in Gramsci's phrase. And thus the great eighteenth-century landscapes and country houses will lead a century later to the "wealthy and class-divided city" of London: "This version [Conan Doyle's representation of London as Sherlock Holmes's domain] of a glittering and dominant metropolitan culture had enough reality to support a traditional idea of the city, as a centre of light and learning, but now on an unprecedented scale. The cultural centralization of England was already at this time more marked, at every level, than in any comparable society" (229).

To speak of the canon is to understand this process of cultural centralization, a direct consequence of imperialism and the globalism we still live with today. The privilege of the great work is that it sits at the center of the center and can therefore either touch or include the historical experience of peripheral, marginal, or eccentric lives, albeit in a reduced or scarcely visible form. Criticism in the global setting spun together by imperialism affords a whole series of possibilities, especially if we take seriously the historical experience of decolonization, with its enabling perspectives and resourceful readings as an extension of the struggle to be heard, and to be a realized part of what T. S. Eliot calls "the whole consort dancing together."

I do not want to be understood as suggesting that you have to be a member of a formerly colonized or disadvantaged minority group in order to do interesting and historically grounded literary scholarship. When such notions of insider privilege are advanced they have to be rejected out of hand as perpetuations of the exclusions one should always oppose, a sort of racism or nationalism by imitation, which in this book I have criticized both in supposedly privileged or "objective" observers like Naipaul and Orwell, both of them renowned for the transparency and "honesty" of their style, and in social insiders like Walter Lippmann. Like all style, "good" or transparent writing has to be demystified for its complicity with the power that allows it to *be there*, whether at the center or not.

Moreover, the study of literature is not abstract but is set irrecusably and unarguably within a culture whose historical situation influences, if it does not determine, a great deal of what we say and do. I have been using the phrase "historical experience" throughout because the words are neither technical nor esoteric but suggest an opening away from the formal and technical toward the lived, the contested, and the immediate, which in these essays I keep returning to again and again. Yet I am as aware as anyone that the dangers of an empty humanism are quite real, that simply asserting the virtues of classical or humanistic norms in the study of literature is to feed an agenda that is determined to weed out and possibly eliminate any mention of transnational experiences such as war, slavery, imperialism, poverty, and ignorance that have disfigured human history—and discredited the humanism that left responsibility for those evils to politicians and Others. In a forthcoming book on humanism in America I hope to develop this idea and to affirm the continued relevance of humanism for our time. The point here, however, is that at present the study of literature has gone in two opposed and in my opinion ridiculously tendentious directions: one, into a professionalized and technologized jargon that bristles with strategies, techniques, privileges, and valorizations, many of them simply verbal or "postmodern" and hence lacking in engagement with the world, or two, into a lackluster, ostrich-like, and unreflective pseudo-healthiness that calls itself "traditional" scholarship. Historical experience, and in particular the experience of dislocation, exile, migration, and empire, therefore opens both of these approaches to the invigorating presence of a banished or forgotten reality which in the past two hundred years has dominated human existence in an enormous variety of ways. It is this general and particular experience that my own kind of criticism and scholarship in this book are trying to reclaim, understand, and situate.

I should add that I have tried to deal with music as a particularly rich and, for me, unique branch of aesthetic experience. Several essays in this book are either about musical subjects or discuss music in ways that are, I think, linked to my other interests. As someone whose life-long association with Western classical music has included performance, musicology, and criticism, I have always regretted that modern culture seems to have isolated music away from the other arts, with the result that most educated people are far more at ease talking about cinema, photography, art, dance, or architecture than they are with Bach or Schoenberg. Yet music's extraordinary disciplinary rigor, its capacity for plurality of voice, for expressiveness, for a whole range of performative possibilities, for a fascinating though sometimes arcane capacity to internalize, refer to, and go beyond its own history, have compelled my attention and have sharpened as well as deepened my other, more superficially worldly concerns. In this sort of wonderfully problematic cross-fertilization between the musical and the immediacies of ordinary experience my model has been Adorno, an impossible example to follow but one whose brilliant musical intelligence makes him utterly unique among the great philosophical and cultural thinkers of our time.

I must now conclude by being considerably more specific about my own experience, and how that enters into (very often indirectly or unwittingly) so much of what is in the thirty-five years of this book. Elsewhere I have not spared my readers a rather substantial body of writing on the question of Palestine, the fate of the Palestinian people, and of course the whole ensemble of contemporary politics that has

absorbed them and their fate. In this book, however, Palestine appears from time to time as a theme (not until more than halfway through), although its influence is felt earlier, often in an incompletely grasped and formulated way. There is first of all the sheer fact of Palestine as a deeply, some might say inordinately significant geographical territory, a subject for imaginative, ideological, cultural, and religious projection, but also the site of an ongoing conflict for control. In my own experience Palestine has always been identified partly elegiacally, partly resolutely with dispossession and exile, whereas for so many others it is known principally as Israel, an "empty" land returned to according to biblical fiat. At the core, then, there is an irreconcilable, antinomian conflict embodied in the land.

Second, there is the sense of dissonance engendered by estrangement, distance, dispersion, years of lostness and disorientation—and, just as important, the precarious sense of expression by which what "normal" residents find easy and natural to do requires in exile an almost excessive deliberation, effort, expenditure of intellectual energy at restoration, reiteration, and affirmation that are undercut by doubt and irony. I have found that the greatest difficulty to be overcome is the temptation to counter-conversion, the wish to find a new system, territory, or allegiance to replace the lost one, to think in terms of panaceas and new, more complete visions that simply do away with complexity, difference, and contradiction. Whereas the critical task for the exile in my view is to remain somehow skeptical and always on guard, a role I have directly associated here and in my Reith Lectures (*Representations of the Intellectual*) with the intellectual vocation, which also refuses the jargon of specialization, the blandishments of power, and—just as much to the point—the quietism of non-involvement. Those essays in this book that are connected to debates in literary theory, anthropology, area studies (Orientalism), and, further afield, matters having to do with journalistic or artistic narrative, the art of the piano, popular culture, and particularly Arabic literature have drawn on the same kind of intellectual position of affiliation maintained in conjunction with critique.

What I have found myself looking for in our age of the politics of ethnic identity and passionate conviction are alternative communities that have emerged from the experience of exile with a great deal of

their memory and their private subjectivity still preserved, as John Berger and Jean Mohr so beautifully show, despite the extinction of privacy all around them. In this too, Palestine has played a role. Because Palestine is uncomfortably, indeed scandalously, close to the Jewish experience of genocide, it has been difficult at times even to pronounce the word *Palestine*, given that entire state-supported policies by enormous powers were dedicated to making sure that the name, and more so the memory and aspiration—to say nothing of the often startling similarity of namelessness and rejection—simply did, would, could not exist. But we are after all a coherent people, and I have found a universal meaning in the experiences on behalf of Palestinian rights, whether because liberal human rights discourse, otherwise so eloquent about all other rights, has stood in embarrassed silence before Palestine, looking the other way, or because Palestine provides the test-case for a true universalism on such matters as terror, refugees, and human rights, along with a real moral complexity often bypassed in the rush to various nationalist assertions.

It would, however, be a real mistake if this book were read as delivering an extended political message. On the contrary, much of the material here is presented as essentially in contrast to politics, that is, in the realm of the aesthetic, even though (as Jacqueline Rose indicates in her wonderfully suggestive phrase "states of fantasy," with its emphasis on the notion of a state) the interchange between politics and aesthetics is not only very productive, but endlessly recurring. And pleasurable as well. For how else can one appreciate dancers like Tahia Carioca or film stars like Johnny (Tarzan) Weissmuller except as figures expressing the mobility, the uncoopted and unadministered force, of what political life hasn't totally absorbed? But it would be disingenuous not to admit that the Palestinian experience seems retrospectively to have predisposed my own critical attention in favor of unaccommodated, essentially expatriate or diasporic forms of existence, those destined to remain at some distance from the solid resting-place that is embodied in repatriation. Therefore the essay form has seemed particularly congenial, as have such exemplary figures for me as Conrad, Vico, and Foucault.

Thus, as a cause, as a geographic, local, original experience, Palestine for me provided affinities with, say, Conrad's radical exilic vision, or

with the lonely exceptionalism of a Foucault and a Melville. But I should mention also that in the last few years my political experience underwent two major changes, one due to severe illness, which obliged me to leave the activist world of political struggle, and the other due to the defanging and the (in my opinion) terrible transformation of what was a secular, critical, and hopeful movement for liberation and change into a miserably confined, sordidly run West Bank/ Gaza entity as a result of the "peace process." I have written too much about this journalistically to rehearse any of my arguments here. Suffice it to say that Palestine casts an altered shadow over those later essays in the book having to do with questions of interpretation, education, and what I call "the politics of knowledge." I wouldn't at all call the result of the change resignation or even detachment (which I think I've always had), though I would say that the change in situation does accommodate my sense of how perspective in the Nietzschean sense is less a matter of choice than of necessity. In any event, I have been so specific here about the influence of Palestine because I have long wanted to acknowledge intellectually its importance and universality that go well beyond the regional and the local. Besides, we all know how concerns from one area of life impinge silently and unasked on others.

I have argued that exile can produce rancor and regret, as well as a sharpened vision. What has been left behind may either be mourned, or it can be used to provide a different set of lenses. Since almost by definition exile and memory go together, it is what one remembers of the past and how one remembers it that determine how one sees the future. My hope in this book is to demonstrate the truth of this, and to provide my readers with the same pleasure I derived from using the exile's situation to practice criticism. And also to show that no return to the past is without irony, or without a sense that a full return, or repatriation, is impossible.

1

Labyrinth of Incarnations:
The Essays of Maurice Merleau-Ponty

According to Emile Bréhier, the distinguished philosopher and historian of philosophy, the major task faced by French thinkers of the early twentieth century was to re-situate man in what he aptly describes as "the circuit of reality." The theories of which Bergson and Durkheim, for example, were heirs had isolated man in a limbo, in order that "reality," or whatever was left when man was lifted aside, could be studied. Mechanism, determinism, sociologism: a variety of sometimes simple and sometimes ingenious keys kept unlocking doors that led further away from what philosophers like Gabriel Marcel and Jean-Paul Sartre were later to call "lived"—as opposed to general, universal, abstract or theoretical—"life." The discrediting of these "isms," which began as a useful polemic, has, since the middle 1930s, become a sophisticated and frequently tangled strand of intricate philosophizing, not without its moments of fatuous elegance (at which the French are masters) but more frequently studded with works of enduring importance. Whether it calls itself Marxism, existentialism, or phenomenology, the thought of this period (from about 1936 onward) almost always concerns itself with *concrete situations*—a key phrase—rather than with abstractions, with precise methodology but not with universal principles. Somehow, it manages also to be highly adventurous and speculative and yet markedly anti-theoretical, a paradox that keeps occurring to the reader for whom antitheses of this sort are still novel and troubling. Moreover, even the Marxists (the best of them, that is) join in attacking the doctrine of simple causation, a doctrine that satisfies no one and often arouses ridicule because of its pallid rigidity. All in all, causation, abstract theory, and "unsituated" discussion are as irrelevant as possible to the generality of recent French thought. Their uselessness to this thought is best illustrated by the way in which Zeno's paradox of Achilles and the tortoise is invalidated by actual motion.

The fall of France in 1940 considerably strengthened the impulse to discredit mechanistic or reductive philosophy, and generated an impatience with a sort of ossified precision that seemed incapable of touching man. What had previously been a debate between professional philosophers turned into almost national reaction to a social, spiritual, moral, and even military posture that was simply not ready for the brutalities of history. In a sense, the mode of philosophy changed from inbred professionalism to humanistic amateurism. The war caught up and made overt what had been stirring beneath the surface of French life, the conflict between what M. Bréhier calls the stability of principles and the shifting variety of human experience. Like the Maginot Line, these fixed principles buckled as the waves of an onrushing and terrible experience assaulted them with catastrophic effect. It is ironic, of course, that German thought—that of Marx, Edmund Husserl, and Martin Heidegger in particular—played a considerable part in the intellectual turnabout. For what these philosophers brought to the attention of their French disciples was an awareness that the starting point of any philosophical enterprise is man's own life, which can neither be left unexamined nor conveniently herded under some theoretical rubric. A corollary to this notion is one with which current Anglo-Saxon philosophy, normally hostile to the style of Continental philosophizing, concurs: the central importance of language to human experience. In a sense, philosophy has passed from the study of economic-behavioral-psychological man to the study of linguacentric man. Immanence—or the meaning embedded in human, lived reality—is now the central theme of French philosophy, and in the work of Maurice Merleau-Ponty it has received extraordinarily rich, passionate, and complex treatment.

Like his long-time friend Jean-Paul Sartre, Merleau-Ponty was a prewar *normalien* who then did the usual tour of pedagogic duty at a provincial lycée before military service in 1939. During the war, he worked with the Resistance while teaching philosophy at the Lycée Carnot. In 1945, with Sartre, he founded *Les Temps Modernes* and contributed unsigned as well as signed political and philosophical articles to it until the two men broke with one another: their friendship, according to Sartre, was difficult and very often strained. Sartre, incidentally, wrote a remarkable portrait of Merleau-Ponty just after the latter's death in 1961; not only is it the most interesting and personal study of Merleau-Ponty but it is Sartre at his best, complex and clear at the same time, full of sympathy and a kind of baffled understanding for his problematic subject. One wonders how two such different men could have been friends for so long (Sartre suggests coyly that what kept them together was his great respect for Merleau-Ponty—who, he says, had achieved maturity and had "learned history" sooner than his fellows). They complement each other: Sartre with his expansive genius, pushing out in form after form, restlessly exploring one literary and philosophic mode after another; Merleau-Ponty with his brooding, concentrated power of mind, gathering in his experience and his thoughts, his writing becoming more and more dense, its texture thicker and tighter. Both are great synthesizers, but Sartre's style is essentially centrifugal, Merleau-Ponty's centripetal. Their disagreement in 1950 reached a climax during the Korean war. Merleau-Ponty, ever a stoic realist, became convinced that words meant nothing (he said he would commit suicide now by going to New York to work as an elevator boy). Naked force had been let loose. Sartre, though plainly discouraged, was still hopeful that voices could be raised in protest and discussion.

Between 1945 and 1953, Merleau-Ponty taught for a time in Lyons, and at the Sorbonne. In 1953, he was made professor at the Collège de France; the chair he was given—he was the youngest man ever named to it—had previously been held by Bergson and by Etienne Gilson. Merleau-Ponty died suddenly in 1961 at the age of fifty-three, his work, at least as he had sketched out its future outlines, only begun. His death came eight years after his mother's, when, by his own admission to Sartre, one-half of his life had been destroyed. Furthermore, he claimed never to have recovered from an incomparable childhood. Sartre surmises that Merleau-Ponty's incurable dislike of the philosophy that is practiced as an elevated survey probably was derived from his desire to investigate man's preconscious history, his natal attachments to the world. This is not as fanciful a conjecture as it sounds. For Merleau-Ponty's central philosophic position, insofar as one can be articulated for him, is that we are in and of the world before we can think about it. Perception, to which he devoted his major philosophic labors, is a crucial but complex process that reasserts our connection with the world and thereby provides the basis for all our thought and meaning-giving activity. This, put very simply, is what makes him a phenomenologist. His aim is to rediscover experience at the "naïve" level of its origin, beneath and before the sophisticated encroachments of science. Phenomenology approaches experience as a novelist or poet approaches his subject, from within, but it is not at all anti-scientific; on the contrary, its aim is to put science on a proper footing and to restore it to experience.

On the surface, Merleau-Ponty's life seems to have been relatively uneventful, and therefore of little interest to the student of his thought. But, as Werner Jaeger showed in his magistral study of Aristotle, one of the most significant aspects of a philosopher's work is the connection between the development of his thought and the tenor of his life. Merleau-Ponty's earliest works were published as his thesis for the *docteur ès lettres* in 1945: *The Structure of Behavior* and *Phenomenology of Perception*. These large, careful, laborious volumes, filled with recondite examples from science (physics, biology, and psychology), were an attempt to free the mind from the bonds of pure empiricism at one extreme, and idealism at the other. These two doctrines subsumed what Merleau-Ponty took to be the major fallacies of philosophy. Empiricism argued the sufficiency of practical observation and experiment, but was forced to resort to extra-empirical concepts to unify and give meaning to the results of these observations. A neurosis, for instance, can't be understood merely by adding together all its symptoms, since a neurosis is something more than the sum of its parts: it is a working whole, or *Gestalt*, in action. Idealism, on the other hand, taught the primacy of abstract wholes that pertain to some realm of which, by definition, we can have no experience, and the ascendancy of mind over matter. Merleau-Ponty confutes this latter belief by attention to the body's crucial role in our experience. Truth, he concludes, is based on what is real—and that is our perception of the world: perception becomes "not presumed true," but may be "defined as access to truth." He goes on to say, in *Phenomenology of Perception*, that "the world is not what I think, but what I live through. I am open to the world, I have no doubt that I am in communication with it, but I do not possess it; it is inexhaustible. 'There is a world,' or rather: 'There is the world'; I can never completely account for this ever-reiterated assertion in my life." Merleau-Ponty's efforts to account for the assertion are the positive aspect of the two volumes: he shows how human reality can best be understood in terms of behavior (action given form) which is neither a thing nor an idea, neither entirely mental nor entirely physical. Instead of rushing from one absolute incompatibility to another, torn between them, his mode of thought is dialectical, weaving among realities without absolutes. His philosophy thus took as its province what he was later to call "the constantly experienced moment."

The two works clearly pertain both to the war experience and to the immediate postwar years. Whatever remained of "pure" thought, "pure" morality, "pure" anything, he wrote a little later, was unlearned; "we learned a kind of vulgar immoralism, which is healthy." His task was to open men to their experience—they had been, like their country, virtually raped by history. One thinks of Yeats's "Leda" sonnet and then of Merleau-Ponty struggling to muster knowledge equal to the power of so devastating an experience. It was no longer a question of finding ways to churn up new secrets about man—which is the characteristic prejudice of late nineteenth-century philosophy and psychology. With his usual uncanny precision, André Malraux has one of the characters in his *Les Noyers de l'Altenburg,* a wartime novel, reject classical (and presumably Freudian) psychology exactly because man's secrets have nothing to do with man's humanity. Merleau-Ponty's thought is best understood not as a way of uncovering new truths about man but as a way of intensifying participation in human experience. One does not read his work to discover what one had not known before. Instead, one is readmitted from distraction to one's own experience, as is the case when one reads Proust (an author from whom Merleau-Ponty quotes a great deal). There is also a curious resemblance here to the Platonic doctrine of recollection. This is why, as I suggested earlier, philosophy ceases to be a privileged, professional activity to which only initiates are admitted; the language, the techniques, the biases ought to be available to all, for we are amateurs together, subjected to contingency, to "the metamorphoses of fortune," to "facticity," and to death.

Almost everything that Merleau-Ponty wrote after 1945 was originally cast in essay form—big books, with their forced systematic unity that draws one further into its clutches, were less open to the vagaries of human experience. His penchant for shorter forms is reminiscent of Wittgenstein's, for whom writing was less a delivery of finished thought than a series of moments fully embedded in experience. In the *Tractatus*, Wittgenstein mirrors Merleau-Ponty's wonder at the world's presence in and around us: "Not *how* the world is, is the mystery, but *that* it is." (Interestingly, Georg Lukács, who admits the sincerity of Merleau-Ponty's work, upbraids him for his "mystical" attitude to history and reality.)

The great themes of Merleau-Ponty's essays are language, art, psychology, and politics, and the three major volumes form part of the integral translation of his work undertaken in an extraordinary project at Northwestern University Press.[1] The earliest essays, those in *Sense and Non-Sense,* date from between 1945 and 1947. Those in *Signs* are later efforts from 1958 on, and those in *The Primacy of Perception* contain not only some early pieces but also the last work published during his lifetime, "Eye and Mind." (Between *Sense and Non-Sense* and *Signs,* he wrote two volumes of political philosophy with particular attention to contemporary Marxism: *Humanism and Terror* and *The Adventures of Dialectic.* In 1964, a volume gleaned from his notes, *Visible and Invisible,* appeared in Paris.) His very earliest essays excepted, Merleau-Ponty's style of exposition in these volumes is novel and at first hard to fathom. For he disdains point-by-point logic, preferring instead to explore his theme laterally and obliquely, in a manner strikingly reminiscent of R. P. Blackmur's—whose interest in "gesture" Merleau-Ponty shares. This style is consistent with his belief that philosophy, or serious discourse, is "as real as the world of which it is a part," and is "the act whereby we take up this unfinished world in an effort to complete and conceive it." Unlike Sartre's assertion that we are condemned to freedom, Merleau-Ponty's quieter realism illustrates that we are condemned to *meaning;* in all its aspects, our life is our way of giving meaning to the brute fact of existence. This analysis is a more sober version of Gerard Manley Hopkins' exuberant "the world is bursting with meaning." Thus, in a wonderful phrase, Merleau-Ponty speaks of the world's prose, by which he means not that we are a tabula rasa on which the world writes, but that we express the world, its sense and non-sense, what is visible and what we experience even if it is invisible—for expression and gesture are the basic human prerogatives.

> Finally, we find that the perceived world, in its turn is not a pure object of thought without fissures or lacunae; it is rather, like a universal style shared in by all perceptual beings. . . . Before our undivided existence the world is true; it exists. The unity, the articulation of both are intermingled. We experience it in a truth which shows through and envelops us rather than being held and circumscribed by our mind.

Yet, we are *condemned* to meaning, and this is the other side of the coin, in much the same way that Joseph K. in *The Trial* is enmeshed in the Parable of the Law, forced to spin meaning after meaning for it, challenged endlessly by its seemingly inexhaustible possibilities. Merleau-Ponty offers no single meaning to existence because he is, as he has been called by one of his critics, a philosopher of ambiguity; Sartre comments a little wryly that Merleau-Ponty lived between a thesis and an antithesis, always unwilling to go to a definite synthesis. Yet, in a recent book on Roland Barthes and *"la nouvelle critique,"* Serge Doubrovsky laments the loss to the intellectual world of Merleau-Ponty's great synthesizing powers.

The fact of the matter is, I think, that Merleau-Ponty's language is itself the synthesis, however tenuous or difficult, for which Sartre looked. In his studies of perception, Merleau-Ponty had all but obliterated the distinction between mind and matter, as well as all the comforting and helpful antinomies with which philosophy had previously kept itself apart from the more vulgar categories of life: form and content, spirit and body. He discerned instead structures and forms that inhere in human behavior. As he said in one of his most telling phrases, perception not only involves the thinking body but also the incarnated mind. In what is his most original contribution to psychology, Merleau-Ponty demonstrates that we use our body to know the world; space and time are not abstractions but almost-entities that we haunt and inhabit. The body is not an object that receives impressions which the mind then translates in its function as a subject: on the contrary, existence is the dimension of what he calls compresence.

Properly speaking, then, perception is an activity that clarifies a primordial way of being, a being that lies beneath the level of intelligible discourse. Perception, quite literally, is the way human existence comes into being. In his essay called "The Primacy of Perception," Merleau-Ponty casts his thought as follows:

> The experience of perception is our presence at the moment when things, truths, values are constituted for us; that perception is a nascent *logos;* that it teaches us, outside all dogmatism, the true conditions of objectivity itself; that it summons us to the tasks of knowledge and action. It is not a question of reducing human knowledge to sensation, but of assisting at the birth of this knowledge, to make it as sensible as the sensible, to recover the consciousness of rationality. This experience of rationality is lost when we take it for granted as self-evident, but is, on the contrary, rediscovered when it is made to appear against the background of non-human nature.

There cannot be one absolute meaning for existence, since that would presume the intellectualist distinction between transcendent meaning and human existence that Merleau-Ponty decries. His writing does not *interpret* in the usual sense, for then it would have to be *about* something; rather, it is already in the dimension of meaning ("we are condemned to meaning"), and its primary job is the articulation of that *already present* immanence. Not how the world is but that it is. Therefore, says Merleau-Ponty, "expressing what exists is an endless task." There is a close connection between his manner of discourse and the critical stance of Susan Sontag, whose attitude "against interpretation" more militantly puts the French thinker's case; both write in and for the period after "the end of ideology."

The two incipient dangers of a philosophy like this are, first, the sheer difficulty of interpreting a language that makes no concessions, and, second, a kind of laissez faire attitude to all human activity and to ethics and politics in particular. Merleau-Ponty succumbs to the first danger from time to time, but never to the second. The introduction to *Signs,* for example, is scarcely decipherable because it is so much like a long conversation already in progress when it begins and not really concluded by the time it is supposedly over. Terms of reference are not always clear, and allusions to people, incidents, and passages in unnamed works lurk everywhere. One hastens to add, however, that it is possible to make out the larger drift of everything Merleau-Ponty wrote because his is the prose of the world in which we now live. From Husserl he borrows the word *Lebenswelt,* a useful neologism coined by the German phenomenologist to designate the life-world, or life-context and life-situation, of an individual. Merleau-Ponty's answer to charges against his blatant subjectivity is always that subjectivity is itself a universal, which means that intersubjectivity, or the whole of all existing subjectivity, is the only transcendent value.

> By myself I cannot be free, nor can I be a consciousness or a man; and that other whom I first saw as my rival is my rival only because he is myself. I discover myself in the other, just as I discover consciousness of life in consciousness of death, because I am from the start this mixture of life and death, solitude and communication, which is heading towards its resolution.

He clearly rejects what Herbert Marcuse has called one-dimensional man on the same grounds that made him in 1950 sharply criticize the Marxists with whose thought he had hitherto sympathized. To allow things to go as they are, whether or not commanded from above by a rationalized and monolithic superstructure, is bad faith. It means the surrender of the distinctively human activity of conscious perception, and hence the resignation of our task "to complete and conceive" the world. He reiterates time and again in his essays that the "broad lines of history," at least as the Marxists see them, do not determine every single episode in history. "Every historical undertaking is something of an adventure since it is never guaranteed by any absolutely rational structure of things. . . . Our only recourse is a reading of the present which is as full and as fruitful as possible, which does not prejudice its meaning, which even recognizes chaos and non-sense where they exist, but which does not refuse to discern a direction and an idea in events where they appear." Still, like Sartre, he freely appreciated (in the essay "Marxism and Philosophy") what he called Marx's realistic existentialism, his dialectical mode, and the human order for which he spoke. The final ambiguity between human effort and the inner logic of history was, however, entirely necessary to Merleau-Ponty's thought. The clarity and superb insight with which he treats Montaigne and Machiavelli in *Signs* testify to the vital polarity between human self-examination and political realism on which his courageous posture is built.

Sartre's description of Merleau-Ponty's attitude is "smiling moroseness"; at other times, perhaps wishing to balance seriousness with humor, he speaks of Merleau-Ponty's charming *"gaminerie."* Neither description, of course, does justice to Merleau-Ponty's greatest achievement as a philosopher of language (he was the first contemporary French philosopher of stature to examine language with any seriousness and profundity) and of art—and as Husserl's most imaginative student. Many months of independent research in the Husserl Archives in Louvain convinced Merleau-Ponty that Husserl, contrary to what had been thought, underwent a decisive change in mid-career. Previously a philosopher whose hope had been the formulation of a universal eidetic (or ideal essence) of mind and language, Husserl, according to Merleau-Ponty, came to realize that the clue to philosophical research was the whole man, considered in his existential situation, his *Lebenswelt.* From believing that a universal grammar could be discovered, Husserl passed to the belief that one's concern ought to be the "speaking subject," since there is no such thing as a language that one does not use (the only languages we know are the ones we *can* use). Language (or *"langage,"* as it is called by the French to distinguish it from *"langue,"* and to suggest all forms of human articulation) is man's principal expressive mode, and, as Merleau-Ponty writes in *Sense and Non-Sense,* it must *surround* each speaking subject, like an instrument with its own inertia, its own demands, constraints, and internal logic, and must nevertheless remain open to the initiatives of the subject (as well as to the brute contributions of invasions, fashions and historical events), always capable of the displacement of meanings, the ambiguities, and the functional substitutions which give this logic its lurching gait. Perhaps the notion of *gestalt*, or structure, would here perform the same service it did for psychology, since both cases involve ensembles which are not the pure manifestations of a directive consciousness, which are not explicitly aware of their own principles, and which nevertheless can and should be studied by proceeding from the whole to the parts.

Structure, I think, here corresponds to Wittgenstein's notion in the *Philosophical Investigations* of the "forms of life" which provide language with its inner ontology and rules. Merleau-Ponty's attention to structure, which he more accurately calls infrastructure (and which has since created a minor intellectual industry in France called *le structuralisme*), owes its existence to an imaginative combining of Ferdinand Saussure's linguistics with Husserl's later philosophy. Saussure had argued that "signs [words] do not signify anything, and that each one of them does not so much express a meaning as mark a divergence of meaning between itself and other signs." In short, words are diacritical. Each of the national languages, and by analogy each individual's own idiom, is an indirect language that refers not to objects but to a complex structure ("no Platonic idea") which is the total lived and organized reality of whoever uses the language. Philosophy ought really to be a study of language—a point of view one appreciates when one reads thinkers as different in aim as Heidegger, whose work is an exploration of one German's inner reality, Wittgenstein, or the Anglo-American linguistic analysts. The study of language becomes a study in the semiology (as C. S. Peirce called it) of a given society. It has been left to such brilliant speculators as Roman Jakobson and Claude Lévi-Strauss to show how linguistic structures correspond to kinship systems and to the regulating structure of social exchange. Confronted with a phenomenon like magic, Merleau-Ponty writes in *Signs*, the investigator must think his way into the phenomenon, reading or deciphering it. And this reading always consists in grasping the mode of exchange which is constituted between men through institutions, through the connections and equivalences they establish, and through the systematic way in which they govern the use of tools, manufactured or alimentary products, magical formulas, ornaments, chants, dances, and mythical elements, as a given language governs the use of phonemes, morphemes, vocabulary, and syntax. This social fact, which is no longer a massive reality, but an efficacious system of symbols or network of symbolic values, is [in] . . . the depths of the individual.

Spoken language is only one of a series of concentric circles that surround man in society, for kinship systems, mythology (as Barthes and Lévi-Strauss have shown), political ideas, even household objects are varieties of human expression that correspond to each other and to language. A fully fledged culture—fully situated, that is, in existence—has what Merleau-Ponty and Sartre call a semantic thickness about it. (Here, phrases from linguistics are made to extend beyond a narrowly linguistic frame of reference in order to accentuate the notion that human society is a web of inner bonds.) Thickness suggests the density of human experience felt not only spatially but temporally, the kind of "matter" Henry James so eloquently bewailed the lack of in America when he wrote about Hawthorne. Literature and culture, Merleau-Ponty says in *Sense and Non-Sense,* are "defined as the progressive awareness of our multiple relationship with other people and the world, rather than as extramundane techniques." The individual writer, he adds in *The Primacy of Perception,* "is himself a kind of new idiom, constructing itself, inventing new ways of expression, or diversifying itself according to its own meaning." Roland Barthes' book, *Le degré zéro de l'écriture,* examines the degrees of difference possible for a writer in different societies, and it is an interesting fact that in his later books he turns to semiology, acknowledging his debts not only to Jakobson, Saussure, Lévi-Strauss, and Peirce, but also to Merleau-Ponty.

Society, then, is a true labyrinth of incarnations, to use one of Merleau-Ponty's phrases from "Eye and Mind," the richness of which it is possible to suggest in written language. A "labyrinth" because of a complexity that has no discernible end or beginning, and an "incarnation" because implicit gestural language and outward expression are inseparable, united as man himself is in an indissoluble bond between body and soul. Philosophy, as Merleau-Ponty learns it from Husserl, holds together the human sciences, for it is

> the taking over of cultural operations begun before our time and pursued in many different ways, which we now "reanimate" and "reactivate" from the standpoint of our present. Philosophy lives from this power of *interesting* ourselves in everything that has been and is attempted in the order of knowledge and of life, and of finding a sharable sense in it, as if all things were present to us through our present. The true place of philosophy is not time, in the sense of discontinuous time, nor is it the eternal. It is rather the "living present" *(lebendige Gegenwart)*—that is, the present in which the whole past, everything foreign, and the whole of the thinkable future are reanimated.

These words realize and clarify Vico's in *The New Science,* where history and culture are shown to be made by man and therefore the first subjects of scholarly enterprise. Merleau-Ponty is linked to the great tradition of European radical humanism in which, as he says in *Sense and Non-Sense,* man, not Prometheus or Lucifer, is the hero.

Art is the human activity about which Merleau-Ponty speaks in terms of a unique joy. He says in *Sense and Non-Sense* that "the joy of art lies in showing how something takes on meaning—not by referring to already established and acquired ideas but by the temporal and spatial arrangements of elements." Among human faculties, he attaches the greatest importance to sight, for he is convinced that the major advances in art as well as philosophy are made when man *sees* more of what is there. Like Ruskin's work, whose program was to show the relevance of seeing well to the spirit of his time, Merleau-Ponty's essays on film and on Cézanne distinguish the fundamental projects animating the visual arts. In the work of a painter like Cézanne, art is "being present at the fission of Being from the inside." In his superb essay on "Cézanne's Doubt" (which with "Eye and Mind" puts Merleau-Ponty's art criticism alongside Malraux's, Gombrich's *Illusion and Reality*, and Rilke's Rodin books), he treats the most philosophic of painters as if Cézanne were a phenomenologist assisting, in his work, at the very birth of meaning: "Cézanne simply expressed what they [the faces and objects as he saw them] wanted to say." Cézanne's doubt is the essential human difficulty—and Merleau-Ponty's own—of living at and acknowledging the point where so many opposites converge, where the meaning of our reality is at once threatened and asserted: Now. "Essence and existence, imaginary and real, visible and invisible—a painting mixes up all our categories in laying out its oneiric universe of carnal essences, of effective likenesses, of mute meanings." The doubt, however, persists, and his final words on Cézanne profoundly reflect on Merleau-Ponty's own unfinished work, and that inherent yet necessary incompleteness of all human endeavor which is the basis of humanism:

> Yet it was in the world that he had to realize his freedom with colors upon a canvas. It was on the approval of others that he had to wait for the proof of his worth. That is the reason he questioned the picture emerging beneath his hand, why he hung on the glances other people directed toward his canvas. That is the reason he never finished working. We never get away from life. We never see our ideas or our freedom face to face.

Sense and Sensibility

E. D. Hirsch divides criticism into two moments, of which the first is intuitive and deeply sympathetic, the second reflexive and logical. Presumably, criticism as art and criticism as science. He focuses his own book, *Validity in Interpretation,* exclusively on the second moment, although he seems unwilling to note how the first moment always influences the second. Nevertheless, his demand for a logical method for weighing evidence about verbal statements, and a means to secure validity, is a fair one. What it involves is that the critic turn himself on the work he criticizes, asking himself questions that will either legitimize his statements about the work or, hopefully, correct them; in either case, he makes himself aware of what he is doing. Works of literature, Hirsch argues, have a meaning that is neither arbitrary nor changeable, and it is to his great credit that he recognizes the vast difficulties of construing the meaning not only of a work but of meaning itself. Consequently his book argues painstakingly (and rather drily) for a very modest "hermeneutic," in which intention (in Husserl's sense of the word) or meaning, as opposed to significance, is common to every use of language. Even nonsense has meaning, albeit nonsensical meaning. In literature, the broadest category of intention is genre: each literary utterance belongs to a "type" that performs a definable task, so that we can understand *Paradise Lost* because it is an epic which will always fulfill specific social and historical expectations. Hirsch proposes little that is more definite than this, for he is prudently hamstrung by a couple of limitations: (1) "there are no general rules which are at once general and practical," and (2) there are "no rules for generating insights." The rest of the time he spends in useful groundwork: making distinctions between meaning and significance, attacking relativism, generalizing about verbal meaning and probability.

Hirsch's most interesting observation is that in criticism "to understand is to understand as necessary." I doubt that his modesty will let him associate this remark made about the end of a critic's logical job of work with Heidegger writing about Hölderlin. For his essays on the poet are, Heidegger says, his method of showing how Hölderlin is a "necessity of thought," a series of actions that are necessary for the mind to perform. Hirsch might characteristically demand validation for such a project, yet when we read Poulet or Blackmur validation is simply in the necessary beauty of their understanding of literature, which to them is the crux of thought. Criticism is notorious for its imperialism, carried out in the name of understanding: method swallowing work, argument dividing to conquer and variety colonized into periods and "ages." By contrast, Poulet's wish is to *prolong* literature in his criticism, Blackmur's to reveal literature taking, in Henry James's phrase, from "the enormous lap of the actual." Criticism is therefore a way of living up to and living with literature. Inner conversion rather than public quarrel. We may say that such criticism flies too close to art, yet both are the more interesting for it, I think, and doubtless criticism is less concerned with accuracy as a result. Fiction makes its own canon of accuracy, however, to which Hirsch is too impervious, for even in criticism there are two cultures.

One can solicit Heidegger only at the beginning of any appreciation of the work of Blackmur and Poulet; their work is too richly distinctive, each in its own way, each now almost an institution (without enough acclaim though), to herd under a general rubric. That their criticism requires the attention we give art is of course very debatable. Certainly except for a handful of fine essays, notably by J. Hillis Miller on Poulet and by Joseph Frank and John Crowe Ransom on Blackmur, most critics have not been convinced that such criticism requires much attention. Furthermore, the idioms Blackmur and Poulet employ are notoriously problematic. Neither man is given to strident polemic, nor to "pieces" written with the left hand. Poulet's criticism and, even though it is misleadingly dumped in with New Criticism understood as explication, Blackmur's seem intensely to play to the reader's imaginative awareness. For theirs is an enterprise whose aim is nothing less than the reconstruction of experience apprehended from the point of its origin to its incarnation in form, or literature. So delicate an undertaking, which Blackmur has called bringing literature to performance, supposes an ultimate talent for closeness to the animating experience that goes into literature. Hillis Miller has spoken of Poulet's "quietistic" explorations into a writer's consciousness, and Joseph Frank of Blackmur's sentences as "ideated sensations": both styles reflect the care taken in preserving a sense of literature as highly nuanced and as intimate as possible. (Interestingly, Blackmur's unique classroom mode, as described by Arthur Gold, one of Blackmur's Princeton students, was to demonstrate how one becomes intimate with literature.) For all their differences then, Poulet and Blackmur are virtuous in their devotion to a writer's experience, and virtuosos in their gift for handling and representing that experience.

The costs of such criticism are necessarily high. Blackmur irritates with his hedging, his hidden ball play, as one critic called it, that neither wholly delivers a point nor lets it go. His wit is gnarled and capricious, his continuity often a mystery. Poulet's tone suggests the voice of literature itself, as if each writer he discusses is simply an idea momentarily illuminated by a cosmic consciousness. Unkindly, a twentieth-century Circumlocution Office (Blackmur) and Monsieur Teste (Poulet). Yet a price more than worth it. Blackmur's aphorisms that epitomize a writer's energy, the special genius that combines "unconscious skills of apprehension and gradual intimacy" with a deep immersion in the ways of "bourgeois humanism," the talent for theorizing that never loses its grip on the "rich irregularity of things"; Poulet's enormous tact in the choice of quotations, his ability to describe a consciousness revealing itself to itself as "pure instantaneousness," the extraordinary working together in his essays of a heedless abstraction with an almost shocking particularity. Neither plays what

Blackmur calls "the game of research." And each reads literature like his autobiography written at the time of happening.

It never will cease to amaze, I think, how it is that the closeness and intimacy that Poulet and Blackmur convey can be so greatly different in tone. Poulet's books, of which *The Metamorphoses of the Circle* is only the third to be translated, are always concerned with a theme—time, space, the circle—treated in the work of a series of writers. The given writer's initial moment of self-consciousness, his Cartesian *cogito,* will imply the kind of interior life that he will continue to lead thereafter: man is given only the instant, says Poulet in *Le Point de Départ* (1964), and then the mind creates duration whose "true direction is that which goes from the isolated instant to temporal continuity." Poulet's method is to attribute measurable dimension to a writer's style, which is the writer's consciousness translated into the duration of language. Hence Poulet can study changes in interior space and time, changes in the cosmology of style and consciousness, as evidence of the history of sensibility. In *The Metamorphoses of the Circle* Poulet chooses the circle as a Kantian *ding-an-sich,* its perfection and inviolability providing an aloof model for minds whose chief purpose, Poulet claims, is to achieve plenitude, horizon, and centrality. (A recent *TLS* review of Poulet's work put him down sarcastically for these "fancy" unrealities, but I do not find it hard to imagine that the mind can be interested, even obsessively, in space and time.) Thus in eighteen chapters, four of which examine whole periods and fourteen that explore individual writers, he enters into contact with specific consciousness, a contact that is direct and which is mediated only by the mind's effort to see its own center and circumference. For the circle—as Poulet shows in each chapter—is an image for understanding the mind's dialectical sense of its own existence: the center is mind's identity, the circumference its sequential progress through time, the area its way of inhabiting space and the whole figure its final coherence.

Between the Middle Ages and the Baroque period consciousness passes from an image of itself as the spherical analogy of God's perfect circular wholeness to an indulgent delight in the mind's free concentration and expansion from circle to circumference and back again. The eighteenth century, "a relativist century," feels thought as "pure sinuosity," creating its own occasional centers like a series of spider webs. Chapters on Rousseau, Lamartine, and the Romantics reveal the mind's gradual defensive withdrawal into a center whose strength is its alienation from others, because in reaching beyond itself it discovers the hostility of others—Rousseau—or insubstantiality—Lamartine. Brilliant chapters on Balzac, Flaubert, Mallarmé, and James alternate with unsatisfyingly vague essays on Nerval and Vigny. The triumph happens also to be the book's longest essay, on Amiel, the Swiss diarist. Here we discover the validation of Poulet's method, for nowhere more than in a writer whose concern is "pure consciousness" can we see how clearly thought's processes aspire to the mathematical exactness of zero, point, circumference, and area. Despite the awesome length of his diary (fifty thousand plus pages) Amiel becomes quite literally the "brief abstract" of mind, an attenuated chronicle of interior history; a man-made circle that compels, *implicates,* all other minds into its curves. Amiel, I think, is Poulet's archetype; every other chapter translates Amiel's ascetic exercises—Poulet reminds us that Amiel was singularly inept at "the dreary intercourse" of everyday life—into a fuller, though less perfect, idiom of self-consciousness.

Poulet asks us to believe that consciousness can be grasped as a pure texture, as an irreducible medium. He deals only with a writer's total *oeuvre,* rarely with individual works. History is read as consciousness slowly filling itself out, like some vast geometric pattern realizing itself in reality. It ought to be remarked also how much Poulet's general scheme of literary history adheres to our conventional understanding of it, but even though he speaks of the medieval sense of wholeness and of romantic alienation he gives us an uncannily precise tracing of the figures in history's carpet. God, presumably, is totality, the fulfillment of which goes on apace. Behind, or underneath, all activity is the desire for completion, and if Poulet's quiet essays seem unconcerned with the brute facts of existence it is because his criticism is an essentializing activity. One may wish to disagree with him, but in the absence of everything but the virtuality of consciousness the conflicts of ordinary experience, as we encounter them in Edmund Wilson, say, or in Erich Auerbach, seem completely foreign. For all its tremendous complexity Poulet's work is like an Olympian daydream (Coleridge's phrase for *Clarissa*), its voice unvaryingly deliberate as it turns out one author after another like emptied receptacles. His text is Maurice

Blanchot's description of literature: "the experience whereby consciousness discovers its being in its inability to lose consciousness." With Poulet, in fine, we see what Shelley meant when he referred to the "intense inane"; it is one of the mind's necessary poles, though its untempered fineness drives us in the other direction.

Blackmur is our best guide on that vacillating journey between Poulet's metaphysics and "what holds us, what keeps us, what moves us." All of Blackmur's work can be viewed as an effort to grasp the rich variety of experience as it bends and surges either toward form (thought) or toward pure behavior (actuality). To discover the "deep, underlying form" in behavior is the task of literature, specifically of fiction, and most specifically in the master nineteenth-century novelists, of whom James was Blackmur's spiritual mentor. Whereas Poulet sees consciousness aspiring to the condition of mathematics, Blackmur prefers to do his "sums" in criticism: his "digits," as he called them, are analysis, comparison, elucidation, and judgment. He is a lively abacus of all our critical and imaginative skills. What quickens the pulse of Blackmur's work is a skepticism learned from Montaigne, what Blackmur called "having a marginal mind for the play and interest of it," which holds to a sense of radical imperfection in both imagination and intellect. This is one reason, incidentally, why Blackmur's essays are fiendishly hard to write about. So shot through is his work with provisionality that statement about his work is virtually misrepresentation. The value of Blackmur is in the reading of his Tory anarchy.

The irony is that Blackmur is almost always talking about, and attempting, representation. *A Primer of Ignorance,* a selection of essays culled by Frank out of Blackmur's writing between 1943 and 1959, is the representation of Blackmur's intimacy, "the sense of which is the only primer of [our, his] ignorance." Intimacy, first of all, with *Anni Mirabiles,* the literature of 1921–1925: with the sensuality of its poetry, with the absence in it of "predictive form," and the lack in it of a recognizable principle of composition. The writers he deals with are fully appropriated by his sensibility, and certainly his knack for inventing quirky, yet superb, titles for his essays and unparalleled epitomes for his authors is a sign of how assimilated modern literature had become to his idiom. In subsequent essays he plays with problems of the intellect and imagination in modern society (the logos in the catacomb) and with the prevailing symptoms of the American pathology. Henry Adams and Henry James are poignant witnesses to the "expense of greatness" in America.

The concluding paragraph of Blackmur's warm essay on Allan Tate shows Blackmur at his generous, and epitomizing, best. There the achievement of a man of letters "unwilling to surrender his intelligence or his sense of the human condition as its chief regular informing agent," is turned into a symphony of interweaving themes associated with Tate's work. What especially characterizes the passage (which is far too long to quote) is Blackmur's use of "terms," words that are the focus of Blackmur's criticism and the gestures of his mind: they fix the contours of his reason and imagination even as they describe the object (in this case Tate) of his critique. For, he wrote in "My Critical Perspective," published in Japan in 1959 and not found in the present volume,

> intellectual formulation is the great convenience for ordering the experience of the mind, and the cause of the imperfections of the mind and even greater convenience for stepping in the guise of generalization or hypothesis when there is not enough experience to go around; which is how you lead from the known to the unknown in any field, I suppose. Or again, if either art or criticism, if either imagination or intellect, were relatively perfect, we should have no trouble and no problem and the staring inadequacies of either in respect to the other would long since have disappeared.

The staring inadequacies of imagination in respect to intellect secure Blackmur's terms: they appear then to belong inevitably together. To theorizing intellect belong administration, convention, formulation, and bourgeois humanism (defined as "the treasure of residual reason in live relation to the madness of the senses"); to representative imagination belong the faculties of "incarnating" the madness of the senses, "the lap of the actual," the "under-momentum" of life that gives gesture to language. Action is common to both reason and imagination, and in art each ought to borrow from the other. Technique is imagination aspiring to reason; form is reason aspiring to imagination. Knowledge is "a fall from the paradise of undifferentiated sensation." The two sets of terms dance together in *A Primer of Ignorance,* each set "radically imperfect" alone, and Blackmur choreographs them ambitiously to embrace literature, politics, society. He notes, for example, the tendency of Americans to use technique so well as to leave out the informing subject—this in connection with his impressions of American ballet. Yet this tendency seems designed to counter the force in twentieth-century letters that gives precedence to thought *arising out of the senses,* rather than to thought out of the reason. Thus one set of terms—those related to the representative imagination—rebel, and instead of seeking their control in reason, look to their own activity for control. Poetry in the twentieth century becomes an irregular metaphysics, and subsequently a secret craft, the novel a "technique of trouble" and sciences like psychology "mistake the conditions of our struggle for its object." Conversely, political agencies administer without governing, and society becomes a catacomb without spirit. History is a creative lie. The intellectual, like Adams, finds intellectual "harmony" in the twelfth-century world; the artist, James, is lost in "the country of the blue," for which there is no equivalent in reason. Artist and intellectual are makers of rival creations.

Alone, reason constricts; alone, imagination is chaos. On the one hand, prison, on the other, "painful unlearning" and "a special kind of illiteracy." So regular is Blackmur's sense of provisionality, however, that even in the supreme partnership of art the two generate more uncertainty. Even if in his essays one feels that intelligible terms tend finally to dissolve like sugar in hot tea, Blackmur himself survives the momentary sense of his terms. He quotes Ophelia's "To have seen what I have seen, see what I see" with special pertinence: art rises beyond intelligibility into a kind of stunned, yet clear, awareness. This is why two of Blackmur's favorite sayings are Croce's "art gives theoretic form to our feelings," and Maritain's "art bitten by poetry longs to be freed from the control of the reason." What else is this but art acting as reason (Croce) and art acting as imagination (Maritain)? And when in his essays he works the two maxims together, it is criticism behaving like art. Between them then Poulet and Blackmur show us life translated into literature. One, life's resolution into a book of world consciousness, fully immanent and always moving toward certain realization; the other, life's irresolution in essays that mock realization and represent the stutters of our imperfections. James said that the house of fiction has many windows, to which we add that criticism has many eyes with which to see; its unique poignancy is that criticism sees from *this* side of fiction, though in reading Blackmur and Poulet we cannot often be sure.

3

Amateur of the Insoluble

Writing was the first human activity to acquire a more or less permanent chronicle of its history. During the past century and a half, when all other human functions—psychological, biological, political, social, economic, cultural—were submitted to the austere revisions that transformed them into their own antitypes, writing alone escaped. For if it was not the instrument of critique, it was at least its absolute bearer. With everything else around it rethought and rewritten, writing now seems to be undergoing its own revolution from within, largely because it has the leisure, as well as the loneliness, to be freed of other business. The newest knowledges have not fully availed themselves of linear script: this is especially true in physics, mathematics and biology, even in linguistics. Modern literature has converted a dependence on writing into a method for isolating writing from what is natural, forcing it consequently to be haunted by problems that challenge its legitimacy, its intelligibility, and especially its continuity. Literally understood, the radical movement in literature and philosophy makes of writing an acquired mannerism whose performance, whose characteristic gesture, is based on the desire to leave the page for the healthier spaces of "life," the desire not to be written. The difficulty of poets like Mallarmé and Eliot, for instance, is that their writing does not want to be a text. Our fury as readers is that we watch words that wish not to be on a page, or words that want to be read before their appearance on the page, or words that *happen* to be on a page. Self-repugnance, originality, and chance—these are the signs by which writing reveals how it has turned on itself.

Writing therefore is a visible, but dissatisfied, barrier between language as a totality, and speech: this is perhaps a minimum description. The genres, like poetry, drama, fiction, are prior dreams, but only the essay (strictly speaking, an attempt) can be realized with the slenderest and the most naive projection: the essential grammatological hope of inscribing words on a page. The poet *wants* a poem; the essayist merely sets out to write an essay, and if he manages the least discourse he need not necessarily have succeeded, but he will have tried: hence his essay, whereas the poet cannot safely say whether he made the poem he wanted. In *The Soul and Its Forms,* the obscure, proleptic book that inaugurates Lukács' philosophical career, he reflects that in the essay its form becomes its fate, yet since the essay's form is basically an idea of hesitating trial and of provocation, rather than of completed achievement, there is no fate in the essay. Plato, according to Lukács, is the primal essayist, and the form of his work is Socrates' life, which is not a tragic one crowned with a true end, but an ironic life terminated by arbitrary intrusion. The center of the Platonic essay is the Idea: anterior to any of its manifestations, abstract, colorless, without extension, ungraspable. For the modern essayist, however, I think there is only the idea of writing itself, at best a biography of fading traces of thought, at worst a problematic stimulant to thought.

Along with only one other of the forms of writing the essay can afford to make no concessions to narrative description—it has no image in mind but itself—and to forsake what Hopkins called pitch, or utterly faithful accuracy, in the interests of play. Montaigne comes to mind immediately, also Oscar Wilde. In the modern perspective their essays are expatriations from things (as Wilde has one of his characters say, "things exist only to be argued about") and explorations in a language whose written version surprises by its wit, invention, sheer novelty. Writing, in other words, that delights in the mere fact of its being written cleverly, as if by a child first learning to scratch words on a page, seeing them as pretty and strangely meaningful bursts of script that transgress the unrelieved blankness of the paper. The epigram and the aphorism in the essay are what characters are to a play, or what philology is to literature. The subject of the essay does not exist beforehand, and neither does the subject go on existing after it—the subject is neither predictive nor prolonged beyond the essay, yet the subject is a choice made, as E. M. Cioran puts it, for "a break with the quietude of Unity." Thus some of his own essays, collected and translated under a title *(The Temptation to Exist)*[1] that preserves the essay's primitive hesitancy, "advance, dissociated from [their own] footsteps," and what they undertake is to give "knowledge without information." Cioran's project in writing coexists admirably with what he calls "the essential tendency of the modern mind": "to pulverize the *acquired*."

Such a project does not of course enhance the coherence of Cioran's work. Nevertheless, he is an exquisitely intelligible writer who "prowls around the Absolute," preferring what he calls the fragility of subtlety to wholehearted sincerity that might obscure the very finest points. He cannot really be read consecutively, since his prose (to which Yeats's image of a fly struggling in marmalade is very suited) accomplishes turn after turn of dense thought that seems always to leave the reader elsewhere. Yet the vigilance of his writing is an expression of his, and his writing's, consciousness, and that is explicitly based on self-hatred. For what is the pulverization of the acquired but a desire to destroy the closest and the most intimate of our gained possessions, the self? "It is from self-hatred that consciousness emerges, hence it is in self-hatred that we must seek the point of departure of the human phenomenon. I hate myself: I am absolutely a man." When he charges us "to become a source, an origin, a starting point . . . to multiply by all means our *cosmogonic moments*," he urges us to convert our misanthropy into energy, and into spectacle. A desire consequently to be interesting is saturated with hatred, although interest is productive. Cioran's characteristic idiom then forges together consciousness (which includes being interesting, and hating it) with the production of thought and prose (which includes a wish to pulverize, and the means to work that end). As a form of provocation his writing deposits the reader into a maelstrom of discomforts. Here is an image from an essay ("The Evil Demiurge"), which appeared in the Summer 1967 issue of

the *Hudson Review,* that analogically turns back on the prose that delivers it: "We find it inadmissible that a god, *or for that matter a man,*
could issue from a round of gymnastics consummated by a groan."

Cioran is peculiar enough to be a case, but not an example. His pages
are dotted with impossible words like abulia, presbyopic, succedanea,
aporia, mirific, obnubilation, incivism. Development, for example, is foreign to him, just as he is studiously foreign, actually and metaphysically,
in everything he does. He is a Rumanian who writes French which, in
Richard Howard's translation, comes over in English with very much the
same jerky intellectual queerness. The essays that have been published
over the past five years in the *Hudson Review* (translated by Marthiel
Mathews and Frederick Brown) emerged from other collections, but
bearing the same marks of what Cioran calls the hybrid intellectual: a
talent for "voyeurism of the void," the incapacity to emulate Eastern or
mystical abstraction, the distraction that keeps his rages from final nihilism. He has written on Joseph de Maistre, Machiavelli, utopias, but
above all on decomposition. Most of all, he thinks, he suffers from the
inability "to take place." Like Rameau's nephew he sees the world, and
his writing therefore acts out, a series of positions taken—but only for a
short while. Then he abandons them all since "meaning," he avers, "is
beginning to date." Inescapably the predicament returns him to an
awareness of the impasse of writing itself:

> If today's artist takes refuge in obscurity, it is because he can no
> longer create with *what he knows.* The extent of his information
> has turned him into a commentator, an Aristarchus without il-
> lusions. To safeguard his originality he has no recourse save an
> excursion into the unintelligible. He will therefore abandon
> the facts inflicted on him by an erudite and barren age. If he is
> a poet, he discovers that none of his words, in its legitimate ac-
> ceptation, has a future; if he wants them to be viable, he must
> fracture their meaning, court impropriety. In the world of
> Letters as a whole, we are witnessing the capitulation of the
> Word which, curiously enough, is even more exhausted than
> we are. Let us follow the descending curve of its vitality, sur-
> render to its degree of overwork and decrepitude, espouse the
> process of its agony. Paradoxically, it was never so free before;

its submission is its triumph: emancipated from reality, from experience, it indulges in the final luxury of no longer expressing anything except the ambiguity of its own action.

Such a view of language makes it rather difficult to summarize systematically Cioran's own thought, although he is plainly a man of very strong dislikes, which include himself, other writers, and the novel preeminently. His attacks on Christianity, and on St. Paul in particular, are unlike Nietzsche's in that, first of all, they see the religion only as a bundle of depressing contradictions and, second of all, they cannot forgive Christianity for being *passé*. For Cioran, however, the premise of his withering criticism is not as it was for Marx in the criticism of religion, but rather in the attack upon time and history. Here Cioran rejoins the radical critique of writing of which I spoke earlier. For writing is a moving image of time: every word and letter is an addition to previous writing just as—to force the parallel a little closer—every moment adds to the prior sum. Whether as writer or as man, the urge to *add to*, which Cioran identifies as the demiurge in man, is a disease, the result "of centuries of attention to time":

> Instead of letting it erode us gradually, we decided to go time one better, to add to its moments *our own*. This new time grafted onto the old one, this time elaborated and projected, soon revealed its virulence: objectivized, it became history, a monster we have called up against ourselves, a fatality we cannot escape, even by recourse to the formulas of passivity, the recipes of wisdom.

In whatever we do, or write, we are acting against ourselves by remembering, rewriting (though digressively) the tired script of history. Thus "when a writer's gifts are exhausted, it is the ineptitude of a spiritual director that comes to fill the blanks of his inspiration." Such a man then is "a spoiler suspended between speech and silence." Most writing is fraudulent, a mask for the void behind it, and the novelist, because his fictions are the most exorbitant, is "an archeologist of absence."

The greatest justice that can be done Cioran is to apply these strictures to his own writings, to let his thought think against itself. His relish for extreme statement, as I suggested earlier, is always indulged;

one statement first animates, then precipitates steps toward a new statement, equally extreme—this is what Cioran himself calls "the idolatry of becoming." The essays are a biography of movements, in the way that an oscillograph conveys a version of music that is not the music itself. To be "up against itself at last," as he claims his work to be, means that Cioran's essays instead toss about at a remove from everything they attempt to touch. He puts it very well:

> We breathe too fast to be able to grasp things in themselves or to expose their fragility. Our painting postulates and distorts them, creates and disfigures them, and binds us to them. I bestir myself, therefore I emit a world as suspect as my speculation which justifies it; I espouse movement, which changes me into a generator of being, into an artisan of fictions, while my cosmogonic verve makes me forget that, led on by the whirlwind of acts, I *am* nothing but an acolyte of time, an agent of decrepit universes.

A victim of its own temporal fixation, Cioran's writing is reduced to a particularly energetic variety of what Roland Barthes has called writing at the zero degree.

I find it difficult therefore to agree with Susan Sontag (who has provided a set of valiant, but not always pertinent, notes as an introduction) when she claims Cioran for the tradition of Novalis, Rilke, and Kafka. On the contrary, he seems a mocking ghost of all traditions, which in effect means that he mocks all writing in some of the same ways that Jacques Derrida, for example, has closed the world of writing by treating it as *mere* writing. Even less—and here Sontag curiously implies this while stating the opposite—does Cioran resemble John Cage, for whom a kind of joyous freedom, *jouissance,* underlies every one of his efforts in either prose, music, or silence. Cioran, by his own admission, is "a fanatic *without convictions,*" firmly, even hysterically, committed to the amateurism of the insoluble. His prose is perfect for what it does, and it is airless as well: like the Europe he characterizes mercilessly, the prose becomes more interesting as it masters the art of surviving itself. His highest praise is bestowed on the Jews, for they, he thinks, have always represented what in a sense his writing wishes to accomplish, "failure on the move."

Cioran is to the essay what Borges, I think, is to fiction. That is, when we read both writers we are constantly in the presence of the mask and of the apocryphal utterance, one undercutting the other, and so on until we are tired out by the unceasing game. Borges' fable and what Cioran calls "abstract autobiography" are pretexts by which, as Cioran goes on to say, the writer "can continue to cry out: 'Anything, except my truths!'" We might call this the insomniac stage of writing, and were it not for the preservation of ironic hauteur, the stage seems a needless punishment. Yet the sustained pose of such a style—detached from and yet thoroughly implicated in its revulsions—gives one pause. For after all writing has triumphed, with

> the universe reduced to the articulations of the sentence, *prose as the unique reality,* the word self-absorbed, emancipated from the object and from the world: a sonority-in-itself, cut off from the exterior, the tragic ipseity of a language bound to its own finitude.

4

A Standing Civil War

Twenty years ago it appeared to Roger Stéphane in his *Portrait de l'aventurier* that men like T. E. Lawrence, André Malraux, and Ernst von Salomon were of a type now neither possible nor effective in a world given over entirely to large collectivities. The solitary adventurer who incarnated and performed a private metaphysic of action had been succeeded by the political militant. In his Preface to Stéphane's book Sartre took issue with this view, refusing to believe, he said, in the dichotomy of the subordinate militant and the egoistical adventurer. True, there could be no more Lawrences. But the contemporary militant had to summon the adventurer's virtues to the political task by connecting in his person what Sartre called "constituted" reason (a political goal formulated into discipline by a Party) with dynamic "constituting" reason (self-conscious, self-critical, even negative human activity). This, Sartre admitted, was a vicious circle; yet, he went on to conclude, even as one force seemingly cancelled out the other, *man* emerged, and this emergence makes as well as dignifies the *human* as no simple role can.

As a forecast of the revolutionary-adventurer like Che or Régis Debray, this formula is interesting, at least as it murkily concedes that politics somehow is not all. There is an almost intransigent human residue left after the political role is filled, and the persistence of this mysterious, attractive quality still grips the imagination: this is true of Che and Debray. Nevertheless, with such men it is for the most part possible to reconcile the abiding charisma with a very definite political position taken and sacrificed for. So in some way an adventurer's spirit is required for a militant program of the sort they advocated. In the case of Lawrence, however, what has now become abundantly, even bewilderingly, clear is how great the disparity was between his extraordinary human means, whether exercised or not, and the ends they appeared to serve. With Lawrence the great question is, *what was he about;* since no definite aim seems to have been his from start to finish except perhaps the cultivation, and subsequent stalemating within himself, of a variety of contradictory gifts. The life-adventure was, to use Sartre's term, entirely "constituting," although without a constituted resolution. In a series of profound letters to Lionel Curtis in the spring of 1923 Lawrence proved, he said, that man was "a civil war"; the "end of this," he continued, "is that man, or mankind, being organic, a natural growth, is unteachable." Elsewhere Lawrence made the metaphor more personal: he himself was "a standing civil war"; and when in *Too True to be Good* Shaw called a character based on Lawrence Private Napoleon Alexander Trotsky Meek, the name alone was meant to convey Shaw's perception that his model contained forces in nearly desperate contradiction to one another. No wonder Lawrence took the strange view that "conscience in healthy men is a balanced sadism."

To say, in Irving Howe's vulgar description, that Lawrence had "a load on his mind" is to cheapen what makes him truly interesting. Lawrence's was a case of vital forces in conflict with themselves, not of a heavy philosophy weighing down a life. He is the best example I know of a special but extreme form of life: the decentered one. Within himself Lawrence assembled tendencies that were highly developed, but he seemed unable to make one permanently dominant over and central to the others. This is one reason why E. M. Forster calls him a "joy for experts"—psychological, political, moral, biographical, or literary—all trying to find what central thing explains him. In attempting to discover and fix him in some place, if only a conceptual one, the experts have missed, I think, what Forster so sensitively noted about Lawrence when Lawrence was at his most accessible, in the cottage he owned at Cloud's Hill. There Lawrence could "reject intimacy without impairing affection":

> I don't know whether I'm at all conveying in these remarks the atmosphere of the place—the happy casualness of it; and the feeling that no one particularly owned it. T. E. had the power of distributing the sense of the possession among all the friends who came there. When Thomas Hardy turned up, for instance, as he did one sunny afternoon, he seemed to come on a visit to us all, and not especially to see his host. Thomas Hardy and Mrs. Hardy came up the narrow stairway into the little brown room and there they were—the guests of us all. To think of Cloud's Hill as T. E.'s home is to get the wrong idea of it. It wasn't his home, it was rather his *pied-à-terre,* the place where his feet touched the earth for a moment, and found rest.

In each of the different activities he practiced Lawrence could devise a *pied-à-terre* for himself. One of the strongest impressions that his *Letters* give is how great his skill was at *seeming* to inhabit a field of endeavor. We see him writing as the professional Arabist, the revolutionary, the intelligence expert, the imperialist politician, the classical archeologist, the classical scholar, the military tactician and administrator, the social critic, the literary critic, the historian, and above all the writer haunted by his own writing—in each of these he found a *pied-à-terre,* and yet in no one did he completely rest and in no one did he completely take possession. R. P. Blackmur goes so far as to say that "Lawrence never produced a character, not even his own."

One way of dealing with the problem that I raised above (what was Lawrence about?) is to try to decide where Lawrence as a phenomenon *took place.* The latest such effort ingenuously gives away its mission in its title[1]—as if to suggest that there, in his *secret* lives, Lawrence can be pinned down—and after "revealing" in a styleless prose a series of often sensational secrets (most of them hinted at, and even exposed, in other works on Lawrence), concludes pointlessly by quoting his epitaph. In many ways Knightley and Simpson (young though they are) are the culmination of almost fifty years of playing the Lawrence-hunting game. In their instance, however, the redoubtable research services of the *London*

Sunday Times were placed at their disposal: no stone left unturned, documents here printed for the first time, interviews conducted in far-away places. The journalistic clichés of self-congratulation, problem solving, and relentless sleuthing are legion. But as psychologists of Lawrence, or as literary critics, they don't—I must borrow Leavis's stern evaluation of C. P. Snow—begin to exist. Their politics, too, must be as baffling to them as they are to me.

What have they really contributed? Two things: one, a view of the precise extent to which Lawrence was enmeshed in a series of imperial dealings and double-dealings with the Near East, and two, the description of an elaborate ritual of flagellation devised by Lawrence shortly after he had extricated himself from the Arabian adventures. The first contribution amply documents the hypocrisy, arrogance, and cynicism of the European powers when dealing with the "brown dominion": as a background to the daily catastrophe enacted in the Near East today the British and French connivances told by the authors filled me with helpless rage. What they simply report, they do well. As to the exact nature of and motive for Lawrence's role, we are left unsatisfied. At first an imperialist, trained by D. G. Hogarth at Oxford on war games and military scholarship, he was a member of the imperialist version of the Cambridge Apostles. As tactician and go-between during the Anglo-Arab alliance that began in 1916, he played a crucially important role. (There is a dissenting Arab version, most persuasively set forth in Suleiman Mousa's *T. E. Lawrence: An Arab View,* Oxford, 1967, that depicts Lawrence as Richard Aldington did—as a liar and a subtle braggart.) The point to be made firmly is that Lawrence was useful in getting the Arabs to a position where they could be *nationally* identified and then pushed around by the Franco-British *entente.* By then, however, Lawrence had characteristically foresworn the whole business: that conclusion, or resolution, to his work he could not tolerate. In reality Lawrence had no politics to speak of: he did have an incredibly exact sense of places and persons, in particular Arabia and the Arabs. More than that, he hated the French irrationally, and apprehended vague, unsettling forces around him. But when it came to the meaning of his work with the Arabs—after it was all over—he could only summarize imaginatively. He put it in this way in the suppressed opening chapter of *The Seven Pillars of Wisdom:*

In these pages the history is not of the Arab movement, but of me in it. It is a narrative of daily life, mean happenings, little people. Here are no lessons for the world, no disclosures to shock peoples. It is filled with trivial things, partly that no one mistake for history the bones from which some day a man may make history, and partly for the pleasure it gave me to recall the fellowship of the revolt. We were fond together, because of the sweep of the open places, the taste of wide winds, the sunlight, and the hopes in which we worked. The morning freshness of the world-to-be intoxicated us. We were wrought up with ideas inexpressible and vaporous, but to be fought for. We lived many lives in those whirling campaigns, never sparing ourselves; yet when we achieved and the new world dawned, the old men came out again and took our victory to re-make in the likeness of the former world they knew. Youth could win, but had not learned to keep: and was pitiably weak against age. We stammered that we had worked for a new heaven and a new earth, and they thanked us kindly and made their peace.

After having been in the midst of the whole imbroglio Lawrence was contented with whatever arrangements Churchill (then Colonial Secretary) made. The Arabs were driven out of Damascus by the French, Iraq and Transjordan were created and endowed upon Feisal and Abdullah respectively, and the ambiguously promised Palestine held in mandate by the British. Nowhere do Knightley and Simpson imply, as they should have, that Lawrence's failure of impulse, his almost hysterical retreat from schemes he concocted (like the one involving the Arabs and the Zionists, who were to supply money at 6 percent) was rooted in his congenital desire to remain always the lonely exception to all plans and men and customs. Here is the pattern in two sentences from *The Seven Pillars:* "I had learned to eat much one time; then to go two, three, or four days without food; and after to over eat. I made it a rule to avoid rules in food; and by a course of exceptions accustomed myself to no custom at all." Nor can one account for this circuit of self-foiling ("I accustomed myself to no custom at all") as due simply to the exigencies of desert warfare. Lawrence wrote the following in a letter of 1923:

I consume the day (and myself) brooding, and making phrases and reading and thinking again, galloping mentally down twenty divergent roads at once, as apart and alone as in Barton Street in my attic. I sleep less than ever, for the quietness of night imposes thinking on me: I eat breakfast only, and refuse every possible distraction and employment and exercise. When my mood gets too hot and I find myself wandering beyond control I pull out my motor-bike and hurl it top-speed through these unfit roads for hour after hour. My nerves are jaded and gone near dead, so that nothing less than hours of voluntary danger will prick them into life: and the "life" they reach then is a melancholy joy at risking something worth exactly 2/9 a day.

The unceasing inner ferment of his later life had developed from his young man's habit of doing remarkable, unexplained things. He rode bicycles uphill and walked them downhill, he would not eat anything on certain days, he learned how to read a newspaper upside down, he knew more (and showed it) about certain subjects than anyone else. He could draw forth compliments of the highest sort from professionals (Liddell Hart compared Lawrence with Marlborough as a brilliant soldier, Lord Wavell said that no one knew more about military history than Lawrence, Churchill acknowledged Lawrence as a very great man, Shaw and E. M. Forster were enthusiastic admirers of his writing) without ever turning himself into a professional.

To some of his friends he admitted that after becoming so terribly famous as a Prince of Mecca a deeper disquiet took him over utterly. This is apparent during the course of *The Seven Pillars*, in which as narrator and prime mover, Lawrence becomes narrator and actor slowly being destroyed by a sense of consuming deceit. He describes, in the book's most notorious chapter, how after being captured by the Turks at Deraa he was forced to submit to torture and rape, as if in punishment for the game he was playing. Knightley and Simpson go over the incident meticulously: was Lawrence, as he admitted to Charlotte Shaw, really buggered? They cannot be sure, but there is no doubt that Lawrence acted later *as if* he had lost what he called his "bodily integrity." The weird arrangement he made with a young Scotsman, John Bruce, to have himself periodically beaten according to orders given by a mysterious Old Man (an invention) ran concurrently with the "mind-suicide" he devised for himself by enrolling in the ranks first of the RAF, then the Tank Corps, then finally the RAF again. Knightley and Simpson are scarcely equipped to do more than tell this story in gross narrative sequence, this story of inner ravagement. They construct a plausible scheme whereby Lawrence subordinated himself to various admired individuals during different periods of his life, but the scheme still does not explain his psychology. For his mode of experience was as much trial by ordeal as it was submission to authority; and overriding both was determined eccentricity. He seemed fascinated by irregulars like Roger Casement, and planned *The Seven Pillars* as a "titanic" book, i.e., big and thoroughly exceptional. He made three or four strong emotional attachments during his life, to a young Arab (probably the S. A. to whom *The Seven Pillars* was dedicated in a cryptic poem), to D. G. Hogarth, and then to Charlotte Shaw (Mrs. G. B. S.), but all of them were of course incapable of development.

One fact about Lawrence has always to be dealt with: his illegitimacy. No critic has ever disputed that as a young boy Lawrence found out that his parents were unmarried, and all have gone on to assume that the discovery wounded him permanently. Knightley and Simpson hedge their ideas about this with some reservations, but in the main they concur. In an otherwise perceptive paper on Lawrence, the Boston psychiatrist John E. Mack (*The American Journal of Psychiatry*, February 8, 1969) suggests that the "profound impact" of his illegitimacy on the young Lawrence was in the main detrimental. Mack does not go far enough, I think. It was the very essence of Lawrence's self to transform this primal weakness into the basis of his deliberate singularity. We can assume that he was shocked at the discovery, but what he did with the discovery—obviously a revelation to him of something that weakened him psychically (not socially as Mack says)—was to convert it into a strength. An illegitimate son is in everything but legal and religious status a real son: every bit of evidence that Mack gives portrays the relation between Lawrence and his mother as a very strong one. Lawrence felt her to be "rather wonderful: but very exciting." Yet he resented, and in fact prevented, her invasion of his integrity. Two things emerge then: a sense of isolation and strength, and second, a gift for extracting from others (initially from his mother) the devotion he deserved *as if* he were a regular, that is a legitimate, object of devotion. The two are inter-connected, for isolation is enforced by illegitimacy, and strength that only lends itself provisionally to either a cause or a person can develop independent of permanent ties. The tie especially to be avoided was the maternal one and all its analogues: that is, any tie that would make Lawrence appear as anything but self-born, self-originating. In relation to his family, to his country, to the Arabs, to most of his friends, this is exactly the way Lawrence stood: strong, alone, and only *as if* one of them.

It is very difficult to carry off that sort of attitude in one's work as a writer. The ties between an author and his writing are definite (he is the final *authority,* no matter what the fiction). Lawrence's complex relations to his writing ultimately centered around the extent to which he did well as an author, the extent to which he was able to translate "the everlasting effort to write" into the best prose. The fastidiousness of his care was astonishing, rivalling that of Flaubert or James; and the prose itself is nothing if not worked and re-worked, sometimes into a terrifying density. Even so he often masked his care in the as-if technique of his personal life. On August 23, 1922, he shrugged himself off to Edward Garnett:

> Don't call me an artist. I said I'd like to be, and that book *The Seven Pillars* is my effort in the manner of an artist: as my war was a decent imitation of soldiering, and my politics chimed well with the notes of politicians. These are all good frauds, and I don't want you to decorate me, for art, over the book in which I explode my legend as man-of-war and statesman!

He was more candid ten years later in a letter to Ernest Altounyan:

> Writing has been my inmost self all my life, and I can never put my full strength into anything else. Yet the same force, I know, put into action upon material things would move them, make me famous and effective. The everlasting effort to write is like trying to fight a feather-bed. In letters there is no room for strength.

And at a late moment (Chapter 99) in *The Seven Pillars* he says the following:

It was a hard task for me to straddle feeling and action. I had had one craving all my life—for the power of self-expression in some imaginative form—but had been too diffuse ever to acquire a technique. At last accident, with perverted humour, in casting me as a man of action had given me a place in the Arab revolt, a theme ready and epic to a direct eye and hand, thus offering me an outlet in literature, the technique-less art. Whereupon I became excited only over mechanism.

What attracted Lawrence to the act of writing was what paradoxically frustrated him, although he was able to recognize how perfectly writing itself, viewed either as tight order, as mechanism, or as having no conclusive force over things, was an analogy for his own personality. The author assumes a voice and a manner that will give him command over his matter only as long as he does not doubt his own authority. When in *The Seven Pillars* Lawrence begins to be primarily conscious of playing a part, of being just an agent, with the Arabs—from that moment he becomes an unwilling transcriber of events. The capture at Deraa exposes his masquerade, and he is punished for it. From then on the author is the victim of his writing, a project, like the Arab revolt, which must be completed despite his efforts to withdraw. Lawrence's failure as a sincere man is balanced by a fanatical sincerity in rendering his own hypocrisy. In short, a standing civil war.

Lawrence's two main works, *The Seven Pillars of Wisdom* (1922) and *The Mint* (1936), are stages in his consciousness of this process. In the first book he is the builder of a movement and the architect of a war: when Damascus is liberated the "house is completed." During the work, however, Lawrence discovers that what he is building is a monument to betrayed hopes (from the Arab viewpoint), and a structure of hypocrisy (his own). That he completes the work at all reveals to him how wedded he is to an effort that dooms him completely to surviving as a triumph of inauthenticity. "For him," André Malraux writes, "art insensibly supplanted action. The Arab epic became in his mind the medium for a grandiose expression of human emptiness."[2] In the next work, which corresponds to the last part of his life, Lawrence has given himself up entirely to a machine that mints replicas; his role is no longer that of author-initiator, but of author transformed into common coin. The two books together then portray the destiny of an exceptional individuality, committed simultaneously to its own subjection and to a unique record of that subjection.

The gradually filled out account of Lawrence's life that we get in books such as Knightley and Simpson's is not, I think, going to make the man's special psychology become more accessible. In the end Lawrence's mind took writing as its province, there to begin, to flourish for a while, and die. Or, as he once said, to represent "the truth behind Freud." For in writing, exceptionality—Lawrence's goal—can be maintained even as normal human ties and relations (even those between a man and himself) dissolve. It was Lawrence's human tragedy that his exceptionality formed itself into a circle of pitiless antitheses, barely held in check by the desire to articulate them in prose. Again Malraux:

> The subject of the book he believed he was writing had become the struggle of a being lashed without mercy by the scorn which he felt for certain appeals of his own nature, by a fatality acknowledged, with terrible humiliation, as a permanent failure of his will,—against the passionate resolution of this same being to kill his demon with great conquering strokes of lucidity. *I wrote my will across the sky in stars . . .*

Lawrence will not endure as guerrilla fighter, political militant, or even psychological oddity. But as a writer for whom writing replaced character with a dynamic of ceaseless and self-nullifying activity, he will remain exemplary. The body was held in contempt ("I have wished myself to know that any deliberate exercise of display of the body is prostitution; our created shapes being only our accidents until by taking pleasure or pains in them we make them our fault"), the mind was rebellious in an originality that admitted no progenitor. His final province, "the processes of air," overcame even his personality, until he could *write* from isolation into a fellowship as intimate as it was distant:

> We race over in the first dawn to the College's translucent swimming pool, and dive into the elastic water which fits our bodies closely as a skin:—and we belong to that too. Everywhere a relationship: no loneliness any more. *(The Mint)*

5

Arabic Prose and Prose Fiction After 1948

Reading is inevitably a complex, comparative process. A novel in particular, if it is not to be read reductively as an item of sociopolitical evidence, involves the reader with itself not only because of its writer's skill but also because of other novels. All novels belong to a family, and any reader of novels is a reader of this complex family to which they all belong. *How* they belong, however, is a very difficult problem to settle in cases where the novel in question is not in the central Western European or American tradition. In that tradition there is a recognizable genealogy, going as far back as *The Odyssey* and *Don Quixote,* but concentrated primarily in the eighteenth, nineteenth, and the main part of the twentieth centuries. What we have become accustomed to is the novel as a line to which non-European or non-American novels in the modern period offer puzzling alternatives. Are these novels "imitations" (which, minus the euphemism, means colonial copies of "the great tradition")? Are they original works in their own right? Are they neither?

Such alternatives, I think, confuse us more than they help us to read with understanding. Comparing novels of equal merit but from different traditions cannot mean, and never has meant, judging one over the other as more original or more of a copy. All literature, in a certain narrow mimetic sense, is a "copy" of something; originality is really the art of recombining the familiar. And this is precisely the premise upon which the novel is based. Not only do novels "imitate" reality, but they also imitate each other: this is the natural condition of their existence and the secret of their persistence as a form. But if the Western European novel has a long linear genealogy linking its members to each other (in ways we shall presently examine), in the more recent novelistic traditions, of which the Arabic is one, both the history and the structure of the form are different. The difference is primarily a matter of the form's existence (shorter in the Arabic novel, which effectively begins in this century), of the circumstances of history, and of the aesthetic method.

In a short introduction of this kind one can scarcely begin to take in all these differences; nor, for that matter, can one expect to treat the Arabic novel with the detail or care it requires. But I shall try to suggest first how the Arabic novel in its history and development redistributes, or disperses, the conditions under which the Western European novel has existed. This will take up the opening part of my discussion, after which I shall describe the exigencies of contemporary Arabic prose, particularly those operating after 1948. I hope thus to provide the reader with some historical and aesthetical service when he compares, as he must, Arabic writing with other sorts.

In the two and a half centuries of its existence the Western European novel has been the creation of both a particular historical development and the rise, then the triumph, of the middle class. Not less an institution for all the intricacies of its method, the variety of its subject matter, the powerful entrancement of its psychological and aesthetical structures, and the sheer detail of its vision, the novel is the most time-bound and circumstantial as well as the most universal of all postclassical literary forms. Yet history *in* the novel and history *of* the novel—what the novel in Stendhal's image reflects of life as in a mirror and what the novel's own internal history as a form of literature is—these are very different things.[1] The first, I think, is a constant pressure: every novelist is of his time, however much his imagination may take him beyond it. Each novelist articulates a consciousness of his time that he shares with the group of which historical circum-

stances (class, period, perspective) make him a part. Thus even in its irreducible singularity the novelistic work *is itself* a historical reality—one
whose articulation is doubtless more fine, more circumstanced and idiomatic with regard to its moment, than other human experiences.
Narrative, in short, is the historical mode as it is most traditionally understood. But what makes it possible to distinguish Marx's *The Class
Struggles in France* from Flaubert's *L'Education sentimentale*—both works
whose subject is the 1848 revolution—is the history of the type of narrative incorporated within the narrative. Marx's belongs eccentrically
to a tradition of analysis and polemic taken in part from journalism;
Flaubert's, no less eccentric in its own way, no less polemic, stands
squarely within an institutional tradition, the novel's, whose language,
pressures, and audience Flaubert assumes—and puts to work on his behalf—as Marx cannot assume for his work.

Between the middle of the eighteenth century and, roughly, the first
third of this century, to write a novel meant that it was impossible for
the novelist to ignore the history and tradition of the form. I put the
statement in this negative way in order to emphasize the extraordinarily fertile polarity existing within each good novel: the polarity between the claims of the novel's internal history and those of the
novelist's individual imagination. In no small measure to write a novel
was, for Dickens, Eliot, Flaubert, Balzac, to have received and further
sustained the institution of prose fiction. Just as their subject matter
is frequently a variation on the family romance, with a hero or heroine
attempting to create his or her own destiny against the bonds of
family, so too the great classical novels of the nineteenth century are
themselves a massive aesthetic dynasty to which even the most powerful imaginations are necessarily apprentices or children. The relation
of Tolstoy to Stendhal, or of Dostoevski to Balzac and Dickens, exactly
illustrates the manner in which even the most original imaginations
considered themselves heirs of an aesthetic past that they were extending into their own times. Thus each novel imitates not only reality
but also every other novel. It was *because of* his imagination that
Tolstoy could benefit from, by imitating, the novel's own history as
represented to him by Stendhal; for the particular marvel of prose fiction was its power to employ creatively its own genealogy over and over.
This is especially true of every great novel, whose novelty was (perhaps

surprisingly) in making the transmitted institutions of prose fiction serve as a defense against the unmediated urgency either of individual imagination or of the historical moment. Since, as Lukács has said, "the novel is the epic of a world that has been abandoned by God," then "the mental attitude of the novel is virile maturity, and the characteristic structure of its matter is discreteness, the separation between interiority and adventure."[2] The novel's secular world is maintained by an author whose maturity depends on distinctions, inherited from the novel's history, between pure subjective fantasy and pure factual chronicle, between directionless brooding and an unlimited episodic repetition.

In all these ways, then, time—or rather temporality grasped in the complex ways I have been discussing—is the novel's life: as historical moment and as history of the form, temporality makes the world's pressure amenable to verbal structure. Yet such a life in Western Europe and, to a certain extent, in nineteenth-century America has enjoyed the broad support of readers and critics. They too contribute to the novel as an institution. From Fielding's digressive essays on the novel in his novels, through Sterne's technical brilliance, through Stendhal's and Balzac's critical work, and on into the commentary and metacommentary of such writers as Proust, Henry James, and James Joyce, the novel has employed novelists as critics. Moreover it has produced critics both professional and amateur—one remembers Dickens' avid periodical subscribers who always knew what it was they wanted from the novelist—sustaining the discipline, and the reality, of the form. This interplay between reader and writer has been unique in prose fiction: it has its origin perhaps in Part Two of Cervantes' *Don Quixote*, where the errant protagonist encounters men and women who have read Part One and expect—indeed, demand—certain actions from him. In one sense readers of fiction through the years of its maturity have played almost as great a role in the form's flourishing as have the writers.

A dramatically different situation obtains in the history of the modern Arabic novel. The twentieth-century novel in Arabic has a variety of forebears, none of them formally and dynastically prior and useful as, say, in the rather directly useful way that Fielding antedates Dickens. Arabic literature before the twentieth century has a rich assortment of narrative forms—*qissa, sira, hadith, khurafa, ustura, khabar, nadira, maqama*—of which no one seems to have become, as the European novel did, the major narrative type. The reasons for this are extremely complex, and they cannot occupy us here (elsewhere I have speculated on one reason for this difference between Arabic-Islamic and European prose fiction: whereas the former literary tradition views reality as plentiful, complete, and divinely directed, the latter sees reality as radically incomplete, authorizing innovation, and problematic).[3] The fact remains, however, that there is a modern Arabic novel which, during the twentieth century, has undergone numerous and interesting transformations. Today it has produced a very wide variety of talents, styles, critics, readers, all mostly unknown or deliberately ignored outside the Middle East; surely the ruling Western obsession with Arabs exclusively (or nearly so) as a political problem is largely to blame for this lamentable failure in knowledge. There is less of an excuse for this failure today, as Trevor Le Gassick's sensitive translations (e.g., of Naguib Mahfouz' *Midaq Alley,* Halim Barakat's *Days of Dust*) and those by Denys Johnson-Davies begin to gain the currency they surely deserve.[4]

Yet the peculiarly fascinating background of issues formal and issues historical and psychological faced by the contemporary Arabic novelist needs some elucidation, particularly if one takes the period after 1948, and that after 1967, as shaping an intelligible historical period for the novelistic imagination. Particularly also if this period is considered as constitutive of the common subject matter presented to any and all writers in the Arab East, not simply novelists, during the past quarter century. Even more particularly if the course of the European novel is kept in mind as a *comparative fact* with which the Arabic novel *produces* valuable differences. I shall try to present this period, then, with its two great demarcations in 1948 and 1967, from the point of view of any Arab wishing to write. Allowing for a modicum of opportunism and bad writing during the years since 1948, I believe that Arabs who wrote (novels, plays, poetry, history, philosophy, political polemic, etc.) undertook a fundamentally heroic enterprise, a project of self-definition and autodidactic struggle unexampled on such a scale since World War II. Consider first the setting that offered itself as historical moment. After decades of internal struggle against political chaos and foreign domination, a struggle in which politico-national identity was still at its most precarious initial stage—with religion, demography, modernity, language en-meshed confusingly with each other—Arabs everywhere were forced ad-ditionally to confront as their own problem, taking an especially provocative form, one of the greatest and still unsolved problems of Western civilization, the Jewish question. To say that 1948 made an ex-traordinary cultural and historical demand on the Arab is to be guilty of the crassest understatement. The year and the processes which it culmi-nated represent an explosion whose effects continue to fall unrelentingly into the present. No Arab, however armed he was at those and later mo-ments by regional or tribal or religious nationalism, could ignore the event. Not only did 1948 put forth unprecedented challenges to a collec-tivity already undergoing the political evolution of several European cen-turies compressed into a few decades: this after all was mainly a difference of detail between the Arab East and all other Third World countries, since the end of colonialism meant the beginning and the tra-vail of uncertain national selfhood. But 1948 put forward a monumental enigma, an existential mutation for which Arab history was unprepared.

An Egyptian might say that the events of 1948 pressed on the Palestinian Arab the most closely; so too might an Iraqi, a Lebanese, a Sudanese. Yet no Arab could say that in 1948 he was in any serious way detached or apart from the events in Palestine. He might reasonably say that he was shielded from Palestine; but he could not say—because his language and his religious, cultural tradition implicated him at every turn—that he was any less a loser, an Arab, as a result of what happened in Palestine. Furthermore nothing in his history, that is, in the repertory or vocabulary provided to him by his historical experi-ence, gave him an adequate method for representing the Palestine drama to himself. Arab nationalism, Islamic traditionalism, regional creeds, small-scale communal or village solidarities—all these stopped short of the general result of Zionist success and the particular expe-rience of Arab defeat. No concept seemed large enough, no language precise enough to take in the common fate. What happened could not be put down to a flaw in the Arab character (since no such character was ever articulated), nor to a divine decree against the faithful, nor to a trivial accident in a faraway place.

The magnitude of such events is indicated, I think, in one of the words most usually employed to describe them, the Arabic word *nakba*.

Its most celebrated use is in the title of Constantine Zurayk's 1948 book, *Ma'na al-nakba* [The meaning of the disaster];[5] yet even in Zurayk's work, which advances an interpretation of the Zionist victory as a challenge to the whole of Arab modernity, another of the meanings of *nakba* is in play. For the word suggests in its root that affliction or disaster is somehow brought about by, and hence linked by necessity to, deviation, a veering out of course, a serious deflection away from a forward path. (This incidentally is in marked contrast to another, less commonly employed word for 1967: *naksa,* which suggests nothing more radical than a relapse, a temporary setback, as in the process of recovery from an illness.) The development of Zurayk's argument in his book led him, as it was to lead many other writers since 1948, to interpret *al-nakba* as a rupture of the most profound sort. It is true that Zionism exposed the Arabs' disunity, lack of technological culture, political unpreparedness, and so on; more significant, however, was the fact that the disaster caused a rift to appear between the Arabs and the very possibility of their historical continuity as a people. So strong was the deflection, or the deviation, from the Arabs' persistence in time up to 1948, that the issue for the Arabs became whether what was "natural" to them—their continued national duration in history—would be possible at all.

There is an interesting paradox here, and it is one that would inform Arab writing thereafter. Zurayk was saying in fact that the deviation was so strong as to put the Arabs, as a people, in historical question. Yet he was also saying that the disaster had revealed to the Arabs that their history had itself not yet made of them a nation. So from the perspective of the past, the Arabs would seem to have swerved from the path toward national identity, union, and so on; from the perspective of the future, the disaster raised the specter of national fragmentation or extinction. The paradox is that both of these observations hold, so that at the intersection of past and future stands the disaster, which on the one hand reveals the deviation from *what has yet to happen* (a unified, collective Arab identity) and on the other reveals the possibility of *what may happen* (Arab extinction as a cultural or national unit). The true force then of Zurayk's book is that it made clear the problem of the *present,* a problematic site of contemporaneity, occupied and blocked from the Arabs. For the Arabs to act knowingly was to *create* the present, and this was a battle of restoring historical continuity, healing a rupture, and—most important—forging a historic possibility.

It is for all these reasons that a very high premium is placed, in Zurayk's argument, upon what he called the creative elite. The elite's role, essentially considered, was to articulate the present in the precise historical and realistic terms which, as we have seen, the disaster threatened with obliteration. To speak or to write in Arabic was to articulate not only the lingua franca but also the reality—the possibility of an Arab contemporaneity—very precariously held within the present. Without referring back to Zurayk's book of 1948, Anwar Abdel Malek, the Egyptian sociologist, powerfully elaborated on the nature, and the language, of struggle. As recently as the seventies, Abdel Malek was arguing that Arab-Islamic civilization, although prey to economic and political imperialism, was most seriously endangered, in the long run, by its susceptibility to cultural imperialism, the principal feature of which was to impose on the Arabs a sort of impediment whose purpose was to prevent direct ties between them and Asia and Africa. Unless Arab culture, employing the full resources of its *specificity* (the word has great urgency for Abdel Malek), could participate freely in its own self-making, it would be as if it did not exist.[6]

In such a context, then, the role of any writer who considered himself seriously engaged in the actuality of his time—and few writers during the period since 1948 considered themselves otherwise engaged—was, first of all, as a producer of thought and language whose radical intention was to guarantee survival to what was in imminent danger of extinction. Beginning with the Egyptian Revolution of 1952, the rise of movements of national liberation provided opportunities for a dialectical vision in which the crises of the present would become the cornerstones of the future. Writing therefore became a historical act and, according to the Egyptian literary critic Ghali Shukri, after 1967, an act of resistance. If before 1948 the Arab novel could be described *sui generis* as a novel of historical recapitulation, then after 1948 it became a novel of historical and social development.[7] This is especially evident in the Egyptian novel. Even though a so-called romantic (i.e., sentimental, backward-looking) alternative existed for writers such as Yusuf el-Siba'i, the large theme of most Egyptian novels after 1948 was, as Shukri observed, the near-tragic conflict between a protagonist and some "outside" force.[8] The imperatives for the writer were to increase the refinement and detail of his portrayals; or, as Raja al-Naqqash phrased in a polemical letter to Nazik al-Mala'ikah (the Iraqi poet), writing was not and could not be free: it had to put itself at life's service. This was another way of identifying the writer's role directly with the problematics of Arab contemporaneity.[9]

The Arab writer's role was further aggravated by the internal conflict he experienced between his particular regional identity and his transregional or Arab-Islamic ambition. Yet even in such vastly different assertions of regional identity as Hussayn Fawzi's work on Egyptian civilization, or Said Aql's on Lebanese poetics, or in the ideologies of such movements as the Syrian Nationalist party and the Ba'ath, there remained, always, the web of circumstance that enmeshed every Arab, from Algeria to the Gulf. So strong was it—as I described it above in terms of a paradoxical present—that the primary task seemed always to be one of *making* the present in such a way as, once again, to *make* it in touch with past authenticity and future possibility. The past is usually identified with loss, the future with uncertainty. But as for the present, it is a constant experience, a *scene* to be articulated with all the resources of language and vision. Even when the writer's aim is to render the present as disaster, the more so after the war of 1967, it is the *scene* as the irreducible form of the present which the writer must affirm.

Here we must remark another complexity. Just as there is no traditional Arab novel, there is no real Arab drama, or at least no long-standing and unbroken dramatic tradition. There are considerable dramatic attainments, however—mostly, as is the case with the novel, of the period after World War I. So here, too, when one speaks of a scene, there is a kind of eccentricity implied, unique to the writer in Arabic. What the dramatic and prose scene have in common, first of all, is the sense of *contested space*. Whether it is a page or the proscenium arch theater, the writer fills it with language struggling to maintain a presence. Such an attitude leads to very definite technical and aesthetic consequences. If the unit of composition is the scene, and not the period (prologue, middle, end, in the Aristotelian sense), then the connection between scenes is tenuous. There is a tendency in fact to episodism, and the repetition of scenes, as if the rhythmic succession of scenes can become a substitute for quasi-organic continuity. It is a striking fact that the principal successes of artistic prose and drama, even from before 1948—for example, Taha Hussayn's *Al-ayyam,* Tawfiq al-Hakim's *Yawmiyat na'ib fil aryaf,* the comedies of Naguib al-Rihani, the films of Kamal Salim and Niyazi Mustapha, the works of Khalil Gibran, Jabra Jabra's novella *Surakh fi laylin tawil*—are formally a succession of scenes held together more in the style of a journal than in that of the Aristotelian model. Unlike the journal, however, these works are built out of discretely shaped scenes in which a continuous play of substitutions takes place; entrances and appearances, for instance, play the role of ontological affirmation. Conversely, absences and exits seem to threaten extinction or a quasi death. To be in a scene is to displace extinction, to substitute life for the void. Thus the very act of telling, narrating, uttering, guarantees actuality; here the Islamic tradition of the *isnad* (support, witness) is vitalized and put to a definite aesthetic purpose.

The author's persona is very frequently the *spectator,* engaged enough in what he is telling about to be a character, disengaged enough to be able to point out the abuses, the comedy or melodrama of what is taking place before him in the narration. Tawfiq al-Hakim's persona often speaks of *masrah al-hayat* ("the theater of life"), which is less a figure of speech than an aesthetic method. Each episode is a scene of enactment whose importance is revealed to be not that it took place (all of the scenes are scenes of habitual occurrences) but that it is being recorded and being narrated to someone; in the action of narration and transmission, the habitual is exposed for the often lurid abuse of humanity that it is. Even the abuse itself conforms to the pattern. Once, for example, the narrator is told a story—an episode within an episode—by a doctor who, after being summoned to a poor village patient, discovers her lying on her back with a baby's arm protruding from her womb. He learns from the old midwife that after the fetus' death three days before, she stuffed the woman's womb with straw, and the two of them waited patiently under God's protection *(sitr rabbuna).*[10] Since the woman has died, and since *sitr* means literally to disguise or shelter with a screen or curtain, the entire episode doubles over itself as it sets in motion, through narrative enactment, the interplay of scene, substitution, recurrence, absence, death, and, finally, scene again.

The emphasis on scenes therefore is intensified, is made more urgent, after 1948: a scene formally translates the critical issues at stake in the Arab world. This is not a matter of proving how literature or writing *reflects* life, nor is it confirmation of an allegorical interpretation of Arab reality: for, unfortunately, these approaches to modern Arabic writing are endemic to most of the very scarce Western analyses of the literature.[11] What is of greater interest is how the scene *is itself* the very problem of Arabic literature and writing after the disaster of 1948: the scene does not merely reflect the crisis, or historical duration, or the paradox of the present. Rather, the scene *is contemporaneity* in its most problematic and even rarified form. In no place can one see this more effectively than in prose directly concerned with the events in Palestine. Here is the opening scene of Ghassan Kanafani's novella *Rijal fil shams,* certainly his finest work and one of the subtlest and most powerful of modern novellas.

> Abu Qais laid his chest on the dirt wet with dew. Immediately the earth began to throb: a tired heart's beats, flooding through the sand grains, seeping into his very innermost being . . . and every time he threw his chest against the dirt he felt the same palpitation, as if the earth's heart had not stopped since that first time he laid himself down, since he tore a hard road from the deepest hell toward an approaching light, when he once told of it to his neighbor who shared the cultivation of a field with him, there on the land he had left ten years ago. His reply was derision: "What you hear is the sound of your own heart plastered to the earth." What tiresome malice! And the smell, how does he explain that? He inhaled it, as it swam through his brow, then passed fadingly into his veins. Every time he breathed as he lay supine he imagined himself drinking in the smell of his wife's hair as she had stepped out after bathing it in cold water. . . . That haunting fragrance of a woman's hair, washed in cold water and, still damp, spread out to dry, covering her face. . . . The same pulse: as if a small bird was sheltered between your cupped palms.[12]

The scene continues as Abu Qais slowly awakens to a realization of his exact surroundings, somewhere near the estuary of the Tigris and the

Euphrates; he is there awaiting arrangements to be made to take him illegally into Kuwait, where he hopes to find work. As in the passage quoted above, he will "understand" his location, and the scene's setting in the present, by way of a recollection out of his past: his teacher's voice, in a Palestinian village schoolhouse, intoning the geography lesson, a description of the estuary. Abu Qais' own present is an amalgam of disjointed memory with the gathering intrusive force of his intolerable situation: he is a refugee, with a family, forced to seek employment in a country whose blinding sun signifies the universal indifference to his fate. We will discover that the approaching light is a proleptic reference to the novella's final episode: along with two other Palestinian refugees, Abu Qais is being smuggled into Kuwait in the empty belly of a tanker-truck. The three of them are left in the truck while the border inspection is being negotiated. Under the sun the three die of suffocation, unable even to give a sign.

This passage is one of the numerous scenes into which the work is divided. In almost every one, the present, temporally speaking, is unstable and seems subject to echoes from the past, to synaesthesia as sight gives way to sound or smell and as one sense interweaves with another, to a combination of defensiveness against the harsh present and the protection of some particularly cherished fragment of the past. Even in Kanafani's style—which seems clumsy in my translation, but I thought it important to render the complex sentence structure as exactly as I could—one is unsure of the points in time to which the center of consciousness (one of the three men) refers. In the passage above, "every time" blends into "since that first time," which also seems to include, obscurely, "there on the land he had left ten years ago." Those three clauses are dominated figuratively by the image of tearing a road out of darkness toward the light. Later, during the main part of the novella, we will remark that much of the action takes place in the dusty street of an Iraqi town where the three men, independent of each other, petition, plead, bargain with "specialists" to take them across the border. The main conflict in the book therefore turns about that contest in the present: impelled by exile and dislocation, the Palestinian must carve a path for himself in existence, which is by no means a "given" or stable reality for him. Like the land he left, his past seems broken off just before it could bring forth fruit; yet the man has family, responsibilities, life itself to answer to, in the present. Not only is his future uncertain; even his present situation increases in difficulty as he barely manages to maintain his balance in the swirling traffic of the dusty street. Day, sun, the present: those are at once there, hostile, and goads to him to move on out of the sometimes misty, sometimes hardened protection of memory and fantasy. When the men finally move out of their spiritual desert into the present, toward the future which they reluctantly but necessarily choose, they will die—invisibly, anonymously, killed in the sun, in the same present that has summoned them out of their past and taunted them with their helplessness and inactivity.

For Kanafani a scene is centrally the convenience given to the writer by the general novelistic tradition; what he uses in order to present the action, therefore, is a device which, displaced from the tradition that can take it for granted, ironically comments on the rudimentary struggles facing the Palestinian. He must make the present; unlike the Stendhalian or Dickensian case, the present is not an imaginative luxury but a literal existential necessity. A scene barely accommodates him. If anything, then, Kanafani's use of the scene turns it from a novelistic device which anyone can recognize into a *provocation*. The paradox of contemporaneity for the Palestinian is very sharp indeed. If the present cannot be "given" simply (that is, if time will not allow him either to differentiate clearly between his past and his present or to connect them, it is because the disaster, unmentioned except as an episode hidden within episodes, prevents continuity), it is intelligible only as *achievement*. Only if the men can manage to pull themselves out of limbo into Kuwait can they *be* in any sense more than mere biological duration, in which earth and sky are an uncertain confirmation of *general* life. Because they must live—in order ultimately to die—the scene prods them into action, which in turn will provide writer and reader with the material for "fiction." This is the other side of the paradox: a scene is made for the novel, but out of material whose portrayal in the present signifies the psychological, political, and aesthetic result of the disaster. The scene *provokes* Abu Qais; when he achieves action because of it, he has made a readable document and, ironically, the inevitability of his extinction. The distances between language and reality are closed.

As I have said, the immediacy of Kanafani's subject matter tends to give his scenes their subtly provocative character. Yet between 1948 and 1967 some of the same urgency informs other work using the scenic method as I have described it. In Naguib Mahfouz' fiction, certainly the most magisterial of novelistic achievements in the Arab world, whether in the *Trilogy* (1956–57) or *Awlad Haritna* (1959) or the collections of short stories, episodism is everywhere apparent. The scene dramatizes *periodicity*, that is, the active historical process by which Arab reality, if it is to have existential status, must form itself. That reality's intermittent nature, which in Mahfouz' postnaturalistic phase of the early sixties has been called *al-wujudiyah al-waqi 'iyah* ("realistic existentialism"),[13] developed more and more insistently into an aesthetic of minimalism and shattering effect; its complement was, I think, the quasi-Hegelian comic drama—or rather *dramatism,* since the play was in a sense the subject of the play—*Al-farafir* (1964), by Yousef Idriss. There are similarities also between these works and Hussayn Fawzi's *Sindibad misri,* subtitled *Jawlah fi rihab al-tarikh* [Travels through the expanses of history]. Hussayn himself speaks of the cinematic techniques he uses in a book whose aim, he says, could not have been achieved before 1952: to show how Egypt is a maker of civilizations. Hussein's method is episodic, so that each incident selected as an illustration of Egypt's character is a scene confirming Egypt's historical destiny as its own self-maker.

It is worth mentioning digressively that no one who has seen an Arabic "popular" film from before 1967 can have failed to notice the central, and sometimes seemingly irrelevant, presence of the cabaret or theater scene. Nor in the popular Rihani stage comedies is the carefully prepared scene of verbal attack *(radh),* rather like a human cockfight, any less *de rigueur.* Such scenes are often dismissed as catering to some vague mass cult (of voyeurism? lower-class sensationalism?), while their obvious connection with the preciously refined *maqama* tradition passes unnoticed. This tradition is the one of formal storytelling (out of which *A Thousand and One Nights* develops), among whose characteristics is the dramatization of the tale's telling. Under the influence of a highly important event that is incompletely understood and difficult to apprehend aesthetically, the story-telling tradition tends to become highly self-conscious; the event is 1948, and art turns back on itself to become meta-art. The scene is the location of the nexus between art and its objects: it knits time and character together in an exhibited articulation. Pushed to the surface thus, articulation guarantees survival, as Scheherazade's nightly recital in *The Arabian Nights* postpones her own death. The impending, or surrounding, disaster is displaced by a human duration continuously being made; the effect is not unlike the technique in Conrad's narratives, where an important event seems always to require the setting up of a narrative occurrence such as men swapping yarns, a circle of friends listening to a story-teller, and so on.

Gamal Abdel Nasser was to make the Pirandellian motif in all this very explicit. Arab history, he wrote in his *Philosophy of the Revolution*, was like a role in search of an actor to play it or, in the terms I have been using, like a scene in search of a drama. These metatheatrical images force history into two temporalities: one, that of actuality in which the disaster has taken place, a temporality of discontinuity or rupture; and, two, a temporality constituting the scene as a site for a restorative history. Thus *that* something gets articulated, constituted, and set tends to be more important than *what* is articulated: this is a common enough motif in modern literature, where the conditions of drama or narrative are in some ways more important than the subject of narration. According to Abdullah Laroui this also happens to coincide with a motif in the history of Islam, which, he speculates, is seductive because system and structure compel individualized acts into patterns.[14]

The tension between system and occurrence underlies the tension between scene and the drama of which it is a part. For Arabic prose after 1948 the political issue underlying this tension is everywhere latent. It means, for example, that there may be no whole linking these parts, no "Arab" idea, identity, history, collectivity, destiny, drama, novel giving the diachrony of scene-events any synchronic intention, aim, structure, meaning. The present may after all be *only* that, perhaps not a consequence of the past and certainly not a basis for the future. I raise this cluster of problems here in order to emphasize the investigative character of Arabic writing during the post-1948 period. For problematic doubts did not mean stupefaction. All the evidence we have points to wide-ranging intellectual and aesthetical activity. My point is that the formal characteristics which I have been describing do not merely reflect passively on the problems: they are those problems in a very privileged, engrossing way. Thus the sustained tension between the present and either the past or the future creates the scene which, in turn, is (not a reflection of) the present in a form of raised tension with the past and the future. The dialectic is constant, and enriching.

The effects of the war of 1967 predictably were to recall 1948. Zurayk, for instance, published a book entitled *Ma'na al-nakba mujada-dan* [The meaning of the disaster renewed]. The scene was transformed from a theatrical one into an arena of fairly immediate gladiatorial struggle. The relations between spectator and action were variously redefined now. In some post-1967 works, notably those by Sadek al-Azm—and even though he was writing philosophical and/or political polemic it is hard to overlook the sheer theatricality of his performance—the author entered the arena, identified the combatants, and engaged them.[15] Such an optic took it that the war of 1967 was the first truly international war fought by the Arabs in modern times. This was a war fought as much in the media as on the battlefields; the struggle was felt to be *immediately historical* because it was fought simultaneously in the scenes created by actuality and those created by television, radio, newspapers.

In this sense everything about the war was historical, just as, according to Lukács, the Napoleonic wars for the first time in European history had engaged the masses in a truly international way.[16] Hitherto wars had been distant and exclusively the affair of armies. Now everyone was involved. Everything thought or written about the war had the status of historical act; whether as a soldier, a writer, or an ordinary citizen, the Arab became part of a scene which, in the case of al-Azm, was claimed to have been largely the creation of passivity, backwardness, the mediations of custom, religion, and ossified tradition. Therefore the only progressive role to be played was that of an activist-author forcing the Arab to recognize his role in the struggle. No one could be, or really ever was, a spectator: the present was not a project *to be* undertaken; it was now. Whether he discussed the *fahlawi* personality, or the consternation caused in Egypt by the visitation of the Virgin, al-Azm saw the Arabs fighting themselves, and, whether they admitted it or not, he was going to prove it to them by fighting them.

The didactic, even pedantic, quality of al-Azm's prose should be seen as part of a burgeoning general interest in precision. The Egyptian critic Shukry Ayyad has said that beyond the first cries of anguish and denial after June 10, writers began to make it their task to render the exact detail of everyday life. They hoped thus to diagnose those causes of the defeat that could be remedied. Yet Ayyad believed that a perhaps unforeseen effect of such writing was actually to intensify the anguish *(qalaq)* of modern man in the technological age. Some writers therefore treat Arab reality as a marvelous enigma *(lughz bari')* to be deciphered; others draw attention to the aesthetic skill with which reality was being portrayed.[17] And indeed the proliferation of "absurdist" drama and narrative testifies to Ayyad's point. In Raymond Gebara's *Taht ri'ayit zaqqur* the scene is an occasion for mockery; as in al-Azm's work, quotations from "correct" sources are employed as starting points for sarcastic dissociation. Hamlet becomes a whining Arab boy, and so on. Yet unlike al-Azm's writing as a whole, which has an active intellectual integrity, Gebara's aesthetic of self-deprecating quotation conceals quietism of the most extreme sort. And it is this quietism that finally makes for the differences between intellectual activism and absurdist pastiche; the former is self-criticism based on revolutionary presupposition; the latter is not. Al-Azm's books are linked directly to the political importance of radical analysis and of radical movements, the Palestinian groups in particular. In their verbal form, as well as in their fate, intellectual activism and absurdist pastiche are rejections of the present: for both, the scene is most usefully understood as immediate history in spite of Arab failure. Thus a new paradox, one that turns the Arab into a world-historical individual because of his specialized talent for ineptitude, is born.

Since 1967, however, there has been no unanimity on the principal thesis which that disaster supposedly proved, the existence of a collective Arab identity. While it is true that the war involved the Arabs as a whole, the very particularism spurring the writer to capture every detail of life also led him to make precise differentiations between, say, local experience and collective experience. In a curious way, therefore, the rise in prominence of Palestinian writers after 1967 (Mahmoud

Darwish, Samih el-Kassem, Kana-fani, Fadwa Touqan, and others), a tendency which accompanied the enormous dissemination of political interest in specifically Palestinian activity, was only one aspect of the change that also produced a more intense focus upon the distinctions between the varieties of Arab experience. This, I think, is notably true in Egypt. Certainly the most brilliant writing produced during the past generation, Mahfouz' collection of short stories and playlets *Taht al-mizalla* (1969), was written in the months immediately following the 1967 June War. As with most of Mahfouz' other work, the collection is composed of short scenes, although now the scene has a special new character: instead of being part of a prospective continuity in the making, each individual scene is shot through with the desolation of extreme, and hence Egyptian, loneliness. The scene therefore is a sort of national clinical process. Things take place with the utmost medical clarity, yet their general opacity, their terrifying impingement on every ordinary citizen, their defiance of ordinary, lay understanding, the swift succession of inexplicably triggered events, all these cut off the action (always minutely Egyptian) from understanding or, more interestingly, from the possibility of a universal Arab explanation.

Mahfouz' world turns Egypt into a vast hospital whose boundaries are the various military fronts, and whose patients are, equally, soldiers and citizens. The author presents his cases silently; no explanations or apologies are given. A curious, perhaps obsessive, theme in this collection as well as in Mahfouz' 1973 novel of no-war no-peace Egypt, *Hubb taht al-matar,* is the cinema. The scenes in which films are being made, where directors are being sought for their help in solving some specially difficult problem of interpretation, in which citizens are seen changing into actors, are common. When Egyptian involvement in Palestine or Yemen is mentioned, it is always by way of journalism or the cinema. Arab problems must be mediated by the layers of Egyptian reality that surround everyday life like the walls of a clinic, or the protection of a cinema studio.

Hanging over all the writing produced after 1967 is, nevertheless, the sense of profound disappointment. This is true of Mahfouz' work, of Halim Barakat's fiction, of al-Azm's polemics, and, indeed, of all those works either portraying or explaining the sudden speed of the disaster, its astonishing surprise, and the catastrophic lack of Arab resistance.

No Arab can have been immune from the feeling that his modern history, so laboriously created—scene by scene—would prove so easy to brush aside in the test. The almost incredible outpouring of print after 1967 suggests a vast effort at reconstructing that history and that reality. Of necessity the first stage is the one represented in Barakat's fiction, the one that corresponds to the stage of disillusion whose classic will always be Flaubert's *L'Education sentimentale*, the great Parisian example of post-1848 European disappointment. Like Flaubert, Barakat, in *Days of Dust*, examines responses in Beirut to an Arab political calamity which ought to be understood in terms of failure, not in those of an enemy's victory. Unlike Flaubert, Barakat shows a genuine kindness to his cast of actors; he has none of Flaubert's bitter indictment of an entire generation. Whereas in *L'Education sentimentale* sentiment and fantasy are associated with the impotent failure at which Frederic Moreau and Deslauriers finally arrive, in Barakat's novel sentiment is employed to heighten the human poignancy of the disaster. For Barakat disappointment and dislocation can always be made intelligible if they are commented on with reference to justificatory passion. The images of sea and fire, as well as the sequences using the *Flying Dutchman* figure, are instruments of clarification employed to increase the disaster's universality, and its tragic shades.

Barakat's use of the scene shares with Mahfouz' technique the interest in intense particularity; indeed, it shares with Barakat's classic study (done jointly with Peter Dodd) of the 1967 Palestinian refugee exodus, the practiced sociologist's focus on those minutiae of everyday life that compose man's large-scale activity.[18] Yet Barakat's scene is dominated by the almost hateful sequence of six days. This short succession of moments dominates the action off-stage, but in the novel Barakat amplifies these days into a wide-ranging geographical and emotional voyage. His blurring of space-time distinctions, the montage effect of rapid scene-change, the carefully chosen cross-section of characters from Beirut to Amman to the West Bank, all these argue a sometimes uncertain balance between the social scientist's deliberateness and the novelist's inventiveness. Unlike both Flaubert and Mahfouz, Barakat takes, I think, a decidedly softer position on Arab contemporaneity in the throes of a major disaster. For him, the scene is an arena for continual struggle. Even though Arab history is a repetition of

Biblical history, Barakat's principal character, Ramzy, judges it also as a field for potential victory. There is none of that bitter attitude toward repetition that animates Flaubert's work or Marx's *18th Brumaire of Louis Napoleon* or, for that matter, Mahfouz' post-1967 work. For in the end Barakat is a novelist of good will; and this is his interest.

If I say good will and not vision, I mean this as no negative judgment of Barakat. As his latest sociological work shows, he is increasingly concerned with what seems to be an inherent resistance in particular Arab societies to coherent unity.[19] Good will is genuine patriotic involvement truly baffled by the complexity of forces flowing through, but not wholly composing, everyday Arab reality. Perhaps no novelist today can undertake a synoptic view—or at least not with the instruments hitherto developed from the novel. In Europe and America it is true that the novel played a crucial (and even conservative) role in the coalescing of society around itself. Yet that role was confined primarily to the nineteenth century; the authoritative vision of realistic fiction was superseded in a way by the new knowledge available in psychology, sociology, ethnology, and linguistics. The Arab writer confronts the very complex interweaving of society and contemporary knowledge with an even more complex mixture of styles, backgrounds, and predilections. The novelist will doubtless register his own crisis as a novelist facing the subject matter and its challenges. But in this task he starts from the same point as every other Arab intellectual; that point is nothing other than the forward position leading forward, the region's collective reality. Ultimately, then, the crises of Arab writers are precisely, and more so than elsewhere, those of the society at large. As this recognition is increasingly diffused, the unsung heroic role played by the Arab writer since 1948 will surely receive its due acknowledgment. In the meantime one can do no less than read with the care and urgency of an involved writer.

6

Between Chance and Determinism:
Lukács's *Aesthetik*

Béla Királyfalvi's *The Aesthetics of György Lukács* is a welcome attempt to deal mainly with Lukács's last major work, a two-volume systematic philosophy of art, *Die Eigenart des Aesthetischen* (1963). Despite the *Aesthetik*'s Goethean grandeur—for near the end of his life Lukács had come to think in terms of health, normality, and majestic ripeness, which is one reason he does not seem current—it is still not well known in the West. Királyfalvi has examined the Hungarian versions of Lukács's Marxist works (without telling us how they differ, if at all, from the German texts; as a result the choice of purely Hungarian works seems rather an arbitrary and unexplained one) and written a solidly reliable account. The main points of Lukács's argument in the *Aesthetik* are very well covered.

What one misses, however, are two important elements. The first is some recognition that Lukács proceeds as much by concrete example and analysis as he does by philosophic generality. Királyfalvi's précis is denuded of almost any of Lukács's suggestive insights into specific works of art. Another lack is Királyfalvi's regrettable, but not wholly unjustified, decision to confine analysis to Lukács's Marxist works.

Lukács is interesting not only as a Marxist, but also for the kind of Marxism he produced, which was eccentric and, with regard to his own pre-Marxist period, eclectic and inclusive. To this aspect of Lukács, Királyfalvi is not sensitive.

Yet as the first book-length work in English to deal with a full-scale Marxist and contemporary aesthetic philosophy, Királyfalvi's book completes an important first phase. Now we need to know more about Lukács's antecedents in the German philosophic and literary culture of the late nineteenth century, his association with Hungarian artists (mentioned by Királyfalvi); and most important, we need to study the themes, motifs, and images that unify his work over almost six decades. For even Lukács's misreadings and misunderstandings are interesting, and are an integral part not only of Marxist but of Western culture. Nevertheless, as a presence in those cultures Lukács offers his reader a problematic mass of writing.

This has now been as worked-over as it profitably can be for evidence of its author's political bad faith, moral cowardice, compromises with Stalinism, attacks against himself, and so on. George Lichtheim's strictures against Lukács at least did not prevent him from trying to analyze here and there the substance of the man's philosophy and criticism; but even then one's impression was that what seemed to matter most was not Lukács's work but whether or not one approved not so much of his politics as of his political and moral style. The main suggestion was that, reprehensibly, he survived every difficulty, but it was also implied that communist behavior ought to be judged by moral standards never applicable to capitalists.

No one has carried moral disapproval of Lukács further in the direction of intellectual terrorism than the rancorous G. Zitta, whose *Georg Lukács' Marxism* (1964) traces every evil everywhere unilaterally back to Lukács's Marxist dialectic. Recently, and especially with G. H. R. Parkinson's excellent collection, *Georg Lukács: The Man, His Work, and His Ideas* (1970), an intellectually serious view of Lukács has begun to emerge. His technique of seeming to support and then survive Stalinism no longer obscures his achievements. Many, if still not most, of the major works have been translated into English, so that at last the Anglo-American reader will know more about Lukács's intelligence than that it was partial to Balzac and realism.

   Still, Lukács's reputation and influence since his death in 1971 are sadly and ironically lacking in effect upon modern critical discourse. How is it that the militant intellectual inventor of the very conceptions of prototype, vanguard, and precursor is really nowhere to be found among contemporary critics whose watchword is prophetic avant-gardism and radical adversary intellectualism? Something decidedly unglamorous about Lukács has survived—in circles where formalism, structuralism, and deconstruction are discussed, he will seem out of place mainly for his heavy thematic pedagogy, his apparently blind inclinations to rate even Heinrich Mann over Kafka, his repetition, frequent inexactness, and nineteenth-century mustiness. Only George Steiner understood and wrote in 1960 on the drama of Lukács's work, although Steiner could not anticipate the poignancy of Lukács's admission to Hans Heinz Holz in 1967 that Hector, "the man who suffered a defeat, was in the right and was the better hero," and was in fact "a determinant for my entire later development."

   In literature Lukács stood always for the nineteenth century. His culture was Hector's—as opposed to that of Achilles, which was modish, intense, victoriously short-lived. Nietzsche and Schopenhauer for Lukács were regrettable irrationalists, sadly exemplary and reactionary modernists. Go through the reams of Lukács's pages and you will realize that what mattered to him at bottom were not eccentrics but the big writers, Shakespeare, Goethe, Marx, Hegel, Balzac, Tolstoy, and the high settled culture that produced them. He seemed incapable of being led to writers who shattered literary values, like Rousseau or Artaud, since his was the culture of complex, but ascertainable and uniformly transmittable, laws. Almost nowhere, after the First World War, did Lukács speak of what it is like to read or experience an author, or of what impresses and disorientates one in a given novel. Nevertheless, his criticism and philosophy span almost all the area now settled on by critical discourse: representation, reflection, reification, reception, epistemic unity, dynamism in the artwork, sign-systems, the relations of theory with practice, the problems of the "subject" or, as he put it in the title of an early untranslated article, "Die Subjekt-Objekt Beziehung in der Aesthetik." Like Kenneth Burke's, Lukács's criticism arches over these central problems without seeming to help other critics; both Lukács and Burke indefatigably have made all their work too explicit, too finished in a way, for ideas or suggestions to spill down into the mainstream. Such work therefore represents what is believed to be an unvarying value: in Burke's case a quirky, homemade and fabulous eclecticism, in Lukács's, barely surviving the Cold War, an unflinching Marxism.

Certainly he was a bulldog Marxist. No political or cultural or literary instance after his conversion in the early 1920s was too subtle or recondite for him to draw a Marxist lesson from it. Occasionally one feels this as an impoverishment of the instance; normally, however, it is the reverse. The essay on Hölderlin in *Goethe und seine Zeit* is surprising in its range of human sympathy and political understanding. Rescuing Hölderlin from George, Gundolf, Dilthey, and National Socialism, Lukács then reconnects the poet's "belated Jacobinism" with Hegel and the French Revolution. Instead of the precursor of irrational mysticism Hölderlin is authenticated as the unique poet without successors that Lukács believes him to be. Here, as frequently, Lukács's taste impels him to what ungenerous commentators would call trimming, by which Marxism is trickily altered to accommodate temperamental affinities for a given writer. Maybe—but why is it always assumed that Marxism is rigidly stupid, or that Marxism is (as it was not for Lukács) only a crude *imprimatur* on some aspects of culture?

It seems fairly clear now to say that Marxism for Lukács was not merely a collection of truths, nor even a method of analysis, but a sort of necessity, first for correcting, then for transforming and conducting, his relations with the world. Nothing can be more moving, surely, than the themes of yearning *(Sehnsucht)* and unfocused irony in his early works before his conversion to Marxism. The combination in them of Kant and Kierkegaard, with their influence on Lukács's masterful but essentially retrospective analyses of the lyric, drama, essay, and novel, were tempered, however, by his grasp of the Socratic Plato, an idealistic, passionate seeker whose romantic tendencies were controlled by the discontinuities of his life and his mode (the essay), as well as the prevailing ironic comedy of his examples. Yet the idea of Socrates as an antidote to unrestricted emotion is strengthened implicitly by Lukács's discovery of prospective time, even as he seemed to be mired in the hopeless moral dilemmas of the early twentieth century.

Near the end of the first essay (1910) in *Die Seele und die Formen,* Lukács begins to speak of a great aesthetic event which, when it comes, will render essay and essayist powerless, for all their clarity, autonomy, and vision. Nonetheless, the essay itself "seems justified as a necessary means to the ultimate end, the penultimate step in this hierarchy." Here are the three dimensions of time of which Lukács, more even than Georges Poulet, and before Heidegger, was the philosopher and poet, the technician of its pathos: an unrecoverable, yearned-for unity in the past, an intolerable disjunction between present ideals and present actualities, an all-conquering and all-destroying future. Loss, alienation, and obliteration. What after 1918 Marxism did for Lukács was not really to transform this triad of temporal phases, but rather to give the intellectual a discipline (the dialectic) and a place (the essay) by and in which to observe, manage, and clarify them. Instead of being subject to them, he objectifies them, but only in writing. Whether discussing the novel or the proletariat, Lukács was actually discussing the coincidence of a particular moment of these three phases with the particular form, static or dynamic, of its understanding by consciousness. Lessing and Marx taught him to disentangle these coincidences from the apparent disorder of events.

Consider the main problematics, even the idioms, to which Lukács gave currency. Most of them have less to do centrally with history than with marginality and eccentricity vis-à-vis history, or with imputations about and potentialities in history. Hence reification, proletariat class consciousness, alienation, totality. In his work in the mid-1920s, Lukács was also fascinated by the disjunction between the vegetative (or natural) world and human life. Marxism dramatized and specialized the reflections of time and history in human awareness. Lukács's Marxist writing located the existentially unsatisfying quality of time—its total mediacy, its corrosive ironies, its unending proleptic features—and fixed it in identifiable categories. Yet whenever Lukács discussed reality, and desirable moments in reality such as the unity of subject and object, he seemed at a remove from it, reflecting on its reflections. At best, he seemed to imply, Marxism for him regulated an interchange between the individual or group intellect and brute actuality; it did not overcome barriers; it dissolved them by formalizing them almost infinitely, just as (paradoxically) proletarian consciousness truly existed when a dehumanized atomism had both dismembered and postponed all human solidarity. Only Marxist dialectic heavily freighted with Hegel could cope with such rarefaction and negation; only language used in such a way as to signify, and *be* the very way in which time was a form of absence, not presence, could translate these predicaments. "History is the history of the unceasing overthrow of the objective forms that shape the life of man."

In part, Lukács's combination of dogmatism with evasiveness was a result. His involvement with politics throughout his career never had the focus of, say, Gramsci's until 1930, and Gramsci was the only other non-Russian Marxist theoretician with Lukács's intellectual scope and power. But whereas Gramsci had Italian culture, the Italian Communist Party, and *Nuovo Ordine,* despite his later isolation and his quarrels with the Comintern, Lukács was intermittently in and out of Hungary, Hungarian, German, Germany, the Soviet Union, and numerous journals, institutes, and academies all over Eastern and Western Europe. Both men definitely were members of an adversary culture, but it has never been easy to identify Lukács with an objective situation or movement within that culture, nor even to predict where— figuratively speaking—he was going to be next.

I would call Lukács's movements para-Hegelian, since they always moved not so much between antitheses and syntheses but away from immediacy and toward a constantly future "totality." Consider this passage from *History and Class Consciousness:*

> If the attempt is made to attribute an immediate form of existence to class consciousness, it is not possible to avoid lapsing into mythology: the result will be a mysterious species-consciousness (as enigmatic as the "spirits of the nations" in Hegel) whose relation to and impact upon the individual consciousness is wholly incomprehensible. It is then made even more incomprehensible by a mechanical and naturalistic psychology and finally appears as a demiurge governing historical movement.
>
> On the other hand, the growing class consciousness that has been brought into being through the awareness of a common situation and common interests is by no means confined to the

working class. The unique element in its situation is that its surpassing of immediacy represents an *aspiration towards society in its totality* regardless of whether this aspiration remains conscious or unconscious for the moment.

The logic here is Hegelian in its dynamism, but more radical and political both in its substance and in its pointing to the future than Hegel, and still more radical and surprising than anyone (except the despised Nietzsche) in its thrust into totality. This, Lukács said, would happen by means of "the dialectical process by which immediacies are constantly annulled and transcended."

With the total intellectualism of such writing (and how carefully Lukács avoids power or taking power) goes a certain blankness. By that I mean simply that the core of the argument about class consciousness can neither be proved nor disproved. It expresses not so much a law as an ontological predilection for annulment and transcendence as movements of life. It does not clearly show improvement in the lot of a miserable proletariat; and it has little affective force. Rather Lukács seems, like Mann's Aschenbach, to be thinking of stress (a closed fist) relieved by another movement (an open fist), except that annulment and transcendence for Lukács are dialectical terms for total tension and total aspiration which are themselves inherent in his universe. Here again Marxism regulates for Lukács; it holds him in check so that these total opposites do not fly off into the blue. Class consciousness, something one does not possess but tries to achieve, is the discrete social discipline of which history is the cosmic illustration.

As he grew older Lukács added another regulatory impulse to his work—the technique of repudiation allied with the habit of republishing what was being repudiated. This is no doubt part of a constant revision within his work that one would expect from so formidably self-reflective a writer as Lukács. So far as I know, no one has studied the repudiations systematically; I myself have never been able to understand the 1967 preface to *History and Class Consciousness,* nor the 1926 review of Moses Hess, in which Lukács attacked himself in Hess for his "idealist dialectic." Do such critiques recur at specifiable moments in the career? Do they really cancel out, embellish, or extend the arguments to which they are addressed, such as the one about nature being a social category? Are they always attempts by Lukács to make himself seem more orthodox? Are they imaginative requirements of the dialectic itself? Do they not demonstrate how auto-critique is another form of insistence, another text in the unending series of commentaries upon commentaries, of reflections on reflections, by which Lukács kept himself alive?

These are especially relevant questions when we come to Lukács's aesthetics. From start to finish art for Lukács is reflection: of man, of society, of itself. Depending on which moment in the career one chooses, Lukács is arguing more strongly for one over the other of these three as the object of art's reflection. A nice dialectical symmetry can be observed in those emphases. At the beginning of his career he was concerned with genres reflecting, in a sense, on themselves; as he treated it, the novel could be understood at so clarified a level of generality as to be virtually speaking of itself to itself. At the end of his career he returns to the *ansich* in aesthetics, but, as he says in the foreword to his *Aesthetik* (1963), with radically opposed methods and attitudes.

Now the main category of art, its proper or inherent identity *(Eigenart)* so far as a rigorous aesthetics is concerned, is speciality, particularity, concreteness *(Besonderheit);* but this is neither magical, religious, nor transcendentally unknowable. It is connected with man's wholeness, and with history, objectively and subjectively. In between these diametric early and late poles, Lukács has fleshed out the principal outlines of an ambitious Marxist critical practice.

The main features of this are well enough known. They include his work on realism, modernism, irrationalism, existentialism, the historical novel, as well, of course, as his numerous treatments of tendentiousness in art. Yet what is especially significant about the late aesthetics is how Lukács recapitulates and resolves his major theses from the 1930s, 1940s, and 1950s. The old disdain for vulgar causation and unrefined mimetic directness remains. Impatience with modernist irrationality, alienation, idealism (in all its guises) is strengthened. Allegory is attacked, as is consumerism. The notions of extensive and intensive totality are refined and deepened. Yet totality has now become the category through which art overcomes infinite mediation, and it puts Lukács firmly in contact, for once, with bodily reality without embarrassment or hedging and with an idea of "freedom from class society." These are impressive reprises of early themes. Novelties are an extended discussion of language (with the interesting invention of *Das Signalsystem I,* a good indication of how aware Lukács was of semiotics) and a resolution of what Agnes Heller has called "the false dilemma of receptivity." On the other hand, the sections on music, film, ornamental art are of debatable value. Yet the spirit of the work, its anthropocentric, anthropomorphic current carrying forward Aristotelian criticism, is hopeful and bears the evident imprint of Ernst Bloch, whose influence, along with Max Weber's, Lukács frankly acknowledges.

As an achievement Lukács's *Aesthetik* is next to matchless in this century. One thinks of Croce, or in literature of Ingarden's *Das Literarische Kunstwerk.* There are no Marxist analogies, although as far as applications of Marxist principles go Lucien Goldmann's *Le Dieu caché* still towers over the field. Goldmann was a student and disciple of Lukács. Very few writers are as focused as Lukács on the centrality and inclusiveness of the aesthetic experience, or on its potential for engaging the whole man, society, and ennobling conceptions of work. Lukács tries to deal with everything as few would dare. What gives him the confidence, I think, is neither his erudition nor a simple Marxist orthodoxy. One factor is the realization hinted at broadly everywhere in the two volumes that aesthetic behavior, being as it is a *type* (this is Weber) of human activity, *can represent* human totality; art need not *be* everything if it can typify one symbolic aspect of the whole. This, we might say, is Lukács making abstract mediation and marginality over into sensuous immediacy by virtue of the aesthetic sign and the semiologic power of aesthetic form. Second, there is a wholly controlled dialectic between the artwork and its circumstances: this dialectic is Lukács's major achievement after years of experiment, and it allows him to steer confidently between determinism and chance as forces building the artwork. In other words, Lukács has been able to systematize the processes by which reality *gets into* and *is reflected by* art. Temporality by then seems infinitely less problematic than before.

7

Conrad and Nietzsche

Conrad and Nietzsche were disaffected and yet admiring students of Schopenhauer. Each was temperamentally in agreement with Schopenhauer's pessimistic philosophy, although each—in similar ways—was critical of its principal arguments. Nietzsche did not believe that the Will was blind, nor did he think that it was simply a Will to live. Rather he saw the Will as inclining always to the acquisition of power; so too Conrad, for whom such men as Kurtz, Gould and Nostromo were nothing if not willful and deliberately egoistic overreachers. What troubled Nietzsche about Schopenhauer was the latter's weakening before the amoral picture of the world he had drawn. Whereas Nietzsche acknowledged life's uncompromising and inescapable disdain for either man or morality, he felt that his once-revered teacher had devised a cowardly retreat from life by preaching stoic withdrawal. Nietzsche's repeated statements of this criticism are echoed by Conrad's treatment of Heyst in *Victory,* whose code of philosophic disengagement from life is articulated only to be violated by Lena, Schomberg, Mr Jones, and the others. These, plus a lifelong interest in Wagner, are part of a common cultural patrimony shared by Nietzsche and Conrad.

There are a number of superficial resemblances between the Professor in *The Secret Agent* and what is often referred to as the extreme nihilism of Nietzsche's philosophy. As the embodiment of an attitude uniting a total moral purity with the will to absolute destruction, the Professor, it is true, seems like one result of Conrad's interest in radical paradoxes of human character—a result perhaps refined, or even inspired, by a reading of Nietzsche. In his letter of October 26, 1899, to Garnett (written before *The Secret Agent*) Conrad speaks of having received a copy of Garnett's essay on Nietzsche;[1] so far as I know Conrad simply mentions the essay twice and never again refers to it. But from his tone—for instance, the passing reference to Nietzsche in "The Crime of Partition"—it is arguable that Conrad was familiar with Nietzsche as the author of such ideas as the will to power, the Overman, and the transvaluation of all values. There may be more circumstantial evidence of actual borrowings to show how Conrad not only read but made use of Nietzsche, but turning it up is not what I consider to be the most interesting or useful way of considering the two writers together. Rather, they are best read in terms of a common tradition of which Nietzsche, always determined to spell things out in the smallest detail, is in many ways the apogee. That such a tradition exists is a fact of European literature and thought, and even though Conrad is a good deal less explicit about it than Nietzsche, I think that one can find evidence for it in the fiction nonetheless.

Since my main concern is with showing similarities and affinities between the two writers, I can only touch rather inadequately on the methodological and historical question of why and in what manner Conrad and Nietzsche together belong to this tradition. In other words, everything I shall write here might very well be put into serious doubt by any rigorous attempt to define the common field of play inhabited by Conrad and Nietzsche. Even to say that they both inhabit a common field is, at least for Conradian criticism, to say something fairly unusual. Conrad has been systematically treated as everything *except* a novelist with links to a cultural and intellectual context. His politics, aesthetics, and morality have been analyzed not as the products of thought, with roots in an intellectual ambiance, but rather as a series of accidents that happened to a Pole writing in England between the nineties and 1924. Why this critical failure is so, for a novelist whose cultural range is after all so impressively vast, is a subject for analysis in itself. Here I shall limit myself to describing the connections between Conrad's and Nietzsche's thought, connections quite interesting enough for their own sake.

For want of a better label to give the tradition to which I referred above, I shall call it the radical attitude toward language. For Nietzsche, no less than for Conrad, the life of language was the first fact of the writing life, of what Conrad named the life of "the worker in prose." In his early work, for example a set of notebooks dating from January to July 1875, Nietzsche used the title "philologist" to apply to great artists and thinkers capable of seeing and articulating the sharpest truths, Goethe, Leopardi, Wagner, Schopenhauer. As his thought developed through the late seventies and up to 1888, Nietzsche returned constantly to the connection between the characteristics of language as a form of human knowledge, perception, and behavior, and those fundamental facts of human reality, namely will, power, and desire. All through the great series of works he produced from *Human, All Too Human* (1878), through *The Gay Science* (1882), *Thus Spake Zarathustra* (1883-92), *Beyond Good and Evil* (1886), *Genealogy of Morals* (1887), *Twilight of the Idols* (1889), up to and including the extraordinary set of posthumously published notes entitled *The Will to Power* (1883-1888), Nietzsche examined language for its concealed duplicity, and its alliance with power and rank, which he called perspective. As early as 1873 he described truth in linguistic terms as follows:

> What, then, is truth? A mobile army of metaphors, metonyms, and anthropomorphisms—in short, a sum of human relations, which have been enhanced, transposed, and embellished poetically and rhetorically, and which after long use seem firm, canonical, and obligatory to a people: truths are illusions about which one has forgotten that this is what they are; metaphors which are worn out and without sensuous power; coins which have lost their pictures and now matter only as metal, no longer as coins.[2]

Nietzsche's moral and historical transvaluations depend very greatly upon insights such as this, which are a form of perspectival interpretation, treating language as a tyrannical epistemological system.

Although he developed this position, with all its complex self-irony (since Nietzsche was perfectly aware that his own work too was a perspectival fact of language) beyond any other writer, the position itself is not original with Nietzsche. Rather one ought to see it as a logical development out of the new philology of the early nineteenth century, and of course out of the so-called higher criticism of the Bible later in the century. Nietzsche's affiliations with his philological antecedents are too detailed to list here, but one main line of descent from them can be pointed out. That is the discovery—made by numerous investigators including Bopp, Grimm, von Humboldt, and the two Schlegels—that there is no such thing as a first, or original, language, and nor is there a first text. All human utterances are connected to each other, but not genealogically as to a first language (most commonly believed to be the Hebrew spoken by God and Adam in Eden); the connections between utterances are formal, lateral, adjacent, complementary, systematic. In short, every utterance is a controlled, disciplined, rule-coordinated variation on some other utterance. While it is unique to human beings, language is an order of repetition, of creative repetition, not of original speech. Thus every utterance interprets a prior utterance, is an interpretation of an interpretation which no longer serves. More urgently still Nietzsche saw human history as a battle of interpretations; for since man exists without hope of getting to the first link in the chain of interpretations he must present his own interpretation as if it were a secure meaning, instead merely of one version of the truth. By doing so he forcibly dislodges another interpretation in order to put another in its place. The struggle between interpretations historically grasped is what Nietzsche considered the genealogy of *morals* to be all about. As to the function of interpretation in a world of increasing becoming, Nietzsche has this to say in 1885–1886:

> "Interpretation," the introduction of meaning—not "explanation" (in most cases a new interpretation over an old interpretation that has become incomprehensible, that is now itself only a sign). There are no facts, everything is in flux, incomprehensible, elusive; what is relatively most enduring is—our opinions.[3]

The extent to which such a view was carried by Nietzsche can be gathered from the section subtitled "Our new 'infinite'" of *The Gay Science:*

But I should think that today we are at least as far from the ridiculous immodesty that would be involved in decreeing from our corner that perspectives are permitted only from this corner [Nietzsche here rejects the position that takes all other positions as mere interpretation, implying that this one is truth and not interpretation]. Rather the world has become "infinite" for us all over again, inasmuch as we cannot reject the possibility that *it may include infinite interpretations.*[4]

If from one point of view therefore language heightens the "pathos of distance"[5] between the user and brute reality, from another point of view language makes common, betrays, coarsens human experience. Nietzsche's thesis from *The Birth of Tragedy* on was that *melos* is a more authentic expression of reality than *logos*. The more highly developed consciousness is, the more likely then that language will exceed simple communication between men (need and distress cause men to want to communicate, and this desire increases to a point where the power of communication is really an accumulated subtlety exceeding actual need) and will be poor with regard to the "incomparably personal, unique, and infinitely individual."[6]

This difficult paradox, that language is at once excess and poverty, stands very near the heart of Nietzsche's work and, I believe, plays a considerable role in Conrad's handling of narrative language and technique. This view of language as perspective, interpretation, poverty, and excess is the first of three ways in which Conrad and Nietzsche can be brought together. Elsewhere I have commented on Conrad's habit of employing reported, or secondary, speech by which to convey the tale;[7] in this he is like Nietzsche averring that all language is an interpretation of an interpretation. Moreover, the transformation of narrative time from the linear to, in Conrad's major work, the multiple, bears witness to Nietzsche's general obsession with the past, and to the observation made in *Wir Philologen* that man is "a multiplication of many pasts."[8] Yet despite this conviction such Conradian narrators as Marlow are always reminding their audience that what is being said can never capture the true essence of the action that took place. Though Conrad's stated aesthetic rested on his avowal to make the reader see, with few exceptions what the reader remembers is a sustained effort to make words tell, even as it is frequently evident that words are ultimately inadequate, so special and eccentric is the experience.

I do not think it is incorrect to understand the peculiar genius of Conradian narrative—especially in such standard-setting works as *Heart of Darkness*—as in many ways arriving at a number of the same discoveries formulated by Nietzsche. Of course Conrad's tone is rarely like Nietzsche's; no one should underestimate the difference between the startling aphoristic gaiety cultivated by Nietzsche and Conrad's frequent solemnity and affected garrulity, which often seems at a loss for exactness. (There are occasional similarities: for example, the *Schadenfreude* of "An Outpost of Progress" or the cutting sarcasm of *The Secret Agent*.) Yet to be stopped by the difference is no more correct than speaking indiscriminately of their common nihilism. Both writers are too uncommonly detailed in their technique and in the presentation of their views for that. But what has often passed for an adequate literary account of the Conradian, or for that matter the Jamesian, interest in narrative presentation, the use of multiple point of view, the overlaying of one narrative by another, the enveloping of an inner by an outer frame—all this seems, I think, better accounted for when Nietzsche's work is read as relying upon a set of working attitudes toward language shared in common with Conrad. And of these attitudes the one seeing utterance as inevitably and endlessly leading to another, without recourse to a single originating or unequivocally privileged first fact—this is, I think, the major point in common. What matters in Conrad is what Nietzsche called interior "polyphony of effort."[9] Kurtz and Jim and Nostromo are finally no more important than the meditation and the reflection and the language they stimulate. They are posited in a way as fundamentally unknowable. It is left for the narrative to deliver them, not in themselves, but as they are from many perspectives. Narrative does not explain, it introduces plural meanings where none had been before—at the heart of darkness. One passage from *The Gay Science* describes the Conradian enterprise in *Heart of Darkness*.

> What is originality? *To see* something that has no name as yet and hence cannot be mentioned although it stares us all in the face. The way men usually are, it takes a name to make

something visible for them. Those with originality have for the most part also assigned names.[10]

What Marlow does in the tale is precisely—or as precisely as he can—to name something which has no name; he does this in order for it to be seen. This too is Kurtz's distinction at the end: to have judged, identified, named the horror even if that horror is less a thing than a thing said. The economic literalness of how Conrad does this is remarkable indeed, the more so I think in that it resembles Nietzsche's way too. More often than not Conrad's narratives are delivered by men whose professional standpoint in life is learned, contemplative, even medical in the sense that a physician is a doctor whose compassion includes the capacity for understanding as well as the perspective seeing humanity as an affliction. These narrators, reporters, conveyors of special insights not only tell a story but also inevitably create an audience even as they fashion their tale: *Lord Jim* and *Heart of Darkness* are perfect examples, with their select group of listeners, and their carefully devised barriers between one or another temporal, declarative, and physical level. Is not this exactly a major fact of Conrad's style, this elaborate strategy for the controlled play of meaning in language, this scenic design for utterances delivering and withholding "original" truths? Here is Nietzsche discussing the process:

> One does not only wish to be understood when one writes; one wishes just as surely *not* to be understood. It is not by any means necessarily an objection to a book when anyone finds it impossible to understand: perhaps that was part of the author's intention—he did not want to be understood by just "anybody." All the nobler spirits and tastes select their audience when they wish to communicate; and choosing that, one at the same time erects barriers against "the others." All the more subtle laws of any style have their origin at this point: they at the same time keep away, create a distance, forbid "entrance," understanding, as said above—while they open the ears of those whose ears are related to ours.[11]

Yet even to those "related" ears there are mysteries which Conrad's language does not finally reveal, for all its effusiveness and breadth.

His narratives are dotted with disclaimers such as "there are no words for the sorts of things I wanted to say." These, I think, are appeals from *logos* to *melos,* from what Nietzsche called the net of language to a lyrical domain that words cannot penetrate. "We have emancipated ourselves from fear of reason, the ghost that haunted the eighteenth century: we again dare to be absurd, childish, lyrical—in one word: 'we are musicians.' "[12] The virtuosity of Conrad's language, even when it has offended critics by its untidy sprawls and rhetorical emptiness, regularly carries with it eloquent indications that language is not enough. "Compared with music all communication by words is shameless; words dilute and brutalize; words depersonalize; words make the uncommon common."[13] The lyrical evocativeness of the scene between Marlow and Kurtz's intended unmistakably gestures toward that mysterious musical realm of intoxication, unreason, and danger:

> . . . and the sound of her low voice seemed to have the accompaniment of all the other sounds, full of mystery, desolation, and sorrow, I had ever heard—the ripple of the river, the soughing of the trees swayed by the wind, the murmurs of the crowds, the faint ring of incomprehensible words cried from afar, the whisper of a voice speaking from beyond the threshold of an eternal darkness.[14]

The second rapprochement between Nietzsche and Conrad is their sense of intellectual adventure and with it, their discovery of the inevitable antitheses everywhere to be found in human existence. In Conrad, the form of his tales enacts the dialectic between two opposed impulses, one, that of what Nietzsche calls the man who wants knowledge, and who "must again and again abandon the *terra firma* where men live and venture into the uncertain"; and two, "the impulse which desires life [and which] must again and again grope its way toward a more or less secure place where it can find a purchase."[15] In *The Mirror of the Sea* Conrad described these impulses as landfall and departure, experiences of the sea with obvious pertinence to such excursions into the unknown as *Heart of Darkness,* or such willful adventures as those of Jim and Nostromo and returns to "civilization" and life as are contained in Marlow's retrospective ruminations.

But even this dual movement from one antipode to the other is rooted in the sort of logic formulated in linguistic terms that makes the violent postscript of Kurtz's report not so unacceptable an aberration as it appears. In *Beyond Good and Evil* Nietzsche argued that the distinctions between such qualities as good and evil or such concepts as cause and effect are "pure concepts, that is to say . . . conventional fictions for the purpose of designation and communication—*not* for explanation."[16] A better way of understanding these concepts is by psychology—Nietzsche everywhere employs psychology in conjunction with metaphors of depth and penetration—which alone can enter the place where one can see how values are *created* by strength of will, no matter how contradictory is the material from which they are made. Words bear evidence of this kind of creation; at no point can a word be said necessarily to refer to a fixed concept or object like "good" or "reasonable." Similarly, Marlow's journey into the heart of darkness is everywhere characterized by dislocations in psychological sense caused by the displacement of habitual values, objects, meanings from one place to another. At bottom, literally, much of the strangeness in the tale is attributed to Kurtz, whose power has been precisely to create free from the logical, social, and grammatical constraints holding back everyone else. This is also Jim's achievement in Patusan. Language—as Nietzsche first found out in his early studies of Greek civilization—enables the cohabitation of total opposites, as when it is possible for a modern philologist to envision Greek tragedy as one aspect of Wagner's artwork of the future. Underneath words seethes a potential will to power, bringing forward evil with knowledge or an insight such as "and this also was one of the dark places of the earth." Nietzsche's thesis, argued for the first time in *Human, All Too-Human,* is that the sheer honesty of the free spirit pays no heed to conventions separating things or words from their opposite. Every coin has another face; this must be acknowledged, just as Kurtz's light of progress is sustained at exactly the same level and with the same degree of intensity as the darkness.

It would be inadvisable, I think, to call this second rapprochement between Conrad and Nietzsche their common nihilism. For one, Nietzsche's nihilism is no simple thing; indeed, he makes numerous distinctions between types of nihilism, between pessimism, romanticism, decadence, and nihilism, and it is altogether unclear to me whether even in Book One, "European Nihilism," of *The Will to Power* he applies the adjective "nihilistic" to himself. There is not much doubt on the other hand that both he and Conrad believed the world to be devoid of anything except spectacular value. Such a belief, to quote Nietzsche, is "the last form of nihilism . . . [and] includes disbelief in any metaphysical world and forbids itself any belief in a *time* [as opposed to *becoming*] world. Having reached this standpoint, one grants the reality of becoming as the *only* reality, forbids oneself every kind of clandestine access to afterworlds and false divinities—but *cannot endure this world though one does not want to deny it.*"[17] As to the world itself, there is a striking resemblance, not accidental I am sure, between Conrad's famous letters to Cunningham Graham, dated December 20, 1897, and January 14, 1898, on the knitting machine, and this last item in *The Will to Power*:

> This world: a monster of energy, without beginning, without end; a firm, iron magnitude of force that does not grow bigger or smaller, that does not expend itself but only transforms itself; as a whole of unalterable size, a household without expenses or losses, but likewise without increase or income; enclosed by "nothingness" as by a boundary; not something blurry or wasted, not something endlessly extended, but set in a definite space as a definite force, and not a space that might be "empty" here or there, but rather as force throughout, as a play of forces and waves of forces, at the same time one and many, increasing here and at the same time decreasing there; a sea of forces flowing and rushing together, eternally changing, eternally flooding back, with tremendous years of recurrence, with an ebb and a flood of its forms; out of the simplest forms striving towards the most complex, out of the stillest, most rigid, coldest forms towards the hottest, most turbulent, most self-contradictory, and then again returning home to the simple out of this abundance, out of the play of contradictions back to the joy of concord, still affirming itself in this uniformity of its courses and its years, blessing itself as that which must return eternally, as a becoming that knows no satiety, no

disgust, no weariness: this, my *Dionysian* world of the eternally
self-creating, the eternally self-destroying ... without goal. ...
This world is the will to power—and nothing besides! And you your-
selves are also this will to power—and nothing besides![18]

Nietzsche had expressed similar views in *The Gay Science*, section 109,
cautioning against attributing "aesthetic anthropomorphisms"—that
is, "order, arrangement, form, beauty, wisdom"—to the world.[19]

So far as the writer is concerned such a view of the world entails no
simple acceptance of it, but rather an acknowledgment that values are
created, just as words in a text are also created, by human force.
Conrad's confession that writing for him was the conversion of force
into words bears this acknowledgment out. A more problematic consequence, however, is that a highly patterned many-leveled narrative
structure of the type I discussed earlier is also an act of will, in which
the care expended upon making the structure firm runs the risk of
being effaced when the distinctions sustaining the structure collapse
into equals. This occurs notably in the final sentences of *Heart of
Darkness* where Conrad uses exactly the same words to describe the setting at the Thames estuary that he had used for the African scenes. In
other words, we can find instances of repetition whose function is to
reduce the difference between one value, one place or time and another, to an absolute identity. In *Nostromo*, for example, all the men—
for all their differences in character and temperament—are slaves of
the recurrent power of the silver mine.

This alternation between difference and repetition brings me to my
third and final instance of the similarity between Conrad and Nietzsche. Conrad's narratives for the most part (this is especially true of the
earlier work up till *Under Western Eyes*) flirt quite deliberately with
enigma and "inconclusive experience." What starts out as a tale bearing
hope for some conclusion, some teleology, turns out either not to reveal
the secrets for which the reader searches, or to minimize the distinction
between the exceptional, masterful egoistic hero and "us," the comparatively herd-like remainder of mankind. In both cases of course Conrad's method, I said earlier, is to employ reported, or secondary, speech.
Such a narrative tactic has the effect of transforming novelty into recurrence; as Nietzsche said, "the great dice game of existence ... must

pass through a calculable number of combinations."[20] Here both Nietzsche and Conrad are part of a very pervasive nineteenth-century European tradition of philosophic repetition to be found in Kierkegaard, Marx, and later, Freud; paradoxically, there are as many different philosophies of repetition as there are philosophers describing repetition, so it would be wrong to impose a strict identity of views upon Conrad and any one of the others. But what demands notice is this tendency in Conrad—and in Nietzsche insofar as his view of the world as repeatable force coincides with Conrad's—to move his characters and his narrative structures unceasingly from a reliance on novelty, exceptionality, egoism, exoticism to a perspective where after all they are repetitive instances of some common, all too-human pattern. So in *Heart of Darkness* we recognize that the tale's difficulty is precisely the unmediated co-presence in it of the untoward and the altogether unprecedented, with the familiar, the habitual, and the ordinary. This co-presence is situated on every level, on that of action, language, and character. How much of Marlow's discomfiture in Africa is due to seeing, for example, routine office duties performed in the remotest jungle as if in a London office. The narrative pries the habitual from its normal surroundings and applies it to new ones, which in turn must be apprehended and described by a language telling us that things are not so different after all: must we not remember that here is another one of Marlow's "inconclusive experiences," that "this also was one of the dark places of the earth," and so on?

"There are moments when one's past came back to one, as it will sometimes when you have not a minute to spare to yourself; but it came in the shape of an unrestful and noisy dream, remembered with wonder amongst the overwhelming realities of this strange world of plants, and water, and silence."[21] The alternation is typically Conradian: from present, to past, to present again—never forward into the dawn, as we would have moved in Nietzsche's case. Whereas Nietzsche attached the greatest explicit importance to conceiving eternal recurrence as an aspect of the future, Conrad's obsession with the past kept him in a tighter orbit of past and present, one repeating the other without respite. The two great European writers separate at this point. One can speculate that Conrad's deepest commitment as a writer is to the narrative form, which of itself finds the recurrence of past and present normal and congenial. Nietzsche, the superb aphorist who worked in the mode of LaRochefoucauld, Chamfort, and Lichtenberg, uses language to thrust and probe further from what is expected, despite the wholly admitted belief in eternal recurrence. Conrad is the less daring of the two, although—and this is one of those seeming contradictions of art that Nietzsche was a genius enough to appreciate, even as he denigrated the novel—he is no less of a European event than his contemporary Nietzsche. No one could have written such works as *Heart of Darkness,* with their suggestive dramatization of changes in state of mind, and have not been sensitively attuned to the whole psychological culture of late nineteenth-century Europe. It is hard to fault Conrad, as D. H. Lawrence did, for not going far enough. After all, both Conrad and Nietzsche permanently modified our confident sense of aesthetic and psychological direction. Why it was done differently by a novelist and a philosopher and how it was done are questions that should not be confused. But as we answer both questions separately we cannot deny *that* it was done.

Vico on the Discipline of Bodies and Texts

Although Vico's style is a very learned and bookish one, what it frequently describes is quite physical. With the adjective "poetic," for example, Vico was able to bring into *The New Science* a fairly wide repertoire of passionate, and sometimes violent, physical behavior, including copulation, bodily abuse of many sorts, and such outdoor activities as planting, building, and traveling. His *Autobiography* begins and ends with two remarkable physical descriptions that impress upon the reader a sense of Vico's existence as having had an unmistakable bodily tone, in spite of his cerebral career. First he tells us that as a boy of seven he fell head first from the top of a ladder; having recovered, despite the doctor's discouraging prognosis that he would either die or become an idiot, Vico consequently acquired a melancholy and irritable temperament. The last thing he tells about himself is that his *New Science* gave him the enjoyment of life, liberty, and honor, achieved because he enjoyed adversity, which presented him with "so many occasions for withdrawing to his desk, as to his high impregnable citadel to meditate and to write further works which he was wont to call 'so many noble acts of vengeance against his detractors.' "[1] Thus in *The New Science* Vico writes in a scholarly way about human history whose features are clear in matrimony, agriculture, war, burial, and festivity; and similarly in his *Autobiography* Vico sees his personal intellectual history as understandable in terms of not always ennobling physical behavior. Both works quite openly rub the philologists' and philosophers' noses in what Yeats calls "the uncontrollable mystery on the bestial floor."

Yet what usually goes with these physical and bodily experiences is some attempt at control over them. Vico's notions about education illustrate this perfectly. Education deals with the young, who are lively, energetic animals. Instead of advocating a program that breaks the young temperament, Vico encourages instead the enhancement of its best qualities while—he says in *The New Science* (338)[2]—reducing them to duty (the original says "di ridurre in ufizio," which suggests putting to work, making responsible and settled). The same view, that man educates himself and thus begets his own history and society by bridling his physical passions, enables Vico to construct his vivid account of the earliest, youthful stages of human "gentile" existence. As for such relatively abstract products of intellect as meaning, that comes when words "are carried from bodies and from the properties of bodies" and made to serve a stable signifying purpose (237). Vico is everywhere deliberately playing upon the physical, material bases of human reason, and not only because he knows that discipline really begins when you make a method out of giving the body civilized things to do, but also because the body's outlines seem always to interpose themselves between his eyes and the books he either reads or writes. So rather than dispel the body he emphasizes its presence to himself and to others, as, like a trained soldier, it transforms walking into marching, or sitting into combat alert. There is a perfect epitome of this early in the *Autobiography*. As a boy

> during the summer, he would sit down at his desk at nightfall; and his good mother, after rousing from her first slumber and telling him for pity's sake to go to bed, would often find that he had studied until daybreak. This was a sign that as he grew older in the study of letters he would vigorously maintain his reputation as a scholar.[3]

Vico's predilection for associating youth and physical vitality with the important first stages of human existence is dramatically symbolized by his giants. Their size and impressive presence to his mind's eye is the first characteristic of what he would call poetic or heroic man. Indeed, as we know from his oration on the heroic mind, it was extended exertion like that of a gymnast, and prolonged self-discipline like that of a clerical ascetic, and the good flowing from those which he associated with heroism, not necessarily what we would call either nobility or bravery. When he came to organizing his *New Science* he could not relinquish his hold upon the body; the "elements" he enumerated at the outset will "course" through the book like blood in animate bodies. Gradually the vision of an animal body associates itself with notions of animation, as well as with the whole complex of words having to do with life (*anima, animare, ingegno,* and so forth), and with notions of disciplined movement, of which *corso* and *ricorso* are obviously the principal ones. Thus Vico's writing itself is enlivened when rarefied realms—such as truth or meaning—are shown to have those physical bases which conventional scholarship all but eliminates. His etymological habits are a form of "retro-signification" that drives meanings back to the bodies from whence originally they came.[4] This is anti-Cartesian atavism with a vengeance.

The cost of this to Vico's didactic aims in *The New Science* is perhaps too high. No reader needs to be reminded of how peculiarly organized the book is, nor of how eccentric in the alternation of opacity with blinding force, of directness with interminable and digressive detail, is its style. For that I think we must blame not only Vico's lonely, eccentric originality, but also his insight that there is always something outside mere logical sense to be engaged and dealt with when human reality is discussed. This is the body, whose untidy, immediate, sprawling largeness becoming intelligent and fit for social history is Vico's real subject. Vico inevitably seems not to be in full control of what he says, nor to be fully aware of what he is all about. This is partly because the body is his source of knowledge, a body, it is true, diminished in its original size, compelled into discipline, educated into intelligent behavior. The anthropomorphization of knowledge, against which Nietzsche was later to rebel, is Vico's project, even if civilization progresses (if that is the word) from the body to impersonal institutions. Yet in writing about this progress Vico's unhappy style also communicates a loss of immediacy, as if the prolixity of descriptive language trying to recapture the bodily directness of "poetic" thought were a demonstration of mind trying unsuccessfully and inelegantly to recover glad animal movement.

For the literary critical theorist of today Vico's type of atavism is usefully suggestive in other ways. We are too comfortable I think with the idea of a literary text as inhabiting a dimensionless, uncircumstanced, and even sexless element, purged of every worldly evidence except the sovereignty of its author, vulnerable to the whimsy of ingenious interpretation and system building.[5] Vico's way with texts is principally to push them back into the human struggles from which they emerge. But no less important is Vico's methodological anti-theorizing. If he forces one to see the gross physical circumstances from which a text emerges— remember how he says that "fables in their origin were true and severe narrations, when *mythos,* fable, was defined as *vera narratio.* But because they were originally for the most part gross, they gradually lost their original meanings, were then altered, subsequently became improbable, after that obscure, then scandalous, and finally incredible . . . [and] were received by Homer in this corrupt and distorted form" (814)—he is also perfectly capable of knowing that the rarefying or theorizing of texts is inevitable. He recognizes that no matter how much the atavist reveals about a text's physical origins, the theorist will begin by disregarding the text's "incredible" subject-matter in order to concentrate happily on its form, or its figures, or *his* form and figures. Rather than simply opposing this formalistic prejudice, Vico shows that it too has a history, that theoretical reflection was once something else, just as Homer's poems too were not always believed to be the work "of a calm, cultivated, and gentle philosopher" (828).

The New Science is everywhere a reminder that scholars hide, overlook, or mistreat the gross physical evidences of human activity, including their own. Yet what surprises one, I think, is Vico's tolerant attitude toward either theory or systems, particularly, but not exclusively, rationalistic ones. He suspects them both, but we cannot say that he disdains either. Neither does he feel that the happy theorist or inspired system builder is patently mistaken just because each is more concerned with *his* ideas at the expense of whatever in the text might contradict them. Vico was too strong an egotist to make that criticism; certainly he believed that forceful observation and theorizing were acts of personal power, for which canonical authority or institutional prestige were no substitute. What he sees in a theory or a system, however, is paradoxically its capacity, or not, for assimilating physical detail, which either lights it up (as when Vico himself theorizes about the true Homer and Dante and adds physical details to these bloodless fictions) or does not (as when Vico says that there is no hope of getting to first principles from books written directly out of the conceit of nations or of scholars [330]). For Vico it is one thing for theory or systems as forms of reflective mental fiction to take in, or even engender, contradicting sense impressions. It is quite another for a theory to harden into institutional obstinacy, which must be circumvented or modified at all costs.

Yet even the most fanatically believed-in conceits, however, are not neglected by Vico. He is sagely aware that if it is true that ideas can become rigid obsessions it is no less true that they were once passionate imaginings stemming from responses to physical existence. A canonical text, venerated blindly as an unchanging document by university professors, *can still be made to appear* a historical and dynamic process, as Vico showed with Roman Law. The important thing is to *persuade* students that this dynamic, passionate history exists, and Vico was not a professor of eloquence for nothing. But we begin to sense here how thin the dividing line is between *what is* and *what can be made to be* in Vico's work. He rarely pronounces on the limits of "invention," going so far in fact as to heap on the smallest point mountains of semi-bogus etymological evidence. Like his "first theological poets" seeing Jove everywhere, Vico gives animate substance to everything. Retranslated *Iovis omnia plena* might just as well be "Vico floods all things with passion." We will be less impressed with the evidence cited by Vico on the origins of names (433) than we will be by his virtuosity in marshalling disparate bits of learning into a coherent, if factitious, argument. The discipline of such arguments is to be found in how poetically inspiring they are, and Vico must take credit for that, not some reusable scientific method.

Its claims to scholarship and rigor notwithstanding, *The New Science* therefore seems to legitimize not impersonal method but personal inspiration, and a particularly unscrupulous one at that. What matters to Vico in short is not what evidence is *there*, but rather what evidence you can invent, or put there, or "find" topically, quite apart from whether it is scientifically true or completely understood. *Verum* and *factum* are genuinely interchangeable for Vico. The use of a theory is what it enables one to produce in the way of physical evidence, just as Vico's incredible productivity with the allegorical emblem for his work engenders meanings for it no other person was likely to find in it. The famous maxim about how knowing is making leaves the expected sequence or even dialectic of knowledge in a shambles. What is important about theory is not what it can explain, but how much it can assimilate, which turns out to be the same as how much one can produce from it, despite contradictions or logic.

I seem to have reversed my first point about Vico's atavistic method. From seeing his work as an attempt to force theory back into gross physical beginnings, I now have him using theory instead to manufacture a whole private vision of things, in much the same way he uses the adjective "poetic" to pull one "state" after another from out of his scholarly imagination. In the first case with which I began this essay, theory or system—and I shall use the two words to mean an abstract "seeing" or explanation from above of a mass of experiences—are forced to encounter the body, which they have ignored. Thus the academy is sent back to the huts and forests for its instruction: atavism. In the second case, a theory or system in the hands of an imperious intellect like Vico's encounters a petrified landscape which it proceeds to move by filling the space with activity and objects: invention.

I do not believe that we increase our esteem for Vico by arguing that these two seemingly antithetical attitudes, one atavistic, the other frankly creative, are reconcilable. His reader must do the reconciling, if that can be done. My impression is that Vico liked both ways of dealing with history and used them both without being able to forge a made-up *via media,* a concession to logical argument. He seems quite at ease with contradiction, which is not to say, however, that he was careless of making meaning: quite the contrary. To the contemporary critic he is most interesting as a maker of meaning,[6] as a disciplinarian of meaning for whom *intelligence,* like a body dancing, is a very particular activity. If now we follow Vico's demonstrations of how intelligence works, and how language operates, we can arrive, I think, at a useful scheme for understanding how at least one kind of meaning, textual meaning, is compatible with Vico's atavism and with his "creative" method. For Vico's interest in discipline, which is *The New Science*'s manifest subject, has more to do with discipline as the text's existence in culture than as the critic's method. But this will be clear from what I will be saying.

Vico quotes Aristotle's observation, *Nihil est in intellectu quin prius fuerit in sensu.* Then he adds: "the mind uses intellect when, from something it senses, it fathers something which does not fall under the senses; and this is the proper meaning of the Latin verb *intelligere*" (363). As some commentators have pointed out,[7] Vico's use of the word *intelligence* has at least two different meanings, and this is important for Vico's theory of the relation between epistemology and institutional development. Yet early in *The New Science,* in the section on *Poetic Wisdom* which is where *intelligere* is defined above, Vico is doing something of relevance to the critic of texts for whom the questions of theory and physical evidence, of real evidence versus made-up evidence, of method versus inspiration are important. *Intelligere* is an activity out of which a discipline can develop. This is where we can begin now to appreciate Vico's insight into humanistic discipline, where the problem of theory and practice too often degenerates into one sort of institutional or mentalistic excess or another.

Vico is concerned with what happens to sense impressions in the mind given the overwhelming preponderance of body. He associates intelligence with a kind of escape-and-rescue operation, by which the mind gathers and holds on to something that does not fall under the senses, even though that "something" could not come into being without the body and sense experience. *Intelligence* turns out to be a later word for *divinare,* prohibited amongst the Hebrews, but the source of all wisdom amongst the gentile nations. The difference between *intelligere* and *divinare* is not fully clear, yet Vico seems consistent in associating intelligence with modern philosophers, divination with the barbaric poets. One is an operation of intellect, the other of will and desire, but at bottom both take out something more than a sense impression from a sense experience. They take it out and they maintain it, which necessarily gives it a different form. The sum total of all these "something mores" is commanded by wisdom, acting through the agency of disciplines whose job it is to recover these "something mores" for use by wisdom.

Now we must see how Vico applies this to the production of the first ideas, which were myths of course, and ultimately to the making of coherent sign-systems, or texts. The greatest as well as the first feat of mythical divination is Jove, King, "father of men and gods." He is the central poetic figure, the first powerful coherence of signs to emerge out of the primitive imagination as it encounters a natural occurrence—thunder clap—of overpowering sensuous force. What in this occurrence is not assimilable to the senses is "something more," a nameless force the senses can neither identify nor control, but which nevertheless must be identified and controlled. Why? Vico does not say, except allusively, why that need is felt, yet his choice of details for Jove's attributes gives a certain number of clues. "The first men, who spoke by signs, naturally believed that lightning bolts and thunder claps were signs made to them by Jove; whence from *nuo,* to make a sign, came *numen,* the divine will, by an idea more than sublime and worthy to express the divine majesty" (397). Here too we note the sense impression and something more: the making of a sign, *nuo,* followed by what escapes from, extends the sign past the immediate sense experience of making it, *numen.* A little later Vico demonstrates how Jove the savior, *Soter,* receives the epithet *Stator,* "stayer or establisher." This parallels two other Jovian labels, *optimus* and *maximus.* Thus simultaneously Vico describes the creation of Jove by man, as well as the distancing of that creation from the immediate sense impression out of which it derived. Here we must note that *numen, Soter, Stator, optimus,* and *maximus* are details, and follow an order, that are Vico's own; Jove certainly had all these distinctions, but Vico puts them together on his own in what is an unconventional way.

All this is not a theory of linguistic origins, but it can act as a theory of any linguistic sign system or object which acquires a certain presence and duration. In making a sign or in believing one is made to you, you are involved in more than the exchange of vivid sense impression: so Vico says. The first men "naturally believe" that the claps and bolts were signs made to them because *they* speak by signs, yet nowhere does Vico say how they got into the habit of using signs among themselves: it is merely natural. What is *not* natural, but poetic—the difference is

crucial—is the ascription of *nuo* to the thunder clap, which subsequently draws forth the idea of *numen*. For their own sign language *nuo*
is presumably enough: the sign is immediately consumed in use. But
to locate a stable meaning to which one can revert, they must impute
numen to a sign in the same way that they convert an unprecedented
natural occurrence into a sign for them. Vico's description is difficult
to follow very closely since he shifts back and forth from seeing the
primitives as makers of Jove to seeing them as Jove's subjects; the
point, of course, is that by making Jove they implicate themselves in
his realm. This mutually limiting network is not only religious, but as
Vico says, it is cultural and civil, and it has a certain persistent discipline to it.

What matters to the historian of culture are not random occurrences
but enduring events, events that have a continuing historical, material,
and recoverable existence in human society. The great storm produces
a sign of Jove in the primitive mind, but more important, it produces a
way for the sign to save the memory and to last a great deal longer and
more productively than noise and light usually do. The genius of this
formulation for the world of cultural documents is that it does two
things. First, it makes the sign and the sense impression coterminous
but not reducible "naturally" to each other. Second, it associates the
sign's preservation equally a) with its having been saved from the immediacy of sense (its negative aspect) and b) with the sign's staying or
establishing of its own mode of disciplined persistence (its positive aspect). These things do not happen naturally; they occur when the
senses cannot control everything before them. Similarly, I would argue
that for us to speak of language as willing, preserving, or establishing
itself is to speak of *how* a text is in time and space, *where* it is in time and
space, *what* it is being in time and space *for*.

To the theoretician of a text such descriptions bring to mind those
worldly institutions by which a text maintains itself and for which it
plays a role. In other words, the appearance, dissemination, circulation, preservation, currency, recurrency, and disappearance of a text
are principal functions of a text, as much as are the physical circumstances of its production, its internal coherence, and the possible
meanings derived from it. The whole didactic effort of Vico's understanding of what texts are drives us to realize that by investigating the

text's more-than-sensuous dimension, its disseminative and staying capacities, we are no longer talking about a simple world in which evidence is either there or not there. The same is true of language, since signs are not simple presences but creating and created networks of relations. For the literary theorist, then, the text's being is not natural, just as after the first men engender Jove neither they nor Jove simply *are*. Jove is bound to them as much as they are to him. The text is in culture as is its reader; neither text nor reader is "free" arbitrarily to produce meaning since, as we said earlier, both are part of a regulating network that exists whenever and wherever texts, like any group of signs, exist.

Therefore the discipline of a text is how the immediacy from which it originally derived is translated into permanence and transmitted in and by culture. Jove is born not just as a more-than-human god, but as a father. He produces everything else, including his rivals, yet the whole network, like that of a text holding in its readers and even its most willful interpretive distorters,[8] inheres in the still larger network, which after all is material, historical human society. For Vico the world of men is like a text, and vice versa. Both come from the body in an act of inspired divination by which inert objects, random marks, become sign systems; as sensuous immediacy is lost intellectual and aesthetic powers are gained: Jove, like the great sacred text, becomes *optimus* and *maximus*. Out of these divine-royal-paternal texts—and how powerfully Vico saw that for both its readers and its author the text fills the world—come the institutions of culture, of readers and writers of more texts. Thus a new body develops, a distorted new *politeia* (371), of diminished stature when compared with the giant forms from which originally it came, as *Ius* is a contraction of *Ious* (398). In this new textual *corpus* Vico the philologist found a discipline which is more, rather than less, rigorous for its physical antecedents and beginnings. When Vico spoke of the "concrete and complex order of human civil institutions" (1026), it is this discipline he had in mind.

Tourism among the Dogs

Legally deprived of extensive quotation from Orwell's work, Peter Stansky and William Abrahams have nevertheless pressed on not only to finish a two-part biography, entitled *Orwell: The Transformation,* which they began in 1972 when *The Unknown Orwell* was published, but also to bring to an end their study of British writers in the thirties who were involved in the Spanish Civil War. (*Journey to the Frontier,* 1966, was about John Cornford and Julian Bell.) Not that more facts, more analyses of his mind and work, would have prevented Orwell's provinciality, his narrow view of life, his cheerless reporting from coming through, as indeed those things come through here in this carefully admiring, small-scaled study.

The case *for* him could not be made better than Stansky and Abrahams make it, that is, with his stubborn professionalism and the "natural" white style he perfected winning out in the hierarchy of virtues over his supposed political savvy or intellectual conscience. They make no attempt to hide Orwell's astonishingly apolitical awareness of his world—Gordon Comstock, the hero of *Keep the Aspidistra Flying,* they remark, is "only fitfully aware of the hundreds of thousands of unemployed . . . and he is equally indifferent to any sort of political solution to the evils of the money world from which he is in flight"—nor to pretend that as a novelist he is on a level with Kipling, much less a successor to Lawrence, Joyce, or Conrad. Their Orwell has his limits emphasized, and those are considerable.

After a surprisingly clumsy first paragraph that dances unconvincingly around the metamorphosis of Eric Blair into George Orwell, Stansky and Abrahams go on with great skill to depict the transformation in terms of an emerging, rather modest career, from *Down and Out in Paris and London* (1933) to Orwell's Spanish entrance and exit (1936–1937), which produced *Homage to Catalonia* and his famous commitment to democratic socialism. He gives up teaching, gets married, writes reviews and essays, does a set of well-received books, travels to the northern mining country, wanders among down-and-outers, goes to Spain in search of raw experience, he and his wife acquire a modest house, he takes up again with old Etonian friends: those are the high spots of his life to 1937, patiently, even elegantly chronicled and shrewdly set forth by Stansky and Abrahams. Definitely not a heroic, and not quite an anti-heroic, life. A few disheartening patterns emerge, however.

Orwell's sustained political writing career coincides not with his down-and-out years, nor with his brief interest in the concrete experience of imperialism *(Burmese Days),* but with his re-admission to and subsequent residence inside bourgeois life. Politics was something he observed, albeit as an honest partisan, from the comforts of bookselling, marriage, friendship with other writers (not by any means with the radicals used as material for *The Road to Wigan Pier* and *Homage to Catalonia,* then dropped), dealing with publishers and literary agents. It is this milieu that nurtured and always inhibited his politics. Despite it he has been given credit for a kind of overall political sanctity and cultural prescience. Out of it grew the later social patriotism which, as Raymond Williams has shown in his excellent little study of Orwell, blocked any serious political analysis of "England Your England." Even the homey terms that were usually Orwell's preference over genuinely historical or theoretical explanation—"England in a phrase: a family with the wrong people in control"—derive from this essentially humdrum background.

In other words, Orwell needed to surround himself with a familiar atmosphere that eliminated all worries before he could formulate a position; where but in the center of a social setting that, minus children, restored all the ingredients of a nice family romance could his anxieties be calmed? In *Down and Out* he makes a revealing admission about the nature of the worry that plagued him. Once you hit absolute bottom, he says, there comes a sense that "you have talked so often of going to the dogs—and well, here are the dogs, and you have reached them, and you can stand it. It takes off a lot of anxiety." *Not standing it*—"it" being the psycho-moral strain of falling apart completely, losing your identity as defined for you by where you come from and where most of the time you know (as Orwell certainly knew from membership in the lower-upper-middle class) you can return. Surely the removal of this last option causes the peculiar dread experienced by Winston Smith during his final ordeal in *1984*, the more so after having lost the cosy sanctuary he shared with Julia above Mr Charrington's shop. Just as surely, the off-stage presence of home and the possibility of a phone call for money to Eric Blair's Aunt Nellie constitute the narrator's bad faith when he was a *plongeur* in Paris or a tramp in England.

In *The Unknown Orwell* Stansky and Abrahams speak of Orwell's having successfully blocked "from his consciousness the invented or synthetic character of the [down and out] experience," yet they are too perspicacious to deny that his true reality anchored, gave privileged strength to, his tourism among the dogs. Compare Genet with Orwell and the point is not even arguable. Thus when Orwell became an overtly political writer in the middle thirties the risks of politics were handled from the perspective of someone who very definitely felt, and really was, at home *somewhere*. Hence the peculiar force of Stansky and Abrahams's tautology, "Orwell belonged to the category of writers who write." And could afford to write, they might have added. In contrast they speak of George Garrett, whom Orwell met in Liverpool, a gifted writer, seaman, dockworker, Communist militant, "the plain facts of [whose] situation—on the dole, married and with kids, the family crowded into two rooms—made it impossible for him to attempt any extended piece of writing."

Orwell's writing life then was from the start an affirmation of unexamined bourgeois values. There is nothing the matter with that, but it was always being overshadowed and hidden by the adventurous content of Orwell's material, which had the effect of persuading his readers that he spoke as one of the oppressed. True, he had courage and humanity, but, we must now say, he also had security and protection. Stansky and Abrahams make it possible to see Orwell's political excursions as tours in the garden, not as travels abroad, nor as the harrowing exposures to real politics for which he has been celebrated. And the famous style emerges in this excellent picture as a technical achievement, not the result of political trial by fire.

His style's human and political costs, in what he cut away or refused ever to confront, are troubling to think about, though. Stansky and Abrahams give evidence simultaneously of Orwell's retrospective doctoring of his past, and of his downright foolishness about the contemporary scene. A fuller account of this is to be found in Raymond Williams's book on Orwell. What Orwell said when he wrote for Ukrainian readers of *Animal Farm* about his alleged commitment to socialism in 1930 is plainly an untruth, made the more reprehensible not only because Stansky and Abrahams show that he had no notion of socialism until much later, but also because we catch him unaware in 1935 "that Hitler intended to carry out the programme of *Mein Kampf.*" Far from having earned the right to denounce socialism *from within* Orwell had no knowledge either of Marx or of the massive Marxist and socialist traditions; moreover he consistently referred to English radicals as "the pansy Left," and seemed totally uninterested in any social or economic analysis that was neither journalistic (like his) nor anti-Marxist. When he was not verbally abusing people he considered opponents or competitors, he was holing up as a reviewer of more or less unchallenging books. Stansky and Abrahams thus provide an earlier complement for Isaac Deutscher's damaging account of the later Orwell, his insularity being a turn from cosmopolitan or radical modernism to an ideology of the middle-brow "our way of life" variety, which in the United States at least has been dressed up as "neo-conservatism."

Nor is this all. Stansky and Abrahams state, more, alas, than they demonstrate, that in his happy marriage to Eileen O'Shaughnessy Orwell was less defensive and barbed in his attitudes than before. Yet apart from the dubious idyll enacted in The Stores, Wallington, what do Stansky and Abrahams really let us see? Eileen cooking the whole day. Eileen typing manuscripts. Eileen there to provide Orwell with support in Spain. The result for her (again Stansky and Abrahams are coolly devastating) was the sheer fatigue that caused her death. Most relationships seem to have made considerably fewer demands on Orwell than on his friends.

What then is the *literary* history narrated in *Orwell: The Transformation?* Surely the consolidation of Orwell's plain style as it reported without unnecessary adornment the views of a decent man. Many good things have justifiably been said about this style, although it is curious how they have often tended to prevent other things from also being said. For instance, the plain reportorial style coerces history, process, knowledge itself into mere events being observed. Out of this style has grown the eye-witness, seemingly opinion-less politics—along with its strength and weakness—of contemporary Western journalism. When they are on the rampage, you show Asiatic and African mobs rampaging: an obviously disturbing scene presented by an obviously concerned reporter who is beyond Left piety or right-wing cant. But are such events events only when they are shown through the eyes of the decent reporter? Must we inevitably forget the complex reality that produced the event just so that we can experience concern at mob violence? Is there to be no remarking of the power that put the reporter or analyst there in the first place and made it possible to represent the world as a function of comfortable concern? Is it not intrinsically the case that such a style is far more insidiously unfair, so much more subtly dissembling of its affiliations with power, than any avowedly political rhetoric? And more ironically still, aren't its obsessive fantasies about indoctrination and propaganda likely to promote exactly that "value-free" technocracy against which one might expect plainness and truth to protest? That such questions arise out of an account of Orwell only until 1937 fairly suggests the skill with which Stansky and Abrahams have done it.

10

Bitter Dispatches from the Third World

There is a suggestive scene in one of V. S. Naipaul's early essays that has him in a garden in British Guiana, asking the name of a flower whose scent is familiar but whose name he doesn't know. An elderly lady answers: "We call it jasmine." Then *he* reflects: "So I had known it all those years! To me it had been a word in a book, a word to play with, something removed from the dull vegetation I knew. . . . But the word and the flower had been separate in my mind for too long. They did not come together." A year later, in 1965, he writes that "to be a colonial is to be a little ridiculous and unlikely," and this is directly reflected in the clearly etched but on the whole gentle comedy about being an English-speaking East Indian from the West Indies, as numerous characters (including Naipaul himself) in Naipaul's early prose are. Having the language but with it a different tradition—like reading Wordsworth without ever having seen a daffodil, like the young Hindu in Port of Spain, Trinidad, who "takes up his staff and beggar's bowl and says that he is off to Benares to study"—is part of the same general discordance, "the play of a people who have been cut off."

There are many aspects of this fate which Naipaul has explored in autobiographical as well as fictional terms. His novels, for example, have developed the meanings lying coiled up in his own past, meanings which, like the verbal ambiguities in the word "Indian," don't easily go back to some unquestioned origin or source. Fiction has therefore been that "play" of "adjustments" made when a remembered India fell away for East Indians after World War II: "A new people seemed all at once to have been created," Naipaul wrote in *The Overcrowded Barracoon,* and their life was "like listening to a language I thought I had forgotten [although it] gave that sensation of an experience that has been lived before." But, he adds, "fleetingly, since for the colonial there can be no true return." Nevertheless, there was plenty to explore in the interim, the quite literal fictional space between lost origin and present scene; hence the exotic fun, the sensitive embarrassment, the odd fantasy and creative mimicry of characters from Ganesh, the mystic masseur *(The Mystic Masseur),* to Biswas *(A House for Mr. Biswas).*

Yet the possibility of anger, desperate bewilderment, and bitter sarcasm has always lurked in Naipaul's work, because the possibility derived as much from his compromised colonial situation as it did from what, as a result, he wrote about. His subject was extraterritoriality—the state of being neither here nor there, but rather in-between things (like the tropical jasmine and its name) that cannot come together for him; he wrote from the ironic point of view of the failure to which he seems to have been resigned.

Beginning in the early 1970s, however, this in-betweenness occasioned an increasingly bitter and obsessive strain in Naipaul's writing. Consider as a telling case the final section of *In a Free State* (1971). Naipaul is in Luxor in 1966 watching an Egyptian senselessly camel-whipping some poor children, while a couple of Italian tourists film the scene.

A year later, of course, the June war will break out, so there is something vaguely ominous about the event. Suddenly he makes a decision: he confronts the bully, saying, "I will report this to Cairo," then, having succeeded in stopping the cruelty, he retreats, feeling "exposed, futile." He gets no satisfaction from accomplishing his end because he is haunted by the overall loss of "innocence . . . the only pure time, at the beginning, when the ancient artist, knowing no other land, had learned to look at his own and had seen it as complete." Egypt, like

India, or Trinidad, or all the Third World, presents the modern colonial writer with no such innocence or completion, no satisfactory return when he comes back to his roots. Worse yet, he begins to suspect that those roots in "the beginning" were little more than "a fabrication, a cause for yearning, something for the tomb."

Whether the sense of consequently being locked into a world of reflections and inauthentic replicas rests principally for Naipaul on a metaphysical or a political discovery is not an answerable question: what is certain, to the reader of *Guerrillas* (1975) and *India: A Wounded Civilization* (1977), is that politics and metaphysics support each other. Quite deliberately in the process he becomes a peregrinating writer in the Third World, sending back dispatches to an implied audience of disenchanted Western liberals, not of presumably unteachable colonials. Why? Because he exorcises all the 1960s devils—national liberation movements, revolutionary goals, Third Worldism—and shows them to be fraudulent public relations gimmicks, half native impotence, half badly learned "Western" ideas. Most important, Naipaul can now be cited as an exemplary figure from the Third World who can be relied on always to tell the truth about it. Naipaul is "free of any romantic moonshine about the moral claims of primitives or the glories of blood-stained dictators," Irving Howe said in a *Times* review of *A Bend in the River* (1979), and this supposedly without "a trace [in him] of Western condescension or nostalgia for colonialism."

Not surprisingly, then, Naipaul is the perfect witness for *The New York Review of Books,* where he can be counted on to survey the Third World (with scarcely any other Third World testimony to challenge him), its follies, its corruption, its hideous problems. To say that Naipaul resembles a scavenger, then, is to say that he now prefers to render the ruins and derelictions of postcolonial history without tenderness, without any of the sympathetic insight found, say, in Nadine Gordimer's books, rather than to render that history's processes, occasional heroism, intermittent successes; he prefers to indict guerrillas for their pretensions rather than indict the imperialism and social injustice that drove them to insurrection; he attacks Moslems for the wealth of some of their number and for a vague history of African slave trading, thus putting aside many centuries of majority struggle and complex civilization; he sees in today's Third World only counterfeits of the First World, *never* such things as apartheid or the wholesale American devastation of Indochina. Because he is so gifted a writer— and I write of him with pain and admiration—he can therefore produce such effusions as this from Elizabeth Hardwick (note her elisions, the misleading phrase "lack of historical preparation," which suggests that the Third World's real problem is in not being liberal or white, regardless of how much severer was the "preparation" provided by colonial domination): "Reading his work . . . one cannot help but think of a literal yesterday and today, of Idi Amin, the Ayatollah Khomeini, of the fate of Bhutto. These figures of an improbable and deranging transition come to mind because Naipaul's work is a creative reflection upon a devastating lack of historical preparation, upon the anguish of whole countries and people unable to cope."

The homely intransitive "unable to cope" gives away what the liberal American finds in Naipaul: Africa, Asia, and Latin America suffer from self-inflicted wounds, they are their own worst enemies, their contemporary history is the direct result of seeking, but not finding, a suburban bourgeois therapy for their difficulties. But if this is not really Naipaul's epistle to Hampstead and the Upper West Side, what *does* he give? There isn't real analysis in his essays, only observation, or to put it differently, he does not explain, he only regrets sarcastically. His novels are of a piece with this. *A Bend in the River* takes place in an Africa drenched in memories of departed colonialists replaced by an invisible Big Man whose doings are unreservedly irrational and gratuitous. In the meantime he manages to unsettle a small group of hybrid Indian Moslems like Salim, the novel's sensitive protagonist, who, with no place to go and nothing to do, see the world taken over by rich Arabs and ridiculous savages. For his portrait of "wounded" India, Naipaul resorts to an almost hysterical repetition of how the place has no vitality, no creativity, no authenticity; read the book's last half and you will not believe that this, in its turgid denunciations of a poor country for not measuring up, is the great Naipaul everyone has been extolling.

The Return of Eva Peron is mostly a collection of *New York Review* essays (1972–1975), all of them, except the last one, which is on Conrad, about debased imitations of some already fallen idol. "Michael X and the Black Power Killings in Trinidad" is what the novel *Guerrillas* was based on, the story of a black adventurer using black power ideas for his own meretricious ends in a Trinidad where "racial redemption is as irrelevant for the Negro as for everyone else." The result is a bloody climax representing, like Jimmy Ahmed's demise, "a deep corruption" that "perpetuates the negative, colonial politics of protest" as well as the media and public relations hold on things. Whatever perspicacity there is in Naipaul's deft narrative is betrayed, however, by his analogy of Michael X to O'Neill's Emperor Jones, the ravaged and misled Pullman porter who returns to the jungle. His use of Jones's atavism in the essay and in *Guerrillas* neatly disproves Irving Howe's hasty pronouncement that Naipaul contains no trace of "Western condescension." For indeed, Michael X is seen through deeply condescending and offended *Western* eyes, through which slips not even a momentary flicker of compassion.

The similarity in motif between the essays on Uruguay and Argentina on the one hand, and Mobutu's Zaire on the other, is that in all three places the past has vanished, and has been supplanted either by outlandish parodies of modernity or by a vacancy of the sort likely to produce Borges's peculiar epic memories and the Peron phenomenon. What I find revealing is that Naipaul assumes first of all that the only "past" that counts in Africa or South America is essentially European (hence to be regretted for its disappearance), and second, that *all* attempts to deal with both a multilayered past as well as the present are bound to lead to ridiculous mimicry, tyranny, or some combination of both. So great has the pressure of Western ideas become in Naipaul that any sympathetic feelings he might have had for the things he sees have been obliterated. There is no life in what he writes about—only hard "lunacy, despair." What is not European can only be borrowed from Europe, further enforcing colonial distortion and dependency. The "great African wound" is somehow equivalent to "the African need for African style and luxury." Sex (always badly handled in Naipaul's work) emerges in Latin America as buggery (*machismo*) lovemaking in "the small hole," to use the phrase from *Guerrillas*).

For so assertive and all-seeing an observer, Naipaul is curiously remiss in not having much to say about the role of class in postcolonial societies. Surely more allowances than his must be made for the differences between colonial elites and the masses they dominate. Moreover, there is no good reason for him to avoid comment on the European-American role in Zaire, or in Argentina for that matter. Nowhere in his own reading of the metropolitan West, therefore, did Naipaul establish contact with currents that might have transformed his anger and help-lessness into something less constricting, more helpful than bitterness. Instead, he relies on a European tradition of supposedly direct obser-vation, which has always been dangerously quick to elevate disen-chanted impressions into sweeping generalization. Used *against* native colonial societies by imperialist-minded Westerners, from Lamartine to Waugh, it has justified racial stereotypes and colonialism. Used by a na-tive against other natives it has tended to produce more dependence, self-disgust, collaboration, apathy.

Finally, Naipaul reads Conrad (who "had been everywhere before me") so as to allay his "political panic." Here was an author who had seen "the new politics [of] half-made societies that seemed doomed to remain half-made." Conrad was "the writer who is missing a society," like Naipaul himself; yet unlike today's novelists he did not give up his "interpretive function" when "the societies that produced the great novels of the past [had] cracked." He goes on *meditating*, again like Naipaul, on peripheral societies making and unmaking themselves. But what Naipaul does *not* see is that his great predecessor exempted neither himself nor Europe from the ironies of history readily seen in the non-European world. Certainly there are African, Asian, and Latin American savages in Conrad's novels, but more important, there are Kurtz, and Charles Gould, and of course all the characters in *The Secret Agent*. London, Conrad says in *Heart of Darkness*, is no less a "dark place" than the Congo. No one can draw a self-bolstering European patriotism out of Conrad and claim at the same time to be reading what Conrad *actually* wrote.

That Naipaul does so in effect tells us more about him and his blocked development than any confession. He is in the end too re-markable and gifted a writer to be dismissed; he will be used again, perhaps even by such as Senator Daniel Patrick Moynihan, when the inconveniences of the Third World are to be attacked. One can be sure that when he travels to the rest of the Islamic world, postrevolutionary Iran in particular will seem as stupid, violent, and half-made as Zaire.

The more interesting questions are when will his fundamental position become clear to him and when, consequently, will he see himself with less bad faith than he now sees himself and his fellow colonials. Whether that vision can in his case produce a good novel is not exclusively an aesthetic puzzle, just as whether he will then amuse the audience that now regards him as a gifted native informer is also not mainly an aesthetic question. But he will, almost certainly, come to fuller appreciation of human effort and he will be a freer, more genuinely imaginative writer along the way. Perhaps then the jasmine and its name will remain apart in his mind at less cost to the poor natives who have been helping to pay his emotional bill.

11

Grey Eminence

Walter Lippmann (1889–1974) was probably the most powerful and famous American journalist of this century, a fact confirmed many times over in Ronald Steel's extraordinarily fine biography, *Walter Lippmann and the American Century*. The only son of very well-off German-Jewish parents, Lippmann had a sheltered and privileged childhood in New York, "learning Latin and Greek by gaslight and riding a goat cart in Central Park" before going off to Harvard, where his classmates included John Reed, T. S. Eliot, and Conrad Aiken. From birth to death, Fortune—in the form of knowing nearly everyone who counted and being able to defend at least two sides of every major public issue of his time—always favored him. The list of his friends, his associates, the things he did ("worked as a legman for Lincoln Steffens . . . debated socialism with Bernard Shaw and H. G. Wells . . . became the éminence grise to Woodrow Wilson's own alter ego, Colonel House"), the presidents, kings, and leaders he knew, the great events he witnessed at very close quarters, the papers, books, and journals he produced, the careers he espoused or helped, the ideas, issues, problems he encountered and illuminated, is positively awesome, and, as Steel says justly, "gave him an enormous power over public opinion." Yet Lippmann never held office; although substantial, his wealth did not command direct control over industry or finance capital; he had many influential friends, but never a school or movement behind him. The only thing he did ("only" being a most inadequate word here) was, as he put it, to assist his American readers in making an "adjustment to reality."

Somewhere fairly close to raw power of the kind generals, captains of industry, and politicians have, and well above the vast majority of mankind, was where Lippmann stood. He was in, without being fully of, the American Establishment. One of Steel's accomplishments is to portray this Establishment, so unlike its European counterparts, with rare skill; compared with the recent *The American Establishment* by Leonard and Mark Silk, Steel's portrait is far more effective precisely because, like Lippmann himself, Steel understands that what matters is how it is animated, what a master of its contradictions and conjunctures can manipulate in it, and not only what, stated as if it were something for which a Cook's Tour could be arranged, it is. Lippmann's achievements and his eminence derive less from opportunism than from his principled belief in the necessity of balance and realism, which of course are the very code words of American Establishment beliefs. You hold all the cards, ultimately, if you have the power; Rockefellers, Lamonts, Morgans, Roosevelts, people the political landscape from right to liberal left; the main thing, therefore, is not simply to exclude or include, but in the final analysis to *incorporate* all positions even as you make one position dominant, the "realistic" one. And this is what Lippmann rationalized—the appearance, and actually more than that, the *conviction*, of realism.

Before World War One he was a radical socialist. He dropped that for muckraking journalism. Then he shifted to liberalism, to pragmatism (whose philosophical elements he had picked up while studying under William James), and then finally to national prominence as a pundit who wrote regularly for the *New Republic*, the *New York World*, the *Herald Tribune*, the *Washington Post*, and *Newsweek*. The keynote of his manner throughout his career was dispassionate impartiality, which was doubtless responsible both for his reputation as a man above politics and for his "remarkable facility for not straying too far from the thrust of public opinion." Here particularly, guiding the reader through the labyrinthine turns of a career intimately connected with U.S. public policy before, during, and after World War One, the Depression, the New Deal, World War Two, and Vietnam, Steel is masterful. He ferrets out the emotional component in Lippmann's attitude to issues and to people (his love for Theodore Roosevelt and De Gaulle, his support for and his opposition to Al Smith, F. D. R., and Wilson, his noble disenchantment with L. B. J. over Vietnam, which led him to entertain I. F. Stone at his house), and then clearly outlines Lippmann's public views, reducing neither his personal commitments to his stated positions, nor his carefully formulated philosophy to his emotional peculiarities.

On the other hand, Steel does seem to be too cautious, given the vastly tempting evidence he puts forward in so scrupulous a way. True, he knew Lippmann and spent many years writing the book, and true also that he is a biographer, after all, not a polemicist. But surely there are explicit connections to be made between Lippmann's ambivalence toward his own Jewishness and his lesser ambivalence toward authority: this is indirectly exemplified in the way his sympathy for Sacco and Vanzetti was overridden by a need to congratulate President Lowell of Harvard (who with some associates wrote the report that condemned the two men to death) for doing a "disagreeable duty bravely." Similarly, Steel does not sufficiently analyze Lippmann's notions about the importance of wealth and fame, thereby failing to contrast his celebrated, often-proclaimed journalistic ethic of liberalism and disinterestedness with his record of rarely offending any one of the powerful Establishment figures who patronized him. There are also ellipses in Steel's otherwise satisfying account of Lippmann's friendships with Bernard Berenson and Felix Frankfurter, two men whose rise in celebrity and subsequent symbolic value for the largely WASP Establishment parallels Lippmann's own. Perhaps, too, there could have been more said about Lippmann's unpleasantly constricted personal life, and about his second wife, who before Lippmann won her had been married to Hamilton Fish Armstrong, editor of *Foreign Affairs,* and one of Lippmann's closest friends, and who quite simply turned away from him during his illnesses: this, Steel says unconvincingly, was an instance of her inability to "handle" suffering. But what might such human lapses, ultimately caused by him and frequently present in the midst of all Lippmann's closest relationships, tell us about the general aura of coldness, distance, and emotional inadequacy radiated by his life and work? Steel does not say.

None of these insufficiently investigated matters is, I believe, merely a detail in the otherwise exemplary career Lippmann fashioned for himself during "the American century." Each with its disturbing significance belongs crucially to some aspect of his biography and of his country, which, as Steel says, acquired dominance in the twentieth century. Balance and disinterestedness, for example, derive less from fairness and human concern than from the world-view of a class for whom the Atlantic West and the unquestioned power of privilege and wealth provided the focus of vision, and from a condescending view of humanity at large. Consonant with this, Lippmann upheld the principle of racial quotas in immigration, thought the inhabitants of the Caribbean "inferior races," and was bored and uncomfortable with the Third World. In 1938, European Jews were to him aspects of an "overpopulation" problem. A "surplus" number (presumably those who were not otherwise to be interned or killed) could be shipped off to Africa, he suggested grandiosely. He considered the idea of interning Japanese-Americans a congenial one, just as (with his friend Berenson) he found Hindu art, like Hindu people, loathsome and terrifying.

Even though Steel is surely correct to say that Lippmann was neither a philosopher nor a system-builder, but a skeptic who "could analyze situations with finesse and give off brilliant flashes of illumination," Lippmann's painstakingly cultivated public prominence tells an important story about the consistent social role he played. In providing so much material about this as a sort of running accompaniment to the main story, Steel's book will, I think, be enduringly valuable. Consider, it asks, what it means for a man to make a career out of politics and journalism, yet to appear to have been unsullied by either of them. Consider again the career of a man whose view of the mass audience he wrote for was patronizing at best, contemptuous at worst. Or there is the story of a man who was admired by nearly everyone as a towering intellectual, yet who—except for his opposition to the Vietnam War—could not sustain a position which he considered, on grounds of conscience, to be right.

This is an American career best understood initially in Italian terms. Lippmann is Gramsci's organic intellectual; he caters to the powers of civil society in the sophisticated manner of Castiglione's courtier; his social authority is acquired like that of Croce (a lay pope, Gramsci said), whose adroit mastery of disseminative techniques and rhetorical strategies gave him the ascendancy and popularity normally denied so mandarin a figure. Thereafter, the Italian analogies no longer serve and have to be replaced by the appropriately American characteristics that help to explain his successes. Lippmann was in part a secular evangelist representing the cult of expertise and realism. He belongs equally to McLuhan's media world and to the network of prominent Eastern clubs, universities, corporations, and government. Pulsating with compelling tenacity through everything he wrote was the ideological doctrine allowing a lone voice the authority to "express America" with the unanimity of national consensus: the roots of this extend back to the Puritan notion of an errand in the wilderness.

The result in personal terms is extraordinarily depressing to contemplate. Steel's book is uncompromising in this regard. Few political writers more than Lippmann stripped the self of its ties to community, family, and personal loyalty, in order to enhance the claims of a "national" interest. He perfected the idea that democracy was to be celebrated for (rather than by) the masses by people who knew better, experts who were members of a "specialized class," "insiders" who instructed everyone else in what was good or bad. And who better than Lippmann shrouded raw American power in the mystifying clouds of altruism, realism, and moralism, from which the country as a whole has yet to escape, while its unparalleled capacity for good and evil has scarcely begun to be controlled or understood?

Lippmann, in short, was the journalist of consolidation. For him, what mattered was the status quo: he elaborated it, he was tempted by and he succumbed to it, he sacrificed his humanity to it. Childless, shedding and acquiring friends and attitudes with alarming frequency and poise, allowing his writing only very rarely to express the uncertainty and human frailty that Steel convinces us he often felt, Lippmann articulated the "national interest" as if only his insider's view was responsibly serious. Hence his ultimate public influence and his ultimate superficiality as a commentator on the world. This is Steel's assessment:

> He believed that America's cold war policies were essentially defensive, that it had acquired its informal empire by "accident," and that the problem was primarily one of execution rather than of conception. He criticised the policy-makers, but rarely what lay behind their conception. Thus when he returned from India in late 1949 he could write that Asians need not choose sides in the cold war because they could remain sheltered by the world power balance and "the tacit protection of a friendly state which dominates the highways of the globe in order to protect the peace of the world." Not for another 15 years [until his disenchantment with Johnson's Vietnam policy: he would then be seventy-five years old] would he question whether that dominant state really had such "friendly" motives.

Although it is commonplace to berate radical writers on American politics for their naiveté and lack of realism, Steel's Lippmann is the one who appears unrealistic, even naive. Randolph Bourne, I. F. Stone, H. L. Mencken, C. Wright Mills, and Lincoln Steffens had few illusions about power: Lippmann made an early compromise with it, and never again looked at it without at the same time prettifying it, or at least screening it from genuine demystification. This, one surmises, was partly due to vanity, partly to a kind of amazingly self-confident thoughtlessness. Never was he without the appearance of seriousness, however. Even the many vignettes of Lippmann's personal life provided by Steel show him solemnly *preserving* himself (worrying about his weight, buying the right kind of suit, seeing the right people, staying at the right hotels, sticking to an inflexible schedule of work, rest, and self-improving travel), and almost never exposing himself to the realities on which he was an expert. Wit and irony seem totally absent from his life. His one great emotional experience seems to have been the courting of Helen Armstrong, an episode rendered with great refinement by Steel: thereafter it is the sense of orderly comfort pervading Lippmann's existence that takes over. When he feuds with L. B. J. over Vietnam—clearly his finest hour for Steel, who endures his subject's heaviness of bearing with admirable patience—one is grateful for the old man's spunk, as well as bothered by the fact that Lippmann's opposition to the garrulous Texan was the result, not only of anger at a reckless military policy, but of personal pique. "Seduction and Betrayal" is Steel's title for the episode.

On what was Lippmann's realism based? We must rule out the disenchantment that may come with deep reflection on experience, just as we must rule out serious scholarship or learning. He cannot be said ever to have tried to identify the sources of U.S. foreign policy, or even to have investigated the conceptual framework in which the nation carried on its business at home and abroad. Certainly he did not live politics as someone responsible to a constituency: he never became a technical expert at running a political apparatus, encountering human resistances, fashioning new tactics as a result. No: he was a realist only so far as opinion was concerned. His skill was in using his considerable resources to maintain himself before the public, to gain an impressive social authority, and, for fifty years, to keep it. One can respect that achievement, which is a formal and social one, more easily than most of the intellectual or moral ones which have been claimed for him by his admirers.

Lippmann's career thus exemplifies his country's choice of the *style* of reassuring authority over any concrete message or social vision. Why else do people still speak of Walter Cronkite as a Presidential candidate if it is not because of what Lippmann pioneered as a reliable media personality? The important thing for a European to understand about Lippmann is that he had the prestige of an Orwell, a Sartre, or a Silone, a much wider audience than all of them together, without at any time actually having an intellectual's mission.

To consider Lippmann's case as an instance of the *trahison des clercs* is to apply canons of judgment where they are not completely pertinent. The relevant attitude is, I think, an investigative one. How did the ever-expanding contemporary information apparatus (of which the mass media are a branch) grow to such an extent as almost to swallow whole the intellectual's function? How do a career and a status like Lippmann's get sustained entirely by opinion: without necessary reference to reality or truth (most people, for example, never seemed to test Lippmann and other "insiders" or experts against what *really* takes place in the world) or to principle? And, finally, what have the Western media done in creating personalities and worlds of opinion operating paradoxically in full, ostensibly free public view according to esoteric laws of their own? Has the modern journalist so effectively become mankind's unacknowledged legislator?

12

Among the Believers

In his new book *Among the Believers: An Islamic Journey*, Naipaul the writer flows directly into Naipaul the social phenomenon, the celebrated sensibility on tour, abhorring the post-colonial world for its lies, its mediocrity, cruelty, violence, and maudlin self-indulgence. Naipaul, demystifier of the West crying over the spilt milk of colonialism. The writer of travel journalism—unencumbered with much knowledge or information, and not much interested in imparting any—is a stiff, mostly silent presence in this book, which is the record of a visit in 1979–1980 to Iran, Pakistan, Malaysia, Indonesia. What he sees he sees because it happens before him and, more important, because it confirms what, except for an occasionally eye-catching detail, he already knows. He does not learn: *they* prove. Prove what? That the "retreat" to Islam is "stupefaction." In Malaysia Naipaul is asked: "What is the purpose of your writing? Is it to tell people what it's all about?" He replies: "Yes, I would say comprehension." "Is it not for money?" "Yes. But the nature of the work is important."

Thus Naipaul travels and writes about it because it is important, not because he likes doing it. There is very little pleasure and only a bit more affection recorded in this book. Its funny moments are at the expense of

Muslims, wogs after all, who cannot spell, be coherent, sound right to a worldly-wise, somewhat jaded judge from the West. Every time they show their Islamic weaknesses, Naipaul the phenomenon appears promptly. A Muslim lapse occurs, some puerile resentment is expressed, and then, *ex cathedra*, we are given a passage like this:

> Khomeini required only faith. But he also knew the value of Iran's oil to countries that lived by machines, and he could send the Phantoms and the tanks against the Kurds. Interpreter of the faithful, he expressed all the confusion of his people and made it appear like glory, like the familiar faith: the confusion of a people of high medieval culture awakening to oil and money, a sense of power and violation and a knowledge of a great new encircling civilization. It was to be rejected: at the same time it was to be depended on.

Remember that last sentence and a half, for it is Naipaul's thesis as well as the platform from which he addresses the world: the West is the world of knowledge, criticism, technical know-how, and functioning institutions, Islam its fearfully enraged and retarded dependant, awakening to a new, barely controllable power. The West provides Islam with good things from the outside, for "the life that had come to Islam had not come from within." Thus the entire existence of 800,000,000 people is summed up in a phrase, and dismissed. Islam's flaw was at

> its origins—the flaw that ran right through Islamic history: to the political issues it raised it offered no political or practical solution. It offered only the faith. It offered only the Prophet, who would settle everything—but who had ceased to exist. This political Islam was rage, anarchy.

After such knowledge what forgiveness? Very little obviously. The Islamic characters encountered by Naipaul, those half-educated schoolteachers, journalists, sometime revolutionaries, bureaucrats, and religious fanatics, they exude little charm, arouse scant interest or compassion. One, yes, one person only, an Indonesian poet, suggests some nobility and intelligence. Carefully set and dramatized, Naipaul's descriptions, however, invariably tend to slide away from the specific into the realm of the general. Each chapter ends with some bit of sententiousness, but just before the end there comes a dutiful squeezing out of Meaning, as if the author could no longer let his characters exist without some appended commentary that aligns things clearly under the Islam/West polarity. Conversation made in a Kuala Lumpur hotel in the company of two young Muslims and a book left by one of them with Naipaul, are suddenly instances of "Islam" (uncritical, uncreative) and the "West" (creative, critical).

It is not just that Naipaul carries with him a kind of half-stated but finally unexamined reverence for the colonial order. That attitude has it that the old days were better, when Europe ruled the coloreds and allowed them few silly pretensions about purity, independence, and new ways. It is a view declared openly by many people. Naipaul is one of them, except that he is better able than most to express the view perhaps. He is a kind of belated Kipling just the same. What is worse, I think, is that this East/West dichotomy covers up a deep emptiness in Naipaul the writer, for which Naipaul the social phenomenon is making others pay, even as a whole train of his present admirers applauds his candor, his telling-it-like-it-is about that Third World which he comprehends "better" than anyone else.

One can trace the emptiness back a few years. Consider, for instance, "One Out of Many," a deft story published in *In a Free State* (1971). At the very end of the tale Santosh, the Bombayan immigrant to Washington, watches the city burn. It is 1968: blacks run amuck and, to Santosh's surprise, one of them scrawls *Soul Brother* on the pavement outside his house. "Brother to what or to whom?" Santosh muses. "I was once part of the flow, never thinking of myself as a presence. Then I looked in the mirror and decided to be free. All that my freedom has brought me is the knowledge that I have a face and have a body, that I must feed this body and clothe this body for a certain number of years. Then it will be over." Disavowal of that admittedly excited community of sixties revolutionaries is where it begins. Seeing oneself free of illusion is a gain in awareness, but it also means emptying out one's historical identity. The next step is to proceed through life with a minimum number of attachments: do not overload the mind. Keep it away from history and causes; feel and wait. Record what you see accordingly, and cultivate moral passions.

The trouble here is that a mind-free body gave birth to a super-ego of astonishingly assertive attitudes. Unrestrained by genuine learning or self-education, this persona—Naipaul the ex-novelist—tours the vulnerable parts of his natal provenance, the colonial world he has been telling us about via his acquired British identity. But the places he visits are carefully chosen, they are absolutely safe, places no one in the liberal culture that has made him its darling will speak up for. Everyone knows Islam is a "place" you must criticize. *Time* did it, *Newsweek* did it, the *Guardian* and the *New York Times* did it. Naipaul wouldn't make a trip to Israel, for example, which is not to say that he wouldn't find rabbinical laws governing daily behavior any less repressive than Khomeini's. No: *his* audience knows Israel is OK, "Islam" not. And one more thing. If it is criticism that the West stands for, good— we want Naipaul to criticize those mad mullahs, vacant Islamic students, cliché-ridden revolutionaries. But does he write *for* and *to* them? Does he live among them, risk their direct retaliation, write in their presence so to speak, and does he like Socrates live through the consequences of his criticism? Not at all. No dialogue. He snipes at them from the *Atlantic Monthly* where none of them can ever get back at him.

What is the result? Never mind the ridiculous misinformation (on page 12, for example, he speaks absurdly of loyalty to the fourth imam as responsible for the Shia Iranian "divergence") and the potted history inserted here and there. The characters barely come alive. The descriptions are lackadaisical, painfully slow, repetitious. The landscapes are half-hearted at best. How can one learn about "Islam" from him? Without the languages, he talks to the odd characters who happen by. He makes them directly representative of "Islam," covering his ignorance with no appreciable respect for history. On the first page we are told that Sadeq "was the kind of man who, without political doctrine, only with resentments, had made the Iranian revolution." An unacceptable exaggeration. Millions of Iranians, not just the Sadeqs and the Khomeinis, but the Shariatis, Taleqanis, Barahenis, and many many more poets, clerics, philosophers, doctors, soldiers—they made the revolution. All one has to do is to look at Nikki Keddie's *Roots of Revolution: An Interpretive History of Modern Iran* (Yale, 1981) to find out what doctrines and persons made the revolution. But no, Naipaul petulantly says, it was just resentment. Doubtless he hasn't dreamed of the possibility that the same *Hajji Baba* by James Morier which he quotes to assert the fanatical religious gullibility of Iranians was translated into Iranian early in this century by Mirza Habib Esfhani and in this version, according to Professor Keddie, the book is more critical of "Iran's faults than the original."

Little of what took place in 1979 is mentioned here. Naipaul's method is to attack Islamic politics without taking account of what its main currents and events are. In Pakistan Zia's much-resented, much-resisted (U.S.-assisted) assault on Pakistani civil society is nearly invisible to Naipaul. Indonesian history is the Japanese occupation, the killing of "the communists" in 1965, and the present. The massacres of East Timor are effaced. Iran is portrayed as a country in the grip of hysteria; you would not know from Naipaul that a tremendous post-revolutionary battle, occurring while he was there, continues to go on. All this to promote an attitude of distant concern and moral superiority in the reader.

Despite its veneer of personal impressionism, then, this is a political book in intention. On one level Naipaul is the late twentieth-century heir of Henry MacKenzie, who in *The Man of Feeling* (1771) averred that "every noble feeling rises within me! every beat of my heart awakens a virtue—but it will make you hate the world! No . . . I can hate nothing; but as to the world—I pity the men of it." That these men happen to be brown or black is no inconvenience on another level. They are to be castigated for not being Europeans, and this is a political pastime useless to them, eminently useful for anyone plotting to use Rapid Deployment Forces against "Islam." But then Naipaul isn't a politician: he's just a Writer.

13

Opponents, Audiences, Constituencies, and Community

Who writes? For whom is the writing being done? In what circumstances? These, it seems to me, are the questions whose answers provide us with the ingredients making for a politics of interpretation. But if one does not wish to ask and answer the questions in a dishonest and abstract way, some attempt must be made to show why they are questions of some relevance to the present time. What needs to be said at the beginning is that the single most impressive aspect of the present time—at least for the "humanist," a description for which I have contradictory feelings of affection and revulsion—is that it is manifestly the Age of Ronald Reagan. And it is in this age as a context and setting that the politics of interpretation and the politics of culture are enacted.

I do not want to be misunderstood as saying that the cultural situation I describe here caused Reagan, or that it typifies Reaganism, or that everything about it can be ascribed or referred back to the personality of Ronald Reagan. What I argue is that a particular situation within the field we call "criticism" is not merely related to but is an integral part of the currents of thought and practice that play a role within the Reagan era. Moreover, I think, "criticism" and the traditional academic humanities have gone through a series of developments over time whose beneficiary and culmination is Reaganism. Those are the gross claims that I make for my argument.

A number of miscellaneous points need to be made here. I am fully aware that any effort to characterize the present cultural moment is very likely to seem quixotic at best, unprofessional at worst. But that, I submit, is an aspect of the present cultural moment, in which the social and historical setting of critical activity is a totality felt to be benign (free, apolitical, serious), uncharacterizable as a whole (it is too complex to be described in general and tendentious terms), and somehow outside history. Thus it seems to me that one thing to be tried—out of sheer critical obstinacy—is precisely *that* kind of generalization, *that* kind of political portrayal, *that* kind of overview condemned by the present dominant culture to appear inappropriate and doomed from the start.

It is my conviction that culture works very effectively to make invisible and even "impossible" the actual *affiliations* that exist between the world of ideas and scholarship, on the one hand, and the world of brute politics, corporate and state power, and military force, on the other. The cult of expertise and professionalism, for example, has so restricted our scope of vision that a positive (as opposed to an implicit or passive) doctrine of noninterference among fields has set in. This doctrine has it that the general public is best left ignorant, and the most crucial policy questions affecting human existence are best left to "experts," specialists who talk about their specialty only, and—to use the word first given wide social approbation by Walter Lippmann in *Public Opinion* and *The Phantom Public*—"insiders," people (usually men) who are endowed with the special privilege of knowing how things really work and, more important, of being close to power.[1]

Humanistic culture in general has acted in tacit compliance with this antidemocratic view, the more regrettably since, both in their formulation and in the politics they have given rise to, so-called policy issues can hardly be said to enhance human community. In a world of increasing interdependence and political consciousness, it seems both violent and wasteful to accept the notion, for example, that countries ought to be classified simply as pro-Soviet or pro-American. Yet this classification—and with it the reappearance of a whole range of cold war motifs and symptoms (discussed by Noam Chomsky in *Towards a New Cold War*)—dominates thinking about foreign policy. There is little in humanistic culture that is an effective antidote to it, just as it is true that few humanists have very much to say about the problems starkly dramatized by the 1980 Report of the Independent Commission on International Development Issues, *North-South: A Programme for Survival.* Our political discourse is now choked with enormous, thought-stopping abstractions, from terrorism, Communism, Islamic fundamentalism, and instability, to moderation, freedom, stability, and strategic alliances, all of them as unclear as they are both potent and unrefined in their appeal. It is next to impossible to think about human society either in a global way (as Richard Falk eloquently does in *A Global Approach to National Policy* [1975]) or at the level of everyday life. As Philip Green shows in *The Pursuit of Inequality,* notions like equality and welfare have simply been chased off the intellectual land-scape. Instead a brutal Darwinian picture of self-help and self-promotion is proposed by Reaganism, both domestically and internationally, as an image of the world ruled by what is being called "productivity" or "free enterprise."

Add to this the fact that liberalism and the Left are in a state of in-tellectual disarray and fairly dismal perspectives emerge. The challenge posed by these perspectives is not how to cultivate one's garden despite them but how to understand cultural work occurring within them. What I propose here, then, is a rudimentary attempt to do just that, notwithstanding a good deal of inevitable incompleteness, overstate-ment, generalization, and crude characterization. Finally, I will very quickly propose an alternative way of undertaking cultural work, al-though anything like a fully worked-out program can only be done collectively and in a separate study.

My use of "constituency," "audience," "opponents," and "commu-nity" serves as a reminder that no one writes simply for oneself. There is always an Other; and this Other willy-nilly turns interpretation into a social activity, albeit with unforeseen consequences, audiences, con-stituencies, and so on. And, I would add, interpretation is the work of intellectuals, a class badly in need today of moral rehabilitation and social redefinition. The one issue that urgently requires study is, for the humanist no less than for the social scientist, the status of *information* as a component of knowledge: its sociopolitical status, its contemporary fate, its economy (a subject treated recently by Herbert Schiller in *Who Knows: Information in the Age of the Fortune 500*). We all think we know what it means, for example, to *have* information and to write and interpret texts containing information. Yet we live in an age which places unprecedented emphasis on the production of knowledge and information, as Fritz Machlup's *Production and Distribution of Knowledge in the United States* dramatizes clearly. What happens to information and knowledge, then, when IBM and AT&T—two of the world's largest corporations—claim that what they do is to put "knowledge" to work "for the people"? What is the role of humanistic knowledge and information if they are not to be unknowing (many ironies there) partners in commodity production and marketing, so much so that what humanists do may in the end turn out to be a quasi-religious concealment of this peculiarly unhumanistic process? A true secular politics of interpretation sidesteps this question at its peril.

At a recent MLA convention, I stopped by the exhibit of a major university press and remarked to the amiable sales representative on duty that there seemed to be no limit to the number of highly specialized books of advanced literary criticism his press put out. "Who reads these books?" I asked, implying, of course, that however brilliant and important most of them were they were difficult to read and therefore could not have a wide audience—or at least an audience wide enough to justify regular publication during a time of economic crisis. The answer I received made sense, assuming I was told the truth. People who write specialized, advanced (i.e., New New) criticism faithfully read one another's books. Thus each such book could be assured of, but wasn't necessarily always getting, sales of around three thousand copies, "all other things being equal." The last qualification struck me as ambiguous at best, but it needn't detain us here. The point was that a nice little audience had been built and could be routinely mined by this press; certainly, on a much larger scale, publishers of cookbooks and exercise manuals apply a related principle as they churn out what may seem like a very long series of unnecessary books, even if an expanding crowd of avid food and exercise aficionados is not quite the same thing as a steadily attentive and earnest crowd of three thousand critics reading one another.

What I find peculiarly interesting about the real or mythical three thousand is that whether they derive ultimately from the Anglo-American New Criticism (as formulated by I. A. Richards, William Empson, John Crowe Ransom, Cleanth Brooks, Allen Tate, and company, beginning in the 1920s and continuing for several decades thereafter) or from the so-called New New Criticism (Roland Barthes, Jacques Derrida, et al., during the 1960s), they vindicate, rather than undermine, the notion that intellectual labor ought to be divided into progressively narrower niches. Consider very quickly the irony of this. New Criticism claimed to view the verbal object as in itself it really was, free from the distractions of biography, social message, even paraphrase. Matthew Arnold's critical program was thereby to be advanced not by jumping directly from the text to the whole of culture but by using a highly concentrated verbal analysis to comprehend cultural values available only through a finely wrought literary structure finely understood.

Charges made against the American New Criticism that its ethos was clubby, gentlemanly, or Episcopalian are, I think, correct only if it is added that in practice New Criticism, for all its elitism, was strangely populist in intention. The idea behind the pedagogy, and of course the preaching, of Brooks and Robert Penn Warren was that everyone properly instructed could feel, perhaps even act, like an educated gentleman. In its sheer projection this was by no means a trivial ambition. No amount of snide mocking at their quaint gentility can conceal the fact that, in order to accomplish the conversion, the New Critics aimed at nothing less than the removal of *all* of what they considered the specialized rubbish—put there, they presumed, by professors of literature—standing between the reader of a poem and the poem. Leaving aside the questionable value of the New Criticism's ultimate social and moral message, we must concede that the school deliberately and perhaps incongruously tried to create a wide community of responsive readers out of a very large, potentially unlimited, constituency of students and teachers of literature.

In its early days, the French *nouvelle critique,* with Barthes as its chief apologist, attempted the same kind of thing. Once again the guild of professional literary scholars was characterized as impeding responsiveness to literature. Once again the antidote was what seemed to be a specialized reading technique based on a near jargon of linguistic, psychoanalytic, and Marxist terms, all of which proposed a new freedom for writers and literate readers alike. The philosophy of *écriture* promised wider horizons and a less restricted community, once an initial (and as it turned out painless) surrender to structuralist activity had been made. For despite structuralist prose, there was no impulse among the principal structuralists to exclude readers; quite the contrary, as Barthes' often abusive attacks on Raymond Picard show, the main purpose of critical reading was to create new readers of the classics who might otherwise have been frightened off by their lack of professional literary accreditation.

For about four decades, then, in both France and the United States, the schools of "new" critics were committed to prying literature and writing loose from confining institutions. However much it was to depend upon carefully learned technical skills, reading was in very large measure to become an act of public depossession. Texts were to be unlocked or decoded, then handed on to anyone who was interested. The resources of symbolic language were placed at the disposal of readers who it was assumed suffered the debilitations of either irrelevant "professional" information or the accumulated habits of lazy inattention.

Thus French and American New Criticism were, I believe, competitors for authority within mass culture, not other-worldly alternatives to it. Because of what became of them, we have tended to forget the original missionary aims the two schools set for themselves. They belong to precisely the same moment that produced Jean-Paul Sartre's ideas about an engaged literature and a committed writer. Literature was about the world, readers were in the world; the question was not *whether* to be but *how* to be, and this was best answered by carefully analyzing language's symbolic enactments of the various existential possibilities available to human beings. What the Franco-American critics shared was the notion that verbal discipline could be self-sufficient once you learned to think pertinently about language stripped of unnecessary scaffolding: in other words, you did not need to be a professor to benefit from Donne's metaphors or Saussure's liberating distinction between *langue* and *parole*. And so the New Criticism's precious and cliquish aspect was mitigated by its radically anti-institutional bias, which manifested itself in the enthusiastic therapeutic optimism to be observed in both France and the United States. Join humankind against the schools: this was a message a great many people could appreciate.

How strangely perverse, then, that the legacy of both types of New Criticism is the private-clique consciousness embodied in a kind of critical writing that has virtually abandoned any attempt at reaching a large, if not a mass, audience. My belief is that both in the United States and in France the tendency toward formalism in New Criticism was accentuated by the academy. For the fact is that a disciplined attention to language can only thrive in the rarefied atmosphere of the classroom. Linguistics and literary analysis are features of the modern school, not of the marketplace. Purifying the language of the tribe—whether as a project subsumed within modernism or as a hope kept alive by embattled New Criticisms surrounded by mass culture—always moved further from the really big existing tribes and closer toward emerging new ones, comprised of the acolytes of a reforming or even revolutionary creed who in the end seemed to care more about turning the new creed into an intensely separatist orthodoxy than about forming a large community of readers.

To its unending credit, the university protects such wishes and shelters them under the umbrella of academic freedom. Yet advocacy of *close reading* or of *écriture* can quite naturally entail hostility to outsiders who fail to grasp the salutary powers of verbal analysis; moreover, persuasion too often has turned out to be less important than purity of intention and execution. In time the guild adversarial sense grew as the elaborate techniques multiplied, and an interest in expanding the constituency lost out to a wish for abstract correctness and methodological rigor within a quasi-monastic order. Critics read each other and cared about little else.

The parallels between the fate of a New Criticism reduced to abandoning universal literacy entirely and that of the school of F. R. Leavis are sobering. As Francis Mulhern reminds us in *The Moment of Scrutiny*, Leavis was not a formalist himself and began his career in the context of generally Left politics. Leavis argued that great literature was fundamentally opposed to a class society and to the dictates of a coterie.

In his view, English studies ought to become the cornerstone of a new, fundamentally democratic outlook. But largely because the Leavisites concentrated their work both in and for the university, what began as a healthy oppositional participation in modern industrial society changed into a shrill withdrawal from it. English studies became narrower and narrower, in my opinion, and critical reading degenerated into decisions about what should or should not be allowed into the great tradition.

I do not want to be misunderstood as saying that there is something inherently pernicious about the modern university that produces the changes I have been describing. Certainly there is a great deal to be said in favor of a university manifestly not influenced or controlled by coarse partisan politics. But one thing in particular about the university—and here I speak about the modern university without distinguishing between European, American, or Third World and socialist universities—does appear to exercise an almost totally unrestrained influence: the principle that knowledge ought to exist, be sought after, and disseminated in a very divided form. Whatever the social, political, economic, and ideological reasons underlying this principle, it has not long gone without its challengers. Indeed, it may not be too much of an exaggeration to say that one of the most interesting motifs in modern world culture has been the debate between proponents of the belief that knowledge can exist in a synthetic universal form and, on the other hand, those who believe that knowledge is inevitably produced and nurtured in specialized compartments. Georg Lukács' attack on reification and his advocacy of "totality," in my opinion, very tantalizingly resemble the wide-ranging discussions that have been taking place in the Islamic world since the late nineteenth century on the need for mediating between the claims of a totalizing Islamic vision and modern specialized science. These epistemological controversies are therefore centrally important to the workplace of knowledge production, the university, in which *what* knowledge is and how it ought to be discovered are the very lifeblood of its being.

The most impressive recent work concerning the history, circumstances, and constitution of modern knowledge has stressed the role of social convention. Thomas Kuhn's "paradigm of research," for example,

shifts attention away from the individual creator to the communal restraints upon personal initiative. Galileos and Einsteins are infrequent
figures not just because genius is a rare thing but because scientists are
borne along by agreed-upon ways to do research, and this consensus encourages uniformity rather than bold enterprise. Over time this uniformity acquires the status of a discipline, while its subject matter becomes
a field or territory. Along with these goes a whole apparatus of techniques, one of whose functions is, as Michel Foucault has tried to show
in *The Archaeology of Knowledge,* to protect the coherence, the territorial
integrity, the social identity of the field, its adherents and its institutional presence. You cannot simply choose to be a sociologist or a psy-
choanalyst; you cannot simply make statements that have the status of
knowledge in anthropology; you cannot merely suppose that what you
say as a historian (however well it may have been researched) enters historical discourse. You have to pass through certain rules of accreditation, you must learn the rules, you must speak the language, you must
master the idioms, and you must accept the authorities of the field—determined in many of the same ways—to which you want to contribute.

In this view of things, expertise is partially determined by how well
an individual learns the rules of the game, so to speak. Yet it is difficult to determine in absolute terms whether expertise is *mainly* constituted by the social conventions governing the intellectual manners of
scientists or, on the other hand, mainly by the putative exigencies of
the subject matter itself. Certainly convention, tradition, and habit
create ways of looking at a subject that transform it completely: and
just as certainly there are generic differences between the subjects of
history, literature, and philology that require different (albeit related)
techniques of analysis, disciplinary attitudes, and commonly held
views. Elsewhere I have taken the admittedly aggressive position that
Orientalists, area-studies experts, journalists, and foreign-policy specialists are not always sensitive to the dangers of self-quotation, endless repetition, and received ideas that their fields encourage, for
reasons that have more to do with politics and ideology than with any
"outside" reality. Hayden White has shown in his work that historians
are subject not just to narrative conventions but also to the virtually
closed space imposed on the interpreter of events by verbal retrospec-
tion, which is very far from being an objective mirror of reality. Yet

even these views, although they are understandably repugnant to many people, do not go as far as saying that everything about a "field" can be reduced either to an interpretive convention or to political interest.

Let us grant, therefore, that it would be a long and potentially impossible task to prove empirically that, on the one hand, there could be objectivity so far as knowledge about human society is concerned or, on the other, that all knowledge is esoteric and subjective. Much ink has been spilled on both sides of the debate, not all of it useful, as Wayne Booth has shown in his discussion of scientism and modernism, *Modern Dogma and the Rhetoric of Assent.* An instructive opening out of the impasse—to which I want to return a bit later—has been the body of techniques developed by the school of reader-response critics: Wolfgang Iser, Norman Holland, Stanley Fish, and Michael Riffaterre, among others. These critics argue that since texts without readers are no less incomplete than readers without texts, we should focus attention on what happens when both components of the interpretive situation interact. Yet with the exception of Fish, reader-response critics tend to regard interpretation as an essentially private, interiorized happening, thereby inflating the role of solitary decoding at the expense of its just as important social context. In his latest book, *Is There a Text in This Class?*, Fish accentuates the role of what he calls interpretive communities, groups as well as institutions (principal among them the classroom and pedagogues) whose presence, much more than any unchanging objective standard or correlative of absolute truth, controls what we consider to be knowledge. If, as he says, "interpretation is the only game in town," then it must follow that interpreters who work mainly by persuasion and not scientific demonstration are the only players.

I am on Fish's side there. Unfortunately, though, he does not go very far in showing why, or even how, some interpretations are more persuasive than others. Once again we are back to the quandary suggested by the three thousand advanced critics reading each other to everyone else's unconcern. Is it the inevitable conclusion to the formation of an interpretive community that its constituency, its specialized language, and its concerns tend to get tighter, more airtight, more self-enclosed as its own self-confirming authority acquires more power, the solid status of orthodoxy, and a stable constituency? What is the acceptable humanistic antidote to what one discovers, say, among sociologists, philosophers, and so-called policy scientists who speak only to and for each other in a language oblivious to everything but a well-guarded, constantly shrinking fiefdom forbidden to the uninitiated?

For all sorts of reasons, large answers to these questions do not strike me as attractive or convincing. For one, the universalizing habit by which a system of thought is believed to account for everything too quickly slides into a quasi-religious synthesis. This, it seems to me, is the sobering lesson offered by John Fekete in *The Critical Twilight*, an account of how New Criticism led directly to Marshall McLuhan's "technocratic-religious eschatology." In fact, interpretation and its demands add up to a rough game, once we allow ourselves to step out of the shelter offered by specialized fields and by fancy all-embracing mythologies. The trouble with visions, reductive answers, and systems is that they homogenize evidence very easily. Criticism as such is crowded out and disallowed from the start, hence impossible; and in the end one learns to manipulate bits of the system like so many parts of a machine. Far from taking in a great deal, the universal system as a universal type of explanation either screens out everything it cannot directly absorb or it repetitively churns out the same sort of thing all the time. In this way it becomes a kind of conspiracy theory. Indeed, it has always seemed to me that the supreme irony of what Derrida has called logocentrism is that its critique, deconstruction, is as insistent, as monotonous, and as inadvertently systematizing as logocentrism itself. We may applaud the wish to break out of departmental divisions, therefore, without at the same time accepting the notion that one single method for doing so exists. The unheeding insistence of René Girard's "interdisciplinary" studies of mimetic desire and scapegoat effects is that they want to convert all human activity, all disciplines, to one thing. How can we assume this one thing covers everything that is essential, as Girard keeps suggesting?

This is only a relative skepticism, for one can prefer foxes to hedgehogs without also saying that all foxes are equal. Let us venture a couple of crucial distinctions. To the ideas of Kuhn, Foucault, and Fish we can usefully add those of Giovanni Battista Vico and Antonio Gramsci. Here is what we come up with. Discourses, interpretive communities, and paradigms of research are produced by intellectuals, Gramsci says, who can either be religious or secular. Now Gramsci's implicit contrast of secular with religious intellectuals is less familiar than his celebrated division between organic and traditional intellectuals. Yet it is no less important for that matter. In a letter of August 17, 1931, Gramsci writes about an old teacher from his Cagliari days, Umberto Cosmo:

> It seemed to me that I and Cosmo, and many other intellectuals at this time (say the first fifteen years of the century) occupied a certain common ground: we were all to some degree part of the movement of moral and intellectual reform which in Italy stemmed from Benedetto Croce, and whose first premise was that modern man can and should live without the help of religion . . . positivist religion, mythological religion, or whatever brand one cares to name. . . .[2] This point appears to me even today to be the major contribution made to international culture by modern Italian intellectuals, and it seems to me a civil conquest that must not be lost.[3]

Benedetto Croce of course was Vico's greatest modern student, and it was one of Croce's intentions in writing about Vico to reveal explicitly the strong secular bases of his thought and also to argue in favor of a secure and dominant civil culture (hence Gramsci's use of the phrase "civil conquest"). "Conquest" has perhaps a strange inappropriateness to it, but it serves to dramatize Gramsci's contention—also implicit in Vico—that the modern European state is possible not only because there is a political apparatus (army, police force, bureaucracy) but because there is a civil, secular, and nonecclesiastical society making the state possible, providing the state with something to rule, filling the state with its humanly generated economic, cultural, social, and intellectual production.

Gramsci was unwilling to let the Vichian-Crocean achievement of civil society's secular working go in the direction of what he called "immanentist thought." Like Arnold before him, Gramsci understood that if nothing in the social world is natural, not even nature, then it must also be true that things exist not only because they come into being and are created by human agency (*nascimento*) but also because by coming into being they displace something else that is already there: this is the combative and emergent aspect of social change as it applies to the world of culture linked to social history. To adapt from a statement Gramsci makes in *The Modern Prince*, "reality (and hence cultural reality) is a product of the application of human will to the society of things," and since also "everything is political, even philosophy and philosophies," we are to understand that in the realm of culture and of thought each production exists not only to earn a place for itself but to displace, win out over, others.[4] All ideas, philosophies, views, and texts aspire to the consent of their consumers, and here Gramsci is more percipient than most in recognizing that there is a set of characteristics unique to civil society in which texts—embodying ideas, philosophies, and so forth—acquire power through what Gramsci describes as diffusion, dissemination into and hegemony over the world of "common sense." Thus ideas aspire to the condition of acceptance, which is to say that one can interpret the meaning of a text by virtue of what in its mode of social presence enables its consent by either a small or a wide group of people.

The secular intellectuals are implicitly present at the center of these considerations. Social and intellectual authority for them does not derive directly from the divine but from an analyzable history made by human beings. Here Vico's counterposing of the sacred with what he calls the gentile realm is essential. Created by God, the sacred is a realm accessible only through revelation: it is ahistorical because complete and divinely untouchable. But whereas Vico has little interest in the divine, the gentile world obsesses him. "Gentile" derives from *gens,* the family group whose exfoliation in time generates history. But "gentile" is also a secular expanse because the web of filiations and affiliations that composes human history—law, politics, literature, power, science, emotion—is informed by *ingegno,* human ingenuity and spirit. This, and not a divine *fons et origo,* is accessible to Vico's new science.

But here a very particular kind of secular interpretation and, even more interestingly, a very particular conception of the interpretive situation is entailed. A direct index of this is the confusing organization of Vico's book, which seems to move sideways and backward as often as it moves forward. Because in a very precise sense God has been excluded from Vico's secular history, that history, as well as everything within it, presents its interpreter with a vast horizontal expanse, across which are to be seen many interrelated structures. The verb "to look" is therefore frequently employed by Vico to suggest what historical interpreters need to do. What one cannot see or look at—the past, for example—is to be divined; Vico's irony is too clear to miss, since what he argues is that only by putting oneself in the position of the maker (or divinity) can one grasp how the past has shaped the present. This involves speculation, supposition, imagination, sympathy; but in no instance can it be allowed that something other than human agency caused history. To be sure, there are historical laws of development, just as there is something that Vico calls divine Providence mysteriously at work inside history. The fundamental thing is that history and human society are made up of numerous efforts crisscrossing each other, frequently at odds with each other, always untidy in the way they involve each other. Vico's writing directly reflects this crowded spectacle.

One last observation needs to be made. For Gramsci and Vico, interpretation must take account of this secular horizontal space only by means appropriate to what is present there. I understand this to imply that no single explanation sending one back immediately to a single origin is adequate. And just as there are no simple dynastic answers, there are no simple discrete historical formations or social processes. A heterogeneity of human involvement is therefore equivalent to a heterogeneity of results, as well as of interpretive skills and techniques. There is no center, no inertly given and accepted authority, no fixed barriers ordering human history, even though authority, order, and distinction exist. The secular intellectual works to show the absence of divine originality and, on the other side, the complex presence of historical actuality. The conversion of the absence of religion into the presence of actuality is secular interpretation.

Having rejected global and falsely systematic answers, one had better speak in a limited and concrete way about the contemporary actuality, which so far as our discussion here is concerned is Reagan's America, or, rather, the America inherited and now ruled over by Reaganism. Take literature and politics, for example. It is not too much of an exaggeration to say that an implicit consensus has been building for the past decade in which the study of literature is considered to be profoundly, even constitutively nonpolitical. When you discuss Keats or Shakespeare or Dickens, you may touch on political subjects, of course, but it is assumed that the skills traditionally associated with modern literary criticism (what is now called rhetoric, reading, textuality, tropology, or deconstruction) are there to be applied to *literary* texts, not, for instance, to a government document, a sociological or ethnological report, or a newspaper. This separation of fields, objects, disciplines, and foci constitutes an amazingly *rigid* structure which, to my knowledge, is almost never discussed by literary scholars. There seems to be an unconsciously held norm guaranteeing the simple essence of "fields," a word which in turn has acquired the intellectual authority of a natural, objective fact. Separation, simplicity, silent norms of pertinence: this is one depoliticizing strain of considerable force, since it is capitalized on by professions, institutions, discourses, and a massively reinforced consistency of specialized fields. One corollary of this is the proliferating orthodoxy of separate fields. "I'm sorry I can't understand this—I'm a literary critic, not a sociologist."

The intellectual toll this has taken in the work of the most explicitly political of recent critics—Marxists, in the instance I shall discuss here—is very high. Fredric Jameson has recently produced what is by any standard a major work of intellectual criticism, *The Political Unconscious*. What it discusses, it discusses with a rare brilliance and learning: I have no reservations at all about that. He argues that priority ought to be given to the political interpretation of literary texts and that Marxism, as an interpretive act as opposed to other methods, is "that 'untranscendable horizon' that subsumes such apparently antagonistic or incommensurable critical operations [as the other varieties of interpretive act] assigning them an undoubted sectoral validity within itself, and thus at once cancelling and preserving them."[5] Thus Jameson avails himself of all the most powerful and contradictory of contemporary methodologies, enfolding them in a series of original readings of modern novels, producing in the end a working through of three "semantic horizons" of which the third "phase" is the Marxist: hence, from *explication de texte,* through the ideological discourses of social classes, to the ideology of form itself, perceived against the ultimate horizon of human history.

It cannot be emphasized too strongly that Jameson's book presents a remarkably complex and deeply attractive argument to which I cannot do justice here. This argument reaches its climax in Jameson's conclusion, in which the utopian element in all cultural production is shown to play an underanalyzed and liberating role in human society; additionally, in a much too brief and suggestive passage, Jameson touches on three political discussions (involving the state, law, and nationalism) for which the Marxist hermeneutic he has outlined, fully a negative as well as a positive hermeneutic, can be particularly useful.

We are still left, however, with a number of nagging difficulties. Beneath the surface of the book lies an unadmitted dichotomy between two kinds of "Politics": (1) the politics defined by political theory from Hegel to Louis Althusser and Ernst Bloch; (2) the politics of struggle and power in the everyday world, which in the United States at least has been won, so to speak, by Reagan. As to why this distinction should exist at all, Jameson says very little. This is even more troubling when we realize that Politics 2 is only discussed once, in the course of a long footnote. There he speaks in a general way about "ethnic groups, neighborhood movements . . . rank-and-file labor groups," and so on and quite perspicaciously enters a plea for alliance politics in the United States as distinguished from France, where the totalizing global politics imposed on nearly every constituency has either inhibited or repressed their local development (p. 54). He is absolutely right of course (and would have been more so had he extended his arguments to a United States dominated by only two parties). Yet the irony is that in criticizing the global perspective and admitting its radical discontinuity with local alliance politics, Jameson is also advocating a strong hermeneutic globalism which will have the effect of subsuming the local in the synchronic. This is almost like saying: Don't worry; Reagan is merely a passing phenomenon: the cunning of history will get him too. Yet except for what suspiciously resembles a religious confidence in the teleological efficacy of the Marxist vision, there is no way, to my mind, by which the local is necessarily going to be subsumed, cancelled, preserved, and resolved by the synchronic. Moreover, Jameson leaves it entirely up to the reader to guess what the connection is between the synchrony and theory of Politics 1 and the molecular struggles of Politics 2. Is there continuity or discontinuity between one realm and the other? How do quotidian politics and the struggle for power enter into the hermeneutic, if not by simple instruction from above or by passive osmosis?

These are unanswered questions precisely because, I think, Jameson's assumed constituency is an audience of cultural-literary critics. And this constituency in contemporary America is premised on and made possible by the separation of disciplines I spoke about earlier. This further aggravates the discursive separation of Politics 1 from Politics 2, creating the obvious impression that Jameson is dealing with autonomous realms of human effort. And this has a still more paradoxical result. In his concluding chapter, Jameson suggests allusively that the components of class consciousness—such things as group solidarity against outside threats—are at bottom utopian "insofar as all such (class-based) collectivities are *figures* for the ultimate concrete collective life of an achieved Utopian or classless society." Right at the heart of this thesis we find the notion that "ideological commitment is not first and foremost a matter of moral choice but of the taking of sides in a struggle between embattled groups" (pp. 291, 290). The difficulty here is that whereas moral choice is a category to be rigorously de-Platonized and historicized, there is no inevitability—logical or otherwise—for reducing it completely to "the taking of sides in a struggle between embattled groups." On the molecular level of an individual peasant family thrown off its land, who is to say whether the desire for restitution is exclusively a matter of taking sides or of making the moral choice to resist dispossession. I cannot be sure. But what is so indicative of Jameson's position is that from the global, synchronic hermeneutic overview, moral choice plays no role, and, what is more, the matter is not investigated empirically or historically (as Barrington Moore has tried to do in *Injustice: The Social Basis of Obedience and Revolt*).

Jameson has certainly earned the right to be one of the preeminent spokesmen for what is best in American cultural Marxism. He is discussed this way by a well-known English Marxist, Terry Eagleton, in a recent article, "The Idealism of American Criticism." Eagleton's discussion contrasts Jameson and Frank Lentricchia with the main currents of contemporary American theory which, according to Eagleton, "develops by way of inventing new idealist devices for the repression of history."[6] Nevertheless, Eagleton's admiration for Jameson and Lentricchia does not prevent him from seeing the limitations of their work, their political "unclarity," their lingering pragmatism, eclecticism, the relationship of their hermeneutic criticism to Reagan's ascendancy, and—in Jameson's case especially—their nostalgic Hegelianism. This is not to say, however, that Eagleton expects either of them to toe the current ultra-Left line, which alleges that "the production of Marxist readings of classical texts is class-collaborationism." But he is right to say that "the question irresistibly raised for the Marxist reader of Jameson is simply this: How is a Marxist-structuralist analysis of a minor novel of Balzac to help shake the foundations of capitalism?" Clearly the answer to this question is that such readings won't; but what does Eagleton propose as an alternative? Here we come to the disabling cost of rigidly enforced intellectual and disciplinary divisions, which also affects Marxism.

For we may as well acknowledge that Eagleton writes about Jameson as a fellow Marxist. This is intellectual solidarity, yes, but within a "field" defined principally as an intellectual discourse existing solely within an academy that has left the extra-academic outside world to the new Right and to Reagan. It follows with a kind of natural inevitability that if one such confinement is acceptable, others can be acceptable: Eagleton faults Jameson for the practical ineffectiveness of his Marxist-structuralism but, on the other hand, meekly takes for granted that he and Jameson inhabit the small world of literary studies, speak its language, deal only with its problematics. Why this should be so is hinted at obscurely by Eagleton when he avers that "the ruling class" determines what uses are made of literature for the purpose of "ideological reproduction" and that as revolutionaries "we" cannot select "the literary terrain on which the battle is to be engaged." It does not seem to have occurred to Eagleton that what he finds weakest in Jameson and Lentricchia, their marginality and vestigial idealism, is what also makes him bewail their rarefied discourse at the same time that he somehow accepts it as his own. The very same specialized ethos has been attenuated a little more now: Eagleton, Jameson, and Lentricchia are literary Marxists who write for literary

Marxists, who are in cloistral seclusion from the inhospitable world of real politics. Both "literature" and "Marxism" are thereby confirmed in their apolitical content and methodology: literary criticism is still "only" literary criticism, Marxism only Marxism, and politics is mainly what the literary critic talks about longingly and hopelessly.

This rather long digression on the consequences of the separation of "fields" brings me directly to a second aspect of the politics of interpretation viewed from a secular perspective rigorously responsive to the Age of Reagan. It is patently true that, even within the atomized order of disciplines and fields, methodological investigations can and indeed do occur. But the prevailing mode of intellectual discourse is militantly antimethodological, if by methodological we mean a questioning of the structure of fields and discourses themselves. A principle of silent exclusion operates within and at the boundaries of discourse; this has now become so internalized that fields, disciplines, and their discourses have taken on the status of immutable durability. Licensed members of the field, which has all the trappings of a social institution, are identifiable as belonging to a guild, and for them words like "expert" and "objective" have an important resonance. To acquire a position of authority within the field is, however, to be involved internally in the formation of a canon, which usually turns out to be a blocking device for methodological and disciplinary self-questioning. When J. Hillis Miller says, "I believe in the established canon of English and American Literature and the validity of the concept of privileged texts," he is saying something that has moment by virtue neither of its logical truth nor of its demonstrable clarity.[7] Its power derives from his social authority as a well-known professor of English, a man of deservedly great reputation, a teacher of well-placed students. And what he says more or less eliminates the possibility of asking whether canons (and the imprimatur placed upon canons by a literary critic) are more methodologically necessary to the order of dominance within a guild than they are to the secular study of human history.

If I single out literary and humanistic scholars in what I am saying, it is because, for better or worse, I am dealing with texts, and texts are the very point of departure and culmination for literary scholars. Literary scholars read and they write, both of which are activities having more to do with wit, flexibility, and questioning than they do with solidifying ideas into institutions or with bludgeoning readers into unquestioning submission. Above all it seems to me that it goes directly against the grain of reading and writing to erect barriers between texts or to create monuments out of texts—unless, of course, literary scholars believe themselves to be servants of some outside power requiring this duty from them. The curricula of most literature departments in the university today are constructed almost entirely out of monuments, canonized into rigid dynastic formation, serviced and reserviced monotonously by a shrinking guild of humble servitors. The irony is that this is usually done in the name of historical research and traditional humanism, and yet such canons often have very little historical accuracy to them. To take one small example, Robert Darnton has shown that

> much of what passes today as 18th century French literature wasn't much read by Frenchmen in the 18th century. . . . We suffer from an arbitrary notion of literary history as a canon of classics, one which was developed by professors of literature in the 19th and 20th centuries—while in fact what people of the 18th century were reading was very different. By studying the publisher's accounts and papers at [the Société Typographique de] Neufchatel I've been able to construct a kind of bestseller list of pre-revolutionary France, and it doesn't look anything like the reading lists passed out in classrooms today.[8]

Hidden beneath the pieties surrounding the canonical monuments is a guild solidarity that dangerously resembles a religious consciousness. It is worth recalling Michael Bakunin in *Dieu et l'état:* "In their existing organization, monopolizing science and remaining thus outside social life, the *savants* form a separate caste, in many respects analogous to the priesthood. Scientific abstraction is their God, living and real individuals are their victims, and they are the consecrated and licensed sacrificers."[9] The current interest in producing enormous biographies of consecrated great authors is one aspect of this priestifying. By isolating and elevating the subject beyond his or her time and society, an exaggerated respect for single individuals is produced along with, naturally enough, awe for the biographer's craft. There are similar distortions in the emphasis placed on autobiographical literature whose modish name is "self-fashioning."

All this, then, atomizes, privatizes, and reifies the untidy realm of secular history and creates a peculiar configuration of constituencies and interpretive communities: this is the third major aspect of a contemporary politics of interpretation. An almost invariable rule of order is that very little of the *circumstances* making interpretive activity possible is allowed to seep into the interpretive circle itself. This is peculiarly (not to say distressingly) in evidence when humanists are called in to dignify discussions of major public issues. I shall say nothing here about the egregious lapses (mostly concerning the relationship between the government-corporate policymakers and humanists on questions of national and foreign policy) to be found in the Rockefeller Foundation-funded report *The Humanities in American Life*. More crudely dramatic for my purposes is another Rockefeller enterprise, a conference on "The Reporting of Religion in the Media," held in August 1980. In addressing his opening remarks to the assembled collection of clerics, philosophers, and other humanists, Martin Marty evidently felt it would be elevating the discussion somewhat if he brought Admiral Stansfield Turner, head of the CIA, to his assistance: he therefore "quoted Admiral Turner's assertion that United States intelligence agencies had overlooked the importance of religion in Iran, 'because everyone knew it had so little place and power in the modern world.'" No one seemed to notice the natural affinity assumed by Marty between the CIA and scholars. It was all part of the mentality decreeing that humanists were humanists and experts experts no matter who sponsored their work, usurped their freedom of judgment and independence of research, or assimilated them unquestioningly to state service, even as they protested again and again that they were objective and nonpolitical.

Let me cite one small personal anecdote at the risk of overstating the point. Shortly before my book *Covering Islam* appeared, a private foundation convened a seminar on the book to be attended by journalists, scholars, and diplomats, all of whom had professional interests in how the Islamic world was being reported and represented in the West generally. I was to answer questions. One Pulitzer Prize–winning journalist, who is now the foreign news editor of a leading Eastern newspaper, was asked to lead the discussion, which he did by summarizing my argument briefly and on the whole not very accurately. He concluded his remarks by a question meant to initiate discussion: "Since you say that Islam is badly reported [actually my argument in the book is that "Islam" isn't something to be reported or nonreported: it is an ideological abstraction], could you tell us how we should report the Islamic world in order to help clarify the U.S.'s strategic interests there?" When I objected to the question, on the grounds that journalism was supposed to be either reporting or analyzing the news and not serving as an adjunct to the National Security Council, no attention was paid to what in everyone's eyes was an irrelevant naiveté on my part. Thus have the security interests of the state been absorbed silently into journalistic interpretation: expertise is therefore supposed to be unaffected by its institutional affiliations with power, although of course it is exactly those affiliations—hidden but assumed unquestioningly—that make the expertise possible and imperative.

Given this context, then, a constituency is principally a clientele: people who use (and perhaps buy) your services because you and others belonging to your guild are certified experts. For the relatively unmarketable humanists whose wares are "soft" and whose expertise is almost by definition marginal, their constituency is a fixed one composed of other humanists, students, government and corporate executives, and media employees, who use the humanist to assure a harmless place for "the humanities" or culture or literature in the society. I hasten to recall, however, that this is the role voluntarily accepted by humanists whose notion of what they do is neutralized, specialized, and nonpolitical in the extreme. To an alarming degree, the present continuation of the humanities depends, I think, on the sustained self-purification of humanists for whom the ethic of specialization has become equivalent to minimizing the content of their work and increasing the composite wall of guild consciousness, social authority, and exclusionary discipline around themselves. Opponents are therefore not people in disagreement with the constituency but people to be kept out, nonexperts and nonspecialists, for the most part.

Whether all this makes an interpretive *community*, in the secular and noncommercial, noncoercive sense of the word, is very seriously to be doubted. If a community is based principally on keeping people out and on defending a tiny fiefdom (in perfect complicity with the defenders of other fiefdoms) on the basis of a mysteriously pure subject's inviolable integrity, then it is a religious community. The secular realm I have presupposed requires a more open sense of community as something to be won and of audiences as human beings to be addressed. How, then, can we understand the present setting in such a way as to see in it the possibility of change? How can interpretation be interpreted as having a secular, political force in an age determined to deny interpretation anything but a role as mystification?

I shall organize my remarks around the notion of *representation,* which, for literary scholars at least, has a primordial importance. From Aristotle to Auerbach and after, mimesis is inevitably to be found in discussions of literary texts. Yet as even Auerbach himself showed in his monographic stylistic studies, techniques of representation in literary work have always been related to, and in some measure have depended on, social formations. The phrase "la cour et la ville," for example, makes primarily *literary* sense in a text by Nicolas Boileau, and although the text itself gives the phrase a peculiarly refined local meaning, it nevertheless presupposed both an audience that knew he referred to what Auerbach calls "his social environment" and the social environment itself, which made references to it possible. This is not *simply* a matter of reference, since, from a verbal point of view, referents can be said to be equal and equally verbal. Even in very minute analyses, Auerbach's view does, however, have to do with the *coexistence* of realms—the literary, the social, the personal—and the way in which they make use of, affiliate with, and represent each other.

With very few exceptions, contemporary literary theories assume the relative independence and even autonomy of literary representation over (and not just from) all others. Novelistic verisimilitude, poetic tropes, and dramatic metaphors (Lukács, Harold Bloom, Francis Ferguson) are representations to and for themselves of the novel, the poem, the drama: this, I think, accurately sums up the assumptions underlying the three influential (and, in their own way, typical) theories I have referred to. Moreover, the organized study of literature—*en soi* and *pour soi*—is premised on the constitutively primary act of literary (that is, artistic) representation, which in turn absorbs and incorporates other realms, other representations, secondary to it. But all this institutional weight has precluded a sustained, systematic examination of the coexistence of and the interrelationship between the literary and the social, which is where representation—from journalism, to political struggle, to economic production and power—plays an extraordinarily important role. Confined to the study of one representational complex, literary critics accept and paradoxically ignore the lines drawn around what they do.

This is depoliticization with a vengeance, and it must, I think, be understood as an integral part of the historical moment presided over by Reaganism. The division of intellectual labor I spoke of earlier can now be seen as assuming a *thematic* importance in the contemporary culture as a whole. For if the study of literature is "only" about literary representation, then it must be the case that literary representations and literary activities (writing, reading, producing the "humanities," and arts and letters) are essentially ornamental, possessing at most secondary ideological characteristics. The consequence is that to deal with literature as well as the broadly defined "humanities" is to deal with the nonpolitical, although quite evidently the political realm is presumed to lie just beyond (and beyond the reach of) literary, and hence *literate,* concern.

A perfect recent embodiment of this state of affairs is the September 30, 1981, issue of *The New Republic.* The lead editorial analyzes the United States' policy toward South Africa and ends up supporting this policy, which even the most "moderate" of Black African states interpret (correctly, as even the United States explicitly confesses) as a policy supporting the South African settler-colonial regime. The last article of the issue includes a mean personal attack on me as "an intellectual in the thrall of Soviet totalitarianism," a claim that is as disgustingly McCarthyite as it is intellectually fraudulent. Now at the very center of this issue of the magazine—a fairly typical issue by the way— is a long and decently earnest book review by Christopher Hill, a leading Marxist historian. What boggles the mind is not the mere coincidence of apologies for apartheid rubbing shoulders with good Marxist sense but how the one antipode includes (without any reference at all) what the other, the Marxist pole, performs unknowingly.

There are two very impressive points of reference for this discussion of what can be called the national culture as a nexus of relationships between "fields," many of them employing representation as their technique of distribution and production. (It will be obvious here that I exclude the creative arts and the natural sciences.) One is Perry Anderson's "Components of the National Culture" (1969);[10] the other is Regis Debray's study of the French intelligentsia, *Teachers, Writers, Celebrities* (1980). Anderson's argument is that an absent intellectual center in traditional British thought about society was vulnerable to a "white" (antirevolutionary, conservative) immigration into Britain from Europe. This in turn produced a blockage of sociology, a technicalization of philosophy, an idea-free empiricism in history, and an idealist aesthetics. Together these and other disciplines form "something like a closed system," in which subversive discourses like Marxism and psychoanalysis were for a time quarantined; now, however, they too have been incorporated. The French case, according to Debray, exhibits a series of three hegemonic conquests in time. First there was the era of the secular universities, which ended with World War I. That was succeeded by the era of the publishing houses, a time between the wars when Gallimard-NRF—agglomerates of gifted writers and essayists that included Jacques Rivière, André Gide, Marcel Proust, and Paul Valéry—replaced the social and intellectual authority of the somewhat overproductive, mass-populated universities. Finally, during the 1960s, intellectual life was absorbed into the structure of the mass media: worth, merit, attention, and visibility slipped from the pages of books to be estimated by frequency of appearance on the television screen. At this point, then, a new hierarchy, what Debray calls a mediocracy, emerges, and it rules the schools and the book industry.

There are certain similarities between Debray's France and Anderson's England, on the one hand, and Reagan's America, on the other. They are interesting, but I cannot spend time talking about them. The differences are, however, more instructive. Unlike France, high culture in America is assumed to be above politics as a matter of unanimous convention. And unlike England, the intellectual center here is filled not by European imports (although they play a considerable role) but by an unquestioned ethic of objectivity and realism, based essentially on an epistemology of separation and difference. Thus each field is separate from the others because the subject matter is separate.

Each separation corresponds immediately to a separation in function, institution, history, and purpose. Each discourse "represents" the field, which in turn is supported by its own constituency and the specialized audience to which it appeals. The mark of true professionalism is accuracy of representation of society, vindicated in the case of sociology, for instance, by a direct correlation between representation of society and corporate and/or governmental interests, a role in social policymaking, access to political authority. Literary studies, conversely, are realistically *not* about society but about masterpieces in need of periodic adulation and appreciation. Such correlations make possible the use of words like "objectivity," "realism," and "moderation" when used in sociology or in literary criticism. And these notions in turn assure their own confirmation by careful selectivity of evidence, the incorporation and subsequent neutralization of dissent (also known as pluralism), and networks of insiders, experts whose presence is due to their conformity, not to any rigorous judgment of their past performance (the good team player always turns up).

But I must press on, even though there are numerous qualifications and refinements to be added at this point (e.g., the organized relationship between clearly affiliated fields such as political science and sociology versus the use by one field of another unrelated one for the purposes of national policy issues; the network of patronage and the insider/outsider dichotomy; the strange cultural encouragement of theories stressing such "components" of the structure of power as chance, morality, American innocence, decentralized egos, etc.). The particular mission of the humanities is, in the aggregate, to represent *noninterference* in the affairs of the everyday world. As we have seen, there has been a historical erosion in the role of letters since the New Criticism, and I have suggested that the conjuncture of a narrowly based university environment for technical language and literature studies with the self-policing, self-purifying communities erected even by Marxist, as well as other disciplinary, discourses, produced a very small but definite function for the humanities: to represent humane marginality, which is also to preserve and if possible to conceal the hierarchy of powers that occupy the center, define the social terrain, and fix the limits of use functions, fields, marginality, and so on. Some of the corollaries of this role for the humanities generally and literary criticism in particular are that the institutional presence of humanities guarantees a space for the deployment of free-floating abstractions (scholarship, taste, tact, humanism) that are defined in advance as indefinable; that when it is not easily domesticated, "theory" is employable as a discourse of occultation and legitimation; that self-regulation is the ethos behind which the institutional humanities allow and in a sense encourage the unrestrained operation of market forces that were traditionally thought of as subject to ethical and philosophical review.

Very broadly stated, then, noninterference for the humanist means laissez-faire: "they" can run the country, we will explicate Wordsworth and Schlegel. It does not stretch things greatly to note that noninterference and rigid specialization in the academy are directly related to what has been called a counterattack by "highly mobilized business elites" in reaction to the immediately preceding period during which national needs were thought of as fulfilled by resources allocated collectively and democratically. However, working through foundations, think tanks, sectors of the academy, and the government, corporate elites according to David Dickson and David Noble "proclaimed a new age of reason while remystifying reality." This involved a set of "interrelated" epistemological and ideological imperatives, which are an extrapolation from the noninterference I spoke about earlier. Each of these imperatives is in congruence with the way intellectual and academic "fields" view themselves internally and across the dividing lines:

1. The rediscovery of the self-regulating market, the wonders of free enterprise, and the classical liberal attack on government regulation of the economy, all in the name of liberty.
2. The reinvention of the idea of progress, now cast in terms of "innovation" and "reindustrialization," and the limitation of expectations and social welfare in the quest for productivity.
3. The attack on democracy, in the name of "efficiency," "manageability," "governability," "rationality," and "competence."
4. The remystification of science through the promotion of formalized decision methodologies, the restoration of the authority of expertise, and the renewed use of science as legitimation for social policy through deepening industry ties to universities and other "free" institutions of policy analysis and recommendation.[11]

In other words, (1) says that literary criticism minds its own business and is "free" to do what it wishes with no community responsibility whatever. Hence at one end of the scale, for instance, is the recent successful attack on the NEH for funding too many socially determined programs and, at the other end, the proliferation of private critical languages with an absurdist bent presided over paradoxically by "big name professors," who also extoll the virtues of humanism, pluralism, and humane scholarship. Retranslated, (2) has meant that the number of jobs for young graduates has shrunk dramatically as the "inevitable" result of market forces, which in turn prove the marginality of scholarship that is premised on its own harmless social obsolescence. This has created a demand for sheer innovation and indiscriminate publication (e.g., the sudden increase in advanced critical journals; the departmental need for experts and courses in theory and structuralism), and it has virtually destroyed the career trajectory and social horizons of young people within the system. Imperatives (3) and (4) have meant the recrudescence of strict professionalism for sale to any client, deliberately oblivious of the complicity between the academy, the government, and the corporations, decorously silent on the large questions of social, economic, and foreign policy.

Very well: if what I have been saying has any validity, then the politics of interpretation demands a dialectical response from a critical consciousness worthy of its name. Instead of noninterference and specialization, there must be *interference,* a crossing of borders and obstacles, a determined attempt to generalize exactly at those points where generalizations seem impossible to make. One of the first interferences to be ventured, then, is a crossing from literature, which is supposed to be subjective and powerless, into those exactly parallel realms, now covered by journalism and the production of information, that employ representation but are supposed to be objective and powerful. Here we have a superb guide in John Berger, in whose most recent work there is the basis of a major critique of modern representation. Berger suggests that if we regard photography as coeval in its origins with sociology and positivism (and I would add the classic realistic novel), we see that

> what they shared was the hope that observable quantifiable facts, recorded by experts, would constitute the proven truth

that humanity required. Precision would replace metaphysics; planning would resolve conflicts. What happened, instead, was that the way was opened to a view of the world in which everything and everybody could be reduced to a factor in a calculation, and the calculation was profit.[12]

Much of the world today is represented in this way: as the McBride Commission Report has it, a tiny handful of large and powerful oligarchies control about ninety percent of the world's information and communication flows. This domain, staffed by experts and media executives, is, as Herbert Schiller and others have shown, affiliated to an even smaller number of governments, at the very same time that the rhetoric of objectivity, balance, realism, and freedom covers what is being done. And for the most part, such consumer items as "the news"—a euphemism for ideological images of the world that determine political reality for a vast majority of the world's population—hold forth, untouched by interfering secular and critical minds, who for all sorts of obvious reasons are not hooked into the systems of power.

This is not the place, nor is there time, to advance a fully articulated program of interference. I can only suggest in conclusion that we need to think about breaking out of the disciplinary ghettos in which as intellectuals we have been confined, to reopen the blocked social processes ceding objective representation (hence power) of the world to a small coterie of experts and their clients, to consider that the audience for literacy is not a closed circle of three thousand professional critics but the community of human beings living in society, and to regard social reality in a secular rather than a mystical mode, despite all the protestations about realism and objectivity.

Two concrete tasks—again adumbrated by Berger—strike me as particularly useful. One is to use the visual faculty (which also happens to be dominated by visual media such as television, news photography, and commercial film, all of them fundamentally immediate, "objective," and ahistorical) to restore the nonsequential energy of lived historical memory and subjectivity as fundamental components of meaning in representation. Berger calls this an alternative use of photography: using photomontage to tell other stories than the official sequential or ideological ones produced by institutions of power. (Superb examples are Sarah Graham-Brown's photo-essay *The Palestinians and Their Society* and Susan Meisalas' *Nicaragua*.) Second is opening the culture to experiences of the Other which have remained "outside" (and have been repressed or framed in a context of confrontational hostility) the norms manufactured by "insiders." An excellent example is Malek Alloula's *Le Harem colonial*, a study of early twentieth-century postcards and photographs of Algerian harem women. The pictorial capture of colonized people by colonizer, which signifies power, is reenacted by a young Algerian sociologist, Alloula, who sees his own fragmented history in the pictures, then reinscribes this history in his text as the result of understanding and making that intimate experience intelligible for an audience of modern European readers.

In both instances, finally, we have the recovery of a history hitherto either misrepresented or rendered invisible. Stereotypes of the Other have always been connected to political actualities of one sort or another, just as the truth of lived communal (or personal) experience has often been totally sublimated in official narratives, institutions, and ideologies. But in having attempted—and perhaps even successfully accomplishing—this recovery, there is the crucial next phase: connecting these more politically vigilant forms of interpretation to an ongoing political and social praxis. Short of making that connection, even the best-intentioned and the cleverest interpretive activity is bound to sink back into the murmur of mere prose. For to move from interpretation to its politics is in large measure to go from undoing to doing, and this, given the currently accepted divisions between criticism and art, is risking all the discomfort of a great unsettlement in ways of seeing and doing. One must refuse to believe, however, that the comforts of specialized habits can be so seductive as to keep us all in our assigned places.

14

Bursts of Meaning

The standard objection to John Berger's criticism of the visual arts is that it is too sentimental, too earnest. Leftist critics in particular tend to find Berger mushy and vague, despite his obviously rigorous position on the social functions of art in capitalist (or socialist) society. Such objections, however, seem to me both inaccurate and uninteresting, given Berger's deliberate style of commentary and its remarkably suggestive, as well as original, accomplishments.

Nevertheless, Berger is not easy to digest, partly because he has a great deal to say in his stream of essays, books of criticism, film scripts, and novels, and partly because he says it in unusual ways. He relies on no single method, although he takes from various semiologists and iconographers the better things they have to offer. He is that rare being, an unorthodox Marxist who doesn't feel the need to construct a massive new theoretical framework to account for the unforeseen complexities of late capitalism. His knowledge of art history, philosophy, and literature, like his acute political sense, is sophisticated without being heavy or obtrusive. The best thing about him, though, is his relentless striving for accessible truths about the visual arts—

their ambiguity, memorial enchainments, half-conscious projections, and irreducibly subjective force.

Berger has been typecast as an English eccentric who has chosen to live among peasants in a particularly rough and mountainous area of France. A closer look at his recent work, however, reveals a more systematic, philosophical, and political project than the rather empirical cast of his prose suggests. His interest in the peasant life he discusses in *Pig Earth,* for example, is intensified by the fact that such life is now threatened with extinction. Similarly, his studies of Picasso, photography, and "ways of seeing" attempt to rescue the valuable in art from the false reputations, advertising clichés, and routine judgments that might otherwise triumph. Berger's project is to distinguish the authentic from the merely successful, and to save the former from the ravages of the latter.

Another Way of Telling is perhaps his most ambitious work along these lines: for the first time he offers an explicit and sustained account of art's positive uses in a setting hostile to art as felt experience. Berger's co-author is the great Swiss photographer Jean Mohr, with whom he produced such classics as *A Fortunate Man* and *A Seventh Man. Another Way of Telling* begins with a series of personal reflections by Mohr on his art; next is Berger's extended essay, "Appearances," on the meaning of photographs and photo-sequences; followed by "If each time . . .," a section containing 150 photographs by Mohr, carefully arranged and centered around the life of an elderly French peasant woman. Berger returns with "Stories," a few pages on the relationship between prose narratives and the order of visual succession. The book ends with an absolute masterpiece of a photograph by Mohr opposite a short poem by Berger: photograph and poem together produce another way of telling about the reality of an old peasant, this one a man, facing a day's chores at an ungodly morning hour. Narrative has been replaced by constellations of experience (what Gerard Manley Hopkins would have called bursts of meaning) that convey the privacy as well as the context of the old man's life.

This rather schematic account cannot do this rich book justice. The photographs that accompany Mohr's ruminations on his artistic practice are extraordinary both as pictures and as accompaniment to the text. This is especially true of two sets of photographs. One consists of pictures of a blind Indian girl who, while listening to Mohr make animal sounds, breaks out into a shatteringly beautiful smile; a moment later we see her lapsing back into lonely repose. The second set is of hungry Indonesian children running alongside Mohr's train, hands outstretched yet receiving nothing. He says that they became an obsession with him, a feeling echoed by the children's fugitive grace, despite their emaciated bodies and unnaturally bright eyes.

But at the heart of the book is, I think, an argument *against* linear sequence—that is, sequence construed by Berger as the symbol of dehumanizing political processes. For Mohr and Berger, the contemporary world is dominated by monopolistic systems of order, all engaged in the extinction of privacy, subjectivity, free choice. According to Berger, this state of affairs is a consequence of the violent conflation of time with History—objective, official, real—that occurred as part of industrialization in the nineteenth century. "Public photography" reduces a man weeping or "a door or a volcano" to a statistic, a recordable fact, a commodity. Subjectivity, whose last social function is "the individual consumer's dream," is forcibly attenuated:

> From this primary suppression of the social function of subjectivity, other suppressions follow: of meaningful democracy (replaced by opinion polls and market-research techniques), of social conscience (replaced by self-interest), of history (replaced by racism and other myths), of hope—the most subjective and social of all energies (replaced by the sacralization of Progress as Comfort).

In control systems and in scientific investigations, photographs supply identity and information respectively. In advertising or journalism, photographs are used *as if* they belonged to the same order of truth as science or control systems; the communications industry would like to press viewers into accepting the photograph as evidence either of buyable goods or of immutable reality. Buy this product because it will make you happy; the poor are sick and hungry, and that's the way it is.

In fact, because of its peculiar status as a quotation from reality containing traces of the historic world, the photograph bears an ambiguity within itself that is not so easily co-opted. As a "way of telling," the historical model not only objectifies the world; it also forces on it "the principle of historical progress." This, Berger says, does "a deep violence" to subjective experience by coercing reality into linear forms that narrate progress—thus eliminating the timeless, the dead, superstition, embedded conservatism, eternal laws, fatalism, and the like. Private photographs, however, those "fragile images, often carried next to the heart or placed by the side of the bed, are used to refer to that which historical time has no right to destroy." Every photograph, therefore, is the result of a choice (of the instant to be photographed), although its meanings depend on the viewer's ability to lend it a past and a future, to reinsert the discontinuous instant into a durational continuum. The photograph's ambiguity can thus be either acknowledged—at which point interpretive words supplied for the photograph lift it from the level of fact to the level of suggestion and ideas—or denied, in which case it is subject to "the opportunism of corporate capitalism."

To read or interpret photographs, then, is to unite the human expectation of coherence with the language of appearances. The richer the photograph in quotation, the broader the scope for creative interpretation and the more the photographic instant achieves "another kind of meaning." This new kind of meaning is born when "confronting the event [the subject of the photograph] extends and joins it to other events, thus widening [the photograph's] diameter." All this, like a stone in water, breaks the one-directional flow of sequential narratives decreeing that what journalists, government discourse, and scientific experts say is History, whereas the private subjective experience is not. Photographs are therefore potentially insurrectionary, so long as the language interpreting them does not, like most semiological discourse, become "reductive and disapproving."

Berger's language is neither. No one can more ably turn frozen surfaces into tractable worlds, "appropriated by reflection, permeated by feelings." And no one has so persuasively made it possible to read a sequence of photographs—in this particular case, the set of 150 that radiate out from one humble peasant life—as a "field of coexistence like the field of memory." In destroying the notion of sequence, Berger allows one to see mutual "energies of attraction" between photographs, so that, as he says, the ambiguity of photographs "at last becomes true." And this ambiguity, of course, is another way of telling about human life.

Berger and Mohr answer directly and eloquently to the need for some leftist alternative to an almost incredibly successful capitalist culture, whose inhuman sequences of order—newspaper columns, TV news narratives, official expertise—assume a silently complacent constituency. Their work derives from Walter Benjamin in some ways (Benjamin also preferred the episodic, deliberately un-booklike collection of pieces, seeing such "inconspicuous forms" as better suited to influence "active communities" than "the pretentious, universal gesture of the book") and from Marcuse in others. The frankly libertarian and optimistic bias of Berger's style, however, is his alone.

And yet, for all its brilliance, *Another Way of Telling* leaves me with a certain skepticism. True, the media, advertising, and the "experts" have cornered the market on "objective truth." Even truer, the oppositional culture has in the main been co-opted almost beyond redemption; impotence is the leftist intellectual's common lot today. But the rediscovery of subjectivity as a social value, and of time and timelessness as embodied in a photograph, are feeble bulwarks against the encroaching sea of cement. As passionately as Ruskin, Berger seems to believe that a proper schooling of the visual faculties will make for a more effective counter-hegemonic cultural practice.

Two questions are left unanswered by Berger's work. First, can one really undertake aesthetic/intellectual projects in the private sector, so to speak, and then launch out from there directly into politics? Unlike Lukács and Gramsci, Berger fails to deal with the power of ideology to saturate culture. There can be no unilateral withdrawal from ideology. Surely it is quixotic to expect photographic interpretation to serve some such purpose.

The second question is the central one of oppositional politics—what to do? Photography, Berger says, deals with memory and the past. What of the future? Even if he wishes to deal only with cultural politics, *Another Way of Telling* demands a further step which Berger does not take: connecting his aesthetics with action. It is a measure of Berger's achievement as a writer that for him that step wouldn't be hard to take.

Egyptian Rites

Egypt isn't just another foreign country; it is special. Everyone has some acquaintance with it, whether through photographs of Abu Simbel, busts of Nefertiti, school courses in ancient history, or images of Anwar Sadat on television. Historical characters—Cleopatra, Ramses, Tutankhamen, among many—have been drafted for service in mass culture, and they continue to exist and function as symbols of passion, conquest, and wealth complicated by an exotic remoteness that remains attractive in the late twentieth century. Yet curiously, because these figures have such a clearly outlined yet eccentric status, in their isolated distance from anything truly familiar, they also remind us how small and selective is our knowledge of Egypt, which, after all, is a real place with real people possessing a real history. Nevertheless, Western representations of Egypt have a history too, one that doesn't always coincide with Egyptian representations of Egypt.

This is to be kept in mind as we try to unravel the dense symbolic web encircling the Metropolitan Museum's new Egyptian wing and the film series that has accompanied its opening, along with some occasionally adroit but often uninteresting commentary from the Met's staff of Egyptologists. Much has been written and said about these pharaonic treasures. Yet what hasn't been articulated is just as significant and certainly as telling. Above all we mustn't accept the notion that the fascination with what is Egyptian is merely perennial and stable. In fact, the taste for Egypt and the images that derive from it are part of the political history of our time, as changeable and shifting in their meaning as any other of the icons with which our ideological perspectives are propped up.

Egypt's astonishing historical continuity of thousands of years of recorded existence has regularly attracted European travelers, visionaries, artists, and conquerors, from Herodotus, Caesar, and Alexander to Shakespeare, Napoleon, and Flaubert. Then came the Americans—Cecil B. De Mille, David Rockefeller, Henry Kissinger. Its strategic closeness to Europe and the East has made Egypt a highly prized and much sought after imperial possession: the roll call of civilizations that constructed foreign policies around Egypt is virtually unparalleled in world history, although the Atlantic West and the Arab world together have played the dominant part in this continuing drama.

As a result, then, we can speak intelligibly and correctly of a battle not only *for* Egypt, but also for the right to depict Egypt. On the one hand, there is the Egypt whose symbolic, cultural, and political identity, while African, is nevertheless essentially Western, in which the country's ancient grandeur and modern significance come together in ways that are British, French, German, Italian, or American. On the other, there is the Egypt whose Islamic and Arab roles are in frequent conflict with its Western representations, which have often stressed the country's remote (therefore more attractive) past at the expense of its actual present. In the contemporary phase of this conflict Egyptians themselves have been divided in ways that are both surprising and interesting, since in the age of mass international communications they too have become participants in the contest over Egypt's identity.

Yet everyone who has ever been to Egypt or, without actually going there, has thought about it somewhat is immediately struck by its coherence, its unmistakable identity, its powerful unified presence. All sorts of reasons have been put forward for Egypt's millennial integrity, but they can all be characterized as aspects of the battle to represent Egypt, which somehow remains itself, aloof and yet inviting, distant and still accessible. To contemporary Arabs, for example, Egypt is quite simply the only *real* Arab country, society, people; in comparison, all the others are an odd assortment of badly put together postcolonial countries sorely lacking in the kind of genuine nationality that Egypt has. For in Egypt, it is argued, there are real institutions, real traditions, real civil dynamics; the crude posturings of puerile colonels and mafialike political parties are not long tolerated there, as much because Egyptian history instantly makes them look silly as because the celebrated Egyptian ironic wit—flowing confidently from the country's assumed historical continuity—wears them down. To Egypt has therefore gone the role of leader, naturally and irresistibly. It is one index of Gamal Abdal Nasser's Arab success and Anwar Sadat's failure that the former understood and exploited Egypt's Arab role, whereas the latter rejected it totally. And so in the Arab world the efforts made to regain (or shun) Egypt since Nasser's death in 1970 are implicit in daily political life.

But these matters are tangential where Egyptology and Egyptological interests are concerned. These are usually portrayed as European, Western activities. This is of course true up to a point, but it is also true that the nature of Egyptology is to some degree less about Egypt than it is about Europe. Consider that for almost two millennia European scientists, philosophers, painters, musicians, and poets created a fantastic myth about Egypt—its hieratic mysteries, its fabulous gods, its age-old wisdom—without even being able to decipher hieroglyphics, the language in which ancient Egypt recorded its own history. Mozart's masonic fantasies about Egyptian rites in *The Magic Flute,* for example, were no more inaccurate than the disquisitions of all the philologists and scholars who pronounced on the secrets of Egypt's past. Then in 1822, using the Rosetta Stone as text and guide, Champollion decoded hieroglyphics in one of the most brilliant cryptographic discoveries of all time. From then on Egyptology was put on a more scientific basis, which, it must immediately be added, corresponded exactly with the era of high European imperialism. Thus it is perfectly fitting that the most readable and interesting of recent books on the history of Egyptology should be entitled *The Rape of the Nile* (by Brian Fagan).

As it emerges from the pages of Fagan's book, Egyptology's past is not an attractive one, and gives new meaning to Walter Benjamin's aphorism that "there is no document of civilization which is not at the same time a document of barbarism, [barbarism that] also taints the manner in which it was transmitted from one owner to another." For whereas Egypt joined the Arab and Muslim world with its conquest by Amr ibn-As in 639 A.D., none of the great nineteenth-century European archaeological pioneers had anything but contempt or ignorance to show for that aspect of Egypt. During this period, however, some European scholars and travelers also developed an interest in modern Egypt, the greatest cultural result of which was Edward Lane's classic *The Manners and Customs of the Modern Egyptians* (1836). Nevertheless, the country was mainly available as a place to be ransacked for treasures and imposing ruins, a great many of which found their way into the major European museums. Although it was part of the Ottoman Empire, for most of the nineteenth century Egypt was in everything but name a European annex, traveled and raided—scientifically and enterprisingly—at will. Men like Belzoni and Mariette (Verdi's librettist for *Aida*) were heroic workers who endured unimaginable hardships in Upper Egypt as they unearthed, traded in, and transported a vast number of important finds; and Mariette in addition was a genuine scholar who, in the words of the catalogue for the huge Egyptian exhibit at the 1867 Paris Exposition, rescued ancient Egypt for Europe.

Nonetheless, their methods were those of marauding pirates encouraged both by a string of feeble and corrupt Macedonian Circassian-Albanian viceroys (whose last fruit was King Farouk) and by a profitable network of European museums, speculators, traders, and scholarly societies. Thus Egypt was bankrupt and lost title to the Suez Canal, as well as to an enormous bulk of its archaeological treasure by the time it was occupied by England in 1882. In stark contrast, the major European cities were decorated with imposing ancient Egyptian monuments showing off a languid imperial splendor, their museums exhibiting Egyptian materials that ranged from the minuscule to the gigantic. Yet, at the same time, an air of melancholy seemed to hang over those splendid Egyptological fragments. Somehow their funerary tone and the fact that their aesthetic was a neutralizing combination of embalmment and aggrandizement seemed also to highlight, or at least comment on, nineteenth-century archaeology's inability to integrate rapacity with human interest. There is no more concrete equivalent of that inability than Flaubert's novel *Salammbô*.

And still the passion for ancient Egypt continued, given additional impetus by Howard Carter's discovery of Tutankhamen's tomb in 1922. To Europeans and Arabs, Egypt at mid-century was, however, becoming a more problematic place. It was a palimpsest of conflicting actualities, overlapping cultural spheres, tense political rivalries.

I spent a good part of my youth there, and I can recall more vividly than any of my other early experiences the sense of a dangerously rich environment in which the whole place was steeped. The British occupation was nearing its end, Arab nationalism was beginning its big postwar rise, the currents of Islamic resistance were frequently and violently in evidence, and interfused with them all was Egypt's ungraspably long past, pharaonic, Hellenistic, Coptic, Fatimid, Mameluke, Ottoman, European. Cairo then was a wonder of places to grow up in, with spacious European boulevards and manicured suburbs—the products of what seemed to be a harmonious imperial vision drawing out responses from the city's innate majesty—adjoining colorful Arab and Islamic vistas populated by a rich variety of human types that spilled out of Egypt into the neighboring region. To the south the pyramids hovered, visible in delicate outline on the horizon. I saw my first *Aida* in the very same Cairo Opera House for which Verdi wrote it, an ornate small-scale model of the Garnier Opera in Paris; a traveling Italian company did an annual winter season in Cairo and Alexandria to a mixed audience of Europeans, smart Egyptians, and adaptable Levantines. Hardly half a mile away lay the great treasures of the Cairo Museum, supervised in its construction by Mariette and Maspero, a hulk so overcrowded and dusty as inevitably to suggest the irrelevance into which Ramses, Horus, and Isis (who lived on in modern Egypt only as Coptic first names), Akhnaton and Hatshepsut had fallen.

America's Egypt has very little in common with all this. Egypt is of course a polar opposite, an Old World with which the early American connections were at bottom romantic, mythological, or, if you prefer, ideological—not colonial, historical, or political in an ongoing concrete sense. While the British and French were excavating the Nile Valley, the Americans (among them Emerson, Melville, and Whitman) appropriated Egypt and its hieroglyphic culture as a mythical emblem which, the scholar John Irwin has written, was "various enough to sustain almost any interpretation that man projected on it in the act of knowing." The Metropolitan Museum of course acquired (and during the early 1960s flooded the buyers' market with) a large collection of miscellaneous objects, the biggest of which is the Temple of Dendur, entire. Until the postwar period, American travelers, some archaeologists, scholars, missionaries, and merchants were in Egypt, but there was never the large-scale investment there that characterized the centuries-old European presence.

This was to change, as the British and French ceded their Eastern empires to the United States, which now embarked on an on-again, off-again romance with Egypt that the Met's exhibition halls—more neutral, minus the national context provided by European excavations—and its feature film series curiously but accurately symbolize. Cecil B. De Mille's *Cleopatra* (1934), an odd amalgam of one Shaw and two Shakespeare plays, was shot in Hollywood; Claudette Colbert was ill throughout the shooting, but, as if that wasn't enough of a problem, the historical models used for the film are unclear, improvised, stylistically unintegrated. Little attempt seemed to have been made to ground *Cleopatra* in anything particularly Egyptian, or for that matter, historical, and the verbal idiom seems always to be alluding to rather than saying something. As one character puts it impatiently to Mark Antony, "You and your 'friends, Romans, and countrymen'!"

Unbearably heavy, earnest, and long, *The Ten Commandments* (1956) emanates from a different world altogether. There is first neither the loose suggestiveness of *Cleopatra*, nor the floating but quite effective atmospherics of another "Egyptian" 1930s film, *The Mummy*. Every statement in *The Ten Commandments* is italicized; its scenes are soggy with significance and authenticity, so much so that one spill-off from the film was a book, *Moses and Egypt* (1956), purporting to show how all the film's details were "true" and historical, firmly anchored in the Bible and other unimpeachable sources: "to accomplish the vast research work for the film, 950 books, 984 periodicals, 1286 clippings and 2964 photographs were studied." It is difficult to know how much of this is bad faith, how much naiveté. For, secondly, *The Ten Commandments* is saturated with an ideology that no amount of sources and historical accuracy can dispel. De Mille himself was an ultraconservative literalist whose penchant for vulgar spectacle and titillating fleshiness served to promote a world view perfectly in harmony with John Foster Dulles's. Certainly his biblical films were an aspect of the American passion for origins, historical myths by which we explain ourselves with reference to a past that dignifies and makes sense of us. But the fact that Moses is played by the emphatically American Charlton Heston herds the Bible into line with an American national ego whose source is no less than God. It is perhaps worth recalling that whereas European countries sought their national myths of origin in Greco-Roman or Norse mythology, we have sought ours, like the Founding Fathers, in selected portions of the Old Testament, whose bloodthirsty righteousness and un-self-conscious authoritarianism are both powerful and (to me at least) deeply unattractive.

Charlton Moses is also the American abroad, telling the devious wogs of the third world that "our" way is the right way, or there'll be hell to pay. Two years before *The Ten Commandments* was released, the Egyptian revolution had occurred, and, in its early days, it teetered between the Soviet bloc and the United States as arms suppliers; this was also the period when Egypt's new rulers (headed by General Naguib, who figureheaded the government whereas Gamal Abdal Nasser was really in control) were seeking some sort of working relationship with the United States. Perhaps inadvertently, De Mille's vision posed the issues with a realism that so angered the Egyptian government that it banned the film, which had been shot on location. On the one hand, there was a WASP Old Testament prophet who led his people following God and Conscience into a Promised Land conveniently empty of any inhabitants; on the other stood his scheming, vaguely Oriental foster brother (Yul Brynner) who had it in for Hebrews (and by extension Americans). Egypt was an oppressor, Hebrews were heroes. In the context of the time, with the creation of Israel barely six years old and the Suez invasion a few months in the future, De Mille, like Dulles, seemed to be warning Egypt that nationalism not vindicated by God and America was evil and would therefore be punished. Moreover, by some quick telescoping of history, America *included* Israel, and if that meant that Egypt was therefore excluded, then so much the worse for Egypt. The fact that Charlton Moses returns from his sojourn in the desert equipped with all sorts of technological tricks (a magic staff, the ability to work miracles, parting the Red Sea) simply underlined the point to contemporary Egyptians that Israel and America possessed modern techniques for dominating nature and other societies.

Like *The Egyptian,* another film of the same period shown in the Met's current series, *The Ten Commandments* is a historico-biblical epic at serious cross-purposes with itself, designed to render history beyond politics. The blaring trumpets, the vast scale, the cast of thousands, the insufferably posturing characters are made to coexist both with a dialogue that is hopelessly flat, dull, and spoken with a variety of different accents, as well as with a series of scenes designed to show audiences that people back then were human, small scale, "like us." Clearly these attempts at familiarity and hominess carry over into one of the Met's catalogues for the Egyptian exhibits, organized around the notion that everyday life in the ancient world actually did occur, and we can identify with it. Yet the overall effect is that of history rendered by displacement, not by accuracy, memory produced as a branch of forgetting and not as genuine recollection. This is an attitude to the past that makes sense only as an attitude of the present, an imperial view of reality that is unlike classical European colonialism, based instead on an imagined view of how the Other can be interpreted, understood, manipulated. It derives from an imperial power that is still at a very great distance from the realities it seeks to control, and while in a sense it removes from the past much of its inaccessibility and strangeness, it also imparts to the world out there a peculiar, if hypnotic, unreality.

Underlying the contemporary American interest in ancient Egypt is therefore, I think, a persistent desire to bypass Egypt's Arab identity, to reach back to a period when things were assumed to be both simple and amenable to the always well-intentioned American will. It is not an exaggeration to view the media, government, and public love affair with Sadat as part of the same desire; for as Mohamed Heikal says in his brilliant new book about Sadat, *Autumn of Fury* (Random House), the assassinated president-for-life of Egypt aspired to the role of contrite and reformed pharaoh which America was all too prepared for him to play. His policies, after all, were a vindication of *The Ten Commandments'* ideology: make peace with Israel, acknowledge its existence, and all will be well. If, in the process, Sadat lifted Egypt out of the present into an imagined timelessness, like an inspired moviemaker (or a dutiful provincial who believed in history as De Mille wished it), it would be "the Arabs" (as in fact Sadat used to say) who would be the losers. Never was such an attitude more dearly bought. He was assassinated by men who thought they represented the true, i.e., Islamic and Arab, Egypt, and he was unmourned by the vast majority of his compatriots, who, Heikal says, were part of his lost constituency, "the constituency which was naturally his as President of Egypt—the Arab world." Heikal continues:

> Sadat was the first Egyptian Pharaoh to come before his people armed with a camera; he was also the first Egyptian Pharaoh to be killed by his own people. He was a hero of the electronic revolution, but also its victim. When his face was no longer to be seen on the television screen it was as if the eleven years of his rule had vanished with a switch of the control knob.

Not surprisingly, then, the Met's Egyptian wing and its film series silently illustrate a larger phenomenon—the difficulty of dealing with Arab and Islamic Egypt. This is an Egypt represented by Abdal Nasser, a third world leader and popular nationalist who, unlike Gandhi, has not yet found a place in the canon of acceptable nonwhite heroes. He governed Egypt and, in a sense, the Arab world from 1952 till his death in 1970, and although he had many opponents in the region (not least the Saudi Arabians), it is ruefully and quite uselessly acknowledged that much of the mediocrity, corruption, and degeneration of the Arabs today exists because he hasn't been around to prevent it.

Nasser was never popular in the West and indeed could be considered its archetypal foreign devil. To some this is a true index of how successfully he stood up to imperialism, despite his disastrous military campaigns, his suppression of democracy at home, his overrhetorical performances as maximum leader. Nasser was the first modern Egyptian leader to make no claims for himself on the basis of caste or blood, and the first to transform Egypt into the major Arab and third world country. He sheltered the Algerian FLN, he was a leader at the Bandung Conference, and along with Nehru, Tito, and Sukarno, a pioneer of the Non-Aligned Movement. Above all, he changed Egypt irrevocably, a fact that Sadat seemed incapable of contending with. How much of this history has never reached the mass Western audience can be gauged by looking at the films dealing with Egypt that come from the period. Apart from the pharaonic and biblical epics, Egypt serves as a backdrop for a Western suspense story *(Death on the Nile),* or a location for European love stories *(Valley of the Kings),* and World War II history *(The Desert Fox);* I know of only one film that tried to reconcile itself to modern Egypt, Gregory Ratoff's *Abdullah's Harem,* an amusing, somewhat coarse caricature of Farouk's last days, which it is said was produced with the active encouragement of Egypt's new revolutionary government.

Excluded from mass culture except as political events dictated its presence, contemporary Egypt was—like so much of the third world—fixed within an ideological consensus. Its appearances were regulated accordingly: Egyptians were war-like, their leaders bloodthirsty, their existence a collective anonymous mass of ugly, poverty-stricken, and fanatical mobs. Sadat of course changed all that, to his credit, although it is highly arguable that the present media fix on Egypt as big and peace-loving (otherwise a cipher) is much of an improvement. True, Egyptian political rhetoric and propaganda under Nasser were strident and, true also, the state dominated life to a very great extent, as it still does. But things were going on that one should be prepared to admit might be of some interest to an American audience not completely brainwashed or transistorized. There is the tiniest suggestion of this other Egypt in the Met's current series, Shadi Abdelsalam's *The Night of Counting Years* (1969), which is presented anomalously as a film if not about ancient Egypt, then about Egyptology.

Abdelsalam's film is deeply political and utterly topical and, I am afraid, will be dismissed as a rather heavy and brooding film about life among the monuments of the Upper Nile. The plot is simple: alarmed at the trade in antiquities, the government's archaeological commission, under Maspero, a Frenchman, sends an expeditionary force up the Nile headed by a young native archaeologist whose job is to investigate and put an end to the thefts. The time is 1881. Meanwhile we are introduced to a tribe of austere Upper Egyptians whose traditional livelihood depends on their knowledge of secret pharaonic burial places, from which they extract treasure that is sold to a middleman. When the film opens, one of the tribe's elders has just died, and his two sons are initiated into the secret. Both are repelled by their people's complicity in this sordid trade. One of the brothers is assassinated when his protests threaten the tribe; the other, Salim, finally communicates the secret to the Cairo archaeologist, who thereupon removes the cache of mummies and treasure for transport to Cairo. Salim is terrifyingly alone when the film closes.

If they are looking for insights into archaeology, viewers of this film will be disappointed, just as it is likely that they will miss the connection between the film's gloomy atmosphere and the last years of Nasser's regime, a period of disenchantment, introverted pessimism, and, in the arts, a good deal of oblique political criticism. Abdelsalam said in a 1971 interview that when he made the film he was given much trouble by the Egyptian central state bureaucracy, and certainly the sense of hostility and alienation felt by the film's tribespeople toward the "effendis" from Cairo seems to duplicate the director's own feelings. But in addition, there are several forces in conflict throughout the film; all of them are highlighted by the date of the film's setting, just one year before the British occupation, which, transposed to 1969, prefigures the end of Nasser's fiery anti-imperialism and the onset of an American domination of Egypt consummated by Sadat.

First is the presence of foreign experts, like Maspero, whose ideas about Egyptian priorities (museum artifacts rather than peasant livelihoods) are dominant. Second, the Cairo class of modernizing elites—archaeologists, traders, policemen—who live in collaboration with Europe, and against their own people. Third, the population of piously Islamic peasants; their traditional occupation is conducted with ritual dignity, but it happens to be nothing less than grave robbery. Fourth, of course, is the consciousness represented by Salim, acutely aware of what is wrong and right, but unable to make any decisions that do not also bring unfortunate consequences: thus for him to live as a dutiful son is to break the law, but to turn his people in is to collaborate with the hated Cairo authorities. The fact that everyone speaks a deliberate classical Arabic, rather than any of the spoken dialects, transforms the dialogue from a language of communication into a language of impersonal exhibition.

This, Abdelsalam seems to be saying, is the Egypt that goes on under its official rhetorical blanket of Arabism. His film therefore is like a matrix of the major problems in which modern Egypt is involved, and out of which many more questions arise than answers. The country's European heritage doesn't jibe with its Arab actuality, its pharaonic past is too remote from its modern Islamic culture for it to be any more than an object of trade, the state's allegedly principled loyalty to the splendors of ancient Egypt is brutal in its effect upon daily life, and if, like Salim, one tries sincerely to reconcile the demands of conscience with the social realities of modern life, the results are going to be disastrous. Questions: can Egypt's Arab role—during the 1967 war or the Yemen campaign—be of much relevance either to the country's impoverished majority or to its incredibly old pharaonic past? Which Egypt is, so to speak, the right one? How can modern Egyptians disentangle themselves enough from the world system commanded by the West (symbolized by Maspero and his Cairo associates) to pay attention to their own prerogatives without at the same time living in a fossilized pattern of arid, unnourishing barter?

These are some of the things suggested by the film, but the point I'd like to conclude with is that in its New York setting, as one of the items celebrating the Met's new Egyptian wing, *The Night of Counting Years* will probably seem like an odd and perhaps dismissable bit of local color. During the amiable lecture that preceded the Met's screening of *The Egyptian,* the presiding curator remarked that the fourteenth-century B.C. courtesan Nefer, played in the film by Bella Darvi, anachronistically addressed her servants in Armenian. This drew a titter from the audience. But in a sense a solitary Egyptian film about Egypt—presented at the Met alongside Cecil B. De Mille's extravaganzas and row after row of mute archaeological specimens—might in fact be the same kind of intrusion as Nefer's inappropriate Armenian jabberings. On the other hand, it might serve to allude to another reality, only barely evident elsewhere in the commemorative exercises.

16

The Future of Criticism

There is a particularly desolate, perhaps even inappropriate quality to a topic like "the future of criticism" when proposed for the occasion commemorating Eugenio Donato's sad death. Criticism exists only because critics practice it. It is neither an institution nor, strictly speaking, a discipline. In the case of its exceptional practitioners like Donato, there is an urgent and irreducible bond between what critics do and who they are, and this bond cannot otherwise be reproduced, codified, or transmitted as "criticism" *tout court.* But because one acutely feels the loss of a critical style or voice as distinctive as Donato's—particularly given that his major theme was the irrecoverability of history and the melancholy inevitability of representation as memory, literature, and prophecy—there is justification for representing criticism as *having* a future, as much because Donato's work will have an important place in it, as because, writing against the grain of what he discovered and the fact of his death, critics need to affirm the future as something more than the continuity of a profession.

The activity of doing or practicing criticism can be said to have a future in two senses. First, there is the future of a particular kind of criticism, a future intrinsic to that kind of work as opposed to all other varieties, in which certain problems are posited and then tackled by the critic with the aim—in the future—of arriving at a certain set of goals. To take a pair of classic cases, we can say that John Livingstone Lowes set out to read Coleridge in such a way as finally to be able to know everything significant there was to be known about the sources and the meanings of the poet's richest verse; similarly, F. R. Leavis read English fiction in order to be able to discover within it a dominatingly great, as opposed to a minor or simply noteworthy, tradition. Such critical activities set not only discrete and finite goals that can be accomplished within one or two works of criticism, but also larger goals that may include the production of many more works of that particular type and the transformation of idle readers into active believers in, practitioners of, a certain kind of criticism.

Now the second sense in which criticism has a future is social and contextual, that is, a future whose form and setting are extrinsic to the practice of criticism considered as activity having internal norms. We must assume, first of all, that critics always exist and function in some place, even when they work in a fundamentally solitary and intransigent mode. Theodor Adorno and R. P. Blackmur—to take two of the most individualistic and recalcitrant critics of this century—can be and indeed have been characterized as doing their work within various contexts and settings despite their self-consciously stubborn distance from anything limiting the autonomy of their work. It is worth remembering Adorno's rule of thumb that in the contemporary world cultural forms that appear most distant from society—for example, the lyric, and dodecaphonic music—are the best places to see the imprint as well as the distortions of society upon the subject, "convex to concave," Fredric Jameson has perceptively said. Thus, both in its extroverted and introverted forms, criticism is a social activity occurring in several either very well-defined or less defined places. As examples of the former there are the classroom, the newspaper review, the scholarly and professional society; as examples of the latter there are such things as the mind of the age, its taste, political ideologies, national or class structures. Most, but by no means all, criticism cannot easily be confined to one place, just as it is also true that some forms of criticism are more prominent than others at the same time. The worldly aspects of criticism aspire, I think more or less uniformly, to hegemony in

Gramsci's sense of the word, and if it is also true to say that not every critic is as ambitious as, say, Matthew Arnold or T. S. Eliot in their openly proselytizing moments, the very act of doing criticism entails a commitment to the future, more particularly, a commitment to appearing in, making a contribution to, or in various other ways forming and affecting the future.

Although I have separated them analytically, these intrinsic and extrinsic aspects of criticism's future are dialectically interwoven, and together they regulate, even if they do not absolutely command, the field of activity to which critics look forward generally in the course of doing their work. Having said that, I think it is useful to suggest another pair of characterizations according to which we can further refine our expectations of the future. (I realize, by the way, that the history of criticism is dotted with characterizations and typologies of the sort I am about to offer: the habit of classification itself seems inherent in the very structure of critical self-consciousness.) My immediate source is a longish paragraph in Walter Benjamin's beautiful essay "The Image of Proust" *(Illuminations)*. In discussing Proust's radical self-absorption, Benjamin describes the man's tremendous loneliness and his consequent dislike of friendship. Yet the persistence of Proust's unquenchable desire for conversation is still to be explained, since this desire in fact co-exists quite noticeably with Proust's solitary egoism. Benjamin's speculation is that Proust wished company, but no physical contact; he pointed at things, but wanted no touching.

Benjamin's typology here is attractive. Literature, he says, is of two types—the directive *(die weisende)* and the touching *(die berührende)*. Proust's writing is an instance of the first, Péguy's of the second; whereas Proust points to, explains, analyzes things, he does so, according to Ramon Fernandez, with "depth, or, rather, intensity . . . always on his side, never on that of his partner." Writers like Péguy on the other hand are interested in moving closer to their readers, getting together, converting or collaborating with readers.

If these terms are shifted to the domain of criticism, it might be possible to say that the aim of some forms of criticism is to exemplify, do, embody a certain kind of activity without in the least attempting to produce effects of disciplehood or doctrine in the reader. Quite clearly Adorno's work is the most extreme form of this combination of distance and performance that we have; like Proust he points to things, but he does so in the modes afforded him by negative dialectics, obsessively and, it seems, untiringly. Yet he cannot be paraphrased nor, in a sense, can he be transmitted: the notion of an Adorno *fils* is quite laughable. This then is essayistic and algorithmic criticism, and insofar as its future effects are concerned, they are what can be called oppositional and secular.

The second type of criticism is the equivalent of Péguy's touching mode: criticism that openly seeks the assent and identification with it of its readers. Most of the great critical systematizers are touchers; they want you to take what they have to offer and use it elsewhere, over and over again preferably. Their work is codifiable and detachable; it travels in place and time gaining or losing in strength and effectiveness according to situation, period, practitioner. This is *systematic* criticism. If the form of the first kind is the essay, the form of this is the doctrine out of which books are made.

The permutations of the four terms I've just described—intrinsic and extrinsic goals, essayistic and systematic modes of critical work—are invitingly numerous, although there isn't much point in working out all the combinations. So let us proceed immediately to concrete circumstances in order to see what the actual future terrain for criticism is. Perhaps it is worth saying first that the domain of mass culture is likely to enlarge, almost definitely at the expense of what criticism has traditionally been associated with: the domain of elite culture. A corollary is the dramatic downward shift in literacy or, if you prefer, a dramatic alteration in the standards defining levels of accepted literacy. The trend has been in unmistakable evidence since the early years of this century, with the consequence, I believe, of rendering marginal what most academic critics do, at least so far as expanding their audience is concerned. On the other hand, even though a considerable retreat from the theoretical enthusiasm of the early nineteen-sixties has taken place, it is certainly true that literary criticism itself is much less insular than it ever has been. Thanks to the efforts of pioneers like Eugenio Donato, philosophy, linguistics, psychoanalysis, sociology and anthropology are in fruitful dialogue with the hermeneutic and philological practice of interpreting literary texts, so much so that most people aspiring to the condition of critics are directly exposed to the winds of interdisciplinary thought. Nevertheless—and here the socio-institutional realities assert themselves—new, and I would argue, extremely assertive divisions of labor have come down between critics. These, I think, are limiting if one believes, as I do, that critical energies are optimally realized not in systematic or doctrinal modes which tend to solidify the status of criticism as a packaged commodity, but in the salutary intransigence of oppositional criticism whose function is radically secular, investigative, and relentlessly mobile. Donato's work, I think, was essentially of the latter sort. And the force of the kind of criticism he practiced has been registered elsewhere in powerful ways, nowhere more usefully than in the continuing pressures exerted against privileges or authority granted to aesthetic and cultural texts on the basis of class, race, or gender. The Eurocentric vision of culture has been somewhat eroded; the claims of feminism, of Europe's Others, of subaltern cultures, of theoretical currents running counter to the rule of affirmatively dominant pragmatism and empiricism have been felt and will not be ignored.

From these circumstances certain conclusions can be drawn. If criticism is principally an intellectual and rational activity, situated in the world, it must obviously find its home somewhere. Is that locale the literary department? To some degree, literary departments play a necessary conservative or curatorial role since they maintain, elucidate and modify canons, although even this formerly neutral function is now a highly contested issue. But the liberating intercourse between fields of which I spoke a moment ago suggests an opening out from a preservative horizon to an investigative one. If so, then criticism is a response at least as much to the discrepancies and dissonances of human experiences, as it is to its routinely compartmentalized stabilities. As inscribed in various discourses and disciplines, these discrepancies comprise the material competing with the texts whose cultural authority and interpretive richness have traditionally constituted the main focus of literary scholarship: the problem for criticism is what to do about this potentially disorienting confrontation.

Let me describe this problematic in less abstract and even more limited terms. The intellectual correlative of political upheaval during the late sixties was the shaking-up of traditional humanism that was given by what were considered outré theoretical approaches making their claims felt; thus what semiotics and structuralism achieved was radical revision in, for example, the notion of how a text works, how its author's function was conceived, how it could—or could not—be read. Such changes, no one needs to be told, occurred right across the board but, I should like to add, they were assimilated too readily on the one hand, and spurned too categorically by defenders of traditional humanism on the other. I don't think it is too much to say that the domestication of critical theory, as much as resistance to it, was undertaken in modes stunningly compliant with the commodity fetishism and market consumerism everyone was at pains to disown. The result has been curious.

If we leave aside those who feel simply that all change is bad, we see the field of criticism divided into many camps—labelled with the names of various critical schools—whose roots are struck in relatively superficial and restricted academic soil, and not in the deeper social and ideological matter that may originally have nurtured them. Now I would certainly not want to say that the academy ought to become a sort of brief abstract or immediate microcosm of society. But there is a difference, I believe, between an academic attention that flattens, cosmetizes, and blandly assimilates social experience, and an attention no less academic that preserves, heightens, and interprets the great dissonances and discrepancies informing social, historical, and aesthetic forms. In America, the relative absence of either an indigenous socialist or a traditional philological culture has minimized interest in social discrepancy, while promoting models of effective power taken from managerial experience.

And so the gates are now open, and the barriers between disciplines, rhetorically and actually, are down. The future of criticism or the critical function is, I believe, to be exercised in the traffic between cultures, discourses and disciplines, rather than in the appropriation, systematization, management, and professionalization of any one domain. This statement of what the future is of course indicates a preference for the essayistic over the systematic and doctrinal, but more important is the certainty that criticism based on the impulse to dominate and hold previously gained positions is, no matter the ingenuity and energy of elaboration, much less likely to be responsive to the future than to variously ornamented extensions of the past and present.

This brings me to my other main idea about the future of criticism, this one emanating from the intrinsic pressures I mentioned at the outset. Every act of criticism is always literally tied to a set of social and historical circumstances; the problem is in specifying or characterizing the relationship, not merely in asserting that it exists; then the critic goes on actively to choose between competing social tendencies. All criticism is postulated and performed on the assumption that it is to have a future; ideally then, intrinsic goals, such as more complete interpretations of X or Y genre or author, might be connected to such extrinsic aims as a change in or enhancement of society. Rarely, however, are connections of such scope and range made.

Very well then—who is to do the specifying, characterizing and choosing if not the critic? No matter how rarified the type of criticism, it seems to me incumbent on critics not to lose or efface but to clarify and reflect upon the social traces of their work. This is so in the end because as a social and rational intellectual activity criticism is, properly speaking, an interventionary and, in Gramsci's phrase, a potentially *directive* phenomenon. This is today more rather than less true, for reasons that have become explicitly self-evident whether one inhabits metropolitan (post-industrial, late-capitalist) regions, states of the socialist bloc, or peripheral (third-world, post-colonial) territories. In all these polities, it is the critical consciousness that is threatened by the institutions of a mass society whose aim is nothing less than a political quiescence assuring the citizenry's "governability" (to use the current word). Yet, as I said, there is a marked reticence about extending intrinsic critical goals out toward the social polity enfolding and to some degree enabling critical practice as a form of resistance. To conceive of criticism as first and last playing a service or management role in the culture industry is therefore to diminish its potential as well as actual importance too drastically. Yet to think of criticism principally as a competitor within that industry of the so-called creative arts, is both to reify and mystify precisely those distinctions between art and criticism being called into question by the elevation of criticism to priority. In any event, controversy over the status of criticism tends in a backward-looking way to occlude and postpone the equally relevant question of its destiny or future.

There are few exceptions to this habit of *not* thinking about the future in recent theoretical writing about the function of criticism. One noteworthy exception is Adorno writing in his last publication that "the relationship of subject and object would lie in the realization of peace among men as well as between men and their Other. Peace is the state of distinctness without domination, with the distinct participating in each other." Another instance is Raymond Williams writing in "The Tenses of the Imagination," that "we usually still hesitate between tenses: between knowing in new ways the structures of feeling that have directed and now hold us, and finding in new ways the shape of an alternative, a future, that can be genuinely imagined and hopefully lived."

What connects these two passages about the future to each other is not simply the common accent on hopeful alternatives and the human distinction and concreteness dialectically preserved, rather than blotted out, in the future. It is the emphasis on non-dominative and non-coercive modes of life and knowledge as essential components of the desired future. Note that Adorno and Williams signal no nostalgic return to some original and unmediated state of plenitude. That both men as critics tie this particular image of the future to critical praxis suggests a choice that many may find uncongenial, as well as too utopian, or too presumptuous, although any reader of Donato's astringent critiques of romantic disillusionment may see the choice offered as logically entailed by those very same critiques. My own notion is that both the image and its direct relationship to criticism are fundamentally implicit in all but the most cynical readings of recent critical and intellectual history. And, I would add, as much as our images of our discipline's past, images of the future, abductible (in Peirce's sense of the word) or inferrable from the present—however much these images are left unarticulated or implicit—shape what we do in the present.

17

Reflections on Exile

Exile is strangely compelling to think about but terrible to experience. It is the unhealable rift forced between a human being and a native place, between the self and its true home: its essential sadness can never be surmounted. And while it is true that literature and history contain heroic, romantic, glorious, even triumphant episodes in an exile's life, these are no more than efforts meant to overcome the crippling sorrow of estrangement. The achievements of exile are permanently undermined by the loss of something left behind forever.

But if true exile is a condition of terminal loss, why has it been transformed so easily into a potent, even enriching, motif of modern culture? We have become accustomed to thinking of the modern period itself as spiritually orphaned and alienated, the age of anxiety and estrangement. Nietzsche taught us to feel uncomfortable with tradition, and Freud to regard domestic intimacy as the polite face painted on patricidal and incestuous rage. Modern Western culture is in large part the work of exiles, émigrés, refugees. In the United States, academic, intellectual and aesthetic thought is what it is today because of refugees from fascism, communism, and other regimes given to the oppression and expulsion of dissidents. The critic George Steiner has even proposed the perceptive thesis that a whole genre of twentieth-century Western literature is "extraterritorial," a literature by and about exiles, symbolizing the age of the refugee. Thus Steiner suggests:

> It seems proper that those who create art in a civilization of
> quasi-barbarism, which has made so many homeless, should
> themselves be poets unhoused and wanderers across language.
> Eccentric, aloof, nostalgic, deliberately untimely . . .

In other ages, exiles had similar cross-cultural and transnational visions, suffered the same frustrations and miseries, performed the same elucidating and critical tasks—brilliantly affirmed, for instance, in E. H. Carr's classic study of the nineteenth-century Russian intellectuals clustered around Herzen, *The Romantic Exiles*. But the difference between earlier exiles and those of our own time is, it bears stressing, scale: our age—with its modern warfare, imperialism, and the quasi-theological ambitions of totalitarian rulers—is indeed the age of the refugee, the displaced person, mass immigration.

Against this large, impersonal setting, exile cannot be made to serve notions of humanism. On the twentieth-century scale, exile is neither aesthetically nor humanistically comprehensible: at most the literature about exile objectifies an anguish and a predicament most people rarely experience first hand; but to think of the exile informing this literature as beneficially humanistic is to banalize its mutilations, the losses it inflicts on those who suffer them, the muteness with which it responds to any attempt to understand it as "good for us." Is it not true that the views of exile in literature and, moreover, in religion obscure what is truly horrendous: that exile is irremediably secular and unbearably historical; that it is produced by human beings for other human beings; and that, like death but without death's ultimate mercy, it has torn millions of people from the nourishment of tradition, family, and geography?

To see a poet in exile—as opposed to reading the poetry of exile—is to see exile's antinomies embodied and endured with a unique intensity. Several years ago I spent some time with Faiz Ahmad Faiz, the greatest of contemporary Urdu poets. He was exiled from his native Pakistan by Zia's military regime, and found a welcome of sorts in strife-torn Beirut. Naturally his closest friends were Palestinian, but I sensed that, although there was an affinity of spirit between them, nothing quite matched—language, poetic convention, or life-history. Only once, when Eqbal Ahmad, a Pakistani friend and a fellow-exile, came to Beirut, did Faiz seem to overcome his sense of constant estrangement. The three of us sat in a dingy Beirut restaurant late one night, while Faiz recited poems. After a time, he and Eqbal stopped translating his verses for my benefit, but as the night wore on it did not matter. What I watched required no translation: it was an enactment of a homecoming expressed through defiance and loss, as if to say, "Zia, we are here." Of course Zia was the one who was really at home and who would not hear their exultant voices.

Rashid Hussein was a Palestinian. He translated Bialik, one of the great modern Hebrew poets, into Arabic, and Hussein's eloquence established him in the post-1948 period as an orator and nationalist without peer. He first worked as a Hebrew language journalist in Tel Aviv, and succeeded in establishing a dialogue between Jewish and Arab writers, even as he espoused the cause of Nasserism and Arab nationalism. In time, he could no longer endure the pressure, and he left for New York. He married a Jewish woman and began working in the PLO office at the United Nations, but regularly outraged his superiors with unconventional ideas and utopian rhetoric. In 1972 he left for the Arab world, but a few months later he was back in the United States: he had felt out of place in Syria and Lebanon, unhappy in Cairo. New York sheltered him anew, but so did endless bouts of drinking and idleness. His life was in ruins, but he remained the most hospitable of men. He died after a night of heavy drinking when, smoking in bed, his cigarette started a fire that spread to a small library of audio cassettes, consisting mostly of poets reading their verse. The fumes from the tapes asphyxiated him. His body was repatriated for burial in Musmus, the small village in Israel where his family still resided.

These and so many other exiled poets and writers lend dignity to a condition legislated to deny dignity—to deny an identity to people. From them, it is apparent that, to concentrate on exile as a contemporary political punishment, you must therefore map territories of experience beyond those mapped by the literature of exile itself. You must first set aside Joyce and Nabokov and think instead of the uncountable masses for whom UN agencies have been created. You must think of the refugee-peasants with no prospect of ever returning home, armed only with a ration card and an agency number. Paris may be a capital famous for cosmopolitan exiles, but it is also a city where unknown men and women have spent years of miserable loneliness: Vietnamese, Algerians, Cambodians, Lebanese, Senegalese, Peruvians. You must think also of Cairo, Beirut, Madagascar, Bangkok, Mexico City. As you move further from the Atlantic world, the awful forlorn waste increases: the hopelessly large numbers, the compounded misery of "undocumented" people suddenly lost, without a tellable history. To reflect on exiled Muslims from India, or Haitians in America, or Bikinians in Oceania, or Palestinians throughout the Arab world means that you must leave the modest refuge provided by subjectivity and resort instead to the abstractions of mass politics. Negotiations, wars of national liberation, people bundled out of their homes and prodded, bussed or walked to enclaves in other regions: what do these experiences add up to? Are they not manifestly and almost by design irrecoverable?

We come to nationalism and its essential association with exile. Nationalism is an assertion of belonging in and to a place, a people, a heritage. It affirms the home created by a community of language, culture, and customs; and, by so doing, it fends off exile, fights to prevent its ravages. Indeed, the interplay between nationalism and exile is like Hegel's dialectic of servant and master, opposites informing and constituting each other. All nationalisms in their early stages develop from a condition of estrangement. The struggles to win American independence, to unify Germany or Italy, to liberate Algeria were those of national groups separated—exiled—from what was construed to be their rightful way of life. Triumphant, achieved nationalism then justifies, retrospectively as well as prospectively, a history selectively strung together in a narrative form: thus all nationalisms have their founding fathers, their basic, quasi-religious texts, their rhetoric of belonging, their historical and geographical landmarks, their official enemies and heroes. This collective ethos forms what Pierre Bourdieu, the French sociologist, calls the *habitus,* the coherent amalgam of practices linking habit with inhabitance. In time, successful nationalisms consign truth exclusively to themselves and relegate falsehood and inferiority to outsiders (as in the rhetoric of capitalist versus communist, or the European versus the Asiatic).

And just beyond the frontier between "us" and the "outsiders" is the perilous territory of not-belonging: this is to where in a primitive time peoples were banished, and where in the modern era immense aggregates of humanity loiter as refugees and displaced persons.

Nationalisms are about groups, but in a very acute sense exile is a solitude experienced outside the group: the deprivations felt at not being with others in the communal habitation. How, then, does one surmount the loneliness of exile without falling into the encompassing and thumping language of national pride, collective sentiments, group passions? What is there worth saving and holding on to between the extremes of exile on the one hand, and the often bloodyminded affirmations of nationalism on the other? Do nationalism and exile have any intrinsic attributes? Are they simply two conflicting varieties of paranoia?

These are questions that cannot ever be fully answered because each assumes that exile and nationalism can be discussed neutrally, without reference to each other. They cannot be. Because both terms include everything from the most collective of collective sentiments to the most private of private emotions, there is hardly language adequate for both. But there is certainly nothing about nationalism's public and all-inclusive ambitions that touches the core of the exile's predicament.

Because exile, unlike nationalism, is fundamentally a discontinuous state of being. Exiles are cut off from their roots, their land, their past. They generally do not have armies or states, although they are often in search of them. Exiles feel, therefore, an urgent need to reconstitute their broken lives, usually by choosing to see themselves as part of a triumphant ideology or a restored people. The crucial thing is that a state of exile free from this triumphant ideology—designed to reassemble an exile's broken history into a new whole—is virtually unbearable, and virtually impossible in today's world. Look at the fate of the Jews, the Palestinians, and the Armenians.

Noubar is a solitary Armenian, and a friend. His parents had to leave Eastern Turkey in 1915, after their families were massacred: his maternal grandfather was beheaded. Noubar's mother and father went to Aleppo, then to Cairo. In the middle-sixties, life in Egypt became difficult for non-Egyptians, and his parents, along with four children, were taken to Beirut by an international relief organization. In Beirut, they lived briefly in a pension and then were bundled into two rooms of a little house outside the city. In Lebanon, they had no money and they waited: eight months later, a relief agency got them a flight to Glasgow. And then to Gander. And then to New York. They rode by Greyhound bus from New York to Seattle: Seattle was the city designated by the agency for their American residence. When I asked, "Seattle?," Noubar smiled resignedly, as if to say, better Seattle than Armenia—which he never knew, or Turkey, where so many were slaughtered, or Lebanon, where he and his family would certainly have risked their lives. Exile is sometimes better than staying behind or not getting out: but only sometimes.

Because *nothing* is secure. Exile is a jealous state. What you achieve is precisely what you have no wish to share, and it is in the drawing of lines around you and your compatriots that the least attractive aspects of being in exile emerge: an exaggerated sense of group solidarity, and a passionate hostility to outsiders, even those who may in fact be in the same predicament as you. What could be more intransigent than the conflict between Zionist Jews and Arab Palestinians? Palestinians feel that they have been turned into exiles by the proverbial people of exile, the Jews. But the Palestinians also know that their own sense of national identity has been nourished in the exile milieu, where everyone not a blood-brother or sister is an enemy, where every sympathizer is an agent of some unfriendly power, and where the slightest deviation from the accepted group line is an act of the rankest treachery and disloyalty.

Perhaps this is the most extraordinary of exile's fates: to have been exiled by exiles—to relive the actual process of up-rooting at the hands of exiles. All Palestinians during the summer of 1982 asked themselves what inarticulate urge drove Israel, having displaced Palestinians in 1948, to expel them continuously from their refugee homes and camps in Lebanon. It is as if the reconstructed Jewish collective experience, as represented by Israel and modern Zionism, could not tolerate another story of dispossession and loss to exist alongside it—an intolerance constantly reinforced by the Israeli hostility to the nationalism of the Palestinians, who for forty-six years have been painfully reassembling a national identity in exile.

This need to reassemble an identity out of the refractions and discontinuities of exile is found in the earlier poems of Mahmoud Darwish, whose considerable work amounts to an epic effort to transform the lyrics of loss into the indefinitely postponed drama of return. Thus he depicts his sense of homelessness in the form of a list of unfinished and incomplete things:

> But I am the exile.
> Seal me with your eyes.
> Take me wherever you are—
> Take me whatever you are.
> Restore to me the colour of face
> And the warmth of body
> The light of heart and eye,
> The salt of bread and rhythm,
> The taste of earth . . . the Motherland.
> Shield me with your eyes.
> Take me as a relic from the mansion of sorrow.
> Take me as a verse from my tragedy;
> Take me as a toy, a brick from the house
> So that our children will remember to return.

The pathos of exile is in the loss of contact with the solidity and the satisfaction of earth: homecoming is out of the question.

Joseph Conrad's tale "Amy Foster" is perhaps the most uncompromising representation of exile ever written. Conrad thought of himself as an exile from Poland, and nearly all his work (as well as his life) carries the unmistakable mark of the sensitive émigré's obsession with his own fate and with his hopeless attempts to make satisfying contact with new surroundings. "Amy Foster" is in a sense confined to the problems of exile, perhaps so confined that it is not one of Conrad's best-known stories. This, for example, is the description of the agony of its central character, Yanko Goorall, an Eastern European peasant who, en route to America, is shipwrecked off the British coast:

> It is indeed hard upon a man to find himself a lost stranger helpless, incomprehensible, and of a mysterious origin, in some

obscure corner of the earth. Yet amongst all the adventurers shipwrecked in all the wild parts of the world, there is not one, it seems to me, that ever had to suffer a fate so simply tragic as the man I am speaking of, the most innocent of adventurers cast out by the sea.

Yanko has left home because the pressures were too great for him to go on living there. America lures him with its promise, though England is where he ends up. He endures in England, where he cannot speak the language and is feared and misunderstood. Only Amy Foster, a plodding, unattractive peasant girl, tries to communicate with him. They marry, have a child, but when Yanko falls ill, Amy, afraid and alienated, refuses to nurse him; snatching their child, she leaves. The desertion hastens Yanko's miserable death, which like the deaths of several Conradian heroes is depicted as the result of a combination of crushing isolation and the world's indifference. Yanko's fate is described as "the supreme disaster of loneliness and despair."

Yanko's predicament is affecting: a foreigner perpetually haunted and alone in an uncomprehending society. But Conrad's own exile causes him to exaggerate the differences between Yanko and Amy. Yanko is dashing, light, and bright-eyed, whereas Amy is heavy, dull, bovine; when he dies, it is as if her earlier kindness to him was a snare to lure and then trap him fatally. Yanko's death is romantic: the world is coarse, unappreciative; no one understands him, not even Amy, the one person close to him. Conrad took this neurotic exile's fear and created an aesthetic principle out of it. No one can understand or communicate in Conrad's world, but paradoxically this radical limitation on the possibilities of language doesn't inhibit elaborate efforts to communicate. All of Conrad's stories are about lonely people who talk a great deal (for indeed who of the great modernists was more voluble and "adjectival" than Conrad himself?) and whose attempts to *impress* others compound, rather than reduce, the original sense of isolation. Each Conradian exile fears, and is condemned endlessly to imagine, the spectacle of a solitary death illuminated, so to speak, by unresponsive, uncommunicating eyes.

Exiles look at non-exiles with resentment. *They* belong in their surroundings, you feel, whereas an exile is always out of place. What is it like to be born in a place, to stay and live there, to know that you are of it, more or less forever?

Although it is true that anyone prevented from returning home is an exile, some distinctions can be made among exiles, refugees, expatriates, and émigrés. Exile originated in the age-old practice of banishment. Once banished, the exile lives an anomalous and miserable life, with the stigma of being an outsider. Refugees, on the other hand, are a creation of the twentieth-century state. The word "refugee" has become a political one, suggesting large herds of innocent and bewildered people requiring urgent international assistance, whereas "exile" carries with it, I think, a touch of solitude and spirituality.

Expatriates voluntarily live in an alien country, usually for personal or social reasons. Hemingway and Fitzgerald were not forced to live in France. Expatriates may share in the solitude and estrangement of exile, but they do not suffer under its rigid proscriptions. Émigrés enjoy an ambiguous status. Technically, an émigré is anyone who emigrates to a new country. Choice in the matter is certainly a possibility. Colonial officials, missionaries, technical experts, mercenaries, and military advisers on loan may in a sense live in exile, but they have not been banished. White settlers in Africa, parts of Asia and Australia may once have been exiles, but as pioneers and nation-builders, they lost the label "exile."

Much of the exile's life is taken up with compensating for disorienting loss by creating a new world to rule. It is not surprising that so many exiles seem to be novelists, chess players, political activists, and intellectuals. Each of these occupations requires a minimal investment in objects and places a great premium on mobility and skill. The exile's new world, logically enough, is unnatural and its unreality resembles fiction. Georg Lukács, in *Theory of the Novel*, argued with compelling force that the novel, a literary form created out of the unreality of ambition and fantasy, is *the* form of "transcendental homelessness." Classical epics, Lukács wrote, emanate from settled cultures in which values are clear, identities stable, life unchanging. The European novel is grounded in precisely the opposite experience, that of a changing society in which an itinerant and disinherited middle-class hero or heroine seeks to construct a new world that somewhat resembles an old one left behind forever. In the epic there is no *other* world, only the finality of *this* one. Odysseus returns to Ithaca after years of wandering; Achilles will die because he cannot escape his fate. The novel, however, exists because other worlds *may* exist, alternatives for bourgeois speculators, wanderers, exiles.

No matter how well they may do, exiles are always eccentrics who *feel* their difference (even as they frequently exploit it) as a kind of orphanhood. Anyone who is really homeless regards the habit of seeing estrangement in everything modern as an affectation, a display of modish attitudes. Clutching difference like a weapon to be used with stiffened will, the exile jealously insists on his or her right to refuse to belong.

This usually translates into an intransigence that is not easily ignored. Willfulness, exaggeration, overstatement: these are characteristic styles of being an exile, methods for compelling the world to accept your vision—which you make more unacceptable because you are in fact unwilling to have it accepted. It is yours, after all. Composure and serenity are the last things associated with the work of exiles. Artists in exile are decidedly unpleasant, and their stubbornness insinuates itself into even their exalted works. Dante's vision in *The Divine Comedy* is tremendously powerful in its universality and detail, but even the beatific peace achieved in the *Paradiso* bears traces of the vindictiveness and severity of judgment embodied in the *Inferno*. Who but an exile like Dante, banished from Florence, would use eternity as a place for settling old scores?

James Joyce *chose* to be in exile: to give force to his artistic vocation. In an uncannily effective way—as Richard Ellmann has shown in his biography—Joyce picked a quarrel with Ireland and kept it alive so as to sustain the strictest opposition to what was familiar. Ellmann says that "whenever his relations with his native land were in danger of improving, [Joyce] was to find a new incident to solidify his intransigence and to reaffirm the rightness of his voluntary absence." Joyce's fiction concerns what in a letter he once described as the state of being "alone and friendless." And although it is rare to pick banishment as a way of life, Joyce perfectly understood its trials.

But Joyce's success as an exile stresses the question lodged at its very heart: is exile so extreme and private that any instrumental use of it is ultimately a trivialization? How is it that the literature of exile has taken its place as a *topos* of human experience alongside the literature of adventure, education, or discovery? Is this the *same* exile that quite literally kills Yanko Goorall and has bred the expensive, often dehumanizing relationship between twentieth-century exile and nationalism? Or is it some more benign variety?

Much of the contemporary interest in exile can be traced to the somewhat pallid notion that non-exiles can share in the benefits of exile as a redemptive motif. There is, admittedly, a certain plausibility and truth to this idea. Like medieval itinerant scholars or learned Greek slaves in the Roman Empire, exiles—the exceptional ones among them—do leaven their environments. And naturally "we" concentrate on that enlightening aspect of "their" presence among us, not on their misery or their demands. But looked at from the bleak political perspective of modern mass dislocations, individual exiles force us to recognize the tragic fate of homelessness in a necessarily heartless world.

A generation ago, Simone Weil posed the dilemma of exile as concisely as it has ever been expressed. "To be rooted," she said, "is perhaps the most important and least recognized need of the human soul." Yet Weil also saw that most remedies for uprootedness in this era of world wars, deportations, and mass exterminations are almost as dangerous as what they purportedly remedy. Of these, the state—or, more accurately, statism—is one of the most insidious, since worship of the state tends to supplant all other human bonds.

Weil exposes us anew to that whole complex of pressures and constraints that lie at the center of the exile's predicament, which, as I have suggested, is as close as we come in the modern era to tragedy. There is the sheer fact of isolation and displacement, which produces the kind of narcissistic masochism that resists all efforts at amelioration, acculturation, and community. At this extreme the exile can make a fetish of exile, a practice that distances him or her from all connections and commitments. To live as if everything around you were temporary and perhaps trivial is to fall prey to petulant cynicism as well as to querulous lovelessness. More common is the pressure on the exile to join—parties, national movements, the state. The exile is offered a new set of affiliations and develops new loyalties. But there is also a loss—of critical perspective, of intellectual reserve, of moral courage.

It must also be recognized that the defensive nationalism of exiles often fosters self-awareness as much as it does the less attractive forms of self-assertion. Such reconstitutive projects as assembling a nation out of exile (and this is true in this century for Jews and Palestinians) involve constructing a national history, reviving an ancient language, founding national institutions like libraries and universities. And these, while they sometimes promote strident ethnocentrism, also give rise to investigations of self that inevitably go far beyond such simple and positive facts as "ethnicity." For example, there is the self-consciousness of an individual trying to understand why the histories of the Palestinians and the Jews have certain patterns to them, why in spite of oppression and the threat of extinction a particular ethos remains alive in exile.

Necessarily, then, I speak of exile not as a privilege, but as an *alternative* to the mass institutions that dominate modern life. Exile is not, after all, a matter of choice: you are born into it, or it happens to you. But, provided that the exile refuses to sit on the sidelines nursing a wound, there are things to be learned: he or she must cultivate a scrupulous (not indulgent or sulky) subjectivity.

Perhaps the most rigorous example of such subjectivity is to be found in the writing of Theodor Adorno, the German-Jewish philosopher and critic. Adorno's masterwork, *Minima Moralia,* is an autobiography written while in exile; it is subtitled *Reflexionen aus dem beschädigten Leben (Reflections from a Mutilated Life).* Ruthlessly opposed to what he called the "administered" world, Adorno saw all life as pressed into ready-made forms, prefabricated "homes." He argued that everything that one says or thinks, as well as every object one possesses, is ultimately a mere commodity. Language is jargon, objects are for sale. To refuse this state of affairs is the exile's intellectual mission.

Adorno's reflections are informed by the belief that the only home truly available now, though fragile and vulnerable, is in writing. Elsewhere, "the house is past. The bombings of European cities, as well as the labour and concentration camps, merely precede as executors, with what the immanent development of technology had long decided was to be the fate of houses. These are now good only to be thrown away like old food cans." In short, Adorno says with a grave irony, "it is part of morality not to be at home in one's home."

To follow Adorno is to stand away from "home" in order to look at it with the exile's detachment. For there is considerable merit in the practice of noting the discrepancies between various concepts and ideas and what they actually produce. We take home and language for granted; they become nature, and their underlying assumptions recede into dogma and orthodoxy.

The exile knows that in a secular and contingent world, homes are always provisional. Borders and barriers, which enclose us within the safety of familiar territory, can also become prisons, and are often defended beyond reason or necessity. Exiles cross borders, break barriers of thought and experience.

Hugo of St. Victor, a twelfth-century monk from Saxony, wrote these hauntingly beautiful lines:

> It is, therefore, a source of great virtue for the practised mind to learn, bit by bit, first to change about invisible and transitory things, so that afterwards it may be able to leave them behind altogether. The man who finds his homeland sweet is still a tender beginner; he to whom every soil is as his native one is already strong; but he is perfect to whom the entire world is as a foreign land. The tender soul has fixed his love on one spot in the world; the strong man has extended his love to all places; the perfect man has extinguished his.

Erich Auerbach, the great twentieth-century literary scholar who spent the war years as an exile in Turkey, has cited this passage as a model for anyone wishing to transcend national or provincial limits. Only by embracing this attitude can a historian begin to grasp human experience and its written records in their diversity and particularity; otherwise he or she will remain committed more to the exclusions and reactions of prejudice than to the freedom that accompanies knowledge. But note that Hugo twice makes it clear that the "strong" or "perfect" man achieves independence and detachment by *working through* attachments, not by rejecting them. Exile is predicated on the existence of, love for, and bond with, one's native place; what is true of all exile is not that home and love of home are lost, but that loss is inherent in the very existence of both.

Regard experiences as if they were about to disappear. What is it that anchors them in reality? What would you save of them? What would you give up? Only someone who has achieved independence and detachment, someone whose homeland is "sweet" but whose circumstances make it impossible to recapture that sweetness, can answer those questions. (Such a person would also find it impossible to derive satisfaction from substitutes furnished by illusion or dogma.)

This may seem like a prescription for an unrelieved grimness of outlook and, with it, a permanently sullen disapproval of all enthusiasm or buoyancy of spirit. Not necessarily. While it perhaps seems peculiar to speak of the pleasures of exile, there are some positive things to be said for a few of its conditions. Seeing "the entire world as a foreign land" makes possible originality of vision. Most people are principally aware of one culture, one setting, one home; exiles are aware of at least two, and this plurality of vision gives rise to an awareness of simultaneous dimensions, an awareness that—to borrow a phrase from music—is *contrapuntal*.

For an exile, habits of life, expression, or activity in the new environment inevitably occur against the memory of these things in another environment. Thus both the new and the old environments are vivid, actual, occurring together contrapuntally. There is a unique pleasure in this sort of apprehension, especially if the exile is conscious of other contrapuntal juxtapositions that diminish orthodox judgment and elevate appreciative sympathy. There is also a particular sense of achievement in acting as if one were at home wherever one happens to be.

This remains risky, however: the habit of dissimulation is both wearying and nerve-racking. Exile is never the state of being satisfied, placid, or secure. Exile, in the words of Wallace Stevens, is "a mind of winter" in which the pathos of summer and autumn as much as the potential of spring are nearby but unobtainable. Perhaps this is another way of saying that a life of exile moves according to a different calendar, and is less seasonal and settled than life at home. Exile is life led outside habitual order. It is nomadic, decentered, contrapuntal; but no sooner does one get accustomed to it than its unsettling force erupts anew.

18

Michel Foucault, 1927–1984

According to the medical bulletin published in *Le Monde,* Michel Foucault died at 1:15 P.M. on June 25 in Paris's Hôpital de la Salpetrière of neurological complications following acute septicemia. Framing the announcement was an extraordinary array of tributes grouped under a page-one, two-column headline, "La mort du philosophe Michel Foucault." The lead article was by Pierre Bourdieu, Foucault's distinguished colleague at the Collège de France. It is difficult to imagine so concentrated and estimable a degree of attention paid to any other contemporary philosopher's death, except in France and in Foucault's case, which despite the difficulty and intransigence of his philosophic and historical work even drew a memorial tribute from the prime minister. Why this was so explains the enormous loss represented by Foucault's death, as it also says something about the startling yet sustained force and influence of his thought.

He is best understood, I think, as perhaps the greatest of Nietzsche's modern disciples and, simultaneously, as a central figure in the most noteworthy flowering of oppositional intellectual life in the twentieth-century West. Along with Sartre and Merleau-Ponty, Georges Canguihelm, Jean-Pierre Vernant, Lucien Goldmann, Althusser,

Derrida, Lévi-Strauss, Roland Barthes, Gilles Deleuze, and Bourdieu himself, Foucault emerged out of a strange revolutionary concatenation of Parisian aesthetic and political currents, which for about thirty years produced such a concentration of brilliant work as we are not likely to see again for generations. In what amounted to a genuine upheaval in modern thought, the barriers between disciplines and indeed languages were broken, then the fields separated by these barriers were reshaped literally from beneath the surface to their most complex superstructures. Theory, images of astonishing fecundity, and vast formal systems—to say nothing of idioms that seemed barbarous at first, but soon became fashionable—poured out from these figures, whose ancestry was again a contradictory amalgam of the academic and the insurrectionary. All seemed to have been deeply affected by Marx and (individually to a greater or lesser degree) by Freud; most were rhetorical tacticians, as well as obsessed by language as a way of seeing, if not actually constituting, reality; many were influenced by university courses and almost legendary teachers—the names of Bachelard, Dumezil, Benveniste, Hyppolite, and Kojève (whose famous lectures and seminars on Hegel seemed to have formed an entire generation) recur with frequency—as much as they were influenced by surrealist poets and novelists like André Breton and Raymond Roussel, as well as by the maverick writer-philosophers Georges Bataille and Maurice Blanchot. Yet all of these Parisian intellectuals were deeply rooted in the political actualities of French life, the great milestones of which were World War II, the response to European communism, the Vietnamese and Algerian colonial wars, and May 1968. Beyond France, it was Germany and German thought that mattered most, rarely the work of British or American writers.

Even in this unprecedentedly exceptional company, Foucault stood out. For one, he was the most wide-ranging in his learning: at once the most concrete and historical, he was as well the most radical in theoretical investigation. For another, he seemed the most committed to study for its own sake ("le plaisir de savoir" in Bourdieu's phrase for him) and hence the least Parisian, the least modish, fashionable, or backbiting. More interestingly, he covered huge expanses of social and intellectual history, read both the conventional and the unconventional texts with equal thoroughness, and still seemed never to say routine or unoriginal things, even when in the last part of his career he had a tendency to venture comically general observations. He was neither simply a historian, a philosopher, nor a literary critic, but all of those things together, and then more still. Like Adorno, he was rigorous, uncompromising, and ascetic in his attitudes, although unlike Adorno his obscurities had less to do with his style, which was brilliant, than with the grippingly large, often obscure, theoretical and imaginative suggestions about culture, society, and power toward which his entire oeuvre tended.

In short, Foucault was a hybrid writer, dependent on, but in his writing beyond, the genres of fiction, history, sociology, political science, or philosophy. He therefore imparts a certain deliberate extraterritoriality to his work, which is for that reason both Nietzschean and postmodern: ironic, skeptical, savage in its radicalism, comic and amoral in its overturning of orthodoxies, idols, and myths. Yet in Foucault's most impersonal prose, one can still hear a distinctive voice ringing through; it is not accidental that he was a master of the interview as a cultural form. Thus the old acceptable demarcations between criticism and creation do not apply to what Foucault wrote or said, just as they do not apply to Nietzsche's treatises, or to Gramsci's *Prison Notebooks*, Barthes's writing generally, Glenn Gould's piano and verbal performances, Adorno's theoretical or autobiographical fragments, John Berger's work, Boulez's, or Godard's. This is by no means to say that Foucault's histories, for example, have no historical validity or accuracy, but it is to say that—like the others I have mentioned—the form and concern of these histories as artifacts require principal attention as self-aware, mixed-genre performances in the present, full of learning, quotation, and invention.

A number of themes therefore recur in Foucault's work from inception to end, although there are at least three distinct phases to his intellectual career. But first the themes, which are better grasped as constellations of ideas, rather than as inert objects. An insistently durable chain of conflicts marks everything Foucault studied and wrote about, and which his famous archaeologies and Nietzschean genealogies attempted to describe. In the beginning he seems to understand European social life as a struggle between, on the one hand, the marginal, the transgressive, the "different," and, on the other, the acceptable, the "normal," the generally social, or "same." Out of this are born (and the metaphors of parturition and biological sequence are important to Foucault's conception of things) various attitudes which later develop into institutions of "discipline" and confinement that are constitutive of knowledge. Hence, we get the birth of the clinic, prison, or the asylum, the institutions of medical practice, penal science, or normative jurisprudence. These in turn produce resistance to and consequently changes in the very same institutions, until—and this is a grim insight formulated by the later Foucault—prisons and hospitals are seen as factories for producing delinquency and illness respectively. Thereafter Foucault argues that power insinuates itself on both sides of the sequence, within institutions and sciences, and eruptively and as a form of attractive but usually co-opted insurrectionary pressure, in the collectivities and individuals doomed to confinement and the production of knowledge—the mad, the visionary, the delinquent, the prophets, poets, outcasts, and fools.

Another major constellation of ideas present from start to finish in Foucault's work is knowledge *(savoir)* itself. He studied its origins, its formation, its organization, its modes of change or stability, always responsive to its massive material presence, its reticulated complexity, its epistemological status, as well as to its minutest detail. His "archaeologies" were purposely intended not to resemble studies in the sociology of knowledge. Instead he was, in his words, attempting to turn history against itself, to "sever its connection to memory, its metaphysical and anthropological model, and construct a countermemory—a transformation of history into a totally different form of time."

Between himself and knowledge, Foucault therefore developed an evolvingly complex and ambivalent attitude, and here we ought to make quick reference to the three phases of his career. In his earliest large works—*Madness and Civilization* (1961; English translation 1965) and *The Order of Things* (1966; English translation 1970) (the rather approximate relationship between the translations and their French originals, titles as well as texts, is an index of how erratic were Foucault's English translations)—is the enthusiastic, "relentlessly erudite" researcher, digging up documents, raiding archives, rereading and demystifying canonical texts. Later, in period two, in *The Archaeology of Knowledge* (1969: English translation 1972) and *The Discourse on Language*

(1970; English translation 1971), he stands away from knowledge, spinning out a whole systematic apparatus so as to do to knowledge what knowledge does to *its* material. During this period knowledge is, so to speak, taken apart and redisposed into Foucault's terminology: this is when words like "archive," "discourse," "statement," "enunciative function," fill his prose as a way not so much of signalling a French obsession for precise classification, as of controlling, making productive his emerging hostility to knowledge as a kind of transparent mental prison. Yet, paradoxically, the overall bias of Foucault's work remains rational, dispassionate, calm. But with *Discipline and Punish* (1975; English translation 1977), which emerges directly from Foucault's work on behalf of prisoners, and *The History of Sexuality* (1976: 1978), whose basis in the vicissitudes of Foucault's own sexual identity is notable, knowledge has clearly been transformed into an antagonist. To it he pessimistically attaches power, as well as the ceaseless, but regularly defeated, resistance to which it gives rise.

At the heart of Foucault's work is, lastly, the variously embodied idea that always conveys the sentiment of otherness. For Foucault, otherness is both a force and a feeling *in itself,* something whose seemingly endless metamorphoses his work reflects and shapes. On a manifest level, as I said, Foucault wrote about deviation and deviants in conflict with society. More interesting, however, was his fascination with everything excessive, all those things that stand over and above ideas, description, imitation, or precedent. This fascination was in back of his anti-Platonism, as well as his unwillingness to tilt with critics (except for occasional sardonic forays against critics—George Steiner comes quickly to mind—who insisted on calling him a structuralist). What he was interested in was, he said in *The Archaeology,* "the more" that can be discovered lurking in signs and discourses but which is irreducible to language and speech; "it is this 'more,'" he said, "that we must reveal and describe." Such a concern appears to be both devious and obscure, yet it accounts for a lot that is specially unsettling in Foucault's writing. There is no such thing as being at home in his writing, neither for reader nor for writer. Dislocations, a dizzying and physically powerful prose (for example, the description of torture that opens *Discipline and Punish,* or the quieter, but more insidiously effective pages on the death of man in *The Order of Things*), the uncanny ability to invent whole fields of investigation: these come from Foucault's everlasting effort to formulate otherness and heterodoxy without domesticating them or turning them into doctrine.

This is Nietzsche's legacy operating at a deep level in the work of a major twentieth-century thinker. All that is specific and special is preferable to what is general and universal. Thus, in a memorable interview, Foucault showed his preference for the "specific" as opposed to the "universal" intellectual, for the thinker who like himself worked at the concrete intersection of disciplines rather than for the great pontificators (perhaps Sartre and Aron were intended) who presumed to command the whole culture. However alienated, estranged, or commodified it may have been then, the present and its concerns dictated the imperatives of study and its ethics to Foucault. Neither identity in the object, nor the author's identity, neither object nor subject, were as important to him as the fugitive energies making up human, or even institutional, performances in the process of taking place. Hence the almost terrifying stalemate one feels in his work between the anonymity of discourse and "discursive regularity," on one side, and on the other side, the pressures of "infamous" egos, including Foucault's own, whose will to powerful knowledge challenges the formidable establishment of impersonal rules, authorless statements, disciplined enunciations. At the same time that he was immersed, perhaps even immured in archives, dossiers, and manuscripts, Foucault seems paradoxically to have stimulated himself and his audience to a greater degree of sovereign authority, as if to illustrate his own thesis that power produces resistance, and resistance new forms of power.

The middle phase of his career was, I think, energized by the events of May 1968 which, for the first time, impelled Foucault to serious methodological reflection. This is also when he gave his first interviews, using them to advance ideas that he would later elaborate in *The Archaeology of Knowledge*. His philosophy of power also originated in the late sixties as perhaps he began to understand both the limits of insurrectionary rebellion and the extent of the domains regulated imperceptibly by the laws of discourse. Curiously, although he was already tending to the almost Schopenhauerian pessimism and determinism of his late work, Foucault's essays during the sixties and early seventies can be read as an expression of pleasure in the variety, the density and energy, of aesthetic and intellectual projects. The pieces on Bataille, Flaubert, Deleuze, Hölderlin, Magritte, and Nietzsche, which date from this period (some were collected and sensitively annotated by Don Bouchard in *Language, Counter-Memory, Practice*) are to some readers his finest work, essays in the truest sense of the word, brilliant without being overbearing.

The pivotal work, however, was an inaugural lecture at the Collège de France, *L'Ordre du discours,* given in the spring of 1970. Here he set forth his program of research and lectures at France's premiere academic institution. In typical fashion he addressed his audience across the centuries, as it were, outlining projects on nothing less than truth, rationality, and normality in a voice that was simultaneously Beckettian in its gnomic ellipses and Renanian in its portentous sonority. At roughly the same time he took on Derrida, who must have seemed to him to have become his major domestic competitor for intellectual ascendancy. Even if we allow for Foucault's clearly genuine fear that an ahistorical laissez-faire attitude was being licensed by the school of deconstruction, there is an edge and a derisive scorn to his words about Derrida that were not typical of him, as if in striking he had to strike definitively at the man who was otherwise affiliated with him by virtue of a common antimythological, anticonservative project. To the best of my knowledge Derrida did not respond to Foucault, a mark of compunction and restraint which led, I believe, to a gradual healing of the rift between them.

It is too early to disentangle the numerous threads of Foucault's interests, antinomian, often violent, always provocative and political, that proliferated during the seventies. He became a celebrated author and a lecturer much in demand all over the world. His courses at the Collège drew large audiences, to whom he returned the compliment by actually preparing his lectures, always researching them exhaustively, delivering them with appropriate formality and respect in the best tradition of the *cours magistrale.* His work on behalf of prisoners and penal reform matured and was completed during this period, as were his related—but highly eccentric—attitudes toward psychiatry and revolution. These, naturally enough for an intellectual with his sociopsychological trajectory, were embodied in the hostility he frequently evinced for the work of Freud and Marx, authors without whom Foucault himself would have been unthinkable. But it is a fact that his socially anomalous personality and his immense gifts made Foucault suspicious of his own genealogy. He was therefore a self-born man, choosing his predecessors carefully, like Borges's Kafka, effacing some of his life's biological, intellectual, and social traces with great care and effort. He was even more careful with his contemporaries, distancing himself in the course of time both from the Maoist currents of the sixties, and the worst excesses of the *nouveaux philosophes,* who were generally respectful of him as they were not of the other great Parisian idols.

In the last phase of his career Foucault's interests narrowed from investigations of the generally social aspects of confinement as reflected in the "microphysics" of power, to ruminative histories of sexual identity. In other words, he shifted his attention from the constitution of the human as a social subject, knowable through the detail of disciplines and discourses, to human sexuality, knowable through desire, pleasure, and solicitude. Even so, his very last project changed considerably from what he had said it would be in the first volume of his *History of Sexuality.* By the time the next two volumes (*L'Usage des plaisirs* and *Le Souci de soi*) appeared after a hiatus of eight years, in the year of his death, he had completely reconceived the project, and had gone back to classical Greece and Rome, there to discover how "individuals were led to focus attention on themselves, to discover and acknowledge themselves as subjects of desire, playing with the relationship between different aspects of themselves which would allow them to discover the truth of their being in desire, whether it was construed as natural or depraved."

What caused this particular and overdetermined shift from the political to the personal was, among other things, the effect of some disenchantment with the public sphere, more particularly perhaps because he felt that there was little he could do to affect it. Perhaps also his fame had allowed a considerable relaxation in the formidable, and the formidably public, regimen of erudition, production, and performance he had imposed on himself. It was noticeable that he was more committed to exploring, if not indulging, his appetite for travel, for different kinds of pleasure (symbolized by his frequent sojourns in California), for less and less frequent political positions. It was never-

theless sad to think of him as yet another "progressive" who had succumbed to the blandishments of often hackneyed pronouncements
against the Gulag and on behalf of Soviet and Cuban dissidents, given
that he had in the past so distanced himself from any such easy political formulas.

Yet we can also speculate that characteristically Foucault had made
the change via an unusual experience of excess, the Iranian revolution.
He had been one of the first Westerners to look into what he called the
"spiritual politics" of the Shi'ite opposition to the Shah. He discovered
in it just that entirely collective, involuntary excessiveness that could
not be herded under conventional rubrics like "class contradictions"
or "economic oppression." The ferociously murmuring and protracted
energy he discerned in the Iranian revolution attracted him to it for a
while, until he saw that its victory had brought to power a regime of
exceptionally retrograde cruelty. It was as if for the first time
Foucault's theories of impersonal, authorless activity had achieved
contemporary and visible realization, and from that he recoiled with
understandable disillusion.

A truly intelligent man, Foucault had a world reputation
at the time of his death. What all his readers will surely remember is
how in reading him for the first time they felt a particular shock at encountering so incisive and interesting a mind which, with one elec-
trical burst after another, stages ideas with a stylistic flair no other
writer of Foucault's depth and difficulty possessed. In so productive
and exhaustive a researcher, it was remarkable that his books, even the
very long ones, tended always to the aphoristic, and his mastery of the
art of making crisp negative distinctions in series of threes and fours
(e.g., "archaeology" is neither the history of ideas, nor intellectual history, nor the history of mind) rarely tired one out: on the contrary,
they exhilarated and stirred the reader. Yet in the English-speaking
world he was most influential among literary theorists who, alas, dis-
sected and redissected his methodologies and paid little attention to
his histories.

On the other hand, his weaknesses were quite marked even though,
I think, they did not seriously mar the quality and power of his fundamental points. The most striking of his blind spots was, for example, his insouciance about the discrepancies between his basically

limited French evidence and his ostensibly universal conclusions. Moreover, he showed no real interest in the relationships his work had with feminist or postcolonial writers facing problems of exclusion, confinement, and domination. Indeed, his Eurocentrism was almost total, as if "history" itself took place only among a group of French and German thinkers. And as his later work became more private and esoteric in its goals, he seemed even more unrestrained in his generalizations, seeming by implication to scoff at the fussy work done by historians and theorists in the fields he had disengaged from their grasp.

But whether Foucault is read and benefited from as a philosopher or as a superb intelligence riskily deploying language and learning to various, often contradictory ends, his work will retain its unsettling, antiutopian influence for generations to come. His major positive contribution was that he researched and revealed "technologies" of knowledge and self that beset society, made it governable, controllable, normal, even as these technologies developed their own uncontrollable drives, without limit or true rationale. His great critical contribution was to dissolve the anthropological models of identity and subjecthood underlying research in the humanistic and social sciences. Instead of seeing everything in culture and society as ultimately emanating either from a sort of unchanging Cartesian ego, or a heroic solitary artist, Foucault proposed the much juster notion that all work, like social life itself, is collective. The principal task therefore is to circumvent or break down the ideological biases that prevent us from saying that what enables a doctor to practice medicine or a historian to write history is not mainly a set of individual gifts, but an ability to follow rules that are taken for granted as an unconscious a priori by all professionals. More than anyone before him Foucault specified rules for those rules, and, even more impressively, he showed how over long periods of time the rules became epistemological enforcers of what (as well as how) people thought, lived, and spoke. If he was less interested in how the rules could be changed, it was perhaps because as a first discoverer of their enormously detailed power he wanted everyone to be aware of what disciplines, discourses, *epistemes,* and statements were *really* all about, without illusion.

It is almost too neat an irony, however, that Foucault died in the very hospital, originally a mental institution, now a hospital for neurological disorders, he had researched for his *Histoire de la folie*. This is eerie and depressing, as if his death confirmed Foucault's theses on the symbiotic parallelism between what was normal and what was pathological, rational and irrational, benign and malignant. A more striking irony was that the philosopher of the death of man, as Foucault was sometimes called, should seem to be, at the time of his own death, the very example of what a truly remarkable, unmistakably eccentric and individual thing a human life really is. Much more than a French public figure, Foucault was an intellectual with a transnational vocation. Instead of easy denunciation, he brought to the job of exposing the secret complicities between power and knowledge the patient skepticism and energetic fortitude of philosophic seriousness. And he was stylish and brilliant to boot.

19

Orientalism Reconsidered

The problems that I'd like to take up each derive from the general issues addressed in *Orientalism*. The most important of these are: the representation of other cultures, societies, histories; the relationship between power and knowledge; the role of the intellectual; the methodological questions that have to do with the relationships between different kinds of texts, between text and context, between text and history.

I should clarify a couple of things at the outset. First, I use the word "Orientalism" less to refer to my book than to the problems to which my book is related; I shall be dealing with the intellectual and political territory covered both by *Orientalism* (the book) as well as by the work I have done since. Second, I would not want it to be thought that this is an attempt to answer my critics. *Orientalism* elicited a great deal of comment, much of it positive and instructive; a fair amount of it was hostile and in some cases abusive. But the fact is that I have not digested and understood everything that was written or said. Instead, I have grasped those questions raised by my critics which strike me as useful in focusing an argument. Other observations, like my exclusion of German Orientalism, which no one has given any reason for me to have *included*, have frankly struck me as superficial, and there seems no point in responding to them. Similarly, the claim made by some, that I am ahistorical and inconsistent, would have more interest if the virtues of consistency, whatever may be intended by the term, were subjected to rigorous analysis; as for my ahistoricity, that too is a charge weightier in assertion than in proof.

As a department of thought and expertise, Orientalism of course involves several overlapping aspects: first, the changing historical and cultural relationship between Europe and Asia, a relationship with a 4,000-year-old history; second, the scientific discipline in the West according to which, beginning in the early nineteenth century, one specialized in the study of various Oriental cultures and traditions; and third, the ideological suppositions, images, and fantasies about a region of the world called the Orient. The common denominator among these three aspects of Orientalism is the line separating Occident from Orient, and this, I have argued, is less a fact of nature than it is a fact of human production, which I have called imaginative geography. This, however, does not mean that the division between Orient and Occident is unchanging, nor that it is simply fictional. It is to say—emphatically—that, as with all aspects of what Vico calls the world of nations, the Orient and the Occident are facts produced by human beings, and as such must be studied as integral components of the social, and not the divine or natural, world. And because the social world includes the person or subject doing the studying as well as the object or realm being studied, it is imperative to include them both in any consideration of Orientalism. Obviously enough, there could be no Orientalism without, on the one hand, the Orientalists, and on the other, the Orientals.

This is, in reality, a fact basic to any theory of interpretation, or hermeneutics. Yet there is still a remarkable unwillingness to discuss the problems of Orientalism in the political or ethical or even epistemological contexts proper to it. This is as true of professional literary critics who have written about my book as it is of the Orientalists themselves. Since it seems to me patently impossible to dismiss the truth of Orientalism's political origin and its continuing political actuality, we are obliged on intellectual as well as political grounds to investigate the resistance to the politics of Orientalism, a resistance symptomatic precisely of what is denied.

If the first set of questions is concerned with the problems of Orientalism reconsidered from the standpoint of local issues like who writes or studies the Orient, in what institutional or discursive setting, for what audience, and with what ends in mind, the second set of questions takes us to a wider circle of issues. These are issues raised initially by methodology. They are considerably sharpened by questions as to how the production of knowledge best serves communal, as opposed to sectarian, ends; how knowledge that is non-dominative and non-coercive can be produced in a setting that is deeply inscribed with the politics, the considerations, the positions, and the strategies of power. In these methodological and moral reconsiderations of Orientalism, I shall quite consciously allude to similar issues raised by the experiences of feminism or women's studies, black or ethnic studies, socialist and anti-imperialist studies, all of which take for their point of departure the right of formerly un- or mis-represented human groups to speak for and represent themselves in domains defined, politically and intellectually, as normally excluding them, usurping their signifying and representing functions, overriding their historical reality. In short, Orientalism reconsidered in this wider and libertarian optic entails nothing less than the creation of objects for a new kind of knowledge.

I should return to the local problems I mentioned first. The hindsight of authors not only stimulates in them a sense of regret at what they could or ought to have done but did not; it also gives them a wider perspective in which to comprehend what they did. In my own case, I have been helped to achieve this broader understanding by nearly everyone who wrote about my book, and who saw it—for better or worse—as being part of current debates, contested interpretations, and actual conflicts in the Arab-Islamic world, as that world interacts with the United States and Europe. In my own rather limited case, the consciousness of being an Oriental goes back to my youth in colonial Palestine and Egypt, although the impulse to resist its accompanying impingements was nurtured in the post–Second World War environment of independence when Arab nationalism, Nasserism, the 1967 War, the rise of the Palestine national movement, the 1973 War, the Lebanese Civil War, the Iranian Revolution and its horrific aftermath, produced that extraordinary series of highs and lows which has neither ended nor allowed us a full understanding of its remarkable revolutionary impact. It is difficult to try to understand a region of the world whose principal features seem to be that it is in perpetual flux, and that no one trying to comprehend it can, by an act of pure will or of sovereign understanding, stand at some Archimedean point outside the flux. That is, the very reason for understanding the Orient generally, and the Arab world in particular, was first, that it prevailed upon one, beseeched one's attention urgently, whether for economic, political, cultural, or religious reasons, and second, that it defied neutral, disinterested, or stable definition.

Similar problems are commonplace in the interpretation of literary texts. Each age, for instance, re-interprets Shakespeare, not because Shakespeare changes, but because, despite the existence of numerous and reliable editions of Shakespeare, there is no such fixed and nontrivial object as Shakespeare independent of his editors, the actors who played his roles, the translators who put him in other languages, the hundreds of millions of readers who have read him or watched performances of his plays since the late sixteenth century. On the other hand, it is too much to say that Shakespeare has no independent existence at all, and that he is completely reconstituted every time someone reads, acts, or writes about him. In fact, Shakespeare leads an institutional or cultural life that among other things has guaranteed his eminence as a great poet, his authorship of thirty-odd plays, his extraordinary canonical powers in the West. The point I am making here is a rudimentary one: that even so relatively inert an object as a literary text is commonly supposed to gain some of its identity from its historical moment interacting with the attentions, judgments, scholarship, and performances of its readers. But this privilege was rarely allowed the Orient, the Arabs or Islam, which separately or together were supposed by mainstream academic thought to be confined to the fixed status of an object frozen once and for all in time by the gaze of western percipients.

Far from being a defense either of the Arabs or of Islam—as my book was taken by many to be—my argument was that neither existed except as "communities of interpretation," and that, like the Orient itself, each designation represented interests, claims, projects, ambitions, and rhetorics that were not only in violent disagreement, but also in a situation of open warfare. So saturated with meanings, so overdetermined by history, religion and politics are labels like "Arab" or "Muslim" as subdivisions of "The Orient" that no one today can use them without some attention to the formidable polemical mediations that screen the objects, if they exist at all, that the labels designate.

The more such observations are made by one party, the more routinely they are denied by the other. Anyone who tries to suggest that nothing, not even a simple descriptive label, is beyond or outside the realm of interpretation is almost certain to find an opponent saying that science and learning are designed to transcend the vagaries of interpretation, and that objective truth is, in fact, attainable. This claim was more than a little political when used against Orientals who disputed the authority and objectivity of an Orientalism intimately allied with the great mass of European settlements in the Orient. At bottom, what I said in *Orientalism* had been said before me by A. L. Tibawi, by Abdullah Laroui, by Anwar Abdel Malek, by Talal Asad, by S. H. Alatas, by Frantz Fanon and Aimé Césaire, by Sardar K. M. Pannikar and Romila Thapar, all of whom had suffered the ravages of imperialism and colonialism, and who, in challenging the authority, provenance, and institutions of the science that represented them to Europe, were also understanding themselves as something more than what this science said they were.

The challenge to Orientalism, and the colonial era of which it is so organically a part, was a challenge to the muteness imposed upon the Orient as object. Insofar as it was a science of incorporation and inclusion by virtue of which the Orient was constituted and then introduced into Europe, Orientalism was a scientific movement whose analogue in the world of politics was the Orient's colonial accumulation and acquisition by Europe. The Orient was, therefore, not Europe's interlocutor, but its silent Other. From roughly the end of the eighteenth century, when the Orient was rediscovered by Europe, its history had been a paradigm of antiquity and originality, functions that drew Europe's interests in acts of recognition or acknowledgment but *from* which Europe moved as its own industrial, economic, and cultural development seemed to leave the Orient far behind. Oriental history—for Hegel, for Marx, later for Burkhardt, Nietzsche, Spengler, and other major philosophers of history—was useful in portraying a region of great age, and what had to be left behind. Literary historians have further noted in all sorts of aesthetic writing and figurative portrayals that a trajectory of "Westering," found for example in Keats and Hölderlin, customarily saw the Orient as ceding its historical preeminence and importance to the world spirit moving westward away from Asia and toward Europe.

As primitivity, as the age-old antetype of Europe, as a fecund night out of which European rationality developed, the Orient's actuality receded inexorably into a kind of paradigmatic fossilization. The origins of European anthropology and ethnography were constituted out of this radical difference, and, to my knowledge, as a discipline, anthropology has not yet dealt with this inherent political limitation upon its supposedly disinterested universality. This is one reason Johannes Fabian's book, *Time and the Other: How Anthropology Constitutes Its Object*, is both unique and important. Compared, say, with the standard disciplinary rationalizations and self-congratulatory clichés about hermeneutic circles offered by Clifford Geertz, Fabian's serious effort to redirect anthropologists' attention back to the discrepancies in time, power, and development between the ethnographer and his/her constituted object is all the more remarkable. In any event, what for the most part got left out of the discipline of Orientalism was the very history that resisted its ideological as well as political encroachments. That repressed or resistant history was now returned in the various critiques and attacks upon Orientalism, as a science of imperialism.

The divergences between the numerous critiques of Orientalism as ideology and praxis are very wide nonetheless. Some attack Orientalism as a prelude to assertions about the virtues of one or another native culture: these are the nativists. Others criticize Orientalism as a defense against attacks on one or another political creed: these are the nationalists. Still others criticize Orientalism for falsifying the nature of Islam: these are, grosso modo, the believers. I will not adjudicate between these claims, except to say that I have avoided taking stands on such matters as the real, true, or authentic Islamic or Arab world. But, in common with all the recent critics of Orientalism, I think that two things are especially important—one, a methodological vigilance that construes Orientalism less as a positive than as a critical discipline and therefore makes it subject to intense scrutiny, and two, a determination not to allow the segregation and

confinement of the Orient to go on without challenge. My understanding of this second point has led me entirely to refuse designa-
tions like "Orient" and "Occident."

Depending on how they construed their roles as Orientalists, critics
of the critics of Orientalism have either reinforced the affirmations of
positive power in Orientalism's discourse or, much less frequently alas,
engaged Orientalism's critics in a genuine intellectual exchange. The
reasons for this split are self-evident: some have to do with power and
age, as well as institutional or guild defensiveness; others have to do
with religious or ideological convictions. All are political—something
that not everyone has found easy to acknowledge. If I may use my own
example, when some of my critics agreed with the main premises of my
argument, they still tended to fall back on encomia to the achievements of what Maxime Rodinson called "la science orientaliste." This
self-serving view lent itself to attacks on an alleged Lysenkism lurking
inside the polemics of Muslims or Arabs who lodged a protest with
"western" orientalism. This preposterous charge was made despite the
fact that all the recent critics of Orientalism have been quite explicit
about using such "western" critiques as marxism or structuralism in
an effort to override invidious distinctions between East and West, between Arab and western truth, and the like.

Sensitized to the outrageous attacks upon an august and formerly
invulnerable science, many certified professionals whose division of
study is the Arabs and Islam have disclaimed any politics at all, while
vigorously pressing an ideologically intended counter-attack. I should
mention a few of the more typical imputations made against me so
that you can see Orientalism extending its nineteenth-century arguments to cover an incommensurate set of late twentieth-century eventualities. All of these derive from what to the nineteenth-century mind
is the preposterous situation of an Oriental responding to
Orientalism's asseverations. For unrestrained anti-intellectualism, unencumbered by critical self-consciousness, no one has quite achieved
the sublime confidence of Bernard Lewis. His almost purely political
exploits require more time to mention than they are worth. In a series
of articles and one particularly weak book—*The Muslim Discovery of
Europe*—Lewis has been busy responding to my argument, insisting
that the western quest for knowledge about other societies is unique,

that it is motivated by pure curiosity, and that, in contrast, Muslims were neither able nor interested in getting knowledge about Europe, as if knowledge about Europe was the only acceptable criterion for true knowledge. Lewis's arguments are presented as emanating exclusively from the scholar's apolitical impartiality, whereas he has become a widely rated authority for anti-Islamic, anti-Arab, Zionist, and Cold War crusades, all of them underwritten by a zealotry covered with a veneer of urbanity that has very little in common with the "science" and learning Lewis purports to be upholding.

Not quite as hypocritical, but no less uncritical, are younger ideologues and Orientalists like Daniel Pipes. His arguments, as demonstrated in his book *In the Path of God: Islam and Political Power,* would appear to be at the service not of knowledge but of an aggressive and interventionary state—the United States—whose interests Pipes helps to define. Pipes speaks of Islam's anomie, its sense of inferiority, its defensiveness, as if Islam were one simple thing, and as if the quality of his either absent or impressionistic evidence were of the most secondary importance. His book testifies to Orientalism's unique resilience, its insulation from intellectual developments everywhere else in the culture, and its antediluvian imperiousness as it makes its assertions and affirmations with little regard for logic or argument. I doubt that any expert anywhere in the world would speak today of Judaism or Christianity with quite that combination of force and freedom that Pipes allows himself about Islam. One would also have thought that a book about Islamic revival would allude to parallel and related developments in styles of religious insurgence in, for example, Lebanon, Israel, and the United States. Nor is it likely that anyone anywhere, writing about material for which, in his own words, "rumor, hearsay, and other wisps of evidence" are the only proof, will in the very same paragraph alchemically transmute rumor and hearsay into "facts," on whose "multitude" he relies in order "to reduce the importance of each." This is magic quite unworthy even of high Orientalism, and although Pipes pays his obeisance to imperialist Orientalism, he masters neither its genuine learning nor its pretense at disinterestedness. For Pipes, Islam is a volatile and dangerous business, a political movement intervening in and disrupting the West, stirring up insurrection and fanaticism everywhere else.

The core of Pipes's book is not simply its highly expedient sense of its own political relevance to Reagan's America, where terrorism and communism merge into the media's image of Muslim gunners, fanatics and rebels, but its thesis that Muslims themselves are the worst source for their own history. The pages of *In the Path of God* are dotted with references to Islam's incapacity for self-representation, self-understanding, self-consciousness, and with praise for witnesses like V. S. Naipaul who are so much more useful and clever in understanding Islam. Here, of course, is the most familiar of Orientalism's themes—they cannot represent themselves, they must therefore be represented by others who know more about Islam than Islam knows about itself. Now, it is often the case that you can be known by others in different ways than you know yourself, and that valuable insights might be generated accordingly. But that is quite a different thing than pronouncing it as immutable law that outsiders ipso facto have a better sense of you as an insider than you do of yourself. Note that there is no question of an *exchange* between Islam's views and an outsider's: no dialogue, no discussion, no mutual recognition. There is a flat assertion of quality, which the western policy-maker, or his faithful servant, possesses by virtue of his being western, white, non-Muslim.

Now this, I submit, is neither science, nor knowledge, nor understanding: it is a statement of power and a claim for absolute authority. It is constituted out of racism, and it is made comparatively acceptable to an audience prepared in advance to listen to its muscular truths. Pipes speaks to and for a large clientele for whom Islam is not a culture but a nuisance; most of Pipes's readers will, in their minds, associate what he says about Islam with the other nuisances of the 1960s and 1970s—blacks, women, post-colonial Third World nations that have tipped the balance against the United States in such places as UNESCO and the UN, and for their pains have drawn forth the rebuke of Senator Moynihan and Mrs. Kirkpatrick. In addition, Pipes—and the rows of like-minded Orientalists and experts he represents as their common denominator—stands for programmatic ignorance. Far from trying to understand Muslims in the context of imperialism and the revolt of an abused, but internally very diverse, segment of humanity, far from availing himself of the impressive recent works on Islam in different histories and societies, far from paying some attention to the immense advances in critical theory, in social science, in humanistic research, and in the philosophy of interpretation, far from making some slight effort to acquaint himself with the vast imaginative literature in the Islamic world, Pipes obdurately and explicitly aligns himself with colonial Orientalists like Snouck Hurgronje and shamelessly pro-colonial renegades like V. S. Naipaul.

I have talked about Pipes only because he serves to make some points about Orientalism's large political setting, which is routinely denied and suppressed in the sort of claim proposed by its main spokesman, Bernard Lewis, who has the effrontery to disassociate Orientalism from its 200-year-old partnership with European imperialism and associate it instead with modern classical philology and the study of ancient Greek and Roman culture. It is worth mentioning that this larger setting comprises two other elements, namely, the recent prominence of the Palestinian movement and the demonstrated resistance of Arabs in the United States and elsewhere against their portrayal in the public realm.

The question of Palestine and its fateful encounter with Zionism, on the one hand, and the guild of Orientalism, its professional caste-consciousness as a corporation of experts protecting their terrain and their credentials from outside scrutiny, on the other hand, together account for much of the animus against my critique of Orientalism. The ironies here are rich. Consider the case of one Orientalist who publicly attacked my book, he told me in a private letter, not because he disagreed with it—on the contrary, he felt that what I said was just—but because he had to defend the honor of his profession! Or, take the connection—explicitly made by two of the authors I cite in *Orientalism,* Renan and Proust—between Islamophobia and anti-Semitism. Here, one would have expected many scholars and critics to have seen the conjuncture, that hostility to Islam in the modern Christian West has historically gone hand in hand with, has stemmed from the same source, has been nourished at the same stream as anti-Semitism, and that a critique of the orthodoxies, dogmas, and disciplinary procedures of Orientalism contributes to an enlargement of our understanding of the cultural mechanisms of anti-Semitism. No such connection has ever been made by critics, who have seen in the critique of Orientalism an opportunity for them to defend Zionism, support

Israel, and launch attacks on Palestinian nationalism. The reasons for this confirm the history of Orientalism, for, as the Israeli commentator Dani Rubenstein has remarked, the Israeli occupation of the West Bank and Gaza, the destruction of Palestinian society, and the sustained Zionist assault upon Palestinian nationalism have quite literally been led and staffed by Orientalists. Whereas in the past it was European Christian Orientalists who supplied European culture with arguments for colonizing and suppressing Islam, as well as for despising Jews, it is now the Jewish national movement that produces a cadre of colonial functionaries whose ideological theses about the Islamic or Arab mind are implemented in the administration of the Palestinian Arabs, an oppressed minority within the white-European-democracy that is Israel. Rubenstein notes with some sorrow that the Hebrew University's Islamic studies department has produced every one of the colonial officials and Arab experts who run the Occupied Territories.

Another irony should be mentioned in this regard: just as some Zionists have construed it as their duty to defend Orientalism against its critics, there has been a comic effort by some Arab nationalists to see the Orientalist controversy as an imperialist plot to enhance American control over the Arab world. According to this implausible scenario, the critics of Orientalism are not anti-imperialists at all, but covert agents of imperialism. The logical conclusion from this is that the best way to attack imperialism is not to say anything critical about it. At this point, I concede that we have left reality for a world of illogic and derangement.

Underlying much of the discussion of Orientalism is a disquieting realization that the relationship between cultures is both uneven and irremediably secular. This brings us to the point I alluded to a moment ago, about recent Arab and Islamic efforts, well-intentioned for the most part, but sometimes motivated by unpopular regimes, who, in drawing attention to the shoddiness of the western media in representing the Arabs or Islam, divert scrutiny from the abuses of their rule. Parallel developments have been occurring in UNESCO, where the controversy surrounding the world information order—and proposals for its reform by various Third World and socialist governments—has taken on the dimensions of a major international issue. Most of these disputes testify, first, to the fact that the production of knowledge, or information, of media images is unevenly distributed: its main centers are located in what, on both sides of the divide, has been polemically called the metropolitan West. Second, this unhappy realization, on the part of weaker parties and cultures, has reinforced their grasp of the fact that, although there are many divisions within it, there is only one secular and historical world, and that neither nativism, nor divine intervention, nor regionalism, nor ideological smokescreens can hide societies, cultures, and peoples from one another, especially not from those with the force and will to penetrate others for political as well as economic ends. But, third, many of these disadvantaged post-colonial states and their loyalist intellectuals have, in my opinion, drawn the wrong conclusions, which are that one must either attempt to impose control upon the production of knowledge at the source, or, in the worldwide media market, attempt to improve, enhance, ameliorate the images currently in circulation without doing anything to change the political situation from which they emanate and by which they are sustained.

The failings of these approaches are obvious: one need not belabor such matters as the squandering of immense amounts of petro-dollars for short-lived public relations scams, or the increasing repression, human-rights abuses, outright gangsterism that has taken place in many Third World countries, all of them occurring in the name of national security, and occasionally of fighting neo-imperialism. What I do want to talk about is the much larger question of what is to be done, and how we can speak of intellectual work that isn't merely reactive or negative.

One of the legacies of Orientalism, and indeed one of its epistemological foundations, is historicism, that is, the view propounded by Vico, Hegel, Marx, Ranke, Dilthey, and others, that if humankind has a history, it is produced by men and women and can be understood historically, at given epochs or moments, as possessing a complex but coherent unity. So far as Orientalism in particular and the European knowledge of other societies in general have been concerned, historicism meant that the one human history uniting humanity either culminated in or was observed from the vantage point of Europe or the West. What was neither observed by Europe nor documented by it was, therefore, "lost" until, at some later date, it too could be incorporated by the new sciences of anthropology, political economics, and linguistics. It is out of this later recuperation of what Eric Wolf has called people without history that a still later disciplinary step was taken: the founding of the science of world history, whose major practitioners include Braudel, Wallerstein, Perry Anderson, and Wolf himself.

But along with the greater capacity for dealing with—in Ernst Bloch's phrase—the non-synchronous experiences of Europe's Other has gone a fairly uniform avoidance of the relationship between European imperialism and these variously constituted and articulated knowledges. What has never taken place is an epistemological critique of the connection between the development of a historicism which has expanded and developed enough to include antithetical attitudes such as ideologies of western imperialism and critiques of imperialism, on the one hand, and, on the other, the actual practice of imperialism by which the accumulation of territories and population, the control of economies, and the incorporation and homogenization of histories are maintained. If we keep this in mind, we will remark, for example, that in the methodological assumptions and practice of world history—which is ideologically anti-imperialist—little or no attention is given to those cultural practices, like Orientalism or ethnography, affiliated with imperialism, which in genealogical fact fathered world history itself. Hence, the emphasis in world history as a discipline has been on economic and political practices, defined by the processes of world historical writing, as in a sense separate and different from, as well as unaffected by, the knowledge of them which world history produces. The curious result is that the theories of accumulation on a world scale, or the capitalist world system, or lineages of absolutism (a) depend on the same percipient and historicist observer who had been an Orientalist or colonial traveler three generations ago; (b) they depend also on a homogenizing and incorporating world historical scheme that assimilated non-synchronous developments, histories, cultures, and peoples to it; and (c) they block and suppress latent epistemological critiques of the institutional, cultural, and disciplinary instruments linking the incorporative practice of world history with, on one hand, partial knowledges like Orientalism, and on the other, with continued "western" hegemony of the non-European, "peripheral" world.

The problem is once again historicism and the universalizing and self-validating that has been endemic to it. Bryan Turner's important little book, *Marx and the End of Orientalism,* went a great distance toward fragmenting, dissociating, dislocating, and decentering the experiential terrain covered at present by universalizing historicism. What he suggests, in discussing the epistemological dilemma, is the need to go beyond the polarities and binary oppositions of marxist-historicist thought (voluntarisms v. determinism, Asiatic v. western society, change v. stasis) in order to create a new type of analysis of plural, as opposed to single, objects. Similarly, in a series of studies produced in interrelated and frequently unrelated fields, there has been a general advance in the process of breaking up, dissolving, and methodologically as well as critically reconceiving the unitary field ruled hitherto by Orientalism, historicism, and what could be called essentialist universalism.

I shall give examples of this dissolving and decentering process in a moment. What needs to be said about it immediately is that it is neither purely methodological nor purely reactive in intent. You do not respond, for example, to the tyrannical conjuncture of colonial power with scholarly Orientalism simply by proposing an alliance between nativist sentiment buttressed by some variety of native ideology to combat them. This, for example, has been the trap into which many Third World and anti-imperialist activists fell in supporting the Iranian and Palestinian struggles, and who found themselves either with nothing to say about the abominations of Khomeini's regime or resorting, in the Palestine case, to the time-worn cliches of revolutionism and rejectionary armed-strugglism after the Lebanese debacle. Nor can it be a matter simply of recycling the old marxist or world-historical rhetoric, whose dubious accomplishment is merely the re-establishment of the intellectual and theoretical ascendancy of the old, by now impertinent and genealogically flawed, conceptual models. No: we must, I believe, think in both political and theoretical terms, locating the main problems in what Frankfurt theory identified as domination and division of labor. We must confront also the problem of the absence of a theoretical, utopian, and libertarian dimension in analysis. We cannot proceed unless we dissipate and redispose the material of historicism into radically different pursuits of knowledge, and we cannot do that until we are aware that no new projects of knowledge can be constituted unless they resist the dominance and professionalized particularism of historicist systems and reductive, pragmatic, or functionalist theories.

These goals are less difficult than my description sounds. For the reconsideration of Orientalism has been intimately connected with many other activities of the sort I referred to earlier, and which it now becomes imperative to articulate in more detail. Thus, we can now see that Orientalism is a praxis of the same sort as male gender dominance, or patriarchy, in metropolitan societies: the Orient was routinely described as feminine, its riches as fertile, its main symbols the sensual woman, the harem, and the despotic—but curiously attractive—ruler. Moreover, Orientals, like housewives, were confined to silence and to unlimited enriching production. Much of this material is manifestly connected to the configurations of sexual, racial, and political asymmetry underlying mainstream modern western culture, as illuminated respectively by feminists, by black studies critics, and by anti-imperialist activists. To read, for example, Sandra Gilbert's brilliant recent study of Rider Haggard's *She* is to perceive the narrow correspondence between suppressed Victorian sexuality at home, its fantasies abroad, and the tightening hold on the nineteenth-century male imagination of imperialist ideology. Similarly, a work like Abdul Jan Mohammed's *Manichean Aesthetics* investigates the parallel but unremittingly separate artistic worlds of white and black fictions of the same place, Africa, suggesting that even in imaginative literature a rigid ideological system operates beneath a freer surface. Or in a study like Peter Gran's *The Islamic Roots of Capitalism,* which is written out of an anti-imperialist and anti-Orientalist, meticulously researched and scrupulously concrete historical stance, one can begin to sense what a vast invisible terrain of human effort and ingenuity lies beneath the frozen Orientalist surface formerly carpeted by the discourse of Islamic or Oriental economic history.

There are many more examples of analyses and theoretical projects undertaken out of impulses similar to those fueling the anti-Orientalist critique. All of them are interventionary in nature, that is, they self-consciously situate themselves at vulnerable conjunctural nodes of ongoing disciplinary discourses where each of them posits nothing less than new objects of knowledge, new praxes of humanist activity, new theoretical models that upset or, at the very least, radically alter the prevailing paradigmatic norms. One might list here such disparate efforts as Linda Nochlin's explorations of nineteenth-century Orientalist ideology as working within major art-historical contexts; Hanna Batatu's immense restructuring of the terrain of the modern Arab state's political behavior; Raymond Williams's sustained examination of structures of feeling, communities of knowledge, emergent or alternative cultures, patterns of geographical thought (as in his remarkable *The Country and the City*); Talal Asad's account of anthropological self-capture in the work of major theorists, and his own studies in the field; Eric Hobsbawm's new formulation of "the invention of tradition" or invented practices studied by historians as a crucial index both of the historian's craft and, more important, of the invention of new emergent nations; the work produced in re-examination of Japanese, Indian, and Chinese culture by scholars like Masao Miyoshi, Eqbal Ahmad, Tariq Ali, A. Sivanandan, Romila Thapar, the group around Ranajit Guha *(Subaltern Studies)*, Gayatri Spivak, and younger scholars like Homi Bhabha and Partha Mitter; the freshly imaginative reconsideration by Arab literary critics—the *Fusoul* and *Mawakif* groups, Elias Khouri, Kamal Abu Deeb, Mohammad Bannis, and others—seeking to redefine and invigorate the reified classical structures of Arabic literary tradition, and, as a parallel to that, the imaginative works of Juan Goytisolo and Salman Rushdie, whose fictions and criticism are self-consciously written against the cultural stereotypes and representations commanding the field. It is worth mentioning here, too, the pioneering efforts of the *Bulletin of Concerned Asian Scholars,* and the fact that twice recently, in their presidential addresses, an American Sinologist (Benjamin Schwartz) and Indologist (Ainslee Embree) have reflected seriously upon what the critique of Orientalism means for their fields, a public reflection as yet denied Middle Eastern scholars. Perennially, there is the work carried out by Noam Chomsky in political and historical fields, an example of independent radicalism and uncompromising severity unequaled by anyone else today; or in literary theory, the powerful theoretical articulations of a social, in the widest and deepest sense, model for narrative put forward by Fredric Jameson; Richard Ohmann's empirically arrived-at definitions of canon privilege and institution in his recent work; revisionary Emersonian perspectives formulated in the critique

of contemporary technological and imaginative as well as cultural ideologies by Richard Poirier; and the decentering, redistributive ratios of
intensity and drive studied by Leo Bersani.

In conclusion, I should try to draw them together into a common endeavor which can inform the larger enterprise of which the critique of
Orientalism is a part. First, we note a plurality of audiences and constituencies; none of the works and workers I have cited claims to be
working on behalf of One audience which is the only one that counts,
or for one supervening, overcoming Truth, a truth allied to western (or
for that matter eastern) reason, objectivity, science. On the contrary, we
note here a plurality of terrains, multiple experiences, and different
constituencies, each with its admitted (as opposed to denied) interest,
political desiderata, disciplinary goals. All these efforts work out of
what might be called a decentered consciousness, not less reflective and
critical for being decentered, for the most part non- and in some cases
anti-totalizing and anti-systematic. The result is that instead of seeking
common unity by appeals to a center of sovereign authority, methodological consistency, canonicity, and science, they offer the possibility
of common grounds of assembly between them. They are, therefore,
planes of activity and praxis, rather than one topography commanded
by a geographical and historical vision locatable in a known center of
metropolitan power. Second, these activities and praxes are consciously
secular, marginal, and oppositional with reference to the mainstream,
generally authoritarian systems against which they now agitate. Third,
they are political and practical in as much as they intend—without necessarily succeeding—the end of dominating, coercive systems of knowledge. I do not think it too much to say that the political meaning of
analysis, as carried out in all these fields, is uniformly and programmatically libertarian by virtue of the fact that, unlike Orientalism, it is
based not on the finality and closure of antiquarian or curatorial
knowledge, but on investigative open analysis, even though it might
seem that analyses of this sort—frequently difficult and abstruse—are in
the final count paradoxically quietistic. We must remember the lesson
provided by Adorno's negative dialectics, and regard analysis as in the
fullest sense being *against* the grain, deconstructive, utopian.

But there remains the one problem haunting all intense, self-
convicted, and local intellectual work, the problem of the division of

labor, which is a necessary consequence of that reification and com-modification, first and most powerfully analyzed in this century by Georg Lukács. This is the problem, sensitively and intelligently put by Myra Jehlen for women's studies, whether, in identifying and working through anti-dominant critiques, subaltern groups—women, blacks, and so on—can resolve the dilemma of autonomous fields of experi-ence and knowledge that are created as a consequence. A double kind of possessive exclusivism could set in: the sense of being an excluding insider by virtue of experience (only women can write for and about women, and only literature that treats women or Orientals well is good literature), and second, being an excluding insider by virtue of method (only marxists, anti-orientalists, feminists can write about economics, Orientalism, women's literature).

This is where we are at now, at the threshold of fragmentation and specialization, which impose their own parochial dominations and fussy defensiveness, or on the verge of some grand synthesis which I, for one, believe could very easily wipe out both the gains and the op-positional consciousness provided by these counter-knowledges hith-erto. Several possibilities propose themselves; I shall conclude simply by listing them. A need for greater crossing of boundaries, for greater interventionism in cross-disciplinary activity, a concentrated aware-ness of the situation—political, methodological, social, historical—in which intellectual and cultural work is carried out. A clarified political and methodological commitment to the dismantling of systems of domination which since they are collectively maintained must, to adopt and transform some of Gramsci's phrases, be collectively fought, by mutual siege, war of maneuver, *and* war of position. Lastly, a much sharpened sense of the intellectual's role both in the defining of a context and in changing it, for without that, I believe, the critique of Orientalism is simply an ephemeral pastime.

20

Remembrances of Things Played: Presence and Memory in the Pianist's Art

Pianists retain a remarkable hold on our cultural life. There are the crowd-pleasing "superstars" as well as a somewhat lesser order of pianists who nevertheless have sizable followings. Recordings enhance and amplify our involvement in what the performing pianist does: they may evoke memories of actual recitals—live audiences coughing and clapping, live pianists playing. Why do we seek this experience? Why are we interested in pianists at all, given that they are a product of nineteenth-century European culture? And further, what makes some pianists interesting, great, extraordinary? How, without being either too systematic or absurdly metaphysical, can we characterize what it is that sustains the distinguished pianist before us, claiming our attention, bringing him or her back to us year after year?

For although there is an immense piano repertory, there is little in it that can be called new; the world of the piano is really a world of mirrors, repetitions, imitations. And what actually gets performed is a relatively small part of the repertory—Beethoven, Schubert, Chopin, Schumann, Liszt; some Debussy and Ravel; some Bach, Mozart, and Haydn. Alfred Brendel has said that there are only two performing traditions with regard to the piano: one built on the works of Chopin and a few related composers, the other and richer one made up of the works of Central European composers from Hamburg to Vienna, and from Bach to Schoenberg. A pianist who attempts to build a career performing the works of, say, Weber, MacDowell, Alkan, Gottschalk, Scriabin, or Rachmaninoff usually ends up as little more than a peripheral artist.

My own enjoyment of today's pianism, an enjoyment involving not only the pianist's presence but also my ability to play the instrument and to reflect on what I play and hear, is pointed toward the past. That is to say, to a large degree it is about memory. That my pleasure should be so strongly linked to the past (more specifically, my understanding of it) is not hard to understand. Despite the energetic immediacy of their presentation, pianists are conservative, essentially curatorial figures. They play little new music, and still prefer to perform in the public hall, where music arrived, via the family and the court, in the nineteenth century. It is private memory that is at the root of the pleasure we take in the piano, and it is the interesting pianist who puts us in touch with this pleasure—who gives the recital its weirdly compelling power.

On March 23 and March 31 of this year, Maurizio Pollini performed at Carnegie Hall and Avery Fisher Hall. Pollini, a Milanese, is forty-three years old, and from the very beginning his career has been extraordinary: at the age of eighteen he won the Warsaw Chopin Competition, the first non-Slav to do so. His programs for the New York recitals—Beethoven and Schubert in the one, Schumann and Chopin in the other—were the typically Pollinian mix of familiar, even hackneyed, pieces (the "Moonlight" Sonata, Chopin's "Funeral March" Sonata) and difficult and eccentric works (the Schubert Sonata in C Minor and Schumann's last piano work, the *Gesänge der Frühe*, written during, and some would say exemplifying, the final stage of his mental illness). More important than the programs, though, was the way Pollini demonstrated once again that he is an *interesting* pianist, one who stands out in the enormous crowd of first-rate pianists filling the New York concert agenda.

To begin with there is Pollini's technical prowess, which comes across as neither glib facility nor tedious heroic effort. When he plays especially difficult pieces like the Chopin Etudes or one of the complex

Schumann or Schubert compositions, you do not automatically remark on how cleverly he has solved the music's challenge to sheer dexterity. His technique allows you to forget technique entirely. Nor do you say, This is the *only* way Chopin, or Schubert, or Schumann ought to sound. What comes through in all of Pollini's performances is an *approach* to the music—a direct approach, aristocratically clear, powerfully and generously articulated. By this I also mean that you are aware of him encountering and learning a piece, playing it supremely well, and then returning his audience to "life" with an enhanced, and shared, understanding of the whole business. Pollini doesn't have a platform manner, or a set of poses. What he presents instead is a totally unfussy *reading* of the piano literature. Several years ago I saw him, jacketless, and with the score before him, perform Stockhausen's intransigently thorny *Klavierstück X;* I could perceive in his playing some of the marginality and playful anguish of the composition itself—music that takes itself to limits unapproached in the work of other contemporary composers.

Even when Pollini does not achieve this effect—and many have remarked on his occasionally glassy, tense, and hence repellent perfection—the expectation that it will occur in another of his recitals remains vivid. This is because there is for the listener the sense of a career unfolding *in time.* And Pollini's career communicates a feeling of growth, purpose, and form. Sadly, most pianists, like most politicians, seem merely to wish to remain in power. I have thought this, perhaps unfairly, of Vladimir Horowitz and Rudolf Serkin. These are men with tremendous gifts, and much dedication and energy; they have given great pleasure to their audiences. But their work today strikes me as simply going on. This can also be said about fine but much less interesting pianists like André Watts, Bella Davidovitch, Vladimir Ashkenazy, and Alexis Weissenberg. But you could never say that Pollini's work just goes on, any more than you could say that about the work of Alfred Brendel; nor could you so neatly write off Sviatoslav Richter or Emil Gilels or Arturo Benedetti Michelangeli or Wilhelm Kempff. Each of these pianists represents a project unfolding *in time,* a project that is about something more than playing the piano in public for two hours. Their recitals are opportunities to experience the exploration, interpretation, and, above all, reinterpretation of a major portion of the pianistic repertory.

All pianists aspire to be distinctive, to make an impression, to have a unique aesthetic and social imprint. This is what we call a pianist's "personality." But pianists are thwarted in their desire to sound "different" by the fact that audiences today take for granted a very high level of technical competence. It is assumed that pianists will be sophisticated performers, and that they will get through the Chopin or Liszt Etudes flawlessly. Thus pianists must rely on the equivalent of special effects to establish and sustain their pianistic identities. Ideally, a listener should be able to recognize the sound, style, and manner of an individual pianist, and not confuse them with those of other pianists. Still, resemblances and comparisons are crucial to the outlines of any interesting signature. Thus we speak of schools of pianists, disciples of one or another style, similarities between one Chopin specialist and another.

No contemporary pianist more brilliantly established himself through an extraordinarily distinctive identity than Glenn Gould, the Canadian pianist who died in 1982 at the age of fifty. Even Gould's detractors recognized the greatness of his gifts. He had a phenomenal capacity to play complicated polyphonal music—preeminently Bach's—with astonishing clarity and liveliness. Andras Schiff has rightly said of Gould that "he could control five voices more intelligently than most [pianists] can control two."

Gould's career was launched with a stunning recording of Bach's *Goldberg Variations,* and so rich was his pianistic resourcefulness that one of the last records he made was still another *Goldberg* interpretation. What is remarkable is that the 1982 version is very different from the earlier one—and yet it is patently the work of the same pianist. Gould's interpretation of Bach was meant to illustrate the music's richness, not simply the performer's ingenuity—without which, of course, Bach's fertile counterpoint would not have emerged in so startlingly different a way in the second recording. Gould's performances of Bach—cerebral, brilliantly ordered, festive, and energetic—paved the way for other pianists to return to the composer. Gould left the recital stage in 1964 and confined himself to recording. But a string of other pianists, all of them influenced by Gould—Andras Schiff, Peter Serkin, Joao Carlos Martins, Charles Rosen, Alexis Weissenberg—have become known for performing the *Goldberg Variations.* Gould's

Bach playing caused a seismic (by pianistic standards) shift in ideas about performance. No longer would Bach be ignored in favor of the standard repertory—Beethoven, Chopin, Liszt, Brahms, Schumann. No longer would his work be treated as inoffensive "opening" material for recitals.

Gould's playing was noteworthy for more than mere keyboard virtuosity. He played every piece as if he were X-raying it, rendering each of its components with independence and clarity. The result was usually a single beautifully fluid process with many interesting subsidiary parts. Everything seemed thought out, and yet nothing sounded heavy, contrived, or labored. Moreover, he gave every indication, in all that he did, of being a mind at work, not just a fleet pair of hands. After he retired from the concert stage Gould made a number of records, television films, and radio broadcasts that attest to his resourcefulness beyond the keyboard. He was at once articulate and amiably eccentric. Above all, he always surprised. He never contented himself with the expected repertory: he went from Bach to Wagner to Schoenberg; back to Brahms, Beethoven, Bizet, Richard Strauss, Grieg, and Renaissance composers like Gibbons and Byrd. And, in a perverse departure from the tradition of playing only those composers and pieces one likes, Gould declared that he *didn't* like Mozart, then proceeded to record all of his sonatas, playing at exaggerated speeds and with unlovely inflections. Gould presented himself to the world meticulously. He had a sound all his own; and he also had arguments about all kinds of music, arguments that seemed to find their way into his playing.

Of course intelligence, taste, and originality do not amount to anything unless the pianist has the technical means to convey them. In this respect, a great pianist is like a great tennis player, a Rod Laver or a John McEnroe, who can serve strongly, volley accurately, and hit perfect ground strokes—every day, against every opponent. We should not underestimate the degree to which we respond to a fine pianist's *athletic* skill. The speed and fluency with which Josef Lhevinne could play thirds and sixths; the thundering accuracy and clangor of Horowitz's octaves; the rhythmic dash and chordal virtuosity of Alicia de Larrocha's Granados and Albéniz; Michelangeli's transcendentally perfect rendering of Ravel's *Gaspard de la Nuit;* Pollini's performance of Beethoven's *Hammerklavier,* with its finger-bending fugue and its meditative slow movement; Richter's strong but ethereally refined performances of Schumann, especially the long episodic pieces like the *Humoresque*—all these, in their bravura and virtuosic elaboration, lift the playing of the notes above the ordinary. These are physical achievements.

But the intelligent audience cannot be satisfied by what might be called loud-and-fast playing. There is virtuosity of style, too, in Brendel's Beethoven performances, where we feel intellect and taste allied with formidable technical command; or in Murray Perahia's Schubert, where a gentle singing line is supported by a superbly controlled chordal underpinning; or in Martha Argerich's sinuous filigree work in a Chopin scherzo. Similarly, the resolution of great musical complexity holds our interest, whether we find it in Charles Rosen's performances of Elliott Carter, in Jerome Lowenthal's performances of Bartók concertos, or in the incandescent purity of Edwin Fischer's Bach or Mozart. Above all, the pianist must physically shape sounds into form—that is, into the coherent interlocking of sonority, rhythm, inflection, and phrasing that tells us: *this* is what Beethoven had in mind. It is in this way, at such a moment, that the composer's identity and the pianist's are reconciled.

Pianists' programs are put together with greater or lesser degrees of thought and skill. While I would not go to hear an unknown pianist only because he or she has an interesting program, I would also not go to hear a distinguished pianist offering an obvious or carelessly put together program. One looks for programs that appear to *say* something—that highlight aspects of the piano literature or of performance in unexpected ways. In this, Gould was a genius, whereas Vladimir Ashkenazy, his very gifted near-contemporary, is not. Ashkenazy first announced himself as a "romantic" pianist specializing in Chopin, Liszt, and Rachmaninoff, and he confirms his prowess in that field every time he plays. Yet his programs do not reveal new meanings or new connections, at least not those of the sort Gould revealed when he linked Bach and Richard Strauss, or Sweelinck and Hindemith (the contrapuntal elaborations of the latter two composers, similar in their learned determination and often graceless length, occur almost three centuries apart).

Some programs are interesting because they present the audience with a narrative. This narrative may be conventional, moving historically from Bach or Mozart to Beethoven, the Romantics, and then the moderns. Or a program may have an inner narrative based on evolving forms (sonatas, variations, fantasies), tonalities, or styles. Of course, it is the pianist who makes the narrative come alive, consolidates its lines, enforces its main points.

Each of Pollini's programs last March focused on a pair of near-contemporary composers: Beethoven and Schubert in the March 23 recital, Schumann and Chopin in the performance on March 31. In both recitals the older composer was represented by works whose formal structures are "free"—Beethoven's two Op. 27 sonatas, which he described as *quasi una fantasia,* and Schumann's *Gesänge der Frühe* and *Davidsbündlertänze,* made up of loosely connected mood pieces. The younger composers were represented by two kinds of works: a shorter, rigorously symmetrical piece, intended as a *divertissement* but revealing a strong minor-key pathos (Schubert's C Minor Andante, Chopin's Scherzo in C-sharp Minor), and a major sonata (Schubert's late Sonata in C Minor, Chopin's Sonata No. 2 in B-flat Minor) that recalled the episodic material featured earlier. Thus Pollini's programs made clear the rigorously structured, almost Bach-like logic in Beethoven's and Schumann's free, or "fantastic," forms, as well as the way in which Schubert's and Chopin's sonatas, in the grip of a great musical intelligence, almost overflow their formal restrictions. The "almost" is a tribute to Pollini's restraint in observing the significant, if small, difference between fantasy and sonata in the early Romantic idiom. It hardly requires saying that such complete satisfaction as offered by Pollini's consummately demonstrative but unpretentious performances is very rarely found.

Most programs are divided into halves, each with its own introduction and climax. It is rare for a program not to end with a bang, although pianists generally make some effort to link the fireworks with the rest of the performance. Usually this is done by including something substantial—a big Chopin group, for example—as a way of impressing the audience with the pianist's power. Encores, in my opinion, are appalling, like food stains on a handsome suit. They serve to illustrate that the art of building a program is still a primitive one. In fact, the typical program, constructed out of little more than the most simple-minded contrasts (a reflective piece followed by a showy one), is often a reason for *not* attending a recital.

Some pianists tend to put together didactic programs—all the Beethoven or Schubert sonatas, for example. Last March, at the Metropolitan Museum, Andras Schiff did an especially noteworthy sequence of three Bach recitals, culminating in the *Goldberg Variations*. The first pianists to attempt such programs were Ferruccio Busoni and Anton Rubinstein, whose recitals offered a history of piano music on a truly heroic scale. All-Chopin or all-Schumann recitals are not in themselves arresting, in part because they are not that uncommon, but the sequence of sixteen concerto performances presented by Artur Rubinstein in the 1960s *was* interesting. While the performances were noteworthy in illuminating the various transformations of the concerto form, that was not the chief source of their power. What was so gripping was the spectacle of a feat combining aesthetic range and athletic power and spanning a number of weeks.

But such interesting programming is rare. Most pianists plan their recitals around a repertory stamped by their predecessors, hoping—generally without any basis, in my opinion—to capture the music for themselves. What aesthetic identity can a pianist possibly have if he allows himself to be billed as "the new Schnabel" or "the twentieth-century Tausig"? Even worse are those who try to imitate the sounds of the one pianist who for half a century has been the model of dynamic and, I would say, strident pianism, Vladimir Horowitz. None has succeeded, in part at least because Horowitz himself has gone on playing.

Adding to the limitations of the pianistic repertory is the fact that most of the piano literature is very familiar and pretty well fixed: the notes are written down and, in almost all cases, the pieces have been recorded. Thus to play the four Chopin ballades, as Emanuel Ax recently did at Carnegie Hall, is not just to play the pieces, but to *replay* them. The hope is that the pianist does so with variations that reveal his or her imagination and taste—and that show no sign of copying others or distorting the composer's text. Most interesting pianists, even when working through a conventional program, give the impression that their playing of a piece is also a commentary on it, much as an essay on a great novel is a commentary, and not simply a plot summary. A successful performance of the Schumann Fantasy, such as Pollini's, makes the listener feel two disparate things *together*: you feel that this is the work Schumann wrote; and you feel that Pollini, in responding to its infinitely variable rhythmic and rhetorical impulses, accents, phrases, pauses, and inflections, is *commenting* on the piece, giving us his version of it. Thus do pianists make their statements.

The world of pianism is a curious amalgam of "culture" and business. Some would argue that the cultural context (no less than the ticketseller's booth) is a distraction from the *sound* of the pianist. But that view too easily dismisses as distractions some of the circumstances that actually stimulate what we would term interesting pianism. The very prominence of modern pianists is in fact a result of the fraying, described fifty years ago by Theodor Adorno, of the connection between the three essential threads of music making: the composition and production of music, its reproduction or performance, and its consumption. Most pianists have no time for contemporary music; conversely, not much music is being written with the piano in mind. The public is saturated with mechanically reproduced music. Moreover, musical literacy is no longer a requirement for the educated person. As a result, audiences are by and large removed from the acts of playing and composing.

Musical competitions, which were established as a way of launching virtuoso careers, have also contributed to specialization. Most of these contests are run by an odd assortment of philanthropists, musicians, and concert managers, and they have tended to foster a kind of pianistic triumphalism. To those like myself who are aghast at what takes place in most competitions, this triumphalism brings to mind the world of sports, where amphetamines and steroids are routinely taken to improve performance. Occasionally pianists will survive the paranoid atmosphere that is a feature of all competitions. The pianism of these few is not ruined by their having to adopt the bravura techniques and pared-down and neutral style favored by juries. Pollini is one of the survivors, in part, I believe, because after he won the Warsaw Chopin Competition he did not immediately go on tour to launch a "major career." Instead he spent several years studying and, not incidentally, maturing as a pianist. When I speak of survival I am not suggesting that prizewinners fizzle out after a while. The roster of successful prizewinners and competition pianists is very large: Ashkenazy, Malcolm Frager, and André Michel Schub come to mind. What I am suggesting is that hardly any of them do interesting work.

"Star" pianists command great fees, and when this money is combined with the income from their records it can amount to a sizable fortune. Some pianists seem to benefit from the system: their success allows them to play less often, to take sabbaticals, to learn new (and riskier) material. In general, however, there seems to be a scramble for more concerts, better recording contracts, greater "opportunities." The stars struggle to maintain their positions and lesser luminaries try desperately to move up a rung. All this results in little pleasure for the mass audience, although it produces much profit for the agents, middlemen, and media manipulators.

There is not much hope that composer, performer, and listener will once again work together—without the distraction of recording deals and prizes—in a real community, the kind of community for which the Bach family has always served as an attractive model. Nor is the public likely to become less susceptible to hype and commercialism. But there *are* signs, both within the piano world and outside it, that many people feel the need to reestablish links between piano playing and other human activities, so that the mindless virtuosity of the whizbang pianist might be superseded by something more interesting. Certainly Pollini's success has something to do with this, as does Brendel's. And Glenn Gould, in everything he did, expressed dissatisfaction with piano playing as such: his project was an attempt to connect pianism with the larger society.

All of this is evidence of a pianism trying to break out of its intellectual silence, its fetishes and rituals, its "beautiful" sounds and athletic skill. We will always admire those sounds, that skill; and we will always take pleasure in listening to pianists perform the standard repertory. But the experience of the piano is intensified when it is joined to the other experiences in which we find nourishment.

How do pianists transport us from the performance itself to another realm of significance? Listen to the records of Sergei Rachmaninoff. Rachmaninoff fairly bristles with interest; everything he does strikes us as an intervention into a piece of music that would otherwise be a score dead on the page. We feel there is a point he is trying to make. In playing the Schumann *Carnaval,* for example, he makes us aware of the composer working the piece out, bringing it to statement; and yet the chaos of Schumann's merely private vision is plainly in evidence. We feel the same thing about the playing of Alfred Cortot.

This sort of pianism is not simply a matter of taking risks, playing at outrageously fast tempi, introducing highly inflected lines. Rather—and this is the central matter—such pianism draws us in because its processes are apparent, compelling, intelligently provoking. The same point can be made negatively. There is nothing less stimulating than a pianist whose sole concern is perfection, perfection of the sort that causes one to say: How perfect is this playing. The emphasis on winning prizes certainly encourages such an aesthetic of "accomplishment," as does the desire to remove from the performance everything but the pianist's dazzling finger-work. Put differently, piano playing that seems so finished as to be solely about itself (the work of the formidable Josef Lhevinne comes to mind) pushes the listener away and isolates the pianist in that sterile environment reserved for "pros."

The kind of playing that engages me is playing that lets me in, so to speak: the pianist, by the intimacy of his or her playing, makes me feel that I would want to play that way too. The work of Dinu Lipatti, who turned out burningly pure performances of Mozart and Chopin, exudes that sense, as does the work of a relatively obscure school of British pianists—Myra Hess, Clifford Curzon, the great Solomon, and the equally fine Benno Moiseiwitsch. Today Daniel Barenboim, Radu Lupu, and Perahia carry on in that vein.

One could argue that the social essence of pianism is precisely the opposite: it *ought* to alienate and distance the public, thereby accentuating the social contradictions that gave rise to the virtuoso pianist, the preposterous result of the overspecialization of contemporary culture. But this argument ignores what is just as apparent, and no less a result of the alienation produced by consumerism—namely, the *utopian* effect of pianistic performances. For the performer traffics between composer and listener. And insofar as performers do this in ways that involve us as listeners in the experience and processes of performing, they invite us into a utopian realm of acute awareness that is otherwise inaccessible to us. Interesting pianism, in short, breaks down the barriers between audience and interpreter, and does so without violating music's essential silence.

When a performance taps into its audience's subjective time, enriches it and makes it more complex, it becomes more than a couple of hours of good entertainment. Here, I think, is the essence of what can make the piano and pianists interesting. Each listener brings to a performance memories of other performances, a history of relationships with the music, a web of affiliations; and all of this is activated by the performance at hand. Every pianist does this differently. Gould seemed actually to invent himself and his playing; it was as if he had no antecedents. The counterpoint seemed to speak to you directly, intelligently, vividly, forcing you to leave your ideas and experiences in abeyance. Pollini, on the other hand, lets you hear in his Schumann not only the composer's episodic genius but also the performances of other pianists—Michelangeli, for instance—from whom Pollini has learned, and gone beyond. The intellectual rigor of both pianists compares, in strength and cogency, with the prose of a first-rate discourse.

Thus the greatest pianists somehow bridge the gap between the unnaturally refined, rarefied world of the recital stage and the world of music in human life. Surely we have all been tremendously moved by a piece of music, and have imagined what it must be like to feel compelled to perform it, to be disturbed into expressing it aloud, to be urged into articulating it, note by note, line by line. It is this experience which the best pianists can stimulate: the conviction of their playing, the beauty and nobility of their sound, make me feel what I might feel were I able to play as they can.

This is not at all a matter of the performer meeting one's expectations. Just the opposite: it is a matter of the performer giving rise to expectations, making possible an encounter with memory that can be expressed only in music performed this way, now, before one.

Many years ago in Europe I heard the great German pianist Wilhelm Kempff perform. To my knowledge Kempff has played in America only once recently, a Carnegie Hall recital about ten or twelve years ago which was not very successful. He has not been much celebrated in this country, overshadowed perhaps by lesser contemporaries such as Wilhelm Backhaus and Serkin. Kempff's music has a unique, singing tone, and his playing, like Gould's, is unusual in not bearing the imprint of his teachers, or of other pianists. What you do hear in his playing is an unfolding interpretation. Kempff is someone for whom technique has been subordinated to discovery, for whom the piano is an instrument sharpening perception, rather than delivering perfectly fashioned sounds. This is true of all of his work, from the rigorous counterpoint of the terminal fugue in Beethoven's Op. 110 to the fantastic, broken energy of Schumann's *Kreisleriana*.

The surface finish of Kempff's playing never impresses us with either its assertiveness or its strength. Rather, we are aware of him bringing a literal reading of the notes to its fulfillment, much the way, over a longer period of time, we learn a piece of music, grow to understand it, and finally know it, as the beautiful phrase has it, "by heart."

To understand what I mean, listen to Kempff's 1976 performance of Bach's "Jesu, Joy of Man's Desiring." Most people know this piece from Dinu Lipatti's transparent and pure recording. But while Lipatti uses Myra Hess's transcription, Kempff uses his own, thereby heightening the intimacy of his performance. Bach's work is a serene elaboration of chorale melody with a sinuous triplet obbligato, which Lipatti renders in a legato encompassing infallibly stated inner voices; this execution is envied by most other pianists. Yet the listener is always aware of one effect or another claiming his attention. This is especially apparent when one compares Lipatti's interpretation with that of Kempff. By the time Kempff reaches the final statement of the chorale tune, obbligato and melody have been expanded to embrace the pianist's lifetime of attention to Bach's music. The disciplined line of the performance reaches its conclusion without pious triumphalism or trite melancholy. The music's outward evidence and inner movement are experienced as two forms articulated together. And we realize that while much of the pianistic enterprise as we know it—through playing (if we play), and through listening—takes place in the public sphere, its fullest effects are felt in a private sphere of memory and association which is the listener's own. This sphere is shaped, on the one hand, by the enveloping sphere of performances, patterns of taste, cultural institutions, aesthetic styles, and historical pressures, and, on the other, by far more personal pleasures.

I am speaking here of the quite considerable musical world that was explored and illuminated by Proust in *A la recherche du temps perdu* and by Thomas Mann in *Doktor Faustus*, those extraordinary monuments to the convergence of literary, musical, and social modernism. It is an indication of how powerfully the three spheres still interact that Glenn Gould seemed to be the embodiment of Mann's Adrian Leverkuhn, and that the robust theatricality of Artur Rubinstein's pianism seems to come straight out of the salons and *musicales* of Proust's Hôtel de Guermantes in the Faubourg Saint-Germain.

That the corporate world of the music business has replaced bohemia and the *beau monde* as the environment for concert music tells us of marketable commodities, yes; but it also testifies to the durability of a tradition served and often ennobled by the contemporary pianist, who, when he or she functions on the level attained by Pollini, attests to that tradition's variety and seriousness.

The greatest performances provide the invaluable restatements and forceful interpretations of the essay, a literary form overshadowed by the grander structures of epic and tragedy. The essay, like the recital, is occasional, re-creative, and personal. And essayists, like pianists, concern themselves with givens: those works of art always worth another critical and reflective reading. Above all, neither pianist nor essayist can offer final readings, however definitive their performances may be. The fundamental sportiness of both genres is what keeps them honest, as well as vital. But there is an irreducible romance to the pianist's art. It is suggested by the underlying melancholy in Schumann's *Humoresque* and Chopin's Ballade in F Minor; by the lingering authority of legendary pianists—Busoni, Eugen d'Albert, Franz Liszt, Leopold Godowsky—with magical names; by the sonorous power that can encompass the solidest Beethoven and the most slender Fauré; by the curious, almost audible mixture of dedication and money circulating through the recital's atmosphere.

21

How Not to Get Gored

Readers of American writing have been struck by the prevalence of what Dwight Macdonald once called "how-to-ism." This is not simply a matter of guides to gadgetry, or to cooking, or to doing things like dieting, marrying wealth, and achieving peace of mind, although writing on all these subjects is more plentiful in America than anywhere else. What I have in mind is the practical, instructional attitude which is to be found in a great many canonical works of high literature: *Moby Dick,* for instance, can be seen as a manual of what to do if you want to go whaling, as well as an encyclopedia of everything pertaining to ships and the sea. Cooper's novels are full of practical hints about forest and Indian life, Twain is stuffed with South-Western and Mississippi River lore, as is *Walden* of New England nature and Faulkner of the South; in Henry James the tendency takes the form of connoisseurship. In all these cases the implication is that reality cannot stand on its own, but requires the services of an expert to convey or unlock its meaning. The converse of this is no less true, that Americans seem interested not so much in reality as in how to approach and master it, and for this expert guidance is necessary.

A useful way of understanding this peculiar structure of perception is to see it as a substitute for the feeling of historical depth and continuity. To foreground information and expertise is in many ways to say that what matters can be pushed up to the surface, and that history, insofar as it is out of easy reach, is better forgotten or, if it can't be forgotten, ignored. Experience of the here-and-now—the relevant—is therefore given priority. To the extent that the writer is able to provide such experience, to that extent his or her claims are felt as important, urgent, impressive. As a result, in no other literature is the writer so much a performing self, as Richard Poirier has observed, and in no other literature is such a premium placed on raw data and its virtuoso delivery.

The American interest in "fact" derives from the same complex of attitudes. One can see it not only in the regularly contemptuous dismissal of opinion and interpretation, but also in the much more interesting cult of "objectivity" and expertise, the spread of consultancy as a profession, and the institutionalization of the "news," which in America, it is believed, has been definitively separated from the burden of subjectivity. By the late twentieth century the commodification, packaging, and merchandising of reality which constitute the knowledge industry have come to predominate almost to the exclusion of actual content. Note, for instance, that documentary films are not really popular in America (unless they are English) and are rarely made, whereas twenty-four-hour news channels are increasing in number. The assumption underlying the worship of news is that a tight little product, billed as pure "information" with all opinion removed and flashing across our vision for no longer than thirty seconds per item, is convincing beyond question. That this form of news is "fact" few people will dispute: what gets excluded is the tremendously sophisticated process of selection and commodification which makes bits of information into unassailable "fact."

The continued pressure of such attitudes on American literature and society makes for genuine eccentricity in both. The great American classics are not, I believe, comparable to either the French or the English, which are the product of stable, highly institutionalized and confident cultures. In its anxieties, its curious imbalances and deformations, its paranoid emphases and inflections, American literature is like its Russian counterpart, although it would be impossible to extend these analogies into matters of political style.

In such an unusual setting it is not surprising to discover that one of the greatest American books of the twentieth century is Hemingway's *Death in the Afternoon,* first published in 1932. Hemingway's reputation is now somewhat in eclipse, although the effect of his stylistic innovations on other writers continues. Remembered for his macho divagations (and to a certain extent discredited because of them), Hemingway was always a relentless expert and purveyor of expertise on such interesting subjects for early twentieth-century Americans as war, Europe, fishing, hunting, bohemia, and bullfighting. Departing from the almost incredible purity of line and severity of vision in his earliest short stores, Hemingway's later fiction is regularly disturbed by displays of knowledge, showy bundles of information. He seems to have had one eye turned toward an audience eager for news about the world of cafés, about Paris, World War One, Pamplona, Biarritz, and in his writing he took pains to convert his style of living into knowledgeability—with very mixed results. For my generation, the post-war Hemingway had already become Papa—tiresome as well as unsufferably affected. Until, that is, in 1959, he contracted for, and subsequently published in *Life* Magazine, a series on the summer-long competition between the two greatest of living Spanish bullfighters, Antonio Ordoñez and Luis Miguel Dominguin. Then the magisterial qualities of *Death in the Afternoon* were recalled.

Death in the Afternoon has the patient manner of a mammoth treatise on the art not so much of bullfighting—which Hemingway considered as having arrived at a state of decadent elaboration—as of killing specially bred fighting bulls. In the process, Hemingway also offers an idiosyncratic history of Spain and of Spanish culture, as well as an impressive grammar of the gestures, rituals, emotions, and methods associated with the *corrida de toros.* The book is intended as an explanation (but by no means a justification) of what Hemingway regards as an exclusively male art form, not a sport. His mannerisms are often annoying—as when he invents an objecting woman with whom he carries on a hopelessly arch series of verbal duels—and his zeal for explanation often goes unchecked. What turns the book into a triumph is his ability to enter and master an alien world, engaging his reader with characters and even bulls, much as Tolstoy, it was said, could make us feel what it is like to be a horse.

The massive edifice of *Death in the Afternoon* stands, like a tower on a rock, on top of Hemingway's obsession with death. Bullfighting is the art of sustaining, prolonging, and containing the encounter with death, the matador's arsenal of *veronicas, pasos naturales,* and *recibiendos* lifting the slaughter of a brave animal into a structured display of exposure to and mastery over death, sculpted and clarified into three acts by such conceits as *suerte, dominio,* valor, and honor. In its intensity and power, there is very little like this book in Hemingway's other work, and it seems to me essential for understanding what he might have been capable of had he not been so successful as a writer of grown-up boys' stories laden with outdoor and wine-drinking expertise. The impression he gives is of a haunted man whose cultural—and no doubt actual—incapacity for aestheticizing the experience of death is remedied in the act of describing how the Spaniards do it through the *corrida.* Rarely in modern literature, except perhaps in writers like Kafka, does one come across such a studious rendering of the mechanics of ritualized suffering: as you read in *Death in the Afternoon* of the finer points of picadoring, of the various types of *cornada,* of TB and syphilis as diseases of matadors, you will be reminded of the Hunger Artist or the machine in "The Penal Colony"; and nowhere else do words like "nobility" and "elegance" have so lurid and yet so compelling an aura.

The 1959 *Life* articles were to form the climax to Hemingway's return to Spain and bullfighting in 1953, after a long gap. The magazine published only a fraction of the hundred thousand words Hemingway wrote; and the present publishers have restored some but not all of what he had intended to be the account of "the destruction of one person [Dominguin] by another [Ordoñez] with all the things that led up to and made it." In several ways, therefore, *The Dangerous Summer* is a retrospective work that re-establishes continuity with Hemingway's earlier days. First, there is the return to Spain, where, Hemingway tells us, even the border guards now know him and his books. There is little indication here of Hemingway's being much troubled by Franco's politics, which is a way of saying that the work's cloistral narrowness excludes most things except the summer's main event, a *mano a mano* between the two great rivals. Second, there is Hemingway's revival of interest, after the death of Manolete in 1949, in the art of killing bulls. Ordoñez is not only a brilliant fighter: he is also the son of Cayetano, the matador whose work in the ring had been described with such admiration in *The Sun Also Rises*. Hemingway regards the son as a better fighter than the father, and indeed as a vindication of the art itself, now fallen into disrepair and dishonesty as a result of cowardice, greed, and the ignorance of spectators.

The Dangerous Summer contains within its covers not only the account of a contest between the two greatest living matadors but a couple of other contests as well. One is between bullfighting then and bullfighting now: the first a remembered but vanished art, impermanent because confined to a couple of hours on Sunday afternoons, but given presence and actuality in the prose of Hemingway's earlier masterpiece; the second, a contemporary version of the first, struggling to gain distinction through the bravery and skill of two men who rise to eminence in a setting of underbred cowardly bulls with shaved horns, of greedy managers and mediocre fighters. The other, deeper contest is between the earlier Hemingway and the later: the earlier a man obsessed with the *corrida* as tragedy, with Spain and truth, with writing and death, with the possibility of rescuing some practical knowledge from a metaphysical drama that symbolized the tyrannical passage of time, for whom great bullfighting and clear prose represented a similar triumph; the later, a world-famous writer more celebrated than his material, tired, yet courageously risking self-repetition and self-parody as he seeks to resurrect dead impulses, forgotten gestures, true qualities buried beneath commercialism, hangers-on, and a somnolent, degenerate Spain. Nevertheless, he starts the book with a cocky assurance—even if we allow for the edgy, awkward reference to Mary:

> It was strange going back to Spain again: I had never expected to be allowed to return to the country that I loved more than any other except my own and I would not return so long as any of my friends there were in jail. But in the spring of 1953 in Cuba I talked with good friends who had fought on opposing sides in the Spanish Civil War about stopping in Spain on our way to Africa and they agreed that I might honourably

return to Spain if I did not recant anything that I had written and kept my mouth shut on politics . . .

By 1953 none of my friends were in jail and I made plans to take my wife Mary to the *feria* at Pamplona and then to proceed to Madrid to see the Prado and after that, if we were still at large, to continue on to Valencia for the bullfights there before getting our boat to Africa. I knew that nothing could happen to Mary since she had never been in Spain in her life and knew only the very finest people. Surely, if she ever had any trouble they would rush to her rescue.

Ordoñez is the victor of the manifest contest between the two matadors. Dominguin is reduced at the end to mechanical fighting and repeated injury—these are the main signs of his defeat. But this is a relative matter, for which English-speaking readers are quite dependent on Hemingway. What I know of pre-Manolete bullfighting I know from Hemingway, but I did see a fair number of *corridas* in the sixties, enough to realize that Hemingway was right to say that the art of killing bulls had been displaced by a cult of the glamorous bullfighter, just as in music the art of composing had been displaced by the virtuoso conductor or performer. If you saw El Cordobes, Paco Camino, El Viti and the others in the sixties, you would have to say that they were brave and often spectacular fighters, but with the possible exception of El Viti, none of them brought to mind the "classical" *faenas* reported by Hemingway and others during the golden age. The only exception was Ordoñez, whom I saw in 1966, most memorably at a minor *feria* in Badajoz, a dusty and mercilessly sun-beaten town in Estremadura. Even if you disliked bullfighting, it would have been hard not to have been jolted out of your seat by his authority, by the way he dominated the *corrida,* and the severe grace, economy, and fearlessness which he brought to what Hemingway brilliantly called a great matador's education of the bull into the moment of truth.

Perhaps because I remember Ordoñez so vividly, I was convinced by *The Dangerous Summer* that he had beaten Dominguin and, more interestingly, re-established a continuum between the early days and these. In Valencia, Ordoñez did a *faena* that "had the beautiful flow of the water as it curves over the crest of a dam or a falls." For anyone who cares about such things, *The Dangerous Summer* is obligatory if repetitive reading, the chronicle of journeys up and down Spain, of fights in Bilbao, Valencia, Malaga, Aranjuez, of restaurants, hotels, hospitals, and *fincas*. Atmosphere and the color of the Spanish *ferias,* yes—but also patient, often ungainly description of bulls, *veronicas,* and various styles of fighting.

The hidden core of the book, however, is the other contest, between early and late Hemingway. As a subject of expertise, bullfighting for Hemingway had had one strikingly clear advantage: there was an absolute correspondence between its basis—"the formal *corrida,*" he reminds us in *The Dangerous Summer,* is based on the bull's complete "innocence of previous contact with a man on foot"— and the fact that he was the first American to write about it at such length and with such knowledge. Moreover, the time-period for killing a bull should never extend beyond fifteen or twenty minutes, for after that the bull learns to distinguish between an artfully deployed cape and the solid reality of a man's body. Thus bullfighting is not only a highly specialized art, but also an extremely limited site of intensity, irreversible in its processes, precisely calibrated in its space for maneuver, totally restricted in its morbid conclusion. No wonder Hemingway ends *Death in the Afternoon* on a somber note of loss and achievement, attuned to the notion that "I know things change now and I do not care." What he did was to write an unsatisfactory book with regard to the real-life *corrida*—"not enough of a book"—but an expertly wrought whole just the same: "The great thing is to last and get your work done and see and hear and learn and understand; and write when there is something that you know; and not before; and not too damned much after . . . It is not enough of a book, but still there were a few things to be said. There were a few practical things to be said."

Hemingway's return to bullfighting then is repetition, and Ordoñez's brilliance a consolidation of the earlier lore and practical appreciation of the form contained in *Death in the Afternoon*. The difference is that *The Dangerous Summer* much more insistently features Hemingway himself, a personality welcomed and to some extent whored after by those in bullfighting circles. In 1959, American expertise, which had once derived from "innocence of contact," has become a very jaded thing. Hemingway the character, with his wine-drinking chums, his chauffeur-driven Lancia, his vanity (Dominguin and Ordoñez are described as killing bulls in the most difficult manner "for me"), his captive women, his hotels and servitors, intrudes everywhere. He resembles Howard Cosell, the famous American sports broadcaster, interviewing, and to some extent wooed by, Muhammad Ali. The proposition that Wimbledon is really played for Dan Maskell would be no odder than the following passage from *The Dangerous Summer*'s final pages, based on the often repeated notion that Ordoñez requires Hemingway for his art to be complete (Ordoñez, we are told earlier, would kill the bull "to please me"):

> Then he swung around and looked at the crowd and the surgeon's look was gone from his eyes and his face was happy about the work he had done. A bullfighter can never see the work of art that he is making. He has no chance to correct it as a painter or a writer has. He cannot hear it as a musician can. He can only feel it and hear the crowd's reaction to it. When he feels it and knows that it is great it takes hold of him so that nothing else in the world matters. All the time he is making his work of art he knows that he must keep within the limits of his skill and his knowledge of the animal. Those matadors are called cold who visibly show that they are thinking of this. Antonio was not cold and the public belonged to him now.

The innocence is gone from such descriptions, except as a recollection of an earlier, purer time when the correspondence between expert and reality was more urgent and equal, and when the writer's performance was driven by the need for the aesthetic experience of mortality. In *The Dangerous Summer* the pressures of *Life*'s commission seem to have transformed Hemingway into a self-conscious middleman, his repetitions and garrulousness edited down to a pastiche of his famous earlier self. The audience isn't there to participate: it is there to watch him getting Ordoñez and Dominguin to acknowledge him as the Old Man, and thereby help him to earn his money, even though, he says, "I had lost much of my old feeling for the bullfight." It is a sign of Hemingway's ambiguous fate in this book that he survives as a well-known aficionado paying tribute to Ordoñez, and as an exhausted writer whose posthumous work calls the reader's attention back to his strongest past performance.

Yet a curious inconclusiveness, a kind of situationless disorientation, settles upon the reader. Why was the book published now and not, say, shortly after Hemingway's death? Who is it addressed to? Was it intended as an effort to restore Hemingway's reputation, or to gain new attention for him? The book provides no answer to these questions and will remain, I think, a dislocated addendum to Hemingway's earlier writing: the expertise offered by an expert witness who has gone on "too damned much after." What stands revealed here is the great problem of American writing: that the shock of recognition derived from knowledge and converted into how-to-ism can only occur once, cannot be sustained. The second time around, it is dragged into the market, where the homogenizing processes turn out neither art nor knowledge, but the merest "product."

22

Foucault and the Imagination of Power

By the time power had become an explicit and central theme in his work in the early seventies, Foucault had already spelled out his theory of discourse and discourse analysis in *L'Ordre du discours* and *L'Archéologie du savoir*. While they looked forward to what he would later write, both of these works built and elaborated upon still earlier work, his archaeological studies in *Histoire de la folie*, *Les Mots et les choses*, and *Naissance de la clinique*. What is, I think, deeply compelling about the continuity of Foucault's early with his middle works is his highly wrought presentation of the order, stability, authority, and regulatory power of knowledge. For him *les choses dites* are objects placed on the registers of knowledge much as formations of soldiers are located tactically and strategically on fields of battle. When Borges says, "I used to marvel that the letters in a closed book did not get mixed up and lost in the course of a night," it is as if he were providing Foucault with the start of a historical quest, to understand how statements acquired not only their social and epistemological status, but their specific density as accomplished work, as disciplinary convention, as dated orthodoxy.

Thus Foucault's view of things was, as he implied to the journal *Hérodote* in 1976,[1] spatial, which makes it somewhat easier to understand his predilection for the analysis of discontinuous but actual spaces, territories, domains, and sites—libraries, schools, hospitals, prisons— rather than, as one would expect in a historian, a tendency to talk principally about continuities, temporalities, and absences. It is probable that Foucault's admirably un-nostalgic view of history and the almost total lack in it of metaphysical yearning, such as one finds in heirs to the Hegelian tradition, are both ascribable to his geographic bent. So marked is this in Foucault, and so deeply linked to his vision of statements as carefully fashioned extensions of institutions and instruments of governance, that it is usefully elucidated by someone who, although in a different and much earlier tradition than Foucault, resembles him in many ways, Ibn Khaldun, the great fourteenth-century Arab historiographer and philosopher. In the *Muqadimah* Ibn Khaldun says that the science of history is unique because while related to rhetoric and civil politics it is different from both. He thus sees the historian's task as work taking place between rhetoric, on the one hand, and civil politics, on the other. This, it seems to me, describes Foucault's analytical attitude uncannily well: statements for him carry more weight than ways merely of speaking either convincingly or not, and these statements are also somewhat less in authority than the direct pronouncements of someone in governmental power.

The difference between Ibn Khaldun and Foucault is no less instructive. Both men—Ibn Khaldun more—are worldly historians who understand, and perhaps even appreciate, the dynamics of secular events, their relentless pressure, their ceaseless movement, their elusive complexity which does not permit the luxury of easy moral classification. And both are unlike Hobbes in that they respect and suspiciously admire the drive toward coherent order which characterizes human discourse as well as the historian's craft. Ibn Khaldun's vision of social order is what he calls *'asabiyah* (usually translated as "group solidarity"); Foucault's is "the order of discourse," *l'ordre du discours*. Yet Ibn Khaldun's perspective is such that history for him is composed of social life cycles describing movements from origin, to ascendancy, to decline, and rise again that occur within various polities, each of which is organized around the greater or lesser degree of *'asabiyah* within it. Foucault's perspective, however, is that in the modern period to which he belongs there is an unremitting and unstoppable expansion of power favoring the administrators, managers, and technocrats of what he calls disciplinary society. Power, he writes in his last phase, is everywhere. It is overcoming, co-opting, infinitely detailed, and ineluctable in the growth of its domination. The historical tendency that seems to me to have held Foucault in its grip intellectually and politically in his last years was one he perceived—incompletely, I think—as growing ever more coherent and unidirectional, and it is this tendency that carried him over from the differentiations and subtleties within power in *L'Ordre du discours* and *L'Archéologie du savoir* to the hypertrophied vision of power in later works like *Surveiller et punir* and volume 1 of *L'Histoire de la sexualité*.

Many of the people who admire and have learned from Foucault, including myself, have commented on the undifferentiated power he seemed to ascribe to modern society. With this profoundly pessimistic view went also a singular lack of interest in the force of effective resistance to it, in choosing particular sites of intensity, choices which, we see from the evidence on all sides, always exist and are often successful in impeding, if not actually stopping, the progress of tyrannical power. Moreover, Foucault seemed to have been confused between the power of institutions to subjugate individuals, and the fact that individual behavior in society is frequently a matter of following rules and conventions. As Peter Dews puts it: "[Foucault] perceives clearly that institutions are not merely imposed constructs, yet has no apparatus for dealing with this fact, which entails that following a convention is not always equivalent to submitting to a power . . . But without this distinction every delimitation becomes an exclusion, and every exclusion becomes equated with an exercise of power."[2]

Although we shouldn't indulge ourselves in the practice of saving Foucault from himself in order to make self-interested use of him, there is some value in trying to understand why he went as far as he did in imagining power to be so irresistible and unopposable. I shall suggest that there are other images of power, contemporary with Foucault's, that do much to modulate and complement his. But it is sensible to begin by asking the beginning questions, why imagine power in the first place, and what is the relationship between one's motive for imagining power and the image one ends up with. Consider these four possibilities. You think about power (1) to imagine what you could do if you had power; (2) to speculate about what you would imagine if you had power; (3) to arrive at some assessment of what power you would need in order to vanquish present power, and instate a new order or power; (4) to postulate a range of things that cannot be imagined or commanded by any form of power that exists at present.

It seems to me that Foucault was mainly attracted to the first and second possibilities, that is, to thinking about power from the standpoint of its actual realization, not of opposition to it. The third and fourth possibilities are insurgent and utopian. Foucault's emphasis, for example, upon the productivity of power, its provocative inventiveness and generative ingenuity, invigorated his analyses of how disciplines and discourses get things done, accomplish real tasks, gather authority. Similarly, his descriptions of lonely prophetic figures like de Sade and Nietzsche are interesting because of the way their outrageous and even preposterous pressures on rationality are absorbed and institutionalized almost routinely by the very structure one might have thought they had permanently disabled.

In short Foucault's imagination of power is largely *with* rather than *against* it, which is why the third and fourth possibilities do not seriously interest him as matters of either moral choice or rationalized political preferences. I wouldn't go as far as saying that Foucault rationalized power, or that he legitimized its dominion and its ravages by declaring them inevitable, but I would say that his interest in domination was critical but not finally as contestatory or as oppositional as on the surface it seems to be. This translates into the paradox that Foucault's imagination of power was by his analysis of power to reveal its injustice and cruelty, but by his theorization to let it go on more or less unchecked. Perhaps this paradox is rooted in the extreme isolation one senses in Foucault's efforts, the discomfort both with his own genius and with an anonymity that does not suit him, as he gives voice to both in the effacements of self that accompany the brilliant rhetorical display occasioned by his self-presentation (an inaugural *leçon* at the Collège de France) that opens *L'Ordre du discours*.

Still there is no doubt at all that Foucault is nevertheless extraordinarily brilliant as a visionary of power who calls forth in his reader a whole gamut of responses testifying not so much to the rightness of Foucault's reports but to alternative visions of power not entirely suppressed or obliterated by his work, but stimulated and enlivened by it. Against the heedless impersonal efficiency of power there is, first of all, the inflection introduced by C. Wright Mills, whose attack on the banality and irresponsibility of corporate managers will not be silenced by the notion that a micro-physics of power has eliminated classical ideas about ruling classes and dominant interests:

> In so far as there is now a great scatter of relatively equal balancing units, it is on the middle levels of power, seated in the sovereign localities and intermittent pressure groups, and coming to its high point within the Congress. We must thus revise and relocate the received conception of an enormous scatter of varied interests, for, when we look closer and for longer periods of time, we find that most of these middle-level interests are concerned merely with their particular cut, with their particular area of vested interest, and often these are of no decisive political importance, although many are of enormous detrimental value to welfare. Above this plurality of interests, the units of power—economic, political, and military—that count in any balance are few in number and weighty beyond comparison with the dispersed groups on the middle and lower levels of the power structure . . .
>
> . . . Those having real power in the American state today are not merely brokers of power, resolvers of conflict, or compromisers of varied and clashing interest—they represent and indeed embody quite specific national interests and policies.[3]

Secondly, to the extent that modern history in the West exemplifies for Foucault the confinement and elision of marginal, oppositional, and eccentric groups, there is, I believe, a salutary virtue in testimonials by members of those groups asserting their right of self-representation within the total economy of discourse. Foucault is certainly right—and even prescient—in showing how discourse is not only that which translates struggle or systems of domination, but that for *which* struggles are conducted, "le pouvoir dont on cherche à s'emparer."[4] What he seemed not quite as willing to grant is, in fact, the relative success of these counter-discursive attempts first to show the misrepresentations of discursive power, to show, in Fanon's words, the violence done to psychically and politically repressed inferiors in the name of an advanced culture, and then afterwards to begin the difficult, if not always tragically flawed, project of formulating the discourse of liberation.

We may finally believe with Foucault and Lyotard that the great narratives of emancipation and enlightenment are over, but I think we must remember more seriously what Foucault himself teaches, that in this case, as in many others, it is sometimes of paramount importance not so much *what* is said, but *who* speaks. So that it can hardly pass muster that having once declared the "assujettissement du discours," the same source that does so erases any opportunity for adversarial responses to this process of subjugation, declaring it accomplished and done with at the start. The work of Fanon himself, Syed Alatas, Abdallah Laroui, Panikkar, Shariati, Mazrui, novelists like Ngugi and Rushdie—all these as well as the enormously powerful adversarial work of feminists and minority cultures in the West and in the Third World amply record the continuing attraction to libertarian struggle, for which I have gathered Foucault and others in his camp felt either resignation or spectatorial indifference after the Iranian revolution. I must also mention that to describe these counter-discursive efforts simply as non-systemic in Wallerstein's phrase is, I think, to negate precisely the force in them that I am certain Foucault would have understood, the *organized and rationalized* basis of their protest. So that while granting them non-systemic force on one level, we would have to grant on another level the limits of our imagination of *their* power and organizing principles, and thus that they imagine things that we have no easy way of grasping.

Finally—to return to more familiar arenas of struggle—Foucault's unmodulated minimization of resistance provokes allusion to the formation in writers like Gramsci and Raymond Williams of an emergent or alternative consciousness allied to emergent and alternative subaltern groups within the dominant discursive society. I mention them because their work and the work of the Frankfurt School theorists, like Foucault's, accords a paramount place to ideology and culture critique, although they place a quite different, altogether more positive emphasis upon the vulnerability of the present organization of culture. For Gramsci and Williams, the analysis of discursive power is made coeval with an image of what we could describe as contingent power, the principle of whose constitution is that, since it is constructed by humans, it is therefore not invincible, not impervious to dismantling, not unidirectional. Even if we leave aside the complexities of Gramsci's philosophy and the political organization it entails, as well as what he calls "the conquest of civil society," there is the theoretical insistence, against Foucault, of a guaranteed insufficiency in the dominant culture against which it is possible to mount an attack. Williams says that "however dominant a social system may be, the very meaning of its domination involves a limitation or selection of the activities it covers, so that by definition it cannot exhaust all social experience, which therefore always potentially contains space for alternative acts and alternative intentions which are not yet articulated as a social institution or even project."[5]

I wouldn't want to conclude simply by appearing to turn these comments and others against Foucault's notions of power. For in fact the great invigoration of his work, in its extremism and its constant savaging of limits and reifications, is its disquieting recollection of what, sometimes explicitly but often implicitly, it leaves out, neglects, circumvents, or displaces. The problematic of the relationship between subjectivity and ideas of justice, for example, or the category of the aesthetic as a negation of power, or of genealogical and critical history as interventionary activities within the network of discourses of knowledge—all these are suggested through a kind of antithetical engagement, by Foucault's imagination of power. But nowhere is this engagement more gripping than in the conflict between Foucault's archaeologies and social change itself, which it must remain for his students, like ourselves on such occasions, to expose and if possible to resolve.

23

The Horizon of R. P. Blackmur

Not an inch measure nor a yard stick, but a compass bearing: the focus of scope, great enough initially to absorb any amount of attention, wide enough eventually, one thinks, to command a full horizon.

—R. P. BLACKMUR

Few things in intellectual or aesthetic life are more unattractive and dispiriting, and yet more common, than the orthodoxy to which a vital and significant performance can be reduced by a programmatic admiration and uncritical codification. Flaubert's *Dictionnaire des idées reçues* is of course the parodic monument to such a fall, but so too on a modest and quotidian level are the definitions, tags, markers employed to theatricalize and grasp the work of critics, particularly those whose writings are perceived as influential. To think of Matthew Arnold and T. S. Eliot, for example, is virtually impossible without getting past a whole set of by now automatic labels like "the best that has been thought and said" or "dissociation of sensibility." The irony, of course, is that such labels give currency to work whose density might otherwise render it unread, although we should also

allow that a direct connection does in fact exist between populariza-
tions of Eliot and Arnold and their intention to make their ideas prevail.

Some usually unstated (or unstatable) balance between critical performance and critical influence can be found at the heart of every
major critic's work. The critic feels, and even intends, the balance,
without being able to say whether it works. This is not just a matter of
empirical verification, of actually trying to ascertain whether readers
find, for example, that insights delivered by a given critic are useful or
practical for them; nor is it a matter of calculated strategy by which the
critic launches a few slogans while also reserving a part of his thought
for really difficult work. Critics write, of course, in order to be read; to
change, refine, or deepen understanding; to press evaluation and revaluation. Yet rare are the critics for whom criticism is its own justification, and not an act for the gaining of adherents or for the persuasion
of larger and larger audiences. Rarer still are critics whose work at its
center cradles the paradox that whatever criticism urges or delivers
must not, indeed cannot, be replicated, reproduced, re-used as a lesson
learned and then applied.

Even among such a tiny minority of critical practitioners R. P.
Blackmur occupies a position of intransigent honor. Not that he does
not teach. Rather what he teaches, or whatever his reader gains access
to, appears to be incidental to the main department of his concern.
His earliest essays in critical explication were exploratory and way-
ward, marked by the frank amateur's enthusiasm, the autodidact's
diligence, the private reader's inwardness. Much of the time he
seemed to locate himself at the source of the poet's creativity, as it deployed forms, idioms, figures to negotiate the disorder of modernity.
Blackmur was especially sensitive to the dangers besetting modern
poetry in an inattentive culture, dangers stemming from a felt incompleteness and lack of support in the environment that drew the
poet (and by implication the critic) to the invention of machinery or
of a system whose job it was to supplement poetry with the rigor, the
stability, the discipline of universal order. Like the early Lukács, such
poets—among them Yeats, Eliot, and Pound—regarded with nostalgia
a lost age of integrated life, thereby condemning themselves in the
present to overcoming what Eliot called "the immense panorama of
futility and anarchy which is contemporary history."[1] This they could

do themselves by providing various therapies for the afflictions of modernity in the form of insights or systems that gave coherence on the one hand, but repelled readers on the other. Blackmur's seminal point of departure therefore was this fact, perceived not as a disability but as an enabling condition of great modern poetry:

> It is almost the mark of the poet of genuine merit in our time—the poet who writes serious works with an intellectual aspect which are nonetheless poetry—that he performs his work in the light of an insight, a group of ideas, and a faith, with the discipline that flows from them, which taken together form a view of life most readers cannot share, and which, furthermore, most readers feel as repugnant, or sterile, or simply inconsequential.[2]

The difficulty the reader experienced with the great moderns resided only partly in the esoteric language, complex homemade schemes, and what Blackmur was later to call the "irregular metaphysics" on which these writers depended; difficulty also derived from the reader's negative reactions to them, which Blackmur was one of the first to recognize as an obstacle purposely designed by the writer. Modernism therefore was like a customs barrier erected to force through the bits of modern life that could be shaped by technique and the symbolic imagination into aesthetic order, and it was also a way to compel readers to pay out parts of their full being as humans in order, perhaps, to gain a new sort of aesthetic insight. This technique worked in odd ways and, as Blackmur was to show in *Language as Gesture,* very often it did not work at all. Yeats expected too much from magic, Hardy from his "ideas," the late Eliot from his Christianity, Stevens from his abstract fictions, and Pound from his "intellectual attitudes."

Unlike Arnold and Eliot, however, Blackmur did not see his role as suited principally to emphasize the modernist writer's failures, and consequently, the reader's feelings of repugnance, sterility, and inconsequence. What he constantly kept referring to instead was the imagination, which, when it was employed to decode modernist instincts, he called the provisional imagination, an energy rather than an organ, as it wrestled with the passage from "life" to "art." Thus, he wrote, "criticism keeps the sound of . . . footsteps live in our reading, so that we understand both the fury in the words and the words themselves."[3] This is one of the many definitions of criticism scattered throughout Blackmur's work; it is typical of them all in that inflections and emphases are on processes, energies, turbulences. Criticism took from modernism the struggle to get matter into language ("getting into" is one of Blackmur's most frequent idioms), although it was of course the critic's job to do the work over, and to see whether or not life actually made it into art, how much was exacted by technique and aesthetic ingenuity, how little or how much that was necessarily left out could be recalled, or at least felt, in what poetic language delivered.

No one who has read Blackmur will fail to be impressed by how hard he worked at giving his chosen writers their due. He is without question the finest, the most patient and resourceful explicator of difficult literature produced in mid-twentieth-century America; he ranks with such differently virtuosic European readers as William Empson and Georges Poulet, although unlike them he is not deflected into the antinomian stabilities provided even by categories like "ambiguity" or "human time." For all his sporty quirkiness Blackmur took seriously the central polarity of nineteenth- and twentieth-century high culture, the one theme that provided continuity for him from romanticism up through modernism: the relationship between "Life" and "Art." Because he saw the relationship between this pair of terms as encompassing every possibility from opposition to absolute correspondence, he read poetry, fiction, and criticism as processes giving provisional resolution to the differences and similarities between art and life. Criticism for him therefore dramatized and re-performed the mediations by which art and the symbolic imagination actualized life, but of its very nature criticism also undermined itself. It did not define ideas, taste, and values so much as it set them back into the Moha, "the vital, fundamental stupidity of the human race,"[4] from which as art or as Numen they then emerged. Criticism is best seen as a provisional act, as perhaps even a temporary deformation of and deflection from literature, which itself is approximate, tentative, irresolute. "Literature," Blackmur writes in the title essay of *The Lion and the Honeycomb*, "is one of our skills of notation of the incarnation of the real into the actual."[5]

The consistency of Blackmur's criticism is that from the beginning to the end of his career he read literature as secular incarnation, a word he used frequently to represent the powers of life to reappear in art, or, as he spoke of it in reference to *Anna Karenina,* "the bodying forth in aesthetic form by contrasted human spirits of 'the terrible ambiguity of an immediate experience.'"[6]

It was enough for him to take stock of literary actuality—incarnating, realizing the real, whether that was society, culture, the unconscious human behavior. Beyond that, he said, "the mind acknowledges that the force behind art exists outside art, and also that the work of art itself almost gets outside art to make a shape—a form of the forms—of our total recognition of the force that moves us."[7]

The deliberateness of Blackmur's language, its studied *lenti* and detours should not, however, obscure its remarkable generalities, its frequently imprecise terminology, its plainly impressionistic dependence on the vocabulary of theology and mysticism. In Blackmur, there is a surprising concordance between the great technical proficiency in deciphering modernism, and the lesser homegrown (because random and unpredictable) bourgeois humanism in a churchyard. It is as if the idiom of I. A. Richards were constantly being drawn back toward, and then soaked in, the subjectivity of Montaigne, amplified by, say, what could be imputed to such differently Christian writers as Dante and Maritain. Blackmur's terms allusively map a field, however; they do not hold down things, or territories. He speaks of soul, spirit, art, artist, society, and life, with familiarity, not with the decorum of a trained cleric. Then, suddenly, he moves into the verse of a finely calibrated poet like Marianne Moore in order to register with astonishing precision the nature of her actuality, as it gets formulated in a line: "She resorts, or rises like a fish, continually to the said thing, captures it, sets it apart, points and polishes it to bring out just the special quality she heard in it. Much of her verse has the peculiar, unassignable, indestructible authority of speech overheard—which often means so much precisely because we do not know what was its limiting, and dulling, context."[8]

This combination of precision and allusiveness, of relentless poetic accuracy and often sloppy soul-mongering, is, I think, of the very essence of Blackmur's genius. He should be read as constantly reinscribing his fidelity to the discipline and the impurity of serious intellectual work, in which one eye is kept on a repeatedly invaded and turbulent world, while the other eye follows the processes of aesthetic composition with an unswerving interest in its redemptive and extraworldly ambitions. The result is a criticism whose "labor is to recapture the imaginative burden and to avoid the literal like death."[9]

Not surprisingly then, Blackmur is the least influential, the least doctrinal, the least serviceable (in the base sense of the word) of the New Critics, a group of eminent interpreters with whom he has always been associated. Conversely, no one of them—not Ransom, nor Tate—had his range or anything like his power. His intellectual world was as much European, classical, and metropolitan as Erich Auerbach's or T. S. Eliot's, but without Auerbach's narrative and relational explicitness or his capacity by training and conviction to enact philological presentations like *Mimesis,* and without Eliot's conservative sense of tradition or his austere canonizations of European monuments. The point to be made here is that unlike all the other New Critics Blackmur *could* make use of Auerbach and Eliot in ways that emphasized either their wildness or their interesting shortcomings, despite their weighty authority. He sensed in Eliot's work its unappeasable restlessness, which ran directly counter to its Anglo-Catholic proclamations; in Auerbach's readings of Pascal and Flaubert he commended the man's fine erudition and his account of the *topoi,* by which these authors placed life into literature, even as Auerbach gave "too little credit to the actual material that got into the work with their aid." What Auerbach forgot, according to Blackmur, is

> that every writer who survives is constantly wrestling with a burden of actual experience by no means amenable to anything but disposition (disponibleness) by the method. Thus he [Auerbach] not only missed but denied the wrestling, swindling authority of life itself, apart from all categories, in the series of images that lead to the whiff of all human ill in Emma's soul—a whiff looking out its home in the smoking stove, creaking door, sweating walls, damp floor, and above all in the odor of the food; and missed, too, our chance at that whiff

while Emma pecks at the hazel nuts or marks on the oil cloth—
those creases that come and go—with her knife. No; for him it
is *bêtise à la bête*, with a further cruel judgment in Flaubert's
style. That was Auerbach's; and it is true that he has made it
present; it must be taken account of.[10]

The return to a generous assessment of the great *Philolog* at the end
of this otherwise critical passage is characteristic of Blackmur, as
much his style as the impressive appeal in what precedes it to the
minute details of everyday life so grindingly actual in Flaubert's
prose. (It is worth mentioning that Emma's tongue reaching deep
into the bottom of the glass from which she licks the very last drop is
one of the recurring motifs in Blackmur's criticism: it signifies "a
touch of the actual" used by the major artists to "put in" and to "leave
out" just enough of instinct and institutions in the representations of
reality.)[11] But the closer we look at Blackmur's work the more we shall
find that back-and-forth restlessness, that oscillating and shuttling
between text and reality which, in his one major attempt at a theory
of literature, he called "between the Numen and the Moha," that
transforms his work from the mere explication, to the *performance*, of
literature. Wherever Blackmur finds a reification, a hard definition, a
system, a strident tone, an overly busy label, a conception forced into
overwork, a scheme running on by itself, there he methodically introduces the "uncontrollable mystery on the bestial floor." To the claims
of Auerbach's seminar, given at Princeton in 1949, there was opposed
not only Flaubert's stubbornly middle-class Emma imported by
Blackmur into the discussion so as to provoke Auerbach, but also the
presence of Ernst Robert Curtius, hardly less trained and formal than
the author of *Mimesis*, but a man who was "relative to Auerbach, a
deep anarch of the actual. Every blow he struck at Auerbach was
meant to break down the formulas whereby we see how unlike things
are like. . . . He understands why it is that the textbooks *must be wrong*:
because they are designed to take care of the reading we do not do: a
legitimate enterprise when provisional, fatal when permanent. . . . It
seemed to me, then, that Curtius was potentially always on the verge
of breaking through into Emma's life itself, or into the moving subject or locus of literature."[12]

As in so many other places in his criticism, Blackmur here outdistances anything we might still recognize as New Criticism. There are not only the concerns about "life" and worldliness, but the tense impatience with any attitude that does not see literature—no matter how well-wrought, how much "itself"—as poised uneasily between anarchy and form. Moreover Blackmur was concerned not just with literature but with the nature of the aesthetic; a true theorist of art, his interests and instruments were theoretical, cultural, social, even political, all of which have appeared to me to be quite unconnected with the comparatively modest, even tight world of New Critical ideology. In trying to understand Blackmur as someone interested in the "moving subject or locus of literature," we should remember that he intended criticism to be as quick, as moving, as theoretical (in the Crocean sense), and as nomadic as literature itself, at the same time that it retained a "tory" cast of form and perceivable order.

Let us now examine the historical and intellectual conjuncture that seemed misleadingly to have aligned Blackmur with the New Criticism, and then let us reappraise his place in American criticism as it appears two decades after his death. Then, finally, we can go on to discuss Blackmur's significance as perhaps the greatest of native American critics produced in the first half of the twentieth century, and certainly one of the very greatest anywhere in the contemporary West.

Blackmur's oddities of background and manner have been noted often enough: they require only the very briefest of rehearsals here. With the exception of Kenneth Burke, Blackmur had the least dependence on formal education of any of his contemporaries who wrote what we might call "high" as opposed to journalistic or popular criticism. This is not only because, obviously enough, he had no formal university training, but because he resolutely made no effort to compensate for that fact. None of his work pretends to scholarly completeness or to exhaustiveness, at the same time that it is both learned and openly grateful to the best that scholarship has to offer. Neither did Blackmur use the word "academic" to stand in for expressions of contempt or dismissal. On the other hand, immediately after he came to Princeton in 1940, he did learn how to exploit the academic world with great success.

Clearly he did not fit easily or comfortably in an academic Department of English, but that is where for the longest part of his intellectual life he functioned, and it is there that he must be evaluated.

What distinguishes Blackmur's style from the very beginning, well before he became a university academic, was the freedom and errantry of his explorations of literature. Biography certainly mattered very little in his critical apparatus, except when he studied Henry Adams; then it mattered too much. Although Blackmur generally focused on the literary text, he was strikingly different from Brooks, Warren, Tate, and Ransom in that he wandered very far afield from it. As we shall see presently, midway through his career he became much more of an intellectual, in the Sartrean or Gramscian sense of the term, than any of the New Critics. Yet he seems to have only guardedly admired Lionel Trilling, and in his consideration of *The Liberal Imagination* had much to criticize in Trilling's elevation of "mind" and "intellect" as models for, and contents of, literature. Trilling, Blackmur said, was too much indebted to Arnold and Freud, "masters" of extremism and power. In his concern with society, power, and mind as regulators of literature, Trilling, according to Blackmur, disregarded "the true business of literature, as of all intellect, critical or creative, which is to remind the powers that be, simple or corrupt as they are, of the turbulence they have to control. There is a disorder vital to the individual which is fatal to society."[13] And this criticism is levied much more harshly against Irving Babbitt's Humanism, a doctrine that made for itself "a mind that was restricted to general ideas, and general ideas that could not refresh themselves, such was the severity of their order in the monkish sense, in the fount of disorder."[14]

As against the official learning and disciplinary rigor either of scholarship or of the committed intellectual, Blackmur occasionally offered a sometimes uninspired blend of turbulent, unfocused, and badly misappropriated doctrine, drawn seemingly at random from his recent reading. Blackmur's slips—there are a fair number of them—cannot be overlooked, because they do really count as signs of the daring logic that governs his overall performance. His rehash of Coleridge and Aristotle towards the end of the essay "The Lion and the Honeycomb" has in it much of the sliding and slipping of someone unable to do much with a general idea like "crisis" ("Turning," Blackmur writes, "is

a kind of decision. *Crisis* is the intellectual act, *and* its occasion, of decision")[15] and equally unable to move from general to specific because he
refuses to let traditions of scholarly argument and intellectual sequence
support him. Consider the following passage from this essay as an example of what I mean, and note how his handling of general ideas falls
either into unconvincing repetitions of what he had said much better
elsewhere, or into the jarring irrelevance of some ridiculously trivial observation that does not help matters at all:

> Mimesis, I take it, is the mind's action, and there is no question
> that, richly understood, any single full mimesis operates in
> deep, but widely variable relation to poetics, dialectic, and
> rhetoric. For myself, I see a sequence or relation whereby the
> mimetic act is the incarnation into actuality of what we can
> grasp of reality; which is the reason why we pay enormous
> salaries and devotion in Hollywood and why in my boyhood
> Bernhardt was the divine Sarah, and which is also a good part
> of the reason for the lasting power—and greatness—of great lit-
> erature.[16]

What remains of this flailing and clutching, however, is the reaching
out and crossing over and, underneath that, the rhythms of chancy investigation governed by Blackmur's finely responsive sense of "the
moving subject or locus of literature." Here, as I said, the effort doesn't
work, but elsewhere it does. Thus if for Blackmur literature was about
movement, if the place of literature was not restricted to a fixed spot
(or *topos*), then it behooved the critic somehow to remain attuned to
that fact, to describe literary experience as a zone rather than as an
inert place—above all, not to remain bound or in any serious way inhibited by the barriers and protocols of academic or literary specialization. Even so, the field was not an open one to Blackmur; he had to
take stock of what styles of writing on literature already existed so that
he could then go on to devise his own mode.

We must try to recall, I think, what Blackmur was offered as a set of
models for writing criticism, most of which he refused. There was first
the academic scholarship produced by the universities; this entailed
editing, textual criticism, historical periodization and, when it was
done as brilliantly as it was by Livingstone Lowes, important studies of

influence and reference. Second, there was the style of criticism perfected by Edmund Wilson, a form of literary portraiture indebted to Sainte-Beuve, versatile, journalistic in its directness and address to the reader, serious and engaging at the same time. This seemed not to have interested Blackmur, probably because narrative lay at its heart, and narrative gave Blackmur very little leeway for the exfoliation of impressions and musings. Third, there was also the nationalistic historiography underpinning the criticism written by Van Wyck Brooks, and this was too programmatic and tense for Blackmur's much more leisurely mode; like the New Critics—and this is why he has always been lumped together with them—he avoided the explicit teleological moralizing that drove Brooks's and Parrington's "ages" of American literature, preferring instead to concentrate on texts. My conjecture is that Blackmur's neglect of F. O. Matthiessen and Perry Miller is traceable back to his discomfort with the earlier generation of tendentious Americanists, although I am certain that had he more carefully read the newer generation he would have favorably noted the difference.

As for the criticism associated with *Partisan Review* or with the New York intellectuals, as they have been called, Blackmur's treatment of Trilling, respectful and interested as it is, nevertheless stands for the larger impatience he had with a critical mode that operated on what he seems to have considered to be the principle of authorization, which took one back all-too-dutifully to Freud, Arnold, Marx, and other critical masters for validation and accreditation. Some of this impatience is much more pronounced in Blackmur's pawing of Granville Hicks, not as formidable or polished an intellect as Trilling, but seen as a representative of politicizations of criticism that were disabling in Blackmur's eyes. Perhaps it is for that reason that Blackmur's avoidance of the English critical scene (always excepting Richards, Eliot, and Empson) is so total; neither Leavis, nor the Bloomsbury group, nor individualistic practitioners like Read and Aldington figure in his mature work at all.

On the other hand it would be too simple to say condescendingly that Blackmur's work is merely provincial; his provinciality was altogether too interesting and self-conscious to be dismissed. He was certainly more aware of European literature than all the above critics except Trilling and Wilson, even if like all of them he was completely unaware of the major schools of twentieth-century Western Marxism, some members of whom, like the early Lukács, Ernst Bloch, Benjamin, and Adorno, he would certainly have found suggestive for their path-breaking aesthetic criticism. Likewise he seemed to have had little working knowledge of French philosophical criticism (the *Nouvelle Revue Française* school, Bachelard, Ramon Fernandez), although I recall from my student days at Princeton the respectful references he made to Marcel Raymond, which were to turn up later in "Anni Mirabiles" (reprinted in *A Primer of Ignorance*); similarly he spoke admiringly of the early Erich Heller.

I mention these gaps and lapses as a way of underlining how thoroughly Blackmur tried to cultivate his own special manner, which he grounded in a kind of studied provinciality, methodically eccentric and outside the main vehicles of critical expression available to him in America during the thirties. His early *Hound and Horn* essays seem to come from direct encounters with poets whose bewildering discontinuity with predecessors is their first characteristic; Blackmur registers their startling achievements without many predispositions except the willingness to be surprised and to follow them, sometimes playfully and at other times sternly, wherever their vocabulary and rhythms take them. More than any other critic in English (more than Eliot, Richards, or Empson, more than the Southern Fugitives) Blackmur's critical *askesis* was to shed as much as possible of his ideological or philosophical beliefs in order to concentrate on poetry as language, not as belief, vision of the world, or truths—which, as I said above, he also studies, but as interferences in poetry. In this view he anticipates some critical attitudes of the 1960s. Hence of course the attractive originality of his voice, and the large spaces created in his essays for patient interpretation and sometimes ingenious speculation. This is the explicative trend or movement embodied by *Language and Gesture*.

Although it contains essays from as early as the thirties, *The Lion and the Honeycomb* (1955) strikes me as opening out Blackmur's critical practice very dramatically. I am not speaking here of a development tied to a later chronological moment in Blackmur's career, but rather to a quite marked attempt occurring right across his work to expand his horizon. Nevertheless one should mention some important events that bear directly on this development in Blackmur's work. First of course is his affiliation with Princeton, which dated from the early forties. A major university thus enabled him to tap its resources, and from it to move out into the world of institutions. Second, is the centrality to him of European modernism as a coherent movement, embodying a set of ideals, a canon of works, and a series of references that predominate in his writing henceforward. Joyce, Mann, Eliot, Yeats, Gide, Pound, Faulkner, Stevens, Kafka are the main figures (except for Rilke, Baudelaire, and Lorca, the absence of major Continental poets is puzzling), and with them came philosophers like Jacques Maritain and Benedetto Croce. Blackmur's major statement on modernism, surprisingly minus an extended consideration of Proust, was formulated in the set of four Library of Congress lectures, "Anni Mirabiles, 1921–25," which remains, I believe, the most sophisticated and brilliant of all the many critical works on modernism, far in advance of its time, dazzling in its close analysis as well as in its general adumbration of the limitations on the artist's role in modern society.

Inevitably, the work on modernism led him back into the nineteenth century to study and write about the great realistic novelists—Flaubert, Dostoevsky, Tolstoy, Stendhal, Melville, Henry James. Some of this work emanated, I believe, from his teaching at Princeton, where I can recall that on occasion he gave public talks, or class lectures as a visitor in various courses taught by colleagues. (One in particular was a bravura and densely associative lecture on *Humphry Clinker,* in which Blackmur's leitmotif was Smollett's predilection for smells!) This communal aspect of his work indicates a much larger concern of Blackmur's years immediately following the end of World War Two, his role as a quasi-public, or in Gramsci's sense an organic, intellectual, involved in the life of society at a fairly high level of integration with it. This is the third important "event," or new bearing, in his critical thought, and since it is quite evident in *The Lion and the Honeycomb,* we should look at it a bit more closely.

The recent publication of Robert Fitzgerald's *Enlarging the Change: The Princeton Seminars in Criticism, 1949–51* provides us retrospectively with the first sustained opportunity to see Blackmur at work as a cultural intellectual. The impressive thing about Fitzgerald's memoir is how in it Blackmur seems to have situated himself at a number of extremely interesting intersections. He was crucially engaged with the early history of the Princeton Institute for Advanced Study, and instrumental in getting Robert Oppenheimer to consider a program in the humanities for the Institute; this was a direct consequence of Blackmur's institutional presence at the University. Secondly, Blackmur was really one of the pioneers in devising an interesting (as opposed to a dead) cultural space to absorb the unhoused energies of that great generation of refugee European philologists that included Auerbach and Curtius. He seems to have sensed—perhaps because of the vantage of his own lack of formal university training—what a formidable background in tradition and learning these refugees carried with them, and how it was imperative in postwar America to give them a direct and appropriate role in intellectual life here. Thirdly, and most importantly, he seems almost instinctively to have understood that the tradition of European bourgeois humanism could not be accommodated to conventional academic demarcations in America, and that an extradisciplinary venue, enabled by foundations and corporations, would be best for acculturating this still lively tradition in the United States. Hence the seminar format, which was later to be institutionalized at Princeton University as the Christian Gauss Seminars in Criticism, certainly the most impressive of such series carried on at an American university.

In all of this Blackmur was the moving figure, helped by his fortunate association with John Marshall of the munificent Rockefeller Foundation. But I do not think that Blackmur's role was mainly entrepreneurial. In saying that culturally and theoretically speaking he stood at a number of intellectual as well as institutional intersections, we are, I think, much closer to a description of his actual role, precisely because his own critical *praxis* had already chosen for itself a sectoral or zonal attitude towards literature and culture. Later, I shall speak of how his attitude derived from, and remained perfectly congruent with, his lifelong commitment to the essay. He had situated himself in a relatively independent position to be able to study literary texts as constantly moving in and charting a novel space between history, society, and the author, a space whose verbal actuality or incarnation was paradoxically both an extension of the real, and a powerfully constituted defense against it. His model for such a critical attitude was Henry James, whose executive powers as a creative writer were matched in their own intellectually distinct form by his critical faculties, as those were exercised most effectively by the public interpretation of his own novels. Blackmur's statement in *The Lion and the Honeycomb* that James's Prefaces were "the most sustained and I think the most eloquent and original piece of literary criticism in existence"[17] was originally made in 1934, but if we try speculatively to reconstruct a rationale for including so exuberant a claim for the Prefaces in a 1955 collection of his essays, we might learn a good deal about the older Blackmur who was developing the Princeton seminars.

In James's asseverations of the novel's value (as an emanation out of its author's "prime sensibility" and its corresponding ability to develop its own moral sense out of its form) Blackmur found statements that offered James a chance to declare his own genius as novelist, and, no less important, "to explain the serious and critical devotion with which he made his Prefaces *a vademecum*—both for himself as the solace of achievement, and for others as a guide and exemplification."[18] Although James did not share Melville's failure as a novelist who relied on imputation from the outside rather than rendering from the inside, he was nevertheless, like his predecessor, an American writer confronting a world of cultural forms fundamentally alien to the new and overburdened sensibility. James's success in the writing of fiction and of a criticism adequate to his practice as a novelist depended on his conception of "underlying form," which gave art its "deep-breathing economy" and its organic texture.[19] This achievement, Blackmur points out, occurs at a time when the "disestablishment of culture" was fully accomplished, and this in turn obligates the artist to the duty of "creating consciousness" laden down with the massive weight of that "whole cultural establishment" no longer carried by social institutions.

America, however, was still tied to Europe, although much sooner than Europe it had moved towards that "formless" mass society in which "the disinheritance but not the disappearance of the individual" had already taken place. How then to accommodate the past, Europe, culture, and the present in an actuality which had at its disposal only consciousness for such a task? Such a dilemma was further underscored by the extreme urgency with which James treated the question of form in the novel. Consequently, Blackmur's consideration of James stressed the relationship between consciousness and form as a social, and not

just an aesthetic, issue. Is there any way, Blackmur says, that we can conceive of how "things are held together in a living way, with the sense of
life going on," now that "there is no longer any establishment, no longer
any formula, and we like to say only vestigial forms, to call on outside of
ourselves?"[20]

I would suggest that this way of phrasing James's predicament is
also the central question of Blackmur's later work. As he articulates
this quandary one can see how Blackmur's reflections on the problem
were a way of linking his actual condition in America—as a teacher,
critic, and cultural force at Princeton right after World War Two—with
his worldly as well as imagined role as an intellectual who has no close
political or social affiliations to carry him along but who nevertheless
feels himself committed to a position of authority and a site of privileged intensity as an heir of the ages. I do not intend any irony here.
Blackmur's postwar criticism is I believe directly tied to a sense of
American responsibility for the world after the dismantling of the old
imperial structures. This sense fueled his most extraordinary essays,
and, alas, the astonishing ignorance and condescension about the
non-Western world in his worst ones. It allowed little or no sympathy
for the problems faced by the new postcolonial states of Africa and
Asia (quite the contrary, as a reading of the first essay in *The Lion and
the Honeycomb*, "Towards a Modus Vivendi," quickly reveals), and it
seems to have blinded him completely to the possibility that Europe's
(and America's) colonial role in the peripheral world was not always up
to the claims of Greco-Roman civilization. But, much more important
for our purposes here, the seriously mulled-over problems of the new
and relatively isolated consciousness impinged on Blackmur's work so
strongly as to enliven his criticism with a skepticism and experimental
alertness that prefigured all the tremendous theoretical changes that
were to occur in American criticism in the decade following his death
in 1965.

So long as Blackmur wrote and acted then, the imperialism latent
in his sense of the American creation of a new consciousness was constantly held back, undercut, reduced by radical doubt and by theoretical self-consciousness. All his portraits of intellectuals and artists in
the world are either morose, severely judgmental, or downright pessimistic: his lifelong fascination with Henry Adams is the strongest

case in point. Unlike Kenneth Burke or the younger but still contemporary Northrop Frye, Blackmur devised no cosmic schemes, had no centralizing or, as the current expression has it, totalizing vision, no completely useful methodological apparatus. "The prescriptive *mortmain*" of codifications of insight were, he thought, especially to be wary of; it is the case now, he said, that there is a "hardening of the mind into a set of unrelated methodologies without the controlling advantage of a fixed body of knowledge, a fixed faith, or a fixed purpose."[21] The created consciousness—his as well as James's—was not really a substitute for fixed knowledge, faith, or purpose, since consciousness was condemned to perceptions and re-perceptions of its vulnerability, its historical situation, and its lucid partiality. Instead of doctrine and fixed method there was a pliant and constantly mobile awareness of the "tory anarchy" provided by art and culture, and in the public sphere, a more complete sense of humanism—without orthodoxy or imposable dogma—than official Humanism allowed:

> The true business of Humanism, since it works from intellectual bias in even its most imaginative moments, and since it takes for itself the function of mediation, is to mediate the ravenings of the intellect; to feel the intellect as elastic, plastic, and absorptive; to feel the experience on which the intellect works as ambiguous, present only provisionally, impinging, vanishing, above and below, known far beyond its own mere grasp; and thus to restore to the intellect its proper sense of strength and weakness in necessity, that in setting up its orders and formulas of order, it is coping with disorder. It should remember that an order is not invalidated by disorder; and that if an order is to become imaginative it must be so conceived as to accommodate disorder, and indeed to desire to do so, to stretch itself constantly to the point where it can envisage the disorder which its order merely names.[22]

Right at the heart of this magnificent passage is the difficult relationship between intellect (one of the forms of consciousness) and experience, in which both parties are in motion, both dependent upon ambiguity, provisionality, opposition. I do not think it is wrong to speak of the form of this apprehension of intellect and experience as fundamentally *theoretical,* in that Blackmur's own subjectivity points away from the restraints and limitations of ego to a zone of activity not empirical or "real" but actual, that is, theoretically possible, and as he was to say in "Anni Mirabiles," "radically imperfect." Thus—here Blackmur fully anticipates that astute combination of assertive reach and deconstructive skepticism basic to twentieth-century theoretical irony from Lukács to Derrida—"each of the modes of the mind avows imperfection by making assertions about its intentions which it neither expresses nor communicates except by convention."[23] And since conventions are recognizably conventional they cannot communicate except by the indirections of the formal, which does no more than "define" (the quotation marks of suppressed doubt are added by Blackmur himself) the indefinable.

The net effect of Blackmur's later work therefore is, I think, that of a negative dialectic, a process by which the stabilities and continuities of twentieth-century capitalism are de-defined, worn back down by a difficult, dissolving prose to the instability which the forms of art, intellect, and society had resorted to when in the first instance they tried to give permanence and shape to their apprehension. The will to explication in his late essays was regularly being displaced by the energies of writing, a disorderly tumble of rhythms unaccommodated by "points," sequential arguments, or narratable reason, morality, or purpose. Blackmur, in short, cannot easily or correctly be reclaimed for traditional humanism, as in a sense the New Critics could be, and he cannot accurately be made to serve the interests of a new institutional or bureaucratic order, as his eccentric affiliations with the academy, the foundations, and the publishing industry might suggest. Is it possible, however, more exactly to describe Blackmur's critical achievements without compromising him more than is absolutely necessary?

The essay form expresses discomposure and incompleteness; its meditative scope is often qualified by the essay's occasional nature (critical essays, after all, are occasioned by an outside event, a book, or a painting); most essays reach back towards the fragment, or the aphorism, rarely towards the book or the treatise. "The essay," says Adorno, "is the critical form par excellence . . . and if the essay is accused of lacking a standpoint and of tending toward relativism because it recognizes no standpoint lying outside itself, then the accusation implicitly contains the conception of truth as something 'ready made,' a hierarchy of concepts." Thus, Adorno continues, the essay is entangled in "un-truth"; moreover,

> the relevance of the essay is that of anachronism. The hour is more unfavorable to it than ever. It is being crushed between an organized science, on the one side, in which everyone presumes to control everyone and everything else, and which excludes, with the sanctimonious praise of "intuitive" or "stimulating," anything that does not conform to the status quo; and, on the other side, by a philosophy that makes do with the empty and abstract residues left aside by the scientific apparatus, residues which then become for philosophy the objects of second-degree operations.[24]

Denis Donoghue is absolutely right to note Blackmur's attachment to the essay's "congenial space," and then to connect that fact with his inability ever to finish his book on Henry Adams.[25] There was something about the definitive closure and size of books that inhibited Blackmur's genius, kept him instead to the smaller, more constitutively open form of the essay. Adorno's comments about the essay form further illuminate Blackmur's quandary, I think. As he meditated the anxious Adams he found himself face to face with the problem of commensuration, of adequacy, synchronization, and congruence: in Henry Adams he beheld the case of a man whose attempts at narrative raised the primal difficulty of all narrativization, which is how to make narrative fit the material at hand, how to make the narrative correspond with history, energy with mind, the individual with society, temporality with sequence. Every encounter with Henry Adams thrust the problem of congruence—of making things fit with each other—to the fore, and this in turn highlighted the tentative nature of Blackmur's own essay, or attempt, to grasp Adams's problem in an adequate form. No ready-made concepts or hierarchies really work in the essay, just as they seemed not to have worked for Adams. And with the apparent consolidation of science and philosophy on either side of Adams, his efforts—like Blackmur's own to understand Adams—seemed anachronistic.

I said earlier that one of Blackmur's themes in his explications of modernism was that necessary effort on the part of readers to employ their "provisional imaginations" as they encountered the often arbitrary and overworked constructs of the great modernists. These great writers furnished the main material for Blackmur's work as he read the contemporary iconology of a post-religious age. I also said that we can distinguish two broad trends in Blackmur's work that are symbolized on the one hand by the explicative and patiently interpretive essays of *Language as Gesture,* and on the other hand by the frankly speculative and theoretically administrative essays of *The Lion and the Honeycomb* and its later companion *A Primer of Ignorance.* (*Eleven Essays in the European Novel* is, in a sense, a synthesis of both trends.) In both instances of course Blackmur's work is congruent with and indistinguishable from the essay form. As we can now survey the whole of Blackmur's writing from the vantage point of the 1980s, after the advent and relative decline of literary theory, the slow emergence of cultural critique, the development of various comparative and contrapuntal approaches to the study of literature in society, we can see with a particular intensity how all the structures of art are either renewed and invigorated by acts of the symbolic imagination or ossified and reduced by the various executive commodifications of the administrative attitude. To have made his readers so extraordinarily aware of these possibilities is a great achievement in itself: but Blackmur did more than that, I think.

In his writing, the critical act itself was not curtained off behind the Archimedean privilege of outside or disinterested judgment. Rather, criticism itself was shown to belong to the very same class as those other activities in which various sorts of constructs, various kinds of released energy, and various brands of dogma were probable consequences of the human imagination acting in alliance with consciousness. To recognize this about Blackmur's criticism is to acknowledge a third, and possibly more elusive and difficult moment in his work, the act of self-criticism which is carefully lodged in and to some degree screened by his analyses not only of Henry Adams, but of those figures like T. E. Lawrence and Swift whom he called "the least abiding writers of magnitude in English." These figures interest Blackmur because in them, he says, "distraught endurance"—the will to go on and on—is not deflected into the positive presence of organizing structures (as in *Ulysses* or *The Magic Mountain*), but is converted by imagination "into a vice and makes stoicism, as Henry Adams called it, a form of moral suicide." How this is done is described by Blackmur in one of the great and, I would suggest, one of the central passages in his work. The following lines should be read not only as a description of T. E. Lawrence but also as a deliberately negative foil for the massive efforts at construction and moral judgment that lie at the heart of the modernist project as it shores up art against ruin. In assessing Lawrence's "only basic" failure to mobilize conviction into "character," in identifying the man's relentless ability to let "the towers of imagination fling up . . . out of quicksand, and stand, firm in light and air," Blackmur was also characterizing that other subterranean, or at least unacknowledged, component of modernism's enormously profitable structures, a component whose service the critic, if he was really to be a critic, uniquely required. This was the dislocating faculty by which criticism "removes the acceptance" of the organizing structures of aestheticized experience, as modernism had employed them, and "leaves the predicament bare":

> In this respect—in this type of sensibility—imagination operates analogously to religion upon the world which both deny; only, if as in Lawrence, the imagination be without religion, the balance of heaven is lacking, the picture projected is incomplete and in an ultimate sense fails of responsibility. It is thus, I think, that we get from Lawrence a sense of unsatisfied excitement, inadequate despair, and the blank extreme of shock. But it is excitement, is despair, is shock; made actual; disturbing us: finding room within us in our own tiding disorder. On the imaginative level, perhaps on the moral level—or on any except the social—order is only a predicament accepted. It is the strength of an imagination like Lawrence's that it removes the acceptance and leaves the predicament bare. The weakness, which is basic only, lies in the absence of any effective anterior conviction to supply a standard of disclosure; and there, it is suggested, is the limitation, chiefly as a dislocated but dominant emotion throughout Lawrence's work.[26]

According to the terms of this description, however, Lawrence could not be transformed into a lesson, a theory, or an example to be applied elsewhere. If the absence of anterior conviction meant anything it was as criticism of the projected, completed, and responsible picture underwriting the "abiding" art of modernism, whose earlier anticipations were the monumental designs of Tolstoy, Flaubert, and Stendhal. And this more radical impulse at the degree zero of writing bore the critic along too, who makes room to speak to us "in our own tiding disorder." Yet, like Lawrence, the critic finds and re-finds the "ultimate inadequacy" that is the result, according to Blackmur, of "the everlasting effort" to write. The startlingly contemporary quality of this formulation is further intensified when we also realize that Blackmur acquires it at exactly the same juncture from which, looking towards art, he perceives, and then refuses, the distant satisfactions of an abiding aesthetic order.

Had this ascetic vantage point been fixed by Blackmur into a position, perspective, or program we might now be reading him only for the results such a critical stance could have permitted him to deliver in one text after another. That he seems to have suspected how dry and predictable the set of readings might be that would result from a reification of his radical and essayistic critical mobility, is perhaps another extraordinary anticipation in his work that even the disciplined skepticism of post-modernist theory can be grooved like a boring train ride into the essay's brief scope and the disenchantments from which its form springs. He seems to have preferred a different regimen altogether, that of criticism as performance, responsive to shifting circumstances, uncertain of its conclusions, prepared always to be solitary and self-limiting, without influence or disciples.[27] To say of such a criticism that it displaced itself from a position of authority to a "focus of scope," is to get some sense of how wide was the horizon of Blackmur's work, and how potentially it can enlarge every critic's scope just to read and engage with his gestures.

24

Cairo Recalled:
Growing Up in the Cultural Crosscurrents of 1940s Egypt

"Since Cairo," I have often said to my mother, "since Cairo" being for both of us the major demarcation in my life and, I believe, in hers. We gave up Cairo in 1963 as a family resident in it for three decades, two parents and their five children, although I had already made my last visit there in 1960; it was fifteen years before I returned as a melancholy tourist who stayed in a Cairo hotel for the first time in his life. A second visit in 1977 might have been to any large third-world city, so sprawling and demographically uncontrolled had Cairo become, its services crippled, its immense mass so dusty and crumbling. I stayed for five days, too unhappy and too sick at heart to last any longer. I left. I had no wish to return, but of course have.

Part of the city's hold over my memory was the clearness of its nearly incredible divisions, divisions almost completely obliterated by Gamal Abdel Nasser when in 1952 he and his free officers overthrew the grotesque reign of King Farouk and assumed power. Nasser made Cairo into what it had principally always been: *the* Arab and Islamic metropolis par excellence. Cairo in Arabic is *al-Qāhira* (the city victorious). While I was growing up in it in the 1940s, a decade earlier, however, its Arab and Islamic dimensions could be ignored and even suppressed, so strong was the hold over the city of various European interests, each of which created an enclave within all the others. Thus there was, of course, British Cairo, whose center was the embassy in Garden City and whose extensions covered academic, juridical, military, commercial, and recreational activities. French Cairo was there too, a useful foil and opposition for its historic colonial competitor, found in schools, salons, theaters, ateliers.

So malleable did the city seem, so open to expatriate colonies existing in separate structures at its heart that there was a Belgian, an Italian, a Jewish, a Greek, an American, and a Syrian Cairo, lesser spheres all of them, each dependent on all the others, each manipulated or indulged by the major colonial power. American Cairo was limited in our awareness to the American University—a minor version of its counterpart in Beirut—the Mission, a mixture of Presbyterian, Baptist, and Evangelical clerics with solid outposts in the form of a church at Ezbekiah (opposite Shepheard's Hotel, a region that also contained the city's well-known red-light district), and in Upper Egypt a school and mission office in the town of Assiut.

We lived about two blocks from the fabled Gezira Club, on an island in the Nile called either Gezira (the Arabic word for island) or Zamalek. The club itself was an enchanted place, quite unlike any sports or country club I've seen anywhere else. It was carved out of the island's center, a pure creation of the colonial imagination: there were polo fields, cricket pitches, a racetrack, football fields, and bowling greens, all grass, all perfectly tended by armies of gardeners whose intensive labors kept the club at a level of beauty and calm designed to reproduce someone's idea of a vast and noble meadow basking in the sun of an English summer's day. In addition, twenty or so squash courts, at least forty red-clay tennis courts, a magnificent pool with a Lido area, a large clubhouse, and gardens made the Gezira, as it was known, a perfect place for sports and meetings, insulated from the outside world of fellahin, bustling casbahs, and generally tiresome realities. White was the prevailing color of dress, and the dozens of dressing-room attendants, suffragis, and "boys" quietly fulfilled the members' requirements of service and smilingly unobtrusive compliance.

At the Gezira one felt English and hence orderly, perhaps even superior. Only the upper ranks in the British army were permitted entry, as were diplomats, wealthy foreign businessmen, and a handful of Egyptian aristocrats. The Gezira encouraged me, I remember, to feel that the logic of the place and what it stood for overruled what to me seemed like the unforgivable messiness of my true reality. Only in *that* Cairo, at that time, could my family and I have made sense, with our carefully subdivided existence and absurdly protected minority status.

Both my parents were Palestinian and Protestant, he from Jerusalem, she from Nazareth. My guess was that both their families had converted in the 1870s or 1880s, my father's from the Greek Orthodox church, my mother's from the Greek Catholic, or Melkite. The Saids became stolidly Anglican, whereas my mother's family—slightly more adventurous—were Baptists, many of whom later studied or taught at places like Baylor and Texas A&M.

Until World War I, Palestine was an Ottoman province, its natives more or less ignored by Constantinople except for taxes and military conscription. In 1911 my father, fresh out of school, ran away from Jerusalem to avoid being drafted to fight for the Turks in Bulgaria. He found his way to the United States and during World War I enlisted in the AEF in the belief that perhaps a unit would be sent to fight Ottomans in Palestine. He ended up in France—wounded and gassed. Two years after war's end he returned, an American citizen, to Palestine and the small family business. Enterprising and immensely energetic, he expanded it to Egypt, and by the early thirties, prosperous and well established, he had married my mother, who had been educated in American mission schools and colleges in Beirut.

So there I was, a Palestinian, Anglican, American boy, English, Arabic, and French speaking at school, Arabic and English speaking at home, living in the almost suffocating, deeply impressive intimacy of a family all of whose relatives were in Palestine or Lebanon, subject to the discipline of a colonial school system and an imported mythology owing nothing to that Arab world among whose colonial elites, for at least a century, it had flourished. Its main tenet was that everything of any consequence either had happened or would happen in the West: insofar as Arabs were concerned, they had to deal with the challenge or the discipline of the West by learning its ways or, where it was impossible to do otherwise, by copying them.

The comic, not to say ironic, results of such a situation for me are only now beginning to be apparent. For the colonial power, as for my schoolteachers and parents, Cairo was assumed to be a potential danger of the extreme sort. Crowds, for example, were believed to be disease-carrying and rabidly nationalistic extremists. Left to itself, native society was supposed to be irreducibly corrupt—lazy, sexually promiscuous, irresponsible, dedicated only to pleasure and sin.

Hence the badly fitting boxes which were placed around me and in which I lived, unconsciously for the most part. My life was generally, if not in every detail, British. I read Enid Blyton, Conan Doyle, Lewis Carroll, Jonathan Swift, Walter Scott, Edgar Rice Burroughs, as well as the Billy Bunter, George Formby, and *Boy's Own* comics, which years later I discovered Orwell had very cleverly analyzed—and I did all this without direct acquaintance either with any of their Arabic equivalents or with the British Isles. I went through British schools in Palestine and Cairo, each of which was modeled on the general idea of a British public school.

Two of these many schools—I was regularly described as a nuisance, a troublemaker, as "misbehaved," so I went through three times as many schools as my sisters, who were models of accomplishment—made the greatest impression on me as a Cairo student: the Gezira Preparatory School (GPS), which I attended for four or five years, and Victoria College, my last secondary school in the Arab world before I came to the United States. The GPS was ruled by a British family whose senior figure, an enormous drunkard of a man, did no teaching and not very much appearing. He was used by his obese headmistress wife to cane misbehaved students like myself, and he did so in a total alcohol-suffused silence. In class we studied all about Kings Alfred and Canute, as well as the Magna Carta; nothing was mentioned about Egypt or the Arabs, except in allusive references here and there to "natives" and later to "wogs." My schoolmates were about half-English and half-cosmopolitan Cairenes—Greeks, Jews, Armenians, Syrians, and a sprinkling of native Muslims and Copts. French, interestingly enough, was treated as a language and culture barely a notch higher than Arabic; French teachers were always a mixture of Greek, Italian, or Armenian, and the effort was conducted with a combination of parsimony and distaste certain to preclude any real knowledge of French. Thus the contempt of one colonial power for another.

By the time I got to Victoria College at age thirteen, I was hopelessly paradoxical to myself. The GPS had convinced me that with a name like Said I should be ashamed of myself but that the Edward part of me should go on and do better, be more English, act more English, that is, "play cricket." Although Victoria College took great pains to turn us all into the "Etonians of the Middle East," as one master put it, the untidy mass of assorted backgrounds and ethnic assertions made daily life in the school (I speak of 1949, 1950, and 1951) a continuous standing war between students and teachers. All of the latter were British, and British near the end of a long colonial tenure in Egypt; all of the former were not. For all kinds of reasons I fit neatly in neither camp, with a sense of misery and discomfort I find completely understandable now but had no way of relieving then.

A large boys school, Victoria College had two branches, one in Alexandria—older, more prestigious, more successful, I think, in homogenizing the students—the other in Cairo. The school was divided into four houses—Frobisher, Drake, Kitchener, and, of course, Cromer. I was a Kitchener boy at the branch in Cairo, which at the time contained such luminaries as Michel Chalhoub (later Omar Sharif) and Zeid el-Rifai (later prime minister of Jordan). You could not, of course, know that such people would go on to success, because VC-Cairo, as it was known, was decidedly not the up-market VC-Alex (whose students included King Hussein of Jordan and Adnan Khasoggi), nor was it the English School, which is where my sisters were enrolled along with much more consistently upper-class Egyptians and all the English boys and girls. I was refused admission there, and so, relegated to the assorted misfits, rogues, and colorful characters of VC-Cairo, I edged my way forward from crisis to crisis, from catastrophe to catastrophe, until I was expelled in 1951, readmitted briefly, and then advised to look elsewhere for a school.

Outside a punishing extracurricular schedule of many sports and piano lessons, I could occasionally touch something of the vast city beyond—teeming with the possibilities of Eastern sensuality and wealth both of which were conducted, so to speak, in European modes.

An annual opera season, an annual ballet season, recitals, concerts by the Berlin and Vienna Philharmonics, major tennis and golf tournaments, regular visits of the Comédie Française and the Old Vic, all the latest American, French, and British films, cultural programs sponsored by the British Council and its continental equivalents—all these filled the social agenda, in addition to countless dances, cotillions, receptions, and balls, and to the extent that I participated in or read about them, I apprehended a sort of Proustian world replicated in an Oriental city whose prevailing authority, the British sirdar, or high commissioner, outranked the ruling monarch, the obese, piggish, and dreadfully corrupt King Farouk, last reigning member of an Albanian-Turkish-Circassian dynasty that began with the considerable éclat of Muhammad Ali in 1805 and ended with Farouk's waddle off to Europe on July 26, 1952.

As I threaded my way through this crowded but highly rarefied cultural maze, my contact with the Cairo that was neither pharaonic nor European was like contact with nature. Everything in my strange minority and paradox-ridden world of privilege was processed, prepared, insulated, confined, except for the native Egyptians I everywhere encountered in fleeting moments of freedom on the streets, in streetcars, movie theaters, demonstrations, and public occasions. And with this quasi-natural life I communicated in the language I have loved more than any—the spoken Cairo dialect of Arabic, virtuosically darting in and out of solemnity, colonial discipline, and the combination of various religious and political authorities, retaining its quick, irreverent wit, its incomparable economy of line, its sharp cadences and abrupt rhythms.

Further away than that stood, I thought, a world I could only dream of perilously, the disorderly palimpsest of Cairo's carnivalesque history, some of which I later recognized in Flaubert and Nerval, but whose astonishingly fluent passages of adventure, sexuality, and magic turn up with a great deal of their raw force in some of the *Thousand and One Nights,* the early novels of Naguib Mahfuz (Cairo's Balzac), the comedies of Naguib el-Rihani (Cairo's Molière), and that endless stream of consciousness which is the Egyptian cinema. A cohabitation of Islamic, Mediterranean, and Latin erotic forms, the latent promiscuity of this semi-underground Cairo, is what I believe I was kept from as I was growing up and what I can easily imagine that the European colonists were attracted to, drew on, and—for their own safety—kept at bay, with their schools, missions, social seasons, and rigid hierarchies of rank and caste. The traffic between Europe and *this* Cairo is what we are beginning to lose, as Nasser's Arabization, Sadat's Americanization, and Mubarak's reluctant Islamization efface its transactions altogether.

I saw the last and for me the best result of the traffic in Ignace Tiegerman, a tiny Polish-Jewish gnome of a man who came to Cairo in 1933, attracted by the city's warmth and possibilities in contrast to what was coming in Europe. He was a great pianist and musician, a wunderkind student of Leschetizky and Ignaz Friedman, a lazy, wonderfully precious and bright-eyed bachelor with secret tastes and unknown pleasures, who ran a Conservatoire de Musique on the rue Champollion just behind the Cairo Museum.

No one played Chopin and Schumann with such grace and unparalleled rhetorical conviction as Tiegerman. He taught piano in Cairo, tying himself to the city's *haute société*—teaching its daughters, playing for its salons, charming its gatherings—in order, I think, to free himself for the lazy indulgence of his own pursuits: conversation, good food, music, and unknown kinds (to me) of human relationships. I was his piano student at the outset and, many years later, his friend. We communicated in an English battered into submission by French and German, languages more congenial to Tiegerman, and after we had abandoned the teacher-student relationship, we would gather together a few stalwarts from Cairo's old days—these were the late 1950s and early 1960s—to play music, talk memory, and put ourselves back in time to when Cairo was more ours—cosmopolitan, free, full of wonderful privileges—than it had become. Although by then I was a Nasserite and a fierce anti-imperialist, it was much easier than supposed to slip back into the style of life represented by Tiegerman's soirées.

Tiegerman died in 1967, a few months after the June War. Although he kept his Polish passport, he was subject to Egyptian residency laws, taxes, and the miscellaneous rigors of Nasser's regime. He chafed under the restrictions but refused to consider moving to Israel. "Why should I go there?" he said rhetorically. "Here I am unique; there many people are like me. Besides," he added, "I love Cairo." During the early 1960s I started seeing him in Kitzbühel, Austria, where he had built himself a tiny cottage in which he had installed an old Broadwood grand and a Pleyel upright. By this time our friendship had become almost totally nostalgic and reminiscent; its bases had shifted to an absent Cairo of splendid people, charming clothes, magnificent parties, all of which had disappeared. My own last symbolic memory of Tiegerman was watching him at his conservatoire listening in 1959 to his most gifted student, a stunningly fluent and accomplished young married woman, a mother of four, who played with her head completely enclosed in the pious veil of a devout Muslim.

Neither Tiegerman nor I could understand this amphibious woman, who with a part of her body could dash through the *Appassionata* and with another venerated God by hiding her face. She never said a word in my presence, although I must have heard her play or met her at least a dozen times. Tiegerman entered her in the Munich piano competition, but she didn't do well in that overheated and cutthroat atmosphere.

Like Tiegerman, she was an untransplantable emanation of Cairo's genius; unlike him, her particular branch of the city's history has endured and even triumphed. For a brief moment then, the conjunction of ultra-European and ultra-Islamic Arab cultures brought forth a highlighted image that typified the Cairo of my early years. Where such pictures have since gone I don't know, but part of their poignancy for me is that I am certain they will never recur.

25

Through Gringo Eyes: With Conrad in Latin America

Joseph Conrad's *Nostromo* is the longest and most complex of his novels. *Nostromo* is also his only extended work to treat Latin America—although like all of Conrad's most memorable writing, it derives its perspectives, characters, and themes from the experience of European imperialism, then at its apogee. To read *Nostromo* again today, as the United States tries clumsily and often brutally to impose its "narrative"—its authorship, plots, and themes—on Latin America (and elsewhere), is to come upon a truly unique earlier text, a text in which one of the explicit subjects is the futility of attempting to control a Latin American country from beyond its borders.

Yet it would be incomplete to read *Nostromo,* which Conrad finished in 1904, simply as a portent of what we have seen happening in our time in Latin America, with its United Fruit companies, despotic colonels, liberation forces, and American-financed mercenaries. For *Nostromo* also foreshadows a gaze—a way of looking at and mediating the Third World. Conrad is the precursor of novelists such as Graham Greene, V. S. Naipaul, and Robert Stone; theoreticians of imperialism such as Hannah Arendt; and of the assorted travel writers and filmmakers whose specialty is bringing home the Third World for analysis, for judgment, or simply for the entertainment of European and North American audiences, with their taste for the "exotic."

If it is true that Conrad would have us see, in *Nostromo*, the San Tomé silver mine and its British and American owners—that is, have us see imperialism—as doomed by impossible ambition, it is also true that Conrad writes as a man in whom a *Western* view of the *non*-Western world is so deeply ingrained that it blinds him to other histories, other cultures, other aspirations. All Conrad can see is a world dominated by the West, and—of equal importance—a world in which every opposition to the West only confirms its wicked power. What Conrad could not see is life lived outside this cruel tautology. He could not understand—or so we would have to conclude from reading him—that places like Latin America (and India and Africa for that matter) also contain people and cultures with histories and ways not controlled by the gringo imperialists and liberal reformers of this world. Nor could he allow himself to believe that all anti-imperialist independence movements were not corrupt and in the pay of puppet masters.

These crucial limitations of vision are as much a part of *Nostromo* as its characters and plot. Seen as a magnificent, darkly ironic, and deeply pessimistic whole—whose main action is the struggle over the fortunes of the San Tomé silver mine in the mythical Latin American country of Costaguana—Conrad's novel embodies much the same paternalistic arrogance of imperialism that it mocks in its characters Charles Gould, the British mine owner, and Holroyd, his American financier. Conrad seems to be saying, we Westerners will decide who is a good or bad native, because all natives have sufficient existence by virtue of our recognition. We created them, we taught them to speak and think, and when they rebel they simply confirm our views of them as silly children, duped by their Western masters. This is, in effect, what we have felt all along about our southern neighbors—we wish independence and justice for them so long as it is the kind of independence and justice that *we* approve. Anything else is simply unacceptable or, more accurately, *unthinkable.*

Conrad was both an anti-imperialist and an imperialist—progressive when it came to rendering the self-confirming, self-deluding corruption of the West's colonial drive; reactionary in his inability to imagine that Costaguana could ever have had a meaningful existence of its own, which the imperialists had violently disturbed. But lest we think patronizingly of Conrad as merely the creature of his own time, we had better note that we today appear to show no particular advance on his views. Conrad was able at least to discern the evil and utter madness of imperialism, something many of our writers and certainly our government is still unable to perceive. Conrad had the wherewithal to recognize that no imperial scheme—including "philanthropic" ones such as "making the world safe for democracy"—ever succeeds.

At the center of Costaguana stands the country's main asset, the San Tomé silver mine, originally a Spanish concern, now controlled by the idealistic Englishman Charles Gould, whose family has had a long association with both the mine and the country. The recent history that Conrad plots so intricately in the novel is mainly about the struggle for control of the mine's wealth, which insinuates its influence into marital life and personal fantasy, but mostly into politics and power. The great Latin American revolutionary Simón Bolívar concluded that the region is fundamentally ungovernable. Conrad cites "the great Liberator" in *Nostromo:* To try to rule it is like ploughing the sea. Typically, and with the unrelenting irony that is his signature, Conrad portrays Costaguana as the place *everyone* tries to rule. It was first a place native to Indian tribes. The Indians capitulate to the Spaniards. Then come the British, who in turn bring the Americans, represented by Holroyd, the San Francisco financier with the mind-set of a missionary. France is represented by Martin Decoud, a native Costaguanan who after some years in Paris has become a journalist and a cynical boulevardier. In addition, there are the Montero brothers, a pair of lazy but opportunistic military men who have spent time in Paris, where they seem to have perfected the arts of conspiracy and of Blanquist insurrection. Italy too has a presence in Costaguana: Giorgio Viola, an elderly Garibaldian who once campaigned with his revered leader in Uruguay but is now an innkeeper in Sulaco; and Gian' Battista Fidanza, known as Nostromo, a Genoese bos'n who slipped ashore after a maritime infraction, and has become the leader of the port's miscellaneous population of stevedores, muleteers, and idle ships' hands.

Told as a series of complicated, sometimes overlapping and digressive flashbacks, *Nostromo* unfolds the story of the struggle waged by

Charles and Emelia Gould, the mine's owners, to maintain the silver works free of local politics, and what they believe to be narrow interests. Conrad's portrait of the couple is devastating—and at times strangely compassionate. Charles is haunted by memories of his Uncle Henry, who was killed by a revolutionary dictator, and of his father, whose fruitless efforts to revive the mine broke his heart. Charles and Emelia bring a new prosperity and power to the silver mine, but in the process of rehabilitating the place they identify their altruistic plans with the mine's prestige and wealth, and use these plans to justify widespread corruption, as well as rule by mercenaries, and the continued oppression of the native population by the Spanish-style local oligarchy.

That is not all. Gould is so determined to retain absolute control of the mine—because, he thinks, he is both incorruptible and above any ignoble or worldly temptations—that he is quite prepared to blow the place up, should it seem to be falling into the wrong hands. How many other fruit, oil, or tin company presidents in the twentieth century have felt that combination of patriarchal solicitude and murderous determination! Gould is totally unable to see how much he is victimized by the silver, whose ultimate masters are the distant imperialists, the mine's financiers. Nor can Gould see how he and his wife, for all their wonderfully selfless aspirations and their loyalty to the country, have atrophied spiritually—he into an aloof symbol of power, she into a kindly fairy godmother whose sole ability to relieve people in acute distress is to listen to their pleas after it is too late to do or undo anything. Together the Goulds sail through life, making deals and ensnaring innocents, realizing their ruthless plans, all the while maintaining their composure against a violent background. So volatile is Costaguana that Conrad's depiction of its history is but a string of dictatorships, coups, and new dictatorships.

Costaguana, at once wealthy and vulnerable to the schemes of indigenous as well as foreign speculators, is therefore meant by Conrad to be typical of Latin America, which is quite different from Africa as a target for imperialism. Africa, in Conrad's view, represents elemental darkness; in it there are only blacks and rapacious or demented whites. On the other hand, Costaguana has "histories," if scattered and incomplete—histories Indian and Spanish, more recently European and American, some religiously inspired, others commercially motivated.

By the end of *Nostromo,* the coastal province of Sulaco—in which the silver mine is situated—has seceded from Costaguana and become an independent state. The place is now more than ever a triumph of neo-colonialism ruled by Gould and Holroyd, and by the local oligarchs who have managed to co-opt even the formerly intransigent bandits and priests. Everyone, in short, is shaped by "material interests."

There was no work of European fiction until *Nostromo,* no authorial vision, that so piercingly and unsparingly captured the imperialist project in Latin America. And no one before Conrad saw that the struggle over the region's prizes (land, fruit, metals, oil) would be so enmeshed in the struggle of ideas—Western attitudes toward the non-European world. Holroyd, the American financier, is not only greedy but infused with the moralistic self-righteousness of a Puritan divine—profits for him are good for Latin American *souls,* much as today we hear politicians proclaim that the security of "our hemisphere" is good for *us* and good for *them.*

As rigorously as Marx, Conrad saw that commodity fetishism can incorporate anything and anyone. Imperialism therefore has the capacity to reproduce itself infinitely. The newly independent state of Sulaco that emerges at the end of *Nostromo* is only a smaller, more tightly controlled and intolerant version of Costaguana, the larger country from which it has seceded and has now displaced in wealth and importance. Conrad perceived that imperialism is a system. *Everything* in the subordinate realm of experience is imprinted by the fictions and follies of the dominant realm.

This is a profoundly unforgiving view, and it has quite literally engendered the equally severe view of Western imperialist illusions that we find, for instance, in Graham Greene's *The Quiet American* or V. S. Naipaul's *A Bend in the River.* The fervent innocence of Greene's Pyle or Naipaul's Father Huismans—men for whom the natives can be educated into "our" civilization—turns out actually to produce murder, subversion, and endless instability in the societies wherein they hope to bring the better things of modern civilization.

Yet works such as these, which are so indebted to Conrad's anti-imperialist irony in *Nostromo,* invariably locate the source of all significant action and life in the West, whose representatives seem at liberty to visit their fantasies and philanthropies upon a mind-deadened

Third World. Without the West, the outlying regions of the world have no life, history, or culture to speak of, no independence or integrity worth representing. When there is something indigenous to be described, it is, following Conrad, unutterably corrupt, degenerate, irredeemable. But whereas Conrad may be forgiven—he wrote *Nostromo* during a period in Europe of largely uncontested imperialist enthusiasms—contemporary novelists (and filmmakers), who have learned his ironies so well, have no excuse for their blindness. They have done their work *after* decolonization; *after* the massive intellectual, moral, and imaginative overhaul and deconstruction of Western representation of the non-Western world; *after* the work of Frantz Fanon, Amilcar Cabral, C. L. R. James, Walter Rodney; *after* the novels and plays of Chinua Achebe, Ngugi Wa Thiong O, Wole Soyinka, Salman Rushdie, Gabriel García Márquez, and many others. Western writers have maintained their biases in the *face* of history.

This is not just a matter of Westerners who cannot feel enough sympathy for foreign cultures, since there are, after all, some artists and intellectuals who have, in effect, crossed over to the other side—Jean Genet, Basil Davidson, Albert Memmi. What is crucial and must be developed is the political willingness to take seriously the alternatives to imperialism, and to grant, in Aimé Césaire's words, that "no race has a monopoly on beauty, on intelligence, on strength, and there is room for everyone at the convocation of conquest."

Whether we read *Nostromo* solely to confirm our habitual suspicions about Latin America, or whether we see in it the lineaments of *our* imperial worldview, capable of warping the perspectives of reader and author equally: *those* are the real alternatives. The world today does not exist as a spectacle about which we can either be pessimistic or optimistic, about which our "texts" can either be ingenious or boring. All such attitudes involve the deployment of power and interests. To the extent that we can see Conrad both criticizing and reproducing the imperial ideology of his time, to that extent we can characterize our own attitudes: the projection, or the refusal, of the wish to dominate, the capacity to damn or the energy to comprehend and engage other societies, traditions, histories.

26

The Quest for Gillo Pontecorvo

A few months ago, on my way back from a trip to Egypt, I made a special detour to Rome to meet director Gillo Pontecorvo. Somewhat tentative in his response to my request for an interview, Pontecorvo nevertheless acceded, and we arranged to meet over Memorial Day weekend at his Rome apartment, in Parioli, an elegant upper-middle-class quarter. He was trying to get his large and untidy-looking dog to relieve himself at the building entrance when I arrived in a driving rainstorm. Luckily, Pontecorvo had decided that the beast would not cooperate (perhaps dog and master sensed my complete lack of enthusiasm for urban pets), so we entered his home forthwith. A smallish, compact man who doesn't look much over fifty-five, Pontecorvo lives in a handsome but decidedly neither grand nor lavish apartment; the ambiance is bourgeois, literate, calm, comfortable. It was a dark day, but no lights were on; books lined one wall; his various (and discolored) prized plaques and statuettes were heaped unassumingly on a high shelf; photographs (Brando was much in evidence) hung here and there; a vast collection of eighteenth-century saints' pictures painted on glass adorned the available wall space. Both Pontecorvo and his flat—I saw no one else there during our discussion—are attractively unassertive, which is strange if one remembers the distinctive, often violent, power of his films. He speaks a serviceable, and occasionally even elegant, French, though the accent and some of the words are strongly Italian (*"si"* for *"oui"* throughout) and the manner sedate but always charming and somehow elusive. His eyes are piercing blue, his ready smile diffident, his tone and patience consistently friendly yet withdrawn.

Pontecorvo's *The Battle of Algiers* (1965–1966) and *Burn!* (1969) are, in my opinion, the two greatest political films ever made. Reclusive and remarkably unprolific, Pontecorvo is now sixty-eight and has not made any widely distributed films since *Burn!* (also known as *Queimada!*); the one (also political) film he made more recently, *Operation Ogro* (1976), was never shown outside Italy and seems not to have done particularly well there. His earlier feature film *Kapo* (1959)—starring Susan Strasberg, Laurent Terzieff, and Emmanuelle Riva—is not well known but was an affecting concentration-camp drama about a young Jewish girl whose family was killed off by the Germans yet who becomes a tough collaborationist *Kapo,* or prisoner-warden, for the Nazis, a fate that isolates and tragically clarifies her doom. *Kapo,* however, never had anything like the effect of Pontecorvo's next two films.

Released a scant three years after Algeria won its independence from France in 1962, and after an especially ugly colonial war, *The Battle of Algiers* did not play in France until 1971. Nevertheless, the film was put up for two Academy Awards, and it won the top prizes for itself and for Pontecorvo at the Venice and Acapulco festivals. It was in many ways *the* great 1960s film, not only because it represented a fairly recent and stirring triumph of insurgency against one of the old empires but also because its spirit was full of resourceful revolutionary optimism, even though violence was at the film's core. The FLN rebels are defeated in the film, but the Algerian people rise again, three years after the French destroy the Casbah rebels in 1958. Pontecorvo records the later triumph lyrically and redemptively, in one of the most remarkable crowd scenes ever put on film, rivaling Eisenstein in its gripping, almost balletic energy. And he shows how the guerrillas who are killed by the French nevertheless live on because of their intelligence, commitment, and—yes—their historical inevitability. None of this, by the way, is corny in the film. Even the French paratrooper colonel, Mathieu, is an attractive and serious man;

as for the film's FLN rebels, with Yacef Saadi (the actual Casbah leader) playing himself in the film, they are nonprofessional Algerians whose authentic passion and suffering come from reliving all-too-recent events, and this transfigures the film's gritty documentary style.

Burn! is a much colder but perhaps more masterful work, more theoretical, more deliberate, extraordinarily prescient and analytical. Marlon Brando plays an early Victorian British agent, William Walker, who encourages, and indeed almost creates, a black leader who leads an insurrection in a sugar-growing Portuguese Caribbean colony. After success, however, Walker returns to England, leaving a black army led by his black disciple, José Dolores, to negotiate a deal with the newly independent Creole planters. Ten years later, and now employed by the British sugar monopoly, Walker returns to the island, where he undertakes a search-and-destroy mission against the persistently rebellious José and his men, who have come to represent a dangerous revolutionary movement against European commercial interests. Although José is, in fact, destroyed, Walker is also killed as he is about to leave the island, stabbed by another young black, another potential José.

Both films now circulate on videocassette, but what happened to Pontecorvo in the two decades since his great prominence has haunted me, not just because I have been curious to know what he's actually done but also because I want to know what he now thinks of those two earlier masterpieces. It has certainly been possible to speculate that his enthusiasm for liberation movements has cooled (although a neocon Pontecorvo is admittedly difficult to imagine) or that the tough purity of his vision at the time blocked him psychologically thereafter. In an age of grotesquely inflated film budgets and widespread mediocrity, why hasn't Pontecorvo been making films? His work, in a sense, made Costa-Gavras possible; many third world directors, from Algeria to India to Latin America and the Middle East, trace much in their cinematography to *The Battle of Algiers* and *Burn!;* the political bite of films like *Salvador, Platoon,* and *Crossfire* owes a considerable debt to Pontecorvo. What does his present silence mean?

Twenty years later, I asked, what did he like about *Battle* and *Burn!,* and what didn't he like? In *Battle,* he said, it was the symphonic structure, the orchestrated power of the film in which a long-suppressed people's struggle for freedom emerged "like a great stream," inevitable, irreversible, triumphant. The interplay in Pontecorvo's language be-tween abstract and musical concepts was effortless and natural; this is surely not the way movie directors speak, I thought to myself, and be-fore long I had forgotten that we were talking about *his* films rather than about a couple of films we had both happened to see and remark upon. Pontecorvo tacitly encouraged and expanded the distance separating us from the films as objects he had made; frequently, he spoke of having forgotten some aspect of the film, and even when he expressed appro-bation, he did it (a paradox) impersonally. What *Battle* represented in his mind now was a collective subject—the phrase he used was *"personnage choral"*—in which the logic of colonialism came up against the logic of nationalism, drawing individuals into one or the other sphere indis-criminately but with a pitiless logic. In trying to represent this, he thinks now that he succeeded.

In *Burn!* he was trying to deal with the next phase, postcolonialism after independence, and how the great successful battle to be free iron-ically led the new states of Africa, the Caribbean, and Asia into new thralldom, new types of dependence on the current imperial powers. I was particularly eager to know what had influenced him as he dealt with this theme, what books, ideas, authors. I drew a blank from him. He had read about Toussaint, for example, but the rest seemed to come from observation and vaguely actual events. "I also heard about the mass suicide of blacks who failed to achieve their freedom," he said. When and where, I asked. "The nineteenth century, I think, somewhere in or perhaps near South America!" he responded with the vagueness of someone more affected by hints than by actual sources. No, he wouldn't change anything in *Burn!*, but he did feel that a rooftop se-quence between the FLN leader Ben M'Hidi and Ali La Pointe in *Battle* should have been struck. "It's much too preachy and didactic," he said of the scene, in which Ben M'Hidi theorizes about how revolutions start with terrorism but then succeed in mobilizing all the people, etc., etc. Pontecorvo's major overall influences for both films was Franz Fanon, first of all *The Wretched of the Earth* and then *A Dying Colonialism*.

I was still uncertain why an Italian filmmaker should make a film about a third world colonial revolution when all around him his com-patriots were concerned only with their own society. He cited as ad-mired confreres not only Rossellini (his favorite) but the Fellini of *8½* and *Orchestra Rehearsal,* as well as Bertolucci (*The Conformist* especially, not *The Last Emperor,* which Pontecorvo didn't believe really came off) and Visconti. So why imperialism and neoimperialism? At this point Pontecorvo became extremely matter-of-fact. "I was a member of the PCI [Italian Communist Party] until 1956, when I quit it," he explained, adding that Hungary had figured in his decision. "Later, I became a left independent. Hence it was logical to treat imperialism." This was the most unsatisfying thing he said. Later, in New York, my friend Eqbal Ahmad told me that he originally met Pontecorvo when both of them, as well as Costa-Gavras, were working for the FLN in the late 1950s. What had been a deep political commitment thirty years ago now seemed an almost academic occurrence.

At only two points in our discussion did Pontecorvo and I disagree strenuously. First, in discussing what I considered to be his "fascinated" portrayal of imperialist villains, both of whom happen to be European—Colonel Mathieu in *Battle* and William Walker in *Burn!*—Pontecorvo claimed that he had to treat them seriously and not as caricatured stereotypes. The logic of their positions needed clarity, and how was he to do this but to present them as rational, serious types; this did not, however, prevent him as director and author from being "against them." I pressed harder. What about the admiring caresses lavished by the camera on Mathieu marching into Algiers? What about Walker as a free superintellectual, rather in the vein of a Kennedy New Frontiersman? Didn't Pontecorvo actually like these people, feel some lingering pleasure in how they operated? "Why," he said, "are you trying to make me agree with you? I don't agree with you," exasperatingly concluding *that* particular line of investigation.

The other disagreement concerned music, which Pontecorvo described as *"l'image sonore,"* for him the second half of every *"image visible."* He spoke with extraordinary beauty of scenes in his films during which dialogue was gradually eliminated to accommodate music that inexplicably but satisfactorily complemented the action. Here he was just as eloquent about Brando, *"ombrageux"* (demanding, difficult), an often petulant man who got bored in Colombia, where *Burn!* was being filmed, and demanded a full-scale removal to Morocco but who also, when Pontecorvo scrubbed five pages of his dialogue to insert a chunk of Bach's cantata *Komm, süsser Tod* in its place, produced a silent gestural performance of such transcendentally expressive acting that even electricians and carpenters present on the set broke out in applause. "Brando," Pontecorvo added, "is the greatest film actor in history." But it is Pontecorvo's passion for music that has always characterized his special aesthetic sense, first as composer (he studied with René Leibowitz in France until lack of money forced him to stop) and then as director, for whom the *image sonore* shaped the scene, making it work along with the *image visible.*

Inevitably, then, I picked up his word "counterpoint" for the special interplay that his great films always seemed to be negotiating between image and music. It indicated an unusual, deliberately complex way of looking at the world, one that I found I was correct in associating with Bach, and indeed with Glenn Gould. *"J'adore Gould,"* he said; Gould, he said, had the uncanny ability to make the bass line sound as if it had been played by another instrument. When I asked if he listened to music a great deal, Pontecorvo said yes, all the time. Which music, I persisted? *"Tout,"* he said, then adding, "but especially Bach, Stravinsky, and Brahms." In fact, he went on to say rather triumphantly, his sons are called Sebastiano, Igor, and Johannes (a physicist, a filmmaker, and a twelve-year-old "who doesn't do well in school"). "Do you really like Brahms?" I asked. "Don't you find him derivative, with far too many notes and not enough music?" "No," he retorted calmly, "I love him, especially the *German Requiem,* which accomplishes the feat of acculturating death to an acceptable human standard."

This line impressed me, although I couldn't really accept it as a description of one of the most turgidly lugubrious pieces ever composed. At this point, with so much expressed enthusiasm and with so impressive a record behind him, it became imperative to get off our disagreement and to ask about what he was doing now. "You mean," he replied rather less euphemistically, "how do I live, given that I do so little?" Suddenly, Pontecorvo's immense fastidiousness surfaced: this was a man who had precise, almost Mallarmé-esque views of art and life, and for whom politics included music, literature, film, images, and ideas bound together contrapuntally, a union in which a certain indirection or understatement was always preferable to italicized or polemical insistence. No wonder, then, that despite the overwhelming force of his anti-imperialist films, there was in them an evident taste for the occasional contradictory current, the violated principle, the expressive detail going against the grain. He had told me earlier that Gramsci was his most important formative influence—how telling that almost the first thing Pontecorvo said to me about Gramsci concerned his "divergences" from the PCI.

"What do I do now?" he repeated. "I should say first that I don't need very much to live. Each of my films gives me enough money for eight or nine years. I read and write constantly, either looking for subjects or actually sketching out treatments." I was curious about his relationship with Franco Solinas, the great scriptwriter, now deceased, who collaborated with him on *Battle* and *Burn!* "He was much better than I at actually producing a script, but although his name was on both films, you will note that mine is there, too, as a writer. I can never make a film unless I do it myself from start to finish." Then, as if to emphasize the exhausting nature of his commitment to work in progress, he exclaimed: "You know, I am impotent, a man incapable of making love, until I find a person with whom I can be totally in love. Unless that happens, I cannot start, much less make, a film at all, and this is why I spend so much time looking, testing, reflecting. Now, for example, I am reading this." He pulled over a large red volume from the other side of the table, Henri Troyat's life of Catherine the Great—"Dino De Laurentiis wants me to make this into a film." His unconvinced tone said it all: this was not a subject for him. Besides, I later discovered that not only is De Laurentiis bankrupt, but, in addition, according to a well-known director I met in London a month later, Pontecorvo really earns his living by making commercials *(caroselli)* for Italian TV!

I probed Pontecorvo a little further: was there no film that he might want to make today? "Yes," he said at last, "there is. I want to make a film about Archbishop Romero of El Salvador. What interests me is how a man who has always remained safely within the limits of the conventional and the established is suddenly converted, suddenly transformed into someone involved in a political cause." He was later to say something similar about Ali La Pointe in *The Battle of Algiers,* another sudden convert to struggle: what interested Pontecorvo there was how Ali's transformation also transformed his shabby history as pimp into a past that was "no longer a scandal." So, too, in a vastly different context, he would focus on the transformation and subsequent assassination of Romero. When I asked at what stage the preparations had arrived, he replied (without much conviction, I think): "I've decided on Gene Hackman [*pronounced "Ackman"*], but I haven't sent him the script yet. I'm working on the finances, which are ready in Europe but as yet incomplete in the United States. There's a general disengagement from politics, not all of it due to Reagan, but mostly having to do with profits. If you were to propose a film revealing that a producer's family was a gang of thieves, he or she would get you the money, so long as it could be demonstrated that such a film could turn a profit."

We branched out from the Romero project to the general problem of political films. "There aren't any," Pontecorvo said. "*Crossfire* was good, *Salvador* wasn't, and Costa-Gavras' films were made a long time ago [this, I thought, was strangely exaggerated] and don't count." Here was shorthand talk, perhaps, for the blockage he experienced after he finished one of his films, as if neither he nor any of the people who had been influenced by his films could actually go anywhere, do anything, say anything. It was as if his own feeling of impotence were writ large on the political scene everywhere. No, he never saw any third world films because, he said definitively, none were shown in Rome. And, on the subject of his own work, he often emphasized his interest in "*vérité*"; what he now saw was wrong with *Kapo* was the blossoming of a love story between the *Kapo* (Susan Strasberg) and a prisoner (Laurent Terzieff). "Too much fiction," he said; "it should have been eliminated." Surprisingly, he added, "I don't like the cinema very much. I don't go to see films really. The only film I liked recently was von Trotta's most recent, and that's it."

Finally, however, I was able to get to what seemed to me to be the logical contemporary extension of the political situations represented in *The Battle of Algiers* and *Burn!* What about the Palestinian uprising, or *intifada*, in the Israeli-occupied territories? I mentioned that a brilliantly vivid account of a day spent in Gaza by a young Palestinian journalist, Makram Makhoul, that had appeared in the Hebrew-language Israeli press reminded me, in its descriptions of the tension and exhilaration among Palestinian militants—"Fear is forbidden here," one of them said—of *The Battle of Algiers*. "Absolutely. I support the Palestinians,"

Pontecorvo said matter-of-factly; "it is a colonial situation." I asked him whether, as a Jew, he felt any reservations about his support for the "other" side. No, he replied quickly, although he went on to give an explanation for why the obvious European film on the Palestinians couldn't be made now. I had suggested earlier that *The Battle of Algiers* was made only as a result of the Algerian victory; surely a similarly successful film would not be possible in instances where victory was either uncertain or apparently impossible. No, he countered, you could make a film that would analyze and clarify the reasons for failure, as well as provide lessons for the future.

Unconvinced, but not a filmmaker myself, I wanted to know why, if not because the struggle was still going on, he didn't see a Palestinian film as an irresistible subject. After all, I went on, Costa-Gavras tried it in *Hannah K.*, even if, we both agreed, the results were interesting but mixed (at best). I then told Pontecorvo that about ten years ago Solinas had come to Beirut looking for a Palestinian theme, had located me as someone to talk to, and had stunned me with his caution, his unwillingness to confront the drama directly (he had wanted to base his script on the letters home of a young Palestinian worker in Germany, "home" being left totally unspecified), his stated fear of Western audiences' reaction to sympathy for the Palestinian cause.

Pontecorvo began, "What makes the situation there more complicated and less clear than France and Algeria"—at which point I interrupted, saying, "But to us, it *is* clear, but there is at the heart of it the comprehensible Israeli psychosis [he meant, I think, fear of extermination, but he also spoke of the fear of encirclement], and this psychosis is a real thing, at work in the majority of Israelis, which prevents them from dealing directly with the claims of Palestinian nationalism." But he also rejected the suggestion that, as a Jew, he felt that the complications perhaps mitigated his solidarity with the Palestinians; rather, he suggested, it was in the nature of film, which requires certain "elementarities," to reduce complexities to levels below that of print. "Film is an extremely unductile medium. On the page, you can be subtle; you can render things with different shades. It's hard to do the same with film." This view tallied with the severity of his vision of struggle in Algeria, where, perhaps following Fanon, he simply took no account in his film of liberals or of the national bourgeoisie: there were only

Algerian militants fighting French occupation, and no good doctors, no tormented and conscience-stricken intellectuals. Knowledge of the struggle was totally contained in the polarity of the radical antagonists. He agreed that an American director would probably have introduced a sprinkling of liberals, to give the film "balance."

Perhaps I was too eager, too importunate and insistent with Pontecorvo. I appeared on his doorstep with only the slenderest of introductions in order (it must have seemed) to pester him with questions about twenty years ago or to preach at him about what he ought to be doing now. An elusive and yet strangely attractive man, he presented me, I think, with a series of paradoxes that may lie at the heart of his long filmic silence after *The Battle of Algiers* and *Burn!* Gripped by indomitable political passions, he sublimates them completely in images and music. An intellectual with a sure grasp of theory and argument, he tolerates the explicit presence of neither in his films. A man whose aesthetic taste is fanatically precise, he apparently manages to do enough hack TV work to keep himself going financially. He understands and, better than anyone, has embodied in film the narrative counterpoint of peoples and histories, yet he seems unwilling to extend the vision from his films into the present. Was Pontecorvo maybe speaking of himself when he described the generalized political disengagement prevalent in today's world?

Perhaps, finally, he means his earlier films to speak for themselves, to remain as the great cinematic documents of the age of empire, which continues today in updated but essentially classic forms. Having spoken with him, I tend now to interpret the ending of *Burn!*—Walker's murder by another rebellious black—as less a statement of confidence in the future than as raising a set of troubling, unanswerable questions: are we once again to repeat the murderous cycle? Is there ever to be a conclusive victory against empire? Does revolutionary violence have the capacity to teach future generations something more than the almost mechanical necessity of violent struggle? Are domination and repression, with the attendant "psychosis," the only likely attitudes between Western-type societies and their "others"?

I had hoped to find help with these questions in going to see Pontecorvo and indeed had assumed that his silence might itself have been an interpretation of current history. But I came away from my visit impressed with the stubbornness of his views, as contained in two great twenty-year-old films—and with the persistence of the questions implied by those films. Pontecorvo himself was now looking elsewhere for inspiration and work, with little certainty (that I could detect) of success, his fidelity to past commitments unimpaired and the challenge of the present still to be met.

Representing the Colonized:
Anthropology's Interlocutors

pas un bout de ce monde qui ne porte mon empreinte digitale
et mon calcanéum sur le dos des gratte-ciel et ma crasse dans le
scintillement des gemmes!

—AIMÉ CÉSAIRE, *Cahier d'un retour au pays natal*

Each of the four main words in the title of these re-
marks inhabits a rather agitated and somewhat turbulent field. It is now
almost impossible, for example, to remember a time when people were
not talking about a crisis in representation. And the more the crisis is
analyzed and discussed, the earlier its origins seem to be. Michel
Foucault's argument has put somewhat more forcefully and more attractively perhaps a notion found in the works of literary historians like
Earl Wasserman, Erich Auerbach, and M. H. Abrams that with the erosion of the classical consensus, words no longer comprised a transparent medium through which Being shone. Instead, language as an
opaque and yet strangely abstract, ungraspable essence was to emerge as
an object for philological attention, thereafter to neutralize and inhibit
any attempt at representing reality mimetically. In the age of Nietzsche,

Marx, and Freud, representation has thus had to contend not only with the consciousness of linguistic forms and conventions, but also with the pressures of such transpersonal, transhuman, and transcultural forces as class, the unconscious, gender, race, and structure. What transformations these have wrought in our notions of formerly stable things such as authors, texts, and objects are, quite literally, unprintable, and certainly unpronounceable. To represent someone or even something has now become an endeavor as complex and as problematic as an asymptote, with consequences for certainty and decidability as fraught with difficulties as can be imagined.

The notion of the colonized, to speak now about the second of my four terms, presents its own brand of volatility. Before World War II the colonized were the inhabitants of the non-Western and non-European world that had been controlled and often settled forcibly by Europeans. Accordingly, therefore, Albert Memmi's book situated both the colonizer and the colonized in a special world, with its own laws and situations, just as in *The Wretched of the Earth* Frantz Fanon spoke of the colonial city as divided into two separate halves, communicating with each other by a logic of violence and counterviolence.[1] By the time Alfred Sauvy's ideas about Three Worlds had been institutionalized in theory and praxis, the colonized had become synonymous with the Third World.[2]

There was, however, a continuing colonial presence of Western powers in various parts of Africa and Asia, many of whose territories had largely attained independence in the period around World War II. Thus "the colonized" was not a historical group that had won national sovereignty and was therefore disbanded, but a category that included the inhabitants of newly independent states as well as subject peoples in adjacent territories still settled by Europeans. Racism remained an important force with murderous effects in ugly colonial wars and rigidly unyielding polities. The experience of being colonized therefore signified a great deal to regions and peoples of the world whose experience as dependents, subalterns, and subjects of the West did not end—to paraphrase from Fanon—when the last white policeman left and the last European flag came down.[3] To have been colonized was a fate with lasting, indeed grotesquely unfair results, especially after national independence had been achieved. Poverty, dependency, underdevelopment, various pathologies of power and corruption, plus of course notable achievements in war, literacy, economic development: this mix of characteristics designated the colonized people who had freed themselves on one level but who remained victims of their past on another.[4]

And far from being a category that signified supplication and self-pity, "the colonized" has since expanded considerably to include women, subjugated and oppressed classes, national minorities, and even marginalized or incorporated academic subspecialties. Around the colonized there has grown a whole vocabulary of phrases, each in its own way reinforcing the dreadful secondariness of people who, in V. S. Naipaul's derisive characterization, are condemned only to use a telephone, never to invent it. Thus the status of colonized people has been fixed in zones of dependency and peripherality, stigmatized in the designation of underdeveloped, less-developed, developing states, ruled by a superior, developed, or metropolitan colonizer who was theoretically posited as a categorically antithetical overlord. In other words, the world was still divided into betters and lessers, and if the category of lesser beings had widened to include a lot of new people as well as a new era, then so much the worse for them. Thus to be one of the colonized is potentially to be a great many different, but inferior, things, in many different places, at many different times.

As for anthropology as a category, it scarcely requires an outsider like myself to add very much to what has already been written or said about the turmoil occurring in at least some quarters of the discipline. Broadly speaking, however, a couple of currents can be stressed here. One of the major tendencies within disciplinary debates during the past twenty or so years has derived from an awareness of the role played in the study and representation of "primitive" or less-developed non-Western societies by Western colonialism, the exploitation of dependence, the oppression of peasants, and the manipulation or management of native societies for imperial purposes. This awareness has been translated into various forms of Marxist or anti-imperialist anthropology, for example, the early work of Eric Wolf, William Roseberry's *Coffee and Capitalism in the Venezuelan Andes,* June Nash's *We Eat the Mines and the Mines Eat Us,* Michael Taussig's *The Devil and Commodity Fetishism in South America,* and several others. This kind of oppositional work is admirably partnered by feminist anthropology (for example, Emily Martin's *The Woman in the Body*, Lila Abu-Lughod's *Veiled Sentiments*), historical anthropology (for example, Richard Fox's *Lions of the Punjab*), work that relates to contemporary political struggle (Jean Comaroff's *Body of Power, Spirit of Resistance*), American anthropology (for example, Susan Harding on fundamentalism), and denunciatory anthropology (Shelton Davis's *Victims of the Miracle*).

The other major current is the postmodern anthropology practiced by scholars influenced by literary theory generally speaking, and more specifically by theoreticians of writing, discourse, and modes of power such as Foucault, Roland Barthes, Clifford Geertz, Jacques Derrida, and Hayden White. I am impressed, however, that few of the scholars who have contributed to such collections as *Writing Culture* or *Anthropology as Cultural Critique*[5]—to mention two highly visible recent books—have explicitly called for an end to anthropology as, for example, a number of literary scholars have indeed recommended for the concept of literature. Yet it is also impressive to me that few of the anthropologists who are read outside anthropology make a secret of the fact that they wish that anthropology, and anthropological texts, might be more literary or literary theoretical in style and awareness, or that anthropologists should spend more time thinking of textuality and less of matrilineal descent, or that issues relating to cultural poetics take a more central role in their research than, say, issues of tribal organization, agricultural economics, and primitive classification.

But these two trends belie deeper problems. Leaving aside the obviously important discussions and debates that go on within discrete anthropological subfields such as Andean studies or Indian religion, the recent work of Marxist, anti-imperialist, and meta-anthropological scholars (Geertz, Taussig, Wolf, Marshall Sahlins, Johannes Fabian, and others) nevertheless reveals a genuine malaise about the sociopolitical status of anthropology as a whole. Perhaps this is now true of every field in the human sciences, but it is especially true of anthropology. As Richard Fox has put it:

> Anthropology today appears intellectually threatened to the same degree that anthropologists have become an endangered species of academic. The professional danger has to do with

the decline in jobs, university programs, research support, and other erosions of the professional status of anthropologists. The intellectual threat to anthropology comes from within the discipline: two disputing views of culture [what Fox calls cultural materialism and culturology], which share too much and argue about too little.[6]

It is interesting and symptomatic that Fox's own remarkable book, *Lions of the Punjab*, from which these sentences have been taken, shares in common with other influential diagnosticians of anthropology's *mal du siècle*—for it is that I think—like Sherry Ortner,[7] that the salutary alternative is a practice based on practice, fortified with ideas about hegemony, social reproduction, and ideology on loan from such nonanthropologists as Antonio Gramsci, Raymond Williams, Alain Touraine, and Pierre Bourdieu. Nevertheless, the impression of a deep sentiment of Kuhnian paradigm-exhaustion persists, with consequences for the status of anthropology that must be, I believe, extraordinarily unsettling.

I suppose there is also some (justified) fear that today's anthropologists can no longer go to the postcolonial field with quite the same ease as in former times. This of course is a political challenge to ethnography on exactly the same terrain where, in earlier times, anthropologists were relatively sovereign. Responses have varied. Some have in a sense retreated to the politics of textuality. Others have used the violence emanating from the field as a topic for postmodern theory. And third, some have utilized anthropological discourse as the site for constructing models of social change or transformation. None of these responses, however, is as optimistic about the enterprise as were the revisionist contributors to Dell Hymes's *Reinventing Anthropology*, or Stanley Diamond in his important *In Search of the Primitive*, an academic generation earlier.

Finally, the word "interlocutors." Here again I am struck by the extent to which the notion of an interlocutor is so unstable as to split quite dramatically into two fundamentally discrepant meanings. On the one hand it reverberates against a whole background of colonial conflict, in which the colonizers search for an *interlocuteur valable*, and the colonized on the other are driven increasingly to more and more desperate remedies as they try first to fit the categories formulated by the colonial authority, then, acknowledging that such a course is doomed to failure, decide that only their own military force will compel Paris or London to take them seriously as interlocutors. An interlocutor in the colonial situation is therefore by definition either someone who is compliant and belongs to the category of what the French in Algeria called an *evolué, notable,* or *caid* (the liberation group reserved the designation of *beni-wéwé* or white man's nigger for the class), or someone who, like Fanon's native intellectual, simply refuses to talk, deciding that only a radically antagonistic, perhaps violent riposte is the only interlocution that is possible with colonial power.

The other meaning for "interlocutor" is a good deal less political. It derives from an almost entirely academic or theoretical environment, and suggests the calm as well as the antiseptic, controlled quality of a thought-experiment. In this context the interlocutor is someone who has perhaps been found clamoring on the doorstep, where from outside a discipline or field he or she has made so unseemly a disturbance as to be let in, guns or stones checked in with the porter, for further discussion. The domesticated result brings to mind a number of fashionable theoretical correlatives, for example, Bakhtinian dialogism and heteroglossia. Jürgen Habermas's "ideal speech situation," or Richard Rorty's picture (at the end of *Philosophy and the Mirror of Nature*) of philosophers discoursing animatedly in a handsomely appointed salon. If such a description of interlocutor appears somewhat caricatural, it does at least retain enough of the denaturing incorporation and cooptation that are, I think, required for such interlocutions to occur. The point I am trying to make is that this kind of scrubbed, disinfected interlocutor is a laboratory creation with suppressed, and therefore falsified, connections to the urgent situation of crisis and conflict that brought him or her to attention in the first place. It was only when subaltern figures like women, Orientals, blacks, and other "natives" made enough noise that they were paid attention to, and asked in, so to speak. Before that they were more or less ignored, like the servants in nineteenth-century English novels, *there,* but unaccounted for except as a useful part of the setting. To convert them into topics of discussion or fields of research is necessarily to change them into something fundamentally and constitutively different. And so the paradox remains.

At this point I should say something about one of the frequent criticisms addressed to me, and to which I have always wanted to respond, that in the process of characterizing the production of Europe's inferior Others, my work is only negative polemic which does not advance a new epistemological approach or method, and expresses only desperation at the possibility of ever dealing seriously with other cultures. These criticisms are related to the matters I've been discussing so far, and while I have no desire to unleash a point-by-point refutation of my critics, I do want to respond in a way that is intellectually pertinent to the topic at hand.

What I took myself to be undertaking in *Orientalism* was an adversarial critique not only of the field's perspective and political economy, but also of the sociocultural situation that makes its discourse both so possible and so sustainable. Epistemologies, discourses, and methods like Orientalism are scarcely worth the name if they are reductively characterized as objects like shoes, patched when worn out, discarded and replaced with new objects when old and unfixable. The archival dignity, institutional authority, and patriarchal longevity of Orientalism should be taken seriously because in the aggregate these traits function as a worldview with considerable political force not easily brushed away as so much epistemology. Thus Orientalism in my view is a structure erected in the thick of an imperial contest whose dominant wing it represented and elaborated not only as scholarship but as a partisan ideology. Yet Orientalism hid the contest beneath its scholarly and aesthetic idioms. These things are what I was trying to show, in addition to arguing that there is no discipline, no structure of knowledge, no institution or epistemology that can or has ever stood free of the various sociocultural, historical, and political formations that give epochs their peculiar individuality.

Now it is true of all the numerous theoretical and discursive revaluations, of which I spoke earlier, that they seem to be looking for a way to escape this embroiling actuality. To develop ingenious textual strategies as a way of deflecting the crippling attacks on ethnographic authority mounted by Fabian, Talal Asad, and Gérard Leclerc:[8] these strategies have comprised one method for slipping past the hopelessly overlapping, impossibly overinterpreted and conflicted anthropological site. Call it the aesthetic response. The other was to focus more or less exclusively on practice,[9] as if practice were a domain of actuality unencumbered by agents, interests, and contentions, political as well as philosophical. Call this the reductively pragmatic response.

In *Orientalism* I did not think it possible to entertain either of those anesthetics. I may have been disabled by radical skepticism as to grand theory and purely epistemological standpoints. But I did not feel that I could give myself over to the view that an Archimedean point existed outside the contexts I was describing, or that it might be possible to devise and deploy an inclusive interpretive methodology that could hang free of the precisely concrete historical circumstances out of which Orientalism derived and from which it drew sustenance. It has therefore appeared to me particularly significant that anthropologists, and not historians for instance, have been among the most unwilling to accept the rigors of this inescapable truth first formulated cogently by Giambattista Vico. I speculate—and I shall say more about this later—that since it is anthropology above all that has been historically constituted and constructed in its point of origin during an ethnographic encounter between a sovereign European observer and a non-European native occupying, so to speak, a lesser status and a distant place, it is now some late twentieth-century anthropologists who say to someone who has challenged the status of that enabling moment, "at least provide me with another one."[10]

This digressive foray will continue a little later, when I return again to what seems to me to be entailed by it, namely, the problematic of the observer, remarkably underanalyzed in the revisionist anthropological currents of which I spoke earlier. This is especially true, I think, in works of resourcefully original anthropologists like Sahlins (in his *Islands of History*) or Wolf (in his *Europe and the People without History*). This silence is thunderous, for me at least. Look at the many pages of very brilliantly sophisticated argument in the works of the metatheoretical scholars, or in Sahlins and Wolf, and you will begin perhaps suddenly to note how someone, an authoritative, explorative, elegant, learned voice, speaks and analyzes, amasses evidence, theorizes, speculates about everything—except itself. Who speaks? For what and to whom? The questions are not pronounced, or if they are, they become, in the words of James Clifford writing on ethnographic authority, matters largely of "strategic choice."[11] The histories, traditions, societies, texts of "others" are seen either as responses to Western initiatives—and therefore passive, dependent—or as domains of culture that belong mainly to "native" elites. But rather than discussing this matter any further, I should like now to return to my excavation of the field surrounding the topic proposed for discussion.

You will have surmised then that neither representation, nor "the colonized," nor "anthropology" and its "interlocutors" can be assigned any very essential or fixed signification. The words seem either to vacillate before various possibilities of meaning or, in some instances, they divide in half. What is most clear about the way they confront us is of course that they are irremediably affected by a number of limits and pressures, which cannot completely be ignored. Thus words like "representation," "anthropology," and "the colonized" are embedded in settings that no amount of ideological violence can dismiss. For not only do we immediately find ourselves grappling with the unstable and volatile semantic ambiance they evoke, but we are also summarily remanded into the actual world, there to locate and occupy if not the anthropological site then the cultural situation in which anthropological work is in fact done.

"Worldliness" is a notion I have often found useful because of two meanings that inhere in it together, one, the idea of being in the secular world, as opposed to being "otherworldly," and two, because of the suggestion conveyed by the French word *mondanite*, worldliness as the quality of a practiced, slightly jaded savoir faire, worldly wise and street smart. Anthropology and worldliness (in both senses) necessarily require each other. Geographical dislocation, secular discovery, and the painstaking recovery of implicit or internalized histories: these stamp the ethnographic quest with the mark of a secular energy that is unmistakably frank. Yet the by now massed discourses, codes, and practical traditions of anthropology, with its authorities, disciplinary rigors, genealogical maps, systems of patronage and accreditation, have been accumulated into various modes of *being anthropological*. Innocence is now out of the question of course. And if we suspect that as in all scholarly disciplines, the customary way of doing things both narcotizes and insulates the guild member, we are saying something true about all forms of disciplinary worldliness. Anthropology is not an exception.

Like my own field of comparative literature, anthropology, however, is predicated on the fact of otherness and difference, on the lively, informative thrust supplied to it by what is strange or foreign, "deep-down freshness" in Gerard Manley Hopkins's phrase. These two words, "difference" and "otherness," have by now acquired talismanic properties. Indeed it is almost impossible not to be stunned by how magical, even metaphysical they seem, given the altogether dazzling operations performed on them by philosophers, anthropologists, literary theorists, and sociologists. Yet the most striking thing about "otherness" and "difference" is, as with all general terms, how profoundly conditioned they are by their historical and worldly context. To speak about "the other" in today's United States is, for the contemporary anthropologist here, quite a different thing than say for an Indian or Venezuelan anthropologist: the conclusion drawn by Jürgen Golte in a reflective essay on "the anthropology of conquest" is that even non-American and hence "indigenous" anthropology is "intimately tied to imperialism," so dominant is the global power radiating out from the great metropolitan center.[12] To practice anthropology in the United States is therefore not just to be doing scholarly work investigating "otherness" and "difference" in a large country; it is to be discussing them in an enormously influential and powerful state whose global role is that of a superpower.

The fetishization and relentless celebration of "difference" and "otherness" can therefore be seen as an ominous trend. It suggests not only what Jonathan Friedman has called "the spectacularization of anthropology" whereby the "textualization" and "culturization" of societies occur regardless of politics and history,[13] but also the heedless appropriation and translation of the world by a process that for all its protestations of relativism, its displays of epistemological care and technical expertise, cannot easily be distinguished from the process of empire. I have put this as strongly as I have simply because I am impressed that in so many of the various writings on anthropology, epistemology, textualization, and otherness that I have read, which in scope and material run the gamut from anthropology to history and literary theory, there is an almost total absence of any reference to

American imperial intervention as a factor affecting the theoretical discussion. It will be said that I have connected anthropology and empire too crudely, in too undifferentiated a way; to which I respond by asking how—and I really mean *how*—and when they were separated. I do not know when the event occurred, or if it occurred at all. So rather than assuming that it happened, let us see whether there is still some relevance to the topic of empire for the American anthropologist and indeed for us all as intellectuals.

The reality is a daunting one. The facts are that we have vast global interests, and we prosecute them accordingly. There are armies, and armies of scholars at work politically, militarily, ideologically. Consider, for example, the following statement, which quite explicitly makes the connection between foreign policy and "the other":

> In recent years the Department of Defense (DoD) has been confronted with many problems which require support from the behavioral and social sciences. . . . The Armed Forces are no longer engaged solely in warfare. Their missions now include pacification, assistance, "the battle of ideas," etc. All of these missions require an understanding of the urban and rural populations with which our military personnel come in contact—in the new "peacefare" activities or in combat. For many countries throughout the world, we need more knowledge about their beliefs, values, and motivations; their political, religious, and economic organizations; and the impact of various changes or innovations upon their sociocultural patterns. . . . The following items are elements that merit consideration as factors in research strategy for military agencies. *Priority Research Undertakings:* (1) methods, theories and training in the social and behavioral sciences in foreign countries . . . (2) programs that train foreign social scientists . . . (3) social science research to be conducted by independent indigenous scientists . . . (4) social science tasks to be conducted by major U.S. graduate studies in centers in foreign areas. . . (7) studies based in the U.S. that exploit data collected by overseas investigators supported by non-defense agencies. The development of data, resources and analytical methods should be pressed so that data

collected for special purposes can be utilized for many additional purposes. . . . (8) collaborate with other programs in the U.S. and abroad that will provide continuing access of Department of Defense personnel to academic and intellectual resources of the "free world."[14]

It goes without saying that the imperial system that covers an immense network of patron and client states, *as well* as an intelligence and policymaking apparatus that is both wealthy and powerful beyond precedent, *does not* cover *everything* in American society. Certainly the media is saturated with ideological material, but just as certainly not everything in the media is saturated to the same degree. By all means we should recognize distinctions, make differentiations, but, we must add, we should not lose sight of the gross fact that the swathe the United States cuts through the world is considerable, and is not merely the result of one Reagan and a couple of Kirkpatricks, so to speak, but is also heavily dependent on cultural discourse, on the knowledge industry, on the production and dissemination of texts and textuality, in short, not on "culture" as a general anthropological realm, which is routinely discussed and analyzed in studies of cultural poetics and textualization, but quite specifically on *our* culture.

The material interests at stake in our culture are very large and very costly. They involve not only questions of war and peace—for, if in general you have reduced the non-European world to the status of a subsidiary or inferior region, it becomes easier to invade and pacify it—but also questions of economic allocation, political priorities, and, centrally, relationships of dominance and inequality. We no longer live in a world that is three-quarters quiescent and underdeveloped. Nevertheless, we have not yet produced an effective national style that is premised on something more equitable and noncoercive than a theory of fateful superiority, which to some degree all cultural ideologies emphasize. The particular cultural form taken by superiority in the context revealed—I cite a typical case—by the *New York Times*'s insensate attack (October 26, 1986) on Ali Mazrui for daring as an African to make a film series about Africans, is that as long as Africa is viewed *positively* as a region that has benefited from the civilizing modernization provided by historical colonialism then it can be tolerated;

but if it is viewed by Africans as still suffering under the legacy of empire then it must be cut down to size, shown as essentially inferior, as having regressed since the white man left. And thus there has been no shortage of rhetoric—for example, Pascal Bruckner's *Tears of the White Man,* the novels of V. S. Naipaul, the recent journalism of Conor Cruise O'Brien—reinforcing *that* view.

As citizens and intellectuals within the United States, we have a particular responsibility for what goes on between the United States and the rest of the world, a responsibility *not* at all discharged or fulfilled by indicating that the Soviet Union is worse. The fact is that we are responsible for, and therefore more capable of influencing, *this* country and its allies in ways that do not apply to the Soviet Union. So we should first take scrupulous note of how—to mention the most obvious—in Central and Latin America, as well as in the Middle East, Africa, and Asia, the United States has replaced the great earlier empires as *the* dominant outside force.

It is no exaggeration to say that looked at honestly the record is not a good one, that is, if we do not uncritically accept the notion that we are entitled to an almost totally consistent policy of attempting to influence, dominate, and control other states whose relevance, implied or declared, to American security interests is supposed to be paramount. United States military interventions since World War II have occurred in every continent, and what we as citizens are now beginning to understand is only the vast complexity and extent of these interventions, the huge number of ways in which they occur, and the tremendous national investment in them. That they occur is not in doubt, all of which is, in William Appleman Williams's phrase, empire as a way of life. The continuing disclosures of Irangate are part of this complex of interventions, although it is worth noting that in little of the immense media and opinion deluge has there been much attention paid to the fact that our Iranian and Central American policies—whether they have to do with the exploitation of a geopolitical opening among Iranian "moderates," or aiding the Contra "freedom-fighters" in overthrowing the legally constituted and elected government of Nicaragua—are nakedly imperialist policies.

Without wishing to spend a great deal of time on this perfectly obvious aspect of U.S. policy, I shall therefore neither cite the cases nor engage in silly definitional polemic. Even if we allow, as many have, that U.S. policy abroad is principally altruistic and dedicated to such unimpeachable goals as freedom and democracy, there is considerable room for a skeptical attitude. For are we not, on the face of it, repeating as a nation what France and Britain, Spain and Portugal, Holland and Germany, did before us? And do we not by conviction and power tend to regard ourselves as somehow exempt from the more sordid imperial adventures that preceded ours precisely by pointing to our immense cultural achievements, our prosperity, our theoretical and epistemological awareness? And, besides, is there not an assumption on our part that our destiny is that we should rule and lead the world, a role that we have assigned to ourselves as part of our errand into the wilderness?

In short, what is now before us nationally, and in the full imperial panorama, is the deep, the profoundly perturbed and perturbing question of our relationship to others—other cultures, other states, other histories, other experiences, traditions, peoples, and destinies. The difficulty with the question is that there is no vantage *outside* the actuality of relationships between cultures, between unequal imperial and non-imperial powers, between different Others, a vantage that might allow one the epistemological privilege of somehow judging, evaluating, and interpreting free of the encumbering interests, emotions, and engagements of the ongoing relationships themselves. When we consider the connections between the United States and the rest of the world, we are so to speak *of* the connections, not outside and beyond them. It therefore behooves us as intellectuals, humanists, and secular critics to grasp the role of the United States in the world of nations and of power, from *within* the actuality, and as participants in it, not as detached outside observers who, like Oliver Goldsmith in Yeats's marvelous phrase, deliberately sip at the honeypots of our minds.

Now it is certainly the case that the contemporary travails of recent European and American anthropology reflect the conundrums and the embroilments of the problem symptomatically. The history of that cultural practice in Europe and the United States carries within it as a major constitutive element the unequal relationship of force between the outside Western ethnographer-observer and a primitive, or at least different but certainly weaker and less developed, non-Western society. In *Kim* Rudyard Kipling extrapolates the political meaning of that relationship and embodies it with extraordinary artistic justice in the figure of Colonel Creighton, an ethnographer in charge of the Survey of India, and also the head of the intelligence services in India, the so-called Great Game to which young Kim belongs. In the recent works of theoreticians who deal with the almost insuperable discrepancy between a political actuality based on force and a scientific and humane desire to understand the Other hermeneutically and sympathetically in modes not always circumscribed and defined by force, modern Western anthropology both recalls and occludes that problematic novelistic prefiguration.

As to whether these efforts succeed or fail, that is a less interesting matter than the very fact that what distinguishes them, what makes them possible is some very acutely embarrassed if disguised awareness of the imperial setting, which after all *is* all pervasive and unavoidable. For, in fact, there is no way that I know of apprehending the world from within our culture (a culture, by the way, with a whole history of exterminism and incorporation behind it) without also apprehending the imperial contest itself. And this I would say is a cultural fact of extraordinary political as well as interpretive importance, because it is the true defining horizon, and to some extent, the enabling condition of such otherwise abstract and groundless concepts like "otherness" and "difference." The real problem remains to haunt us: the relationship between anthropology as an ongoing enterprise and, on the other hand, empire as an ongoing concern.

Once the central wordly problematic has been explicitly reinstated for consideration, at least three derivative issues propose themselves for reexamination together with it. One, to which I referred earlier, is the constitutive role of the observer, the ethnographic "I" or subject, whose status, field of activity, and moving locus taken together abut with embarrassing strictness on the imperial relationship itself. Second is the geographical disposition so internally necessary, historically at least, to ethnography. The geographic motif that is profoundly significant in so many of the cultural structures of the West has routinely been preferred by critics in deference to the importance of temporality. But it is the case,

I believe, that we would not have had empire itself, as well as many forms of historiography, anthropology, sociology, and modern legal structures, without important philosophical and imaginative processes at work in the production as well as the acquisition, subordination, and settlement of space. The point is made illuminatingly in recent but quite disparate books like Neil Smith's *Uneven Development,* or Ranajit Guha's *Rule of Property for Bengal,* or Alfred Crosby's *Ecological Imperialism,* works that explore the ways in which proximity and distance produce a dynamic of conquest and transformation that intrudes on cloistral depictions of the relationship between self and other. In ethnography the exercise of sheer power in exerting control over geography is strong. Third is the matter of intellectual dissemination, the exfoliation of scholarly or mono-graphic disciplinary work from the relatively private domain of the re-searcher and his or her guild circle to the domain of policy making, policy enactment, and—no less important—the recirculation of rigorous ethnographic representations as public media images that reinforce policy. How does work on remote or primitive or "other" cultures, soci-eties, peoples in Central America, Africa, the Middle East, various parts of Asia, feed into, connect with, impede, or enhance the active political processes of dependency, domination, or hegemony?

Two instances, the Middle East and Latin America, provide evidence of a direct connection between specialized "area" scholarship and public policy, in which media representations reinforce not sympathy and understanding but the use of force and brutality *against* native so-cieties. "Terrorism" is now more or less permanently associated in public discourse with Islam, an esoteric religion or culture to most people, but one in recent years (after the Iranian Revolution, after the various Lebanese and Palestinian insurrections) given particularly menacing shape by "learned" discussions of it.[15] In 1986, the appear-ance of a collection of essays edited by Benjamin Netanyahu (then Israeli ambassador to the United Nations), entitled *Terrorism: How the West Can Win,* contained three essays by certified Orientalists, each of whom asseverated that there was a connection between Islam and ter-rorism. What this type of argument produced was in fact consent for the bombing of Libya, and for similar adventures in coarse righteous-ness, given that the public had heard it said by experts in print and on television that Islam was little short of a terrorist culture.[16] A second example concerns popular meaning given the word "Indians" in discourse about Latin America, especially as the association between Indians and terrorism (or between Indians as a backward, unregenerately primitive people and ritualized violence) is cemented. Mario Vargas Llosa's famous analysis of an Andean massacre of Peruvian journalists ("Inquest in the Andes: A Latin American Writer Explores the Political Lessons of a Peruvian Massacre," *New York Times Magazine,* July 31, 1983) is premised on the susceptibility of the Andean Indian to particularly terrible forms of indiscriminate murder; Vargas Llosa's prose is shot through with phrases about Indian rituals, backwardness, gloomy unchangeability, all of them relying on the ultimate authority of anthropological descriptions. Indeed, several prominent Peruvian anthropologists were members of the panel (chaired by Vargas Llosa) that investigated the massacre.

These are matters not just of theoretical but of quotidian importance. Imperialism, the control of overseas territories and peoples, develops in a continuum with variously envisaged histories, current practices and policies, and with differently plotted cultural trajectories. Yet there is by now a sizable literature in the Third World addressing an impassioned theoretical and practical argument to Western specialists in area studies, as well as to anthropologists and historians. The address is a part of the revisionist postcolonial effort to reclaim traditions, histories, and cultures from imperialism, and it is also a way of entering the various world discourses on an equal footing. One thinks of the work of Anwar Abdel Malek and Abdullah Laroui, of people like the Subaltern Studies group, C. L. R. James and Ali Mazrui, of various texts like the Barbados Declaration of 1971 (which directly accuses anthropologists of scientism, hypocrisy, and opportunism) as well as the North-South Report and the New World Information Order. For the most part, little of this material reaches the inner chambers of and has no effect on general disciplinary or discursive discussion in metropolitan centers. Instead, the Western Africanists read African writers as source material for their research, Western Middle East specialists treat Arab or Iranian texts as primary evidence for their research, while the direct, even importunate solicitations of debate and intellectual engagement from the formerly colonized are left largely unattended.

In such cases it is irresistible to argue that the vogue for thick descriptions and blurred genres acts to shut and block out the clamor of voices on the outside asking for their claims about empire and domination to be considered. The native point of view, despite the way it has often been portrayed, is not an ethnographic fact only, is not a hermeneutical construct primarily or even principally; it is in large measure a continuing, protracted, and sustained adversarial resistance to the discipline and the praxis of anthropology (as representative of "outside" power) itself, anthropology not as textuality but as an often direct agent of political dominance.

Nevertheless, there have been interesting albeit problematic attempts to acknowledge the possible effects of this realization on ongoing anthropological work. Richard Price's book *First-Time* studies the Saramaka people of Suriname, a population whose way of staying alive has been to disperse what is in effect a secret knowledge of what they call First-Time throughout the groups; hence First-Time, eighteenth-century events that give the Saramakas their national identity, is "circumscribed, restricted, and guarded." Price quite sensitively understands this form of resistance to outside pressure, and records it carefully. Yet when he asks "the basic question of whether the publication of information that gains its symbolic power in part by being secret does not vitiate the very meaning of that information," he tarries very briefly over the troubling moral issues, and then proceeds to publish the secret information anyway.[17] A similar problem occurs in James C. Scott's remarkable book *Weapons of the Weak: Everyday Forms of Peasant Resistance*. Scott does a brilliant job in showing how ethnographic accounts do not, indeed cannot, present a "full transcript" of peasant resistance to encroachments from the outside, since it is peasant strategy (footdragging, lateness, unpredictability, noncommunication, and so on) not to comply with power.[18] And although Scott presents a brilliant empirical as well as theoretical account of everyday resistances to hegemony, he too undercuts the very resistance he admires and respects by in a sense revealing the secrets of its strength. I mention Price and Scott not at all to accuse them (far from it, since their books are extraordinarily valuable) but to indicate some of the theoretical paradoxes and aporias faced by anthropology.

As I said earlier, and as has been noted by every anthropologist who has reflected on the theoretical challenges now so apparent, there has been a considerable amount of borrowing from adjacent domains, from literary theory, history, and so on, in some measure because much of this has skirted over the political issues for understandable reasons, poetics being a good deal easier to talk about than politics. Yet gradually, however, anthropology is being seen as part of a larger, more complex historical whole, much more closely aligned with the consolidation of Western power than had previously been admitted. The recent work of George Stocking and Curtis M. Hinsley is a particularly compelling example,[19] as is also the case with the very different kinds of work produced by Talal Asad, Paul Rabinow, and Richard Fox. At bottom the realignment has to do, I think, first with the new and less formalistic understanding that we are acquiring of *narrative* procedures, and then second, with a far more developed awareness of the need for ideas about alternative and emergent counterdominant practices. Let me now speak about each of these.

Narrative has now attained the status in the human and social sciences of a major cultural convergence. No one who has encountered Renato Rosaldo's remarkable work can fail to appreciate that fact. Hayden White's *Metahistory* pioneered the notion that narrative was governed by tropes and genres—metaphor, metonymy, synecdoche, irony, allegory, and so on—which in their turn regulated and even produced the most influential nineteenth-century historiographers, men whose historical work had been presumed to advance philosophical and/or ideological notions supported by empirical facts. White dislodged the primacy both of the real and of the ideal; then he replaced them with the astringent narrative and linguistic procedures of universal formal codes. What he seemed unwilling or unable to explain was the necessity and the anxiety for narrative expressed by historians, why, for instance, Jakob Burkhardt and Marx employed narrative (as opposed to dramatic or pictorial) structures at all, and inflected them with differing accents that charged them, for the reader, with quite various responses and burdens. Other theoreticians—Fredric Jameson, Paul Ricoeur, Tzvetan Todorov—explored the formal characteristics of narrative in wider social and philosophical frameworks than White had used, showing at once the scale and the significance of narrative for social life itself. Narrative was transformed from a formal pattern or type to an activity in which politics, tradition, history, and interpretation converged.

As a topic of the most recent theoretical and academic discussion, narrative has of course resonated with echoes from the imperial context. Nationalism, resurgent or new, fastens on narratives for structuring, assimilating, or excluding one or another version of history. Benedict Anderson's *Imagined Communities* drives the point home attractively, as do the various contributors to *The Invention of Tradition,* edited by Eric Hobsbawm and Terence Ranger. Legitimacy and normativeness—for example, in recent discussions of "terrorism" and "fundamentalism"—have either given or denied narratives to forms of crisis. If you conceive of one type of political movement in Africa or Asia as being "terrorist" you deny it narrative consequence, whereas if you grant it normative status (as in Nicaragua or Afghanistan) you impose on it the legitimacy of a complete narrative. Thus *our* people have been denied freedom, and therefore they organize, arm themselves, and fight and get freedom; *their* people, on the other hand, are gratuitous, evil terrorists. Therefore narratives are either politically and ideologically permissible, or not.[20]

Yet narrative has also been at issue in the by now massive theoretical literature on postmodernism, which can also be seen as bearing on current political debate. Jean-François Lyotard's thesis is that the two great narratives of emancipation and enlightenment have lost their legitimizing power and are now replaced by smaller local narratives *(petits recits)* based for their legitimacy on performativity, that is, on the user's ability to manipulate the codes in order to get things done.[21] A nice manageable state of affairs, which according to Lyotard came about for entirely European or Western reasons: the great narratives just lost their power. Given a slightly wider interpretation by situating the transformation within the imperial dynamic, Lyotard's argument appears not as an explanation but as a symptom. He *separates* Western postmodernism from the non-European world, and from the consequences of European modernism—and modernization—in the colonized world.[22] In effect then postmodernism, with its aesthetic of quotation, nostalgia, and indifferentiation, stands free of its own history, which is to say that the division of intellectual labor, the circumscription of praxes within clear disciplinary boundaries, and the de-politicization of knowledge can proceed more or less at will.

The striking thing about Lyotard's argument, and perhaps the very reason for its widespread popularity, is how it not only misreads but misrepresents the major challenge to the great narratives and the reason why their power may now appear to have abated. They lost their legitimation in large measure as a result of the crisis of modernism, which foundered on or was frozen in contemplative irony for various reasons, of which one was the disturbing appearance in Europe of various Others, whose provenance was the imperial domain. In the works of Eliot, Conrad, Mann, Proust, Woolf, Pound, Lawrence, Joyce, Forster, alterity and difference are systematically associated with strangers, who, whether women, natives, or sexual eccentrics, erupt into vision, there to challenge and resist settled metropolitan histories, forms, modes of thought. To this challenge modernism responded with the formal irony of a culture unable either to say yes, we should give up control, or no, we shall hold on regardless: a self-conscious contemplative passivity forms itself, as Georg Lukács noted perspicaciously, into paralyzed gestures of aestheticized powerlessness,[23] for example, the ending of *A Passage to India* in which Forster notes, and confirms the history behind, a political conflict between Dr. Aziz and Fielding—Britain's subjugation of India—and yet can recommend neither decolonization nor continued colonization. "No, not yet, not here," is all Forster can muster by way of resolution.[24]

Europe and the West, in short, were being asked to take the Other seriously. This, I think, is the fundamental historical problem of modernism. The subaltern and the constitutively different suddenly achieved disruptive articulation exactly where in European culture silence and compliance could previously be depended on to quiet them down. Consider the next and more exacerbated transformation of modernism as exemplified in the contrast between Albert Camus and Fanon both writing about Algeria. The Arabs of *La Peste* and *L'Etranger* are nameless beings used as background for the portentous European metaphysics explored by Camus, who, we should recall, in his *Chronique algérienne* denied the existence of an Algerian nation.[25] For his part, Fanon forces on a Europe playing "le jeu irresponsable de la belle au bois dormant" an emerging counternarrative, the process of national liberation.[26] Despite its bitterness and violence, the whole point of Fanon's work is to force the European metropolis to think its history *together with* the history of colonies awakening from the cruel stupor and abused immobility of imperial dominion, in Aimé Césaire's phrase, "mesurée au compas de la souffrance" ["measured by the compass of suffering"].[27] Alone, and without due recognition allowed for the colonial experience, Fanon says, the Western narratives of enlightenment and emancipation are revealed as so much windy hypocrisy; thus, he says, the Greco-Latin pedestal turns into dust.

We would, I believe, completely falsify the shattering novelty of Fanon's inclusive vision—which so brilliantly makes use of Césaire's *Cahier d'un retour au pays natal* as Lukács's *History and Class Consciousness* for its synthesis—if we do not stress, as he did, the amalgamation between Europe and its imperium acting together in the process of decolonization. With Césaire and C. L. R. James, Fanon's model for the postimperial world depended on the idea of a collective as well as a plural destiny for mankind, Western and non-Western alike. As Césaire says, "et il rest à l'homme à conquérir toute interdiction immobilisée aux coins de sa ferveur et aucune race ne possède le monopole de la beauté, de l'intelligence, de la force / et il est place pour tout au rendez-vous de la conquête" ["and man still must overcome all the interdictions wedged in the recesses of his fervor and no race has a monopoly on beauty, on intelligence, on strength / and there is room for everyone at the convocation of conquest"].[28]

Thus: think the narratives through together within the context provided by the history of imperialism, a history whose underlying contest between white and nonwhite has emerged lyrically in the new and more inclusive counternarrative of liberation. This, I would say, is the full situation of postmodernism, for which Lyotard's amnesiac vision has been insufficiently wide. Once again *representation* becomes significant, not just as an academic or theoretical quandary, but as a political choice. How the anthropologist represents his or her disciplinary situation is, on one level, of course, a matter of local, personal, or professional moment. But it is in fact part of a totality, one's society, whose shape and tendency depend on the cumulatively affirmative or deterrent and oppositional weight made up by a whole series of such choices. If we seek refuge in rhetoric about our powerlessness or ineffectiveness or indifference, then we must be prepared also to admit that such rhetoric finally contributes to one tendency or the other. The point is that anthropological representations bear as much on the representer's world as on who or what is represented.

I do not think that the anti-imperialist challenge represented by Fanon and Césaire or others like them has by any means been met; neither have we taken them seriously as models or representations of human effort in the contemporary world. In fact Fanon and Césaire—of course I speak of them as types—jab directly at the question of identity and of identitarian thought, that secret sharer of present anthropological reflection on "otherness" and "difference." What Fanon and Césaire required of their own partisans, even during the heat of struggle, was to abandon fixed ideas of settled identity and culturally authorized definition. Become different, they said, in order that your fate as colonized peoples can *be* different; this is why nationalism, for all its obvious necessity, is also the enemy. I cannot say whether it is now possible for anthropology as anthropology to be different, that is, to forget itself and to become something else as a way of responding to the gauntlet thrown down by imperialism and its antagonists. Perhaps anthropology as we have known it can only continue on one side of the imperial divide, there to remain as a partner in domination and hegemony.

On the other hand, some of the recent anthropological efforts critically to reexamine the notion of culture top to bottom may be starting to tell a different story. If we no longer think of the relationship between cultures and their adherents as perfectly contiguous, totally synchronous, wholly correspondent, and if we think of cultures as permeable and, on the whole, defensive boundaries between polities, a more promising situation appears. Thus to see Others not as ontologically given but as historically constituted would be to erode the exclusivist biases we so often ascribe to cultures, our own not least. Cultures may then be represented as zones of control or of abandonment, of recollection and of forgetting, of force or of dependence, of exclusiveness or of sharing, all taking place in the global history that is our element.[29] Exile, immigration, and the crossing of boundaries are experiences that can therefore provide us with new narrative forms or, in John Berger's phrase, with *other* ways of telling. Whether such novel movements are more easily available only to exceptional vi-sionary figures like Jean Genet or to engaged historians like Basil Davidson, who scandalously criss-cross and transgress the nationally constructed barriers, than to professional anthropologists is not for me to say. But what I want to say in any case is that the instigatory force of such examples is of startling relevance to all the humanities and social sciences as they continue to struggle with the formidable difficulties of empire.

After Mahfouz

Naguib Mahfouz's achievement as the greatest living Arab novelist and first Arab winner of the Nobel Prize has in small but significant measure now retrospectively vindicated his unmatched regional reputation, and belatedly given him recognition in the West. For of all the major literatures and languages, Arabic is by far the least known and the most grudgingly regarded by Europeans and Americans, a huge irony given that all Arabs regard the immense literary and cultural worth of their language as one of their principal contributions to the world. Arabic is of course the language of the Koran, and is therefore central to Islam, in which it has a hieratic, historical and everyday use that is almost without parallel in other world cultures. Because of that role, and because it has always been associated with resistance to the imperialist incursions that have characterized Arab history since the late eighteenth century, Arabic has also acquired a uniquely contested position in modern culture, defended and extolled by its native speakers and writers, belittled, attacked, or ignored by foreigners for whom it has represented a last defended bastion of Arabism and Islam.

During the 130 years of French colonialism in Algeria, for example, Arabic was effectively proscribed as a quotidian language: to a lesser degree, the same was roughly true in Tunisia and Morocco, in which an uneasy bilingualism arose because the French language was politically imposed on the native Arabs. Elsewhere in the Arab *mashriq* Arabic became the focus of hopes for reform and renaissance. As Benedict Anderson has shown, the spread of literacy has spurred the rise of modern nationalism, in the midst of which narrative prose fiction played a crucial role in creating a national consciousness. By providing readers not only with a sense of their common past—for example, in the historical romances of the early twentieth-century novelist and historian Jurji Zaydan—but also with a sense of an abiding communal continuity, Arabic novelists stood squarely wherever issues of destiny, society, and direction were being debated or investigated.

We should not forget, however, that the novel as it is known in the West is a relatively new form in the rich Arabic literary tradition. And along with that we should keep in mind that the Arabic novel is an engaged form, involved through its readers and authors in the great social and historical upheavals of our century, sharing in its triumphs as well as its failures. Thus, to return to Mahfouz, his work from the late thirties on compresses the history of the European novel into a relatively short span of time. He is not only a Hugo and a Dickens, but also a Galsworthy, a Mann, a Zola and a Jules Romain.

Surrounded therefore by politics, and to a very great degree caught up in the contests of the native as well as the international environment, the Arabic novel is truly an embattled form. Mahfouz's allegorical trilogy, *Awlad Haritna* (1959), takes on Islam, and was banned in Egypt when it was about to be published. His earlier Cairo *Trilogy* (1956–1957) traversed the phases of Egyptian nationalism, culminating in the 1952 Revolution, and did so critically and yet intimately as a participant in the remaking of Egyptian society. *Miramar* (1967), his *Rashomon-style* novel about Alexandria, puts a sour face on Nasser's socialism, its abuses, anomalies, and human cost. During the late sixties, his short stories and novels addressed the aftermath of the 1967 war, sympathetically in the case of an emergent Palestinian resistance, critically in the case of the Egyptian military intervention in Yemen. Mahfouz was the most celebrated writer and cultural figure to greet the Egyptian-Israeli peace treaty in 1979, and although his books were banned in Arab countries for a time after that, his reputation as a great writer was too well established to be diminished for long. Even in Egypt the position he took was apparently unpopular, yet he has not only survived the temporary opprobrium but emerged (if anything) more august and admired.

Mahfouz's career is of course distinguished in the Arab world not only because of the extraordinary length of his writing life, but because his work is so thoroughly Egyptian (and Cairene), based as it is on a territorial and imaginative vision of a society unique in the Middle East. The thing about Mahfouz is that he has always been able to depend on the vital integrity and even cultural compactness of Egypt. For all its tremendous age, the variety of its components, and the influences on it—the merest listing of these is inhibitingly impressive: Pharonic, Arab, Muslim, Hellenistic, European, Christian, Judaic, etc.—the country has a stability and identity which have not disappeared in this century. Or, to put it differently, the Arabic novel has flourished especially well in twentieth-century Egypt because throughout all the turbulence of the country's wars, revolutions, and social upheavals, civil society was never eclipsed, its identity was never in doubt, was never completely absorbed into the state. Novelists like Mahfouz had it always there for them, and accordingly developed an abiding institutional connection with the society through their fiction.

Moreover, the main historical and geographical features of the Cairo mapped by Mahfouz have been handed down to the generation of writers who came to maturity in the post-1952 period. Gamal al-Ghitani is like Mahfouz, in that several of his works—for example, his recently translated *Zayni Barakat*[1]—are set in districts like Gamaliyia, which is where Mahfouz's realistic novel *Midaq Alley* is also set. Ghitani considers himself one of Mahfouz's heirs, and the overlap in setting and treatment confirms the generational relationship between the older and the younger man, made more explicit through the city of Cairo and Egyptian identity. For later generations of Egyptian writers Mahfouz offers the assurance of a point of departure.

Yet Mahfouz as, so to speak, patron and progenitor of subsequent Egyptian fiction is not by any means a provincial writer, nor simply a local influence. Here another discrepancy is worth noting. Because of its size and power, Egypt has always been a locus of Arab ideas and movements; in addition, Cairo has functioned as a distribution center for print publishing, films, radio, and television. Arabs in Morocco, on the one hand, Iraq, on the other, who may have very little in common, are likely to have had a lifetime of watching Egyptian films (or television serials) to connect them. Similarly, modern Arabic literature has spread out from Cairo since the beginning of the century; for years Mahfouz was a resident writer at *al-Ahram,* Egypt's and the Arab world's leading daily paper. Mahfouz's novels, his characters and concerns, have been the privileged, if not always emulated, norm for most other Arab novelists, at a time when Arabic literature as a whole has remained marginal to Western readers for whom Fuentes, Garcia Marquez, Soyinka, and Rushdie have acquired vital cultural authority.

What I have sketched so schematically is something of the background assumed when a contemporary, non-Egyptian writer of substantial gifts wishes to write fiction in Arabic. To speak of an "anxiety of influence," so far as the precedence of Mahfouz, Egypt, and Europe (which is where, in effect, the Arabic novel before Mahfouz came from) is concerned, is to speak of something socially and politically actual. Anxiety is at work not only in determining what was possible for a Mahfouz in a fundamentally settled and integrated society such as Egypt, but also in determining what, in a fractured, decentered, and openly insurrectionary place, is maddeningly, frustratingly *not* possible. In some Arab countries you cannot leave your house and suppose that when and if you return it will be as you left it. You can no longer take for granted that such places as hospitals, schools, and government buildings will function as they do elsewhere, or if they do for a while, that they will continue to do so next week. Nor can you be certain that birth, marriage, and death—recorded, certified, and registered in all societies—will in fact be noted or in any way commemorated. Rather, most aspects of life are negotiable, not just with money and social intercourse, but also with guns and rocket-propelled grenades.

The extreme cases in which such eventualities are daily occurrences are Palestine and Lebanon, the first of which simply stopped existing in 1948, and was reborn on November 15, 1988, the second a country that began its public self-destruction in April 1975, and has not stopped. In both polities there are and have been people whose national identity is threatened with extinction (the former) or with daily dissolution (the latter). In such societies the novel is both a risky and a highly problematic form. Typically its subjects are urgently political and its concerns radically existential. Literature in stable societies (Egypt's, for instance) is only replicable by Palestinian and Lebanese writers by means of parody and exaggeration, since on a minute-by-minute basis social life for Lebanese and Palestinian writers is an enterprise with highly unpredictable results. And above all, form is an adventure, narrative both uncertain and meandering, character less a stable collection of traits than a linguistic device, as self-conscious as it is provisional and ironic.

Take first two Palestinian novelists, Ghassan Kanafani and Emile Habibi. Kanafani's seems at first sight the more conventional mode, Habibi's the wildly experimental. Yet in *Rijal fil Sharns* (Men in the Sun, 1963), Kanafani's story of Palestinian loss and death is undermined as a narrative by the novel's peculiarly disintegrating prose, in which within a group of two or three sentences time and place are in such an unrelenting state of flux that the reader is never absolutely certain where and when the story is taking place. In his most complex long narrative *Ma Tabaqqa Lakum* (What Is Left for You, 1966), this technique is taken to such an extreme that even in one short paragraph multiple narrators speak without, so far as the reader is concerned, adequate markers, distinctions, delimitations. And yet so pronounced is the unhappy lot of the Palestinian characters depicted by Kanafani that a kind of aesthetic clarification is achieved when story, character, and fate come jarringly together. In the earlier work, three refugees are asphyxiated in a tanker-truck on the Iraqi-Kuwaiti border; in the later novel, Mariam stabs her abusive and bigamous husband while her brother Hamid faces an Israeli in a mortal encounter.

Habibi's *Pessoptimist* (1974) is a carnivalesque explosion of parody and theatrical farce, continuously surprising, shocking, unpredictable. It makes no concessions at all to any of the standard fictional conventions. Its main character (whose name jams together Pessimism and Optimism) is an amalgam of elements from Aesop, al-Hariri, Kafka, Dumas, and Walt Disney, its action a combination of low political farce, Science Fiction, adventure, and Biblical prophecy, all of it anchored in the restless dialectic of Habibi's semi-colloquial, semi-classical prose. Whereas Kanafani's occasional but affecting melodramatic touches put him within reach of Mahfouz's novels in their disciplined and situated action, Habibi's world is Rabelais and even

Joyce to the Egyptian's Balzac and Galsworthy. It is as if the Palestinian situation, now in its fifth decade without definitive resolution, produces a wildly erratic and free-wheeling version of the picaresque novel, which, in its flaunting of its carelessness and spite, is in Arabic prose fiction about as far as one can get from Mahfouz's stateliness.

Lebanon, the other eccentric and resistant society, has been rendered most typically, not in novels or even stories, but in far more ephemeral forms—journalism, popular songs, cabaret, parody, essays. The Civil War, which officially began in April 1975, has been so powerful in its disintegrating effects that readers of Lebanese writing need an occasional reminder that this, after all, is (or was) an Arabic country, whose language and heritage have a great deal in common with those of writers like Mahfouz. Indeed, in Lebanon the novel exists largely as a form recording its own impossibility, shading off or breaking into autobiography (as in the remarkable proliferation of Lebanese women's writing), reportage, pastiche, or apparently authorless discourse.

Thus at the other limit from Mahfouz is the politically committed and, in his own highly mobile modes, brilliant figure of Elias Khoury, whose earliest important work of fiction, *The Little Mountain* (1977), now appears in English for the first time.[2] Khoury is a mass of paradoxes, especially when compared with other Arab novelists of his generation. Like Ghitany, he is, and has been for at least twelve years, a practicing journalist. Unlike Ghitany—whose gifts for invention and verbal bravura he shares—Khoury has been a political militant from his early days, having grown up as a sixties schoolboy in the turbulent world of Lebanese and Palestinian street politics. Some of the city and mountain fighting of the early days (autumn 1975 and winter 1976) of the Lebanese Civil War described in *The Little Mountain* is based on these experiences. Also unlike Ghitany, Khoury is a publishing-house editor, having worked for a leading Beirut publisher for a decade, during which he established an impressive list of Arabic translations of major Post-Modern Third World classics (Fuentes, Marquez, Asturias).

In addition, Khoury is a highly perceptive critic, associated with the avant-garde poet Adonis and his Beirut quarterly *Mawaqif.* Between them, the members of the *Mawaqif* group were responsible during the seventies for some of the most searching investigations of modernity

and Modernism. It is out of this work, along with his engaged journalism—almost alone among Christian Lebanese writers, he espoused,
from the heart of West Beirut and at great personal risk, the cause of
resistance to the Israeli occupation of South Lebanon—that Khoury
has forged (in the Joycean sense) a national and novel, unconventional,
Post-Modern literary career.

This is in stark contrast to Mahfouz, whose Flaubertian dedication
to letters has followed a more or less Modernist trajectory. Khoury's
ideas about literature and society are of a piece with the often bewilderingly fragmented realities of Lebanon, in which, he says in one of
his essays, the past is discredited, the future completely uncertain, the
present unknowable. For him perhaps the most symptomatic and also
the finest strand of modern Arabic writing derives, not from the stable
and highly replicable forms either native to the Arabic tradition (the
qasidah) or imported from the West (the novel), but from those works
he calls formless—Tawfik al-Hakim's *Diaries of a Country Lawyer*, Taha
Hussein's *Stream of Days*, Gibran's and Nuaimah's writings. These
works, Khoury says, are profoundly attractive and have in fact created
the "new" Arabic writing which cannot be found in the more traditional fictions produced by conventional novelists. What Khoury finds
in these formless works is precisely what Western theorists have called
"Post-Modern": that amalgam principally of autobiography, story,
fable, pastiche, and self-parody, highlighted by an insistent and eerie
nostalgia.

The Little Mountain replicates in its own special brand of formless-
ness some of Khoury's life: his early years in Ashrafiya (Christian East
Beirut, known as the Little Mountain), his exile from it for having
taken a stand with the nationalist (Muslim and Palestinian) coalition,
subsequent military campaigns during the latter part of 1975—in
downtown Beirut and the eastern mountains of Lebanon—and finally
an exilic encounter with a friend in Paris. The work's five chapters thus
exfoliate outward from the family house in Ashrafiya, to which neither
Khoury nor the narrator can return, given the irreversible dynamics of
the Lebanese Civil Wars, and when the chapters conclude, they come
to no rest, no final cadence, no respite. For indeed Khoury's prescience
in this work of 1977 was to have seen a worsening of the situation, in
which Lebanon's modern(ist) history was terminated, and from which

a string of almost unimaginable disasters (the massacres, the Syrian and Israeli interventions, the current political impasse with partition already in place) has followed.

Style in *The Little Mountain* is, first of all, repetition, as if the narrator needed this in order to prove to himself that improbable things actually did take place. Repetition is also, as the narrator says, the search for order—to go over matters sufficiently to find, if possible, the underlying pattern, the rules and protocols according to which a civil war, the most dreadful of all social calamities, was being fought. Repetition permits lyricism, those metaphorical flights by which the sheer horror of what takes place—

> Ever since the Mongols . . . we've been dying like flies. Dying without thinking. Dying of disease, of bilharzia, of the plague . . . Without any consciousness, without dignity, without anything—

is swiftly seen and recorded, and then falls back into anonymity.

Style for Khoury is also comedy and irreverence. For how else is one to apprehend those religious verities for which one fights—the truth of Christianity, for instance—if churches are also soldiers' camps, and if priests, like the French Father Marcel in chapter two of *The Little Mountain,* are garrulous and inebriated racists? Khoury's picaresque ramblings through the Lebanese landscapes offered by civil combat reveal areas of uncertainty and perturbation unthought of before, whether in the tranquility of childhood or in the certainties provided by primordial sect, class, or family. What emerges finally is not the well-shaped, studied forms sculpted by an artist of the *mot juste* (like Mahfouz), but a series of zones swept by half-articulated anxieties, memories, and unfinished action. Occasionally a preternatural clarity is afforded us, usually in the form of nihilistic aphorisms ("the men of learning discovered that they too could loot") or of beach scenes, but the disorientation is almost constant.

In Khoury's writing we get an extraordinary sensation of informality. The story of an unraveling society is put before us as the narrator is forced to leave home, fights through the streets of Beirut and up mountains, experiences the death of comrades and of love, and ends up accosted by a disturbed veteran in the corridors and on the platform of the Paris Metro. The startling originality of *The Little Mountain* is its avoidance of the melodramatic and the conventional; Khoury plots episodes without illusion or foreseeable pattern, much as a suddenly released extraterrestrial prisoner might wander from place to place, backwards and forwards, taking things in through a surprisingly well-articulated earth-language which is always approximate and somehow embarrassing to him. Finally, of course, Khoury's work embodies the actuality of Lebanon's predicament, so unlike Egypt's majestic stability as delivered in Mahfouz's fiction. I suspect, however, that Khoury's is actually a more typical version of reality, at least as far as the present course of the Middle East is concerned. Novels have always been tied to national states, but in the Arab world the modern state has been derived from the experience of colonialism, imposed from above and handed down, rather than earned through the travails of independence. It is no indictment of Mahfouz's enormous achievement to say that of the opportunities offered the Arab writer during the twentieth century his has been conventional in the honorable sense: he took the novel from Europe and fashioned it according to Egypt's Muslim and Arab identity, quarrelling and arguing with the Egyptian state, but always its citizen. Khoury's achievement is at the other end of the scale. Orphaned by history, he is the minority Christian whose fate has become nomadic because it cannot accommodate itself to the exclusionism which the Christians share with other minorities in the region. The underlying aesthetic form of his experience is assimilation—since he remains an Arab, very much part of the culture—inflected by rejection, drift, errance, uncertainty. Khoury's writing represents the difficult days of search and experiment now expressed in the Arab East by the Palestinian *intifadah,* as new energies push through the repositories of habit and national life and burst into terrible civil disturbance. Khoury, along with Mahmoud Darwish, is an artist who gives voice to rooted exiles and the plight of the trapped refugees, to dissolving boundaries and changing identities, to radical demands and new languages. From this perspective Khoury's work bids Mahfouz an inevitable and yet profoundly respectful farewell.

It is an irony and contradiction worth noting by way of an epilogue that Darwish, Khoury, and I met together for the first time in six years at Algiers the other week, to attend the meetings of the Palestine National Council. Darwish wrote the Declaration of Statehood, which I helped re-draft and translate into English. Along with the Declaration, the PNC approved resolutions in favor of two states in historical Palestine, one Arab, one Jewish, whose co-existence would assure self-determination for both peoples. Khoury commented relentlessly, but fondly, as a Lebanese, on what we did, suggesting that perhaps Lebanon might some day be like Palestine. All three of us were present as both participants and observers. We were tremendously moved, of course: yet Darwish and I were worried that our texts were being mutilated by politicians and even more worried that our state was, after all, only an idea. Perhaps the habits of exile and eccentricity could not be changed as far as we ourselves were concerned: but for a short, non-stop-talking spell, Palestine and Lebanon were alive in the texts.

Jungle Calling

Unlike Harpo Marx, Tarzan as played by Johnny Weissmuller was not completely mute, but what he had to say ("Tarzan-Jane") in the twelve films he made between 1932 and 1948 was rather minimal. And even that, on one occasion, was considered too much. The following story appears in Gabe Essoe's *Tarzan of the Movies*:

> Johnny's passion for a straight part can best be illustrated by a story he was especially fond of telling: "I remember once (as Tarzan) I was supposed to point somewhere and say, 'You go.' I must've felt talkative that day because I pointed and said, 'You go quick.' 'Cut,' the director yelled. 'What's the matter, Johnny? We don't want to load this scene with any long speeches. Just do it like it's written.'"

Compare this bit of elegant compression with a speech by Tarzan (whose real identity is John Clayton, Lord Greystoke) in *Tarzan of the Apes* (1912), the first of the Edgar Rice Burroughs novels on the jungle hero:

> "You are free now, Jane," he [Tarzan] said, "and I have come across the ages out of the dim and distant past from the lair of the primeval man to claim you—for your sake I have become a

civilized man—for your sake I have crossed oceans and continents—for your sake I will be whatever you will me to be. I can make you happy, Jane, in the life you know and love best. Will you marry me?"

The surprise is that the original Tarzan—Burroughs's fantasy—is so cultivated, whereas the movie Tarzan is a barely human creature, monosyllabic, primitive, simple. Perhaps for that reason the Weissmuller creation, one of the only serial-film characters of the 1930s not to be rehabilitated and seriously studied by critics, is so little appreciated or remembered. It is as if he, Weissmuller and the Tarzan he played, happened without too much fuss and then disappeared into a well-deserved oblivion. The fact, however, is that anyone who saw Weissmuller in his prime can associate Tarzan only with his portrayal. The stream of comic-book, television, and other movie Tarzans, from Lex Barker and Gordon Scott to Ron Ely and Jock Mahoney, end up being trite variations on a noble theme. Weissmuller's apeman was a genuinely mythic figure, a pure Hollywood product that was built out of Burroughs's Anglophilic and racist fantasy as well as a number of other almost whimsical elements (for example, Tarzan's phenomenal swimming powers, which are nowhere mentioned by Burroughs) that came together in a surprisingly effective way. No one was Tarzan for as long as Weissmuller, and no one since his time could do much more than ring some generally uninteresting changes on the routines he established, grunts, tree swinging, Methodist-like rectitude, and all.

Weissmuller's Tarzan had several Janes, of whom only Maureen O'Sullivan really counted in my opinion. An Irishwoman, O'Sullivan had a British accent, unlike her literary prototype, who was Jane Porter from Wisconsin. As Johnny's first lady she acted with a fresh abandon never equaled since. In the days when films were ruled by an iron law concerning nudity (even belly buttons were not supposed to be seen), O'Sullivan appeared almost naked: there was a notorious scene in *Tarzan and His Mate*, the second Weissmuller film, in which as she dives into the water she sheds her nightgown and quickly reveals a breast. This scene was removed or pared down in subsequent releases, but I am certain that I saw the original version, since the recollection of that astonishing sight on the screen seems definitively imprinted on my memory (or imagination, as the case may be). Between them, Weissmuller and O'Sullivan seem to have had a sexual paradise: he worshiped her; she fretted, scolded, and smiled demurely, but without all the encumbrances of suburban domesticity around them—no lawns to mow, no car pools, no plumbing problems—and in between adventures, they seemed to spend a lot of time making out. What scenes there were of "jungle life," whether those were of swimming or swinging through the trees, or just lying around in their tree house, were shot through with sexual suggestion. After all, they rarely wore any clothes to speak of.

One of the saddest things, therefore, was how their basic loincloth costumes grew progressively from tiny fig leaves to grotesquely large and flappy dowager beach costumes. With that change the sexual motif diminished and the tree house grew larger and more elaborate (the change is obvious in *Tarzan Escapes,* 1936): one could watch the embourgeoisement of the Tarzan family taking place before one's eyes. Three films into the series, Tarzan and Jane "found" a baby son (1939), who was thereafter known as "Boy." (The child, incidentally, was adopted so as not to clutter their sexual paradise with the digressive rituals of childbearing; besides, Jane could not wear her costume or go swimming if she was pregnant.) Then again, over time, we could observe Boy growing into adolescence and subsequently into manhood. After ten years of being Tarzan's son, the actor Johnny Sheffield finally left the family, mainly, it seems, because he had grown too large. He reappeared in another series at another studio as Bomba the jungle boy.

The most interesting thing about Weissmuller was how his portrayal of Tarzan paralleled, but did not really match, the ape-man imagined by Chicago-born Edgar Rice Burroughs (1875–1950), a resolutely minor but prolific talent whose creation was an unimaginable, totally unlikely hodgepodge of polymorphous perversity. Burroughs was obviously influenced by *Robinson Crusoe,* Kipling's Mowgli, and Jack London. For the most part, the heroes of his Tarzan novels are always "grey-eyed," tall Anglo-Saxons; their heroines less emphatically WASP ladies with sinewy, clinging bodies, "feminine" to a fault. The villains are unfailingly males—East European Jews, Arabs, blacks—women being almost completely exempted from evil or sin.

Tarzan is the son of an English aristocrat, Lord Greystoke, and Lady Alice, his wife. They are shipwrecked off the coast of Africa and then killed by a band of apes, one of whom, Kala, has recently lost her child. Kala takes the puling infant from the cabin's debris and turns Tarzan into her surrogate son; as he grows older he is always at a disadvantage, as much because he is hairless and relatively small compared with the other young apes as because he is the butt of the tribe's jokes and abuse. During one of his solitary forays, Tarzan discovers his parents' cabin and laboriously teaches himself to read and write from the books and papers left there. This growing capacity for self-consciousness and knowledge, however, does not relieve him of the ape tribe's unpleasant attentions, until as a young man he is forced to challenge the biggest male, Kerchak, to a fight unto death. Tarzan wins the fight, achieves leadership over the apes, but also realizes that he is not after all an ape. Through clumsily engineered plot coincidences Tarzan meets up with a cousin of his and Jane Porter, as well as with Paul D'Arnot, a French lieutenant who is rescued by Tarzan and gives him a private education to rival John Stuart Mill's. Some of this material appears in the film *Greystoke, a* recent but unsuccessful attempt to revive the Tarzan story.

Over the years Burroughs turned out twenty-eight Tarzan novels, in which the aristocratic ape-man (who marries Jane in novel two, *The Return of Tarzan*) sires a splendid son—John, whose jungle name is Korak—and has every conceivable kind of adventure, each of which concludes with a triumphant reassertion of Tarzan's power, moral force, authority. The interesting thing about Burroughs's creation is that his novels have a system from which he never deviates. Thus Tarzan is always both the savage ape-man (whose forehead scar, the result of his battle with an insubordinate ape in volume one, always turns red when he gets angry) as well as the voluble and learned John Clayton, Lord Greystoke. In the jungle world the anthropoids, men included, are divided into several related species: the Tarmangani, or white men; the Mangani, or great apes; the Bolgani, or gorillas; and Gomangani, or local blacks. Tarzan is often accompanied by a little monkey (not a chimpanzee), Nkima; in one novel he rescues and becomes the friend of a magnificent black-maned lion, Jad-Bal-Ja, who often goes on adventures with him. Most of the jungle animals have names (Tantor the elephant, Histah the snake, etc.) in the ape language that Tarzan learned first; these names are repeated from novel to novel. (An "Ape-English" dictionary is provided in Robert Fenton's book *The Big Swingers*.) Tarzan's wealth as an English lord is ensured by the treasures he finds in the lost city of Opar, to which he returns periodically for the replenishment of his coffers and the renewal of his amorous contacts with the tawny La, the high priestess. He has invincible strength, brilliant intelligence, faithful friends and relatives (he is the honorary king of an entire tribe of natives, thus giving himself the black vote in darkest Africa), and seems absolutely ageless. We discover in a late novel that he has had a fountain of youth available to him in one of his African domains, so that although he has turned ninety he never appears to be more than thirty-five.

The fascinating thing, however, is that Johnny Weissmuller has nothing at all like the complexity of all this, which aside from being almost unimaginable in visual terms is also intended to be incongruous and antithetical intellectually, like Jekyll and Hyde. Weissmuller is far more mysterious than the novelistic Tarzan, who by comparison is a walking genealogical table. Burroughs was a relentless Darwinian who believed that the white man would come out on top no matter how handicapped he was by nature or by the far superior strengths of lower forms of anthropoid life. Indeed, Tarzan's life and adventures are heavily plotted proof of this dictum, that the white man must triumph because, as Burroughs never tires of telling us, he has Reason. On the other hand, Weissmuller's power and origins are almost totally obscure. We are never told where he comes from, or how he got the way he did: of his wonderful strength and authority over the jungle there is no doubt. He has a special affinity for elephants, who frequently come to his aid en masse, something that does not occur in the novels. Only once in the entire film series (*Tarzan and His Mate*, 1934) is Tarzan shown to be the special friend of apes.

An Olympic champion many times over, Weissmuller was considered the greatest swimmer in the first half of the twentieth century. Unlike any of the other movie Tarzans who followed him, however, he was not at all muscle-bound; until he got older and fatter his swimmer's physique blended perfectly with the general mystery of his origins and the source of his power. Everything about Weissmuller was flowing, harmonious, and natural. There were no unsightly bulges on his biceps or across his abdomen, just as his unself-conscious presence in the jungle was undisturbed by residues of a narrative that might have explained his history. Weissmuller's Tarzan was pure existence, a sort of degree zero transmuted into the figure and motions of an Adonis-like man. Moreover, his monosyllabic utterances resonated with no background, no symbolic system, no special significance. In the twelve films he made Weissmuller pronounced only one non-English word—"umgawa"—which was an order barked rather briskly at animals who would then obey his command to do something specific, like push a tree trunk out of the way. On a few occasions "umgawa" was an angry expostulation used for telling Cheetah, Weissmuller's semi-delinquent chimpanzee companion (for whom there is no exact equivalent in the novels), to go away or to behave. Less frequently "umgawa" was a shout directed at the recalcitrant blacks who people the series, either as threatening savages or as cowering and incompetently subservient porters, servants, coolies.

Whereas Burroughs clearly had a worked-out theory about the hierarchy of races, the film Tarzan as represented by Weissmuller was actually *more* complex in his racial attitudes. Everyone who has seen the films remembers that the treatment of blacks is in the main very hostile. Tarzan spends considerable time fighting native tribes who worship strange gods, kidnap, torture, and cannibalize other human beings, and who generally do not observe the assumed norms of human behavior. Several of these groups, such as the Leopard men (*Tarzan and the Leopard Woman,* 1946), are animal worshipers and deviants; others, like the Ganelonis in *Tarzan Escapes* (1936), are emanations of an almost gratuitous evil. Yet Tarzan's relationships with whites, especially those who visit Africa, are uniformly poor. Most often Tarzan suspects them on sight. He regularly confiscates and destroys their cameras and guns, totally distrusts their schemes (even when Jane intercedes on their behalf), and is routinely the victim of their nefarious designs. White men are hunters, they are slave dealers, they traffic in contraband, and, by the time World War II has rolled around, they are Nazi agents. Weissmuller signifies his disapproval of them most basically when he immediately refuses to help them capture wild animals, not only for exhibition but for scientific purposes.

In the one film whose main action is set in the Western (and white) world, *Tarzan's New York Adventure*, Tarzan is shown to be completely at odds with the "normal" world: he cannot wear a suit; he is upset by civilized justice and creates mayhem in a courtroom. He finally eludes the police by diving off the Brooklyn Bridge.

Weissmuller's taciturn opposition to any white outsider does not exactly balance his savagery when dealing with blacks, but at least it is consistent with his general attitude toward the jungle. Although I cannot absolutely vouch for it, I feel practically certain in saying that Tarzan does not actively provoke even the most menacing and appalling of his black antagonists. He encounters them only when for one reason or another he must stray into their territory, and I can recall him saying on one occasion that he would prefer not to do even that. In other words, Weissmuller's position is that of the jungle inhabitant who understands and accepts the system, even when it conflicts with his values or threatens his life. Any intruders or over-reachers are to be opposed and fought because they destroy the finely tuned ecological zero state from which Tarzan himself springs, and which he defends earnestly. So that while Burroughs and the various directors and writers who made the films expressed essentially racist views about "inferior" people, there is an unresolved contradiction between those views and Weismuller's behavior, which is irreducibly hostile not just to unfriendly (but unjustifiably provoked) blacks but to anything that might introduce change into the ensemble of jungle balance.

One of the strangest and most unlikely partial confirmations of my theory comes from Frantz Fanon, the brilliant anti-imperialist author who was born in Martinique, became a psychiatrist, and then joined the Algerian FLN as one of its leading theoreticians of struggle against French colonialism. He died of leukemia in 1961, one year before Algerian independence was achieved, at just about the time his last book, *The Wretched of the Earth* (with a famous preface by Jean-Paul Sartre), was published. In an earlier book, *Black Skins, White Masks* (1952), Fanon spoke about Tarzan in a footnote, noting that when one of the films was seen in Martinique everyone in the audience tended to side with Tarzan against the blacks; the same people seeing the film in France feel their black identity much more acutely and are consequently upset by the sight of a white abusing a lot of natives. Tarzan appears as the racial enemy in one setting, whereas in another he is interpreted as a hero who fights to preserve a natural order against those who disturb it.

This is not to deny that Tarzan's world—or rather the world of Weissmuller—is uncomplicated and dangerous, but to say that Tarzan's powers are always adequate to it. It comes as a small surprise to recall that Weissmuller was preceded by a few other screen competitors, none of whom lasted as long as he did or are remembered with anything like his aura. He was the natural hero in an age of heroes with supernatural or extra-human powers, men like Captain Marvel, Superman, Spiderman, whose relatively boring attraction was that they could do things only dreamed of by ordinary men and women. Weissmuller embodied the man whose entirely human powers allowed him to exist in the jungle with dignity and prestige. This was a matter not just of killing lions and giant snakes (he did that brilliantly) but also of flying through trees like a wonderfully resourceful trapeze artist, or swimming in beautiful lakes (constructed on a back lot in Hollywood) faster than the fastest crocodile, or climbing tremendous heights in bare feet and a loincloth. Surrounded by danger and challenge, Weissmuller was never armed with anything more than a large hunting knife and, on occasion, a lariat plus bow and arrows. In one of the rare ecstatic moments of my early adolescence—I must have been about ten—I recall saying to an older male relative that once in the trees or on his escarpment Weissmuller-Tarzan could hold off twenty or thirty, or maybe even fifty, men on the ground.

Juxtaposed with the wall-to-wall elaborate tackiness of the contemporary world there is an irrelevant beauty to the whole idea of Weissmuller's self-sufficiency and relative silence. Yet I still find it attractively compelling. Remember that Weissmuller seemed to have no life *except* in the Tarzan films. This was before the days of talk shows, of massive television hype, of academic analyses of popular culture. When I saw him in the late 1940s and early 1950s as Jungle Jim—an older, chubbier, and fully clothed man who actually spoke, and seemed to reason, like everyone else—Weissmuller in a sense had already happened and was over. He belonged to the world of Hollywood's fantasy lands: the Orient that was peopled with Jon Hall, Maria Montez, and Sabu (in which Genghis Khan was referred to as "Genghiz Kaahan");

Betty Grable's Hawaii; the roads that led Bob Hope and Bing Crosby to places like Morocco; and Carmen Miranda's Latin America. Weissmuller's African jungle was never filmed on location, but it had a modest integrity, unlike the primitive and mischievous hyperrealism of Schwarzenegger's Conan films, whose relationship (and debt) to Tarzan is similar to the way plastic toys resemble, but are somehow inferior to, wooden toys.

Weissmuller's life after his career as Tarzan was like a grotesque parody of his jungle life—Tarzan lost in civilization, or Tarzan from riches to rags. Four of his five marriages ended in divorce. Most of the money he made was squandered on high living (his drinking problems were notorious), and until his death he was plagued by the IRS. For a time he worked at Caesar's Palace in Las Vegas, but he moved to Fort Lauderdale, where he was honorary curator of the International Swimming Hall of Fame until a series of strokes in the 1970s left him an invalid. In 1984 he died in Acapulco, a short distance from the beach where his last Tarzan movie, the only one shot outside Hollywood, *Tarzan and the Mermaids* (1948), was filmed.

Certainly the Tarzan films and novels readily lend themselves to the disenchantments of Freudian and Marxist analysis. Tarzan is an infantilized "lord of the jungle," a man whose apparent adult authority is actually undermined by his activities as an overgrown child running around in a bathing suit, escaping grown-up responsibility more or less forever. Tarzan is the embodiment of an unresolved (avoided?) Oedipal tension; this is especially true in the films, where Weissmuller's parentage is not even referred to, leading one to suspect that he did away with both father and mother. Nor does Tarzan's jungle world, with its superficially utopian atmosphere of what Marx called "primitive communism," bear up under scrutiny. He exploits everyone—blacks, animals, women—and does precious little besides. Lolling about in the trees is not the same thing as productive work.

Yet before we throw Tarzan completely away as a useless degenerate without either social or aesthetic value, he ought to be given a chance as what in fact he is, an immigrant. Yes, he belongs to the same epoch that produced traveling imperialists like Lawrence of Arabia, Kurtz in Conrad's *Heart of Darkness*, and of course Cecil Rhodes, but despite Hollywood and Burroughs himself, Tarzan is much *less* of a dominant figure than any of those white men. He is vulnerable, disadvantaged, and, because of his lonely silence in the movies, pathetic. Weissmuller's face tells a story of stoic deprivation. In a world full of danger this orphan without upward mobility or social advancement as alternatives is, I've always felt, a forlorn survivor. Quite clearly that is not what Hollywood intended to convey. But it is what still comes through: Tarzan the hero diverted from worldly success and with no hope of rehabilitation, in permanent exile. More unusual still is the fact that Weissmuller's performances as Tarzan are both better and more uncompromising than the novelistic original. Time for a Weissmuller revival.

30

Cairo and Alexandria

Alexandria has always been known as Egypt's second city. It was, until recently, the country's summer capital, and during the first half of this century an elegant seaside resort whose pleasant beaches and plentiful historical sites made a visit there an attractive prospect. I've never been convinced by Alexandria, however; throughout the early part of my life, spent in Egypt, I regarded it as boringly affected and impossibly humid, miles beneath Cairo in splendor and interest. Ever since, I have believed that one is either a Cairo person—Arab, Islamic, serious, international, intellectual—or an Alexandria amateur—Levantine, cosmopolitan, devious, and capricious.

My rather severe formula was put to the test when I visited both cities—Alexandria for the first time in three decades—last May. Partisans of either city could boast of great development and change there. Moreover, I was much more aware now of Cairo and Alexandria as historical, political, and cultural sites than I had been when I lived in Egypt: I had in the past experienced each of them as a stream of smells, sights, and sounds (Alexandria ruled by wind and sea, Cairo by river and desert). Since then Nasser and Sadat had come and gone, the results of the 1967 war and Camp David had been absorbed, and Egypt seemed to me to have fashioned a new regional profile out of its unimaginably long and complex history.

Strangely enough, however, I've never developed a taste for Egypt's Pharaonic past, and on my recent trip it did not even occur to me to visit the Pyramids—though I passed them as I drove out from Cairo to Alexandria on the desert road—or the museum, which has always seemed to me confused, impossibly overcrowded, and poorly lit. Cairo's name in Arabic is Al-Qahirah, or The Victorious, which suggests something of its centrality to Islam and the Arab World. Entry to Egypt from Europe is invariably through Cairo, though the drive into the city from the airport is now jumbled with flyovers and dusty highways. You drive from Heliopolis through Abassiya, a large quarter known for its heavy concentration of military offices and barracks, to Midan el Tahrir (Liberation Square), an enormous space near the center of town around which are arrayed government offices, the American University, bus depots, the unused Arab League building, as well as the Nile Hilton. Everywhere you turn you see masses of people moving turbulently, like a wide current of water forced into a small channel.

And yet, unlike the crowds of New York, Cairenes *en masse* never seem threatening or in any way violent. Stand in Midan el Tahrir for an hour and you see the essential good nature and gentleness of this urban people: the scraggly peasant family alighting from a provincial bus; the group of young men, newspapers furled under their arms, joking together and eating *tirmus* (lupin beans in brine); a handful of elderly Effendis (office workers or government employees), an increasingly large number of *muhaggabat* (veiled women), often walking (improperly) with a young man, and likely in Cairo to have dressed up their veil with a little ornament or feather, or to set it off with a flirtatious lifting of the eyebrows. Across the Kasr el Nil bridge, next to the Hilton, is the district known as Zamalek, at whose heart is the Gezira Sporting Club, a pleasure-garden devised by British colonialism and now a middle-class rendezvous filled to overflowing with tennis and croquet players, swimmers, and enormous families picnicking or lounging near the Lido. They too communicate the comfortable and witty gregariousness which is the essential Cairo note.

When I left Cairo in 1960 it had a population of about three million; today metropolitan Cairo has over fourteen million inhabitants, and so the relative safety one feels in their midst is remarkable. Overcrowding is apparent everywhere, but as a visitor you also feel a sense of space and rest in ways that are theoretically impossible. Walking and loitering, for example, are both considerable pleasures. The city is amply provided with large open spaces like Midan el Tahrir and Abdin, the esplanades and corniches along the Nile, the Ibn Tulun Mosque, the old Zoo in Giza, and the wonderful little grotto and aquarium in Zamalek. Informal rest stations grow up whenever a set of street-food vendors gather together: one has sprung up around the handsome Moorish Garden just across the Kasr el Nil Bridge at the entrance to Zamalek. Here you find carts selling sausages, roast corn, grilled liver, *tirmus,* nuts, sesame cakes, *foul* (stewed fava beans, the national staple), soft drinks, and water. Mill about there for a while (eating is not recommended unless you have built up strong immunity) and you will feel not a spectator but a participant in the life of a city bound together like the many branches of a family.

In other words Cairo is a city of innumerable adjustments and accommodations made over time; despite an equal number of provocations and challenges that might have pulled it apart, it seems to me as coherent as ever, the capital of the nineteenth- and twentieth-century Arab world. The center of modern Cairo (still referred to as *il-balad,* or town) runs from Midan el Ataba (the Square of the Threshold) in the east to Gezira and Dokki in the west. The origins of *il-balad* are colonial. It was constructed in the 1860s during the reign of Khedive Ismail, best known as the ruler who had the Suez Canal built (and for whose Opera House Verdi wrote *Aida*). The architecture of the apartment and office buildings that line streets like Sharia Sherif or Abdel Khalek Sarwat are an odd but still engaging combination of Victorian and Mediterranean, ornately European rather than Arab or Islamic. Ismail imported a Parisian architect to plan and build monuments such as the Ezbekia Gardens, a quasi-Parc Monceau complete with fountains, grotto, elaborate paths and mazes. Like the Opera House (modeled on the Palais Garnier), the Ezbekia Gardens have lost their grandeur, though their tattered and dusty remnants can still be visited if you don't mind the squatters and disorderly human traffic coursing through them. The Opera House mysteriously burned down in the early 1970s and was never reconstructed; a large multi-layered parking structure has been erected on its site in Opera Square. Strangely, though, a new Opera House has been built by the Japanese on Gezira Island, where you can attend performances of *La traviata* by Egyptian and Eastern European singers and instrumentalists.

The colonial city comprises the main downtown area plus Garden City, which is where most of the embassies are to be found, and Gezira Island. As Cairo expanded west and north throughout the twentieth century, whole new districts sprang up, like Mohandeseen (a product of the 1960s) and Madinat el Nasr north of Heliopolis, with little planning or zoning. In old quarters like Agouza, Dokki, and Giza proper, which stretches almost to the foot of the Pyramids, high-rises and ramshackle smaller buildings now jostle each other. Cairo is at least as historically rich in its own way as either Rome or Athens, but you never get the sense of history carefully preserved. Cairo doesn't present itself readily, and its finest spots and moments are either (it would seem) improvised, or surprising in the often spiteful juxtapositions of memory and actuality. The Hilton, for instance, commands one of the finest sites along the Nile (though that stretch of the river has otherwise been disfigured by some insensitive hotel development); and it happens to have been built exactly where the British Kasr el Nil barracks once stood, a long-lasting symbol of European dominance. Unlike the other "name" hotels, the Hilton was begun and completed during Abdel Nasser's administration in the late fifties, when he was still trying to interest the United States in his revolution.

Near the Hilton, whose patio swarms with groups of German, Dutch, and American tourists, is the hulk of the Migama, or Ministry of the Interior, a dreadful eyesore whose labyrinthine corridors and innumerable offices still dishearten unfortunate petitioners; it was originally built thirty years ago to crowd out a Coptic Protestant church whose spire appeared to be too large for what is in effect a minority religion in this primarily Sunni Muslim country. I was further reminded of the peculiar convergence between religious sentiment and overcrowding as I walked by and peered into the old music shop, Papazian, on Sharia Adly—its dark interior unchanged, but its floor-to-ceiling drawers, once full of old seventy-eights and European sheet music, now empty and dusty—and bumped at once into a rather speculatively constructed mosque. It was made of wood and canvas and stretched out from the building entrance, right across the pavement and half-way into the street.

No wonder it's easier for the Western visitor to spend time among the ancient monuments, most of which are either on the outskirts of central Cairo or farther south in Upper Egypt, than in the confusing jumble of a teeming city, in which history is displaced without com-memorative plaques, or allowed to crumble slowly, or left to co-exist with other competing histories. Whichever the case, you don't feel that the curatorial conservation of the past is a top priority for Cairo: a communal interest in things that are useful or serve the present takes precedence. And since the present is overwhelmingly demanding, what with poverty, urban crowding, inadequate resources and unstoppable growth, and since the state is somehow unable to plan for all its in-creasingly well-educated and exigent citizens, Cairo fends for itself, and history must do the same. One of the surprises of my early morning walk along the Nile was a little garden, just a few yards from the Meridien, that dipped off the road toward the river. At the center stood a large unidentified bust of someone vaguely familiar. I had to ask several people before anyone could tell me who it represented: Anwar Sadat, alone and pretty much ignored in a corner of the city he ruled for a decade.

Eastern or native Cairo is a string of wonderfully named quarters (Darb el Ahmar, Bab el Khalq, Sayida Zeinab, Bulaq), each with its own collection of memorials, mosques, architectural marvels, and human interest. None is richer or better preserved than El Gamaliya. The dis-trict has gained in interest recently as the site of many of the novels of Naguib Mahfouz, who was born here. The most interesting walk in Cairo begins at the outskirts of Gamaliya, in the Azhar area, with a visit to the mosque and university, followed by a stop at the Wikalet al-Ghuri, a magnificent medieval hostel (where Mahfouz once worked as a clerk in the office of the Waqf, or Ministry of Islamic Endowments), then into the Khan el Khalili Bazaar and finally down the mile-long length of Shari Mu'izz el Din, a street full of little zigzags.

I walked this route with Mahfouz's most gifted disciple and younger friend, the novelist Gamal el-Ghitani, whose extraordinary novel of intrigue in sixteenth-century Cairo, *Zayni Barakat*, is also set in the Gamaliya district and has recently been published in an English translation. Ghitani's theory about the various turns in the street is psychological: that rather than constructing an endlessly long street in a straight line, the architects broke it up to create a sense of what Ghitani calls *wa'ad bil wusul* (promises of arrival). Just when you think you're at the end, the street veers off sideways and then back in its original direction, deferring the distant trajectory and supplying you with momentary relief.

Mu'izz el Din is lined with wonderful buildings, of which the Qala'un mausoleum and hospital is perhaps the most unusual, Persian-like in its ornate arabesques, Gothic in its spirit, Gaudiesque in its florid excess. But the point to remember here is that all the great Islamic buildings are still in use, and must be experienced as *social* practices, not historical monuments. Ghitani knows all the attendants and custodians, and is a family friend of the man who lives in and keeps the magnificent Suhami house, a seventeenth-century merchant's residence with some of the loveliest *moucharabiya* (wooden lattice work) windows in the whole city. Ghitani referred to these windows, which don't use glass, as "disciplining the sun," to characterize the way their repetitive designs break up and tame the fierce light.

Gamaliya fits (almost too perfectly) within the framework provided by an assimilated Cairo history, something, alas, that Alexandria cannot boast. On the other hand, Alexandria has been written about by Lawrence Durrell, E. M. Forster, Pierre Louys, Cavafy, and Ungaretti, none of whose spirits are much in evidence in today's disappointing and disenchanting Mediterranean port. I spent my few days there hunting for the Alexandria of the past, rather like Stendhal's Fabrice searching for Waterloo. I found next to nothing of it. The city has been abandoned, it would seem, by the middle class. Its once elegant and proud Corniche, which swerves from the Ras el Tin Palace in the west to Montazah Palace in the east—both were used by King Farouk as summer residences—is now a more-or-less continuous traffic jam, and most of the buildings that front it are either peeling disconsolately or have been left unfinished. The great hotels are either empty, like the San Stefano, or, like the downtown Cecil, shabbily uninviting.

E. M. Forster's guidebook is nevertheless useful for its descriptions of old Alexandria—places like the Muhammad Ali Square, still airily expansive, though some of the handsome old buildings like the Banco di Roma have gone. The majestic site of the Serapion Temple is now ringed with tenements, whose main feature is innumerable laundry lines, their clothes fluttering gaily in the wind. There was no one there as I wandered through the temple, near the great pillar of Pompey, in and out of the excavated tombs, sphinxes, baths. The little ticket booth at the entrance to the site is held down by what seems to be a whole corps of veiled young women; they are friendly enough, but seem to know nothing about the temple itself. Much the same is true of the Greco-Roman Museum, a handsome and well-appointed repository of coins, statues, and friezes, staffed by devout young women who neither help nor hinder your sojourn.

While I was in Alex (as the city is often called) I learned that sewage and general waste are simply flooded into the sea off the city's best beaches. Even the Montazah beaches, once among the finest anywhere and now parcelled out into small private lots, are littered with eggshells and orange peel; the odd plastic bottle rides the waves like a forlorn buoy, most certainly *not* marking a site for bathing. Having grown so fast, Alexandria has not coped well with providing municipal services for its population. And so, as the poorer crowds drift in for a week or two in the summer, the more affluent tourists from Cairo have headed west to Alamein, Marsa Matruh, and Agami.

So forlorn is the city without its great foreign communities, so apparently without a mission, so reduced to minimal existence as a cut-rate resort that it filled me with sadness. Crowds mob once-attractive shopping streets like Sharia Sherif, intent on bargains from stores that have been divided and sub-divided into garishly over-stocked slits where cheap shoes and plastic beach toys hang from the ceiling in tasteless abundance. The one or two little islands of Levantine refreshment—the restaurant Santa Lucia, or Pastroudis, the coffee shop frequented half a century ago by Cavafy—are mostly empty. When I stopped for dinner at Santa Lucia I was the only customer except for a nervous little Spanish family who ordered steak and chips and left very quickly. The food was passable but indifferently presented and served.

Sadder still was a chance encounter with a middle-aged Alexandrian acquaintance who had returned to the city a year earlier from Belgium, where she had lived for twenty years. Her father had been ill, she said, and needed to have her nearby, so she left her job and took one in

Alexandria. A month or two later he died, and (for reasons she didn't specify) she simply stayed on. She lived alone in a ten-room apartment filled with the European paintings and knick-knacks of bygone times, trying—impossibly but bravely—to consider herself in the "old" Alexandria. She spoke only French and English, though no one except an occasional visitor like myself knew anything but Arabic.

Her loneliness convinced me that Alexandria was in fact over: the city celebrated by European travelers with decadent tastes had vanished in the middle 1950s, one of the casualties of the Suez war, which drowned the foreign communities in its wake. One of the few meaningful glimpses of the old Alexandria is a little quasi-monument to Cavafy, the great Greek poet and a former Alexandrian resident, that exists more or less secretly on the second floor of the Greek Consulate. The British travel writer Gavin Young had advised me before I left to go to the consulate and ask to see the Cavafy room, but at the time I hadn't paid much heed. Since Alexandria boasts no easily available telephone directory (another sign of its abandonment), I was left to fend for myself when I finally recalled our conversation. It took half a day to find the consulate, though it stands right across from the University of Alexandria Medical School in Chatby, a section of the modern city about a mile west of Montazah.

The consulate clerk, a cross Greek woman with better things to do than to speak to unannounced passersby like myself, told me I couldn't expect to come in just like *that*. When I asked why not, she was slightly taken aback, and then more amiably suggested that I come back in an hour. I didn't leave, for fear that the consulate might disappear; I parked myself on the staircase with the Keeley and Sherrard translation of Cavafy's poetry. After an hour I was shown up to a spacious room in which the Cavafy memorial reposed, unused, unvisited, unconsulted, mostly uncared for. In the bookshelves there were about three hundred volumes of French, English, and Latin works, many of them annotated by the poet, all of them handsomely bound. In the center of the room were several glass cases exhibiting manuscripts, correspondence between Cavafy and other writers (including Marguerite Yourcenar), first editions, and photographs. The bright young Egyptian attendant told me that the small group of chairs and tables came from the Pension Amir, Cavafy's last home in Alexandria. Other visitors to the city have reported that when they went to the Pension Amir, they were approached with offers from people who had "Cavafy furniture" to sell, so one cannot know whether the pieces at the Greek Consulate belonged to the poet or not. Nevertheless, the memorial's melancholy situation, hidden away in a city that has no other recollection of one of the greatest poets of our century, corresponded perfectly with what I had already discovered: that those few parts of Alexandria's colonial past which have not disappeared completely have been consigned to decay.

I returned to Cairo by train the next day. The weather had suddenly turned ugly; Alexandria had grown extremely hot and grey, the sun had disappeared, and the winds had come up from the south. By the time I arrived in late afternoon, a full-fledged sirocco or *khamsin* was upon the capital, but the streets were as lively as always. According to Edmund Keeley, Cavafy had constructed a "sensual city" out of Alexandria, of which nothing remains. No one has ever attempted such a feat in Cairo and it is the better for it. In Cairo you see evidence of many different narratives, identities, histories, most of them only partially there, many of them now either ragged or diminished. But Cairo has not really suffered the amputations Alexandria has. Its busy life is much like the weedlike activity of a Dickens novel, only with an abiding Islamic authority. But you can sense that only if you leave the Cecil B. de Mille and Cook's Tour map. Open yourself instead to Cairo's Fatimid, Ottoman, colonial, and contemporary riches, which, you will soon discover, are far more nourishing than its ancient monuments.

31

Homage to a Belly-Dancer

The greatest and most famous singer of the twentieth-century Arab world was Um Kalthoum, whose records and cassettes, fifteen years after her death, are available everywhere. A fair number of non-Arabs know about her too, partly because of the hypnotic and melancholy effect of her singing, partly because in the worldwide rediscovery of authentic people's art Um Kalthoum is a dominant figure. But she also played a significant role in the emerging Third World women's movement as a pious "Nightingale of the East" whose public exposure was as a model not only of feminine consciousness but also of domestic propriety. During her lifetime, there was talk about whether or not she was a lesbian, but the sheer force of her performances of elevated music set to classical verse overrode such rumors. In Egypt she was a national symbol, respected both during the monarchy and after the revolution led by Gamal Abdel Nasser.

Um Kalthoum's career was extraordinarily long, and to most Arabs it was the highly respectable while very romantic tip of the eroticism typified by the belly-dancer. Like the great singer herself, belly-dancers routinely performed in films, theaters, and cabarets, and on the ceremonial platforms of weddings and other private celebrations in Cairo and Alexandria. Whereas you couldn't really *enjoy* looking at the portly and severe Um Kalthoum, you couldn't do much more than enjoy looking at fine belly-dancers, whose first star was the Lebanese-born Badia Massabni, also an actress, cabaret-owner, and trainer of young talent. Badia's career as a dancer ended around World War Two, but her true heir and disciple was Tahia Carioca, who was, I think, the finest belly-dancer ever. Now seventy-five and living in Cairo, she is still active as an actress and political militant and, like Um Kalthoum, the remarkable symbol of a national culture. Um Kalthoum performed at King Farouk's wedding in 1936, and the lavish party was also Tahia's debut. It gave her a prominence she never lost.

During her heyday as dancer *extraordinaire* Tahia Carioca embodied a very specific kind of sexiness, which she rendered as the most smooth and understated of dancers, and as a highly visible *femme fatale* in Egyptian films. When I looked up the actual number of films she made between the early forties and 1980 I was able to find 190 titles; when I asked her about them in Cairo during the spring of 1989, she couldn't remember the exact figure but opined that the sum was well over 200. Most of her early films included at least one dance number—every Egyptian film that did not pretend to be "high drama" (only a handful did) had to include a song-and-dance routine. This was a formula rather like second-act ballets in nineteenth-century-Paris opera performances: ballets were put on whether or not they fitted the story. In Egyptian films an announcer would suddenly appear on screen and name a singer and dancer; the scene would reveal itself (often gratuitously) to be a nightclub or a large living-room; then an orchestra would strike up the music, and the performance began.

Tahia did such scenes. But they were no more than crude shorthand sketches for her full-scale cabaret performances, the only one of which I actually witnessed I shall forever remember with startling vividness. It took place in 1950. An enterprising schoolmate had discovered that she was dancing at Badia's open-air casino alongside the Nile in Giza (today the site of a high-rise Sheraton), tickets were obtained, and four awkward fourteen-year-olds arrived on the appointed evening at least two hours before she was to begin. The daytime heat of that June day had pretty much dissolved into a balmy, slightly windy evening. By the time the lights went down for the star turn, Badia's was full, all forty or so tables packed with an entirely Egyptian audience of middle-class aficionados. Tahia's partner for the evening was the singer Abdel Aziz Mahmoud, a stolid-looking, bald gentleman in a white dinner-jacket who walked out, planted himself on a wood-and-wicker chair in the middle of the primitive stage, and began to sing to the accompaniment of a small *takhta,* or Arab orchestra, seated off to one side. The song was "Mandil-el-Helou" ("A Pretty Handkerchief"), whose innumerable verses celebrated the woman who draped it, cried into it, decorated her hair with it, on and on for almost a full hour.

There were at least fifteen minutes of this before Tahia suddenly revealed herself a few feet behind the singer's chair. We were sitting about as far from the stage as it was possible to sit, but the shimmering, glistening blue costume she wore simply dazzled the eye, so bright were the sequins and spangles, so controlled was her quite lengthy immobility as she stood there with an entirely composed look about her. As in bullfighting, the essence of the classic Arab belly-dancer's art is not how much but how little the artist moves: only the novices, or the deplorable Greek and American imitators, go in for the appalling wiggling and jumping around that passes for "sexiness" and harem hootchy-kootch. The point is to make an effect mainly (but by no means exclusively) through suggestiveness, and—in the kind of full-scale composition Tahia offered that night—to do so over a series of episodes knitted together in alternating moods, recurring motifs. For "Mandil-el-Helou" Tahia's central motif was her relationship to the largely oblivious Abdel Aziz Mahmoud. She would glide up behind him, as he droned on, appear as if to fall into his arms, mimic and mock him—all without ever touching him or eliciting any response.

Her diaphanous veils were laid over the modified bikini that was basic to the outfit without ever becoming its main attraction. The beauty of her dance was its connectedness: the feeling she communicated of a spectacularly lithe and well-shaped body undulating through a complex but decorative series of encumbrances made up of gauzes, veils, necklaces, strings of gold and silver chains, which her movements animated deliberately and at times almost theoretically. She would stand, for example, and slowly begin to move her right hip, which would in turn activate her silver leggings, and the beads draped over the right side of her waist. As she did all this, she would look down at the moving parts, so to speak, and fix our gaze on them too, as if we were all watching a separate little drama, rhythmically very controlled, re-configuring her body so as to highlight her semi-detached right side. Tahia's dance was like an extended arabesque elaborated around her seated colleague. She never jumped, or bobbed her breasts, or went in for bumping and grinding. There was a majestic deliberateness to the whole thing that maintained itself right through even the quicker passages. Each of us knew that we were experiencing an immensely exciting—because endlessly deferred—erotic experience, the likes of which we could never hope to match in real life. And that was precisely the point: this was sexuality as a public event, brilliantly planned and executed, yet totally unconsummated and unrealizable.

Other dancers might go in for acrobatics, or slithering about on the floor, or modified strip-teasing, but not Tahia, whose grace and elegance suggested something altogether classical and even monumental. The paradox was that she was so immediately sensual and yet so remote, unapproachable, unobtainable. In our severely repressed world these attributes enhanced the impression she made. I especially recall that once she started dancing, and continuing through the rest of her performance, she had what appeared to be a small self-absorbed smile on her face, her mouth open more than is usual in a smile, as if she was privately contemplating her body, enjoying its movements. Her smile muted whatever tawdry theatricality attached to the scene and to her dance, purifying them by virtue of the concentration bestowed on her innermost and most self-abstracted thoughts. And indeed, as I have watched her dancing through at least twenty-five or thirty of her films, I have always found that smile, lighting up the usually silly or affected setting—a still point of the turning world.

That smile has seemed to me symbolic of Tahia's distinction in a culture that featured dozens of dancers called Zouzou and Fifi, most of them treated as barely a notch above prostitutes. This was always evident during periods of Egyptian prosperity, the last days of Farouk, for instance, or when the oil boom brought wealthy Gulf Arabs to Egypt; it was also true when Lebanon was the Arab world's playground, with thousands of girls available for display or hire. Most belly-dancers would appear in such circumstances to go to the highest bidder, the night-club serving as a temporary shop-window.

The pressures of a conservative Islamic culture were to blame for this, as were the distortions produced by uneven development. To be a respectably nubile woman was usually to be destined for marriage without much transition from adolescence; to be young and attractive has therefore not always been an advantage, since a conventional father might for that very reason arrange a wedding with a "mature" and well-off man. If women didn't fall within those schemes, they risked all sorts of opprobrium.

Tahia belongs, not to the easily identified culture of B-girls and fallen women, but to the world of progressive women skirting or unblocking the social lanes. She remained organically linked, however, to her country's society, because she discovered another, far more interesting role for herself as dancer and entertainer. This was the all-but-forgotten role of *almeh* (literally, a learned woman), spoken of by nineteenth-century European visitors to the Orient such as Edward Lane and Flaubert. The *almeh* was a courtesan of sorts, but a woman of significant accomplishments. Dancing was only one of her gifts: others were the ability to sing and recite classical poetry, to discourse wittily, to be sought after for her company by men of law, politics, and literature.

Tahia is referred to as *almeh* in her best film, one of her earliest, *Li'bet il Sit* ("The Lady's Ploy," 1946), which also stars the greatest of twentieth-century Arab actors and comedians, Naguib el-Rihani, a formidable combination of Chaplin and Molière. In the film, Tahia is a gifted young dancer and wit, used by her rascally parents to ensnare men of means. Rihani, who plays an unemployed teacher, is fond of her and she loves him, but she is lured by her parents into a get-rich scheme involving a wealthy Lebanese. In the end, Tahia returns to Rihani—a rather sentimental conclusion of a kind that few of her other films permit themselves. She performs a short but wonderfully provocative dance in the film, but that is meant to be an almost minor affair compared to the display of her wit, intelligence, and beauty.

Subsequently Tahia seems to have been fixed by film directors in a coarser version of this role, which she repeats in film after film. She is the other woman, a counter to the virtuous, domestically acceptable, and much less interesting female lead. Even within those limits, Tahia's talents shine through. You believe she would be more interesting as companion and as sexual partner than the woman who gets married to the leading man, and you begin to suspect that because she is so talented and so sexy, she has to be portrayed as a dangerous woman—the *almeh* who is too learned, too smart, too sexually advanced, for any man in contemporary Egypt. By the fifties Tahia had become the standard woman-as-devil figure in dozens of Egyptian films. In *Shabab Imra'*, considered a later classic, she plays the role of a tough but sexually starved widow who rents a room to a handsome country bumpkin recently come to Cairo as an Azhar student; she seduces and marries him; but when he meets the angelic daughter of a family friend, he awakens from Tahia's Circe-like spell, denounces her, and leaves her for the safe, boring younger woman. In an otherwise undistinguished parable there is one great scene, in which Tahia pulls her young husband away from a street celebration that features a young belly-dancer who has captivated the inexperienced student. Tahia takes him into their house, sits him down, and tells him that she will now show him what real dancing is like. Whereupon she treats him to a private performance that positively smoulders, proving that, middle-aged or not, she still is the finest dancer, the most formidable intellect, and the most desirable sexual object around.

Like many expatriates for whom Tahia was one of the great sexual symbols of our youth, I assumed that she would go on dancing more or less forever. Consider the rude shock when, after an absence from Egypt of fifteen years, I returned there in the summer of 1975 and was told that Cairo's longest-running dramatic hit featured Tahia Carioca and her newest husband, Fayek Halawa, who had also written the play, *Yahya al-Wafd* ("Hooray for the Delegation"). On my second night in Cairo I went to the old Cinema Miami, now an open-air theater, all excitement and sentimental expectation at this rare chance to recover some part of my all-but-buried youth. The play was an overwhelmingly long and vulgar farce about a group of Egyptian villagers who had a delegation of Soviet agricultural experts foisted on them. Relentlessly the play exposed the Russians' rigid unpleasantness (Sadat had thrown out all Russian advisers in 1972) while celebrating the Egyptians' witty deflation of their schemes. It began at about 9:30, but I could only endure two-and-a-half hours (i.e., half) of its idiotic badinage.

No small part in my disillusionment was what had become of Tahia. She had the role of the loudest, toughest village woman, whose prize ram was rented out for breeding purposes (lots of predictable jokes about sexual potency). But it was her appearance and manner that took my breath away. Gone was the tawny seductress, the graceful dancer who was all elegance and perfectly executed gesture. She had turned into a 220-pound swaggering bully; she stood with her hands on her hips unreeling insults, uttering the coarsest of one-liners, the easiest of double-entendres, in an almost unwatchable slapstick style, all of it at the service of what seemed to be the worst kind of opportunistic pro-Sadat, anti-Nasser politics. This was a period when Egyptian policy, moving away from the progressive, Third World and Arab commitments of its post-1954 history under Nasser, was trying to please Henry Kissinger. It saddened me that Tahia and her scrawny little husband should be involved in this kind of thing.

In the fourteen years since that trip to Egypt, bits and pieces of information about Tahia have added complexity to her portrait. A well-known Egyptian sociologist told me, for example, that during the forties and fifties she had been very close to the Communist Party. This, he said, was "the radicalization of the belly-dancers." In 1988 I learned that she appeared in Athens as part of a group of Egyptian and other Arab artists and intellectuals who had signed on to join the Palestinian ship *el-Awda* ("Return") in a symbolic reverse-exodus journey back to the Holy Land. After two weeks of one mishap after another the boat was blown up by the Israeli secret service and the project abandoned. I later heard that Tahia had also emerged as one of the leaders of a very vocal and politically advanced syndicate of cinema actors, directors, and photographers. What then was the truth about the dancer who was now seventy-five and had attained the position of a senior, almost establishment figure in the post-Sadat culture of late twentieth-century Egypt?

Through a friend of Tahia's, the documentary film-maker Nabiha Loutfy, I set up an appointment to see her. She now lives in a small apartment about a block away from where I saw her dance forty years before. She greeted Nabiha and myself with a solemn dignity I had not expected. Dressed in austere black, she was very well made-up, her arms and legs, however, covered in the long sleeves and dark stockings of the pious Muslim woman. She was slightly less large than she had been, and there was no vulgarity. She now communicated a gravity and authority that came from her being much more than just a former belly-dancer. A living legend perhaps, or a famous sage: the *almeh* in semi-retirement. Nabiha addressed her as *Hajja*, the Islamic epithet accorded to elderly women who have made the pilgrimage to Mecca, a designation reinforced not only by her extremely sober mien but by the many pictures of Mecca on the wall and by the Koran plainly in view on a nearby table. As we sat and chatted, her life passed before us in majestic review.

She came from an Ismailia family long active in politics, and her real name is Tahia Mohammed Kraiem. Her paternal uncle was killed by the British, and, she went on proudly, at least three of her family were named Nidal ("Struggle"). Her father had spent time in prisons. She was somewhat Tartuffian when she described her feelings about dancing—like being in a temple, she said—but it was clear as she spoke that she had believed herself to be doing more in her dancing than enticing men like some common *entraîneuse*. "My life as a dancer has been beautiful, and I love it," she said with total conviction. Tahia saw herself—correctly, I believe—as part of a major cultural renaissance, a nationalist revival in the arts based on the liberal independence movement of Saad Zaghloul and his revolution of 1919: the artistic figures included writers like Naguib Mahfouz, Tawfik al-Hakim, Taha Hussein, singers like Um Kalthoum and Abdel Wahhab, actors like Soleiman Naguib and Rihani. As a young girl she had been taught by Badia, who advised her not to hang around night-clubs and bars once she had performed her number. Wistfully she added that she found it very hard to learn to use castanets, but finally managed thanks to Badia, a woman she spoke of with love and veneration.

As the tea and biscuits were brought out I asked her to talk about her political life. Her descriptions were extraordinary, as much because I realized for the first time that she had always been part of the nationalist Left (Nasser, she said, had jailed her in the fifties because she had been a member of the League for Peace, a Moscow front organization) as because she had so low an opinion of Egypt's present leaders. I asked her about the awful *Yahya al-Wafd*. It was considered a Sadatist play, she said, but she saw it mainly as a play about the Egyptian readiness always to think of foreigners "as better than we are." This somewhat unconvincing rationale for what I still thought an obviously self-serving pro-Sadat play led her into a diatribe against her former husband, Fayek Halawa, who, she complained, had dragged her into one disaster after another. "Why," she asked, "do you think I live here and not in my house? He took it and everything in it, including all my pictures and films, leaving me with nothing at all." Pathos quickly gave way to vivacity when I asked her about the United States, which she had visited several times. Once she had even crossed the country by car, a trip she found wonderful. "Liked the people, but hate their government's policy."

For someone who had grown up on Egyptian films without knowing much about their background, and for whom Tahia's dancing was a rich but relatively unexplored memory, talking with this venerable old woman was exhilarating. She was a source of information on a huge variety of subjects, all of it narrated with warmth, humor, and a very attractive irony. At one point her discourse was interrupted by the evening call to prayer, broadcast with an ear-splitting roar from the minaret of a nearby mosque. At once she stopped herself, closed her eyes, extended her arms, palms facing upwards, and recited the Koranic verses along with the muezzin. The moment the prayers were over I burst out with the hopelessly over-determined question I had long held within me, perhaps ever since I saw her dance in 1950. "How many times have you been married, Tahia?" I asked. This was as close as I could come to asking her to connect the sensuality of her dancing (and that incredible smile of hers) with her personal life.

The transformation in her appearance was stunning. She had barely finished her prayers when, in response to my question, she sat up straight, one elbow cocked provokingly at me, the other arm gesturing rhetorically in the air. "Many times," she retorted, her voice taking on the brassiness one associates with a lady of the night. Her eyes and her tone seemed to add: "So what? I've known lots of men." Seeking to get us out of this little impasse, the ever-solicitous Nabiha asked her which of them she had loved, which had influenced her. "None at all," she said harshly. "They were a shabby lot of bastards," a declaration followed by a string of expletives. Far from the resignation and detachment of a prayerful old age, this powerful outburst revealed an individualist and a fighter. And yet one also felt the romantic spirit of a person often de-

ceived, who, given a chance, would fall in love again. Tahia's latest difficulties with a man, the rascally Fayek Halawa, were chronicled in remorseless detail. Our sympathies were fully with her, however, as they
were when she and Nabiha took off after a wealthy film distributor who
was trying to manipulate the syndicate. "Ah, men," she sighed. Her lively
eyes looked at me quizzically.

She knew the patterns and forms of her world, and to a great extent
she had respected them. A dutiful daughter then, a pious older
Muslim now. Yet Tahia was also an emblem of all that was unadministered, uncontrolled, uncoopted in her culture: for such energies the
career of *almeh*, dancer, and actress nonpareil was a perfect resolution.
You could feel the assurance she had brought to her relation with the
centers of authority, the challenge of a free woman. When I went to the
central cinema archive in Cairo the next day to look for photographic
and written material about her, I found only a shambles, a little apartment downtown with more employees than work, more vague designs
to chronicle Egypt's rich artistic history than plans to get the real work
done. Then I saw that Tahia was her own history, largely undocumented but still magisterially present, and subversive to boot.

32

Introduction to *Moby-Dick*

The daring aesthetic beauty and terrifying intensity of *Moby-Dick* have earned it a place of great honor as novel and as remarkable cultural document. No novel in Europe was ever so undomesticated and so unruly in its energies; yet there are few novelistic heroes more clearly memorable, more original and well-fashioned than Captain Ahab. The plot of *Moby-Dick* is Euripidean in its darkly sinuous outlines, and shares with many of the finest works of fiction the unendingly rich and compelling resonance of a quest and pilgrimage story. Its connections to Homer, Dante, Bunyan, Cervantes, Goethe, Smollett are plainly there to be observed and enjoyed. But there are no novels or quest narratives that are so relentlessly declamatory as *Moby-Dick,* whose authors are so bent on instruction, symbolism, preaching, mockery, irony, whose texture and action are so clotted with information, quotation, practical (and impractical) advice, argument, and a wonderfully attractive, hypnotic turgidity.

The greatest and most eccentric work of literary art produced in the United States, *Moby-Dick* communicates on such a variety of levels and through so large an assortment of modes as almost to beggar description or understanding. In his life its author was, however, scarcely as odd as his masterwork, at least on the surface. Herman Melville was born in New York in 1819, the third child and second son of parents who came from distinguished, extremely well-connected families; yet the eight Melville children and their widowed mother endured a life of financial uncertainty, displacement, and constant anxiety that continued for Herman well after his own marriage. He was always a bright, enterprising boy. Even though his education was a limited one, he held various clerical and school jobs and, after a few years of that, took a series of trips across the country, then finally shipped aboard several oceangoing vessels. In 1841 he served on the *Acushnet,* a whaler; later he was seaman on various other ships, including an American warship, the frigate *United States.* Until 1844, therefore, Melville traveled the world, gathering experiences, impressions, and values from sea life and exotic places that were to furnish his written work with an enduring subject matter and personality.

Melville settled his life thereafter on dry land, and seems to have taken up the career of professional writer largely because he did not have any other ready way of earning a living. Besides, his first books (*Typee, Omoo,* and *Mardi*) were largely accounts of his extraordinarily rich travels, mainly in the Pacific, and thus became a natural extension in writing of his life as a sailor. There seemed to be a market for such narratives, and once he had started to write Melville found it a relatively lucrative, not to say successful, enterprise. He married, fathered a child in 1849, and in the same year began work on *Moby-Dick,* which he completed in the latter part of 1851.

When it appeared, the book seems to have had only a muted success. Certainly it did not encourage him to write anything like it ever again, although he continued turning out essays, novels, and poetry until his death in 1891. A fairly well-known writer in his lifetime, Melville was admired by such important literary figures as Nathaniel Hawthorne (to whom *Moby-Dick* is dedicated) and Henry Longfellow. Paradoxically a child of his times—*Moby-Dick,* for example, is steeped in the tremendous social and political debates of the 1850 crisis that presaged the Civil War—Melville was also destined to remain curiously at odds with them. *Moby-Dick* passed from the literary scene during Melville's lifetime and did not really return to a sustained presence for a large audience until the mid-1920s, when it was rediscovered. It has since enjoyed success as the towering work of literature that it is.

A number of Melville's biographers, such as Leon Howard, Newton Arvin, and Michael Paul Rogin, stress the irreducibly American quality of his life and work: its anxious meditations upon and affiliations with the Puritan and familial past, its arguments with legal and political controversies (such as slavery, the Indian heritage, America's connections with the rest of the world), Melville's problematic situation as a writer in a relatively new republic whose literary tradition was as yet unformed and undistinguished. This is all certainly true and it is most interesting. Yet *Moby-Dick*, as I have suggested, is also a book at odds with itself as a novel: this is no less true about Melville as American, since the range, the overreaching, the tremendous energies of this magnificent story of hunting the White Whale spill over national, aesthetic, and historical boundaries with massive force. I suppose it is true to say that only an American could have written *Moby-Dick*, if we mean that only an author as prodigiously endowed as Melville was could also have been, as an American, so obsessed with the range of human possibility. What he enacted in *Moby-Dick* is the encounter between an audacious, rude, and willful force with an elusive, yet unendingly attractive and radically mysterious fate. The more clear in outline and purpose Captain Ahab—Quaker, New England sea captain, tragic hero—becomes, the more driven he is toward the monster albino whale, and the less easily grasped as a historical, national, existential episode the whole thing between the two of them seems.

Seen in this way the Melville of *Moby-Dick* strangely resembles Joseph Conrad, the Anglo-Polish author of *Heart of Darkness* (1902), that eerie novelistic echo of the great American whaling epic. Both Conrad and Melville are writers who were restless in the environments in which they worked, whose explorations of peripheral, unknown, or exotic regions were in fact risky voyages away from everything that is routine or normal, and became investigations of the largely unknown limits of their worlds. As such then their most radical work is in effect a challenge to stable identity itself, in Conrad's case the European and "white" world of his times, in Melville's the American and not completely organized world of the young republic. The difference between them is that whereas Conrad in *Heart of Darkness* wrote about an old imperial enterprise coming to exploit a "new" African territory, Melville wrote about a new action in which the *Pequod* sets forth to discover a very old, much-written-about world of the timeless seas.

An even more interesting similarity that connects Melville to Conrad is the strangeness, the unaccustomed irregularity of their idioms. To read them both is of course to read English, but rarely has English been forced into such self-conscious, shifting, and unpredictable accents. Conrad's sound is the result of writing in a foreign language learned laboriously at age twenty, then employed to describe experiences both exotic and very often nearly indescribable, as for example in "The word 'ivory' rang in the air, was whispered, was sighed. You would think they were praying to it. A taint of imbecile rapacity blew through it all, like a whiff from some corpse."

Melville's prose—and indeed everything about *Moby-Dick* as a strenuously crafted work of literary art—tells of someone always moving away from the expected or the known. In some very profound and affecting way therefore the voyage of the *Pequod* in *Moby-Dick* is something like Melville's own voyage in language and form away from domestic life, into an alternative realm of visionary imagination and entirely novel striving. This is readily evident in such passages as this:

> All that most maddens and torments; all that stirs up the lees of things; all truth with malice in it; all that cracks the sinews and cakes the brain; all the subtle demonisms of life and thought; all evil, to crazy Ahab, were visibly personified, and made practically assailable in Moby Dick. He piled upon the whale's white hump the sum of all the general rage and hate felt by his whole race from Adam down; and then, as if his chest had been a mortar, he burst his hot heart's shell upon it.

We now know that Melville began writing *Moby-Dick* as a tale that considerably depended upon his own youthful experiences as a whaler; this embellished autobiographical mode was after all one he had exploited both well and profitably in his earlier works. At some point in the story, however, a more unusual, hitherto subterranean theme took him over, rather like the way after boarding the *Pequod* at night Captain Ahab remains hidden for many chapters, then emerges to dominate the proceedings definitively. The second effort, sometimes referred to by critics as the second *Moby-Dick,* necessitated a wholly different and much heightened prose, which Melville then introduced retrospectively into what he had already written. The present text of *Moby-Dick* is a result of Melville's grafting and rewriting of the two versions, with all sorts of irregularities and inconsistencies that were never completely taken care of: Bulkington, for instance, belongs to the first version and is supposed to play a significant role there. In the final text he is referred to briefly, then drops out. Curiously, such apparent flaws seem actually to add to Melville's overall effect.

Thus the novel remains the story of the *Pequod* and its motley crew, but it is also a metaphysical search for the absolute, as well as a garrulous, often pedantic course in the technique of whaling, the science of cetology, and the history of whalers and whales. Nor is this all. *Moby-Dick* is dense with allusions to Melville's reading in what he affectingly called "old books." There the range he displays is impressive, as are the innumerable echoes in his prose of the greatest authors he knew, both past and present. Naturally his first point of reference is the King James Bible, along with those mostly seventeenth-century writers—Milton, Bunyan, Thomas Browne, Shakespeare—who derive from the same great cultural period when English was at its most muscular and poetic. He was uniquely impressed with near contemporaries like Byron, Thomas Carlyle, Ralph Waldo Emerson, Alexander Kinglake, and Hawthorne. In addition, all sorts of travel books, sea voyage literature, contemporary political disquisitions, and speeches that he devoured in the meditative internal voyage which the lonely composition of *Moby-Dick* became were fused in with the classical writers Melville venerated.

Melville's distinctive note throughout is his striving for eloquence, which much of his vast reading gave him aplenty. But like so much else, eloquence in *Moby-Dick* is hardly routine. Its exaggerations, its elephantine humor, and its often grotesque rhetoric suggest not the learned scholar but a writer trying restlessly to impress his audience in ways appropriate to a number of contradictory locations, all of them suited both for gripping spectators and for shamelessly impressing in public performance. These locations include the pulpit, lecture hall, tavern, sailors' quarters, political meetings, academic classroom— places where men are accustomed to gather and regale themselves with loudly assertive, sometimes boisterous talk. Most of this is monologic, that is, one speaker holds forth and fairly drowns out everyone else. All of it, I think, is in constant motion, shifting from one sort of effect to another with great power and uncommon effect. Here is an example:

> My hypothesis is this: that the [Sperm Whale's] spout is nothing but mist. And besides other reasons, to this conclusion I am impelled, by considerations touching the great inherent dignity and sublimity of the Sperm Whale; I account him no common, shallow being, inasmuch as it is an undisputed fact that he is never found on soundings, or near shores; all other whales sometimes are. He is both ponderous and profound. I am convinced that from the heads of all ponderous profound beings, such as Plato, Pyrrho, the Devil, Jupiter, Dante, and so on, there always goes up a certain semi-visible steam, while in the act of thinking deep thoughts. While composing a little treatise on Eternity, I had the curiosity to place a mirror before me; and ere long saw reflected there, a curious involved worming and undulation in the atmosphere over my head.

This almost doesn't work, so great is the movement from the seriousness of the beginning to the sentences where "ponderous and profound" are jammed together as "ponderous profound," after which there follows a *very* miscellaneous laundry list, and a mock heroic simile unfolds between the speaker, as author of a "little treatise on Eternity" with "a curious involved worming and undulation" over his head, and the Sperm Whale. One has the sense here of a deflation, from high to low material, but there is also the strong apprehension of uncertainty, as if Melville could not go forward without digression or comic self-consciousness. What we get is a sudden change of site: the orator is displaced from lecture platform to barroom floor. From being a grave scholar or sage he becomes a teller of tall tales. These shifts occur almost nonstop in the novel, but instead of making for exasperation, they provide a good deal of the pleasure, as well as the sensuous excitement of reading *Moby-Dick*.

The reason for this is psychological. Melville asks us to share in the telling of a narrative whose recital causes both apprehension and uncertainty, so unprecedented and uncharted are its main lines. When he gets to the final chase, Melville strips his prose to what is necessary for the fateful convergence of Ahab's obsessive mania with the White Whale's power and fury. All unnecessary mannerisms and tropes are shed: the conflict is revealed in its bare-boned essence. In the meantime, however, as if staving off the blazing excitement of the novel's climactic encounter, Melville wanders around, like the *Pequod* herself, looking, learning, experimenting, laughing, reflecting, preparing, all the while feeling the inevitable prowling pressures of Moby Dick, who must finally be closed with and confronted.

Yet while most of the digressive material is therefore used to defer or delay the inevitable, it derives to some extent from Melville's special narrative persona, what it conceives of itself as doing, how and where in the historical world it represents itself. Of course there is Ishmael, the first-person narrator, to begin with. He appears to us directly at the very outset, pronouncing what is perhaps the most famous opening line in all great fiction: "Call me Ishmael." And his life and exploits— celibate, solemn, melancholy, lonely, and playful, poised on the verge of suicide—frame but do not completely contain the story's actual enunciation. Ishmael is a witness to most of what takes place in *Moby-Dick,* yet he cannot be with Ahab and Starbuck, or with Ahab alone, during those intense, Shakespearean dramatic dialogues and monologues. At such moments, as well as during the novel's riotous displays of erudition, there is Melville himself, bolstering Ishmael, often taking over the narrative flow.

This odd duality in narration, through which Ishmael as main narrator is supplemented by Melville's voice, is related to Melville's conception both of what a novelist is and of what *Moby-Dick*'s story is about. Consider the latter first. Much of the bluster and braggadocio in tone as the novel gets under way aims to assert the vital importance of Nantucket whaling as industry, adventure, achievement. True, there are precedents for this in other nations, yet the narrator asserts that none is quite as grand or important as the Nantucket (and not simply the American) whaler, who is celebrated very vociferously in chapter 14, "Nantucket." There Melville makes it clear that whaling is to Nantucket, and to his story, what empires are to Britain, Russia, and other great centers of power.

"Let America add Mexico to Texas," Ishmael says in an extraordinarily rich passage, and pile Cuba upon Canada; let the English overswarm all India, and hang out their blazing banner from the sun; two thirds of this terraqueous globe are the Nantucketer's. For the sea is his; he owns it, as Emperors own empires; other seamen having but a right of way through it. Merchant ships are but extension bridges; armed ones but floating forts; even pirates and privateers, though following the sea as highwaymen the road, they but plunder other ships, other fragments of the land like themselves, without seeking to draw their living from the bottomless deep itself. The Nantucketer, he alone resides and rests on the sea; he alone, in Bible language, goes down to it in ships; to and fro ploughing it as his own special plantation. *There* is his home; *there* lies his business, which a Noah's flood would not interrupt, though it overwhelmed all the millions in China. He lives on the sea, as prairie cocks in the prairie; he hides among the waves, he climbs them as chamois hunters climb the Alps. For years he knows not the land; so that when he comes to it at last, it smells like another world, more strangely than the moon would to an Earthsman.

Empires are the way of the modern world; an earlier reference to "Alexanders" (of Macedon and of Russia) complements Ishmael's sense in this passage that the world is being divided up by enterprising conquerors. A relative newcomer to the competition for imperial domination, America must make its own, but strikingly different, claim. Whereas other empires control land, America seeks sovereignty over water, and whereas other seamen use the oceans as a way from one landfall to another or as a site on which to do what they do on land (plunder, for instance), only the Americans, and the Nantucketer in particular, live on and derive a living from the sea. All this is the novice imperialist's discourse, carving out a more or less complete, self-sufficient form of life on the sea, so much so that land itself will in time appear to be an alien, unusual element. Ishmael asserts an imperial project whose features are that it can provide both an alternative livelihood for the Nantucketer-American and the potential for an authentically different, even avant-garde sort of achievement.

Of course these hyperbolic statements about the American quest for world sovereignty are playful and should be read mainly in an aesthetic context. Yet no one, no American or non-American who has read this superb novel has ever doubted that in such passages and in Ahab's tremendous quest Melville has very accurately caught something of the imperial motif that runs consistently through United States history and culture. Far from simple and reductive, the discourse of American specialness which Melville so powerfully delivers in the majestically energetic diction of *Moby-Dick* begins with the Puritan "errand into the wilderness" and continues through such doctrines as Manifest Destiny, "making the world safe for democracy," and "the line drawn in the sand." It has inspired the military and economic campaigns that devastated and then sought to rebuild Asia, Latin America, the Pacific, and Europe. Above all American specialness took the country from "white settlement to world hegemony" (in V. G. Kiernan's formula) without prejudice to its moral fervor or its reluctance to change its self-image as an all-conquering force for good in the world. Melville's contribution is that he delivers the salutary effect as well as the destructiveness of the American world presence, and he also demonstrates its self-mesmerizing assumptions about its providential significance.

These considerations jibe very well with Ishmael himself, who is not only a seaman aboard a Nantucket ship but also an outcast orphan, and "isolato." The symbolism of the gifted and the damned plays around him constantly. Along with the renegades, castaways, and mariners who make up the *Pequod*'s crew, Ishmael is therefore far from an imitation of landed imperialists; his is an altogether different and extreme imperiousness with few limits and inhibitions. Melville seems either ambivalent or paradoxical about how exceptional or how typical the whalers are. On the one hand they are meant to be representative of America, the young empire beginning to assert itself among other world empires. On the other, because he is so bent on showing that they are different—and therefore compelled to be more and more different as the story progresses: difference has an internal tendency to intensify and pull away from "sameness"—Melville's "thought-engendering" procedures in the novel further distance Ahab, Ishmael, and the *Pequod* from normalcy, and this in effect puts them beyond human community or even understanding.

Part of *Moby-Dick*'s power—and Melville's own heroism as a writer—comes from the deliberate decision *not* to resolve fully this absolutely fundamental quandary. It is worth reminding ourselves that European novels, for example, were staked on a similar antithesis. Whether Emma Bovary or Robinson Crusoe, fictional protagonists were typical members of the bourgeoisie and unusually, even eccentrically deviant people at the same time; not for them was an average home life or an acceptable career as lawyer or accountant. The whole point of the classical realistic novel was to show that its heroes and heroines belonged to a recognizable social formation, and *also* adventured considerably away from it. For their energy and deviance (the realistic novel, after all, is a very conservative form) the great novelistic heroes are dealt one of two fairly standard fates: either they are reintegrated into society, as in Jane Austen's novels, which routinely end in marriage and property, or they quite simply die, since like poor Emma Bovary they cannot be made to fit.

Melville's seagoing figures in *Moby-Dick* constitute in effect a relentlessly plotted and affirmed American alternative to the European novelistic pattern, which, it needs to be said, was also associated with an imperial project (Crusoe is a settler-colonist, many of Dickens's and some of Balzac's businessmen are traders in the East, Bertha Mason in *Jane Eyre* is from the Caribbean, many of Austen's characters have associations with the navy and colonial trade, Thackeray's Josiah Sedley is a nabob . . . the list is very long). Yet for Melville, America's society was not as settled, established, and patterned as Europe's; nearly everyone in it was, if not an immigrant, traceable to immigrant stock. As Henry James said in his brilliant, affectionately patronizing little treatise on Hawthorne, Americans are necessarily conscious "of not being of the European family, of being placed on the circumference of the circle of civilization rather than at the centre, of the experimental element not having as yet dropped out of their great political undertaking." With "no sovereign, no court, no personal loyalty, no aristocracy, no church, no clergy, no army, no diplomatic service, no country gentlemen, no palaces . . . no literature, no novels, no sporting class—no Epsom nor Ascot," James says that the American writer must fall back either on humor or on a rather limited pastoral style, best for describing "walks in the country, drives in stage-coaches."

Melville was far too ambitious for so genteel and inoffensive a scope. His novel would if necessary invent the novel form anew, would become an irreducibly American variant on the European pattern. His heroes would be outcasts twice over, Americans in flight from Europe *and* from America; Ahab, their leader, would defy all but the grandest, most sublime, and consequently inhuman norms. His manner is always ceremonial, heroic, tremendously dignified, as like a great satanic bishop he baptizes the harpoon in the name of the Devil. Not content with setting up an alternative, entirely male home aboard ship, the crew of the *Pequod* would reorient the entire world, causing Melville to rewrite the whole history of our planet from the whaling viewpoint. As he said in an adulatory review, written while at work on *Moby-Dick,* of Hawthorn's *Mosses from an Old Manse,* the American *was* capable of a distinctive genius, albeit one full of "Puritan gloom" and "the power of blackness." Driving this sublime argument to its conclusion, Melville uses Hawthorne to assert America's cultural independence and does so with an astonishingly imperious, provocative arrogance:

> . . . no American writer should write like an Englishman, or a Frenchman; let him write like a man, for then he will be sure to write like an American. Let us away with this Bostonian leaven of literary flunkeyism towards England. If either must play the flunkey in this thing, let England do it, not us . . . While we are rapidly preparing for that political supremacy among the nations, which prophetically awaits us at the close of the present century; in a literary point of view, we are deplorably unprepared for it . . . Let us boldly contemn all imitation . . . and foster all originality . . . The truth is, that in our point of view, this matter of a national literature has come to such a pass with us, that in some sense we must turn bullies, else the day is lost, or superiority so far beyond us, that we can hardly say it will be ours.

This is strong stuff, and goes some way to explaining the energy, not to say demonism, of Ahab's character, that of an ungodly, godlike man. So that even as the *Pequod* represents an American deviation from the European imperial norm, its master is himself a criminalized (Ishmael's word for him is "usurper") deviation from the deviation. Thus *Moby-*

Dick gives the reader a multiplying series of alternatives to what European novels have provided; each of Melville's alternative characters and situations is an assertion of individuality as well as a representative of a group identity. Ahab is Ahab, *and* a Nantucketer; the *Pequod*'s crew is a highly differentiated set of individuals *and* a representation of America's races, clans, religions; the novel contains an obsessively personal *as well as* a national trajectory.

Rather than resolving the tension, Melville in fact sustains it as long as he can: the *Pequod* continues its journey until it finally meets Moby Dick, closes with the leviathan, and is destroyed by him. At the very end Ishmael returns, principally to affirm his orphanhood and credibly to register his testimony. But the novel's very driven and monumentally unconventional anguish requires further reflection. Much in it is a struggle inward and against restraints: Ahab wants to kill the white whale as embodiment of everything that ails him. Melville's own prose shares the same unforgiving impulse as it drives history, reality, personality, and even cosmology before its monomaniacal gaze. The attitude that Melville best represents as novelist is an undeterred inclusiveness, as befits someone who not only can match Ahab's monomania but—in the figure of Ishmael, the *Pequod*'s last surviving crew member and Melville's narrative alter ego—can also outlive the suicidal captain himself.

It has been said of Richard Wagner's earliest and deservedly forgotten opera that in the first two acts all the characters were killed, which left act III populated exclusively by singing ghosts. Something of the same uninhibited and all-consuming energy courses through *Moby-Dick,* and is most centrally rendered in Ahab's frenzied pursuit of the White Whale. No one can deter Ahab, or prevent him from condemning everyone around him to the same feverish obsession. Ahab compares himself to a train on rails on which his "soul is grooved to run"; even he admits that this is "madness maddened," an insight that gives extraordinary power to the frequently repeated claim that "Ahab is Ahab."

When I said earlier that *Moby-Dick* was, like *Heart of Darkness,* a challenge to the concept of stable identity, I had in mind this combination of manic self-assertion and extinction. Ahab will not stop being Ahab, and the fact that he is not just an obscure eccentric but a grandly heroic person and, on the *Pequod,* an absolute ruler, is Melville's way of showing a sort of executive spirit gone pretty mad. C. L. R. James, the remarkable Caribbean historian and essayist, says in *Mariners, Renegades, and Castaways* that, on one level, Ahab represents the managerial captain of industry bent on American power and success. Yet Melville also admires Ahab and sees in him a convincing example of the new imperialism he ascribes to the United States. There is a clear logic, however, in Melville's dramatization of how once conquest, the assertion of identity, and the single-minded pursuit of a majestic goal are embarked upon no real limits can be set. And the point becomes, I think, that you can neither apply brakes to such a juggernaut nor expect things to remain the same. Everything discrete, clear, distinct is transformed by the energy unloosed in such a drive to fulfillment even unto death or total destruction. To read *Moby-Dick* is to be overwhelmed by Melville's passion at eliminating compromises, middling solutions, anything less than an ultimate will to go forward. Even though he talks mainly about one ship, its master and crew, it is also true that he is unsparing in his intimations that the novel is a national American narrative, a sort of minatory emblem of the *patria*.

But why, finally, such bulk, such almost gargantuan mass for what is after all a work of fiction? A number of possibilities propose themselves. One is that Melville is not only a novelist but also an irrepressible enthusiast. From Carlyle and perhaps also from Swift he learned that if you see your subject from a distinctive point of view you must then go on and see the whole of human history from that angle. Consistency in the basic whaling story of *Moby-Dick* meant for Melville that he had to make everything conform to it consistently. Water is therefore the universal element of the world, its greatest heroes were sailors and fishermen, and on and on. *Moby-Dick* is a cosmology, the *Pequod* not only Noah's ark but also the basic family, as well as Yale and Harvard. The absence of social institutions in America noted by Henry James is turned by Melville into an opportunity to build a new quasi society from scratch. *Moby-Dick,* with its complete course in whaling history and practice, is the greatest how-to-do-it book in American literature. Like Hemingway's *Death in the Afternoon* it combines the autodidactic with the philosophic, producing great bulk by virtue of its zeal. Its classifications of whales, its disquisitions on whiteness and on strategy, its researches in and reconstructions of history, legend, lore, learning amount to little less than a complete epistemology, a how-to-think-about-things book, in which Melville communicates the uncertainty and inventiveness of any great discovery with matchless virtuosity.

Another reason for the acceptable, even necessary density of the novel is that *Moby-Dick* is, as I said, a book about going too far, pressing too hard, overstepping limits. Ahab is distinguished from Starbuck and Stubb, for instance, because unlike them he always looks to the "lower layer." For him surfaces are to be gone beneath, rules to be broken, authority to be addressed with pride and a kind of contemptuous *hauteur*. That Ahab is also a suffering man who has sorrowfully left behind a young wife and family so as to pursue his private obsession makes him more credible, more human perhaps, but no less a giant. With his mutilated body abetted by the insane sanctity and purity of his search for Moby Dick, he is like a wandering Philoctetes: everyone is attracted to and needs him, whereas he in a sense rejects and even disdains them all.

But *Moby-Dick*'s hugeness is, I think, an important aspect of Melville's own altogether prodigious temperament as writer. In the novel he seems to have allowed his most private and dangerous thoughts full expression, although he rarely abandons the discipline of the fiction he has chosen for his narrative labors, the whaling quest itself. One has the sense in reading *Moby-Dick* that Melville went where very few others would have dared; this has given rise to all sorts of interpretations of Ahab's ambitions and of the White Whale's significance: a quarrel with God; a direct confrontation with the unconscious; an experience of pure evil, *angst*, dread, et cetera. These theses are all plausible, and of course encouraged in a sense by Melville, for whom the very existence of an Ahab and a Moby Dick furnish a proper occasion for prophesy, world-historical vision, genius and madness close allied. In its vast spaces and in Melville's blazingly original style, *Moby-Dick* is about (it seems silly to say it this way) the whole world; it willingly incorporates everything, leaving such small matters as resolution, inconsistency, and indeed evaluating the *consequences* of so tremendous and shattering an experience to lesser natures.

There is, in fine, a sort of carelessness about *Moby-Dick* that is, I think, one of the main keys to its imposing magnificence. Along with other great nineteenth-century artists like Balzac, Wagner, and Dickens, Melville is the inventor of a new world. But unlike most of them he is more concerned with making the world than with perfecting or sustaining it. This is why his world in *Moby-Dick* is so remarkably unproductive, so unregenerate and so bachelorlike, so studiously, unforgivingly *male*. Wives and families are left behind. Whaling is an industry kept going entirely by men. Ahab, Moby Dick, Ishmael, and all the others are males, some of whom like Queequeg can sometimes play the role of wives. It is fascinating to note that all of Melville's allusions to the Orient—and the presence in the novel of such people as Fedallah and his Parsee associates—are also all masculine; there are no harems, no gardens of sensual delight here. If Ahab shares somewhat in the Faustian quest, his Gretchen is no Helen but a roughly, boyishly named male animal (Melville's model was a legendary sperm whale called Mocha Dick). There is great poignancy at the end therefore when the *Pequod,* named after an exterminated Indian tribe, goes down like a coffin with its entire crew, leaving Ishmael to be rescued by the "devious-cruising *Rachel.*" Renegades, mariners, castaways, and orphans, the cast of *Moby-Dick* is, as many critics have suggested, a microcosm of America, but an America seen by Melville in very partial, purposely skewed and eccentric terms, the country's deviance intensified with a sort of maniacal deliberation.

Ahab gives no thought to the damage he costs himself *or* the *Pequod.* The last gesture in the narrative is defiant: Tashtego's hand nailing a sky-hawk to the masthead as the satanic ship and all of its crew sink into nothingness. There is a remarkable letter, written by T. E. Lawrence in 1922 to a friend, in which the author of *The Seven Pillars of Wisdom* confessed that he had "collected a shelf of 'titanic' books (those distinguished by greatness of spirit, 'sublimity' of spirit as Longinus would call it): and that they were *The Karamazovs, Zarathustra,* and *Moby Dick.* Well my ambition was to make an English fourth." Elsewhere in his letters Lawrence also described these "big" books as artistic failures, "lacking architecture, the balance of parts, coherence, streamlining"; these, he added, were "books where the authors went up like rockets and burst."

Whatever we may think of Lawrence's own contribution to this selective but distinguished shelf of illiberal, demanding, fiery books, his observations are perspicacious and his choice of adjective, "titanic," brilliant. The Titans were a race of Greek divinities of an earlier generation than such well-known Olympian deities as Zeus, Apollo, and Hera. The most famous of this primitive and intrepid group was Prometheus, whose bravery gave the gift of fire to man and earned him the endless torment of punishment by Zeus. Ahab is referred to several times by Melville in admiring terms as a Promethean figure. Novel and protagonist share the same grandeur and heedlessness: what they accomplish together by way of spectacle and drama can only be done once, is inimitable. As against the imagery of angry death and mourning that concludes the novel, however, we must not forget the ongoing vitality of Moby Dick himself, who swims down and out of sight forever. The whale's undefinable energy and power inform the novel as much as Ahab's tragically undying quest does. What Melville accomplishes is to hold the two in an eternal antithesis, one feeding off, yet resisting the other: Prometheus defying Zeus and the vulture who feeds on his liver without defeating his spirit. The beauty of it is that when we close the book we realize that the whale depends on the man as much as the man on the whale, with neither redemption nor rest for either of them:

> Towards thee I roll, thou all-destroying but unconquering whale; to the last I grapple with thee; from hell's heart I stab at thee; for hate's sake I spit my last breath at thee. Sink all coffins and all hearses to one common pool! and since neither can be mine, let me then tow to pieces, while still chasing thee, though tied to thee, thou damned whale! *Thus*, I give up the spear!

33

The Politics of Knowledge

Last fall I was invited to participate in a seminar at a historical studies center of a historically renowned American university. The subject of the seminar for this and the next academic year is imperialism, and the seminar discussions are chaired by the center's director. Outside participants are asked to send a paper before their arrival; it is then distributed to the members of the seminar, who are graduate students, fellows, and faculty. They will have read the paper in advance, precluding any reading of a lecture to them by the visitor, who is instead asked to summarize its main points for about ten minutes. Then for an hour and a half, there is an open discussion of the paper—a fairly rigorous but stimulating exercise. Since I have been working for some years on a sequel to *Orientalism*—it will be a long book that deals with the relationship between modern culture and imperialism—I sent a substantial extract from the introduction, in which I lay out the main lines of the book's argument. I there begin to describe the emergence of a global consciousness in Western knowledge at the end of the nineteenth century, particularly in such apparently unrelated fields as geography and comparative literature. I then go on to argue that the appearance of such cultural disciplines coincides with a fully global imperial perspective, although such a co-incidence can only be made to seem significant from the point of view of later history, when nearly everywhere in the colonized world there emerged resistance to certain oppressive aspects of imperial rule like theories of subject races and peripheral regions, and the notions of backward, primitive, or undeveloped cultures. *Because* of that native resistance—for instance, the appearance of many nationalist and in-dependence movements in India, the Caribbean, Africa, the Middle East—it is now evident that culture and imperialism in the West could be understood as offering support, each to the other. Here I referred to the extraordinary work of a whole range of non-Western writers and activists, including Tagore, Fanon, C. L. R. James, Yeats, and many others, figures who have given integrity to anti-imperialist cultural re-sistance.

The first question after my brief résumé was from a professor of his-tory, a black woman of some eminence who had recently come to the university, but whose work was unfamiliar to me. She announced in ad-vance that her question was to be hostile, "a very hostile one in fact." She then said something like the following: for the first thirteen pages of your paper you talked only about white European males. Thereafter, on page fourteen, you mention some names of non-Europeans. "How could you do such a thing?" I remonstrated somewhat, and tried to ex-plain my argument in greater detail—after all, I said, I was discussing European imperialism, which would not have been likely to include in its discourse the work of African-American women. I pointed out that in the book I say quite a bit about the response to imperialism all over the world; that point was a place in my argument where it would be per-tinent to focus on the work of such writers as—and here I again men-tioned the name of a great Caribbean writer and intellectual whose work has a special importance for my own—C. L. R. James. To this my critic replied with a stupefying confidence that my answer was not sat-isfactory since C. L. R. James was dead! I must admit that I was non-plussed by the severity of this pronouncement. James indeed *was* dead, a fact that needn't, to a historian, have made further discussion impos-sible. I waited for her to resume, hoping that she might expatiate on what she meant by having suggested that even in discussions of what dead white European males said on a given topic it was inappropriate to confine oneself to what they said while leaving out the work of living African-American, Arab, and Indian writers.

But she did not proceed, and I was left to suppose that she considered her point sufficiently and conclusively made: I was guilty of not mentioning living non-European nonmales, even when it was not obvious to me or, I later gathered, to many members of the seminar, what their pertinence might have been. I noted to myself that my antagonist did not think it necessary to enumerate what specifically in the work of living non-Europeans I should have used, or which books and ideas by them she found important and relevant. All I had been given to work with was the asserted necessity to mention some approved names—which names did not really matter—as if the very act of uttering them was enough. I was also left unmistakably with the impression that as a nonwhite—a category incidentally to which as an Arab I myself belong—she was saying that to affirm the existence of non-European "others" took the place of evidence, argument, discussion.

It would be pointless to deny that the exchange was unsettling. Among other things I was chagrined at the distortions of my position and for having responded to the distortions so clumsily. It did not seem to matter that a great deal of my own work has concerned itself with just the kind of omission with which I was being charged. What apparently mattered now was that having contributed to an early trend, in which Western and European intellectuals were arraigned for having their work constructed out of the suffering and deprivations of so many people of color, I was now allegedly doing what such complicit intellectuals had always done. For if in one place you criticize the exclusion of Orientals, as I did in *Orientalism,* the exclusion of "others" from your work in another place becomes, on one level, difficult to justify or explain. I was disheartened not because I was being attacked, but because the general validity of the point made in *Orientalism* still obtained and yet was now being directed at me. It was *still* true that various Others—the word has acquired a sheen of modishness that has become extremely objectionable—were being represented unfairly, their reality distorted, their truth either denied or twisted with malice. Yet instead of joining in their behalf, I felt I was being asked to get involved in an inconsequential academic contest. I had wanted to say, but didn't, "Is all that matters about the issue of exclusion and misrepresentation the fact that *names* were left out? Why are you detaining us with such trivialities?"

To make matters worse, a few minutes later in the discussion I was attacked by a retired professor of Middle Eastern studies, himself an Orientalist. Like me, he was an Arab, but he had consistently identified himself with intellectual tendencies of which I had always been critical. He now intervened to defend imperialism, saying in tones of almost comic reverence, that it had accomplished things that natives couldn't have done for themselves. It had taught them, among other things, he said, how to appreciate the cuneiform and hieroglyphics of their own traditions. As he droned on about the imperial schools, railroads, hospitals, and telegraphs in the Third World that stood for examples of British and French largesse, the irony of the whole thing seemed overpowering. It appeared to me that there had to be something to say that surrendered neither to the caricatural reductiveness of the two positions by then arrayed against me, and against each other, nor to that verbal quality in each that was determined to remain ideologically correct and little else.

I was being reminded by such negative flat-minded examples of thinking that the one thing that intellectuals *cannot* do without is the full intellectual process itself. Into it goes historically informed research as well as the presentation of a coherent and carefully argued line that has taken account of alternatives. In addition, there must be, it seems to me, a theoretical presumption that in matters having to do with human history and society any rigid theoretical ideal, any simple additive or mechanical notion of what is or is not factual, must yield to the central factor of human work, the actual participation of peoples in the making of human life. If that is so then it must also be true that, given the very nature of human work in the construction of human society and history, it is impossible to say of it that its products are so rarefied, so limited, so beyond comprehension as to exclude most other people, experiences, and histories. I mean further, that this kind of human work, which is intellectual work, is worldly, that it is situated in the world, and about that world. It is not about things that are so rigidly constricted and so forbiddingly arcane as to exclude all but an audience of like-minded, already fully convinced persons. While it would be stupid to deny the importance of constituencies and audiences in the construction of an intellectual argument, I think it has to be supposed that many arguments can be made to more than one audience and in different situations. Otherwise we would be dealing not with intellectual argument but either with dogma or with a technological jargon designed specifically to repel all but a small handful of initiates or coteries.

Lest I fall into the danger myself of being too theoretical and specialized, I shall be more specific now and return to the episode I was discussing just a moment ago. At the heart of the imperial cultural enterprise I analyzed in *Orientalism* and also in my new book, was a politics of identity. That politics has needed to assume, indeed needed firmly to believe, that what was true about Orientals or Africans was *not* however true about or for Europeans. When a French or German scholar tried to identify the main characteristics of, for instance, the Chinese mind, the work was only partly intended to do that; it was also intended to show how different the Chinese mind was from the Western mind.

Such constructed things—they have only an elusive reality—as the Chinese mind or the Greek spirit have always been with us; they are at the source of a great deal that goes into the making of individual cultures, nations, traditions, and peoples. But in the modern world considerably greater attention has generally been given to such identities than was ever given in earlier historical periods, when the world was larger, more amorphous, less globalized. Today a fantastic emphasis is placed upon a politics of national identity, and to a very great degree, this emphasis is the result of the imperial experience. For when the great modern Western imperial expansion took place all across the world, beginning in the late eighteenth century, it accentuated the interaction between the identity of the French or the English and that of the colonized native peoples. And this mostly antagonistic interaction gave rise to a separation between people as members of homogenous races and exclusive nations that was and still is one of the characteristics of what can be called the epistemology of imperialism. At its core is the supremely stubborn thesis that everyone is principally and irreducibly a member of some race or category, and that race or category cannot ever be assimilated to or accepted by others—except as itself. Thus came into being such invented essences as the Oriental or Englishness, as Frenchness, Africanness, or American exceptionalism, as if each of those had a Platonic idea behind it that guaranteed it as pure and unchanging from the beginning to the end of time.

One product of this doctrine is nationalism, a subject so immense that I can treat it only very partially here. What interests me in the politics of identity that informed imperialism in its global phase is that just as natives were considered to belong to a different category—racial or geographical—from that of the Western white man, it also became true that in the great anti-imperialist revolt represented by decolonization this same category was mobilized around, and formed the resisting identity of, the revolutionaries. This was the case everywhere in the Third World. Its most celebrated instance is the concept of *négritude,* as developed intellectually and poetically by Aimé Césaire, Leopold Senghor, and, in English, W. E. B. Du Bois. If blacks had once been stigmatized and given inferior status to whites, then it has since become necessary not to deny blackness, and not to aspire to whiteness, but to accept and celebrate blackness, to give it the dignity of poetic as well as metaphysical status. Thus *négritude* acquired positive Being where before it had been a mark of degradation and inferiority. Much the same revaluation of the native particularity occurred in India, in many parts of the Islamic world, China, Japan, Indonesia, and the Philippines, where the denied or repressed native essence emerged as the focus of, and even the basis for, nationalist recovery.

It is important to note that much of the early cultural resistance to imperialism on which nationalism and independence movements were built was salutary and necessary. I see it essentially as an attempt on the part of oppressed people who had suffered the bondage of slavery, colonialism, and—most important—spiritual dispossession, to reclaim their identity. When that finally occurred in places such as Algeria, the grander nationalist efforts amounted to little short of a reconstructed communal political and cultural program of independence. Where the white man had once only seen lazy natives and exotic customs, the insurrection against imperialism produced, as in Ireland, for example, a national revolt, along with political parties dedicated to independence, which, like the Congress party in India, was headed by nationalist figures, poets, and military heroes. There were remarkably impressive results from this vast effort at cultural reclamation, most of which are well known and celebrated.

But while the whole movement toward autonomy and independence produced in effect newly independent and separate states constituting the majority of new nations in the postcolonial world today, the nationalist politics of identity has nonetheless quickly proved itself to be insufficient for the ensuing period.

Inattentive or careless readers of Frantz Fanon, generally considered one of the two or three most eloquent apostles of anti-imperialist resistance, tend to forget his marked suspicions of unchecked nationalism. So while it is appropriate to draw attention to the early chapters on violence in *The Wretched of the Earth*, it should be noticed that in subsequent chapters he is sharply critical of what he called the pitfalls of national consciousness. He clearly meant this to be a paradox. And for the reason that while nationalism is a necessary spur to revolt against the colonizer, national consciousness must be immediately transformed into what he calls "social consciousness," just as soon as the withdrawal of the colonizer has been accomplished.

Fanon is scathing on the abuses of the postindependence nationalist party, on, for instance, the cult of the Grand Panjandrum (or maximum leader), or the centralization of the capital city, which Fanon said flatly needed to be deconsecrated, and most important, on the hijacking of common sense and popular participation by bureaucrats, technical experts, and jargon-wielding obfuscators. Well before V. S. Naipaul, Fanon was arguing against the politics of mimicry and separatism which produced the Mobutus, Idi Amins, and Saddams, as well as the grotesqueries and pathologies of power that gave rise to tyrannical states and praetorian guards while obstructing democratic freedoms in so many countries of the Third World. Fanon also prophesied the continuing dependency of numerous postcolonial governments and philosophies, all of which preached the sovereignty of the newly independent people of one or another new Third World state and, having failed to make the transition from nationalism to true liberation, were in fact condemned to practice the politics, and the economics, of a new oppression as pernicious as the old one.

At bottom, what Fanon offers most compellingly is a critique of the separatism and mock autonomy achieved by a pure politics of identity that has lasted too long and been made to serve in situations where it has become simply inadequate. What invariably happens at the level of knowledge is that signs and symbols of freedom and status are taken for the reality: you want to be named and considered for the sake of being named and considered. In effect this really means that just to be an independent postcolonial Arab, or black, or Indonesian is not a program, nor a process, nor a vision. It is no more than a convenient starting point from which the real work, the hard work, might begin.

As for that work, it is nothing less than the reintegration of all those people and cultures, once confined and reduced to peripheral status, with the rest of the human race. After working through *négritude* in the early sections of *Cahier d'un retour*, Aimé Césaire states this vision of integration in his poem's climactic moment: "no race possesses the monopoly of beauty, of intelligence, of force, and there is a place for all at the rendez-vous of victory."

Without this concept of "place for all at the rendez-vous of victory," one is condemned to an impoverishing politics of knowledge based only upon the assertion and reassertion of identity, an ultimately uninteresting alternation of presence and absence. If you are weak, your affirmation of identity for its own sake amounts to little more than saying that you want a kind of attention easily and superficially granted, like the attention given an individual in a crowded room at a roll call. Once having such recognition, the subject has only to sit there silently as the proceedings unfold as if in his or her absence. And, on the other hand, though the powerful get acknowledged by the sheer force of presence, this commits them to a logic of displacement, as soon as someone else emerges who is as, or more, powerful.

This has proved a disastrous process, whether for postcolonials, forced to exist in a marginal and dependent place totally outside the circuits of world power, or for powerful societies, whose triumphalism and imperious wilfullness have done so much to devastate and destabilize the world. What has been at issue between Iraq and the United States is precisely such a logic of exterminism and displacement, as unedifying as it is unproductive. It is risky, I know, to move from the realm of interpretation to the realm of world politics, but it seems to me true that the relationship between them is a real one, and the light that one realm can shed on the other is quite illuminating. In any case the politics of knowledge that is based principally on the affirmation of identity is very similar, is indeed directly related to, the unreconstructed nationalism that has guided so many postcolonial states today. It asserts a sort of separatism that wishes only to draw attention to itself; consequently it neglects the integration of that earned and achieved consciousness of self within "the rendez-vous of victory." On the national and on the intellectual level the problems are very similar.

Let me return therefore to one of the intellectual debates that has been central to the humanities in the past decade, and which underlies the episode with which I began. The ferment in minority, subaltern, feminist, and postcolonial consciousness has resulted in so many salutary achievements in the curricular and theoretical approach to the study of the humanities as quite literally to have produced a Copernican revolution in all traditional fields of inquiry. Eurocentrism has been challenged definitively; most scholars and students in the contemporary American academy are now aware, as they were never aware before, that society and culture have been the heterogenous product of heterogenous people in an enormous variety of cultures, traditions, and situations. No longer does T. S. Eliot's idea of the great Western masterpieces enduring together in a constantly redefining pattern of monuments have its old authority; nor do the sorts of patterns elucidated with such memorable brilliance in formative works like *Mimesis* or *The Anatomy of Criticism* have the same cogency for today's student or theorist as they did even quite recently.

And yet the great contest about the canon continues. The success of Allan Bloom's *The Closing of the American Mind*, the subsequent publication of such works as Alvin Kernan's *The Death of Literature*, and Roger Kimball's *Tenured Radicals* as well as the rather posthumous energies displayed in journals like *The American Scholar* (now a neo-conservative magazine), *The New Criterion*, and *Commentary*—all this suggests that the work done by those of us who have tried to widen the area of awareness in the study of culture is scarcely finished or secure. But our point, in my opinion, cannot be simply and obdurately to reaffirm the paramount importance of formerly suppressed or silenced forms of knowledge and leave it at that, nor can it be to surround ourselves with the sanctimonious piety of historical or cultural victimhood as a way of making our intellectual presence felt. Such strategies are woefully insufficient. The whole effort to deconsecrate Eurocentrism cannot be interpreted, least of all by those who participate in the enterprise, as an effort to supplant Eurocentrism with, for instance, Afrocentric or Islamocentric approaches. On its own, ethnic particularity does not provide for intellectual process—quite the contrary. At first, you will recall, it was a question, for some, of adding Jane Austen to the canon of male Western writers in humanities courses; then it became a matter of displacing the entire canon of American writers like Hawthorne and Emerson with best-selling writers of the same period like Harriet Beecher Stowe and Susan Warner. But after that the logic of displacement became even more attenuated, and the mere names of politically validated living writers became more important than anything about them or their works.

I submit that these clamorous dismissals and swooping assertions are in fact caricatural reductions of what the great revisionary gestures of feminism, subaltern or black studies, and anti-imperialist resistance originally intended. For such gestures it was never a matter of replacing one set of authorities and dogmas with another, nor of substituting one center for another. It was always a matter of opening and participating in a central strand of intellectual and cultural effort and of showing what had always been, though indiscernibly, a part of it, like the work of women, or of blacks and servants—but which had been either denied or derogated. The power and interest of—to give two examples particularly dear to me—Tayib Salih's *Season of Migration to the North* is not only how it memorably describes the quandary of a gifted young Sudanese who has lived in London but then returns home to his ancestral village alongside the Nile; the novel is also a rewriting of Conrad's *Heart of Darkness,* seen now as the tale of someone who voyages into the heart of light, which is modern Europe, and discovers there what had been hidden deep within him. To read the Sudanese writer is of course to interpret an Arabic novel written during the late sixties at a time of nationalism and a rejection of the West. The novel is therefore affiliated with other Arabic novels of the postwar period, including the works of Mahfouz and Idriss; but given the historical and political meaning of a narrative that quite deliberately recalls and reverses Conrad—something impossible for a black man at the time *Heart of Darkness* was written—Tayib Salih's masterpiece is necessarily to be viewed as, along with other African, Indian, and Caribbean works, enlarging, widening, refining the scope of a narrative form at the center of which had heretofore always been an exclusively European observer or center of consciousness.

There is an equally complex resonance to Ghassan Kanafani's *Men in the Sun,* a compelling novella about the travails of three Palestinian refugees who are trying to get from Basra in Iraq to Kuwait. Their past in Palestine is evoked in order to contrast it with the poverty and dispossession of which they are victims immediately after 1948. When they find a man in Basra whose occupation is in part to smuggle refugees across the border in the belly of his empty watertruck, they strike a deal with him, and he takes them as far as the border post, where he is detained in conversation in the hot sun. They die of asphyxiation, unheard and forgotten. Kanafani's novella belongs to the genre of immigrant literature contributed to by an estimable number of postwar writers—Rushdie, Naipaul, Berger, Kundera, and others. But it is also a poignant meditation on the Palestinian fate, and of course eerily prescient about Palestinians in the current Gulf crisis. And yet it would do the subject of the work and its literary merit an extraordinary disservice were we to confine it to the category of national allegory, to see in it only a mirroring of the actual plight of Palestinians in exile. Kanafani's work is literature connected both to its specific historical and cultural situations as well as to a whole world of other literatures and formal articulations, which the attentive reader summons to mind as the interpretation proceeds.

The point I am trying to make can be summed up in the useful notion of worldliness. By linking works to each other we bring them out of the neglect and secondariness to which for all kinds of political and ideological reasons they had previously been condemned. What I am talking about therefore is the opposite of separatism, and also the reverse of exclusivism. It is only through the scrutiny of these works *as* literature, as style, as pleasure and illumination, that they can be brought in, so to speak, and kept in. Otherwise they will be regarded only as informative ethnographic specimens, suitable for the limited attention of experts and area specialists. *Worldliness* is therefore the restoration to such works and interpretations of their place in the global setting, a restoration that can only be accomplished by an appreciation not of some tiny, defensively constituted corner of the world, but of the large, many-windowed house of human culture as a whole.

It seems to me absolutely essential that we engage with cultural works in this unprovincial, interested manner while maintaining a strong sense of the contest for forms and values which any decent cultural work embodies, realizes, and contains. A great deal of recent theoretical speculation has proposed that works of literature are completely determined as such by their situation, and that readers themselves are totally determined in their responses by their respective cultural situations, to a point where no value, no reading, no interpretation can be anything other than the merest reflection of some immediate interest. All readings and all writing are reduced to an assumed historical emanation. Here the indeterminacy of deconstructive reading, the airy insouciance of postaxiological criticism, the casual reductiveness of some (but by no means all) ideological schools are principally at fault. While it is true to say that because a text is the product of an unrecapturable past, and that contemporary criticism can to some extent afford a neutral disengagement or opposed perspective impossible for the text in its own time, there is no reason to take the further step and exempt the interpreter from *any* moral, political, cultural, or psychological commitments. All of these remain at play. The attempt to read a text in its fullest and most integrative context commits the reader to positions that are educative, humane, and engaged, positions that depend on training and taste and not simply on a technologized professionalism, or on the tiresome playfulness of "postmodern" criticism, with its repeated disclaimers of anything but local games and pastiches. Despite Lyotard and his acolytes, we are still in the era of large narratives, of horrendous cultural clashes, and of appallingly destructive war—as witness the recent conflagration in the Gulf—and to say that we are against theory, or beyond literature, is to be blind and trivial.

I am not arguing that every interpretive act is equivalent to a gesture either for or against life. How could anyone defend or attack so crudely general a position? I am saying that once we grant intellectual work the right to exist in a relatively disengaged atmosphere, and allow it a status that isn't disqualified by partisanship, we ought then to reconsider the ties between the text and the world in a serious and uncoercive way. Far from repudiating the great advances made when Eurocentrism and patriarchy began to be demystified, we should consolidate these advances, using them so as to reach a better understanding of the degree to which literature and artistic genius belong to and are some part of the world where all of us also do other kinds of work.

This wider application of the ideas I've been discussing cannot even be attempted if we simply repeat a few names or refer to a handful of approved texts ritualistically or sanctimoniously. Victimhood, alas, does not guarantee or necessarily enable an enhanced sense of humanity. To testify to a history of oppression is necessary, but it is not sufficient unless that history is redirected into intellectual process and universalized to include all sufferers. Yet too often testimony to oppression becomes only a justification for further cruelty and inhumanity, or for high-sounding cant and merely "correct" attitudes. I have in mind, for instance, not only the antagonists mentioned at the beginning of this essay but also the extraordinary behavior of an Elie Wiesel who has refused to translate the lessons of his own past into consistent criticisms of Israel for doing what it has done and is doing right now to Palestinians.

So while it is not necessary to regard every reading or interpretation of a text as the moral equivalent of a war or a political crisis, it does seem to me to be important to underline the fact that whatever else they are, works of literature are not merely texts. They are in fact differently constituted and have different values, they aim to do different things, exist in different genres, and so on. One of the great pleasures for those who read and study literature is the discovery of long-standing norms in which all cultures known to me concur: such things as style and performance, the existence of good as well as lesser writers, and the exercise of preference. What has been most unacceptable during the many harangues on both sides of the so-called Western canon debate is that so many of the combatants have ears of tin and are unable to distinguish between good writing and politically correct attitudes, as if a fifth-rate pamphlet and a great novel have more or less the same significance. Who benefits from leveling attacks on the canon? Certainly not the disadvantaged person or class whose history, if you bother to read it at all, is full of evidence that popular resistance to injustice has always derived immense benefits from literature and culture in general, and very few from invidious distinctions made between ruling-class and subservient cultures. After all, the crucial lesson of C. L. R. James's *Black Jacobins,* or of E. P. Thompson's *Making of the English Working Class* (with its reminder of how important Shakespeare was to nineteenth-century radical culture), is that great antiauthoritarian uprisings made their earliest advances, not by denying the humanitarian and universalist claims of the general dominant culture, but by attacking the adherents of that culture for failing to uphold their own declared standards, for failing to extend them to all, as opposed to a small fraction, of humanity. Toussaint L'Ouverture is the perfect example of a downtrodden slave whose struggle to free himself and his people was informed by the ideas of Rousseau and Mirabeau.

Although I risk oversimplification, it is probably correct to say that it does not finally matter *who* wrote what, but rather *how* a work is written and *how* it is read. The idea that because Plato and Aristotle are male and the products of a slave society they should be disqualified from receiving contemporary attention is as limited an idea as suggesting that *only* their work, because it was addressed to and about elites, should be read today. Marginality and homelessness are not, in my opinion, to be gloried in; they are to be brought to an end, so that more, and not fewer, people can enjoy the benefits of what has for centuries been denied the victims of race, class, or gender.

34

Identity, Authority, and Freedom: The Potentate and the Traveler

Several weeks ago, as I was reflecting on what I might say at this occasion, I encountered a friendly colleague, whom I asked for ideas and suggestions. "What is the title of your lecture?" he asked. "Identity, Authority, and Freedom," I replied. "Interesting," he responded. "You mean, therefore, identity is the faculty, authority is the administration, and freedom . . ." Here he paused meaningfully. "Yes?" I asked. "Freedom," he said, "is retirement."

This prescription is altogether too cynical, and in its flippancy reflected what I think both of us felt: that the issue of academic freedom in a setting like this one here in Cape Town is far more complex and problematic for most of the usual formulas to cover with any kind of adequacy.

Not that academic freedom has been a great deal easier to define, discuss, and defend for North American intellectuals. I hardly need to remind you that discussion concerning academic freedom is not only different in each society but also takes very different forms, one version of which in American universities today concerns the nature of the curriculum. For at least the past decade, a debate has been going on between those on the one hand who feel that the traditional curriculum of the liberal arts—in particular the core of Western humanities courses—has been under severe attack, and those on the other side, who believe that the curriculum in the humanities and the social sciences should more directly reflect the interests of groups in society who have been suppressed, ignored, or papered over with high-sounding formulas. For it is a fact that everywhere in the United States, which is after all an immigrant society made up of many Africans and Asians as well as Europeans, universities have finally had to deal with non-Western societies, with the literature, history, and particular concerns of women, various nationalities, and minorities; and with unconventional, hitherto untaught subjects such as popular culture, mass communications and film, and oral history. In addition, a whole slew of controversial political issues like race, gender, imperialism, war, and slavery have found their way into lectures and seminars. To this extraordinary, almost Copernican change in the general intellectual consciousness, responses have often been very hostile. Some critics have reacted as if the very nature of the university and academic freedom have been threatened because unduly politicized. Others have gone further: for them the critique of the Western canon, with its panoply of what its opponents have called Dead White European Males (for example, Aristotle, Shakespeare, and Wordsworth), has rather improbably signalled the onset of a new fascism, the demise of Western civilization itself, and the return of slavery, child marriage, bigamy, and the harem.

In most cases, however, the actual changes in the canon that reflect the interests of women or African or Native Americans have been pretty mild: Western humanities courses now often include Jane Austen or Toni Morrison, and they might also have added novels by Chinua Achebe, García Márquez, and Salman Rushdie. There have been a few extreme cases of silliness: younger teachers and scholars publicly attacking more senior scholars as racists, or pillorying their peers for not being "politically correct." Yet all of this discussion and controversy underlines the general fact that what goes on in school or university is somehow privileged, whether on the one hand it is supposed to appear "above" parochial interests, changes in fashion or style, and political pressure, or on the other hand, whether the university is meant to be engaged intellectually and politically with significant political and social change, with improvements in the status of subaltern or minority populations, and with abuses of power and lapses in morality, which the university must remedy, criticize, and align itself in opposition to.

Although a thousand qualifications and conditions can enter into a discussion of either or both sides, one assumption is common to both: the idea that the status of university or school as well as what goes along with them intellectually and socially is special, is different from other sites in society like the government bureaucracy, the workplace, or the home. I believe that all societies today assign a special privilege to the academy that, whether the privilege exempts it from intercourse with the everyday world or involves it directly in that world, says that unique conditions do, indeed ought to, prevail in it. To say that someone is educated or an educator is to say something having to do with the mind, with intellectual and moral values, with a particular process of inquiry, discussion, and exchange, none of which is encountered as regularly outside as inside the academy. The idea is that academies form the mind of the young, prepare them for life, just as— to look at things from the point of view of the teacher—to teach is to be engaged in a vocation or calling having principally to do not with financial gain but with the unending search for truth.

These are very high and important matters, and for those of us who have made education our life, they testify to the genuine aura surrounding the academic and intellectual enterprise. There *is* something hallowed and consecrated about the academy: there *is* a sense of violated sanctity experienced by us when the university or school is subjected to crude political pressures. Yet, I believe, to be convinced of these genuinely powerful truths is not entirely to be freed of the circumstances— some would call them encumbrances—that impinge on education today, influence our thinking about it, and shape our efforts in the academy. The point I want to make is that as we consider these situational or contextual matters, the search for academic freedom, to which this occasion is so manifestly dedicated, becomes more important, more urgent, more requiring of careful and reflective analysis. So whereas it is universally true that contemporary societies treat the academy with seriousness and respect, each community of academics, intellectuals, and students must wrestle with the problem of what academic freedom in that society at that time actually is and should be.

Let me speak briefly about the two parts of the world that I know most about. In the United States, where I live and work, there has been a distinct change in the academic climate since I was a student a generation ago. Until the late 1960s, it was assumed by most people that what took place within university precincts was removed from any steady, or collaborative, or—in the worst case—collusive association with the world outside. Yet because the experience of war in Vietnam was so powerful, and because there was so much traffic between the academy and the institutions of government and power, the veil was rent, so to speak. No longer was it taken for granted that political scientists or sociologists were sage-like theoreticians or impartial researchers; many of them were discovered to be working, sometimes secretly and sometimes openly, on such topics as counterinsurgency and "lethal research" for the State Department, the CIA, or the Pentagon.

Yet after the university's apartness was seen as an idea to have been abandoned, an equal and opposite set of reactions set in. It became almost a cliché that the university was to be regarded only as an arm of the government, that it reflected only the interests of corporations and establishment power and should therefore be wholly transformed into a place where students would be educated as reformers or revolutionaries. Relevance was the new watchword. And while a new set of materials was introduced into the academy for the first time—I refer once again to women's studies, minority studies, studies that deal with the effect of war, racism, and gender oppression—there did in fact seem to be a new worldliness in the university that denied it the relative aloofness it once seemed entitled to.

As a reaction to all this, academic freedom was the phrase given to the movement that claimed to want to return the university to a now very much regretted sort of impartiality to, and distance from, the everyday world. But here all sorts of exaggerations and polemical distortions were introduced. During the 1980s, the American university was portrayed as being in the possession of a Marxist revolutionary conspiracy. This of course was a ludicrously false notion. Also, the argument put forward in the name of academic freedom claimed that because so many new courses and ideas had been introduced into the traditional curriculum, the university's age-old standards had diminished, had fallen prey to outside political pressures. To restore the university's true freedom from everyday life meant returning to courses, ideas, and values that derived exclusively from the mainstream European thinkers—Plato, Aristotle, Sophocles, Descartes, Montaigne, Shakespeare, Bacon, Locke, and so on. One of the most famous and commercially successful books of the past decade was *The Closing of the American Mind*, a long diatribe against an assorted set of villains, including Nietzsche, feminism, Marxism, and Black Studies; the author of this work, who had been a professor at Cornell University when for a short time the university had been shut down by a group of armed African-American students, was so embittered by his experience that his book argued quite frankly for the university's freedom to educate not large numbers of the deprived and disadvantaged but a small, carefully prepared and instructed elite. The result would be, as the book was quite explicit in explaining, that only a small handful of works by the Greeks and some French Enlightenment philosophers would survive the rigorous tests of inclusion in the newly "liberated" curriculum.

This may sound funny to your ears. I think it does happen to be funny because the prescription for curing the university of its woes, for liberating it from political pressures is in a sense worse than the malady. Surely one would have thought that to use the concept of freedom about the academy is not on the face of it to talk mainly about exclusion but about inclusion, and surely it would seem to be true that the university ought to be the place not where many vigorous and exciting intellectual pursuits should be forbidden but where they ought to be encouraged on as wide a front as possible. I will grant, as everyone must, that the concept of freedom cannot be a license for, as Matthew Arnold put it in another context, entirely doing as one likes. But it must be the case, I think, that advocates of freedom for university communities to undertake intellectual pursuits cannot spend most of their time arguing that only a handful of approved books, ideas, disciplines, and methods are worthy of serious intellectual attention. The realities of social life are viewed in this perspective as sordid and demeaning, although it needs to be noted that professors such as the author of *The Closing of the American Mind* have no difficulty accepting money from corporations and foundations outside the university who happen to espouse their own deeply conservative views. To say of such practices that they represent a double standard is no exaggeration. For you cannot honestly impugn people as enemies of academic freedom just because they welcome worldly concerns into the academy while, when you do more or less the same thing, you consider yourself to be "upholding standards."

An altogether different challenge to the concept of academic freedom is found in national universities in the Arab world, which is where I originally come from. I speak here of most of the large public universities in countries like Jordan, Syria, Iraq, Egypt, Morocco, Saudi Arabia, and other Gulf states. Most of these countries are in fact run by secular governments, although some—like Saudi Arabia—have secular governments with a religious mandate. What is important to understand, however, is that with few exceptions Arab universities are not only nationalist universities but also political institutions, for perfectly understandable reasons. For several centuries, the Arab world has been dominated by Ottoman or European colonialism. National independence for countries like Egypt and Syria, say, meant that young people at last could be educated fully in the traditions, histories, languages, and cultures of their own particular Arab countries. In my own case, for instance, I was educated entirely in British colonial schools in Palestine and Egypt, where all study focused on the history of British society, literature, and values. Much the same was true in the main British and French colonies, such as India and Algeria, where it was assumed that native elites would be taught the rudiments of intellectual culture in idioms and methods designed in effect to keep those native elites subservient to colonial rule, the superiority of European learning, and so forth. Until I was about sixteen I knew a great deal more about the eighteenth-century enclosure system in England than I did about how the Islamic *waqfs* operated in my own part of the world, and—irony of ironies—colonial preconsuls like Cromer and Kitchener were more familiar to me than Haroun al-Rashid or Khalid ibn al-Walid.

When independence was achieved as a result of anti-colonial struggles, one of the first areas to be changed was education. I recall, for instance, that after the Revolution of 1952 in Egypt a great deal of emphasis was placed on the Arabization of the curriculum, the Arabization of intellectual norms, the Arabization of values to be inculcated in schools and universities. The same was true in Algeria after

1962, where an entire generation of Muslims were for the first time entitled and enjoined to study Arabic, which had been forbidden except as a language in mosques while Algeria was considered and ruled as a department of France. It is important to understand, therefore, the passion that went into reclaiming educational territory that for so long had been dominated by foreign rulers in the Arab world, and it is equally important to understand the tremendous spiritual wound felt by many of us because of the sustained presence in our midst of domineering foreigners who taught us to respect distant norms and values more than our own. Our culture was felt to be of a lower grade, perhaps even congenitally inferior and something of which to be ashamed.

Now it would be wrong and even absurd to suggest that a national education based on Arabic norms is in and of itself either trivial or impoverished. The Arab-Islamic tradition is one of the great cultural contributions to humanity, and in the old universities of Fez and al-Azhar as well as the various *madrasas* throughout the Arab world, a rich educational experience has been provided to uncounted generations of students. Yet it is also true to say that in the newly independent countries of the Arab world, the national universities were reconceived, I believe, as (rightly or wrongly) extensions of the newly established national security state. Once again it is clear that all societies accord a remarkable privilege to the university and school as crucibles for shaping national identity.

Yet all too often in the Arab world, true education was short-circuited, so to speak. Whereas in the past young Arabs fell prey to the intervention of foreign ideas and norms, now they were to be remade in the image of the ruling party, which, given the Cold War and the Arab-Israeli struggle, became also the party of national security—and in some countries, the only party. Thus adding to the vastly increased pressure on universities to open their doors to everyone in the new society—an extremely admirable policy—universities also became the proving ground for earnest patriots. Professorial appointments were, as they are in many places in the world today, civil service appointments. Alas, political conformity rather than intellectual excellence was often made to serve as a criterion for promotion and appointment, with the general result that timidity, a studious lack of imagination, and careful conservatism came to rule intellectual practice. Moreover, because the general atmosphere in the Arab world of the past three decades has become both conspiratorial and, I am sorry to say, repressive—all in the name of national security—nationalism in the university has come to represent not freedom but accommodation, not brilliance and daring but caution and fear, not the advancement of knowledge but self-preservation.

Not only did many brilliant and gifted people leave the Arab world in a massive brain-drain, but I would say that the whole notion of academic freedom underwent a significant downgrading during the past three decades. It became possible for one to be free in the university only if one completely avoided anything that might attract unwelcome attention or suspicion. I do not want to make a long, anguished recital of how badly demoralized and discouraged a place the Arab university, in most of its contemporary aspects, has become, but I do think it is important to link its depressed situation with the lack of democratic rights, the absence of a free press, and an atmosphere bereft of well-being and confidence elsewhere in the society. No one can say that these things are not connected to one another, because they so obviously are. Political repression has never been good for academic freedom, and perhaps more important, it has been disastrous for academic and intellectual excellence. My assessment of Arab academic life is that too high a price has been paid in sustaining nationalist regimes that have allowed political passions and an ideology of conformity to dominate—perhaps even to swallow up—civil institutions such as the university. To make the practice of intellectual discourse dependent on conformity to a predetermined political ideology is to nullify intellect altogether.

For all its problems, however, the American academy is a very different place than its counterpart in the Arab world. To suggest that there are any obvious similarities at all would be to misrepresent each seriously. Yet I do not want to celebrate the greater manifest freedom of inquiry, the generally higher level of intellectual attainment, the quite extraordinary range of interests demonstrated in the American academy at the expense of the much more obvious constraints and difficulties in Arab universities, which after everything is said share the fate of many other universities in the Third World. That sort of almost bullying praise of the virtues of Western education today would be too easy and far too simple.

Nevertheless, it is important to show the connection between such different circumstances as those that obtain in the Middle East and in the United States by remarking how it is that in both a very great premium is placed upon the cultural and national *identity* of the education being offered. I spoke earlier about the debate between upholders and opponents of the Western canon in the American university; I also spoke of how in the post-independence, post-colonial Arab universities a great degree of emphasis was placed on the *Arabness* of what was being offered. In both cases, therefore, ordinarily so different and so far removed from each other, one idea—that of national identity—shines through. It is precisely this idea, American and Western in one case, Arab and Islamic in the other, that plays an astonishingly important role as authority and as point of reference in the whole educational process. I want to raise the question of how the central importance and authority given the national identity impinges on and greatly influences, surreptitiously and often unquestioningly, academic freedom—that is, what transpires in the name of academic freedom.

When I discussed earlier how the specific social and cultural circumstances of the academic situation in each society define the problem of academic freedom, national identity was very much what I had in mind. Certainly this is true of a society like that of South Africa, now undergoing a particularly difficult and stressful transformation. But as one looks elsewhere in the world, one finds that many places are experiencing much the same contest of what the national identity is or ought to be. This contest, almost more than anything else, defines the political and cultural situation of the late twentieth century: that as the world grows smaller and more interdependent economically, environmentally, and through the revolution in communications, there is a greater sense that societies interact, often abrasively, in terms of who or what their national identities are. Consider on a global level the importance today of the Western European community as one large cultural block interacting with the Eastern European community and the Soviet Union, with Japan and the United States, and with many parts of the Third World. Similarly, look at the contest between the Islamic world and the West, in which national, cultural, and religious self-images and self-definitions play so powerful a role. To speak of hegemony, attempts at domination, and the control of resources in this global struggle is, I strongly believe, to speak in very accurate (if also melodramatic) terms.

But that is not all. Within societies such as this one and those in other parts of the Western, African, Asian, and Islamic world, there is also a contest as to which concept of national identity ought to prevail. Although this question is principally of philosophical and historical derivation, inevitably it leads one to the urgent political issue of how, given the definition of identity, the society is to be governed. To look closely at the recent history of imperialism and decolonization is to grasp the centrality of the debate. In Algeria, as the works of Frantz Fanon eloquently testify, Algerians were viewed by the French as a subordinate race, fit only for colonial and subaltern status. Even the distinguished humanistic writer Albert Camus, who was a native-born member of the French settler population, embodied the Algerian in his fiction as an essentially nameless, threatening creature; during the late fifties Camus explicitly said in his *Algerian Chronicles* that there was no Algerian Muslim nation. Of course there was. After the liberation in 1962 one of the principal tasks of the FLN was to re-establish the integrity, the centrality, the paramountcy and sovereignty of the Muslim Algerian identity. With the creation of a new governmental structure of Algeria came an educational program focused first on the teaching of Arabic and on Algerian history, formerly either banned or subordinated to programs stressing the superiority of French civilization.

Surely in South Africa much the same dynamic will be and doubtless already is embodied in the nature of the educational program, as the country moves out of apartheid into a new system of democratic, racially unbiased government. However, there are some further points I wish to make about all this, as it has a bearing on the question of academic freedom.

The first is that in a condition in which cultural conflict is, to all intents and purposes, universal, the relationship between the national identity and other national identities is going to be reflected in the academy. The question is how. All cultures teach about themselves, and all cultures naturally assert their supremacy over others. To study the tradition, the masterpieces, the great interpretive methods of a culture inclines members of that culture to reverence, respect, loyalty, and even patriotism. This of course is understandable. But my point is that no culture exists in isolation, and since it is a matter of course that the study of one's own tradition in school and university is taken for granted, we must look at what of *other* cultures, *other* traditions, *other* national communities also is communicated as one's own culture is studied. I should like to argue that if the authority granted our own culture carries with it the authority to perpetuate cultural hostility, then a true academic freedom is very much at risk, having as it were conceded that intellectual discourse must worship at the altar of national identity and thereby denigrate or diminish others.

Let me explain. Historically, every society has its Other: The Greeks had the barbarians, the Arabs the Persians, the Hindus the Muslims, and on and on. But since the nineteenth century consolidated the world system, all cultures and societies today are intermixed. No country on earth is made up of homogenous natives; each has its immigrants, its internal "Others," and each society, very much like the world we live in, is a hybrid. Yet a discrepancy exists at the very heart of this vital, complex, and intermingled world. I have in mind the discrepancy between the heterogenous reality and the concept of national identity, to which so much of education is in fact dedicated. If we recall once again the two examples I gave earlier of debate about what is Western in the American university and of politicization of the Arabness of the Arab university, we will note that in both instances a faltering and outdated concept of a single national identity more or less lords it over the true variety and manifold diversity of human life. In both cases a kind of supernational concept—that of the West in the United States, and that of the Arabs or Islam in countries like Algeria, Syria, and Iraq (each of which has large minority populations)—is pressed into service. This scarcely improves things, since in both a combination of authority and defensiveness inhibits, disables, and ultimately falsifies thought. What finally matters about the West or the Arabs, in my opinion, is not what these notions exclude but to what they are connected, how much they include, and how interesting are the interactions between them and other cultures.

I do not have an easy way of resolving this very serious discrepancy. I do know, nevertheless, that the meaning of academic freedom cannot simply be reduced to venerating the unexamined authority of a national identity and its culture. For in its essence the intellectual life—and I speak here mainly about the social sciences and the humanities—is about the freedom to be critical: criticism *is* intellectual life and, while the academic precinct contains a great deal in it, its spirit is intellectual and critical, and neither reverential nor patriotic. One of the great lessons of the critical spirit is that human life and history are secular— that is, actually constructed and reproduced by men and women. The problem with the inculcation of cultural, national, or ethnic identity is that it takes insufficient note of how these identities are constructions, not god-given or natural artifacts. If the academy is to be a place for the realization not of the nation but of the intellect—and that, I think, is the academy's reason for being—then the intellect must not be coercively held in thrall to the authority of the national identity. Otherwise, I fear, the old inequities, cruelties, and unthinking attachments that have so disfigured human history will be recycled by the academy, which then loses much of its real intellectual freedom as a result.

Now let me speak personally and even politically if I may. Like so many others, I belong to more than one world. I am a Palestinian Arab, and I am also an American. This affords me an odd, not to say grotesque, double perspective. In addition, I am of course an academic. None of these identities is watertight; each influences and plays upon the other. What complicates matters is that the United States has just waged a destructive war against an Arab country, Iraq, which itself had illegally occupied and to all intents and purposes tried to eliminate Kuwait, another Arab country. The United States is also the principal sponsor of Israel, the state that as a Palestinian I identify as having de- stroyed the society and world into which I was born. Israel now ad- ministers a brutal military occupation of Palestinian territories of the West Bank and Gaza. So I am required to negotiate the various ten- sions and contradictions implicit in my own biography.

It should be obvious that I cannot identify at all with the tri- umphalism of one identity because the loss and deprivation of the others are so much more urgent to me. There is some irony in the fact that as I speak as an American to South Africans at a South African university on the subject of academic freedom, the universities and the schools in Palestine are closed and opened by willful and punitive decree of the Israeli military authorities. This situation has obtained since February 1988: during that time, the main universities have been *kept* closed. When you consider that well over two-thirds of the population in Occupied Palestine is made up of people under the age of eighteen, the sheer massive brutality of denying them school and college or university by systematic edict is extraordinary. At the same time, Jewish children and young people freely attend classes in their schools and universities, which are of a decent standard. There is now a generation of Palestinian children virtually being made illiterate, again by Israeli design and programmatic vision. To the best of my knowledge, there has been no really systematic campaign by Western academics and intellectuals to try to alleviate this situation; of course individuals have protested, but Israel continues these and other practices intended to deny, if not altogether to obliterate, the Palestinian national identity, and it does so with little Western objection. Certainly the subsidies from the United States continue and celebrations of Israeli democracy also continue. More to the point I am trying to make here, the Israeli practice of attempting to deny, efface, and otherwise render impossible the existence of a Palestinian national identity except as nameless, disenfranchised "Arab inhabitants" of "Judea and Samaria" (as the West Bank and Gaza are known in official Israeli parlance)—this practice is carried out not just by modern colonialists but by the descendants of a people, the Jews, themselves the victims barely a generation ago of such practices. For the victim to become the victimizer of another people is a reversal of history quite awful to ponder. That this new victimizer has persecuted the very people it dispossessed and exiled, all the while benefiting from munificent Western moral support for Israel, is an appallingly cruel truth.

Why then is it carried out, if not in the assertion of a new national identity and a new nationalism, the Israeli, that decrees the absence of a conflicting (and pre-existing) national identity and nationalism, that of the Palestinian? I cannot and will not try to explain why Israel does this to the Palestinian people. But I can say with understanding and compassion that most Palestinians today who suffer such tribulations naturally long for the day when they can practice their self-determination in an independent state of their own, when Palestinian universities and schools can instruct young people in the history and traditions of Arab culture and in those of the other cultures that make up human history. Surely a majority of South Africans feel the same pain that we do, feel the humiliation and the oppression of seeing our representatives denied their right to represent their people, of our struggle labeled only "terrorism," of our political rights denied, our self-determination endlessly postponed, our collective punishment enacted on a minute-by-minute basis. Is it not a fact that what makes all these things more intensely painful is that they are carried out very often in the name of Western as well as Biblical morality, with its magnificent lineage of sagacity, learning, advancement, and technological proficiency to back it up? How delinquent, how morally repugnant are natives made to feel, that they dare to resist so compelling a cultural identity, that they have the effrontery to call such actions as the closing of schools and universities carried out by such authorities cruel and unjust practices.

To anyone who knows a little about the history of colonialism in the non-European world, these things too will pass. It took dozens of generations, but the British finally did leave India, and after 130 years the French left Algeria, and after a time apartheid will pass. So too for us Palestinians, our oppression will end, and we will have our self-determination, not at the expense of another people, but through a Palestinian state alongside Israel. The challenge is what intellectually and academically do we do with our earned liberation? I pose the question as perhaps the most serious one to be faced not just by those of us who have been on the bottom but by those of us who belong to the side that will at last win liberation.

I would put the question this way: what kind of authority, what sort of human norms what kind of identity do we then allow to lead us, to guide our study, to dictate our educational processes? Do we say: now that we have won, that we have achieved equality and independence, let us elevate ourselves, our history, our cultural or ethnic identity above that of others, uncritically giving this identity of ours centrality and coercive dominance? Do we substitute for a Eurocentric norm an Afrocentric or Islamo- or Arabocentric one? Or, as happened so many times in the post-colonial world, do we get our independence and then return to models for education derived lazily, adopted imitatively and uncritically, from elsewhere? In short, do we use the freedom we have fought for merely to replicate the mind-forged manacles that once enslaved us, and having put them on do we proceed to apply them to others less fortunate than ourselves?

Raising these questions means that the university—more generally speaking the academy, but especially, I think, the university—has a privileged role to play in dealing with these matters. Universities exist in the world, although each university, as I have suggested, exists in its own particular world, with a history and social circumstances all its own. I cannot bring myself to believe that, even though it cannot be an immediately political arena, the university is free of the encumbrances, the problems, the social dynamics of its surrounding environment. How much better to take note of these realities than blithely to talk about academic freedom in an airy and insouciant way, as if real freedom happens, and having once happened goes on happening un-deterred and unconcerned. When I first began teaching about thirty years ago, an older colleague took me aside and informed me that the academic life was odd indeed; it was sometimes deathly boring, it was generally polite and in its own way quite impotently genteel, but what-ever the case, he added, it was certainly better than working! None of us can deny the sense of privilege carried inside the academic sanctum, as it were, the real sense that as most people go to their jobs and suffer their daily anxiety, we read books and talk and write of great ideas, ex-periences, epochs. In my opinion, there is no higher privilege. But in actuality no university or school can really be a shelter from the diffi-culties of human life and more specifically from the political inter-course of a given society and culture.

This is by no means to deny that, as Newman said so beautifully and so memorably,

> the university has this object and this mission; it contemplates neither moral impression nor mechanical production; it pro-fesses to educate the mind neither in art nor in duty; its func-tion is intellectual culture; here it may leave its scholars, and it has done its work when it has done as much as this. It educates the intellect to reason well in all matters, to reach out towards truth, and to grasp it.

Note the care with which Newman, perhaps with Swift, the greatest of English prose stylists, selects his words for what actions take place in the pursuit of knowledge: words like *exercise, educates, reach out,* and *grasp*. In none of these words is there anything to suggest coercion, or direct utility, or immediate advantage or dominance. Newman says in another place,

> Knowledge is something intellectual, something which grasps what it perceives through the senses; something which takes a view of things; which sees more than the senses convey; which reasons upon what it sees, and while it sees; which invests it with an idea.

Then he adds:

> not to know the relative disposition of things is the state of slaves or children; to have mapped out the universe is the boast, or at least the ambition, of philosophy.

Newman defines philosophy as the highest state of knowledge.

These are incomparably eloquent statements, and they can only be a little deflated when we remind ourselves that Newman was speaking to and about English men, not women, and then also about the education of young Catholics. Nonetheless, the profound truth in what Newman says is, I believe, designed to undercut any partial or somehow narrow view of education whose aim might seem only to reaffirm one particularly attractive and dominant identity, that which is the resident power or authority of the moment. Perhaps like many of his Victorian contemporaries—Ruskin comes quickly to mind—Newman was arguing earnestly for a type of education that placed the highest premium on English, European, or Christian values in knowledge. But sometimes, even though we may mean to say something, another thought at odds with what we say insinuates itself into our rhetoric and in effect criticizes it, delivers a different and less assertive idea than on the surface we might have intended. This happens when we read Newman. Suddenly we realize that although he is obviously extolling what is an overridingly Western conception of the world, with little allowance made for what was African or Latin American or Indian, his words let slip the notion that even an English or Western identity wasn't enough, wasn't at bottom or at best what education and freedom were all about.

Certainly it is difficult to find in Newman anything like a license either for blinkered specialization or for gentlemanly aestheticism. What he expects of the academy is, he says,

> the power of viewing many things at once as one whole, of referring them severally to their true place in the universal system, of understanding their respective values, and determining their mutual dependence.

This synthetic wholeness has a special relevance to the fraught political situations of conflict, the unresolved tension, and the social as well as moral disparities that are constitutive to the world of today's academy. He proposes a large and generous view of human diversity. To link the practice of education—and by extension, of freedom—in the academy directly to the settling of political scores, or to an equally unmodulated reflection of real national conflict is neither to pursue knowledge nor in the end to educate ourselves and our students, which is an everlasting effort at understanding. But what happens when we take Newman's prescriptions about viewing many things as one whole or, referring them severally to their true place in the universal system, we transpose these notions to today's world of embattled national identities, cultural conflicts, and power relations? Is there any possibility for bridging the gap between the ivory tower of contemplative rationality ostensibly advocated by Newman and our own urgent need for self-realization and self-assertion with its background in a history of repression and denial?

I think there is. I will go further and say that it is precisely the role of the contemporary academy to bridge this gap, since society itself is too directly inflected by politics to serve so general and so finally intellectual and moral a role. We must first, I think, accept that nationalism resurgent, or even nationalism militant, whether it is the nationalism of the victim or of the victor, has its limits. Nationalism is the philosophy of identity made into a collectively organized passion. For those of us just emerging from marginality and persecution, nationalism is a necessary thing: a long-deferred and -denied identity needs to come out into the open and take its place among other human identities. But that is only the first step. To make all or even most of education subservient to this goal is to limit human horizons without either intellectual or, I would argue, political warrant. To assume that the ends of education are best advanced by focusing principally on *our own* separateness, our own ethnic identity, culture, and traditions ironically places us where as subaltern, inferior, or lesser races we had been placed by nineteenth-century racial theory, unable to share in the general riches of human culture. To say that women should read mainly women's literature, that blacks should study and perfect only black techniques of understanding and interpretation, that Arabs and Muslims should return to the Holy Book for all knowledge and wisdom is the inverse of saying along with Carlyle and Gobineau that all the lesser races must retain their inferior status in the world. There is room for all at the rendezvous of victory, said Aimé Césaire; no race has a monopoly on beauty or intelligence.

A single overmastering identity at the core of the academic enterprise, whether that identity be Western, African, or Asian, is a confinement, a deprivation. The world we live in is made up of numerous identities interacting, sometimes harmoniously, sometimes antithetically. Not to deal with that whole—which is in fact a contemporary version of the whole referred to by Newman as a true enlargement of mind—is not to have academic freedom. We cannot make our claim as seekers after justice that we advocate knowledge only of and about ourselves. Our model for academic freedom should therefore be the migrant or traveler: for if, in the real world outside the academy, we must needs be ourselves and only ourselves, inside the academy we should be able to discover and travel among other selves, other identities, other varieties of the human adventure. But, most essentially, in this joint discovery of self and Other, it is the role of the academy to transform what might be conflict, or contest, or assertion into reconciliation, mutuality, recognition, and creative interaction. So much of the knowledge produced by Europe about Africa, or about India and the Middle East, originally derived from the need for imperial control; indeed, as a recent study of Rodney Murchison by Robert Stafford convincingly shows, even geology and biology were implicated, along with geography and ethnography, in the imperial scramble for Africa. But rather than viewing the search for knowledge in the academy as the search for coercion and control over others, we should regard knowledge as something for which to risk identity, and we should think of academic freedom as an invitation to give up on identity in the hope of understanding and perhaps even assuming more than one. We must always view the academy as a place to voyage in, owning none of it but at home everywhere in it.

It comes, finally, to two images for inhabiting the academic and cultural space provided by school and university. On the one hand, we can be there in order to reign and hold sway. Here, in such a conception of academic space, the academic professional is king and potentate. In that form you sit surveying all before you with detachment and mastery. Your legitimacy is that this is your domain, which you can describe with *authority* as principally Western, or African, or Islamic, or American, or on and on. The other model is considerably more mobile, more playful, although no less serious. The image of traveler depends not on power but on motion, on a willingness to go into different worlds, use different idioms, and understand a variety of disguises, masks, and rhetorics. Travelers must suspend the claim of customary routine in order to live in new rhythms and rituals. Most of all, and most unlike the potentate who must guard only one place and defend its frontiers, the traveler *crosses over,* traverses territory, and abandons fixed positions, all the time. To do this with dedication and love as well as a realistic sense of the terrain is, I believe, a kind of academic freedom at its highest, since one of its main features is that you can leave authority and dogma to the potentate. You will have other things to think about and enjoy than merely yourself and your domain, and those other things are far more impressive, far more worthy of study and respect than self-adulation and uncritical self-appreciation. To join the academic world is therefore to enter a ceaseless quest for knowledge and freedom.

35

The Anglo-Arab Encounter

A massive literature in English now exists in all the many countries that were once British colonies, in many of which (Canada, Australia, New Zealand) English is the *lingua franca;* Ireland and South Africa are similar but not exactly so, with Gaelic and Afrikaans jostling English. In the Indian subcontinent, the British parts of the Caribbean, East and West Africa, literature in English co-exists with literature in other languages, but if we think of Salman Rushdie, Anita Desai, Wilson Harris, Derek Walcott, Chinua Achebe, Ngugi, Wole Soyinka, J. M. Coetzee, and George Lamming we are really talking about an estimably substantial library of English-language but non-English works, by no means peripheral or ignorable. The same is roughly true of former French colonies and Francophone literature, where the paradox of literature in French but directed against colonial France (Fanon, Césaire, Senghor) is still as lively and invigorating as it was when it first appeared one or two generations ago.

The exception, in both the French and to a greater extent the English instance, is the Arab world, once divided unequally between British and French colonialism. In Algeria and Morocco, many distinguished Arab and Muslim writers produce work only in French: Kateb

Yacine, Assia Djebar, Abd el-Kabir el Khatibi, and Tahar ben Jalloun are the names that quickly come to mind. Yet in both those countries political independence from France brought forth new literature in Arabic, with poetry, fiction, criticism, history, political analysis, and memoirs now circulating not only locally but throughout the Eastern Arab world or *mashriq*. There has long been a significant, if uneven, Lebanese literature in French, coexisting with a more impressive Arab production. Some of this Franco-Lebanese literature—for instance the essays of Michel Chiha—had important political consequences, furnishing the Maronite community with a sense of non-Muslim, even non-Arab identity in a predominantly Sunni Arab environment. But this is not to detract from the literary merit of other writers—Georges Shehadé, Etel Adnan, Nadia Tueni, and Salah Stetié among several—whose work in French is no less Lebanese and even Arab.

When it comes to *mashriq* literature in English, the harvest is considerably, puzzlingly, less impressive and coherent. One thinks, for instance, of Edward Atiyeh and George Antonius, men who came to maturity before the Second World War; each produced one central work (Antonius's *The Arab Awakening* remains *the* classic and foundational book on Arab nationalism) but little else. Antonius's daughter, Soraya, has produced two interesting novels in English, but like her father's work, they are isolated examples. In his long career, Jabra Ibrahim Jabra has written only one novel in English, and a handful of fine critical essays, along with his celebrated fiction and poetry in Arabic. A tiny number of Egyptian writers (Wagih Ghali and Magdi Wahba are the main names) have produced an equally small number of literary texts, but that is all. There must be other names here and there, and, of course, there is an appreciable corpus of scholarly works by Arabs in English, but compared with the French North African and Lebanese achievement, the roster is on the whole unimpressive.

Why this should be so, given the length of British tutelage, as well as the estimable schools and English-language universities throughout the Arab world, is something I have never understood. Why did the Franco-Arab cultural encounter give rise to a more developed literary result? Could it be that literary English has been the preserve mainly of isolated members of religious minorities and that, more usually, English has been employed in segregated areas, like administration, the social sciences, and international politics? At the same time, an explosion of literature in the Arabic language has completely overshadowed it, leaving the tiny number of writers in English even more anomalous. Why English and not Arabic is the question an Egyptian, Palestinian, Iraqi, or Jordanian writer has to ask him or herself right off.

Ahdaf Soueif's new novel, *In the Eye of the Sun,* provides a satisfying answer immediately: English serves better when a lot of the material is, so to speak, English, about being in England, having to do intimately with English people and so on. This is not very often a subject (even of episodes) in contemporary Arabic fiction: again, this is curious and surprising. One of the earliest genres of writing in the classical and modern Arab world is about "the Franks," as Europeans were usually called, but almost all this material treats foreigners as exotic, even admirable, curiosities: visited, described, benefited from, it is true, but also looked at very much from the outside. The extraordinary thing about *In the Eye of the Sun* is that Soueif writes of both England and Egypt from within, although for her heroine Asya Ulama (literally translated, Asia [of the] learned clerics) Egypt is the land of her birth, religion, and early education, Britain the land of her post-graduate education, maturity, and intimate expression. In *Aisha,* a collection of stories published in 1983, Soueif focused exclusively on Egyptian life; her English had to negotiate the tricky feat of being idiomatically fluent while dealing with characters who were entirely Arab and Muslim. She was quite successful, but the oddness of the enterprise never wears off.

Asya is a complex hybrid. Her parents are academics (the mother a professor of English at Cairo University), but her upbringing is also traditionally Muslim. Nevertheless, she is educated in English literature and, as the novel opens, is caring for her cancer-stricken maternal uncle Hamid in London: it is mid-1979, and as she muses about her uncle, her mind drifts back to May 1967 when, days before the Arab-Israeli war, he had also been an invalid, the result of a terrible car accident. Those recollections in turn establish themselves as formative for her, and then the novel proper begins, her adolescence, exams, first love affair, the story of her extended family unfolding before us in slow and intimate detail. Unlike *Aisha,* which was set in a sort of apolitical, almost folkloric limbo, *In the Eye of the Sun* takes place against a backdrop of turbulent political history: the shock of the 1967 war; the depredations of the War of Attrition; the advent of Arab socialism; the death of Nasser (this is most memorably and affectionately rendered); Sadat's trip to Jerusalem and the Camp David accords; the bombing of South Lebanon, the emergence of the Palestinian movement, the Israeli occupation of the West Bank and Gaza.

Often these are distant events, a backdrop for relatively inconsequential domestic routine, for instance, or for contrast with the private world of the heroine. Yet just as often politics involve the characters directly. The contrast between Sadat and Nasser is registered in Asya's sense of the former as a sort of bewildering huckster, the latter as a beloved quasi-patriarchal and nationalist symbol. Deena, her younger sister, is married to Muhsin, a young left-wing political activist who is imprisoned under Sadat. Saif, Asya's husband, works in Syrian military intelligence in Damascus. The great bread riots of early 1977 give rise to anxious commentary among Asya and her friends; Eliot Richardson and Robert Murphy are guests at Nasser's funeral, and draw forth the comment from Saif that Sadat will soon start getting closer to the United States. Nowhere is the intersection of private and public history more interesting than when Asya considers the difference between her mother, Lateefa, and herself as each abandons Arabic for English. For Lateefa Mursi, the decision is almost revolutionary, as her generation "seizes" Cairo University from the British, immediately after the revolution of 1952. For Asya, such a triumphalist sense of mission is impossible. She can only experience the need to move away from her job and go to England to get her Ph.D. as something of a parting of the ways between her students and milieu on the one hand and her stubborn selfhood on the other. The politics are entirely psychological, affective, personal. And, in the second half of the novel, they proceed accordingly, getting more intense, at times even labored and stifling.

In the Eye of the Storm is at its powerful best as Soueif slowly explores the appalling limitations of Asya's life as an Arab woman, beset by a strangely prudish and often uncomprehendingly sadistic and repressed husband, Saif Madi, a coarse, sexually overwhelming English paramour, Gerald Stone, and her rebarbative, jargon-filled Ph.D. dissertation on metaphor, which is quoted from rather too often. This

collection of burdens, Asya says, constitutes "the bad bit," a long sequence of choked sexual impulses with Saif, unsatisfying adultery with
Gerald, followed by mercilessly detailed jealousy and torture for her
when the impotent Saif finds out about Gerald. And then there is her
tiresome research, which she does at an unnamed university in the
North of England. Yet, what is quite unique about the novel's second
half is that Asya is revealed to be capable of accepting and living in
both halves (Arabic and English) of her life, were it not that each of
them also rejects a great deal of her. Saif wants her as a dutiful wife (he
refuses to have sex with her before marriage) but gives her none of the
emotional and physical companionship she needs; he beats, harasses,
humiliates, and shames her when they are together after she has been
with Gerald, but can neither be with her as husband nor let her go as
woman. The scenes where he cross-examines her about her sexual relationship with Stone are painful and embarrassing, but they are brilliantly done. Raw, accurate, unendingly searing, Asya's long
association with Saif establishes Ahdaf Soueif as one of the most extraordinary chroniclers of sexual politics now writing. That her pages
are about two Arabs makes them doubly unusual, since fiction,
whether in English or Arabic, has very little that is comparable. Gerald
simply has no comprehension of her background; he neither fully
trusts nor can fully have her. The impasse is only partially relieved as
she works unhappily on her arid dissertation. The novel is therefore
the exploration of a cultural antinomy experienced, as in George
Eliot's novels (cited often), as the stalemate of the individual feminine
consciousness, although in many ways Asya is her own Casaubon.

Is *The Eye of the Sun* an Arabic novel in English? Yes, and not just because the heroine, her family, friends, and background are Arab.
Throughout its subtly illuminated portrait of Asya, Soueif accomplishes the feat of refining a style that is totally amphibious, that is,
not felt as the dutiful English translation of an Arabic original, but unmistakably authentic, stubborn, idiomatic, and, yes, Arab. By turns ornate, telegraphic, allusive, almost comically fluent, barbarous, painful,
lyrical, awkward, and swift, this English is reducible only to Asya, who
is decidedly not a symbol or allegory of the Arab woman, but a fully realized, if impossibly situated, Egyptian sensibility in, but not totally of,
the West.

She is reclaimed for Egypt and Islam in the epilogue when, having rejected both Saif and Gerald, she returns to an almost ritualized Egypt, in which Koranic verses, the songs of Umm Kulthum, pictures of Abdel Nasser, recollections of colonial Cairo being obliterated to construct Sadat's Americanized business center, mingle with family memories and a sense of her own lonely identity as a timeless Egyptian woman. In the novel's final scene Asya comes upon the statue of a Pharaonic woman lying in the sand; an old peasant forbids her to hang around or photograph the statue, but she persuades him to let her do so. As she reflects on the woman's self-possession despite the bleak, not to say incongruous, circumstances, Asya, still unresolved, is given an opportunity to see herself "in the sunlight," an Egyptian woman who has endured the corrosion of modernity and exile, and remained herself.

This is less a conclusion, I think, than a provisional point of rest without phoney balance sheets or, worse, a drawing-up of final statements. *In the Eye of the Sun* is so successful a novel because, although the temptations are always there, Soueif does not in the end fall for the East versus West, or Arab versus European, formulas. Instead, she works them out patiently, and then goes with Asya, who is neither fully one thing nor another, at least so far as ideologies of that sort are concerned. Soueif renders the experience of crossing over from one side to the other, and then back again, indefinitely, without rancor or preachiness. Because Asya is so securely Arab and Muslim, she does not need to make an issue of it. The fine thing, though, is that Soueif can present such a *hegira* as Asya's in English, thereby showing that what has become almost formulaic to the Arab (as well as Western) discourse of the Other need not always be the case. In fact, there can be generosity, and vision, and overcoming barriers, and, finally, human existential integrity. Who cares about the labels of national identity anyway?

36

Nationalism, Human Rights, and Interpretation

Chapter 18 of Samuel Johnson's *Rasselas*, entitled "The Prince Finds a Wise and Happy Man," is an episode in young Prince Rasselas's search for some sort of balance between hopes and ideals on the one hand, human performance and actuality on the other. As anyone who has read *Rasselas* will remember, the work is less a realistic narrative fiction set in the East than it is a long philosophical meditation on the uncertainty of human life, its shifting appearances, the inconstant fortunes that beset every individual, the sorrow and disillusion of ambition, the vanity of pretense and merely rhetorical virtue. The story of the young Abyssinian prince was occasioned by the final illness and death of Johnson's mother in 1759, and so the work is saturated not only with his own generally mournful attitudes, but also with his considerable sense of personal anxiety and guilt. By chapter 17, Rasselas and Imlac, his philosopher friend, have arrived in Cairo, where, Johnson informs us ironically, they "find every man happy."

In this agreeable atmosphere, Rasselas enters a spacious building, where, seated on a stage, is a venerable philosopher held in awe by everyone present for his sagacity, which he delivers in an "elegant diction." His learned discourse elucidates how it is that "human nature is degraded and debased when the lower faculties predominate over the higher; that when fancy, the parent of passion, usurps the dominion of the mind, nothing ensues but the natural effect of unlawful government, perturbation and confusion; that she betrays the fortresses of the intellect to rebels, and excites her children to sedition against reason, their lawful sovereign." As against this the philosopher propounds the rule of reason, reason constant, unafraid, impervious to envy, anger, fear, and even hope. "He exhorted his hearers to lay aside their prejudices, and arm themselves against the shafts of malice or misfortune, by invulnerable patience, concluding, that this state only was happiness."

Imlac warns the enthusiastic Rasselas against such teachers of morality who, he says, "discourse like an angel, but . . . live like men." A few days later Rasselas returns to visit the great sage and finds him "in a room half darkened, with his eyes misty, and his face pale." To the puzzled young prince the philosopher reveals that his only daughter has just died of a fever. Surprised at the man's utter desolation, Rasselas then asks him: "Have you then forgot the precepts . . . which you so powerfully enforced? Has wisdom no strength to arm the heart against calamity?" Such appeals prove unavailing and so, Johnson says, "the prince, whose humanity would not suffer him to insult misery with reproof, went away convinced of the emptiness of rhetorical sound, and the inefficacy of polished periods and studied sentences."[1]

Johnson's novel is filled with such episodes, all of them meditations upon the failings, weaknesses, guilts, and anxieties of the individual. A man of the strictest humanism and philosophical sternness, Johnson represents a classical tradition of fairly pessimistic and skeptical general reflection on the possibilities for development and enlightenment afforded the solitary self. Much of his unencouraging philosophy carries over into Matthew Arnold's work a century later, with the difference that Arnold believes that he has found if not a remedy, then a considerable corrective to human fallibility. This is described in *Culture and Anarchy*, which is commonly thought of by literary and cultural historians as a conservative, if impassioned, account of culture. In my view, however, it is a very rigorous apology for a deeply authoritarian and uncompromising notion of the state. Whatever he says about culture is shown by Arnold to be subjected to the vagaries of the current

English polity, with its fox-hunting and thoughtless upper-class Barbarians, its moralizing and tastelessly bombastic and hypocritical middle-class Philistines, its hopelessly untutored, mindless Populace. Aside from a small number of what he calls Aliens—men of culture who have escaped the depredations of class and can proselytize for "the best that is thought and known"—Arnold places his hopes for culture in the existence of a state, which, he goes on to say, is not a native English concept. He borrows from France and especially Germany for his ideal of the state as the nation's collective best self. And this, he further says, provides a proper framework for regulating and informing individual behavior.

Arnold's cosmopolitan cultural outlook made him one of the few English beneficiaries of continental European thought. Influenced by Renan, Hegel, Michelet, and von Humboldt, Arnold inherits from such figures a tradition of thinking about nations and nationalism that includes a familiar repertory of ideas about the individual national genius, the connection between nations and linguistic as well as mental types, the hierarchy of races, and all sorts of relationships between nationalism and human identity, about which I shall speak in a moment. Yet what I find particularly interesting about Arnold is that in an unmistakably frank, not to say brutally honest, manner he connects his persuasive, even seductive thought about the virtues of culture with the coercive, authoritarian violence of the national state. "The framework of society," he claims, "is sacred . . . because without order there can be no society, and without society there can be no human perfection." What follows in Arnold's argument, which has no equivalent in Dr. Johnson's novel, deserves quotation, even though in later editions of *Culture and Anarchy* he excised the passage. In any event, the general drift remained:

> With me indeed, this rule of conduct is hereditary. I remember my father, in one of his unpublished letters written more than forty years ago, when the political and social state of the country was gloomy and troubled, and there were riots in many places, goes on, after strongly insisting on the badness and foolishness of the government, and on the harm and dangerousness of our feudal and aristocratical constitution of society, and

ends thus: "As for rioting, the old Roman way of dealing with *that* is always the right one; flog the rank and file, and fling the leaders from the Tarpeian Rock!" And this opinion we can never forsake, however much our Liberal friends may think a little rioting, and what they call popular demonstrations, useful sometimes to their own interests and to the interests of the valuable practical operations they have in hand, and however they preach the rights of an Englishman to be left to do as far as possible what he likes, and the duty of his government to indulge him and connive as much as possible and abstain as much as possible from all harshness of repression.[2]

All this is not as far as Arnold goes. He proceeds to identify the state with culture, and both with an inviolate sacredness that must not be touched at all by mere irruptions and demonstrations of protest. "Thus, in our eyes, the very framework and exterior order of the State, whoever may administer the State, is sacred; and culture is the most resolute enemy of anarchy, because of the great hopes and designs of the State which culture teaches us to nourish." Arnold is too sensible to suggest that the state was just a collection of well-endowed individuals filled with good ideas; it had to be developed over time so "as to make the State more and more the expression . . . of our best self, which is not manifold and vulgar, and unstable, and contentious, and ever varying, but one and noble and secure, and peaceful, and the same for all mankind."[3] In such passages the reiterations of nobility and security are as heavy and dogmatically ponderous as the detractions offered by vulgarity and instability are offensive and disturbing.

Even if we allow for Arnold's considerable skill in refining this argument, and if we accept the fact that he is speaking for a sort of ideal rather than on behalf of any realistic realization of his thoughts, his prescriptions very strongly imply that individual failings of the kind encountered over and over by Rasselas might be remedied by this collective best self. He is far from systematic about what he is saying, but it is clear that he means at least to identify various goods with each other in the context not of an international but a national state, namely, England. Moreover, the people, the nation, the culture, and the state he speaks about are his own and are meant to be distinct from those of France, India, or Africa. Arnold's thought and his rhetoric are stamped with the emergence in nineteenth-century Europe of national sentiment. This is so familiar to everyone as to require no further insistence. What does strike me as remarkable, however, is that in the name of order Arnold's ideal state may summarily override individual rights and, indeed, individual lives altogether. There is thus a relatively abrupt shift in register from *Rasselas* to *Culture and Anarchy*. Both begin by treating individual life as improvable by philosophies, norms, values, but of the two only Arnold continues the search upward, so to speak, arriving at a summit of authority and certainty from which he can help individuals by telling them that their quest has been fulfilled collectively for all individuals.

One could march forward from Arnold and end up showing how his ideas lead to Orwell's Big Brother state in *1984* and perhaps even the Stalinist and Hitlerite states of recent memory. That would be, I think, inattentive to Arnold's much more refined notion about the state, that far from being just the monopolist of coercion and violence it is also the repository of our best hopes. The word *best* is crucial here, and only if we take Arnold seriously as really meaning the best—as opposed to the expedient or the best available now—will we grasp the true sinew of his argument. The best is, first of all, a comparative term, even a competitive one. It means a contest fought through and won. It is also not an inclusive but a selective term. It means not all the ideas of the English, but only those that have been left after a lot of other, less good, ideas have been weeded out and discarded. Certainly Arnold's theory of literary critical touchstones demonstrates exactly how the best is to be determined. You read, say, a line from Dante or Sophocles, or Chaucer, and when you put it next to a passage in Wordsworth or Shelley you can see how the seriousness and beauty of the first three outweigh, defeat, the lesser contents of the others. "This idea of art," says Tom Paulin in *Minotaur*, "expresses a secure idea of national grandeur, and it flattens social, political and literary history."[4] On an international scale, therefore, you can say confidently of nations or races that some are more civilized, less provincial than others, whose history you often do flatten. For Arnold, Europe stands at the very top, and despite his unstinting criticism of the English, it was England that he finally preferred to either Germany or France.

In what is still the best account of Arnold's work, Lionel Trilling dismisses Arnold's critics like Leonard Woolf who took him to task for extremely reactionary positions. True, Trilling says, Arnold's vagueness allowed him to ignore or understate the fact that the working class of his time itself held ideas similar to his own about the state as a nation's best self; and true also, the identification of reason with authority can be, as Trilling says, "either disturbing or sterile."[5] But what remains true of Arnold's thought for Trilling is the emphasis upon culture, culture as a corrective to class feeling, as a way of mitigating the abuses of nationalism and provincialism, culture as a way of thinking that would give the growth of the moral life "a fair chance."

Still, it is the unmistakably English and European cast of the culture discussed by Arnold that seems to me striking today. For whatever Arnold harbored in the way of grandly transnational ideas that were free of pettiness and machinery, those ideas were deposited squarely by him inside a notion of identity that was European and English, as opposed to other ones present at the time. In his story "Youth" Conrad describes it as "something inborn and subtle and everlasting. . . . There was a completeness in it, something solid like a principle, and wasteful like an instinct—a disclosure of something secret—of that hidden something, that gift of good or evil that makes racial difference, that shapes the fate of nations." I must not be understood here as saying that Arnold, any more than Conrad, is to be blamed retrospectively for racism and imperialism, since that would be a reductive dismissal not just of Arnold but of virtually all of European culture. The point I am trying to make is that Arnold, more clearly than most, brings together the individual and the collective inside an identifiable and authoritative entity that he calls culture, a culture available with some degree of purposeful striving and hard work to members of the European or British cultural family. The important common term here, which Arnold fortifies with his references to "us" and "we," is a unified common culture intelligible only to those who share a common nationality, language, geography, and history.

Arnold's ideas about culture share with nationalists and patriots of the time a sort of reinforced sense of essentialized and distilled identity, which, in a much later context of twentieth-century genocidal wars and wholesale persecutions, Adorno saw as leading to "identitarian thought." There has been a great deal of attention paid recently to such identities as "Englishness" and "Frenchness," and, in the setting of decolonization, to the authorizing powers of contending identities such as *négritude* and Islam. A fascinating and characteristically powerful analysis in the *London Review* (May 9, 1991) by Perry Anderson of Fernand Braudel's last work, *L'Identité de la France*, makes the essential point, that the concept of national identity differs from that of national character in that the former "has a more selective charge, conjuring up what is inward and essential; rational, implying some element of alterity for its definition; and perpetual, indicating what is continuously the same. . . . Compared with character [here Anderson shifts to the notion of individual identity and character], we might say, identity appears both more profound and more fragile: metaphysically grounded in one way, yet sociologically exposed and dependent in another." It has become appropriate, Anderson suggests, to speak of crises of identity, whereas it is "changes" of character that seem apposite to *that* notion. "Identity," he continues, "always possesses a reflexive or subjective dimension while character can at the limit remain wholly objective, something perceived by others without the agent being conscious of it." The decline of national character studies portends the rise of the discourse of national identity.

Although Anderson brilliantly develops this thesis into an analysis of Braudel and other German, Spanish, French, and English students of national identity, and although he correctly portrays the crisis from which Braudel's work springs as the decline of French identity caused to some degree by the influx of foreigners into late twentieth-century France, Anderson overlooks something about recent concern with national identity that would naturally be perceived by someone who is not European or American. And that is the conjunction of national identity discourse in Europe with the era of classical European imperialism. Much of the literature of colonial justification in France that we associate with names like Jules Harmand, Albert Sarraut, Leroy-Beaulieu, Lucien Fevre, is often structured around a series of contrasting national identities, races, and languages, the point of which is to extract a hierarchy, with France at the top. This procedure is so commonplace, especially in late nineteenth-century European and even American writing, as to pass virtually without notice today. It is also to be found at the heart of the writings on collective psychology pioneered by Gustave Le Bon, but also mobilized by students of languages and primitive mentalities among the early ethnographers and protoanthropologists. So what needs to be added to Anderson's description of Braudel and his background is a sense of how the discourse of national identity was, if not the first, certainly among the most important elements in the armature of power and justificatory zeal posited by imperial theorists and administrators. For behind Arnold's disquisitions on English versus French or German cultural identities was a very elaborate set of distinctions between Europeans and Negroes, Europeans and Orientals, Europeans and Semites, the history of which is pretty constant and pretty unchanging from the 1830s and 1840s to World War II.

One index of how enraging over time this conjunction between European national identity, collective and individual, and the practices of empire can become to a non-European forced to bear their brunt is provided in Aimé Césaire's *Discourse on Colonialism,* published in 1955. You would not call Césaire's language in the *Discourse* either analytic or cool, but he does make the unarguable point that colonization routinely covered unpleasant European practices against people of color with a facade of appeals to the greater civilizational levels attained by the white race; flogging or killing blacks, then, could be interpreted as a case of the lesser identity being exposed to the therapeutic attentions of the higher. When looked at through twentieth-century eyes, particularly those of liberated African and West Indian militants, the claims seem outrageous. As an example, Césaire cites the following lines from Renan's *La Réforme intellectuelle et morale,* which in the European context was for people like Arnold a progressive text, but for Césaire is a direct antecedent of Hitler and Rosenberg:

> The regeneration of the inferior or degenerate races by the superior races is part of the providential order of things for humanity. . . . *Regere imperio populos,* that is our vocation. Pour forth this all-consuming activity onto countries which, like China, are crying aloud for foreign conquest. Turn the adventurers who disturb European society into a *ver sacrum,* a horde like those of the Franks, the Lombards, or the Normans, and

every man will be in his right role. Nature has made a race of workers, the Chinese race, who have wonderful manual dexterity and almost no sense of honor; govern them with justice, levying from them, in return for the blessing of such a government, an ample allowance for the conquering race, and they will be satisfied; a race of tillers of the soil, the Negro; treat him with kindness and humanity, and all will be as it should; a race of masters and soldiers, the European race.... *Let each do what he is made for, and all will be well.*[6]

No one today (not just Césaire) can read such words without a sense of acute horror and revulsion. Yet to the French man and woman or English man and woman of the time these distinctions were an integral part of what constituted Frenchness and Englishness, not only as the French and British vied with each other, but as the two great powers partitioned huge areas and large numbers of people into their colonial territories. It would therefore be nothing short of a historical amputation to excise this material from Renan's writings on what constitutes a nation, or, for that matter, from all those late nineteenth-century writers who contributed so much to the making of a national and cultural identity. The field they worked in, so to speak, was an international and global one; its topography was determined principally by imperial spheres, which in turn were reinforced and reinscribed from within the domestic realm that intellectuals such as Arnold and Renan were so active in shaping; finally and most important there was always the insistence that such national identities homogenized the races and languages that they governed, herding everything under their strict, almost Darwinian rubric. Thus all Orientals were Orientals, all Negroes were Negroes; all had the same unchanging characteristics, and were condemned to the same inferior status.

Yet this was by no means simply a reactionary position, since it included, indeed galvanized, most European liberals as well. Take de Tocqueville and Algeria as an interesting, if disheartening, case in point. He had already made his celebrated observations about America and about American abuses of non-American peoples when knowledge of the continuing French campaign under Bugeaud in Algeria became an issue of public awareness. He had condemned slavery in

America, and perceptively accused white slaveholders of "seeing no incompatibility between their actual role as tyrants and their image of themselves as men of principle." Yet, as Melvin Richter has shown, when it came to extremely harsh French actions against the Algerians, all such observations were deemed inapplicable by Tocqueville himself. He "subordinated historical values to what he judged to be the more urgent imperatives of national interest and international competition."[7] That France in Algeria was engaged in a colonial war against Muslims—members of a different religion and culture—added to Tocqueville's zeal and, as the late Marwan Buheiry reveals in a thorough examination of the man's views about Islam, it impelled him to find in his hostile critique of Islam justification for his support of the genocidal *razzias* and expropriations of land undertaken by the French military: he "wanted to understand the Muslim Algerians in order to better implant a European settler community in North Africa." Therefore,

> Tocqueville judged Islam and found it wanting. He claimed, rather gratuitously, that its principal aim was war. He characterized it as fossilized and especially as decadent without really defining what he meant although he did seem to find the sign in the fact that the Islamic world was unable to resist European domination. The penetrating insights he had [had about] . . . European and North American societies were significantly absent in his consideration of Islam. He never asked how Islamic civilization with its literature, law, and social organization, not only survived the relative collapse in politics, but managed somehow to spread into regions far beyond its epicenter. In short, he failed to appreciate its staying power and spiritual content.[8]

One more thing about Tocqueville. As Richter goes on to show, he and John Stuart Mill admired and respected each other greatly. Their correspondence in 1840 is revealing for what it allowed Tocqueville to explain, by way of appeals to "national pride," about European liberalism when it surveyed the non-European world. Mill, to his credit, demurred even as Tocqueville went on to assert his country's mission to bring "prosperity based on peace, regardless of how that peace is obtained." He was less guarded elsewhere when he spoke admiringly of "the subjection of four-fifths of the world by the remaining fifth." He continued: "Let us not scorn ourselves and our age, the men may be small, but the events are great."⁹ Mill himself did not condone the French theory of *orgueil national,* although for the length of his service at the India Office he opposed self-government for the Indians. In fact, he once said, "The sacred duties which civilized nations owe to the independence and nationality of each other, are not binding towards those to whom nationality and independence are certain evil, or at best a questionable good."¹⁰

Lest these comments quickly degenerate into a list of shame-on-you items of nineteenth-century political incorrectness, let me restate the underlying point. A century after Dr. Johnson, the setting of considerations about human behavior and, more relevant from our standpoint, about reconciling liberal principles with actual behavior is seriously affected by the imperial encounter, that is, by the effect of watching one's own troops putting down the Indian "Mutiny" of 1857, Governor Eyre disciplining his rebellious Jamaican slaves, or Maréchal Bugeaud sacking native villages in pursuit of Emir Abdel Qader's insurgency. There is the tendency to regard things in terms of one's own national side versus "theirs." Uniformly, "theirs" is less culturally valuable and developed, and therefore deserves the inflictions imposed on them by "us," "us" and "ours" being superior in attitude, attainments, and civilizational progress. Perhaps it is that nations occupy the available mental and geographical space so completely as to crowd out other styles of attention (such as compassion and fellow feeling) almost entirely. But it is also the case, I think, that national thought, or thought that is cast in national and essentialist terms, always produces loyalty, patriotism, and the tendency to fabricate excuses and conditions for suddenly turning general liberal principles into a species of irrelevant and jejune footnote. For Arnold, as for Europeans in the age of empire, to identify with one's best self meant identifying also with one's best *power,* a navy or an army as well as a culture and a religion. The competitiveness and bloody-mindedness of the exercise have not always been up to very high standards of decency or concern for human rights.

One thing more about this. Every scheme of education known to me, whether that of victim or victimizer in the imperial contests I have been referring to, purifies the national culture in the process of indoc-trinating the young. No one who studies Spenser, for example, in the various schools of English literature here or in the United States, spends very much time on his appalling attitudes toward the Irish, at-titudes that enter into and inform even his greatest work, *The Faerie Queene*. But the same is true of our interest in writers like Carlyle, Ruskin, Arnold, and Tennyson, with their extraordinarily deprecating and even violent ideas about the lesser races. The curricular study of a national language and literature fairly enjoins an appreciation for that culture that regularly induces assent, loyalty, and an unusually rarefied sense of from where the culture really springs and in what compli-cating circumstances its monuments derive.

This is true not only in the metropolitan West but outside it as well. Young Arabs and Muslims today are taught to venerate the classics of their religion and thought, not to be critical, not to view what they read of, say, Abbasid or *nahda* literature as alloyed with all kinds of po-litical and social contests. Only very occasionally does a critic and poet like Adonis, the brilliant contemporary Syrian writer, come along and say openly that readings of *turath* in the Arab world today enforce a rigid authoritarianism and literalism that have the effect of killing the spirit and obliterating criticism.[11] For his pains, and like so many Arab and Muslim writers, including Salman Rushdie, Adonis is much re-viled and all but exiled.

Or, to move back to the Atlantic world, consider the storm that broke in the United States when within months of each other in 1991, the "West as America" exhibition was mounted at the Smithsonian and Oliver Stone's *JFK* was released. The first ventured the fairly un-complicated proposition that there was a discrepancy between images of the American West circulating in the 1860s and after, and the often violent commercialism and anti-Indian spoliations that really took place. The curators presented a large number of paintings, pho-tographs, and sculptures depicting the Indian as, for example, either noble or violent, and clarified their own critical premises in longish captions explaining how the images were constructed. I attended the exhibition and saw very little that was invidious about it, since, after all, every expanding society necessarily uses violence and a good deal of lying to dress up its conquests. To most, if not all of the official and semiofficial intellectual leaders who commented on the show, such a truism was inadmissible when it came to the authorized image of the United States as an innocent exception to the rules that govern all other countries. That was the premise of the criticism—that America was innocent, and could *not* be guilty of conquest, genocide, and exploitation as other countries were—not the particular accuracy of one or another part of the exhibit. Likewise with the admittedly flawed *JFK*, which brought down on Oliver Stone's ample (and willing) shoulders a heap of abuse from the newspaper of record, and indeed from all the very numerous spokesmen and important intellectuals, pundits, and commentators of record. Here, too, the suggestion of conspiracy in the United States was what offended the patriotic sensibility, as if conspiracy was obvious enough in places like the Middle East, Latin America, and China, for example, but unthinkable for "us."

I don't want to labor the point about the United States too much, except that on occasions like the Gulf War there is a fantastic jump to be observed in the public sphere from the humdrum facts to astonishingly large and finally destructive idealizations of what "we" are all about as a nation. Gone are "our" aggressions in Panama and elsewhere, as well as "our" record of nonpayment of UN dues—to say nothing of flouting Security Council Resolutions that "we" have voted for—and in are trundled the orotund pieties about how "we" must draw a line in the sand and reverse aggression, no matter the cost. As I said, all governments (and especially very powerful imperial ones) babble on about how really moral they are as they do some particularly gangsterish thing. The question I am addressing, however, is how there is appeal for liberals in such rhetoric—from Tocqueville's to George Bush's—which is sanctioned by an education based not on critical appraisal but on venerating the authority of a national culture and a national state. Worse yet, any infringement of the taboo forbidding such criticism leads to censorship, ostracism, imprisonment, severe punishment, and so forth.

To launder the cultural past and repaint it in garish nationalist colors that irradiate the whole society is now so much a fact of contemporary life as to be considered natural. For, as Ernest Gellner shrewdly observes in his book on nationalism, Arnold's vision of a culture coming to dominate the state is based on the homogenization of intellectual space, which, in turn, requires "a high culture [to] pervade the whole of society, define it, and needs to be sustained by the polity. *That* is the secret of nationalism."[12] Thus even though in its early phase nationalism claims to be militating on behalf of "a putative folk culture," the fact is that

> nationalism is, essentially, the general imposition of a high culture on society, where previously low cultures had taken up the lives of the majority, and in some cases of the totality, of the population. It means the generalized diffusion of a school-mediated, academy-supervised idiom, codified for the requirements of reasonably precise bureaucratic and technological communication. It is the establishment of an anonymous, impersonal society, with mutually substitutable atomized individuals, held together above all by a shared culture of this kind [which later in his book Gellner regards as a species of "patriotism"], in place of a previous complex structure of local groups, sustained by folk cultures reproduced locally and idiosyncratically by the micro-groups themselves. That is what *really* happens.[13]

The resulting "homogeneity, literacy, anonymity"[14] of life in the modern nation described by Gellner does not disagree with the account given by Benedict Anderson in his *Imagined Communities,* except that Anderson sees the invention of nationalism as a phenomenon of the new rather than of the old European world. Gellner is not particularly interested in the distinction, since he is less a historian than a theorist. Everyone does it more or less, more or less the same way. What other recent analysts of nationalism often stress, however, is that all the instructive and normative cases are European, since national feeling is basically a European invention. Thus Hans Kohn and Elie Kedourie on the right and, more surprisingly, Eric Hobsbawm on the left. Take, for example, Hobsbawm's strange idea in *Nations and Nationalism Since 1870* that Palestinian nationalism was "created" by "the common experience of Zionism settlement and conquest,"[15] which, in the absence of any cited evidence—and, indeed, with a good deal of evidence belying it—suggests that Hobsbawm's predispositions to locate the germ of all nationalism in Europe are paramount, not nationalism's much more variegated actual history and the many different forms it takes. His Eurocentrism receives an even more peculiar reinforcement when in a later section of his book he tries to explain the lack of serious attention paid to non-European nationalism between the two world wars:

> Virtually all the anti-imperial movements of any significance could be, and in the metropolis generally were, classified under one of these headings: local educated elites imitating European "national self-determination" (as in India), popular anti-Western xenophobia (an all-purpose heading widely applied, notably in China), and the national high spirits of martial tribes (as in Morocco or the Arabian deserts). . . . Perhaps the nearest thing to thought about nationalism inspired by the Third World—outside the revolutionary Left—was a general scepticism about the universal applicability of the "national" concept. . . . *Such reflections were often just,* even though they tended to cause imperial rulers or European settlers to overlook the rise of mass national identification where it did occur, as Zionists and Israeli Jews notably did in the case of the Palestinian Arabs.[16]

So the problems with Western nationalism are replicated in the dependent world according to Hobsbawm, leaving solutions and creative alternative thinking in the Western court, so to speak. Now, granted, the emergence of anti-imperialist nationalism in India, Africa, the Arab world, and the Caribbean led to similar abuses of statism, nationalist chauvinism, and reactionary populism; but was that all it led to? The question is an important one. We must grant that Gellner is right when he says that "having a nation is not an inherent attribute of humanity, but it now has come to appear as such."[17] By the early twentieth century even those peoples in the non-European world who had not enjoyed a day of national independence in years began to speak of self-determination, of independent statehood, of human rights predicated on their identity as a group completely distinct from colonial Britain or France. Yet what has not received the notice it should have from historians of Third World nationalism is that a clear, if paradoxical, antinationalist theme emerges in the writings of a fair number of nationalists who are wholehearted supporters of the national movement itself.

Thus, to cite a small number of examples: Tagore, very much the national poet and intellectual leader of early twentieth-century Indian resistance to the British, condemns nationalism, in his 1917 lectures on the subject, for its state worship, its triumphalism, its militancy. Yet he also remains a nationalist. Césaire in his greatest poem explores *négritude,* hallmark of the African nationalist resistance, and finds it wanting for its exclusivism and *ressentiment.* Similarly, in the writing of C. L. R. James, great historian of what he called "negro revolution" and pan-Africanism, we find that over and over he warns against the nativism that would turn nationalism into a reductive and diminishing rather than a truly liberating effort. And who can miss in Fanon the intensity of his attack on *"mésaventures de la conscience nationale,"* its febrile mimicry of colonial thought and practices, its imprisoning ethic, its brutalizing usurpations? In the annals of Arab nationalism a critique of exclusivism, sectarianism, and provincialism—much of it associated with degradations in Arab and Islamic political life—is steadily present, from early thinkers like Shibley Shumayil to later figures like Rashid Rida, Abdel Rahman al-Bazzaz, Qunstantin Zurayk, and even the resolutely Egyptian Taha Husayn. Finally, in the extraordinary pages of W. E. B. Du Bois's *The Souls of Black Folk,* the repeated warnings against indiscriminate nationalism and reverse racism, the insistence upon careful analysis and comprehensive understanding rather than either wholesale condemnation of whites or futile attempts to emulate some of their methods.

These early twentieth-century critiques of nationalism have been followed by even more sophisticated and acute statements, analyses, and theorizations whose premise is that discussions of nationalism and modernity in the Third World are not immediate reflections of only one authoritative source (for example, the nationalist party viewed as the absolute authority on "loyalty or the opposition to the colonial power"), but rather signposts to a more complex discussion of what Chatterjee calls "the relations between thought, culture and power." In other words, awareness of nationalism from within the anti-imperialist camp requires that the whole matter of interpretation itself be raised. As Partha Chatterjee puts it in *Nationalist Thought and the Colonial World:*

First of all, there is the question of the effectiveness of thought as a vehicle of change. If the imperatives, conditions and consequences of change have been thought out within an elaborate and reasonably consistent framework of knowledge, does this itself indicate that the social potentials exist for the change to occur? . . .

Second, there is the question of the relation of thought to the existing culture of the society, i.e. to the way in which the social code already provides a set of correspondences between signs and meanings to the overwhelming mass of the people. What are the necessary steps when a new group of thinkers and reformers seek to substitute a new code in the place of the old one? . . .

Third, there is the question of the implantation into new cultures of categories and frameworks of thought produced in other—alien—cultural contexts . . .

Fourth, when the new framework of thought is directly associated with a relation of dominance in the cross-cultural context of power, what in the new cultural context are the specific changes which occur in the original categories and relations within the domain of thought? . . .

Finally, all of the above relations between thought and culture have a bearing on still another crucial question—the changing relations of power *within* the society under colonial domination. And here, even if we grant that the social consequences of particular frameworks of thought produced in the metropolitan countries would be drastically different in the colonized culture, i.e. the historical correspondence between thought and change witnessed in the age of Enlightenment in the West would not obtain in the colonized East, we would still have to answer the question, "What are the specific relations between thought and change which do obtain in those countries?"[18]

The gist of these questions is to raise the whole process of interpretation and intellectual rigor and place it at the very center of discussion. For if the history of imperialism reveals a pattern of eloquent cultural discourse modified by and conditioned on national pride and exceptionalism in order to do one's will on non-Europeans, then it must also be true that a decolonizing and reactive nationalism alone is far from a guarantee that the pattern will not be repeated in newly independent states. Is there any place, is there any party, is there any interpretive way to ensure individual freedom and rights in a global-ized world? Does the actuality of nationalities, and not of individuali-ties, furnish any possibility of protection for the individual or the group *from* those nationalities? Who makes the interpretation of rights, and why? A couple of sentences from the final paragraph of Chatterjee's book point a way:

> Much that has been suppressed in the historical creation of post-colonial nation-states, much that has been erased or glossed over when nationalist discourse has set down its own life-history, bears the marks of the people-nation struggling in an inchoate, undirected and unequal battle against forces that have sought to dominate it. The critique of nationalist dis-course must find for itself the ideological means to connect the popular strength of these struggles with the consciousness of a new universality.[19]

Constructing "a new universality" has preoccupied various interna-tional authorities since World War II. Some milestones are, of course, the Universal Declaration of Human Rights, the Geneva Conventions, and an impressive battery of protocols, resolutions, and prescriptions for the treatment of refugees, minorities, prisoners, workers, children, students, and women. All of these explicitly provide for the protection of individuals, regardless of their race, color, nationality, or creed. In addition, a wide range of nongovernmental, national, and interna-tional agencies, such as Amnesty, or the Organization for Human Rights, or the Human Rights Watch committees, monitor and publi-cize human-rights abuses. In all this it is perfectly clear that an under-lying "critique of nationalist discourse" has been taking place, since it is national governments acting in the name of national security who have infringed the rights of individuals and groups who are perceived as standing *outside* the nationalist consensus. Yet to criticize the bru-tality of the Iraqi regime today in the name of universal human rights is by no means to have truly mounted "a critique of nationalist discourse." At roughly the same time that the Iraqi Baath was universally condemned for its oppression of the Kurdish people, the Saudi government unilaterally expelled 800,000 Yemeni workers as vengeance for the Yemeni government's abstention at the UN, that is, its refusal to join in the Security Council resolution pushed through by the United States to go to war against Iraq. After the Gulf War, the Kuwaiti government, which was justly restored to sovereignty by Operation Desert Storm, proceeded to arrest, detain, or expel and harass Palestinians (and other aliens) because, it was argued, the PLO had supported Iraq. Little official condemnation of the Saudi or Kuwaiti governments was recorded in the West.

I cite these paradoxes as a way of emphasizing the continued absence of what Chatterjee calls "a new universality." For in the Western community of nations presided over by the United States, an old, rather than new, nationalist identity has been reinforced, one that derives its ideological resources from precisely the notion of that high culture of which Matthew Arnold and Ernest Gellner both speak. Now, however, it has given itself an internationalized and normative identity with authority and hegemony to adjudicate the relative value of human rights. All the discourse that purports to speak for civilization, human rights, principle, universality, and acceptability accrues to it, whereas as was the case with the Gulf War, the United States managed its fortunes, so to speak, mobilized on its behalf, took it over. We now have a situation therefore that makes it very difficult to construct *another* universality alongside this one. So completely has the power of the United States—under which, in some measure, we all live—invested even the vocabulary of universality that the search for "new ideological means" to challenge it has become, in fact, more difficult, and therefore more exactly a function of a renewed sense of intellectual morality.

This morality can no longer reside comfortably and exclusively in the condemnation of approved enemies—the old Soviet Union, Libya, Iraq, terrorism, and so on. Nor, as the most cursory of surveys will confirm, can it persuasively consist of extolling, in the manner of Francis Fukuyama, the final triumph of the bourgeois liberal state and the end of history. Nor can a sense of the intellectual commitment needed be fulfilled by professional or disciplinary specialization. There has to be a firmer, more rigorous procedure than any of these. For the intellectual, to be "for" human rights means, in effect, to be willing to venture interpretations of those rights in the same place and with the same language employed by the dominant power, to dispute its hierarchy and methods, to elucidate what it has hidden, to pronounce what it has silenced or rendered unpronounceable.

These intellectual procedures require, above all, an acute sense not of how things are separated but of how they are connected, mixed, involved, embroiled, linked. For years, South African apartheid was deemed the problem of a continent both distant and irrelevant to the ordinary pursuit of life in the Western metropolis. The Reagan and Thatcher administrations, for example, opposed the scrupulous enforcement of sanctions against South Africa, preferring instead a policy of "constructive engagement." The assumption was that what took place in South Africa was "their" business, which amounted to approving the domination of a black people by a white minority purporting to be Western, advanced, like "us." It was not until the antiapartheid movement, through organized boycotts, strikes, lectures, and seminars, brought consciousness of apartheid close to the center of Western political discourse that the contradiction between public declarations of support for human rights and the dramatically discriminatory policies of the minority government became untenable. A worldwide campaign against Pretoria, with American and European students demonstrating for divestment of holdings in South African business, took hold, then made its influence felt on South Africa, with results that have produced major political changes inside the country—namely, the release of Nelson Mandela, negotiations between the ANC and the de Klerk government, and so forth.

South Africa in the past two years has been a relative success for human rights. A greater challenge, however, is the contest between Israel and the Palestinian people, a case of particularly inflamed and compelling human rights abuse with which I should like to conclude. When we ask ourselves, "Whose human rights are we trying to protect?"—this, after all, is the question posed by the organizers of this series of Oxford Amnesty Lectures—we need to acknowledge frankly that individual freedoms and right are set irrevocably in a national context.

To discuss human freedom today, therefore, is to speak about the freedom of persons of a particular nationality or ethnic or religious identity whose life is subsumed within a national territory ruled by a sovereign power. It is also true that withholders of freedom, its abusers, also belong to a nation—most often also a state that practices its politics in the name of that nation's best, or most expedient, interests. The difficulty for interpretation politically as well as philosophically is how to disentangle discourse and principle on the one hand from practice and history on the other. Added to that difficulty is the complication in the Palestinian instance of the international dimension of the problem, since historical Palestine itself is no ordinary piece of geography but perhaps more drenched in religious, cultural, and political significance than any on earth.

What has never been in doubt are the actual identities of the opponents in historical Palestine, although a considerable modern campaign on behalf of Zionism has either downplayed or tried to eliminate the very notion of a Palestinian national identity. I mention this at the outset because one of our charges from the organizing committee of these Amnesty Lectures was "to consider the consequences of deconstruction of the self for the liberal tradition." The irony is that the liberal tradition in the West was always very eager to deconstruct the Palestinian self in the process of *constructing* the Zionist-Israeli self. Almost from the very beginnings of the European movement to colonize Palestine on behalf of Zionism, a strain first introduced, I believe, by Balfour has remained the lodestar for Western liberalism. Its classic formulation is provided not in the 1917 Balfour Declaration, but in a comment made by Balfour in a memorandum two years later:

> The contradiction between the letter of the Covenant and the policy of the Allies [the Anglo-French Declaration of 1918 promising the Arabs of former Ottoman colonies that as a reward for supporting the Allies they would have their independence] is even more flagrant in the case of the independent nation of Palestine than in that of the independent nation of Syria. For in Palestine we do not propose even to go through the form of consulting the wishes of the present inhabitants of the country, though the American Commission has been

going through the forms of asking what they are. The four great powers are committed to Zionism and Zionism, be it right or wrong, good or bad, is rooted in age-long tradition, in present needs, in future hopes, of far profounder import than the desires and prejudices of the 700,000 Arabs who now inhabit that ancient land. In my opinion that is right.[20]

Something like this sentiment, with its hierarchical imposition of Zionism on "the desires and prejudices of the 700,000 Arabs" of Palestine, has remained constant for the major figures of Western liberalism, especially after World War II. Think of Reinhold Niebuhr, or Edmund Wilson, or Isaiah Berlin, of the British Labour party, of the Socialist International, of the American Democratic party, of every American president from that party, of every major candidate who has spoken in its name, with the exception of Jesse Jackson, and you have that evaluation maintained and given force. There was hardly a Western liberal during the late 1940s through the 1970s who did not explicitly say that the establishment of Israel in 1948 was one of the great achievements of the postwar era, and did not think it at all necessary to add that this was so for its victors in particular. From the point of view of the survivors of the dreadful massacre of the European Jews it was a central achievement: there is no point at all in denying that. The Jews who came to Palestine were the victims of Western civilization, totally unlike the French military who conquered Algeria, the British felons forced to settle Australia, or those who have ravaged Ireland for several hundred years, or the Boers and the British who still rule in South Africa. But admitting that the difference in identity between Zionists and white settlers in Africa, Europe, Asia, Australia, and the Americas is an important one is not to underplay the grave consequences that tie all the groups together.

An enormous amount of ink has been spilled trying to prove that, for example, Palestine was basically empty before the Zionists came, or that the Palestinians who left in 1948 did so because their leaders told them to, or that, as argued by Cynthia Ozick in the *New York Times* on February 19, 1992, to speak of Palestinian-occupied territories is "cynically programmatic—an international mendacity justified neither by history nor by a normal understanding of language and law." All this amounts to trying to prove that Palestinians do not exist as a national group. Why so many legions of propagandists, polemicists, publicists, and commentators working hard to prove something that were it true would have required hardly any effort at all? What Ozick and company are going on about is that something—namely, the existence of a people with a clear national identity—has stood in the way of the liberal notion, stood in the way and attached itself to Israel as a shadow attaches itself to a person. For in fact the Jewish victims of European anti-Semitism came to Palestine and created a new victim, the Palestinians, who today are nothing less than the victims of the victims. Hardly anything can mitigate the shattering historical truth that the creation of Israel meant the destruction of Palestine. The elevation of a new people to sovereignty in the Holy Land has meant the subjugation, dispossession, and oppression of another.

There is nothing in the repertory of liberalism that condones this, except, of course, its history of making exceptions whenever the going got a little rough, for example, when the French troops undertook a *razzia* or two in Algeria and found Tocqueville willing to excuse them, or when Spenser recommended the virtual elimination of the Irish race, or when Mill ruled that Indian independence should be postponed again and again. Yes, we have come a long way beyond that today, when no one is willing to defend apartheid in a public forum, or when a reasonable semblance of Irish independence has been assured, or when over forty-five states in Africa and at least fifty more elsewhere containing formerly colonized people constitute the new nations.

Look squarely at the Palestinian situation today and what you see fairly beggars one's powers adequately to represent it. You see a nation of over five million people scattered throughout various jurisdictions, without official nationality, without sovereignty, without flag and passport, without self-determination or political freedom. Yet their enemies are still interpreted as having the right to keep them that way and, from the reigning power of the day, to garner the largest amount of foreign aid in the most extensive aid program in history. Words like "democratic" and "Western" flutter around Israel even as the 750,000 Palestinians who are Israeli citizens constitute a little under 20 percent of the population and are treated as a fourth-rate minority called "non-Jews," legally prevented from buying, leasing, or renting land "held in trust for the Jewish people," vastly underrepresented in the Knesset and, for example, given only 1 percent of the education budget, no rights of return, and none of the kinds of entitlement reserved exclusively for Jews. Since 1967, Israel has been in an unrelievedly uncompromising military occupation of the West Bank and Gaza and their almost two million Palestinians. Since the intifada began in late 1987, well over 1,100 unarmed Palestinians have been killed by Israeli troops; over 2,000 houses have been demolished; over 15,000 political prisoners languish in Israeli jails, twice as high per capita as their counterparts under South African apartheid at its worst; twenty-four-hour curfews over the whole of the territories are the rule; over 120,000 trees have been uprooted; schools and universities have been closed for years at a time, and one university, Bir Zeit, has been kept closed for four consecutive years; thousands of acres have been expropriated, whole villages rendered destitute, over 150 settlements established, and about 80,000 Jewish settlers introduced into the heart of Arab population centers, there to live according to laws that allow them to be armed and to kill and beat Arabs with total impunity, all this despite numerous, but alas unenforced, UN resolutions; at least 300 Palestinian leaders have been deported in defiance of the Geneva and Hague conventions; hundreds of books have been banned; the word "Palestine" as well as the colors of the Palestinian flag are forbidden, and when they have been used to decorate a cake or to paint a picture, the offenders have been jailed; punitive taxes are levied against the whole Palestinian population without allowing that population any form of representation or recourse. As for the economy and natural resources, such as water, they are manipulated and exploited by Israel with not the slightest suggestion of proportionality or fairness.

Human rights abuses by the Iraqi and Syrian governments against their own people are certainly appalling. No one can deny that, and no one does. In Israel's case, an extraordinary split exists: here are policies against the Palestinian people that have a forty-four-year-old history, and yet the immense financial, political, and discursive subsidies from Western countries pour in regardless, as if to excuse Israel for what it does. When he spoke against the infamous "Zionism is a form of racism" resolution, which was repealed by the UN last autumn, George Bush summed up the case for repeal in a symptomatic linguistic turn:

Zionism, he said, is not racism because of the suffering of the Jewish people. But what, a Palestinian might ask, if that history of suffering itself had not deterred Zionism from discriminating systematically against the Palestinian people, much as the glory of France did not deter it from decimating the population of Algeria in a few decades? For the truth is that Jewish and Palestinian suffering exist in and belong to the same history: the task of interpretation is to acknowledge that link, not to separate them into separate and unconnected spheres.

Palestine, I believe, is today the touchstone case for human rights, not because the argument for it can be made as elegantly simple as the case for South African liberation, but because it *cannot* be made simple. Speaking as an involved Palestinian, I doubt that any of us has figured out how our particularly trying history interlocks with that of the Jews who dispossessed and now try to rule us. But we know these histories cannot be separated, and that the Western liberal who tries to do so violates, rather than comprehends, both. There is hardly an instance when the connection between freedom and interpretation is as urgent, as literally concrete, as it is for the Palestinian people, a large part of whose existence and fate has been interpreted away in the West in order to deny us the same freedom and interpretation granted Israeli Jews. The time has finally come to join and recognize these two peoples together as indeed their common actuality in historic Palestine already has joined them together. Only then can interpretation be for, rather than only about, freedom.

37

Traveling Theory Reconsidered

In an essay ("Traveling Theory") written several years ago, I discussed the ways in which theories sometimes "travel" to other times and situations, in the process of which they lose some of their original power and rebelliousness. The example I used was Georg Lukács's theory of reification, which is fully explained in the famous fourth chapter of his masterpiece, *History and Class Consciousness*. Underlying my analysis was a common enough bias that, even though I tried to guard against and mitigate its influence, remains in the essay. This bias can be put simply as follows: the first time a human experience is recorded and then given a theoretical formulation, its force comes from being directly connected to and organically provoked by real historical circumstances. Later versions of the theory cannot replicate its original power; because the situation has quieted down and changed, the theory is degraded and subdued, made into a relatively tame academic substitute for the real thing, whose purpose in the work I analyzed was political change.

As a revolutionary in early twentieth-century Hungary, Lukács was a participant in the dramatic social upheavals that in his work he linked to the whole social deformation of alienation, the radical separation of object and subject, the atomization of human life under bourgeois capitalism. To resolve the crisis represented by these things Lukács spoke about "the viewpoint of the proletariat," a dynamic theoretical reconciliation of subject with object that was enabled by getting beyond fragmentation and imagining a revolutionary vision of "totality." *History and Class Consciousness* is full of the agony of life in a brutally capitalist society: the way in which every human relationship and impulse is compelled into "alienated" labor, the bewildering rule of facts and figures with no bonds between people except those of the cash nexus, the loss of perspective, the fragmentation of every experience into saleable commodities, the absence of any image of community or wholeness. When he comes to the remedy for such diminishments and deprivations Lukács presses into service a Marxism that is principally the result of an alteration of consciousness. To be conscious of how widespread is reification—how everything is turned into a "thing"—is for the first time to be aware of the *general* problem of life under capitalism, and for the first time to be conscious of the class of individuals, the proletariat, who are capitalism's most numerous victims. Only in this way can subjectivity understand its objective situation, and this in turn makes possible an understanding of what kept subject and object apart, and how they can be rejoined.

The point I made about all this was that when they were picked up by late European students and readers of Lukács (Lucien Goldmann in Paris, Raymond Williams in Cambridge), the ideas of this theory had shed their insurrectionary force, had been tamed and domesticated somewhat, and became considerably less dramatic in their application and gist. What seemed almost inevitable was that when theories traveled and were used elsewhere they ironically acquired the prestige and authority of age, perhaps even becoming a kind of dogmatic orthodoxy. In the setting provided by revolutionary Budapest, Lukács's theory of the subject-object split and of reification was actually an inducement to insurrectionary action, with the hope that a proletarian perspective in his highly eccentric view of it would see "reality" as eminently changeable because largely a matter of perspective. His later readers regarded the theory as essentially an interpretive device, which is not to take away from their work some considerable and even very brilliant achievements.

What now seems to me incomplete and inadequate in such an account of Lukács's theory and its subsequent travels is that I stressed the reconciliatory and resolvable aspects of his diagnosis. Those who borrowed from Lukács—and for that matter Lukács himself—saw in the reifications imposed epistemologically on the split between subject and object something that could be remedied. For such a view Lukács of course was indebted to Marx and Hegel before him, in whose theories the dialectic between opposed factors was routinely to result in synthesis, resolution, transcendence, or *Aufhebung*. Lukács's particular elaboration (some would say improvement) on the Hegelian and Marxian dialectic was to stress both the extraordinarily widespread infection of all of human life by reification—from the family to professional pursuits, psychology, and moral concerns—as well as the almost aesthetic character of the reconciliation or healing process by which what was split asunder could be rejoined.

In this perhaps more comforting phase of the theory the work of several recent Lukács scholars, chief among them Michael Löwy,[1] is useful. They have shown the powerful influence on the young Lukács, the romantic anticapitalist, of Dostoevsky and Kierkegaard, whose explorations of modern angst found so devastatingly thorough and analytic a realization not only in *History and Class Consciousness* but also in his earlier treatises, *Soul and Form* and *Theory of the Novel*. But, it can be argued, so too can the Kierkegaardian and Dostoevskian influences be found in Lukács's specifically Marxist resolution, or even redemption. As contained in subject-object reconciliation within the largely unreal, projected, or "putative" category of "totality," Lukács's leap from present misery to future healing recapitulates (if it does not actually repeat) the great nineteenth-century irrationalists' leaps of faith.

But what if some of Lukács's readers, totally influenced by his description of reification and the subject-object impasse, did not accept the reconciliatory denouement of his theory, and indeed deliberately, programmatically, intransigently refused it? Would this not be an alternative mode of traveling theory, one that actually developed *away* from its original formulation, but instead of becoming domesticated in the terms enabled by Lukács's desire for respite and resolution, flames out, so to speak, restates and reaffirms its own inherent tensions by moving to another site? Is this different kind of dislocation so powerful as retrospectively to undermine Lukács's reconciliatory gesture when he settles the subject-object tensions into what he calls "the standpoint of the proletariat"? Might we then not call this surprising later development an instance of "transgressive theory," in the sense that it crosses over from and challenges the notion of a theory that begins with fierce contradiction and ends up promising a form of redemption?

Let us return briefly to the early Lukács. In the principally aesthetic works that anticipate *History and Class Consciousness* (1923) he brilliantly examines the relationship between different aesthetic forms on the one hand, and the concrete historical or existential experience from which they derive and to which they are a response. The most famous of these early works is *Theory of the Novel* (1920), premised on the notion that in a world abandoned by God the novel embodies the trajectory of an epic whose hero is either demonic or mad, whose constitutive element is a temporality basically disappointing and demystifying, and whose representative status as the art form of modernity is based on its tremendous constitutive ironies, the irony of "errant souls [adventuring] in an inessential, empty reality," or that of speaking "of past gods and gods . . . to come" but never of what is present, or "the irony [which] has to seek the only world that is adequate to it along the *via dolorosa* of interiority but is doomed never to find it there."[2]

Before he becomes a Marxist, therefore, Lukács's overpowering sense of the disjunctions of modernity (which in his *Logos* essay of 1917 he abstracted into "the subject-object relationship") led him to regard the aesthetic as a site where their contradictions are manageable, and even pleasurable. For this view he is indebted to both Kant and Schiller, although his inflection of the thesis is largely original. Each art form, he says, is itself in a sense the incarnation of a particular phase in the subject-object relationship. The essay, for example, is about heralding a resolution but never giving it; the tragedy is the fatal clash between subjects, and so forth. That the novel has a special privilege in modernity is underscored by its scope, its hero, and (although Lukács never actually says this) by the fact that theoretical discourse (such as his) can express and by its sheer complexity represent the form's quintessential ironies. The transformation in Lukács's politics that occurs after *Theory of the Novel* and in *History and Class Consciousness* is that Marxism, as borne and reflected in "the class consciousness of the proletariat," is explicitly revealed to be the theoretical discourse resolving the subject-object relationship.

Nevertheless, Lukács actually says that that resolution is almost by nature postponed and thus hasn't happened yet. There is an unwonted certainty in his accents that, it must be said immediately, supplies his later work with its gruffly dogmatic authority and assertiveness. Clearly, however, not every reader of Lukács went as far in *that* direction, as the dogged stubbornness of Adorno quite plainly shows. Adorno, I believe, is virtually unthinkable without the majestic philosophical beacon provided by *History and Class Consciousness,* but he is also unthinkable without his own great resistance to its triumphalism and implied transcendence. If for Lukács the subject-object relationship, the fragmentation and lostness, the ironic perspectivism of modernity were supremely discerned, embodied, and consummated in *narrative* forms (the rewritten epics both of the novel and of the proletariat's class consciousness), for Adorno that particular choice was, he said in a famous anti-Lukács essay, a kind of false reconciliation under duress. Much more typical, more in keeping with the irremediably "fallen" character of modernity was "new" music, which, for Adorno, was Schoenberg, Berg, and Webern, *not* Stravinsky and Bartók.

Philosophie der neuen Musik (1948) is a quite spectacular instance of a traveling theory gone tougher, harder, more recalcitrant. In the first place its language is a good deal more difficult to decode even than Lukács's, which in the reification essay of *History and Class Consciousness* had already had a programmatically unattractive density and philosophical obscurity to it. Lukács's choice of the history of classical philosophy—here too the *narrative* of increasing desperation and abstraction was an illustration of subject-object tension unrelieved by reconciliation—was meant to show how deeply alienation had penetrated, and therefore where, in its most abstruse version, it could be analyzed as a pure symptom of the overall *anomie* of modern life. Adorno goes a step further. Modern music, he says, is so marginal, so rarefied, so special an expression as to represent a total rejection of society and any of its palliatives. This is why Schoenberg is such a heroic figure to Adorno. No longer is the composer a figure like Beethoven, who stands for the newly triumphant bourgeoisie, or like Wagner, whose sorcererlike art camouflages the irreconcilability between the aesthetic and the commercial. The twentieth-century composer stands outside tonality itself, proclaiming an art of so totally, irrecusably rebarbative a mode as to reject listeners altogether. Why? Because according to Schoenberg as described by Adorno, "the middle road . . . is the only one which does not lead to Rome."[3]

For indeed the subject-object compromise enacted by Lukács does resemble a middle-of-the-road synthesis; whereas Schoenberg's twelve-tone theory was based upon and, more definitively than any other language, reasserted the impossibility of synthesis. Its premise was dissonance, the subject-object impasse raised to the level of an uncompromisable principle, "forced into complete isolation during the final stage of industrialism" (6). Standing apart from society with a uniquely brooding severity and a remorseless self-control, the new music's loneliness pitilessly showed how all other art had become kitsch, other music ruled by "the omni-present hit tune," "false interpretations and stereotyped audience reaction patterns." These, Adorno said sternly, needed to "be destroyed." Any illusions that the tonality rejected by Schoenberg was somehow natural are rejected: according to Adorno, tonality corresponds to "the closed and exclusive system [of] mercantile society," music submitting to the demands of trade, consumerism, administration. Not for nothing then in a later essay did Adorno attack Toscanini as the *maestro* of conventional music, with its limitless reproducibility, inauthentic perfection, and heartless rhythms contained in the conductor's ironlike dominance and precision.

For Lukács the atomized individual consciousness in surveying its alienation from the product of its own labor desired a kind of healing unity; this was afforded it by "class consciousness," made tenuous, it is true, because, in Lukács's rather circumspect description, consciousness was not empirical or actually and immediately experienceable but "imputable" *(zugerechnetes)*. Such a deferral of the clubby gregariousness normally associated with class feeling undercuts the "vulgar Marxism" that Lukács was so polemically energetic in trying to discredit. But it also allowed him to reharness the aesthetic powers of imagination and projection that had been central to his work before he became a Marxist. "Imputable consciousness" was a daring composite made up not only of what was later to be called Marxist humanism, but in addition borrowing from Schiller's play instinct, Kant's aesthetic realm, and Hans Vaihinger's *als ob*. In all, then, it held a good deal of optimism and even enthusiasm for the promised reconnection of the subject with itself, other subjects, and objects.

None of this is permitted by Adorno in his stirringly bleak account of Schoenberg's emergence and rather repellent triumph. Instead of social relevance Schoenberg's aesthetic chooses irrelevance; instead of amiability the choice is intransigence; instead of antinomian problematics being overcome (a central notion in Lukács's history of classical philosophy) they are vindicated; instead of class consciousness there is the monad; instead of positive thinking there is "definitive negation":

> In the process of pursuing its own inner logic, music is transformed more and more from something significant into something obscure—even to itself. No music today, for example, could possibly speak in the accents of "reward." Not only has the mere idea of humanity, or of a better world no longer any sway over mankind—though it is precisely this which lies at the heart of Beethoven's opera [*Fidelio*]. Rather the strictness of musical structure, wherein alone music can assert itself against the ubiquity of commercialism, has hardened music to the point that it is no longer affected by those external factors which caused absolute music to become what it is. . . . Advanced music has no recourse but to insist upon its own ossification without concession to that would-be humanitarianism which it sees through, in all its attractive and alluring guises, as the mask of inhumanity. (19–20)

Music thus insistently becomes what Lukács's reconciled consciousness has given up—the very sign of alienation which, says Adorno, "preserves its social truth through the isolation resulting from its antithesis to society." Not that this isolation is something to be enjoyed as, say, an 1890s aesthete might have enjoyed the status of arty eccentric. No; in the awareness of an advanced composer that his work derives from such appalling "social roots" as this, there is consequently a recoil from them. So between that awareness and an attitude that "despises [the] . . . illusion of reconciliation" stands new music. Precisely because its constitutive principle is the disjunctive twelve-note series, its harmony a mass of dissonances, its inspiration the remorseless "control" of the composer who is bound by the system's unbreakable laws, music aspires to the condition of theoretical knowledge. Of what? The contradiction.

With this clearly stated, Adorno proceeds resolutely to an account of Schoenberg's career or "progress" (the word is fairly loaded down with irony) from the early expressionist works to the late dodecaphonic masterpieces. As if affectionately recalling and then angrily refuting Lukács, Adorno describes the twelve-tone method in terms taken almost verbatim from the subject-object drama, but each time there is an opportunity for synthesis Adorno has Schoenberg turn it down.

The further irony is that very far from liberating him, Schoenberg's mastery of the atonal technique he invented for escaping "the blind domination of tonal material" ends up by dominating him. The severity, objectivity, and regulatory power of a technique that supplies itself with an alternative harmony, inflection, tonal color, rhythm—in short a new logic for music, the object of the subject's compositional skill—become "a second blind nature," and this "virtually extinguishes the subject" (68–69). In Adorno's descriptions here there is a breathtakingly regressive sequence, a sort of endgame procedure by which he threads his way back along the route taken by Lukács; all the laboriously constructed solutions devised by Lukács for pulling himself out of the slough of bourgeois despair—the various satisfactory totalities given by art, philosophy, Marxism—are just as laboriously dismantled and rendered useless. Fixated on music's absolute rejection of the commercial sphere, Adorno's words cut out the social ground from underneath art. For in fighting ornament, illusion, reconciliation, communication, humanism, and success, art becomes untenable:

> Everything having no function in the work of art—and therefore everything transcending the law of mere existence—is withdrawn. The function of the work of art lies precisely in its

transcendence beyond mere existence. Thus the height of justice becomes the height of injustice: the consummately functional work of art becomes consummately functionless. Since
the work, after all, cannot be reality, the elimination of all illusory features accentuates all the more glaringly the illusory
character of its existence. This process is inescapable. (70)

An even more drastic statement comes later, when Adorno avers as
how the fate of new music in its illusionless self-denial and ossified
self-sacrifice is to remain unheard: "music which has not been heard
falls into empty time like an impotent bullet" (133). Thus the subject-
object antithesis simply disappears, because Adorno has Schoenberg
rejecting even the ghost of achievement and experience. I say it this
way to underscore Adorno's manipulation of Schoenberg, and also to
contrast it with Mann's *Doctor Faustus* (based on Adorno's book), a
tamer version of Adorno's Schoenberg. Mann's hero is an Adornian
emanation, but the novel's technique, especially the presence of
Serenus Zeitblom, the humanist narrator, recuperates and to a degree
saves or domesticates Adrian by giving him the aura of a figure representative of modern Germany, now chastened and perhaps redeemed
for postwar elegiac reflection.

But Lukács's theory has voyaged elsewhere too. Recall that between
Lukács and Adorno there is first of all a common European culture
and more particularly the affinity stemming from the Hegelian tradition to which they both belong. It is therefore quite startling to discover the subject-object dialectic deployed with devastating
intellectual and political force in Frantz Fanon's last work, *The
Wretched of the Earth*, written in 1961, the very year of its author's death.
All of Fanon's books on colonialism show evidence of his indebtedness
to Marx and Engels, as well as to Freud and Hegel. Yet the striking
power that differentiates his last work from, say, the largely Caribbean
setting of *Black Skins, White Masks* (1952) is evident from the unflagging
mobilizing energy with which in the Algerian setting Fanon analyzes
and situates the antinomy of the settler versus the native. There is a
philosophical logic to the tension that is scarcely visible in his previous

work, in which psychology, impressions, astute observation, and an almost novelistic technique of insight and vignette give Fanon's writing its ingratiatingly eloquent inflections.

Two things seem to have happened between *L'An V de la revolution algérienne* (1959), his first collection of essays after he changed his focus from the Caribbean to North Africa, and *The Wretched of the Earth*. One of them, obviously, is that the progress of the Algerian revolution had deepened and widened the gulf between France and its colony. There was a greater drive toward separation between them, the war had become uglier and more extensive, sides were being taken both in Algeria and in the metropolis, with rifts and internecine conflicts in both of the two great hostile encampments. Second—and here I speculate—Fanon seems to have read Lukács's book and taken from its reification chapter an understanding of how even in the most confusing and heterogenous of situations, a rigorous analysis of one central problematic could be relied on to yield the most extensive understanding of the whole. The evidence I have is, to repeat, not firm, but it is worth noting: a French version of Lukács's central work, *Histoire et conscience de classe*, appeared in 1961, in an excellent translation by Kostas Axelos and Jacqueline Bois, published by Editions de Minuit. Some of the chapters had already appeared in *Arguments* a few years earlier, but 1961 was the first time the entire book had made its appearance anywhere at all, ever since Lukács had recanted the book's most radical tenets a generation earlier. In his preface Axelos compared Lukács to Brecht's Galileo, associating him also with those other martyrs to truth, Socrates, Christ, and Giordano Bruno; according to Axelos, the main point for twentieth-century thought, however, was that Lukács's great treatise was expunged from both history and class consciousness, with no visible effects on those working people the book was designed to assist.

How strongly the subject-object dialectic resonated *outside* Europe, and for an audience made up of colonial subjects, is immediately apparent from the opening pages of *The Wretched of the Earth*. The Manicheanism Fanon describes as separating the clean, well-lighted colonial city and the vile, disease-ridden darkness of the *casbah* recalls the alienation of Lukács's reified world. And Fanon's whole project is first to illuminate and then to animate the separation between colonizer and colonized (subject and object) in order that what is false, brutalizing, and historically determined about the relationship might become clear, stimulate action, and lead to the overthrow of colonialism itself. As Lukács put it in his supremely Hegelian 1922 Preface to *History and Class Consciousness*: "It is of the essence of dialectical method that concepts which are false in their abstract onesidedness are later transcended."[4] To this Fanon will answer that there is nothing abstract or conceptual about colonialism, which, as Conrad once said, "mostly means the taking it [land] away from those who have a different complexion or slightly flatter noses than ourselves." Thus, according to Fanon,

> for a colonized people the most essential value, because the most concrete, is first and foremost the land: the land which will bring them bread and, above all, dignity. But this dignity has nothing to do with the dignity of the human individual: for that human individual has never heard tell of it. All that the native has seen in his country is that they can freely arrest him, beat him, starve him: and no professor of ethics, no priest has ever come to be beaten in his place, nor to share their bread with him. As far as the native is concerned: morality is very concrete; it is to silence the settler's defiance, to break his flaunting violence—in a word, to put him out of the picture.[5]

Lukács's dialectic is grounded in *The Wretched of the Earth*, actualized, given a kind of harsh presence nowhere to be found in his agonized re-thinking of the classical philosophical antinomies. The issue for Lukács was the primacy of consciousness in history; for Fanon it is the primacy of geography in history, and then the primacy of history over consciousness and subjectivity. That there is subjectivity at all is be-cause of colonialism—instituted by Europeans who like Odysseus came to the peripheries to exploit the land and its people, and there-after to constitute a new aggressive selfhood—and once colonialism disappears the settler "has no longer any interest in remaining or in co-existing" (45). The subjective colonizer has turned the native into a de-humanized creature for whom zoological terms are the most apt; for the settler the terms used to falsify and palliate his or her repressive presence are borrowed from "Western culture," which whenever it is mentioned "produces in the native a sort of stiffening or muscular lockjaw" (43).

At the same time that Fanon uses the subject-object dialectic most energetically he is quite deliberate about its limitations. Thus, to return to the relationship between the colonial enclave and the native quarter: these "two zones are opposed," says Fanon, "but not in the service of a higher unity. . . . They both follow the principle of reciprocal exclusivity. No conciliation is possible, for of the two terms one is superfluous" (38–39). At the same time that he uses what is a patently Marxist analysis Fanon realizes explicitly that such "analysis should always be slightly stretched" in the colonial situation. For neither the colonist nor the colonized behaves as if subject and object might some day be reconciled. The former plunders and pillages; the latter dreams of revenge. When the natives rise in violent insurrection, it "is not a rational confrontation of points of view. It is not a treatise on the universal, but the untidy affirmation of an original idea propounded as an absolute" (41).

No one needs to be reminded that Fanon's recommended antidote for the cruelties of colonialism is violence: "the violence of the colonial regime and the counter-violence of the native balance each other and respond to each other in an extraordinary reciprocal homogeneity" (88). The logic of colonialism is opposed by the native's equally strict and implacable counterlogic. What operates throughout the war of national liberation is therefore a combative subject-object dialectic whose central term is violence which at brief moments appears to play a reconciling, transfiguring role. True, Fanon says there is no liberation without violence and certainly he admits that there is no "truthful behavior" in a colonial setting: "good is quite simply that which is evil for 'them'" (50). But does Fanon, like Lukács, suggest that the subject-object dialectic can be consummated, transcended, synthesized, and that violence in and of itself is that fulfillment, the dialectical tension resolved by violent upheaval into peace and harmony?

The by now conventional notion about Fanonist violence is exactly that, a received idea, and is a caricatural reduction more suited to the Cold War (Sidney Hook's attack on Fanon being a case in point) than to what Fanon actually says and to how he says it. In other words, Fanon can too easily be read as if what he was doing in *The Wretched of the Earth* was little more than a replication of Lukács, with the subject-object relationship replaced exactly by the colonizer-colonized relationship, the "new class-consciousness of the proletariat," Lukács's synthesizing term, replaced by revolutionary violence in Fanon's text. But that would be to miss Fanon's crucial reworking and critique of Lukács, in which the *national* element missing in *History and Class Consciousness*—the setting of that work, like Marx's, is entirely European—is given an absolute prominence by Fanon. For him, subject and object are European and non-European respectively; colonialism does not just *oppose* the terms and the people to each other. It obliterates and suppresses their presence, substituting instead the lifeless dehumanizing abstractions of two "masses" in absolute uncommunicating hostility with each other. Whereas Lukács saw the subject-object antinomy as integral to European culture, and as in fact its partial symbol, Fanon sees the antinomy as imported from Europe, a foreign intrusion that has completely distorted the native presence. "Thus the history which he [the colonist] writes is not the history of the country which he plunders but the history of his own nation in regard to all that she skims off, all that she violates and starves" (51).

Fanon had made earlier use of the subject-object dialectic in an expressly Hegelian manner; this is most notably evident in *Black Skins,* where he uses the master-slave dialectic to show how the Negro had been turned by racism into an "existential deviation." Yet even there Fanon distinguished the dialectic as Hegel envisioned it for white Europe, and how it might be used by whites against Negroes: "here [in the colonial relationship between races] the master differs basically from the master described by Hegel. For Hegel there is reciprocity; here the master laughs at the consciousness of the slave. What he wants from the slave is not recognition but work."[6] In *The Wretched of the Earth* existential racial relationships have been superseded, in a sense: they are now located and resituated geographically in the colonial setting. And from this derives that "world divided into compartments, a motionless Manicheistic world, a world of statues" (51).

In short, the colonial antinomy can now be reinterpreted as an antagonism between nations, one dominating the other, and in the process actually preventing the other from coming into being. The new complication therefore is nationalism, which Fanon introduces as follows:

The immobility to which the native is condemned can only be called in question if the native decides to put an end to the history of colonization—the history of pillage—and to bring into existence the history of the nation—the history of decolonization. (51)

The unresolvable antinomy is the opposition between two nations which in the colonies cannot be brought to coexist. Fanon matches two sets of terms: pillage and colonization versus the nation and decolonization, and they emerge in the anticolonial struggle itself as absolutely opposed as they were before it began, before the liberation movement was born, before it started to fight, before it challenged the colonizer. The violence of decolonization is no more than an explicit fulfillment of the violence that lurks within colonialism, and instead of the natives being the object of colonial force, they wield it back *against* colonialism, as subjects reacting with pent-up violence to their own former passivity.

Were liberation therefore only to consist in the violence of nationalism, the process of decolonization might be seen as leading inevitably to it, one step along the way. But Fanon's essential point—and here he also rejects Lukács's own resolution—is that nationalism is a necessary but far from sufficient condition for liberation, perhaps even a sort of temporary illness that must be gone through. By the approximate terms of the subject-object antinomy, the natives who reject their reified status as negation and evil take on violence as a way of providing themselves with "a royal pardon" (86): since they stand outside the European class system about which Lukács wrote, colonized natives need an extra measure of rebelliousness to afford them the dubious position of antagonists (their dreams, Fanon remarks, are full of jumping, swimming, running, climbing, as if trying to imagine what it would be like *not* to stay in place). Once antagonists of the colonizers, however, they are only the *opposite* of colonialism: this is why Fanon says that only at an initial stage can violence be used to organize a party. Colonial war is of the colonial dialectic, the replication of some of its mutually exclusive and antagonistic terms on a national level. The opposites reflect each other. For the Europeans this will lead to expulsion; for the native this will mean that national independence will be achieved. Yet both expulsion and independence belong essentially to the unforgiving dialectic of colonialism, enfolded within its unpromising script.

Thereafter Fanon is at pains to show that the tensions between colonizer and colonized will not end, since in effect the new nation will produce a new set of policemen, bureaucrats, and merchants to replace the departed Europeans. And indeed after his opening chapter on violence Fanon proceeds to show how nationalism is too heavily imprinted with the *unresolved* (and unresolvable) dialectic of colonialism for it to lead very far beyond it. The complexity of independence, which is so naturally desirable a goal for all colonized people, is that simultaneously it dramatized the discrepancy between colonizer and colonized so basic to colonialism, and also a discrepancy *(décalage)* between the people and their leaders, leaders who perforce are shaped by colonialism. Thus after the opening chapter on violence, Fanon proceeds to develop the new difficulties of nationalism as it continues the war against colonialism decreed by the subject-object antinomy, while at the same time an entirely new consciousness—that of liberation—is struggling to be born.

It is not until the chapter on "The Pitfalls of National Consciousness" that Fanon makes clear what he has been intending all along: national consciousness is undoubtedly going to be captured by the colonial bourgeois elite, the nationalistic leaders, and far from guaranteeing real independence this will perpetuate colonialism in a new form, a "sterile formalism." Thus, he says, if nationalism "is not enriched and deepened by a very rapid transformation into a consciousness of social and political needs, in other words, into humanism, it leads up a blind alley" (204). Borrowing from Aimé Césaire, Fanon suggests that the necessity is to "invent souls," not to reproduce the solutions and formulas either of colonialism or the tribal past. "The living expression of the nation is the moving consciousness of the whole of the people; it is the coherent, enlightened action of men and women" (204). A few sentences later he states that a national government (the only government ever known!) ought to cede its power back to the people, dissolve itself.

Fanon's radicalism, I think, is and has been since his death too strenuous for the new postcolonial states, Algeria included. The gist of his last work plainly indicts them for this insufficiently visionary response to the colonialist dialectic, from which they have never fully liberated themselves, satisfied as they have been with the imitations and simulacra of sovereignty that they have simply taken over from European masters. But even in this extraordinary turn Fanon relies to some degree on Lukács, although it is a Lukács that had been either rejected or toned down by Lukács himself. So that even for a colonial setting, as he criticized the subject-object reconciliation advocated by *History and Class Consciousness* as the "class consciousness of the proletariat," Fanon takes from Lukács the real dissatisfaction with that resolution that surfaces briefly near the end of the essay on "Class Consciousness," the short essay that precedes the reification chapter. "The proletariat," says Lukács, "only perfects itself by annihilating and transcending itself . . . it is equally [therefore] the struggle of the proletariat against itself" (80).

There is concurrence here between Fanon and this more (and perhaps only momentarily) radical Lukács on the one hand, and between Lukács and Adorno on the other. The work of theory, criticism, demystification, deconsecration, and decentralization they imply is never finished. The point of theory therefore is to travel, always to move beyond its confinements, to emigrate, to remain in a sense in exile. Adorno and Fanon exemplify this profound restlessness in the way they refuse the emoluments offered by the Hegelian dialectic as stabilized into resolution by Lukács—or the Lukács who appeared to speak for class consciousness as something to be gained, possessed, held onto. There was of course the other Lukács which both his brilliant rereaders preferred, the theorist of permanent dissonance as understood by Adorno, the critic of reactive nationalism as partially adopted by Fanon in colonial Algeria.

In all this we get a sense, I think, of the geographical dispersion of which the theoretical motor is capable. I mean that when Adorno uses Lukács to understand Schoenberg's place in the history of music, or when Fanon dramatized the colonial struggle in the language of the manifestly European subject-object dialectic, we think of them not simply as coming after Lukács, using him at a belated second degree, so to speak, but rather as pulling him from one sphere or region into another. This movement suggests the possibility of actively different locales, sites, situations for theory, without facile universalism or over-general totalizing. One would not, could not, want to assimilate Viennese twelve-tone music to the Algerian resistance to French colonialism: the disparities are too grotesque even to articulate. But in both situations, each so profoundly and concretely felt by Adorno and Fanon respectively, is the fascinating Lukácsian figure, present both as traveling theory and as intransigent practice. To speak here only of borrowing and adaptation is not adequate. There is in particular an intellectual, and perhaps moral, community of a remarkable kind, *affiliation* in the deepest and most interesting sense of the word. As a way of getting seriously past the weightlessness of one theory after another, the remorseless indignations of orthodoxy, and the expressions of tired advocacy to which we are often submitted, the exercise involved in figuring out where the theory went and how in getting there its fiery core was reignited is invigorating—and is also another voyage, one that is central to intellectual life in the late twentieth century.

38

History, Literature, and Geography

When I was a graduate student at Harvard in the late fifties, I was employed as a tutor in an elite undergraduate program whose name was "History and Literature." Although there were undergraduates who majored in one or another of the literature departments within History and Literature and a smaller number in it who were in the history department, it was then believed that only a few especially gifted students could handle the two disciplines together. Mercifully, I do not recall a great deal about what as a group the students and tutors of "History and Lit." (as it was called) actually did, but I know that I gave two seminars, one on Thucydides and one on Vico, the idea, I think, being that both writers embodied an approach to history that was literary and an approach to literature that was somehow historical. Aside from that, I recall that the snobbish aura that gave History and Lit. its prestige at Harvard was that our students—who were mostly literary in their interests—were not afraid of, and may even have actually been interested in, literature from a historical standpoint, or literature in its historical context. Paradoxically, however, we were not held in very high esteem by either the Professors of History or the Professors of English. There was something about us that to them seemed either too weak in our methods (such as they were) or too diluted in our focus. Looking back at it I regret to say that they were probably right in both instances.

At the risk of boring you still further with a little more personal rambling, I also recall that after I got my Ph.D. and began to teach at Columbia in 1963, I continued to be dogged by the notion, everywhere current, that history and literature were in fact two quite separate fields of study, and ultimately of experience. I also remember that when I began to write books and articles about philosophy, politics, and later music I earned myself the suspicion, and even the dislike, of professionals in those fields who with good reason saw me as an interloper. I also remember my mother's puzzled question to me time and again when I burdened her with publications by me that patently were not literary in the pure sense. "But Edward," she would say, "I thought your field was literature. Why are you writing or meddling in things that aren't really your line?" This particular complaint became more worried and more hectoring when, for better or for worse, my political writing began to attract attention. This was really a bad business, my mother thought. Go back to literature, was her answer to what she saw as my predicament.

And so it went in my own work for a couple of years more, until, I recall, I began to translate a remarkable essay by Erich Auerbach, whose book *Mimesis* had established itself by 1960 as one of the crucial critical texts of twentieth-century literary study. The essay in question was "Philologie der Weltliteratur (1952)," and it was written and published in Germany after *Mimesis* had appeared; Auerbach uses the occasion to reflect on his own post-war work, the situation of the philologist, and the peculiar entanglement with history that he felt:

> History is the science of reality that affects us most immediately, stirs us most deeply and compels us most forcibly to a consciousness of ourselves. It is the only science in which human beings step before us in their totality. Under the rubric of history one is to understand not only the past, but the progression of events in general; history therefore includes the present. The inner history of the last thousand years is the history of mankind achieving self expression: this is what philology, a historicist discipline, treats. This history contains the records of

man's mighty, adventurous advance to a consciousness of his human condition and to the realization of his given potential; and this advance, whose final goal (even in its wholly fragmentary present form) was barely imaginable for a long time, still seems to have proceeded as if according to a plan, in spite of its twisted course. All the rich tensions of which our being is capable are contained within this course. An inner dream unfolds whose scope and depth entirely animate the spectator [that is, the philologist] enabling him at the same time to find peace in his given potential by the enrichment he gains by having witnessed the drama. The loss of such a spectacle—whose appearance is thoroughly dependent on presentation and interpretation—would be an impoverishment for which there can be no possible compensation. . . . We are still basically capable of fulfilling this duty [that is, the presentation of the spectacle through "collecting material and forming it into a whole"] not only because we have a great deal of material at our disposal, but above all because we have inherited the sense of historical perspectivism which is so necessary for the job.[1]

In this rich description of what in fact is Auerbach's own method as it was so remarkably fulfilled in *Mimesis,* he assigns the philologist the task of collection and presentation. All past written records inherited by us in the present are saturated in the history of their own times; philological work is responsible for examining them. They have a unity which the philologist interprets according to historicist perspectivism. In a sense therefore philology is the interpretive discipline by which you can discern that peculiar slant on things which is the perspective on reality of a given period. Auerbach was Vico's German translator, and the idea he articulates here is indebted to Vico's theory of the unity of historical periods. Vico's new science was the art of reading, say, Homer's poems not as if they were written by an eighteenth-century philosopher, but rather as products of their own primitive time, texts that embody the youth of mankind, the heroic age, in which metaphor and poetry, not rational science and deductive logic, both of which occur only much later, are used to understand and if necessary construct reality. Historicist philology—which is much more than studying the derivation of words—is the discipline of uncovering beneath the surface of words the life of a society that is embedded there by the great writer's art. You cannot perform that act without somehow intuiting, through the use of the historical imagination, what that life *might* have been like, and so, as Dilthey and Nietzsche both suggest, interpretation involves an almost artistic projection of self into that earlier world. Hence, for example, the stunning inner readings of Sophoclean and Euripidean tragedy in *The Birth of Tragedy*, readings which, you recall, incurred the wrath of positivist philosophists like Wilamovitz, for whom words could only be studied with dictionary-like precision.

Auerbach inherits all this in his own training, the likes of which no one today can ever receive. For not only must one have studied all the European languages (Latin, Greek, French, Italian, Spanish, Provençal, etc.), but one must also be able to deal with legal, historical, numismatic, and of course literary texts in all their details and complex special concreteness. But even all this is not enough. One must also have the courage to relive within oneself the whole of human history, as if it were one's own history: in other words, by an act of both creation and self-endowment, the philologist undertakes to assume human history in his/her own work as a spectacle unfolding minutely and patiently in the texts studied. This of course is what makes *Mimesis* the extraordinary work that it is. Each of Auerbach's passages is looked at first as a text to be decoded; then as his angle of vision expands, it is connected to its own age, that age understood as fostering, if not also requiring, a particular aesthetic style. One wouldn't therefore read Flaubert the way Petrocius should be read, not just because they are two different writers working in hugely separated historical periods, but also because their way of apprehending and then articulating the reality of their time is completely different. In the end, however, historical reality is transmuted into a highly idiosyncratic, irreducibly concrete structure of sentences, periods, parataxes, and it is this structure which the philologist tries to render.

And yet *Mimesis* itself is put together episodically: it begins with a reading of Homer and the Old Testament, followed by a whole series of *explication de texte*, from classical antiquity, through the Middle Ages, and stretching forward through the Renaissance, the Enlightenment, and arriving finally in the periods of Realism and Modernism. Although Auerbach makes no concerted attempt to connect the chapters with one another, his underlying theme remains "the representation of reality," which in technical rhetorical terms means the various styles, high, low, and mixed, by which Western writers since antiquity translated reality into sentences. The core of the book, however, is Auerbach's treatment of Dante, who represents the first Western writer to achieve a synthesis in the *Divine Comedy* of the two disparate extremes of classical style: using the figure of Christ, who of course represents a fusion of tragedy and comedy, as a representative of the new middle style, *dolce stil nuovo*, Dante produced a poem whose ambition and indeed subject were nothing less than the unification of past with present and future. And this, in effect, becomes Auerbach's ambition in *Mimesis*, to create a historical vision of the secular world incarnated in language through an unfolding, dramatic interpretation of its entire literature, which Auerbach, in an act of supreme poetic imagination, represents in the various readings.

My interest in Auerbach's method, about which he says next to nothing in *Mimesis* itself, unlocked the system of correspondences between history and literature that is the cornerstone of a whole tradition of regarding temporality as both the repository of human experience, past, present, and future, as well as the mode of understanding by which historical reality can be comprehended. An important preliminary point to be made about this takes us back to the two main words of our conference's title, history and literature. Neither history nor literature are inert bodies of experience; nor are they disciplines that exist out there to be mastered by professionals and experts. The two terms are mediated by the critical consciousness, the mind of the individual reader and critic, whose work (like Auerbach's) sees history and literature somehow informing each other. So the missing middle term between history and literature is therefore the agency of criticism, or interpretation. Auerbach's own background and tradition allowed him the possibility of mediating the two with the techniques of philology, a science for which today there is not, and cannot ever again be, the kind of training provided between the wars in Europe for an Auerbach, or for like-minded polymathic colleagues such as Leo Spitzer, Ernst Curtius, Karl Vossler.

Our generation has been left with criticism, an activity undergoing ceaseless transformation.

In any event, as I said a moment ago, the kind of work done and de- scribed by Auerbach takes as its guarantee an underlying notion of commensurability, or correspondence, or conjuncture between history and literature, which the critic by dint of hard work, the mastery of lots of different texts, and personal vision, can in fact reproduce in his/her work. In this perspective then history and literature exist as temporal activities, and can unfold more or less together in the same element, which is also common to criticism. So whereas he may be one of the finest exemplars of this common unfolding, Auerbach is only one representative of a much larger movement that probably goes back as far as Hegel, whose greatest modern literary theoretician is Georg Lukács, about whom I shall speak in detail presently. If Lukács is the prototypical theorist of aesthetic temporality, then I should like to counterpose him with Antonio Gramsci, whose perspective on the re- lationship between history and culture is mediated and intervened in by a very powerful *geographical* sense. And it is this spatial sense of dis- continuity that complicates and renders far less effective than ever be- fore the possibility of correspondence, congruence, continuity, and reconciliation between different areas of experience. I shall argue that Gramsci's geographical awareness makes it more appropriate for late twentieth-century criticism, which has had to deal with disjunctive formations and experiences such as women's history, popular culture, post-colonial and subaltern material that cannot be assimilated easily, cannot be appropriated and fitted into an overall scheme of corre- spondences.

The Hegelian dialectic, as no one needs to be told, is based on a tem- poral sequence, followed by a resolution between those parts of the se- quence whose relationship was initially based on opposition, contradiction, antitheses. Thus opposition is always destined for rec- onciliation, provided the correct logical process can be instigated. Lukács inherits this basic scheme, but from the beginning of his ca- reer—I refer here to his precocious early book *Die Seele und die Formen*— is also haunted by the possibility that the opposition between one pole and another may be too strong, too stubborn to be resolved in tempo- rality. This is what his early works are really about, the dissonance between dream and reality, which the mere poet or Platonist can do nothing about but which the real artist—the artist as form-giver—can reconcile. Here are a couple of passages chosen almost at random:

> A problem arises when the Platonist's eternal uncertainty threatens to cast a shadow over the white brilliance of the [poet's] verse and when the heaviness of his sense of distance weighs down the poet's soaring lightness, or when there is a danger that the poet's divine frivolity may falsify the Platonist's profound hesitations and rob them of their honesty. . . . A real solution can only come from form. In form alone ("the only possible thing" is the shortest definition of form known to me) does every antithesis, every trend, become music and necessity. The road of every problematic human being leads to form because it is that unity which can combine within itself the largest number of divergent forces, and therefore at the end of that road stands the man who can create form: the artist, in whose created form poet and Platonist become equal.[2]

The beginning point of all of Lukács's analyses is dissonance, that sense of ontological discord between self and other, or as he was later to discuss it, between subject and object. In the study of the novel that immediately followed *Die Seele und die Formen,* he produced an extraordinarily penetrating treatise on the genre itself, which for him became the modern artistic form of expressing and overcoming dissonance par excellence. For the first time he posits a before and an after, the perfectly unified and consonant classical world whose inner nature is expressed in the epic, and the fallen, subsequent world, whose inner nature expresses itself as a gap between various fragments of a fallen being. The former is plenitude and totality; the latter is disintegration and inadequacy. Time in the classical world of plenitude and totality is not a problem, whereas in the modern world it is the problem of temporality, that ironic sense of transcendental distance between subject and object lodged at the very heart of existence. And, says Lukács, it is this sense of transcendental homelessness that produces the novel as a form whose fundamental structural principle is temporality as irony, not as fulfillment or reconciliation. Thus the novel form itself furnishes an aesthetic resolution to the difficulties of modernity, although its complexity as a form, as well as its internal disharmony—after all the novelistic hero, says Lukács, is either a criminal or a madman, and even though the novelist is committed to biography as a vehicle for conveying the hero's life, it cannot really mute or smooth out its fundamental turmoil—is always evident. "The composition of the novel," adds Lukács, "is the paradoxical fusion of heterogeneous and discrete components into an organic whole which is then abolished over and over." As he says a moment later:

> The novel is the epic of a world that has been abandoned by God. The novel hero's psychology is demonic; the objectivity of the novel is the mature man's knowledge that meaning can never quite penetrate reality, but that, without meaning, reality would disintegrate into the nothingness or inessentiality . . . Irony, with intuitive double vision, can see where God is to be found in a world abandoned by God . . . Irony . . . is the highest freedom that can be achieved in a world without God. That is why it is not only the sole possible *a priori* condition for a true, totality-creating objectivity but also why it makes that totality—the novel—the representative art-form of our age: because the structural categories of the novel constitutively coincide with the world as it is today.[3]

The genius of this description of the novel (which is certainly the most brilliant ever offered) is that it shows how as an art form the novel reconciles within itself the internal discrepancies of modern life, and in so doing coincides "with the world as it is today." Moreover, Lukács goes on to show that reconciliation and coincidence are only provisional, since the formal organic whole of the novel is abolished over and over by irony. What makes possible the novel's constitutive aesthetic form, however, is time, which Lukács says about Flaubert's *L'Education sentimentale* gives the meaningless comings and goings of Flaubert's characters their essential quality (*The Theory of the Novel*, 125). So for Lukács time, in all its ironic makings and unmakings, is the core of the great modern art form, the one that most perfectly expresses the transcendental homelessness of contemporary life. Time gives and time takes away. Only *theory*—and hence the meaning of the title of Lukács's treatise—theory in the Hegelian sense of the word can contain both the accomplishments and the ironic dissolutions of form in the novel.

What Lukács seems to have discovered in his theoretical survey of the novel is that whatever reconciliation might be possible between dialectical opposites can only be aesthetic and in the final analysis private. But then all the immense weight and complex pathos of those early years of seeking and desolation finally come to rest in his next, and greatest, work, *History and Class Consciousness*, his first overtly Marxist treatise. He now re-examines the history of consciousness in its purest forms within classical philosophy, whose core problem remains the endlessly reiterated discrepancy, or antinomy, between subject and object. The reconciliation between them that he had found in art is now seen as only one solution along the way, in the period between Kant and Schiller. It is only after Hegel and then Marx that the notion of a dialectic between opposites acquires in Hegel logical force and in Marx sociopolitical force. For the first time historically, then, Lukács says, Marxism provides for the "putative" consciousness that might finally resolve the ontological contradiction that has been sitting at the heart of classical philosophical narrative, and it introduces the very idea of totality which had once been the hallmark of the classical works, but which has since been lost to modernity. If the novel articulates the problem of history as time that offers up no possibility of resolving dissonance, then it is what Lukács now calls "the standpoint of the proletariat" that sees the central problem of reification (reification as dissonance, or disparity and distance between facts or objects hardened into separate irreconcilable identities or antinomies) as resolvable in time through a collective apprehension in consciousness of human history as the history of processes. "History," he says in a famous sentence, "is the history of the unceasing overthrow of the objective forms that shape the life of man."[4]

My reason for going through all this is to illustrate how in Lukács the whole issue of temporality, or rather the temporal apprehension of reality, is given the fullest and most complex philosophical treatment. In the trajectory of his thought from *Die Seele und die Formen*, through *The Theory of the Novel*, to *History and Class Consciousness*, we can read not only a more and more clear philosophical articulation of the problematization of temporality in all its immense pathos and complexity, but also a coming to terms with it in Marxism. Lukács's early Marxism was later repudiated by him as far too radical and dynamic, but for my purposes it expresses a sense of how at least in consciousness it might be possible to treat temporality as a fact at the most fundamental epistemological level: as form, as process, and as putative reconciliation, in which some satisfaction can at last be achieved between the knowing subject and the resistant object through the category of totality. Theodor Adorno attacked Lukács's revolutionary optimism in his essay entitled "Reconciliation under Duress," the duress being the one provided by Lukács's Marxist faith, which Adorno, more skeptical and radical, did not share. Nevertheless, it seems to me that the grandeur of Lukács's criticism is that it is the metaphysical culmination of the Hegelian synthesis applied both to aesthetics and to politics as essentially temporal activities, activities unfolding in time, which while it ironizes and accentuates the dissonances of modern life views them redemptively, as overcoming and resolving them at some future date.

In all sorts of explicit and implicit ways most modern Western literary histories, Auerbach's included, share a similar temporal and redemptive optimism with Lukács. Most of them, however, miss the underlying messianic and ultimately destructive quality of Lukács's vision; what they retain in the way of a sense of concordance between literature and history—the two ultimately supporting and reinforcing each other in a benign temporality—has enabled at least three generations of Western scholarship. It is to be found equally in works directly influenced by Lukács, like Lucien Goldmann's *Le Dieu caché* and those equally powerful and influential Anglo-American works like Ian Watt's *The Rise of the Novel* in which Lukács is at most a shadowy, unacknowledged presence. For all its privacy and complexity the novel as described by Watt is always contained and in the end is perfectly congruent with a history of the bourgeoisie, which itself is congruent with the ascendancy of a new class whose world view is mercantile, individualistic, and enterprising. Goldmann's more directly theoretical work, no less empirically based than Watt's, is in effect a theory of correspondences by which the jagged fragments of Pascal's *Pensées* are carefully and laboriously inserted in an extremely specific and dense history of the Port Royal community, as well as that of the *noblesse de robe*. In both Watt and Goldmann the literary form we are left with is in effect an irreplaceable cornerstone of the general history of the periods in question, one in which all sorts of possible disruptions and dissonances between individual and general are resolved as part of the overall advance of the dominant mainstream.

I am perfectly aware that what I am saying may sound too systematic and reductive, since after all the house of literary history has many windows. But looking at it in this way, it seems to me that a great deal about recent trends in theory and scholarship becomes considerably clearer. Take, as another instance, the whole notion of identity, which is the animating principle of biography, for example, Richard Ellman's famous series of books on Wilde, Joyce, and Yeats, including his symptomatically entitled *The Identity of Yeats*. If we think of literary history as incorporating the lives of major artists, then we must also understand those lives as reinforcing, consolidating, and clarifying a core identity, identical not only with itself, but in a sense with the history of the period in which it existed and flourished. In other words, we read biography not to deconstruct, but to solidify, identity, and where but in temporality does an identity unfold? Trilling's Arnold, Edgar Johnson's Dickens, Bate's Johnson, Painter's Proust, Ehrenpreis's Swift, Martin's Hopkins—all these plus many others too numerous to mention are parts of the finally integral, integrated general structure of historical periods, which the biographies, no matter how complex, rich, and detailed, are enfolded within. Much the same applies to the interpretive studies of poets and novelists, regardless of how revolutionary and innovative they may be, for instance, Harold Bloom's study of Wallace Stevens, or Geoffrey Hartman's pioneering work on Wordsworth. Identity, which is non-contradiction, or rather contradiction resolved, is the heart of the enterprise, and temporality its sustaining element, the essence of its constitutive structure.

I said a moment ago that these trends become clearer if we look at all the immense variety and richness of these studies as belonging to a fundamentally similar way of conceiving the relationship between history and literature. The principal reason for being able to do so, I want now to suggest, is that this particular formation whose most articulated paradigm comes from Lukács as the culmination of a generally Hegelian tradition of focusing on temporality as resolving the threats to identity can be contrasted with a radically different tradition, one for whom Antonio Gramsci serves me here as a great prototype. I'd like to make the case here for Gramsci as having created in his work an essentially geographical, territorial apprehension of human history and society, although like Lukács he is irrecusably attached to the notion of dissonance as a central element in modern consciousness. Unlike Lukács, however, Gramsci seems completely to have escaped the clutches of Hegelianism. Much more of a fox than a hedgehog, he seems to have revelled in particular, and unaccommodated, unhoused rebelliousness against systems. On the other hand, far more than Lukács he was political in the practical sense, conceiving of politics as a contest over territory, both actual and historical, to be won, fought over, controlled, held, lost, gained. Nevertheless, Gramsci, unlike Lukács, whose early *oeuvre* is academic and metaphysical in the best sense, presents truly severe interpretive problems at the level of his text itself.

What are the interpretive problems? They can be broken into two main categories, each reinforcing the other. First, there is the doctrinal one. Some critics argue that because he was so immersed in bourgeois culture and its study, because also in general he seems to have opposed the left-wing of the PCI in its frequent ambitions to take state power, because also his attitude seemed to be one of perhaps reflection and preparation and study (an insufficiently insurrectionary attitude that is), Gramsci was, or expressed, a reformist rather than a revolutionary Leninist philosophy or praxis. Others have gone so far as to say in this vein that Gramsci was essentially a new Crocean. Still others argue that Gramsci was a real insurrectionary revolutionary, and that his views, translated onto the Italian scene, perfectly convey the sense made of contemporary history and praxis by the Comintern. The other category of problems is, for the literary scholar, what we can call the philological one, that is, the condition, the state, and from there, the signifying system of Gramsci's texts.

Gramsci's writings are of three different types: (1) the large set of occasional pieces written by him as a journalist during the period when he was editor of *Ordine nouvo* and additionally when he was a regular contributor of cultural, dramatic, and political criticism to other journals and magazines such as *Avanti* and *Il Grido del Popolo;* (2) Gramsci's writings on questions and topics and writers that preoccupied him throughout his life, and which can be said to form a whole despite the fact that they are distributed more or less all over the place, and cannot really be said, in any one instance, to form a complete or finished work: among these works are the study of Croce, Prodiga, and Machiavelli, the analyses of culture and intellectuals, the great work on the southern (meridionale) question; (3) Gramsci's prison notebooks and letters, a vast collection of fragments, linked, as I said, by Gramsci's powerful and compelling intellect, by his involvement in the working-class movement, by the European resistance to fascism, by his unique fascination with the modern state and its "civil society," by his almost incredible range of miscellaneous reading, by his family and party af-filiations, loves, problems, by his own—I believe central—determination to elaborate, to grapple with, to come to clearer and clearer formula-tions of the role of mind in society. Cutting through the large and fun-damentally disjunct edifice of his work is the never-to-be forgotten fact that Gramsci's training was in philology, and that—like Vico—he un-derstood the profoundly complex and interesting connection among words, texts, reality, and political/social history or distinct physical en-tities.

One can see, even from this very cursory survey of what, in dealing with Gramsci, one has to take into account interpretively speaking. But there are some—no more than a small handful of rules, it seems to me—that can guide our reading of his work as a whole, and especially here and there in the *Prison Notebooks*. Let me try now to enumerate them schematically, as they have to do with a reading of Gramsci, and not with some of the larger, and yet more regional, issues of whether or not he said one thing or another about his party's policy, about gradualism, reformism, etc. I am concerned with Gramsci, that is, as having produced, as being the producer of a certain type of critical consciousness, which I believe is geographical and spatial in its funda-mental coordinates.

1. Gramsci is sensitive to the fact that the world is made up of "ruler and ruled," that there are leaders and led; that nothing in the world is *natural;* and that when it comes to ideas, "they are not spontaneously 'born' in each individual brain."[5] Therefore, everything he writes is based on the presumption that politics and power and collectivity are always involved when culture, ideas, and texts are to be studied and/or

analyzed. More important, this also applies to the writing of texts—such as his own, which are always *situated*.

2. Gramsci is programmatically opposed to two things, from one end to the other of his career: (a) the tendency to homogenize, equalize, mediatize everything, what we can call the temporalizing and homological function by which the whole problem of specificity, locality, and/or identity is reformulated so as to make equivalence; (b) the tendency to see history and society as working according to deterministic laws of economics, sociology, or even of universal philosophy.

3. A great deal of what Gramsci is concerned with is not only the history of an idea or a system of ideas in the world of ruler and ruled, but also the connection between ideas and institutions and classes; and more important, ideas as productions producing not only their coherence and density, but also—and this is where Gramsci is most compelling—their own "aura" (the word is Benjamin's) of legitimacy, authority, self-justification. In other words, Gramsci is interested in ideas and in cultures as specific modes of persistence in what he calls civil society, which is made up of many often discontinuous *areas*.

4. In everything he writes Gramsci is breaking down the vulgar distinction between theory and practice in the interest of a new unity of the two—namely, his notion of concrete intellectual work. Thus everything Gramsci wrote was intended as a contribution to praxis and as a self-justifying theoretical statement: here we can see the consistency of his view in (3) above, that all ideas, all texts, all writings are embedded in actual geographical situations that make them possible, and that in turn make them extend institutionally and temporally. History therefore derives from a discontinuous geography. To a certain extent, and here I speculate, the radically occasional and fragmentary quality of Gramsci's writing is due partially to his work's situational intensity and sensitivity; it is also due to something that Gramsci wanted to preserve, his critical consciousness, which for him, I think, came to mean not being coopted by a system, not in prison, not being coopted even by the system, the history, the density of one's own past writing, rooted positions, vested interests, and so forth. The note, the article in a newspaper, the meditative fragment, the occasional essay, all have their generic constitutive nature going in two opposed directions, so to speak. First, of course, the writings address an immediate problem at hand in all its sit-

uational complexity, as an uneven ensemble of relationships. But second, and going away from the situation out there to the situation of the writer, these occasional disjunctive acts dramatize the physical contingency of the writer himself, that that too is undercut by the momentary nature of his position, that he cannot write for all time, but that he is in a situation compelling him to "prismatic" expression. Gramsci chose these forms then as ways of never finishing his discourse, never completing his utterance for fear that it would compromise his work by giving it the status of a text both to himself and to his readers, by turning his work into a body of *resolved* systematic ideas that would exercise their dominion over him and over his reader.

5. Connected to all this, then, we must remember that most of Gramsci's terminology—hegemony, social territory, ensembles of relationship, intellectuals, civil and political society, emergent and traditional classes, territories, regions, domains, historical blocks—is what I would call a critical and geographical rather than an encyclopedic or totalizingly nominative or systematic terminology. The terms slide over rather than fix on what they talk about; they illuminate and make possible elaborations and connections, rather than holding down, reifying, fetishizing. Most of all, I think Gramsci is interested in using terms for thinking about society and culture as productive activities occurring territorially, rather than as repositories of goods, ideas, traditions, institutions to be incorporated as reconciled correspondences. His terms always depart from oppositions—mind vs matter, rulers vs ruled, theory vs praxis, intellectuals vs workers—which are then contextualized, that is, they remain within contextual control, not the control of some hypostasized, outside force like identity or temporality which supposedly gives them their meaning by incorporating their differences into a larger identity. Like Foucault after him Gramsci is interested in hegemony and power, but it is a much more subtle understanding he has of power than Foucault because it is never abstracted, or even discussed as abstracted from a particular social totality; unlike Foucault's, Gramsci's notion of power is neither occult nor irresistible and finally one-directional. The basic social contest for Gramsci is the one over hegemony, that is, the control of essentially heterogenous, discontinuous, non-identical, and *unequal* geographies of human habitation and effort. There is no redemption

in Gramsci's world, which true to a remarkable Italian tradition of pessimistic materialism (e.g., Vico, Lucretius, Leopardi) is profoundly secular.

What this all does to identity, which you recall is at the core of Hegelian temporality, is to render it unstable and extremely provisional. Gramsci's world is in constant flux, as the mind negotiates the shifting currents of the contest over historical blocks, strata, centers of power, and so on. No wonder then that in the *Prison Notebooks* he spends so much time talking about the different options offered by the war of maneuver and the war of position: an understanding of the historical-social world is so spatially grasped by Gramsci as to highlight the instabilities induced by constant change, movement, volatility. In the final analysis, it is this view that primarily makes it possible for emergent and subaltern classes to arise and appear, given that according to the strictly Hegelian model, the dominant mainstream absorbs dissonance into the problem of change that consolidates the new and reaffirmed identity.

This Gramscian critical consciousness has had very important consequences for literary history and criticism. In the first place it has been far more responsive to the real material texture of socio-political change from the point of view not of what Adorno calls identitarian thought but of fractures and disjunctions that are healed or knitted up temporarily, as a matter of contingency. Take as an instance of this non-identarian viewpoint Raymond Williams's *The Country and the City*. Williams's beginning point is the distinction between two worlds, two geographical entities—urban and rural—whose relationships English literature negotiates, now concentrating on one, now on the other. Thus the tension in romantic literature between rural nature and the emergence of the great industrial metropolis is seen by Williams as going through a remarkable number of changes, from Wordsworth's early expressions of confidence in nature, to his later stress on lonely, dispossessed rural figures (Michael and the Cumberland beggar) to a sense of how the poet of feeling is driven back on himself in order to create from within himself a new abstraction, Man or Humanity; and this movement gives rise to the new green language of country poetry as it is exemplified in Clare principally but also in lesser poets like Bloomfield and Selbourne. On the other hand

Williams's analysis of rural writing is directly related to the emerging complex identity of the modern city, whose "contradictory reality" is composed "of vice and protest, of crime and victimization, of despair and dependence." This is glimpsed of course in Blake and Cobbett, but soon in Dickens, the various so-called industrial novelists, and later, in what Williams marvelously describes as George Eliot's attempts to create in her novels those knowable communities not directly afforded people in the mid- to late-nineteenth century.

In this way then Williams is not a conventional historian of literature, tracking from one period to another with effortless succession. What interests him throughout is the social contest over territory—how estates were acquired so that, for instance, Ben Jonson and Jane Austen each quite differently might write about them. And this will later give rise to the urban businessman, Dombey or Bulstrode, whose activities as powerful impress attests to the presence of a financial or industrial or mercantile form of capitalism. To Williams, quite uniquely among major critics, there is this capacity for seeing literature not as a Whiggish advance in formal and aesthetic awareness, nor as a placid, detached, privileged record of what history wrought and which the institution of literature incorporates with sovereign, almost Olympian prowess, but rather as itself a site of contention within society, in which work, profit, poverty, dispossession, wealth, misery, and happiness are the very materials of the writer's craft, in which the struggle to be clear or to be partisan or detached or committed is in the very nature of the text. Here is Williams on Hardy:

> It is not only that Hardy sees the realities of labouring work, as in Marty South's hands on the spars and Tess in the swede field. It is also that he sees the harshness of economic process, in inheritance, capital, rent and trade, within the continuity of the natural processes and persistently cutting across them. The social process created in this interaction is one of class and separation, as well as of chronic insecurity, as this capitalist farming and dealing takes its course. The profound disturbances that Hardy records cannot then be seen in the sentimental terms of neo-pastoral: the contrast between country and town. The exposed and separated individuals,

whom Hardy puts at the center of his fiction, are only the most developed cases of a general exposure and separation. Yet they are never merely illustrations of this change in a way of life. Each has a dominant personal history, which in psychological terms bears a direct relation to the social character of the change.[6]

Note here the proliferation of spatial terms—the contrast between country and town, the interaction of class and separation, chronic insecurity, the exposed and separated individuals who are instances of a general exposure and separation. All this, Williams goes on a page later, is part of the "difficult mobility" that Hardy, more than most English novelists, tried to render in his work with a success, Williams adds, that centers "his novels in the ordinary processes of life and work" (*The Country and the City*, 211). In his concluding chapters Williams sketches the new geography of high imperialism and decolonization, with their re-figuring of the relationships between peripheries and metropolitan center.

Although one can be critical of his pronounced Anglo-centrism, it has always seemed to me that Williams's great virtue as a critic is that alone of his generation in the United States and Britain he was attuned to the astonishingly productive possibilities of the Gramscian critical consciousness, firmly rooted as that was in the very landscapes, geographies, mobile spaces of a history conceived and interpreted as something more complex and uneven than the Hegelian synthesis had once permitted. I do not mean to say that the various interpretive modes grounded in temporality with which I have, as a form of shorthand, identified with Hegel are to be discarded, or in some way thrown aside. On the contrary, as my enormous interest in and respect for Auerbach testifies, I think it is an absolutely essential thing for us. But what I *do* want to add is that historically the world's geography has changed so definitely as to make it nearly impossible to attempt reconciliations between history and literature without taking account of the new and complex varieties of historical experiences now available to us all in the post-Eurocentric world. Hegel and Auerbach, and of course Lukács, make no secret of their predilection, not to say prejudice, for the centrality of Europe, at the same time that they argue for what they intend as a universal scheme of literary history. But what if the world has changed so drastically as to allow now for almost the first time a new geographical consciousness of a decentered or multiply-centered world, a world no longer sealed within watertight compartments of art of culture or history, but mixed, mixed up, varied, complicated by the new difficult mobility of migrations, the new independent states, the newly emergent and burgeoning cultures? And what if it is now possible for say a specialist in Indian or Arabic literature to look at Western literature not as if the center was Europe, but rather as if his/her optic needed also to include equally India, Egypt, or Syria *and* Europe and America as well? And finally, what if the concept of literature has been expanded beyond texts to the general category of culture to include the mass media and journalism, film, video, rock and folk music, each of which contains its own completely dissonant history of dissent, protest, and resistance, such as the history of student movements, or women's history, or the history of subaltern classes and peoples, the records of whose experience are not to be found in the official chronicles and traditions by means of which the modern state compiles its self-image?

Only an ostrich could possibly ignore the challenges these interruptions open up in the seamless web of an ongoing and calmly unfolding temporal fabric of classical literary history, as for instance rendered in Fredric Jameson's *The Political Unconscious,* which you recall is an effort to synthesize the findings of psychoanalysis, linguistics, and Deleuzian philosophy within a vastly expanded conception of Marxism. I myself do not think that such attempts work, despite the heroism of the endeavor or the brilliance of Jameson's interpretive skills. What he ends up with are beautiful ideal structures, more medieval and scholastic than they are accurate soundings in the turbulence of our time. Neither do the various post-modern theories put forward by J. F. Lyotard and his disciples, with this disdain for the grand historical narratives, their interest in mimicry and weightless pastiche, their unrelenting Eurocentrism.

What then are we to conclude, especially those of us from this part of the world, in Egypt, Arabs for whom the study of European and more particularly English literature has, I still think, a coherence and intellectual validity that should not dissolve in a nativist chorus urging us only to look at our own traditions and ignore all the others. Is there a way for us to understand the connection not simply between history and literature, but between several histories and several literatures? That, I think, is the first step: that even if our focus happens professionally to be English literature, there is no reason why the consideration on critical consciousness which I have been discussing here at length should not be of central concern: do we want to look at English history and literature as forming a closed world whose internal dynamics have gone on undisturbed over eight or nine centuries with no reference to anything but their own resolutely stable and endlessly self-confirming identity? Or rather do we choose to look at English literature and history in the first place as expressing a "difficult mobility" separated and exposed according to the different locales in which the literature actually takes place. Thus the literature of the country house is different from that of the poorhouse, the factory, or the dissenting churches. But not only do we emphasize the differences in locale but we must also, I believe, bring to bear some sense of the counterpoint between England and the overseas territories—including this one—on which its activity, political, commercial, cultural, also impinged. I do not mean, however, studying the image of the Egyptian in British fiction, or looking at travelers in the Middle East, or even Orientalists. Those kinds of study are interesting and important, but they have been done and represent only a beginning approach that is essentially like a first mapping, necessary but not infinitely rich in possibilities. I have in mind two things—although there are several others that one can think of—that strike me as more worth the effort, more likely to make a difference in our overall understanding of the relationship between history and literature.

One is to study the history and literature of England by highlighting, problematizing, emphasizing the outsider's perspective we bring to it by virtue of the fact that we *are* outsiders. In the first place this entails, I believe, stressing not the mainstream but resistance to it as provided not only by the dissenting tradition but by those forces, figures, structures, and forms whose presence derives from outside the establishment mainstream. Two years ago I was particularly impressed by Gaber Asfour's essay in *Alif* on the rhetoric of the oppressed in Arabic literature in which he reads texts for dissimulation, allusion, and oppositional strategies instead of for those affirmations of cultural identity furnished by the establishment, which tends to drive all underground and subversive energies to the margins. As a corollary to this we should try very self-consciously to ask ourselves what a re-thought and re-appropriated canon of English literary history would be like for Arabs: what does growing up and belonging to a great tradition like Arabic specifically prepare us to read and interpret in English literature and history that might not be available to native speakers? I am reminded of Borges's parable "Kafka's Precursors"; each writer creates his own antecedents, he says. What is the English history and literature that leads up not to an English, but to an *Arab* reader? What are the British antecedents for an Arab critic?

Finally, its seems to me that an awareness of history, literature, and geography as I have been discussing them here raises the issue of whether it is culture as the struggle over modernity or over the past that we are struggling to comprehend. Both Lukács and Gramsci saw dissonance and its resolutions as belonging to the present, not to a remote or ideal image of the past. This must also be urgently true for Arabs today, I believe. Modernity *is* crisis, not a finished ideal state seen as the culmination of a majestically plotted history. It is the hallmark of the modern that there are no absolutisms—neither those of power, nor of pure reason, nor of clerical orthodoxy and authority—and in this respect, we must be Arabs engaged with modernity, free of absolutisms.

39

Contra Mundum

A powerful and unsettling book, Eric Hobsbawm's *Age of Extremes* brings to a close the series of historical studies he began in 1962 with *The Age of Revolution: Europe 1789–1848,* and followed in 1975 and 1987 respectively with *The Age of Capital, 1848–1875,* and *The Age of Empire, 1875–1914.* It is difficult to imagine that anyone other than Hobsbawm could have approached—much less achieved—the consistently high level of these volumes: taken together, they represent one of the summits of historical writing in the post-war period. Hobsbawm is cool where others are hot and noisy; he is ironic and dispassionate where others would have been either angry or heedless; he is discriminatingly observant and subtle where on the same ground other historians would have resorted to clichés or to totalistic system. Perhaps the most compelling thing about Hobsbawm's achievement in these four books is the poise he maintains throughout. Neither too innocent nor too knowing and cynical, he restores one's faith in the idea of rational investigation; and in a prose that is as supple and sure as the gait of a brilliant middle-distance runner, he traces the emergence, consolidation, triumph, and eclipse of modernity itself—in particular, the amazing persistence of capitalism (its apologists, practitioners, theoreticians, and opponents) within it.

The four books also record the growth of a world consciousness, both in Hobsbawm himself and in the history he writes. In the 1780s, for example, the inhabited world was known to Europeans only patchily; by the time he gets to the rise of empire a century later, Hobsbawm's subject is Europe's discovery of the rest of the world. Yet the growth of the historian's mind, so to speak, never reduces itself to tiresome self-contemplation. On the contrary, Hobsbawm's solutions to the problems of his own epistemology become part of his quest for knowledge. This emergent global consciousness is at its most memorable in the opening of *The Age of Empire*, where he records the peregrinations of his mother and father—one from Vienna, the other from Britain, both originally from Eastern Europe—and their arrival in Alexandria, which while prosperous, cosmopolitan, and recently occupied by Britain, "also, of course, contained the Arabs." His parents met and married there; Alexandria became Eric's birthplace. This accident of his birth suggests to Hobsbawm that Europe alone can no longer be his subject, any more than his audience can only be academic colleagues. He writes "for all who wish to understand the world and who believe history is important for this purpose," but he does not minimize the fact that as he approaches the present he must deal with that "fuzzy" period he calls "the twilight zone between history and memory; between the past as a generalised record open to relatively dispassionate inspection and the past as a remembered part of, or background to, one's own life."

There is considerable overlap between history and memory in *Age of Extremes*. The period at hand is now Hobsbawm's own lifetime. Although he says that this composite of the public and the private can be understood as the "Short 20th Century" in world-historical terms, the result is necessarily an account that rests on "curiously uneven foundations." The historian is now less a guide than a "participant observer," one who does not, indeed cannot, fully command the historiography of our century. Yet Hobsbawm's disarming admissions of fallibility—he speaks candidly of his ignorance, avowedly controversial views, "casual and patchy" knowledge—do not at all disable *Age of Extremes*, which, as many reviewers have already noted, is a redoubtable work, full of its author's characteristic combination of grandeur and irony, as well as of his wide-ranging scope and insight.

What gives it special appeal is that Hobsbawm himself appears intermittently, a bit player in his own epic. We see him as a fifteen-year-old with his sister on a winter afternoon in Berlin on the day that Hitler becomes Chancellor of Germany. Next he is a partisan in the Spanish Civil War. He is present in Moscow in 1957, "shocked" to see that the embalmed Stalin was "so tiny and yet so all-powerful." He is part of "the attentive and unquestioning multitudes" who listen to Fidel Castro for hours on end. He is a deathbed witness to Oskar Lange's final days, as the celebrated socialist economist confesses that he cannot find an answer to the question: "Was there an alternative to the indiscriminate, brutal, basically unplanned rush forward of the first Five-Year-Plan?" At exactly the time that Crick and Watson were doing their breakthrough work on DNA's structure, Hobsbawm was a Cambridge fellow, "simply unaware" of the importance of what the two men were up to—and in any case, "they saw no point in telling us" about it.

These very occasional glimpses of Hobsbawm the participant lend a special credibility to his account of changes that took place between 1914 and the nineties. One, of course, is that by about 1950 ours had become the most murderous century of all time; this prompts the conclusion that as the century advanced there was "a marked regression in standards" once considered "normal." Torture, murder, and genocide have been officially condoned. To complicate matters, our world is now no longer Eurocentric (even though wealth and power remain essentially Western): the globe is a single unit, a fact already the subject of numerous studies by so-called world system theorists, economists, and historians. But the most drastic transformation of all, Hobsbawm writes, has been "the disintegration of the old patterns of social relationships and with it, incidentally, the snapping of the links between generations, that is to say, between past and present." This gives historians a peculiar relevance since what they do impedes, if it does not altogether prevent, the destruction of the past. Their "business is to remember what others forget." Hence, Hobsbawm says, "my object is to understand and explain *why* things turned out the way they did, and how they hang together."

Three massive blocks constitute his design for this job. Part One, "The Age of Catastrophes," covers the period from World War One through the Second World War to "the end of empires"—that is, the immediate post-war period. Part Two is slightly longer, and is (perhaps ironically) entitled "The Golden Age." It starts with the Cold War, moves through the social, cultural, and economic revolutions of the sixties through to the eighties, glances at the emergence of the Third World, and culminates in a brisk discussion of "real socialism." Part Three, "The Landslide," traces the collapse of most things—the world economy, socialism, the artistic avant-garde—as the story limps to a not particularly cheering conclusion, waiting for the millennium surrounded by poverty and "consumer egoism," all-powerful media, a decline of state power, a rise in ethnic hatred, and an almost total lack of vision. An exhausting and somewhat joyless segment of the trip, this, with Hobsbawm still admirably adroit and rational despite all the catastrophes and declines.

He is at his best identifying and then drawing conclusions from major political and economic trends in the metropolitan West: the rise of socialism and Fascism, life under bureaucratic socialism and advanced capitalism, the fall of the Soviet Union and the end of the Cold War. No one has more chillingly recited the costs of total war and repression than Hobsbawm, and few chroniclers of great power politics have seen them in their folly and waste with a steelier gaze than he. For him the central story of the century is the battle for the hearts and minds of Europeans and (principally North) Americans. He sees the double paradox of capitalism given life by socialism, and of Fascism as belonging not "to an oriental feudalism with an imperial national mission" but "to the era of democracy and the common man." A moment later, as if cautioning against the too rigorous application of his own observation, he remarks that, whereas European Fascism destroyed labor movements, the Latin American fascist élites "they inspired *created* them"; and as anti-Fascism in Europe led to the left, so, too, did anti-colonial movements in Africa and Asia incline to the Western Left, "nursery of anti-imperialist theory."

He is magnificent in charting the progress and indeed the lived texture of socialism, not as theory according to Hegel, Marx, Lukács, or Gramsci, but as a practice dedicated to "universal emancipation, the construction of a better alternative to capitalist society." And it needs pointing out, as he does a moment later, that the devotion and self-sacrifice of individual militants is what kept the thing going, not just the lies and repression of brutally stodgy bureaucracies. "A Russia even more firmly anchored in the past" is how Hobsbawm (unflinchingly) judges "real socialism" as practiced by the Bolsheviks, with "an undergrowth of smaller and larger bureaucrats, on average even less educated and qualified than before." (There isn't enough said, however, about the disappointment later generated in the same committed people, many of whom were mystified by the sudden cancellation of the whole enterprise and the abject and ugly concession to "free market" doctrines that followed.) Hobsbawm's sharp-eyed and demystifying account of the Cold War is similarly trenchant; he writes very effectively of its irrational and gloating lurches, its mindless squandering of resources, its impoverishing rhetoric and ideological corruption, in the United States especially.

His account of the Golden Age in general, to someone a good part of whose life coincides with it, is satisfying and at times very insightful. The descriptions he gives of the rise and progress of the international student movement and of feminism are sober, if only moderately enthusiastic in tone, particularly when he has to keep reminding us that traditional labor—from steel workers to telephone operators—declined in importance, as did the peasantry, which had all but died by the latter third of the century. And there were strange inversions of history as a result: "On city street-corners of Europe small groups of peripatetic Indians from the South American Andes played their melancholy flutes and on the pavements of New York, Paris and Rome black peddlers from West Africa sold trinkets to the natives as the natives' ancestors had done on their trading voyages to the Dark Continent." Or when upper- and middle-class youth start to take on the clothes, music, and language of the urban poor. Strangely absent from this account, however, is the enormous change in popular attitudes to, as well as modes of partaking in, sexuality that begins in the sixties; there is a continuity between this period and the next, in which the new sensibility produced by gays and lesbians, and of course the scourge of AIDS, are central motifs.

Each of Hobsbawm's major claims about periods in world history is provocative and, in the best sense, tendentious. Certainly there is something almost poetically inevitable about the last of his three divisions, "The Landslide": "the history of the twenty years after 1973," he says, "is that of a world which lost its bearings and slid into instability and crisis." What does the slide include? The fall of the Soviet Union and the Eastern European Communist states; the re-division of the world into rich and poor states; the rise of ethnic hatred and xeno-phobic nationalism; guerrilla movements both in the ascendancy and in almost bathetic decline; politics as the art of evasion, and politicians as assuagers rather than leaders; the unprecedented importance of the media as a worldwide force; the rule of transnational corporations; the surprising renaissance of the novel, which in places like Russia, Latin America, and parts of Asia and Africa is an exception to the general eclipse of the major traditional aesthetic genres. Interspersed is a par-ticularly gripping (for the layman at least) chapter on the triumphs and changes in modern science. Hobsbawm gives the best short ac-count of how scientific theory and practice traverse the distance be-tween the laboratory and the marketplace, in the process raising fundamental issues about the future of the human race, now clearly undergoing "a renaissance of barbarism."

His conclusion, laced with understandable fatigue and uncertainty, is scarcely less pessimistic. Most of what he has to say about the *fin de siècle* in his final pages is already perceptible in earlier sections of the book. The general loss of Marxism and of the models for political ac-tion developed in the 1890s is balanced by the bankruptcy of counter-alternatives, principal among them a "theological faith in an economy in which resources were allocated *entirely* by the totally unrestricted market, under conditions of unlimited competition." The worldwide assault on the environment, the population explosion, the collapse of state power, and the appearance of fundamentalist mass movements with "nothing of relevance to say" about the modern world, all these show how "the fate of humanity in the new millennium would depend on the restoration of public authorities." It is clear that Hobsbawm sees little hope in a solution that prolongs either the past or the pres-ent. Both have proved themselves unworthy models.

A very disquieting book this, not only because its conclusions seem so dispiriting but also because, despite one's deep admiration for it as a performance, a muffled quality surfaces here and there in its author's tone, and even at times a sense of self-imposed solemnity that makes it more difficult to read than one would have expected. In part the grandeur of Hobsbawm's project precludes the kind of buoyancy one finds in the brilliantly eccentric earlier books, like *Primitive Rebels* or *Bandits*. For most of the time here he is *so* measured, responsible, serious that the few disputable judgments and questionable facts that turn up in the book seem disproportionately unsettling. Most of them occur in discussions either of the arts or of non-European politics: that is, in areas which he seems to think are mainly derivative and hence inherently less interesting than in the altogether (to him) more important realms of Western politics and economics. At one point he says with quite unmodulated certainty that "the dynamics of the great part of the world's history in the Short 20th Century are derived, not original." He clarifies this by saying something pretty vague about "the élites of non-bourgeois societies" imitating "the model pioneered in the West." The trouble with this, as non-Western historians like the Subaltern Studies group (an influential collective of Indian historians headed by Rangjit Guha, which has been dedicated to the idea that Indian history must be written from the perspective of the real history-makers: the urban masses and the rural poor, not the nationalist élite) have tried to show, is that it leaves out huge gobs of non-élite historical experience which have their own, non-derivative integrity. What about conflicts between nationalist élites and resistant non-élites—in India, China, parts of Africa, the Arab world, Latin America, and the Caribbean? Besides, how can one so easily detach the original from the derivative? As Fanon said, "the entire Third World went into the making of Europe."

It is not just Hobsbawm's occasionally dismissive tone that troubles one but the sense one has of a long-held, quite unexamined decision that in matters non-Western the approved Western authority is to be preferred over less conventional non-Westerners. Hobsbawm registers little awareness that a debate has been raging in Islamic, Chinese, Japanese, African, Indian, and Latin American studies about authority and representation in the writing of history. This debate has often relegated not only traditional authorities but even the questions raised by them to (in my opinion) a well-deserved retirement. In his recent *Nations and Nationalism since 1780* (1990) Hobsbawm expresses an impatience with non-European nationalism which is often quite justified, except that that very impatience also seems to contain a wish not to deal with the political and psychological challenges of that nationalism. I recall with some amusement his characterization there of "Arabian" anti-imperialist nationalism as "the natural high spirits of martial tribes."

Hobsbawm is therefore peculiarly ill-equipped to deal with the rise and ascendancy of "politicised religion," which is surely not, as he implies, an exclusively Muslim phenomenon. The United States and Israel, whose Christians and Jews respectively are in many ways "modern" people, are nonetheless now commanded—or at least deeply affected—by a theologically fervent mentality. The last thing to be said about them, or the Muslims (in the understanding of whose world Hobsbawm is surprisingly banal), is that they "have nothing of relevance to say" about their societies. Barring a few cranks (like the Saudi Arabian cleric who persists in preaching that the world is, and always will be, flat), the contemporary Muslim movements in places like Egypt and Gaza have generally done a better job of providing welfare, health, and pedagogical services to an impoverished populace than has the government. Christian and Jewish fundamentalists also answer to real needs, real anxieties, real problems, which it will not do to brush aside as irrelevant. This blindspot of Hobsbawm's is very surprising. With Terence Ranger, he is a pioneer in the study of "invented tradition," those modern formations that are part fantasy, part political exigency, part power-play. Yet even about this subject, clearly related to the new appearance of religious mass enthusiasm, he observes a mysterious silence in *Age of Extremes*.

The most positive aspect of Hobsbawm's reticence is that it enables his reader to reflect on the problem of historical experience itself. *Age of Extremes* is a magisterial *overview* of twentieth-century history. I accentuate the word "overview" because only rarely does Hobsbawm convey what it was (or is) like to belong, say, to an endangered or truly oppressed class, race, or minority, to a community of artists, to other embattled participants in and makers (as opposed to observers) of a historical moment. Missing from the panorama Hobsbawm presents is the underlying drive or thrust of a particular era. I assume that this is because he thinks impersonal or large-scale forces are more important, but I wonder whether witnesses, militants, activists, partisans, and ordinary people are somehow of less value in the construction of a full-scale history of the twentieth century. I don't know the answer to this, but I tend to trust my own hunch that the view from within, so to speak, needs some reconciling with the overview, some orchestrating and shading.

The absence of these things in turn produces a remarkably jaundiced view of the arts in the twentieth century. First, Hobsbawm seems to believe that economics and politics are determining factors for literature, painting, and music: certainly he has no truck with the idea (which I myself believe in) that the aesthetic is relatively autonomous, that it is not a superstructural phenomenon. Second, he has an almost caricatural view of Western Modernism, which, as far as he is concerned, has not, since 1914, produced an adequate intellectual self-justification, or anything of note, other than Dadaism and Surrealism. Proust apparently counts for nothing after 1914 and neither do Joyce, Mann, Eliot, or Pound. But even if we leave imaginative writers aside—and Hobsbawm's constricting dating system does not help his case—there is good reason to argue that in the arts and disciplines of interpretation, Modernism plays a considerable role. What is Lukács's *History and Class Consciousness* or even Auerbach's *Mimesis* if not Modernist? Or Adorno and Benjamin? And when it comes to trying to understand the often bewildering efflorescence of Post-Modernism, Hobsbawm is stubbornly unhelpful.

The irony here is that both Modernism and Post-Modernism represent crises of historical consciousness: the former a desperate attempt to reconstruct wholeness out of fragments, the latter a deep-seated wish to be rid of history and all its neuroses. In any case the Short 20th Century is, more strikingly and jarringly than any before it, an age of warring interpretations, of competing ideologies, methods, crises. The disciples of Nietzsche, Marx, Freud, the apologists for culture and counter-culture, for tradition, modernity, and consciousness, have filled the air, and indeed space itself, with contestation, diatribe, competing viewpoints; our century has been the age of Newspeak, propaganda, media hype, and advertising. One reason for this—as Gramsci, unmentioned by Hobsbawm, was perhaps the first to appreciate—is the enormous growth in the number and importance of intellectuals, or "mental workers," as they are sometimes called. Well over 60 percent of the GNP in advanced Western societies is now derived from their labor; this has led to what Hobsbawm calls in passing "the age of Benetton," as much the result of advertising and marketing as of the changed modes of production.

In other words, the twentieth century saw, along with the appearance of genocide and total war, a massive transformation of intellectual and cultural terrain. Discussions of narrative moved from the status of story to the hotly debated and fought-over question of the nation and identity. Language, too, was an issue, as was its relationship to reality: its power to make or break facts, to invent whole regions of the world, to essentialize races, continents, cultures. There is therefore something unsatisfyingly unproblematic about Hobsbawm's decision to try to give us facts, figures, and trends shorn not so much of their perspective as of their disputed provenance and making.

Viewed as deliberately standing aside from the interpretative quarrels of the twentieth century, *Age of Extremes* belongs to an earlier, manifestly positivist moment in historiographic practice; its calm, generally unexcited manner takes on an almost elegiac tone as Hobsbawm approaches his melancholy conclusion that history "is no help to prophecy." But as a somewhat younger and far less cautious student of Hobsbawm's other great work, I would still want to ask whether there aren't greater resources of hope in history than the appalling record of our century seems to allow, and whether even the large number of lost causes strewn about does not in fact provide some occasion for a stiffening of will and a sharpening of the cold steel of energetic advocacy. The twentieth century after all is a great age of resistance, and that has not completely been silenced.

40

Bach's Genius, Schumann's Eccentricity, Chopin's Ruthlessness, Rosen's Gift

Charles Rosen's new book is about the group of composers who succeeded the great Viennese Classicists Mozart, Beethoven, and Haydn, and the aesthetic movement they represented. The Post-Classicists emerged for the most part during the period from the death of Beethoven (1827) to the death of Chopin (1849). A substantially expanded version of the Charles Eliot Norton Lectures given at Harvard during 1980-81, *The Romantic Generation,* which follows in the path of its distinguished predecessor *The Classical Style,* is a remarkable amalgam of precise, brilliantly illuminating analysis, audacious generalization, and not always satisfying—but always interesting—synthesis, scattered over more than seven hundred pages of serviceable but occasionally patronizing prose that takes Rosen through a generous amount of mainly instrumental and vocal music at very close range indeed.

What must be said immediately is how well, how enviably well, Rosen knows this music, its secrets, its astonishing harmonic and structural innovations, and the problems and pleasures of its performance: he writes not as a musicologist but as an extremely literate pianist (the book is accompanied by a CD of illustrative extracts played by Rosen) for whom a lifetime of study and public rendition has given the music its very life. Although the book does have its longueurs it is often grippingly, even excitingly, readable. Yet the reader must keep *hearing* the music, since all of Rosen's interesting points relate finally to a revolution of audible effects intended by his three major examples, Chopin, Schumann, and Liszt.

Running through the work is an underlying concentration (*cantus firmus* would be a more appropriate phrase) on the polyphonic genius of Johann Sebastian Bach, and the power of his genius at work in Romantic music that was supposed to be at odds with his learned rigor and fugal mastery. No, it was not, as is often said, Mendelssohn who "discovered" Bach for the nineteenth century, but Chopin, Schumann, Liszt, and before them Beethoven and Mozart, all of whom grew up on the *Well-Tempered Clavier*. Chopin "idolized" Bach; Beethoven was inspired in his third-period works by the preludes and fugues; Liszt and Schumann returned to Bach's work for pointers on how to redistribute piano music contrapuntally in various registers.

Rosen's interest in Bach's presence in Romantic music is an implicit refutation of Glenn Gould's charge that all those composers, like Chopin and Schumann, whose work forms the core of the contemporary pianist's repertoire (which Gould of course both avoided and excoriated) were interested only in *vertical* composition. In perhaps the most interesting section of his book Rosen shows that Chopin—routinely thought of as a swooning, "inspired," small-scale salon composer whose music is basically "effeminate"—is in fact an ingenious contrapuntalist of the most extreme sort, a musician whose affecting surfaces conceal a discipline in planning, polyphony, and sheer harmonic creativity, a composer whose only real rival in the end was someone as different and as grand as Wagner. As Rosen says,

> there is a paradox at the heart of Chopin's style, in its unlikely combination of a rich chromatic web of polyphony, based on a profound experience of J. S. Bach, with a sense of melody and a way of sustaining the melodic line derived directly from Italian opera. The paradox is only apparent and is only felt as

such when one hears the music. The two influences are perfectly synthesized, and they give each other a new kind of power.

According to Rosen, Bach is important in another respect. Although one can analyze the scores of such late contrapuntal masterpieces as the *Art of Fugue* or the *Musical Offering*, it is impossible to hear all the polyphonic effects, which are intended as theoretical, rather than actual, sounds. Eighteenth-century composers like Bach, Mozart, and Handel conceived and annotated their music, Rosen says, to produce "a particular beauty that is only partially related to any imagined performance— an irreducibly inaudible beauty, so to speak." With Beethoven, however, there is an inevitable quality to the sound, which suggests that he "has reached the ideal fusion of conception and realization." But for the Romantics, Schumann in particular, the inaudible, the unplayable, the unimaginable can be incorporated into performance: "it is an essentially Romantic paradox that the primacy of sound in Romantic music should be accompanied, and even announced, by a sonority that is not only unrealizable but unimaginable."

What the core Romantics did therefore was to extend the range of musical composition so as to include not only the inaudible, but also harmonic overtones, new sonorities produced by the pedal, tone color, timbre, register, and spacing, thereby "permanently enlarging the role of sound in the composition of music." At another level their conception of music itself took on new meanings and made possible the invention of distinctive forms influenced by such Romantic literary concerns as the fragment, ruins, and landscape. Precisely because it was imprecise and general (as opposed to discursive language, which was both concrete and exact) music came to be considered the Romantic art par excellence. Rosen makes a number of connections between various Romantic compositions and the ideas of Schlegel, Vico, the physicist Ritter, Senancour, and the traveler and naturalist Ramond de Carbonnières, who in his descriptions of landscapes and glaciers is presented as a major (and completely unknown) anticipator of twentieth-century thought.

There is, alas, a sloppy garrulousness about some of Rosen's exposition: not in his analysis of individual musical pieces, but in his relentless paraphrasing of, and haughty quotation from, intellectual and poetic authorities. All the material will be familiar to readers, say, of M. H. Abrams and Frank Manuel, or, on particular Romantic subjects like ruins, Tom McFarland and others. Rosen rambles on and on, quoting not only translations but even the French and German originals, in displays of erudition that make one extremely impatient. Very rarely are direct inferences drawn from all this cultural background—which is itself unnervingly disconnected from social, economic, and political realities such as the French Revolution, or the advent of industrialization, or the developing interest in economics, as informatively discussed by Albert Hirschmann and Michel Foucault. It is as if, in the best of all possible worlds, Ritter had interesting notions about music and speech, as did Vico, as did Sterne, and Tieck, as finally did Schumann. It is very hard to doubt a community of interest here, but Rosen's method is too casual, too delighted with its own capacity for ferreting out aperçus from diverse writers, for the reader to be left with more than a sense that all those ideas were in the air and somehow made their influence felt in composers' predilections for song cycles, or for the depiction of landscape in their music, or—as Rosen brilliantly shows in the case of Schumann—for the use of fragments as compositional style, giving works like the *Dichterliebe* that sense of half-finished, forlorn desuetude which is uniquely theirs.

Rosen's procedures for the analysis of a cultural period may be too little thought through, too entertained by free-wheeling analogies and "look-at-this" correspondences, too scanting of the immense and very useful scholarship on the material, but they are often stunningly effective for looking at aspects of the Romantic piano and voice literature. He goes much beyond anyone else in revealing the sources of Schumann's amazing eccentricity, which was well-anchored in a whole series of formal practices, and marvelously shows them at work in all the major compositions of the 1830s, the only truly creative decade of Schumann's life. In particular, Rosen does a spectacular job of reading the C major *Fantasie* in terms of Schumann's use of Beethoven's *An die ferne Geliebte,* the great song cycle that bridges his second and late-period styles. No other writer on music has his gift for walking and playing through pieces, pointing out how memory, quotation, observation are given concrete musical realization that extends from the printed score, to the hand on the keyboard, to the pedal, and then is received by the listener's ear.

No wonder then that Rosen can demonstrate that "the song cycle is the most original form created in the first half of the 19th century." And when he shows in detail how such episodic piano works as Schumann's *Davidsbündlertänze* are elaborations of "a musical structure experienced progressively as one moves through it: the disparity of the individual dances reveals the sense of a larger unity only little by little as the series continues," he gets to the heart of a major aesthetic achievement:

> The reappearance of the melancholy second dance is not only a return but more specifically a looking back, as the Romantic travelers delighted to look back to perceive the different appearance of what they had seen before, a meaning altered and transfigured by distance and a new perspective. In Beethoven's instrumental works the return of an initial theme had often been transformed and radically altered by rescoring and rewriting: but in the *Davidsbündlertänze* the *Ländler* [or dance] is apparently unaltered, transformed simply by distance in time and space, by the preceding sonorities, by everything that has taken place since the opening. An age that began with the attempt to realize landscape as music was finally able, in the most radical and eccentric productions of Schumann, to experience music as landscape.

The equation of Schumann's best work with his eccentricity is a matter returned to in the book's final pages. The composer's obsessive sense of detail, Rosen believes, deprived his work of great breadth but made up for it in "hypnotic intensity." I would not myself be so dismissive, not even by implication, of Schumann's symphonies, in particular the superb Second, nor would I scant *Das Paradies und die Peri*, but Rosen's scheme for Schumann is quite inflexible and leaves the chamber music out almost entirely. He argues, for example, that when, after that fruitful decade, Schumann went back to his works to revise them, he always made them worse, not better. By carving out of the oeuvre its most quixotic and certainly its most incandescently eccentric moments Rosen has found a draconian way of dealing with Schumann's peculiar inconsistency of approach and, in the years before his final insanity, the quieting down of his musical ardor. But this is just too schematic and reductive, I think, too impatient with the perceivable outlines of a more various and integrated achievement than Rosen allows.

There are no such intermittences in his account of Chopin: three large chapters on him amounting to two hundred pages are the core of *The Romantic Generation*. Even though there has been some crucial new work on Chopin in the last decade (which Rosen acknowledges), no one has been as disciplined, as well-informed, as discerning, as Rosen, for whom Chopin embodies the paradox of being "the most conservative and most radical composer of his generation." The great thing about these Chopin chapters for a Chopin fanatic like myself is that they can inform and perhaps even change the way he is played. This is particularly true of what Rosen has to say about Chopin's counterpoint (he "was the greatest master of counterpoint since Mozart") and the way an energetic polyphonic strategy that implies three- or four-part writing is at work even in mainly single-line works like the entirely unison, high-velocity last movement of the B flat minor Sonata.

Rosen then proceeds to a truly inspired reading of the Third Ballade in terms of Chopin's adaptation of narrative forms for use in instrumental writing: this allows him to look at the other Ballades as well as the late-period Polonaise-Fantasie and to elucidate them not only according to their amazingly resourceful use of harmonic devices neglected by other composers (the alternation of major and minor modes, the use of related tonalities for coloristic purposes), but also in terms of a heterophony that is as skillful as it is "secret," concealing itself in what may appear to be "soft" or even "sugary" music.

Chopin, Rosen argues extremely persuasively, is in reality not just superbly organized and skilled as few composers have been, but

> ruthless, capable of asking the pianist to try for the unrealizable in delicacy as well as violence. The unrealizable in Chopin, however, is always perfectly imagined as sound. His structures are rarely beautiful or interesting in themselves on paper, as are those of Bach or Mozart (to name his favorite composers): they are conceived for their effect, even if the intended public was a small and very private one in some cases. That is why his long

works have been underestimated: forms like the Third Ballade or the Polonaise-Fantasie appear lopsided on the page. They are justified by performance, although Chopin is among the most difficult of all composers to interpret. His music, never calculated like much of Bach, for solitary meditation, works directly on the nerves of the listener, sometimes by the most delicate and fleeting suggestion, sometimes with an obsessive hammered violence

—as in the concluding pages of the B minor Scherzo.

The theme of Chopin's ruthlessness and "sadism" is developed through a marvelous consideration of the pedagogical techniques embodied (and to some degree derived from Bach) in the *Etudes*. Here as elsewhere Rosen delivers himself of casual observations—on the decline of writing music for the young, on the nature of virtuosity and the pianist's need to bear pain, Chopin's "irony and wit but not a trace of humor"—that sparkle with worldly cleverness and long experience. He is just right, I think, in his account of the Romantic tendency to "morbid intensity," and, in Chopin's case, the ability to transform sentimental clichés of illness or deep, if conventional, feeling into "fierce concentration" rendered more imposing, as in the Nocturnes, "with a profusion of ornamental and contrapuntal detail." A final chapter on what Rosen considers Chopin's "most original and eccentric works"— the Mazurkas—consolidates the main claims for Chopin as "the only composer of his generation who never, after the age of 21, displayed the slightest awkwardness with longer works," or for that matter with short ones. All those features of Chopin's idiom, which include his sources in Polish dance rhythms and Italian opera, as well as his formal and harmonic genius for blurring frontiers between sections, constructing the most inventive thematic transfigurations and returns, are taken by Rosen to constitute a truly distinctive Romantic *style*—the greatest single realization of which is the Barcarolle, a late composition and, in my opinion, Chopin's most magnificent.

It would be difficult to follow the dense, inspired chapters on Chopin with the same level of detail and genuinely turbulent insight, and Rosen doesn't manage it. Not that he isn't full of perspicacious observations on Liszt and Mendelssohn, whom in a backhanded compliment he calls "the inventor of religious Kitsch" in music. (I had always thought of Vivaldi that way!) In fact, he has a great deal to say that is interesting, but the episodic quality of his writing suggests that weariness may have set in. Besides, the categories he has invented for describing Romantic style in Schumann and Chopin seem to have been much harder to apply to others. This is a case of definitions and formulations getting the better of analysis and even taste. Thus the desultory, rather witless chapter on Berlioz, whose work is encapsulated by Rosen in the maddeningly inconsequential one-liner, "it is not Berlioz's oddity but his normality, his ordinariness that makes him great," which produces little more than a series of reluctant admissions that Berlioz may not have been *that* interesting but he could manipulate chord inversions and root positions with surprising skill. It's perhaps relevant that Berlioz was the one member of the Romantic generation who never studied or wrote for the piano; this sets him even further apart for Rosen, who is similarly patronizing about music after 1850.

Except for some unconvincing animadversions on Bellini and Donizetti, both of them composers of a cloying inadequacy, plus a few sound pages on the more gifted Meyerbeer, Rosen doesn't show much interest in Romantic opera: Weber, for instance, isn't mentioned, neither is there much about Rossini's historical music dramas. Early Wagner is left out entirely along with the emergence of the Romantic orchestra, not only in the work of Weber and Berlioz, but also in Mendelssohn (a fleeting reference there) and, more important, Beethoven. Rosen doesn't have to mention everyone and everything— his book is already substantial enough—but it is at the edges and at the beginning of his story that the capriciousness, and the unreflecting closedness of his scheme, make themselves felt. Why, for example, is Beethoven not looked at in his middle and third-period works as an important source of Romanticism rather than a mere indictment of it by virtue of his oeuvre's monumentality? His enabling presence is certainly to be found in Schumann, Mendelssohn, Berlioz, Liszt, and of course Schubert. Only Chopin seems not to have felt his powerful example, but even that resistance highlights the fact that Beethoven was as much a part of Romanticism as in his early period he was of the Classical style.

And in his understandable reluctance to get involved either with the society of which Romanticism was a part, or with cultural theory, Rosen disallows himself insights and concepts exactly where and when in his own argument he might have benefited from them. The Romantic composer's isolation is one of Rosen's themes, yet he does not (at sufficient length) investigate why that isolation should have existed, and the bearing that both the onset of secularism and the end of aristocratic privilege may have had on it.

Rosen is too intelligent not to notice these things (he notes, for example, that Romanticism did not produce religious music, although many composers wrote Requiems), but his rapid allusions simply shut off discussion. Take the extremely vexed question of the relationship between a composer's life and work. He advances the thesis that "the most interesting composers have arranged their lives and their personalities in order to realize their projects and their conceptions most effectively and convincingly," then follows with the unexamined claim that "a purely musical experience is as powerful a sensation as anything outside music." But what is "inside" and "outside" here, and where do lives and personalities end and musical experiences begin? These plonking declarations aren't much of a substitute for a conception, or indeed a theory, of such relationships.

It is hard to disagree completely with the book's summary proposition that Romantic music developed out of an exasperation with rational systems and the Classical hierarchies of genre, but the notion has nowhere near the force contained in Rosen's account of the consequent unpredictability of Romantic composition, of the Romantic attempt "to attain the sublime through the trivial," through the carefully exploited detail, and the eccentric, personal structure. It is the lucidity and resourcefulness of Rosen's remarkably fine analytic examples that will carry readers, not his attempt to legislate general ideas about art and life. On the other hand, the book will certainly change most minds about what Chopin's and Schumann's achievements really were: more important, readers will listen to and play Romantic music with a much more alert understanding than before.

41

Fantasy's Role in the Making of Nations

Late twentieth-century literary criticism is steeped in the hot-house atmosphere of *fin-de-siècle* luxuriance and overabundance. Much, if not all, of this work is of concern to professionals, members of individual schools who engage each other in recondite terminological debates or complicated disputation, too serious and abstract to involve anyone but fellow-acolytes. All of it is urgent, crucial, portentous. Unlike the last *fin de siècle,* wit and playfulness of the sort associated with upper-class dandies fixated on a button-hole or the mysteries of the religious ritual are quite absent. Academic careers rarely admit that sort of play or cultivated whimsy, and today's university departments of literature are staffed with overreachers methodically building careers, critics and scholars whose interest in power, gender, class, race, and the rest appears to transcend the everyday. Most critics who write about criticism belong, whether they like it or not, to Robert Hughes's culture of complaint, although the almost cosmic range of interests gives criticism an air of being too tied up in higher things to have any time for idle complaint.

Thus the Marxist reconfirms Marxism, the deconstructionist deconstruction. One wishes that the whole thing was actually more unsettling, not quite so smug, more likely to get one to forget about one's ideological ties and personal identity in order to think and read differently in novel ways. It is the great virtue of Jacqueline Rose's new book—comprising her 1994 Clarendon Lectures, plus an essay each on Bessie Head and Dorothy Richardson, together with her inaugural lecture at Queen Mary and Westfield College—that in it the reader is bracingly confronted with a genuinely innovative and adventurous style of investigating literary texts. For one, she doesn't give the impression of having written it on a word-processor, pouring out thousands of words with little sweat. Each of her sentences is crafted with a sense of actual experience being articulated in deliberately chosen language. Reading her requires considerable attention to nuance and tone. Although she writes within a recognizable psychoanalytic tradition solidly based in Freud, there is no jargon to get past. Expressions like "trans-generational haunting" occur with some frequency, but they bring clarification and insight, rather than obstacles to understanding or automatic resolution.

For another, Rose's argument is both daring and convincing. The crucial word for her is "fantasy," which is commonly thought of as regressive, in flight from reality, providing what she calls "the dirty tricks of the mind." Rose's point, however, is that fantasy originally arises in Freud's thought during the correspondence with Fleiss, in which the notion is associated with "the question of how subjects tie themselves ethically to each other and enter a socially viable world." Far from fleeing reality, therefore, fantasy, according to Rose, "plays a central, constitutive role in the modern world of states and nations." Moreover, it "always contains a historical reference in so far as it involves, alongside the attempt to arrest the present, a journey through the past." What she consequently tries to do is to connect, or rather maintain, the complex relationship between the State and these ideas of fantasy, reading this troubling, discomposing partnership between the authoritative presence of the institution and the somewhat fugitive but no less informing energies of a "ghostly, fantasmatic" force of imagination, projection, and idealized community, back into a series of modern texts and the political situations from which they derive.

What makes this so apt is that Rose is reacting resourcefully to a set of predicaments (or impasses) in modern critical thought. One is postmodernism, which, she says, in its "vision of free-wheeling identity . . . seems bereft of history and passion." Just so, particularly at a moment when, all over the globe, identities, civilizations, religions, cultures seem more bloodily at odds than ever before. Postmodernism can do nothing to try to understand this. On the other hand, she is also right to say that "identity politics" seems far too caught up in a realism that becomes too private, too soft, and, in the case of identity, too hard, to accommodate the competing solidity of real politics; better the word "state," which "however far it travels . . . always holds its reference to the founding political condition of the modern world." Third, there is nationalism itself, hardly a shrinking violet when it comes to assertiveness and presence, but unwilling in its official narratives to take stock of its own ironies, contradictions, or spiritual demarcations. Insofar as nationalism seems always to intend statehood, Rose uses fantasy as a concept to dismantle the State's major claims for "the total psychic redemption of a people," and, following Freud, to show (in the case of the Jewish people) how "loss, historic deprivation, transmute themselves into necessity, one which soon . . . would entrench itself beyond all negotiable reach." Fourth, there is the secluded quality of much literary attention, for which texts exist in a canon that is removed from anything that seems "foreign" to its national provenance, or that might appear irrelevant to its status as purely literary. Rose chooses writers and texts whose national identity—English, Israeli, South African—tends to be steeped in nationalist fervor, and deftly shows how that is implicated in a whole series of denials, but also in other identities normally thought of as distant.

For her, the principal contest is between stability and fantasy, a basic pattern that shows itself in her hands to be capable of remarkable elaborations, from the literary, to the psychic, the historical, the public, and back again to the private. She is clearly influenced by recent discussion of "imagined communities," though I think she would have benefited a great deal more from Partha Chatterjee's work (both *Nationalist Thought and the Colonial World* and *The Nation and Its Fragments*) than from Benedict Anderson's insubstantial, mostly airy generalizations that try to pass themselves off as theory. More pressing, for her, is the relationship between British and Jewish identities, as the two of them, one settled, the other diasporic, wrestle over her soul. She finds helpful feminist insight also in both Virginia Woolf and Muriel Spark, the former for her "feminized migrancy," the latter for confronting, in *The Mandelbaum Gate,* the challenge of modern statehood, a confrontation already too long deferred. All this comes together in the following passage, which quite remarkably forces the embarrassments of fantasy on to the project of statehood:

> But Israel came into being to bring the migrancy of one people to an end. Uniquely, perhaps, it saw its task as the redemption, not just of that people, but of the horrors of modernity (which is not to ignore the equally strong impulse to give the Jew her play as fully modern citizen). Displacing the Palestinians, it then produced on the spot a new people without statehood, not just by oversight or brutal self-realizing intention, but as if it had symptomatically to engender within its own boundaries the founding condition from which it had fled.

Rose then takes this kind of pattern and begins to trace it in Amos Oz's fiction not simply as writing but as part of a process of laying claim to a land; this in turn allows her to show how territory—that most material and worldly of substances—"can be object and source of its own peculiar form of passion." Some of the thrust of her discussion of Oz is directed against Stanley Fish, who made the fatuous assertion, in a previous set of Clarendon Lectures, that criticism was becoming too political. Rose takes him down by reminding him that claims like his were already political, too enmeshed necessarily in matters over which will, intent, and reason do not easily rule. She reads Oz's novels and his non-fiction as despite themselves revealing "the dangers of certainty," since it is the case that Zionism lays claim to a supposedly barren place and endows it forcibly with meaning and statehood and redemptive status. Far from simply coming down comfortably on the side of dispossession, however, Rose very subtly brings in Palestinian voices—most notably those of Anton Shammas and Raja Shehadeh— to demonstrate the "transgenerational haunting" that occurs when one historical trauma is transmitted and repeated across time, and in unpredictable ways mimes, echoes, counterpoints itself against the confident assertions of the Israeli narrative. A disturbing pattern in Oz's work, she says, is the way he has of undoing "the rhetoric of messianic Israel" by offering a "not less insidious form of apologia for the Israeli state." Thus, the critic's job "is to unpack the points of uncertainty, to follow internally to a single writer the clash of voices pitted, clamouring, against each other in the political world outside." Then she adds with the irony that is latent in this mode of criticism: "But since the terrain and the mind are unsettled, to read in such a way is unlikely to settle the matter."

She is dead set against mechanically substituting one claim for another, however, and in her chapter on Wulf Sachs's *Black Hamlet* she takes the dialectic further by describing the South African psychiatrist's attempt to cross racial lines and identify politically with his black patient, John Chavafambira, even though, as a Jew, Sachs still manages to identify with Israel. Only in the story of Joe Slovo—like Sachs, a Lithuanian Jewish immigrant to South Africa who goes beyond Sachs in openly identifying with black liberation struggle—is there the fulfillment of Sachs's unrealized dream to become "the revolutionary leader of the black people."

The next clarification is Rose's trajectory into Englishness, that political and cultural middle term whose role in both Israel and South Africa is so determining by virtue of its sense of imperial mission. Britain fights the Boers in South Africa and issues the Balfour Declaration that established Israel's first legitimacy. Today, Rose argues, Englishness has been reduced to the mediocre attainments and hollow pretensions of Thatcherite and Majorite Britain. But its former cachet derived from a cultural assumption about what the British identity was at home, and what it should be allowed to be. The line of descent from Matthew Arnold's prescriptions to Kazuo Ishiguro's relentless portrait of the compliant servitor, Stevens, in *The Remains of the Day* is a direct one. The unprotesting butler not only serves Lord Darlington in, as it were, the national interest, but when the Jewish maids are fired and he says nothing, his "muteness marks the spot of what will become the most unspeakable link from British colonialism in Africa to Nazism." We are reminded that Stevens's father, also a butler, had served Darlington's father, and that "the strength [of Ishiguro's novel] is that it is not just Darlington, but a whole class, caste, category of Englishness that is implicated by the novel in the unfolding events."

Weaving together the private and the public, the literary and the political, cultural as well as historical documents, Rose approaches finally the principal ethical question of whether it is possible to speak meaningfully of a "just, lasting, comprehensive settlement" so far as political conflict is concerned. What, in other words, does justice look like, if fantasy is acknowledged as playing an important role in civil life? She is perspicacious in noting at first that each of the novels and writers she has been interested in has had a search for political, moral, historical, even cultural justice as its central concern. The problem, as she sees it, is that demands for justice—after all, the phrase "just, lasting, comprehensive" has been used remorselessly to characterize the current (and deeply flawed) Middle East peace process—demand realization, and preferably realization now. No one whose present misery is acute wants to sit still endlessly for the kind of slow reading, the subtle back-and-forth enacted by Rose as critic and reader, in which fantasy is given its due, allowed to play itself out, even as, of course, injustice is meted out on all sides, in the name of justice. It would be too much to say that Rose succeeds in providing an answer to this quandary; the task is almost super-human in its demands, and in a lecture she can scarcely do more than suggest a few lines of thought. Stripped of desire, for instance, justice becomes tyrannical. Being "good" ends up in a "discouraging chauvinism." Yet opening the demand for justice to the aporias of psychoanalysis in which "the scrutiny of desire" and "the self-perpetuating violence" link the oppressor and the oppressed to each other, is one possibility. But mainly (and here I do not intend a severe criticism) Rose's critical strategy is "to make connections" between the normally disparate realms of states and fantasy, "unavoidable for us all." And in this she succeeds admirably, since there has been very little literary criticism or theory that so convincingly and powerfully makes the connection appear to be so strong and so intellectually and morally attractive.

I would hesitate to suggest that what Rose does so effectively constitutes a method, although it is clear enough that more than most critics she has an extraordinary style. Not the least of her attainments is a kind of worldly confidence, not only in the literary and psychoanalytic materials she handles with such skill, but also in the overall knowledge she has of what it means to inhabit either the South

African worlds of Bessie Head and Wulf Sachs, or the Israeli-Palestinian thicket that ties Amos Oz to Emil Habiby and Raja Shehadeh—a knowledge that is lovingly detailed, sure of its bearings, learned. And these worlds are made more interesting by contrast with their English counterparts. Above all, I think it is her critical intelligence that impresses one the most, not just because it is rare to have a critic accomplish so many fine acts of reading, but also because there is so satisfying a coincidence between her literary attainments and her political consciousness as an intellectual woman with openly declared existential and human affiliations. This isn't a mawkish kind of "personal criticism"—autobiographical meanderings through one's soul—but a capably expressed energy that takes her reader through the moral, cultural, and psychological experiences that matter most to her. That we, too, feel them as important and consequential is a mark of her achievement.

42

On Defiance and Taking Positions

Compared, say, to most African, Asian, and Middle Eastern universities, the American university constitutes a relatively utopian space, where we can actually talk about the boundaries of the academy. In other universities in other parts of the world, of course, the academy is part of the political system and academic appointments are necessarily, very often the case, outright political appointments. This isn't to say, nevertheless, about the American academy that the connections between our world as members of the academy, and the outside world, are not there; they obviously are. The university depends for funding on governments, corporations, foundations, and individuals, and its ties to the larger society are there for us to see and note.

Nevertheless, the first point I want to make is it seems to me that the role of the member of the academy, the teacher, the scholar, the professor, is principally to his or her own field. That is to say, I think that there's no getting away from the fact that, speaking now as a teacher, my principal constituency is made up of my students; and therefore, there is no substitute, no amount of good work on the outside, no amount of involvement, that is a substitute for commitment not only to one's students, but also to the rigors of the discipline in which one finds oneself. Nevertheless, one thing that needs to be observed about this is that there's always the danger of specialization and of what has come to be called professionalization. That is to say, I think that the tendency in the academy to focus upon membership in a guild tends to constrict and limit the critical awareness of the scholar. And this kind of restriction is manifest in a number of things, for example, the use of jargon, specialized language that nobody else can understand. One of my early works—well, perhaps not that early, but it was written, or published, seventeen or eighteen years ago—was a book called *Orientalism,* which took its main subject from the way in which a field, as all fields are, is constituted by its language, though the language itself becomes further and further removed from the experiences and the realities of the subject, in this case the Orient, about which the language was supposed to turn. So the tendency to exclusivist, professionalized, and above all uncritical acceptance of the principal doctrines of one's field is, it seems to me, a great danger within the academy for the professional, for the teacher, for the scholar. And I think, therefore, it's somehow important to balance and maintain a kind of coexistence between the necessities of the field and the discipline of the classroom, on the one hand, and of the special interest that one has in it, on the other, with one's own concerns as a human being, as a citizen in the larger society. For example, I've written a lot about the Middle East, but never in the thirty-six years that I've taught have I ever taught the Middle East. I've always taught Western literature and culture. But necessarily, I think one's work as a scholar is always inflected with one's background, with one's non-academic concern. In my case, for example, it's always been inflected with experiences like exile, like imperialism and the problems of empire, which indeed touch many of the concerns of modern Western literature.

A second point, it seems to me, is to move from the academy to the larger world, and to remind oneself that what we try to—at least what I try to—impart to students isn't so much reverence for authority, or above all for what I say as a teacher (this is, of course, one of the pleasures, prerogatives, if you like, of somebody who teaches in the humanities or let's say the historical sciences, as opposed to the natural sciences), but there is, I think, a terribly important thing that one can teach at the same time that one teaches a field or a subject or a discipline.

That something is a sense of critical awareness, a sense of skepticism, that you don't take what's given to you uncritically. You try to give them the material not with the sense that it's unquestioned and somehow authoritative, but rather to cultivate at the same time what seems to be paradoxically at odds with it, namely, a kind of healthy skepticism for what authorities say. And here it seems to me that clear language and irony are centrally important, not to take refuge—this is something one *can* teach in the classroom—not to take refuge in woolly generalization or jargon or anything that one can hide behind as a way of avoiding a decision and taking a position.

And lastly, connected to this, it seems to me that given the general climate of religious enthusiasm, which I will not call fundamentalism for obvious reasons, it is extraordinarily important in the humanities and the historical sciences to focus on the importance of secularism. Vico's great observation that human beings make their own history, which is central to all the historicizing disciplines, is something that must never be lost sight of.

The third point, then, which has guided me is that as one ventures further outside the academy, it is extraordinarily important to develop a sense not so much of professional vocation, but rather of what I would call intellectual vocation. (And one thing I should say parenthetically is that there are no clear rules for all these things; I mean, there is no manual that tells you how you should behave. There is, of course, history itself, and one's own sense of commitment and principle.) Because the intellectual is not simply a professor, not simply a professional, wrapped in the mantle of authority and special language and special training—which are, of course, terribly important: I'm not trying to put them down. But I think, once you get out of the academy into the larger world, then the intellectual plays a particular role, and this role is essentially—it is perhaps easiest to define it in terms of negatives—an opponent of consensus and orthodoxy, particularly at a moment in our society when the authorities of consensus and orthodoxy are so powerful, and the role of the individual, the voice of the individual, the small voice if you like, of the individual tends not to be heard. So the role of the intellectual is not to consolidate authority, but to understand, interpret, and question it: this is another version of the notion of speaking the truth to power, a point I make in my book

Representations of the Intellectual. I think it is very difficult, once you venture outside of the academy, not to be affected by what seems to me the main issue for the intellectual today, which is human suffering. Indeed, the intellectual vocation essentially is somehow to alleviate human suffering and not to celebrate what in effect does not need celebrating, whether that's the state or the patria or any of these basically triumphalist agents in our society.

To enter into the public sphere means, therefore, not to be afraid of controversy or of taking positions. There's nothing more maddening in our own time than people who say, "Oh no, no, that's controversial; I don't want to do it"; or the habitual trimming refrain, "No, no, I can't sign that because I mean, you know, I may disturb matters and people may think the wrong thing about me." But it seems to me that the entrance into the public sphere means, as the French writer Genet said, that the moment you write something, you are necessarily in the public sphere; you can't pretend that you're writing for yourself anymore. This takes us to issues having to do with the media, namely, public discussion and publication.

Fourth, and I'm just taking very limited examples, it seems to me that one of the major roles today for the intellectual in the public sphere is to function as a kind of public memory; to recall what is forgotten or ignored; to connect and contextualize and to generalize from what appear to be the fixed "truths," let's say in the newspapers or on television, the sound byte, the isolated story, and connect them to the larger processes which might have produced the situation that we're talking about—whether it is the plight of the poor, the current status of U.S. foreign policy, etc. And you understand that what I'm saying is true of intellectuals on the Left or on the Right. It's not a matter of political affiliation, but it's a general, as I say, "public" memory, for which in the generally disconnected and fragmentary public sphere, it falls to the intellectual to make the connections that are otherwise hidden; to provide alternatives for mistaken policies; and to remind an audience, which increasingly thinks in terms of instrumentalization and of what is effective—I mean the great watch word in political language today is pragmatism, *real politik,* all of those kinds of things—to remind the audience of principle, to remind the audience of the moral questions that may be hidden in the clamor and din of the public debate. And finally, as part of this aspect of public memory, to deflate the claims of triumphalism, to remember, as Benjamin says, that history is often written from the point of view of the victor, and that the great procession of victory trails in its wake the forgotten bodies of the vanquished. I think it's important that these kinds of things be part of the role of the intellectual as a public memory in society.

Fifth, it's terribly important since all of us, whether we like it or not, are affiliated with things: we're members of the ACLS, of one or another professional organization; we win awards, which make me deeply suspicious, even the ones that I've won—because I think that the most important thing for the intellectual in the public sphere, beyond the bounds of the academy, is some sort of sense of independence, that you're speaking really with your own voice and from your own sense of conviction, and that you try your best somehow not to collaborate with the centralizing powers of our society. I'm speaking really about this particular moment, when it's very, very easy to join in and become part of those powers, given debates on social policy or foreign policy that are necessarily shaped, to a certain degree, by the government. It strikes me as difficult but necessary to try to be somewhat marginal, rather than to be right in the middle of some office-making policy. It's obviously easy to be a kibitzer and just endlessly make criticisms, but I would say it's almost easier to be in the center of things and to be there passing out judgment. And a more challenging role for the intellectual as I understand him or her, although the intellectual obviously has to be in both places, is to be slightly to one, somewhat distant side of the authorizing and centralizing powers in our society.

And lastly, the sixth point I want to make, is that beyond the boundaries of the academy, there seems to be an absolute necessity to connect oneself, to affiliate oneself, to align oneself with an ongoing process or contest of some sort—the debates over the question of Columbus, the celebrations of Columbus Day or not, the questions raised by Arthur Schlesinger in his book on the disuniting of America, the question of the national history standards. All of these issues require, in the end, not just a little bit of this, a little bit of that, and while I can see, of course, the importance of trying to adjudicate between extreme claims, it doesn't seem to be sufficient for the intellectual just to do that and to keep the discourse simply going; rather, he or she must take a position. And I think there is no better example than one's own example. And so the sense of being part of a process, whether a process of developing a voice, trying to talk about the unheard, or trying to improve the lot of the unfortunate and the oppressed—whatever. There is a sense in being and being also answerable to it, that it isn't just a matter of saying whatever you want without any sense of responsibility or the need to accept criticism and to engage in a debate or a dialogue with this constituency. Of course this also raises the question of what the constituency is. Just to speak from my own experience for a moment, I've always been in this country somebody who is both American and who comes from the Arab world; and I've always felt, especially in recent years, that the sense of really belonging to two cultures or three cultures or different constituencies constantly raises issues that are terribly interesting in and of themselves. I mean, they would give one almost an aesthetic pleasure if one wasn't also victimized by them. How do you address these constituencies? What does it mean actually to *say* something? One example occurred seven or eight years ago at the time of the Salman Rushdie controversy over the *Satanic Verses*. It was important, I felt, for a writer from the Islamic world such as myself to take a position clearly on the side of freedom of expression. But then a few months later I happened to be in the Arab world. I went to Egypt, and there the public position was that the book was banned and was deemed blasphemous. And then I was asked a question about Rushdie at a public gathering, and I was immediately faced with what to do. I mean, do you say a different thing to an audience that's bound to be unsympathetic to your views? Or do you try somehow to maintain the same position but address it, obviously in a different language, to a different constituency? I think the choice was forced on me to take the same position but to try and put it in the language of the place. And that way, I think one of the most exciting things is that you try, then, to create a new constituency. I mean, if an opinion is unpopular, or if something isn't said, then you can try by saying it to create an audience for it where an audience perhaps hadn't existed before.

I conclude by saying that if one tries to follow some of these things outside the academy, unprotected in a sense by it, I think it's likely, particularly if you take seriously the need to stress what is forgotten and what is perhaps unpopular, that popularity and success become moot issues. I don't think you can make a lot of friends that way. And so the whole issue is raised anew as one gets older in life, begins to think about comfortable retirement, and just sort of fading gently into the twilight. But that's very much against my own spirit. I think the proper attitude of the intellectual outside the academy is some sort of defiance. It's very hard to maintain, but I find that it is a source of vitality, and I think, if I may be allowed this final, totally irreverent comment, it is much more important than getting one more award or one more prize.

43

From Silence to Sound and Back Again:
Music, Literature, and History

One of the most effective aspects of Richard Wagner's design for the Bayreuth Festpielhaus is the sunken, completely invisible orchestra pit. His concern was not only to remove a visual distraction for his audience—in every other theater of the time orchestra musicians and conductor were completely visible, interposed as they were rather forcefully, not to say aggressively, between spectators and stage—but also to produce a sound that integrated voices and instruments in a totally unprecedented synthesis. The Bayreuth sound, as it has thereafter been described, is a warm, enveloping, and inclusive one, in which sharp attacks and loud bursts are virtually impossible. Yet to my mind the most magical thing about the Bayreuth sound is how in those operas whose beginning is soft and suggestive, rather than assertive, Wagner enables you to imagine what it must be like to be present at the creation. This is of course especially true of *Das Rheingold, Tristan und Isolde,* and *Parsifal,* music-dramas whose extraordinary intensity is deepened by our apprehension from the first measures that we are entering a special, entirely unique world. The justly celebrated E-flat out of which the Rhine motif develops in *Rheingold* not only gives birth to the system of themes that Wagner develops with systematic force and ingenuity, but also creates a sound-world inhabited by characters and their utterances that is sustained acoustically by orchestra and singers who act according to rules of expression that defy ordinary, or common sense.

Like the characters he created for the *Ring* whose efforts at self-comprehension involve retelling the history of their world, Wagner was much given in his prose works to narrating and renarrating the history of music whose culmination of course he was himself. Not content with letting his music speak for itself, Wagner thus reinforces, buttresses, accompanies his own musical achievement with the story of a purely internal musical development that starts with the Greeks and ends with him. As in Borges's account of Kafka's precursors, Wagner is determined to create his own antecedents from predecessors who seem inevitably to point to him. In the process he also excoriates composers and forms that stood in the way; no one needs to be reminded of his attacks on French and Italian opera, or his uncharitable account of composers like Meyerbeer on whom his own early works depended. But the dialectic of struggle and achievement which is the burden of his recitation required Wagner to counterpose composers with each other, to let one be overcome in his limitations or superseded in achievement by a later one. Thus Haydn, despite his "blithesome freshness" and "a dance ordained by freest fantasy," is limited as Mozart is also by the complete exclusion in their symphonic work of "dramatic pathos." Wagner continues: "so that the most intricate involvements of the thematic motives in a movement could never be explained on the analogy of a dramatic action, but solely by the mazes of an ideal dance, without a suspicion of rhetorical dialectics. Here there is no 'conclusion,' no problem, no solution. Wherefore also these symphonies bear one and all the character of lofty glee."

However inaccurate this somewhat belittling estimate of the two great Viennese composers may have been, it was necessary to Wagner as preparing the way for Beethoven, whom he esteemed as his greatest forerunner. According to Wagner, Beethoven began his career by "opening up the boundless faculty of instrumental music for expressing elemental storm and stress." Nevertheless—and here I summarize an extremely wordy argument filled with totally unverifiable assertions of the kind that Wagner delighted in—nevertheless, even though Beethoven could express every kind of passionate yearning in this tonal language, he could not find contentment and "the endlessness of utterance" which was its logical fulfillment. For that he needed more than pure tones, Wagner says, he needed the word. The metaphor Wagner uses for Beethoven's passage from the purely symphonic world to the new territory charted in his last symphony is that of the artist on the endless sea who, after catching sight of a new world with real men and women in it,

> stanchly . . . threw his anchor out: and this anchor was *the word.* Yet this word was not that arbitrary and senseless cud which the modish singer chews from side to side, as the gristle of his vocal tone; but the necessary, all powerful, and all-uniting word into which the full torrent of the heart's emotions may pour its stream; the steadfast haven for the restless wanderer; the light that lightens up the night of endless yearning: the word that the redeemed world-man cries out aloud from the fulness of the world-heart. This was the word which Beethoven set as crown upon the forehead of his tone creation; and this word was—*"Freude!"* (Rejoice!) . . . And this word will be the language of the *artwork of the future.*

A moment later Wagner even more ecstatically describes the Ninth Symphony as "the redemption of Music," the key to the *universal drama* beyond which "no forward step is possible." One does not have to be a perfect Wagnerite to gather from this that Wagner saw himself as providing the actual universal drama to which Beethoven was only able to adumbrate the skeletal beginning. But that description also quite shrewdly demonstrates how it is that when words are added to music they provide an extremely rich extra dimension, one that appears to sustain itself beyond "the finite *shutting off* of sound." In his predecessors Wagner identified not just a series of distinguished forerunners for himself but more interestingly a common predicament, which is that for all its eloquence and expressivity music is subject to time and to *shutting off,* to silence. To overcome silence, to extend musical expression beyond the final cadence, Beethoven opened up the realm of language whose capacity for explicit human utterance says more on its own than music can. Hence to Wagner the tremendous significance of the eruption of voice and word into the instrumental texture of the Ninth Symphony. What he saw there was a humanized embodiment of language defying the silence of finality and of music itself.

The curious thing about all this is that Wagner focuses exclusively on Beethoven's symphonies. When in 1870 he returned to Beethoven in a centenary study he once again not only bypasses but actually eliminates *Fidelio*, Beethoven's only opera, as important to him. Only the symphonies count for Wagner; in them he seems to have discerned a far more interesting interplay among music, language, and silence than in the one musical and dramatic work that Beethoven wrote and rewrote no fewer than three times. One can only speculate about this lapse, since Wagner was usually an extremely astute, if at times ungenerous, interpreter and philosopher of music. Could it be perhaps that more urgently than the Ninth, *Fidelio* represents and works through precisely that vulnerability to silence and negation that Wagner felt himself (with the Ninth as his antecedent) in the *Ring, Tristan,* and *Parsifal* to have surmounted? Is there something about *Fidelio* that speaks to Wagner's insecurity about his own achievements?

Like Mozart's *Così fan tutte,* to which I believe it is in part a studiously middle-class response, *Fidelio* is a very problematic work. It emerged in the form we see and hear it today in 1814, the result of much agonizing, streamlining, and confusion; so difficult was the process of getting it into acceptable shape that Beethoven always referred to it with exceptional pathos and affection as his favorite child. But a number of things about it are discordant, puzzlingly contradictory. At times, some of its humdrum characters conflict with the elevation and heroism of Leonora and Florestan, her husband. Pizarro, the villainous grandee who has imprisoned Florestan, is monochromatically evil; Ferrando, an emissary of light, is restricted to benevolence and rectitude. Marzelina and Jacquino are Rocco the jailer's daughter and prospective son-in-law; they are minor stock characters of the kind to be found in Beaumarchais. The plot moves from petty intrigue to grand tragedy without a real break. And most puzzlingly Florestan's imprisonment and subsequent release are accomplished, in the case of the former, for unconvincingly obscure reasons, and in the latter, by a deus ex machina that borders on the absurd.

Still *Fidelio*'s overall effect is extremely powerful. It is as if some other, deeper force moves the work and in a subterranean way compels it forward, from the darkness of the prison into the light of day. Its theme is undoubtedly the very constancy and heroism which are the hallmark of Beethoven's middle-period style, and which are premised on the need to celebrate, indeed proclaim jubilantly, the virtuous love of men and women, the victory of light over darkness, and the defeat of injustice and treachery. And yet, *Fidelio* remains problematic, at least in part *because* it ends so triumphantly and noisily. I suspect that what Beethoven could not shake in the opera were traces of a struggle that the sketchy political drama he actually wrote the music for could not compel, could not adequately represent. The clue lies in the first scene of act 2, in which Florestan is discovered in his dark dungeon suffering imprisonment for having once told the truth: "Wahrheit wagt'ich Kühn zu sagen, und die Ketten sind mein Lohn." ("I dared to tell the truth, and chains are my reward.") This infraction and the death sentence he receives are countered by Leonora's heroism on his behalf, whose symbol is the convergence of her rescue (she offers to take the bullet intended for Florestan) with the trumpet call that signals Don Ferrando's arrival.

Florestan is saved, and a few moments later he and all the prisoners are released when Leonora strikes the chains off their wrists. The quickly assembled crowd joins the happy couple and Ferrando in a scene of great rejoicing, which closes in an orgy of C major interplay between soloists and chorus that directly presages the choral movement of the Ninth Symphony (in D major). But the dramatic representation of brotherhood and joy in *Fidelio* exposes, I think, the precariousness of what it is Beethoven is celebrating so vociferously. Florestan's truth is never revealed; the crowd is described as assembled hastily; Leonora and Florestan describe their love as *namenlose*, nameless; and Ferrando's mandate, while providential and benevolent, remains too chancy, too subject to the theatrical machinery that Beethoven engineers so willfully, either to be permanent or a sign that the truth can once again be told without fear of the consequences.

What I am trying to suggest therefore is that on closer examination *Fidelio* is not as assertive and confident as its plot and conclusion—and Beethoven of course—might have wished. The clangorous happiness at the end signifies not so much the return of light but an earnest hope that it might stay a bit longer, that the fickle crowd and the unabashedly opportunistic Rocco might become partisans of truth in the future, and that the great song of joy and togetherness might really prevail. Whereas in fact Beethoven seems to be prolonging this fragile moment of truth (which he is clearly unable to specify) and light as much as he can before the enveloping gloom sets in again, returning Florestan to his darkness, imprisonment, and silence, which have only provisionally been dispelled by the composer's insistent energies. Suddenly this great opera of jubilant certitude appears fraught with considerable doubt. And such doubt also seems to undermine the confident brashness that Wagner discovered in the Choral Symphony and on which he built his own aesthetic. Both Wagner and Beethoven stake their operas on the humanizing effects of drama conceived as rescuing society from the devastations of politics and history. The new man and woman who can sing of love and redemption turn out, however, to be depressingly open in Beethoven's case to vacancy and wishful thinking and in Wagner's case to doubt, evil, cupidity, as well as lonely conspiracy. In this discovery Beethoven seems to have preceded Wagner, who by scanting *Fidelio* can portray himself as being the great pioneer in the entirely positive role struck by the *Ode to Joy,* although of course he continues to venerate the very tormented symphonist on his own terms. No less than Beethoven does in the conclusion to *Fidelio,* Wagner ends the *Ring* cycle with an attempted vindication of redemptive love that is in complete contradiction to the evidence presented in *Rheingold, Walküre, Siegfried,* and *Götterdämmerung* in which love is always mixed with illicit desire, a lust for power, and sheer blind obduracy.

What seems to be going on here is an extraordinary attempt by two great musicians and musical imaginations to forestall the silence, to enhance the staging of creativity and humanistic optimism by pushing back—or rather holding back—the frontiers at which silence threatens its invasion of the stage that their music rules. What I find very moving about these attempts in Beethoven and Wagner is how almost naively they associate life with musical invention, and death, or imprisonment, with silence. It is no accident that both men actually do spend a considerable amount of time dramatizing the underground realm that undermines the shining resoluteness of music and truth: there is Niebelheim in Wagner's case, and Pizarro's dungeon in

Beethoven's. And of course both composers allow us to assume, despite their best intentions, that after the final chords are sounded silence will descend again. In this they are in fact in the same predicament as Shahrazad in the *Thousand and One Nights,* who must continue to tell Shahriar the stories that while away the night and stay the sentence of death imposed on all the king's wives. The continuous sound of the human voice functions as an assurance of the continuity of human life; conversely, silence is associated with death unless, as in the case of Shahrazad, she can prolong life not only by reciting her marvelous tales but also by physically producing a new generation. This she does in the course of her immensely long narration: we learn from the concluding frame that she has had three sons whom she brings to Shahriar as a way of inducing mercy in him. She is successful, and the couple and their children live on happily ever after.

But the fabulous world of the *Arabian Nights,* which is premised on the life-giving attribute of continuous sound, is scarcely that of Beethoven and Wagner, who are involved in a decidedly unfortunate dialectic, without the possibility of permanent redemption and relief. It remained for Thomas Mann's twentieth-century German composer Adrian Leverkühn to finalize the doom implicit in his two forerunners' representation of sound and silence and to declare in the closing pages of *Doktor Faustus* that he was going to "take back" the Ninth Symphony. Leverkühn is a highly allegorized figure—perhaps too allegorical and too highly wrought as a result—who represents post-Reformation Germany, as well as a dominant German culture whose achievement in music, theology, and science or magic seems for many to symbolize the country's disastrous twentieth-century course into National Socialism and self-destruction. Leverkühn's pact with the devil enables him to gain a multidimensional, totally organized and mastered temporality, for which the art of music evolving into Schönberg's dodecaphonic method is the perfect realization. Yet the more successful as an artist Leverkühn becomes, the more humanly disastrous his life. When at Adrian's apogee as a musician his young nephew Echo dies of meningitis, Leverkühn is driven to write a work whose inhumanity, whose cancellation of the human, the good, and the noble, is definitive. The narrator Serenus Zeitblom, a humanist voice whose endless verbal loquacity stands in stark contrast to his friend's increasing concentration of expression, describes the period of Leverkühn's decline into madness and silence as one requiring a *Fidelio* or a Ninth Symphony; and Mann's relentless montage technique superimposed the fate of the composer with Germany's descent into the inarticulate barbarism of World War II.

What Adrian produces instead is *The Lamentations of Doctor Faustus*, "a mammoth variation-piece of lamentation—as such negatively related to the finale of the Ninth Symphony with its variations of exultation." The piece "broadens out in circles, each of which draws the other restlessly after it: movements of large-scale variations, which correspond to the textual units of chapters of a book and in themselves are nothing less than a series of variations. But all of them go back for the theme to a highly plastic, basic figure of notes, which is inspired by a certain passage of the text." In effect then Mann returns sound to its origin in a fertile motif, rather like the ones that Beethoven and Wagner develop so ingeniously and so assertively in their works. Yet in this case Leverkühn's motif for the *Lamentations* is a chromatic row of twelve notes, set to the twelve syllables of "For I die as a good and as a bad Christian." Borrowed of course from Schönberg's system, this device of a basic twelve-note phrase becomes "the basis of all the music— or rather it lies almost as key behind everything and is responsible for the identity of the most varied forms—that identity which exists between the crystalline angelic choir and the hellish yelling in the Apocalypse and which has now become all-embracing: a formal treatment strict to the last degree, which no longer knows anything unthematic, in which the order of the basic material becomes total, and within which the idea of a fugue rather declines into an absurdity, just because there is no longer any free note."

At that point, however, musical language is freed for pure expression: the paradox of Orpheus and Faustus as brothers is at its core, that is, the absolute identity of opposites has occurred, in which Christian and non-Christian merge, and in which sense and nonsense coexist. This explains why echo is employed in Leverkühn's "last and loftiest creation . . . [and] is employed with unspeakably mournful effect." Although readers will find it difficult to imagine such an unheard and unperformed composition, Zeitblom presses on enthusiastically, trying to convey how all the characters of expressivity "have been refined to fundamental types of emotional significance, and crystallized." There is also an effect of immobilization and paralysis since for all its immensely extended articulations the work is riven with an "awful collective silence . . . and dying-away declamations." Zeitblom inevitably returns to recollections of Beethoven's Ninth, so full of energy and joy as a dialectical opposite of Leverkühn's *Lamentations,* which is a "revocation," a summary and final cancellation of humanism.

Nor is this all. Leverkühn's last moments of clarity find him surrounded by a circle of close friends; he has summoned them to his rural Bavarian retreat to hear him speak for the last time in his life, to hear him reveal his compact with the devil, and his descent into perdition. As he declaims what in reality is a résumé of his life, a kind of Shahrazad story in reverse, Adrian weakens considerably, until at last he falls on to his piano, attacking "the keys in a strongly dissonant chord"; "he spread out his arms, bending over the instrument and seeming about to embrace it, when suddenly, as though smitten by a blow, he fell sideways from his seat and to the floor." Never fully conscious again, Leverkühn sinks into a terminal silence at precisely the moment in 1940 at which Germany "was reeling then at the height of her dissolute triumphs, about to gain the whole world by virtue of the one pact she was minded to keep, which she had signed with her blood."

Mann's elaborate fable compresses the decline of sound into the decline of Germany itself. Silence represents not only the end of the humanistic trajectory begun by Beethoven, but also the impossibility of music communicating anything at all except its rigorous internally organized presence and the transfixed mastery of the totally free, totally masterful and yet paralyzed composer. So autonomous has music become with Schönberg (who, translated into words by Adorno, is Mann's reluctant model for Adrian) that it has withdrawn completely from the social dialectic that produced it in the first place. Adorno's account of this negative teleology is found in the densely argued pages of his *Philosophie der Neuen Musik* (1948), an account of Schönberg's epochal significance, and rather mean-spiritedly, of Stravinsky as a kind of forerunner of fascist primitivism. New music symbolizes "the inhumanity of art," which "must triumph over the inhumanity of the world for the sake of the humane." Schönberg's achievement was to have carried music beyond Wagner and even atonality into a new realm of unreconciled intransigence, where melody, rhythm, pitch have transcended

themselves from the pleasant, humane sound of European music before Schönberg into an objectivized set of permutations and counter-
permutations. Unable to say anything at all, new music cannot really be
listened to. By its gnarled constructivism—painstakingly, grimly determined by Schönberg—new music is "the transformation of the composition into nothing more than a mere means for the manufacture of the
pure language of music."

So powerful is music's alienation from society, so difficult and esoteric is its technique, so heedless has it become of anything resembling
an audience, that its reversed course toward silence becomes its raison
d'être, its final cadence:

> It has taken upon itself all the darkness and guilt of the world.
> Its fortune lies in the perception of misfortune; all of its beauty
> is in denying itself the illusion of beauty. No one wishes to be-
> come involved with art—individuals as little as collectives. It
> dies away unheard, without even an echo. If time crystallizes
> around that music which has been heard, revealing its radiant
> quintessence, music which has not been heard falls into empty
> time like an impotent bullet. Modern music spontaneously
> aims towards this last experience, evidenced hourly in mechan-
> ical music. Modern music sees absolute oblivion as its goal. It
> is the surviving message of despair from the shipwrecked.

Mann's final sentences of his account of Leverkühn's last composition
are quite strikingly like this: Zeitblom speaks of the *Lamentations* as
slowly fading, "dying in a pianissimo fermata. Then nothing more: silence and night." Mann gives the whole thing a slightly more positive
dialectical twist than Adorno, for he has Zeitblom remark, "That tone
which vibrates in the silence, which is no longer there, to which only
the spirit hearkens, and which was the voice of mourning, is so no
more. It changes its meaning; it abides as a light in the night."

This, of course, is the classical bourgeois humanist speaking, not
Thomas Mann himself, but whereas Adorno ends his description of
modern music with a severe uncompromising finality that brooks no
palliative—Adorno's own text on Schönberg closes with the extinction
he describes—Mann allows the literary man, Adrian's friend and companion, to transform the silent darkness into "a light in the night." For

Adorno it is the destiny of the new music, which has liberated itself from tonality after Wagner, and since the late Beethoven has in effect been alienated from a consumer, production-driven, and "administered" society, to turn so totally away from sound and reception into silence that it must remain unheard, consigned to "absolute oblivion" so that its resistant, intransigent force can be maintained. Moreover, Adorno took the position that development in new music, which he referred to sarcastically as the phenomenon of "growing old," was strictly speaking impossible. Music had to represent its own self-termination, and consequently its unrelieved silence; any attempt to nurture or coax it into compliance with a society's aesthetic needs has the effect only of cooptation and trivialization.

I have chosen this interrelated series of representations of sound and silence for its rather dramatic coherence, although I have emphasized in it the precariousness and vulnerability to silence, an arc of sound emanating from and then returning to silence, of musical sound. In its instrumental form music is a silent art; it does not speak the denotative language of words, and its mysteriousness is deepened by the fact that it appears to be *saying something*. Verbal representations of musical significance necessarily stress the opposition between sound and nonsound, and in the cases I have been discussing, they try to establish a continuity of sorts between them. Beethoven is a privileged figure for Adorno, who also attaches a great deal of importance to his late phase and what he calls his *spätstil*, as is Schönberg. It is therefore quite possible to see in Beethoven's efforts to induce spoken sound out of music (as in *Fidelio* and the Ninth) something quite similar to Romantic treatments of silence as enabling or making possible the existence of art, more particularly verbal art. Keats's "Ode on a Grecian Urn" opens with an elaborate metaphorical comparison between what is quiet, silent, unheard and what is not, and extends the comparison all through the poem, showing the productiveness of silence and its aesthetic desirability over the poet's sweet but finally inadequate rhyme:

> Thou still unravish'd bride of quietness,
> Thou foster-child of silence and slow time,
> Sylvan historian, who canst thus express
> A flowery tale more sweetly than our rhyme.

By the end of the Ode Keats develops the comparison into a requirement that the actual world of bustle and history be sacrificed to the silence of art:

> What little town by river or sea shore,
> On mountain-built with peaceful citadel,
> Is emptied of this folk, this pious morn?
> And, little town, thy streets for evermore
> Will silent be; and not a soul to tell
> Why thou art desolate, can e'er return.

Having made it into art—the urn as cold and silent pastoral—there can be no return to history for its subjects, although in the next stanza the urn's "silent form, dost tease us out of thought / As doth eternity."

> When old age shall this generation waste,
> Thou shalt remain, in midst of other woe
> Than ours, a friend to man. . . .

Yet in the Ode, art is a mixed thing, neither completely accessible nor completely reassuring. It is cold and remote, yes, but beyond mortality and historical change: "Ah happy, happy boughs! That cannot shed / Your leaves, nor ever bid the spring adieu." And there is something inexhaustible about it, its "happy melodist, unwearied, / Forever piping songs forever new." But there is something strangely, perhaps even mysteriously, unsatisfying about it because, paradoxically, it induces both admiration and pleasure as well as frustration ("That leaves a heart high-sorrowful and cloy'd, / A burning forehead, and a parching tongue") and even pain in the human spectator.

The paradoxes of the Grecian urn tie the work of art to its mortal creator and his world, however great the expense, and however attenuated and finally unspecifiable the pleasures. As an essential component of art, silence symbolizes the difficulty but also the opportunity offered by the realm of the aesthetic. "As for living, our servants will do that for us," said Villiers de l'Isle Adam, a sentiment echoed not only by facile fin-de-siècle dandies, but even by so formidable a figure as

Proust. A work of art, he said, was "un enfant de silence," produced at the expense of everyday intercourse. By the time the American composer John Cage published his book *Silence* in 1961, a considerable devaluation of the privileges of art had taken place such that silence and sound were interchangeable. It was partly Cage's own insurrectionary nature, I suppose, and partly that with the end of World War II—precisely the moment so theatrically represented by Adorno and Mann—all the old classifications, class prerogatives, hierarchies, and traditions of European music had to be scuttled. Cage speaks ebulliently about freedom from "the concept of a fundamental tone," by which he meant of course the tonal system central each in his own way to Beethoven, Wagner, and Schönberg. What the American newcomer welcomed was an age of experimentation in which the production and organization of sound and silence, something and nothing, as he called them, was made experimental, open, limitlessly possible.

Cage saw this as a turning toward nature, away from the musical past, a fearless willingness to admit a new alternative: that art and nature are not opposed, and that sound depends not on what is intended but on what is unintended. Here is how he puts it in a passage from *Silence:*

> But this fearlessness only follows if, at the parting of the ways, where it is realized that sounds occur whether intended or not, one turns in the direction of those he does not intend. This turning is psychological and seems at first to be a giving up of everything that belongs to humanity—for a musician, the giving up of music. This psychological turning leads to the world of nature, where, gradually or suddenly, one sees that humanity and nature, not separate, are in this world together; that nothing was lost when everything was given away. In fact, everything is gained. In musical terms, any sounds may occur in any combination and in any continuity.

Cage's perception is of an order of coexistence, and indeterminacy. There is no opposition between music and silence, nor between art and the unintended. For much of the 1940s and 1950s Cage experimented with all kinds of sound-making equipment—prepared pianos, tape recordings, radio, natural sounds—and a dazzling array of combinatorial techniques, from jazz and zen, to the *Book of Changes* and mathematics. One of his most celebrated works was entitled *4'33", tacit for any inst/insts.;* in some performances it consisted of a pianist coming on stage and sitting absolutely silent at the piano for four minutes and thirty-three seconds. Later works were even less determinate. In 1962 he wrote and performed a composition entitled *o'o* "which involved slicing vegetables, mixing them in a blender, and then drinking the juice."

An appreciable part of Cage's work included an ingenious series of notational innovations whereby graphics, mathematically derived series, and randomly written pages to be used as performers saw fit (*Concert for Piano and Orchestra,* 1958) were employed by Cage virtually to explode the authority of the text, *his* text in particular. I spent a year with Cage in 1967–68 when we were both Fellows at the Institute for Advanced Studies at the University of Illinois. He was a puckish, amusing figure who told me once that he detested, indeed could never listen to, Mozart and Beethoven, but was passionate about Satie and Varèse, the former because he openly mocked classical music, the latter because he "more clearly and actively than anyone else of his generation established the present nature of music. This nature does not arise from pitch relations (consonance-dissonance) nor from twelve tones nor seven plus five (Schönberg-Stravinsky), but arises from an acceptance of all audible phenomena as material proper to music." During that year Cage seemed as interested in collecting mushrooms as he was in music. All of us were supposed to do something like give a lecture or seminar during our year: Cage put on a "performance" in a barn with eight or nine cows, fifteen tape recorders, a mime troupe, miscellaneous instrumentalists scattered all over the structure, and a whole battery of lights and other sounds blaring through dozens of speakers. You walked through for a few minutes if you could stand the din, and then walked out.

Cage's anarchic sense of humor was put to the service of an anti-aesthetic: the idea was to free music from the authoritarianism of Wagner and Schönberg, and to put silence on an equal footing with sound. Banished were Beethoven's anxiety about sustaining music against an enveloping silence, and Webern's refined coerciveness that, according to Adorno, tried "to force the twelve tone technique to speak

. . . his effort to lure, from the alienated, rigidified material of the rows, that ultimate secret which the alienated subject is no longer able to impart to the rows." Instead a space of happy and unanxious freedom was opened up, admitting to it any sound, however randomly produced or encountered, on a par with silence. Cage's idea could only have been generated in America: his relationship with Boulez foundered on the French composer's unwillingness to give up the idea of formal control in the composition of music. As Jean-Jacques Nattiez points out in his introduction to the Boulez-Cage correspondence, the two men differed on the idea of *chance*, which for Cage meant a freewheeling indeterminacy that cheerfully mixed nature, history, politics, "with aesthetic and musical criteria," and for Boulez meant using the aleatory as a way of upsetting stereotypes, but by no means of ceding control of "the mechanism of total serialism."

But it must be remembered that this great debate between musical sound and silence takes place on a stage in which the traffic between one and the other is assumed to originate ontologically, without regard for the historical conditions that make the relationship between sounds and silences possible. Beethoven's Florestan is incarcerated because he spoke an unacceptable truth: we are to suppose, then, that he was once able to speak the truth, and then he was buried in a silent dungeon for having done so. His predicament highlights a more radical one, the case of someone already invisible and unable to speak at all for political reasons, someone who has been silenced because what he or she might represent is a scandal that undermines existing institutions.

There is above all the scandal of a different language, then a different race and identity, a different history and tradition: what this results in is either the suppression of difference into complete invisibility and silence, or its transformation into acceptable, but diametrically opposite, identity. This has a remarkably powerful effect on our understanding and writing of history in which the past is not (and never can be) immediately accessible. The Freudian model for repression is an early instance of the mechanism, although its antecedents—as Freud never tired of showing—are poetic and philosophic. Nietzsche's description of an independent yet largely subterranean Dionysian component given luminous articulation, and distortion, in tragedy is one. Another is to be found in the character of Hamlet, who cannot speak of what it is that drives him, and it is found more interestingly in Ophelia, who begins to be deranged under the pressure of what she has seen, and can no longer speak of: "T'have seen what I have seen, see what I see!" Thus is she "Divided from herself and her fair judgement, / Without the which we are pictures, or mere beasts." Or there is Iago, who having destroyed Othello is shut up back in himself, defying the injunction to speak and explain: "Demand me nothing; What you know, you know: / From this time forth I never will speak word."

Foucault's work from *Histoire de la folie* through *Les Mots et les choses,* *L'Archeologie du savoir,* and *Surveiller et punir* constitutes a set of brilliant explorations of how the historical bases of epistemology either enable, or block, the making of utterances, *enoncés.* Statements traverse the distance between silence and regulated verbal assertion. In Foucault, one can never accede to complete speech or full utterance, or to complete silence, since as students of texts we deal only with language and its representations. Utterance is governed by rules of formation which are difficult to learn, yet impossible to evade; nevertheless, what Foucault called *discourse,* which is the regulated production, exchange, and circulation of utterances (what his English translators render as *statement*), takes on and acquires the appearance of a social authority so complete as to legislate the practice of saying what there is to say, exactly and fully. What is excluded is unthinkable, in the first place, illegal and unacceptable in the second. In his study of the birth of the prison Foucault finds himself explicating what he calls the disciplinary society, in which behavior is regulated by a microphysics of power, whose embodiment he finds in Bentham's Panopticon. The silence of delinquent behavior is made to speak, to expose itself, to order itself before the watchful eye of a silent authoritarian observer, who cannot be seen and is rarely heard to speak: silence and indeed resistance to disciplinary power are gradually eliminated.

Foucault's determinism is partially the result of a kind of political hopelessness which he renders in that extraordinarily heightened style of his as the sadism of an always victorious logic. What it communicates is terminal solitude: no individual can escape it as he—Foucault's subjects are always male—finds himself bound tighter and tighter in a discourse whose aims are to leave nothing unsaid and to leave no one able to make connections except through it, its rules, its habits of confinement, its style of order. For Foucault then the banishment of silence and with it, the sovereignty of statement, amount only to a discipline that is enforced continuously, interminably, monotonously. What puzzles me is not only how someone as remarkably brilliant as Foucault *could* have arrived at so impoverished and masochistically informed a vision of sound and silence, but also how so many readers in Europe and the United States have routinely accepted it as anything more than an intensely private, deeply eccentric, and insular version of history.

This is not to say, of course, that dominance in history is unsustainable: of course it is, but it is far from being the only point of view, or the only history. There has always been a contest, as Benjamin says, between victor and vanquished; history tends to be written from the point of view of the victor. But one of the hallmarks of modern historical consciousness is its interest in what Gramsci called the phenomenon of the subaltern, those whose struggle against the dominant mode has hitherto either been confined to silence or misrepresented in the confident accents of the directive classes. What has made such a work as E. P. Thompson's *Making of the English Working Class* so powerful is that despite that class's defeat, its efforts, its culture, its hidden narratives can be coaxed into eloquence by a historian able to seek them out. Thompson's point, of course, is that the working class was not finally repressed at all because its history was so integral a part of the British history whose academic and historiographical patrons had hitherto scanted it.

After Thompson, however, silence in history becomes even more constitutive to historians of subalternity, and paradoxically more the central subject of the historian's quest. This is particularly true in the case of postcolonial scholars whose affiliation with movements, revolutions, classes, and indeed whole peoples condemned to silence in the regimes of authority and power that misrepresented or dehumanized or simply ignored their validity fuels the new style of writing about them. The hallmark of this historical awakening is Aimé Césaire's great *Discours sur le colonialisme,* whose powerful ringing tones sound a note of sustained rebellious disaffection as

Césaire parades before his reader's ears the racist pronouncements of respectable scholars, intellectuals, thinkers like Renan, Jules Romain, Mannoni, all of whom speak of primitive, irrational, violent, uncultured nonwhites. The point of Césaire's *Discours* is not so much to reveal the silence of these colonized peoples but to shatter their wall-to-wall description, leaving a new space to be filled by peoples who can speak for themselves at last.

Yet for more recent postcolonial historians there is still the fact of colonial silence to be dealt with, not as something that can be filled or animated directly but as something that can only be recovered or adumbrated negatively and deconstructively. Consider Ranajit Guha, founder of the Subaltern Studies group of historians, in his essay "The Prose of Counter-Insurgency." Indian history, he says, was made not by the nationalist elites who were activated and remained in thrall to the colonialist ethos, but by the urban poor and the peasantry whose voices are silent, covered over by a nationalist historiography that has virtually eliminated them. How then to restore the role of these subalterns who have left behind no documents or record? Guha proceeds to analyze a series of nineteenth-century insurgencies, uprisings as they were called, whose profile is available only through what he calls primary, secondary, and tertiary discourses whose effect is on the one hand to silence the content of the actual revolt or on the other to assimilate them to various explanations that eliminate their force as rebellions:

> Historiography has been content to deal with the peasant rebel merely as an empirical person or member of a class, but not as an entity whose will and reason constituted the praxis called rebellion. The omission is indeed dyed into most narratives by metaphors assimilating peasant revolts to natural phenomena: they break out like thunder storms, heave like earthquakes, spread like wildfires, infect like epidemics. In other words, when the proverbial clod of earth turns, this is a matter to be explained in terms of natural history. Even when this historiography is pushed to the point of producing an explanation in rather more human terms it will do so by assuming an identity of nature and culture, a hall-mark, presumably, of a very low

state of civilization and exemplified in "those periodical out-
bursts of crime and lawlessness to which all wild tribes are subject," as the first historian of the Chuar rebellion put it.

He then proceeds to a formal examination of the discourses in whose
interstices we might be able to perceive the rebellious, if still silent natives:

> How did historiography come to acquire this particular blind
> spot and never find a cure? For an answer one could start by
> having a close look at its constituting elements and examine
> those cuts, seams and stitches—those cobbling marks—which
> tell us about the material it is made of and the manner of its
> absorption into the fabric of writing.
>
> The corpus of historical writings on peasant insurgency in
> colonial India is made up of three types of discourse. These may
> be described as *primary, secondary,* and *tertiary* according to the
> order of their appearance in time and their filiation. Each of
> these is differentiated from the other two by the degree of its
> formal and/or acknowledged (as opposed to real and/or tacit)
> identification with an official point of view, by the measure of
> its distance from the event to which it refers, and by the ratio of
> the distributive and integrative components in its narrative.

Guha is no less critical of official nationalism, the plenitude of
whose discourse simply swallows up everything into the Ideal
Consciousness of the Nation, which he rejects as an equal misrepresentation. The practice of subaltern history itself—difficult, rigorous,
unsparing in its ironies and its methods—maintains and yet also interprets the silence. This is also the method used by the Haitian historian Michel-Rolph Trouillot in his book *Silencing the Past: Power and the
Production of History,* a set of essays about the great Haitian slave rebellion that began in 1791 in Saint-Domingue and ended with the declaration of an independent republic in 1804. Trouillot argues that so
unusual, unexpected, and shattering were the effects of the rebellion
that it was virtually unthinkable for Europeans. Subsequent historians
wrote according to what Trouillot calls guild practices, which silenced
the rebellion's eruptive force. And, he continues, the silences continue:

Amazing in this story is the extent to which historians have treated the events of Saint-Domingue in ways quite similar to the reactions of its Western contemporaries. That is, the narratives they build around these facts are strikingly similar to the narratives produced by individuals who thought that such a revolution was impossible.

The net effect of this is maintaining what he calls "the fixity of the past," in which history is reified and solidified into an inaccessible and finally irrecoverable distance which communicates itself to us as silence. Although he does not mention *Heart of Darkness,* Conrad's great literary work is that silence's purest model. Marlow's narrative, indeed Marlow's voice, is all we have as the tale unfolds. Not only are the Africans in the tale limited to indecipherable sound and one or two bursts of substandard speech, but even the commanding figure of Kurtz is forever silenced by the nurturing, reassuringly enigmatic sound of Marlow's narrative. "We live," he says, "as we dream, alone." Silence is transmuted into distance.

But better *that* silence than the hijacking of language which is the dominant note of our age. Postcolonialism has also resulted in the realization of militant nationalism and of nation-states in which dictators and local tyrants speak the language of self-determination and liberation although they are in fact the embodiments of neither one nor the other. There are then the alternatives either of silence, exile, cunning, withdrawal into self and solitude, or more to my liking, though deeply flawed and perhaps too marginalized, that of the intellectual whose vocation it is to speak the truth to power, to reject the official discourse of orthodoxy and authority, and to exist through irony and skepticism, mixed in with the languages of the media, government, and dissent, trying to articulate the silent testimony of lived suffering and stifled experience. There is no sound, no articulation that is adequate to what injustice and power inflict on the poor, the disadvantaged, and the disinherited. But there are approximations to it, not representations of it, which have the effect of punctuating discourse with disenchantment and demystifications. To have *that* opportunity is at least something.

44

On Lost Causes

The phrase "a lost cause" appears with some frequency in political and social commentary: in recent accounts of the Bosnian agony, for example, the British writer Jeremy Harding uses the phrase in passing, as he refers to "the lost cause of Bosnian nationalism" in connection with an analysis of British politics. A lost cause is associated in the mind and in practice with a hopeless cause: that is, something you support or believe in that can no longer be believed in except as something without hope of achievement. The time for conviction and belief has passed, the cause no longer seems to contain any validity or promise, although it may once have possessed both. But are timeliness and conviction only matters of interpretation and feeling or do they derive from an objective situation? That, I think, is the crucial question. Many times we feel that the time is not right for a belief in the cause of native people's rights in Hawaii, or of gypsies or Australian aborigines, but that in the future, and given the right circumstances, the time may return, and the cause may revive. If, however, one is a strict determinist about the survival only of powerful nations and peoples, then the cause of native rights in Hawaii, or of gypsies or aborigines, is always necessarily a lost cause, something both predestined to lose out and, because of belief in the overall narrative of power, required to lose.

But there is no getting round the fact that for a cause to seem or feel lost is the result of judgment, and this judgment entails either a loss of conviction or, if the sense of loss stimulates a new sense of hope and promise, a feeling that the time for it is not right, has passed, is over. Even a phrase like "a born loser" attaches to a person not because of something inherent in that person—which cannot be known anyway—but because a series of events results in the judgment. Narrative plays a central role here. When we say that Jim is a born loser, the phrase is pronounced after Jim's sorry record is presented: he was born to poor parents, they were divorced, he lived in foster homes, he was lured into a life of crime at an early age, and so forth. A loser's narrative is implicitly contrasted with the story of someone who either surmounted all the obstacles (triumph in adversity) or was born in favorable circumstances, developed brilliantly, and won the Nobel Prize in chemistry or physics. When the cause for something is associated with the narrative of a nation or a person, we also employ narrative to present the evidence *seriatim,* and then we make the judgment.

Two other factors need to be stressed: one is the *time* of making the judgment, which usually occurs at an important juncture in the individual's life. I may be about to embark on my sixth marriage, and I have to decide whether I am unfit for wedded life or whether the institution of marriage itself is a lost cause, one that is so hopelessly inconvenient and complicated as never to result even in minimal success. Similarly, one can imagine a great tennis player like John McEnroe at the beginning of the Grand Slam season, trying to decide whether another year of tournaments, an aging body, and a whole crop of new and hungry young players are likely to turn his campaign for more tournament victories into a lost cause. That predicament is more commonly encountered in the life of an individual as he or she nears the end of life, perhaps as the result of serious illness or a failure of capacity or energy due to age. Feeling that one's life is a lost cause as the possibility for cure or continued productivity appears more and more remote is one such instance: giving up on life, becoming withdrawn and dejected, and committing suicide are alternatives when the going gets rough and when we ask ourselves the question can I go on or is it hopeless, hence only despair is the answer. In these instances a cause is not momentous and public, like the survival of a nation or the struggle for national independence, but the sense of urgency may be greater and the stakes may appear to be higher. We are at the point now where genetics may soon make it possible to predict that a person is going to get Alzheimer's or a virulent form of cancer: the bioethical question is whether in the absence of known cures to inform that person that he or she is doomed or to withhold information as a charitable form of letting things be.

The second factor is who makes the judgment, the believer or someone who stands outside the cause, perhaps an active opponent, a professional historian, philosopher, or social scientist, an indifferent onlooker? In the world of political causes a common psychological strategy is for opponents to try to undermine confidence in the cause that opposes them; a battle of wills ensues in which one side attempts to pile up one achievement or "actual fact" after another in the hope of discouraging people on the other side, demonstrating to them that they can have no hope of winning. In such a situation "hearts and minds" have to be won, or must be lost. Antonio Gramsci's political theory of the struggle for hegemony gave this contest a central place in modern politics and explains the motto (taken from Romain Rolland) that he affixed to his journal *L'Ordine nuovo*: "pessimism of the intelligence, optimism of the will." Yet no matter how fraught a situation is, it remains for the person whose cause it is to make the final determination, to keep the initiative, retain the prerogative.

Beginnings, endings, middles—these are the narrative periods or termini at which judgments of victory, success, failure, final loss, hopelessness are made. What I find particularly interesting for my purposes here is the interplay between the private and the public, between what appears to be the intensely subjective and overwhelmingly objective, between the emotional, intensely "gut" feeling and the portentously historical judgment, all of which are entailed in thinking about lost causes. Although we can use the phrase loosely to describe a highly circumscribed personal situation—as in "getting John to give up smoking is a lost cause"—I shall confine myself to situations in which the individual is representative of a more general condition. The word "cause," after all, acquires its force and hearing from the sense we have that a cause is more than the individual; it has the significance of a project, quest, and effort that stand outside individuals and compel their energies, focus their efforts, inspire dedication. Serving the Grail is a cause; acquiring a new car or suit is not. A cause is not often exhausted by the people who serve it, whereas individuals can exhaust themselves in a cause, which is most normally characterized as ahead of one, something greater and nobler than oneself for which great striving and sacrifice are necessary. Alfred Tennyson's "Ulysses" catches this in its last, syntactically very awkward, lines; the aging hero reflects here on the persistence of his will in the service of a cause.

> We are not now and tho' that strength which in old days
> Moved earth and heaven, that which we are, we are—
> One equal temper of heroic hearts,
> Made weak by time and fate, but strong in will
> To strive, to seek, to find and not to yield.

So much of early education in school or family is informed by the need to make young people aware that life is more than self-satisfaction and doing as one likes. Every culture that I know of emphasizes explicitly as well as implicitly the idea that there is more to life than doing well: the "higher things" for which everyone is taught to strive are loyalty to the cause of nation, service to others, service to God, family, and tradition. All are components of the national identity. To rise in the world, that motif of self-help and personal betterment, is routinely attached to the good of the community and the improvement of one's people. As a child growing up in two British colonies and attending colonial schools during the dying days of the empire, I was soon made conscious of the internal contradiction in the stated, albeit divided, program of my education: on the one hand, I was a member of an elite class being educated to serve the cause of my people, to help raise them up and into the privileges of independence, and, on the other, I was not being educated in Arab but in British or European culture, the better to advance the cause of that alien yet more advanced and modern culture, to become intellectually more attached to it than to my own.

After independence the reemergence of euphoric nationalism, with its pantheon of founding fathers, texts, events strung together in a triumphalist story and contained in newly Arabized institutions, reached out and incorporated my generation. The new cause was Arabism itself, al-'urûbah; this came gradually to include the notion of a military-security state, the centrality of a strong army in national development, the idea of a one-party collective leadership (which favored the ideology of the great leader), a deeply critical, perhaps even paranoid suspicion of and obsession with the West as the source of most problems, and, so far as Israel was concerned, hostility combined with a will neither to know nor to have anything to do with the new society and its people. I mention these early causes not so much only as a way of criticizing them—they seemed inevitable at the time, for reasons I do not have the time to go into here—but as a way of marking the distance intellectual elites have traveled since. Today Arabism is supposed to be virtually dead, its place taken by a host of smaller, less causelike nationalisms; Arab leaders are largely drawn from unpopular and isolated minorities and oligarchies, and although there may be a residual anti-Western rhetoric in public discourse, both the state and its institutions have largely now been willingly incorporated into the American sphere. The emergence of an Islamic counter-discourse during the past two decades is due, I think, to the absence of a militant, secular, and independent political vision; hence reversion and regression, the desire to establish an Islamic state with its supposed roots in seventh-century Hijaz.

Another marker of how different things have become is supplied once we contrast Abdel Nasser (the twenty-fifth anniversary of whose death has just been very modestly observed in Egypt and elsewhere) with his arch-rivals King Hussein of the Hashemites and the reigning king of Saudi Arabia. Nasser was a family man, wildly popular, modest, personally incorruptible, culturally a representative of most average Egyptian Sunni Muslims with no property or class privileges to speak of; his rivals (who have outlived him by a quarter of a century) were heads of clans whose names, Hashemites and al-Saud, have been given to the countries they rule. They have come to represent both a feudal conception of rule and fealty to the United States. One of Nasser's most representative and unprecedented acts was to offer to resign on June 9, 1967, after his army's defeat by Israel: this is an unimaginable gesture for any Arab ruler to make today. In any event, it is difficult to discern the presence of a general cause like Arabism in today's Arab world, except for that of Islam. I shall return to this general subject a little later.

The passage from inculcated enthusiasm for higher causes in the young to the disillusionment of age is nevertheless not restricted to modern Middle Eastern history. The aesthetic form of this trajectory is the great realistic novel, one of whose most typical instances is Gustave Flaubert's *Education sentimentale*. Young Frederic Moreau comes to Paris with the ambitions of a provincial youth, determined to succeed in various vocations and causes. He and his friend Deslauriers entertain ideas of becoming prominent literary, intellectual, and political figures, Frederic as the Walter Scott of France, later as its greatest lawyer; Deslauriers has plans to preside over a vast metaphysical system, then to become an important politician. The events of the novel take place during the heady days of the 1848 revolution in Paris, in which upstarts, frauds, opportunists, bohemians, prostitutes, merchants, and, it appears, only one honest man, a humble idealistic worker, jostle each other in an unceasing whirl of dances, horse-races, insurrections, mob-scenes, auctions, and parties.

By the end of the novel the revolution and France have been betrayed (Napoleon III, the cunning nephew of his magnificent imperial uncle, has taken over France) and the two young men have achieved none of their ambitions at all. Frederic "travelled. He came to know the melancholy of the steamboat, the cold awakening in the tent, the tedium of landscapes and ruins, the bitterness of interrupted friendships. He returned. He went into society and he had other loves. . . . His intellectual ambitions had also dwindled. Years went by; and he endured the idleness of his mind and the inertia of his heart" (411). Not a single cause is left. Frederic is visited by a woman he had once loved; he is filled with desire for her, yet restrained by the fear that he might feel disgusted later. He does nothing: *et ce fut tout*, Flaubert says. Deslauriers wanders from job to job and is dismissed from his one chance to serve his country. "After that," Flaubert says, "he had been director of colonization in Algeria, secretary to a pasha, manager of a newspaper, and an advertising agent; and at present he was employed as solicitor to an industrial company" (416).

In his *Theory of the Novel*, Georg Lukács calls *L'Education sentimentale* an instance of the romanticism of disillusion as embodied in the very form of the novel. According to Lukács the novel, unlike the epic, expresses the predicament of a world abandoned by God, in which time is felt as irony, and in which the individual hero strives for what he can never achieve, a correspondence between his idea and the world. In the novel of abstract idealism, which Lukács counterposes against the romanticism of disillusion, the hero is Don Quixote, a prototype of the soul that is narrower than the outside world, and whose main driving impulse is furnished by a demon pushing the individual toward the realization of an ideal or cause:

> The demonism of the narrowing of the soul is the demonism of abstract idealism. It is the mentality which chooses the direct, straight path towards the realisation of the ideal; which, dazzled by the demon, forgets the existence of any distance between ideal and idea, between psyche and soul; which, with the most authentic and unshakable faith, concludes that the idea, because it *should be*, necessarily *must be*, and because reality does not satisfy this *a priori* demand, thinks that reality is bewitched by evil demons and that the spell can be broken and reality be redeemed either by finding a magic password or by courageously fighting the evil forces. (97)

Although most readers would judge Quixote's cause to restore the age of chivalry as a completely lost one, Lukács takes the more audacious step of considering it a partial victory, because Quixote manages "to remain unblemished in the purity of his intent and is also able to transmit some of the radiance of [his] triumphant, though admittedly self-ironising, poetry to [his] victorious opponent" (104). Of course the Don is unsuccessful in restoring Amadis of Gaul and the age of chivalry, but the strength of his conviction is such as even to expose the sordid reality of this extremely unheroic world of ours—with its innkeepers, shepherds, itinerant rogues—to an idealism whose self-conviction and fervor look backward to an age that has disappeared:

> Thus the first great novel of world literature stands at the beginning of the time when the Christian God began to forsake the world; when man became lonely and could find meaning and substance only in his own soul, whose home was

nowhere. . . . Cervantes lived in the period of the last, great and
desperate mysticism, the period of a fanatical attempt to renew
the dying religion from within; a period of a new view of the
world rising up in mystical forms; the last period of truly lived
life by already disoriented, tentative, sophisticated, occult aspirations. (103–104)

The novel, according to Lukács, replaces the epic. Whereas the epic
expresses the religious world of heroes and gods living on a par
with each other, unproblematically and without a trace of self-
consciousness, the novel expresses a fallen world, which God has abandoned. Heroes have been transformed into secular men and women,
subject to the interior dislocations, lostness, and madness of what
Lukács calls "transcendental homelessness." A rift has opened between
Idea and actuality. That is why all the great novelistic figures, from Don
Quixote to Frederic Moreau, cannot really adapt themselves to the secular, historical world because they are haunted by memories of what
they have lost, searching in vain for self-realization and the success of
a cause that cannot be maintained. In this, Lukács and Max Weber—
friends, fellow-members of the Heidelberg circle, sociologists and aes-
theticians—chart the modern world as a place of disenchantment.
Weber says that "the ultimate and most sublime values have retreated
from public life either into the transcendental realm of mystic life or
into the brotherliness of direct and personal human relations" ("The
Vocation of Science," 155). Hence Don Quixote, whose cause has the ef-
ficacity of a private dream with no place to go, or Frederic Moreau and
Deslauriers, failures in everything except in their friendship. Ours is
not a happy, summertime world, but, as Weber says, "a polar night of
icy darkness and hardness" ("The Vocation of Politics," 128).

Yet even in the religious world view that both Weber and Lukács
lament and criticize there exists a patron saint of lost causes, Saint
Jude. During the early years of the Christian era, Jude or Judas was reg-
ularly described as Judas (frater) Jacobi, Judas the brother of James;
along with John the Evangelist the three brothers were disciples of
Jesus, although Jude had the misfortune of being confused with Judas
Iscariot and was therefore known as Jude the Hidden. He and Saint
Simon preached the gospel together in Mesopotamia and were mar-

tyred there. A book on modern pilgrimage says that after Peter and James—Santiago—Jude "ranks third among the apostles as a pilgrimage saint with at least nine European shrines to his credit. Saint Jude also has at least five shrines in North America. The cult of this apostle, who replaced Judas Iscariot among the original group, developed slowly and became important only in the twentieth century" (Nolan, 137). Even to someone like myself who is unpracticed in hagiography, Jude seems a required figure in the economy of the apostolic world. Surrounded as he is by larger-than-life figures—Peter the Rock, John the mystic and theologian, James the patron saint of pilgrims and killer of Moors (Santiago Matamoros)—and overshadowed by the great betrayer Judas Iscariot, Jude the Hidden comes to symbolize all those who have failed in distinction, whose promise has been unrealized, whose efforts and causes have not succeeded. And such a personality ultimately validates the Christian vision of charity and humility: there is a place for everyone, Jude seems to be saying, not just for those who have made it. Interestingly, however, Jude provides a last resort in a religion whose central figure is supposed to be the last resort; for even if one's faith in Christ falters, there is another opportunity afforded the believer by Jude.

It is as a savage attack on any such palliative that Thomas Hardy wrote his last and, in my opinion, his greatest novel, *Jude the Obscure,* first published in 1895. A mediocre young country boy of some sensitivity and admirable if inappropriate ambition, Jude Fawley aspires to better himself from the beginning to the last moment of his experience. We first see him at age ten, taking leave of his schoolmaster who is off to Christminster—a combination of Oxford and Cambridge—to complete his university studies. Jude is infected with the idea that he must try to do the same, and for the remainder of the novel he drifts in and out of Christminster, in search of learning, success, higher purpose. Yet all he encounters is setback, disappointment, and more and more entanglements that lead him into desperate degradation. Whenever he tries to improve his lot in as direct a way as possible he meets impossible resistance. When he acquires a set of Greek and Latin primers in order to teach himself the two classical languages, he realizes that languages cannot be learned simply by reading a book; he then gives up. The two women who enter his life, Arabella and Sue

Bridehead, exhaust him. He goes from job to job, getting poorer and poorer, as each disaster—the suicide of his children, Sue's relationship with Philotson, Jude's early schoolmaster model—humbles him further, especially after he and Sue discover an extraordinarily passionate love between them, for which they both risk and undergo social ostracism and even greater poverty. Jude's death occurs just as the "Remembrance games" take place outside his windows in his impoverished quarters in Christminster; the city and all its religious and educational institutions remain as impervious and insensitive to Jude's basically harmless aspirations now during his final moments as they did when he began his unfortunate career. Hardy orchestrates the pathetic man's last moments by interweaving his singularly pertinent recollections from the Book of Job with the triumphant hurrahs and glorious music of the games:

> "Throat—water—Sue—darling—drop of water—please—O please!"
>
> No water came, and the organ notes, faint as a bee's hum, rolled in as before.
>
> While he remained, his face changing, shouts and hurrahs came from somewhere in the direction of the river.
>
> "Ah—yes! The Remembrance games," he murmured. "And I here. And Sue defiled!"
>
> The hurrahs were repeated, drowning the faint organ notes. Jude's face changed more: he whispered slowly, his parched lips scarcely moving:
>
> *"Let the day perish wherein I was born, and the night in which it was said, There is a man child conceived."*
>
> ("Hurrah!")
>
> *"Let that day be darkness; let not God regard it from above, neither let the light shine upon it. Lo, let that night be solitary, let no joyful voice come therein."*
>
> ("Hurrah!")
>
> *"Why died I not from the womb? Why did I not give up the ghost when I came out of the belly? . . . For now should I have lain still and been quiet. I should have slept: then had I been at rest!"*
>
> ("Hurrah!")

"There the prisoners rest together; they hear not the voice of the op-pressor. . . . The small and the great are there; and the servant is free from his master. Wherefore is light given to him that is in misery, and life unto the bitter in soul?" (Jude, 321)

The point of all this is to ram home the total hopelessness of Jude's condition, and at the same time—this is Hardy's hallmark as an unbeliever—to show that even St. Jude, patron of lost causes, is of no value whatever to Jude Fawley, his modern namesake.

The irony goes well beyond that of the novelists (Cervantes and Flaubert) that I spoke about earlier. Job has displaced Jude in the first place; whereas Don Quixote and Frederic Moreau might have been capable of some attainments, the one a knight, the other a relatively wealthy young man of good education, Jude is incapacitated from the start. Hardy sees to it that both circumstances and his own disabilities undermine everything he does. It is not only that by now God has abandoned the world entirely: it is also that whatever recollection or remnants of an earlier world persist, either they are obliviously mocking of the individual's misery (as when Jude quotes Job without any result of the sort that the biblical figure experiences after his travails; there is no Eliphaz the Temanite to do God's will, offer up seven bullocks and seven rams, and restore Job to happiness and justice) or they are deliberately unredemptive and untherapeutic, like the folk doctor Vilbert or the village wench Arabella, who first attracts Jude's attention by throwing a pig's pizzle at him.

But what Cervantes, Flaubert, and Hardy have in common is that their narratives are mature works, written near the end of their careers at precisely that moment when the individual feels the need for summing-up, making judgments, tallying up the evidence for and against the success of youthful ambitions and aspirations. That they do their summing-up in novels underscores more starkly than usual the underlying ironies and depressing exigencies of the novel form itself, conditioned by experience and the hidden god, to be a narrative in which time ironically exposes the disparity between reality and higher purpose, and in which the individual is really only afforded two on the whole dispiriting alternatives: either one conforms to the sordid practices of the world, thus sacrificing any hope of a noble cause, or one is killed off as Jude, Emma Bovary, and Quixote are killed off. What the novel offers, therefore, is a narrative without redemption. Its conclusion is not the rounded-off closure imputed to a contrite heart as, under the auspices of St. Jude, it re-accepts the final authority of God, but rather the bitterness of defeat, ironized and given aesthetic form it is true, but conclusive nonetheless. So far as idealism is concerned, then, the novel is constitutively opposed. What remains are the ruins of lost causes and defeated ambition.

A lost cause is unimaginable without an adjoining or perhaps parallel victory to compare it with. There are always winners and losers, but what seems to count is how you look at things. A major part of most official culture is dedicated to proving that if, like Socrates, you are put to death for your virtues, which remain intact, you are the victor, your cause has won out, even though, of course, the obvious winners thrive on. "It depends on how you look at it" has something weasely about it, as if the real winner is only a winner in appearances or is so morally inferior as not to be a winner at all. The most devastating refutation of "hm . . . despite all our losses, we have really been the winners, and we live to fight on," is Jonathan Swift's *Gulliver's Travels,* a book that is certainly not a novel but a political satire with an extremely depressing end. Gulliver's voyage to Lilliput locates him in a tiny country where his strength is both an undeniable strength—as when he can entertain the queen's cavalry on his handkerchief—and a curious weakness when he is embroiled in Lilliputian politics and, through an act of quick-thinking rescue, he offends the queen when he urinates on her palace to put out a fire. He is so little a courtier that despite his size and strength he finds himself the victim of a palace plot, the net result of which he tells us is either to blind him or to starve him slowly and painfully to death. He goes to neighboring Blefescu seeking refuge there, but is then the object of an extradition request from Lilliput: he escapes, returns home, but is soon on the ocean again.

He ends up in Brobdingnag, as a tiny little humanoid in a country of giants, where once again neither his comparative agility nor his great experience is much of a help to him. He rather patronizingly tries to convince the king there that Europe is more advanced in both culture and practical politics, believing himself to be a representative of his own species and race as he does so. The king's answer is quite devastating and allows Gulliver not a whit of saving grace: everything noble or good seems, from the Brobdingnagian perspective, to be appallingly depraved:

> . . . you have made a most admirable Panegyrick upon your Country. You have clearly proved that Ignorance, Idleness, and Vice are the proper Ingredients for qualifying a Legislator, That Laws are best explained, interpreted, and applied by those whose Interest and Abilities lie in perverting, confounding, and eluding them. I observe among you some Lines of an Institution, which in its Original might have been tolerable; but these half erased, and the rest wholly blurred and blotted by Corruptions. It doth not appear from all you have said, how any one Perfection is required towards the Procurement of any one Station among you; much less that Men are ennobled on Account of their Virtue, that Priests are advanced for their Piety or Learning, Soldiers for their Conduct or Valour, Judges for their Integrity, Senators for the Love of their Country, or Counsellors for their Wisdom. As for yourself (continued the King) who have spent the greatest Part of your Life in travelling; I am well disposed to hope you may hitherto have escaped many Vices of your Country. But, by what I have gathered from your own Relation, and the Answers I have with much Pains wringed and extorted from you; I cannot but conclude the Bulk of your Natives, to be the most pernicious Race of little odious Vermin that Nature ever suffered to crawl upon the Surface of the Earth. (132)

Nor is Swift done with human illusion, especially of the sort that implies melioristically that a good cause might prevail if the perspective was correct. Having first let Gulliver seem too big, then too small for his context, he thus eliminates the possibility that hidden potential or latent goodness might develop and flourish if the individual was big and idealistic, or small and experienced, relative to the immediate environment. In the final voyage Gulliver becomes a Yahoo, that is, a degenerate savage programmed for lies, duplicity, mendacity, insincerity in a society entirely made up of horses, the Houyhnhnms, whose society produced neither letters nor knowledge of a traditional sort. The plain decency, bland goodness, and inoffensive (if somewhat boring) mores of the Houyhnhnms convince Gulliver that Yahoos—in other words, the human race—represent a totally lost cause, a realization that has no effect on the horses, whose assembly issues an Exhortation condemning Gulliver to exile and deportation. He finally returns to England mortified by his own being and more or less incapable even of enduring the presence of his wife and family. Swift's severity is so uncompromising, Gulliver's reduction in moral status so total, as to disallow any possible relief. There are no winners at all; there is no perspective, or right time, or final moment that permits any sort of redemptive cheer; the whole morass, good cause as well as lost cause, is condemned for the impossible congenital mess that it is. Even W. B. Yeats's "uncontrollable mystery on the bestial floor" is mild and indeed pious by comparison with Swift's strictures on social life in *Gulliver's Travels*.

The implication of Swift's satire is that when the moment for summing-up finally occurs we must be ready to say without the least fudging that human existence simply defeats all causes, good or bad. In the strictness with which he holds this view he belongs in the company of the novelists I have cited, except that he is unkinder and less charitable than they are. Swift, Flaubert, Cervantes, and Hardy allow us to discern how it is that good causes can be represented and defeated; I adduce them as opponents of a world view that is amply available in the Western tradition that claims that in the fullness of time good will prevail and evil will be overcome. I certainly do not have anything in mind that is so simple-mindedly optimistic as the deism lampooned by Voltaire in *Candide*; rather, I am referring to great works of art written by poets and dramatists at the end of their career. The phenomenon of late style is something I have been studying for some years, since it concerns the way in which writers confront mortality in their last works, and how a separate, individualistically inflected *late style* (*Spätstil* or *style tardif*) emerges accordingly. A striking difference is to be observed between two types of late work: those like *The Tempest* and *The Winter's Tale*, or *Oedipus at Colonus*, in which resolution and reconciliation occur, and those like Henrik Ibsen's *When We Dead Awaken* and Euripides' *The Bacchae*, in which all the contradictions and unresolved antinomies of life are left standing, untouched by any sort of autumnal mellowness. According to Theodor Adorno, who is a sort of high priest of late-style gloom—he speaks here of Beethoven's third-period masterpieces—late works are the catastrophes.

What I have so far been discussing is a landscape charted by late works of the decidedly problematic and unreconciled second type, in which every decent intention and each admirable cause goes down to defeat and in effect loses, has no chance. Admittedly, I have been using the realm of the aesthetic to grapple with the nature and constitution of lost causes; these ultimately depend on how one represents the narrative course of a cause from intention to realization, but it is plain that the novel and drama, when they attempt to represent the full struggle between successful and lost causes, also tend to concede that good causes have little chance of success. As a student of literature I find this persuasive, in that a reflective and disabused consciousness is likely to render human reality as particularly hospitable to lost causes, and indeed to lost heroes and heroines. But it is essential to remind ourselves that in their sequentiality, originations, maturity, and death fiction and narrative mirror the process of human procreation and generation, which the novel mocks ironically through its attention to the biographies of its heroes and heroines, the continuity of their lives, and their subsequent maturity, marriage, and death.

But even the disillusionment and lost causes that form so essential a part of the Western narrative tradition seem like incidental things when compared with the Japanese tradition of what in a superb essay Marguerite Yourcenar alludes to as "the nobility of failure," which is the title of Ivan Morris's book on "heroic and violent aspects of the Japanese spirit." As befits the author of *The Memoirs of Hadrian,* Yourcenar elucidates the specific Japanese tradition of portraying and even of enacting the self-obliteration of a hero who is doomed to failure, the prototype for which goes back to the impoverished medieval *samurai,* whose last action is ritual suicide. Morris's book is a chronicle of lost causes, all of them Japanese, all of them represented by him (and fascinatingly by Yourcenar) as interesting "despite or possibly because of its complete uselessness"; the chronicle comes up to Yukio Mishima and the Kamikaze pilots of World War II, whose (to us) appalling self-sacrifice seems a representation of the ancient samurai's spirit, which "had lost its last effulgence there" (82). Yet Yourcenar adds (correctly I think):

> But, on the contrary, love of lost causes and respect for those who die for them seem to me to belong to all countries and all ages. Few escapades are as absurd as that of Gordon at Khartoum, but Gordon is a hero of nineteenth-century British history. Rochejacquelein and "le Garcs" in Balzac's *Les Chouans* are certainly defeated, and their cause with them, unless one considers the few years' reigns of Louis XVIII and Charles X as triumph: they speak no less forcefully to our imagination. The same is true of the Girondins and those sent to the guillotine on 9 Thermidor, whose political views one can hardly say triumphed but who count among the great human myths of the French Revolution. And it is probably much more Waterloo and Saint Helena than Wagram which made Napoleon such a beloved subject for the poets of the nineteenth century. I once caused a Roman emperor whose story I evoked to say that a moment comes when "life, for every man, is an accepted defeat." We all know that, and it is what makes us admire so much those who have consciously chosen defeat and who sometimes have achieved it early on. (83)

Still, there is a difference between the aesthetics of lost causes and the more personal, subjective experience for which no ritual form or ceremony exists. What if we try to grapple with lost causes in the public political world where efforts on behalf of causes actually take place? Is there the same ironized inevitability there, or do subjective hope and renewed effort make a lost cause something to be refused as defeatism? Here I can do no better than to offer my personal experiences as a politically active Palestinian as evidence, particularly as these have crystallized since the watershed Oslo agreement of September 1993.

One of the first things I noticed in the United States when I came here from the Middle East during the 1950s to attend school and university was the white southerner who would refer nostalgically to the Confederacy and speak romantically of the "lost cause" of southern independence, chivalry, nobility of sentiment. "We were defeated by the business ethic," one of them told me at Princeton, although little was ever said about the blacks whose slave labor and systematic oppression were essential to the southern cause. It took the Suez and June War of 1956 and 1967 respectively for me to be convinced that the cause of our people in its effort to regain its land and rights was precariously close to being a lost one. But that realization lasted for only a relatively short time. By the time the Palestinian movement had reemerged in 1968 from the ashes of all three Arab-Israeli wars that I had lived through, I had become much more conscious than before of Palestinians as a people sharing a lot in common with the Vietnamese, Cubans, South Africans, Angolans, and others in the Third World struggling for national liberation. During those heady early years of the revived Palestinian national movement it seemed neither appropriate nor really possible to see ourselves in terms of other dispossessed and forgotten peoples like the Armenians, American Indians, Tasmanians, gypsies, and Australian aborigines. On the contrary, we modeled ourselves on the Vietnamese people, whose resistance to U.S. intervention seemed exactly what we should undertake.

By the end of the decade, phrases like "people's war" and "armed struggle," with lots of passages from Frantz Fanon and Vo Nguyen Giap to back them up, proliferated everywhere in the region where Palestinians undertook their political activity. Yet as I look back on it now, the emphasis was on the symbols of struggle, rather than on organization and mobilization. None of this would have been possible without support from one or another Arab state; Yasir Arafat, who by that time had become the top leader, was a genius at maneuvering between rivals, and between Arab leaders who one day were with him, the next against him. Above all, this was also a period of amazingly plentiful—to call it bountiful would not be an overstatement—oil money; suddenly a whole cadre of individuals emerged who drank only Black Label Scotch whiskey, traveled first-class, drove fancy European cars, and were always surrounded by aides, bodyguards, and hangers-on. In the environment provided by Beirut between 1971 and 1982, when the Palestine Liberation Organization was driven out of the city by the Israeli army, and its leaders exiled to Tunisia, the real, as opposed to the illusory, parallels provided by Vietnam, Cuba, and South Africa were practically impossible to draw. Although only a tiny percentage of

Palestinians actually engaged in armed struggle, and though the casualties sustained by Palestinians were multiples greater than those suffered by Israel, the great campaign for liberation, independence, and the like was pressed, regardless of cost or likelihood of victory.

Looking back over the history of organized Palestinian nationalism during the past several decades, one can now distinguish within it that there were always losers and winners, although in the thick of an ongoing struggle it was difficult to make the distinction. Take as an instance a Palestinian friend and contemporary of mine who, having received an excellent education in the United States, with a Ph.D. from Harvard, got a good teaching job in a West Coast university, but then gave everything up in order to join the movement in Amman in 1968. I saw him regularly until his death in 1976. A man of great dedication and extraordinary principle, he rose in the movement by virtue of his selfless work and his demonstrated service to the ideals of commitment to the Palestinian dispossessed—refugees, camp-dwellers, workers, the disabled; in time he became widely known as a severe, albeit loyal critic of the leadership, its methods, and its dubious alliances. Retrospectively it now seems to me that he had become too much for that leadership, precisely because of his unsullied commitment to the cause, and, although I have no concrete proof of this, I believe that he was sent off on a futile mission in 1976, during the Lebanese Civil War, from which he never returned.

Every political theorist and analyst stresses the importance of hope in maintaining a movement. The world has forgotten that in 1948 Palestinians constituted almost 70 percent of the population of mandatory Palestine; in the years since Jewish immigration had begun on a serious scale, the incoming immigrants had managed to acquire only about 6 percent of the land of the country. Yet during the 1940s and especially after the Second World War—the years of my childhood—very little preparation for or understanding of the situation prevailed; I recall little sense of urgency or alarm at the presence of incoming foreigners from Europe, and little assessment of what their plans might be and how they would execute them. The War of 1948—called Israel's War of Independence—was a catastrophe for Palestinians: two-thirds were driven out of their homes and country, many were killed, all their property was seized, and to all intents and purposes they ceased to exist as a people. I saw this directly in my own family on both my father's and my mother's side, each member of which without a single exception became a refugee, was uprooted and totally disoriented, and still bears the scars of that terrible upheaval. To have lived as a member of a society (admittedly controlled by Britain) where it was possible to own property, maintain a profession or job, raise a family, go to school, pray, farm, and even die as a citizen, one day, and then suddenly on another day not to be able to do that, was for most people I knew a living death. This is the background to the period after the 1967 war that I have been discussing, during which hope for the people as a whole was aroused and seemed to make possible some restoration of Palestinian identity and of actual land.

Hope overrode the enormous obstacles that we faced as a people. Consider these obstacles now. We were the first people whose land had been colonized who were declared persona non grata, were dispossessed, and traces of whose national existence were systematically erased by the immigrants who replaced us. This was no exploitation Algerian-style, nor was it apartheid South African-style, nor was it mass extermination as in Tasmania. Rather we were made not to be there, invisible, and most were driven out and referred to as nonpeople; a small minority remained inside Israel and were dealt with juridically by calling them not "Palestinians" but "non-Jews." The rest officially ceased to exist, and where most of them went in the Arab world the majority were confined to refugee camps, special invidious laws were passed for them, and they became stateless refugees. Internationally and in the Arab world, our history and our national existence either were unrecognized or were treated as a local issue. To live through your own extinction, not permitted even the word "Palestine," while a successor state and people thrived with the world's attention focused on them as pioneers, an island of democracy, miracle state, and so forth, had the programmatic effect of blanking out hope. It was quite ironic that after all the Arab armies were defeated by Israel in 1967—Arab armies whose *raison d'être* was defense against and defeat of Israel—at that very moment there was a resurgence of hope in the idea not so much of restoring but of liberating Palestine as part of a worldwide process taking place in so many parts of the non-European and non-Atlantic world. The Palestinian cause as a universalist cause was thus born at a time when it was possible for us as a people to see ourselves in a different context than the bleak one provided by the defeated Arabs. We saw ourselves as a Third World people, subjected to colonialism and oppression, now undertaking our own self-liberation from domination as well as the liberation of our territory from our enemy.

Yet—to continue the litany of obstacles—we had no territorial base anywhere; where we tried to establish one (e.g., Jordan or Lebanon) we messily disrupted the local polity, came up against armed force, and were subsequently defeated. Moreover, without sovereignty we did not have a base or a haven; this emphasized the fact that most of our people were dispersed exiles, a condition in which geography became our main enemy. To make matters even worse, the Israelis were not the canonical white settlers of Algeria or South Africa. They were Jews—long the classical victims of Western society—with a history of oppression and genocidal attempts against them; they were mainly European, well connected in the countries from which they had emigrated, imbued with an ideological fervor that gave them both solidarity and resourcefulness. Compared with us, they were modern and disciplined, organized, fully capable of collective action. Unlike us, they always had a strategic partner in the greatest power of the day, which after 1967 was the United States. Their diaspora communities—unlike ours, who were mainly impoverished and unorganized refugees—were well established and could maintain a steady flow of support. The contrast between us and them was that between a developed and an underdeveloped people.

Nevertheless, a nation and a movement concerned with something that came to be called the Palestinian cause did emerge with greater and greater definition. For the first time in our modern history we were recognized as a people at the United Nations in 1974. A whole network of institutions dealing with health, education, military training, social welfare, and women's and workers' rights administered by and for Palestinians took hold. In 1988 through the Palestine National Council, of which I was then a member—it was a parliament in exile—we recognized Israel and opted for partition in the land of historical Palestine. A national insurrection called the *intifada* had begun in late 1987 and was to last for four years: it attracted a great deal of attention, and even improved the international image of the Palestinians because of its courage, its willingness frontally to take on Israeli tanks and guns, its capacity for reorganizing society into small, self-sustaining, and independent units that circumvented some but by no means all the depredations of Israeli occupation. Yet during that whole time, Israel pressed on with the building of settlements, with an occupation that was extraordinarily brutal and expensive, with its refusal to recognize Palestinian nationalism. In the world's eyes, and thanks to major blunders of our own, we were known for a long time only as terrorists, although during the *intifada* that designation and Israel's quite favorable image were changed in our favor.

There was certainly an advance in Palestinian consciousness; there was a sense that although we were separated into three entirely discontinuous groups—Israeli Palestinians, inhabitants of the West Bank and Gaza, diaspora Palestinians who made up more than half the total number of our people—we were unified as a people, and regarded as such by an appreciable number of nations; we had now gained the status of a people with a real claim to a homeland. Those were all positive achievements. Nevertheless, every change in the international system since 1982 was turned to advantage by Israel, a real disadvantage for us. The collapse of the Soviet Union and subsequent changes in Eastern Europe, as well as the victory of the U.S. coalition during the Gulf War (where our leadership had made a disastrous miscalculation by siding openly with Saddam Hussein), diminished Palestinian energies, as more people became refugees, and less support was available. Still it was possible to believe that the Palestinian cause continued to represent an idea of justice and equality around which many others could rally. By being for Palestinian rights we stood for nondiscrimination, for social justice and equality, for enlightened nationalism. Our aim was an independent sovereign state, of course. Even though we had lived through our loss, we were able to accept a compromise whereby what we lost in 1948 to Israel (contained within the prewar 1967 lines) would be lost forever, if in return we could have a state in the Occupied Territories. We had assumed (and I do not recall much discussion of this particular option for the future) that our state would have sovereignty, our refugees would have the right of some sort of repatriation or compensation, and our politics would be a distinct advance over those of the Arab states, with their oligarchies, military dictatorships, brutal police regimes.

During the period that was effectively terminated by the Oslo agreement of 1993 I recall quite distinctly that most of the intellectuals, professionals, political activists (leadership and nonleadership), and ordinary individuals I knew well lived at least two parallel lives. The first was in varying degrees a difficult one: as Palestinians living under different jurisdictions, none of them Palestinian of course, with a general sense of powerlessness and drift. Second was a life that was sustained by the various promises of the Palestinian struggle, utopian and unrealistic perhaps, but based on solid principles of justice and, at least since the late 1980s, negotiated peace with Israel. The distorted view of us as a people single-mindedly bent on Israel's destruction that existed in the West bore no relationship at all to any reality I lived or knew of. Most of us, the overwhelming majority, in fact, were most interested in the recognition and acknowledgment of our existence as a nation, and not in retribution; everyone I knew was flabbergasted and outraged that the Israelis, who had destroyed our society in 1948, took our land, occupied what remained of it since 1967, and who bombed, killed, and otherwise oppressed an enormous number of us, could appeal to the world as constantly afraid for their security, despite their immense power relative to ours. Few Westerners took seriously our insecurity and real deprivation: somehow Israel's obsession with its insecurity and need for assurance—with its soldiers beating up Palestinians every day after twenty-eight years of occupation—took precedence over our misery. I vividly recall the anger I felt when I learned that starting in the fall of 1992 under the auspices of the American Academy of Arts and Sciences, an organization of which I was a member, a group of privileged Palestinian intellectuals met with Israeli security officials in secret to begin a discussion of security for settlers and army personnel who would remain in the Occupied Territories should there be some form of Palestinian self-rule arrangement. This was a prelude to Oslo, but the fact that there was an acceptance of the Israeli agenda and a scanting of real Palestinian losses struck me as ominous, a sign that capitulation had already set in. Another sign of capitulation was the efflorescence of Islamic movements whose reactionary message (the aim of which was to establish an Islamic state in Palestine) testified to the secular desperation of the nationalist cause.

Let me skip directly to Oslo and after. The mystery there—indeed, from my viewpoint, the only interesting thing—is how a people that had struggled against the British and the Zionists for over a century (unevenly and without much success it is true) were persuaded—perhaps by the international and regional balance of power, the blandishments of their leaders, the fatigue of long and apparently fruitless struggle—to declare in effect that their hope of real national reconstruction and real self-determination was in effect a lost cause. One of the advantages of so extraordinary a *volte face* is that one can see what is happening against the immediate and also the more distant background. History of course is full of peoples who simply gave up and were persuaded to accept a life of servitude; they are all but forgotten, their voices barely heard, the traces of their life scarcely decipherable. History is not kind to them since even in the present they are seen as losers, even though it is sometimes possible, as Walter Benjamin says, to realize that "whoever has emerged victorious participates to this day in the triumphal procession in which the present rulers step over those who are lying prostrate" (*Illuminations,* 256).

How does the cause of a people, a culture, or an individual become hopeless? We had once believed as a people that there was room for us at the rendezvous of destiny. In the instance I have been discussing, it was certainly true that a collective sentiment developed that the time was no longer right, that now is the period of ascendancy of America and its allies, and that everyone else is required to go along with Washington's dictates. A gradual shift in perspective revealed to the collective consciousness that the cause of Palestinian nationalism, with its earlier yet long-standing and uncompromising position on sovereignty, justice, and self-determination, could no longer be fought for: there had to be a change of strategy whereby the nation now thought of its cause less as something won than as something conceded to it as a defeated people by its opponents and by the international authority. Certainly for Palestinians the sense of isolation among the other Arabs had been growing inexorably. What used to be *the great* Arab cause of Palestine was so diminished that it became a bargaining card in the hands of countries like Egypt and Jordan, who were desperately hard up for American patronage and largesse and therefore tried to position themselves as talking realistic sense to the

Palestinians. Whereas in the past Palestinians gathered hope and optimism from the struggles of other peoples (e.g., the South African battle against apartheid), the opposite became true: *they* were successful because their circumstances were more favorable, and since we did not have the same conditions, we needed instead to become more accommodating. What had once been true for liberation movements was no longer applicable in our case. Soviet help was nonexistent, and besides the times had changed. Liberation was no longer a timely cause—democracy and the free market were, and where better to make application for joining those campaigns than in Washington. The *intifada* had failed to end the occupation, and so a new strategy based on the conviction of loss had to be adopted swiftly and dramatically.

I must confess to you that since the Oslo agreement between Israel and the PLO was announced and then signed in the fall of 1993 I have been trying to understand how it is that a people and its leadership dramatically stepped down and away from the cause of Palestine, which at the very least was to have achieved the recovery of land lost to Israel in 1967, the end of military occupation, annexation, and settlement, and, perhaps most important, the beginnings of a process of real democracy and real self-determination (resources, borders, sovereignty, repatriation, and unity of people in one territory). *That* cause also expressed itself as part of the universal struggle for freedom and equality. Instead:

1. Our consent was given for the first time in liberation history to continued occupation.
2. Our population was redivided—refugees, residents of the West Bank and Gaza, Israeli Palestinians.
3. Israel retained borders and its settlements; it redeployed but kept the army in Gaza and the West Bank and it also held on to Jerusalem, resources, overall security control.
4. Arafat became responsible to Israel, as the local enforcer.
5. He established a dictatorial regime.

To me and every Palestinian I know these agreements signify defeat, not only militarily and territorially but, more important, morally. Our cause had been to refuse and struggle against the injustice inflicted on us as a people. Now we had conceded that we were prepared to exist not as a sovereign people on our land but as a scattered, dispossessed people, some of whom were given municipal authority by the Israelis, with very little to check further Israeli encroachments against us or to prevent violations of the ungenerous pettifogging agreements they tied us into. The American scholar Norman Finkelstein has recently drawn a harrowing portrait of the defeat of the Cherokee Indians and has suggested that a similar fate might now be befalling Palestinians. The sudden transformation of Arafat from freedom-fighter and "terrorist" into an Israeli enforcer and a (relatively welcome) guest at the White House has been difficult for Palestinians to absorb, but I am certain that despite the momentary euphoria and approving media attention that this former symbol of terrorism now benefited from—his strutting presence at the victory celebrations in Washington, his embraces of Yitzhak Rabin and Shimon Peres, John Major and Jacques Chirac, his vision and courage celebrated by pundits and Zionist lobbyists who had formerly dedicated their professional energies to defaming him and his people—despite all this, most Palestinians saw the new Arafat as the symbol of defeat, the very embodiment of a lost cause, now compelled to speak not of Palestinian self-determination but of Israeli security as his top priority.

Arafat also now represented the cancellation of a heritage of loss and sacrifice: his White House speeches, for instance, were profuse with gratitude for Israeli and American recognition, and never once mentioned the land his people had permanently lost, the years of suffering under occupation and in the wilderness, the immense burdens assumed on behalf of the PLO by people who had thought of what they were doing as legitimate support for a just cause. All that was scratched from the record as irrelevant and embarrassing. And when the political failure of a people's cause is so publicly evident, the next best thing to do is to rally round the last remaining symbol of national authority and try to make the best of a bad bargain.

Lost causes can be abandoned causes, the debris of a battle swept aside by history and by the victor, with the losing army in full retreat. In such a situation the collective and the individual still act in concert, agreeing that hopelessness, loss, defeat argue the end of a cause, its historic defeat, the land taken away, the people dispossessed and dispersed, the leaders forced to serve another set of masters. And then the narratives consolidate that decision, tracing—as I have done here—how something that began in hope and optimism ended in the bitterness of disillusion and disappointment. One could argue that no cause is ever totally and irrevocably lost, that personal and collective will can be maintained, and that as, for instance, the Jews were once defeated and destroyed, they were able to return in triumph at a later date. But that, I think, is an extremely rare case. Do many people now believe that the gypsies or the Native Americans can get back what they lost?

But does the consciousness and even the actuality of a lost cause entail that sense of defeat and resignation that we associate with the abjections of capitulation and the dishonor of grinning or bowing survivors who opportunistically fawn on their conquerors and seek to ingratiate themselves with the new dispensation? Must it always result in the broken will and demoralized pessimism of the defeated? I think not, although the alternative is a difficult and extremely precarious one, at least on the level of the individual. In the best analysis of alternatives to the helpless resignation of a lost cause that I know, Adorno diagnoses the predicament as follows. At a moment of defeat:

> For the individual, life is made easier through capitulation to the collective with which he identifies. He is spared the cognition of his impotence; within the circle of their own company, the few become many. It is this act—not unconfused thinking— which is resignation. No transparent relation prevails between the interests of the ego and the collective to which it assigns itself. The ego must abrogate itself, if it is to share in the predestination of the collective. Explicitly a remnant of the Kantian categorical imperative manifests itself: your signature is required. The feeling of new security is purchased with the sacrifice of autonomous thinking. The consolation that thought within the context of collective actions is an improvement proves deceptive: thinking, employed only as the instrument of action, is blunted in the same manner as all instrumental reason. (167–168)

As opposed to this abrogation of consciousness, Adorno posits as an alternative to resigned capitulation of the lost cause the intransigence of the individual thinker whose power of expression is a power— however modest and circumscribed in its capacity for action or victory—that enacts a movement of vitality, a gesture of defiance, a statement of hope whose "unhappiness" and meager survival are better than silence or joining in the chorus of defeated activists:

> In contrast, the uncompromisingly critical thinker, who nei-
> ther superscribes his conscience nor permits himself to be ter-
> rorized into action, is in truth the one who does not give up.
> Furthermore, thinking is not the spiritual reproduction of
> that which exists. As long as thinking is not interrupted, it has
> a firm grasp upon possibility. Its insatiable quality, the resis-
> tance against petty satiety, rejects the foolish wisdom of resig-
> nation. (168)

I offer this in tentative conclusion as a means of affirming the individual intellectual vocation, which is neither disabled by a paralyzed sense of political defeat nor impelled by groundless optimism and illusory hope. Consciousness of the possibility of resistance can reside only in the individual will that is fortified by intellectual rigor and an unabated conviction in the need to begin again, with no guarantees except, as Adorno says, the confidence of even the loneliest and most impotent thought that "what has been cogently thought must be thought in some other place and by other people." In this way thinking might perhaps acquire and express the momentum of the general, thereby blunting the anguish and despondency of the lost cause, which its enemies have tried to induce.

We might well ask from this perspective if *any* lost cause can ever really be lost.

45

Between Worlds

In the first book I wrote, *Joseph Conrad and the Fiction of Autobiography,* published more than thirty years ago, and then in an essay called "Reflections on Exile" that appeared in 1984, I used Conrad as an example of someone whose life and work seemed to typify the fate of the wanderer who becomes an accomplished writer in an acquired language, but can never shake off his sense of alienation from his new—that is, acquired—and, in Conrad's rather special case, admired, home. His friends all said of Conrad that he was very contented with the idea of being English, even though he never lost his heavy Polish accent and his quite peculiar moodiness, which was thought to be very un-English. Yet the moment one enters his writing the aura of dislocation, instability, and strangeness is unmistakable. No one could represent the fate of lostness and disorientation better than he did, and no one was more ironic about the effort of trying to replace that condition with new arrangements and accommodations— which invariably lured one into further traps, such as those Lord Jim encounters when he starts life again on his little island. Marlow enters the heart of darkness to discover that Kurtz was not only there before him but is also incapable of telling him the whole truth; so that, in narrating his own experiences, Marlow cannot be as exact as he would have liked, and ends up producing approximations and even falsehoods of which both he and his listeners seem quite aware.

Only well after his death did Conrad's critics try to reconstruct what has been called his Polish background, very little of which had found its way directly into his fiction. But the rather elusive meaning of his writing is not so easily supplied, for even if we find out a lot about his Polish experiences, friends, and relatives, that information will not of itself settle the core of restlessness and unease that his work relentlessly circles. Eventually we realize that the work is actually constituted by the experience of exile or alienation that cannot ever be rectified. No matter how perfectly he is able to express something, the result always seems to him an approximation to what he had wanted to say, and to have been said too late, past the point where the saying of it might have been helpful. "Amy Foster," the most desolate of his stories, is about a young man from Eastern Europe, shipwrecked off the English coast on his way to America, who ends up as the husband of the affectionate but inarticulate Amy Foster. The man remains a foreigner, never learns the language, and even after he and Amy have a child cannot become a part of the very family he has created with her. When he is near death and babbling deliriously in a strange language, Amy snatches their child from him, abandoning him to his final sorrow. Like so many of Conrad's fictions, the story is narrated by a sympathetic figure, a doctor who is acquainted with the pair, but even he cannot redeem the young man's isolation, although Conrad teasingly makes the reader feel that he might have been able to. It is difficult to read "Amy Foster" without thinking that Conrad must have feared dying a similar death, inconsolable, alone, talking away in a language no one could understand.

The first thing to acknowledge is the loss of home and language in the new setting, a loss that Conrad has the severity to portray as irredeemable, relentlessly anguished, raw, untreatable, always acute—which is why I have found myself over the years reading and writing about Conrad like a *cantus firmus,* a steady groundbass to much that I have experienced. For years I seemed to be going over the same kind of thing in the work I did, but always through the writings of other people. It wasn't until the early fall of 1991, when an ugly medical diagnosis suddenly revealed to me the mortality I should have known about before, that I found myself trying to make sense of my own life as its end seemed alarmingly nearer. A few months later, still trying to assimilate my new condition, I found myself composing a long explanatory letter to my mother, who had already been dead for almost two years, a letter that inaugurated a belated attempt to impose a narrative on a life that I had left more or less to itself, disorganized, scattered, uncentered. I had had a decent enough career in the university, I had written a fair amount, I had acquired an unenviable reputation (as the "professor of terror") for my writing and speaking and being active on Palestinian and generally Middle Eastern or Islamic and anti-imperialist issues, but I had rarely paused to put the whole jumble together. I was a compulsive worker, I disliked and hardly ever took vacations, and I did what I did without worrying too much (if at all) about such matters as writer's block, depression, or running dry.

All of a sudden, then, I found myself brought up short with some though not a great deal of time available to survey a life whose eccentricities I had accepted like so many facts of nature. Once again I recognized that Conrad had been there before me—except that Conrad was a European who left his native Poland and became an Englishman, so the move for him was more or less within the same world. I was born in Jerusalem and had spent most of my formative years there and, before but especially after 1948, when my entire family became refugees, in Egypt. All my early education had, however, been in élite colonial schools, English public schools designed by the British to bring up a generation of Arabs with natural ties to Britain. The last one I went to before I left the Middle East to go to the United States was Victoria College in Cairo, a school in effect created to educate those ruling-class Arabs and Levantines who were going to take over after the British left. My contemporaries and classmates included King Hussein of Jordan, several Jordanian, Egyptian, Syrian, and Saudi boys who were to become ministers, prime ministers, and leading businessmen, as well as such glamorous figures as Michel Shalhoub, head prefect of the school and chief tormentor when I was a relatively junior boy, whom everyone has seen on screen as Omar Sharif.

The moment one became a student at VC one was given the school handbook, a series of regulations governing every aspect of school life— the kind of uniform we were to wear, what equipment was needed for sports, the dates of school holidays, bus schedules, and so on. But the school's first rule, emblazoned on the opening page of the handbook, read: "English is the language of the school; students caught speaking any other language will be punished." Yet there were no native English-speakers among the students. Whereas the masters were all British, we were a motley crew of Arabs of various kinds, Armenians, Greeks, Italians, Jews, and Turks, each of whom had a native language that the school had explicitly outlawed. Yet all, or nearly all, of us spoke Arabic—many spoke Arabic and French—and so we were able to take refuge in a common language in defiance of what we perceived as an unjust colonial stricture. British imperial power was nearing its end immediately after World War Two, and this fact was not lost on us, although I cannot recall any student of my generation who would have been able to put anything as definite as that into words.

For me, there was an added complication, in that although both my parents were Palestinian—my mother from Nazareth, my father from Jerusalem—my father had acquired U.S. citizenship during World War One, when he served in the AEF under Pershing in France. He had originally left Palestine, then an Ottoman province, in 1911, at the age of 16, to escape being drafted to fight in Bulgaria. Instead, he went to the United States, studied and worked there for a few years, then returned to Palestine in 1919 to go into business with his cousin. Besides, with an unexceptionally Arab family name like Said connected to an improbably British first name (my mother very much admired the Prince of Wales in 1935, the year of my birth), I was an uncomfortably anomalous student all through my early years: a Palestinian going to school in Egypt, with an English first name, an American passport, and no certain identity at all. To make matters worse, Arabic, my native language, and English, my school language, were inextricably mixed: I have never known which was my first language, and have felt fully at home in neither, although I dream in both. Every time I speak an English sentence, I find myself echoing it in Arabic, and vice versa.

All this went through my head in those months after my diagnosis revealed to me the necessity of thinking about final things. But I did so in what for me was a characteristic way. As the author of a book called *Beginnings*, I found myself drawn to my early days as a boy in Jerusalem, Cairo, and Dhour el Shweir, the Lebanese mountain village which I loathed but where for years and years my father took us to spend our summers. I found myself reliving the narrative quandaries of my early years, my sense of doubt and of being out of place, of always feeling myself standing in the wrong corner, in a place that seemed to be slipping away from me just as I tried to define or describe it. Why, I remember asking myself, could I not have had a simple background, been all Egyptian, or all something else, and not have had to face the daily rigors of questions that led back to words that seemed to lack a stable origin? The worst part of my situation, which time has only exacerbated, has been the warring relationship between English and Arabic, something that Conrad had not had to deal with since his passage from Polish to English via French was effected entirely within Europe. My whole education was Anglocentric, so much so that I knew a great deal more about British and even Indian history and geography (required subjects) than I did about the history and geography of the Arab world. But although taught to believe and think like an English schoolboy, I was also trained to understand that I was an alien, a Non-European Other, educated by my betters to know my station and not to aspire to being British. The line separating Us from Them was linguistic, cultural, racial, and ethnic. It did not make matters easier for me to have been born, baptized, and confirmed in the Anglican Church, where the singing of bellicose hymns like "Onward Christian Soldiers" and "From Greenland's Icy Mountains" had me in effect playing the role at once of aggressor and aggressed against. To be at the same time a Wog and an Anglican was to be in a state of standing civil war.

In the spring of 1951 I was expelled from Victoria College, thrown out for being a troublemaker, which meant that I was more visible and more easily caught than the other boys in the daily skirmishes between Mr. Griffith, Mr. Hill, Mr. Lowe, Mr. Brown, Mr. Maundrell, Mr. Gatley, and all the other British teachers, on the one hand, and us, the boys of the school, on the other. We were all subliminally aware, too, that the old Arab order was crumbling: Palestine had fallen, Egypt was tottering under the massive corruption of King Farouk and his court (the revolution that brought Gamal Abdel Nasser and his Free Officers to power was to occur in July 1952), Syria was undergoing a dizzying series of military coups, Iran, whose Shah was at the time married to

Farouk's sister, had its first big crisis in 1951, and so on. The prospects for deracinated people like us were so uncertain that my father decided it would be best to send me as far away as possible—in effect, to an austere, puritanical school in the northwestern corner of Massachusetts.

The day in early September 1951 when my mother and father deposited me at the gates of that school and then immediately left for the Middle East was probably the most miserable of my life. Not only was the atmosphere of the school rigid and explicitly moralistic, but I seemed to be the only boy there who was not a native-born American, who did not speak with the required accent, and had not grown up with baseball, basketball, and football. For the first time ever I was deprived of the linguistic environment I had depended on as an alternative to the hostile attentions of Anglo-Saxons whose language was not mine, and who made no bones about my belonging to an inferior, or somehow disapproved, race. Anyone who has lived through the quotidian obstacles of colonial routine will know what I am talking about. One of the first things I did was to look up a teacher of Egyptian origin whose name had been given to me by a family friend in Cairo. "Talk to Ned," our friend said, "and he'll instantly make you feel at home." On a bright Saturday afternoon I trudged over to Ned's house, introduced myself to the wiry, dark man who was also the tennis coach, and told him that Freddie Maalouf in Cairo had asked me to look him up. "Oh yes," the tennis coach said rather frostily, "Freddie." I immediately switched to Arabic, but Ned put up his hand to interrupt me. "No, brother, no Arabic here. I left all that behind when I came to America." And that was the end of that.

Because I had been well-trained at Victoria College, I did well enough in my Massachusetts boarding-school, achieving the rank of either first or second in a class of about a hundred and sixty. But I was also found to be morally wanting, as if there was something mysteriously not-quite-right about me. When I graduated, for instance, the rank of valedictorian or salutatorian was withheld from me on the grounds that I was not fit for the honor—a moral judgment which I have ever since found difficult either to understand or to forgive. Although I went back to the Middle East during holidays (my family continued to live there, moving from Egypt to Lebanon in 1963), I found myself becoming an entirely Western person; both at college and in graduate school I studied literature, music, and philosophy, but none of it had anything to do with my own tradition. In the fifties and early sixties students from the Arab world were almost invariably scientists, doctors, and engineers, or specialists in the Middle East, getting degrees at places like Princeton and Harvard and then, for the most part, returning to their countries to become teachers in universities there. I had very little to do with them, for one reason or another, and this naturally increased my isolation from my own language and background. By the time I came to New York to teach at Columbia in the fall of 1963, I was considered to have an exotic but somewhat irrelevant Arabic background—in fact I recall that it was easier for most of my friends and colleagues not to use the word "Arab," and certainly not "Palestinian," in deference to the much easier and vaguer "Middle Eastern," a term that offended no one. A friend who was already teaching at Columbia later told me that when I was hired I had been described to the department as an Alexandrian Jew! I remember a sense of being accepted, even courted, by older colleagues at Columbia, who with one or two exceptions saw me as a promising, even very promising, young scholar of "our" culture. Since there was no political activity then which was centered on the Arab world, I found that my concerns in my teaching and research, which were canonical though slightly unorthodox, kept me within the pale.

The big change came with the Arab-Israeli war of 1967, which coincided with a period of intense political activism on campus over civil rights and the Vietnam War. I found myself naturally involved on both fronts, but, for me, there was the further difficulty of trying to draw attention to the Palestinian cause. After the Arab defeat there was a vigorous re-emergence of Palestinian nationalism, embodied in the resistance movement located mainly in Jordan and the newly occupied territories. Several friends and members of my family had joined the movement, and when I visited Jordan in 1968, 1969, and 1970, I found myself among a number of like-minded contemporaries. In the United States, however, my politics were rejected—with a few notable exceptions—both by anti-war activists and by supporters of Martin Luther King. For the first time I felt genuinely divided between the newly assertive pressures of my background and language and the complicated demands of a situation in the United States that scanted, in fact despised, what I had to say about the quest for Palestinian justice—which was considered anti-semitic and Nazi-like.

In 1972 I had a sabbatical and took the opportunity of spending a year in Beirut, where most of my time was taken up with the study of Arabic philology and literature, something I had never done before, at least not at that level, out of a feeling that I had allowed the disparity between my acquired identity and the culture into which I was born, and from which I had been removed, to become too great. In other words, there was an existential as well as a felt political need to bring one self into harmony with the other, for as the debate about what had once been called "the Middle East" metamorphosed into a debate between Israelis and Palestinians, I was drawn in, ironically enough, as much because of my capacity to speak as an American academic and intellectual as by the accident of my birth. By the mid-seventies I was in the rich but unenviable position of speaking for two diametrically opposed constituencies, one Western, the other Arab.

For as long as I can remember, I had allowed myself to stand outside the umbrella that shielded or accommodated my contemporaries. Whether this was because I was genuinely different, objectively an outsider, or because I was temperamentally a loner I cannot say, but the fact is that although I went along with all sorts of institutional routines because I felt I had to, something private in me resisted them. I don't know what it was that caused me to hold back, but even when I was most miserably solitary or out of synch with everyone else, I held onto this private aloofness very fiercely. I may have envied friends whose language was one or the other, or who had lived in the same place all their lives, or who had done well in accepted ways, or who truly belonged, but I do not recall ever thinking that any of that was possible for me. It wasn't that I considered myself special, but rather that I didn't fit the situations I found myself in and wasn't too displeased to accept this state of affairs. I have, besides, always been drawn to stubborn autodidacts, to various sorts of intellectual misfit. In part it was the heedlessness of their own peculiar angle of vision that attracted me to writers and artists like Conrad, Vico, Adorno, Swift, Adonis, Hopkins, Auerbach, Glenn Gould, whose style, or way of thinking, was highly individualistic and impossible to imitate, for whom the medium of expression, whether music or words, was eccentrically charged, very worked-over, self-conscious in the highest degree. What impressed me about them was not the mere fact of their self-invention but that the enterprise was deliberately and fastidiously located within a general history which they had excavated *ab origine*.

Having allowed myself gradually to assume the professional voice of an American academic as a way of submerging my difficult and unassimilable past, I began to think and write contrapuntally, using the disparate halves of my experience, as an Arab and as an American, to work with and also against each other. This tendency began to take shape after 1967, and though it was difficult, it was also exciting. What prompted the initial change in my sense of self, and of the language I was using, was the realization that in accommodating to the exigencies of life in the U.S. melting-pot, I had willy-nilly to accept the principle of annulment of which Adorno speaks so perceptively in *Minima Moralia:*

> The past life of émigrés is, as we know, annulled. Earlier it was the warrant of arrest, today it is intellectual experience, that is declared non-transferable and unnaturalisable. Anything that is not reified, cannot be counted and measured, ceases to exist. Not satisfied with this, however, reification spreads to its own opposite, the life that cannot be directly actualised; anything that lives on merely as thought and recollection. For this a special rubric has been invented. It is called "background" and appears on the questionnaire as an appendix, after sex, age and profession. To complete its violation, life is dragged along on the triumphal automobile of the united statisticians, and even the past is no longer safe from the present, whose remembrance of it consigns it a second time to oblivion.

For my family and for myself the catastrophe of 1948 (I was then 12) was lived unpolitically. For twenty years after their dispossession and expulsion from their homes and territory, most Palestinians had to live as refugees, coming to terms not with their past, which was lost, annulled, but with their present. I do not want to suggest that my life as a schoolboy, learning to speak and coin a language that let me live as a citizen of the United States, entailed anything like the suffering of that first generation of Palestinian refugees, scattered throughout the Arab world, where invidious laws made it impossible for them to become naturalized, unable to work, unable to travel, obliged to register and re-register each month with the police, many of them forced to live in appalling camps like Beirut's Sabra and Shatila, which were the sites of massacres 34 years later. What I experienced, however, was the suppression of a history as everyone around me celebrated Israel's victory, its terrible swift sword, as Barbara Tuchman grandly put it, at the expense of the original inhabitants of Palestine, who now found themselves forced over and over again to prove that they had once existed. "There are no Palestinians," said Golda Meir in 1969, and that set me, and many others, the slightly preposterous challenge of disproving her, of beginning to articulate a history of loss and dispossession that had to be extricated, minute by minute, word by word, inch by inch, from the very real history of Israel's establishment, existence, and achievements. I was working in an almost entirely negative element, the non-existence, the non-history which I had somehow to make visible despite occlusions, misrepresentations, and denials.

Inevitably, this led me to reconsider the notions of writing and language, which I had until then treated as animated by a given text or subject—the history of the novel, for instance, or the idea of narrative as a theme in prose fiction. What concerned me now was how a subject was constituted, how a language could be formed—writing as a construction of realities that served one or another purpose instrumentally. This was the world of power and representations, a world that came into being as a series of decisions made by writers, politicians, philosophers to suggest or adumbrate one reality and at the same time efface others. The first attempt I made at this kind of work was a short essay I wrote in 1968 entitled "The Arab Portrayed," in which I described the image of the Arab that had been manipulated in journalism and some scholarly writing in such a way as to evade any discussion of history and experience as I and many other Arabs had lived them. I also wrote a longish study of Arabic prose fiction after 1948 in which I reported on the fragmentary, embattled quality of the narrative line.

During the seventies I taught my courses in European and American literature at Columbia and elsewhere, and bit by bit entered the political and discursive worlds of Middle Eastern and international politics. It is worth mentioning here that for the forty years that I have been teaching I have never taught anything other than the Western canon, and certainly nothing about the Middle East. I've long had the ambition of giving a course on modern Arabic literature, but I haven't got around to it, and for at least thirty years I've been planning a seminar on Vico and Ibn Khaldun, the great fourteenth-century historiographer and philosopher of history. But my sense of identity as a teacher of Western literature has excluded this other aspect of my activity so far as the classroom is concerned. Ironically, the fact that I continued to write and teach my subject gave sponsors and hosts at university functions to which I had been invited to lecture an excuse to ignore my embarrassing political activity by specifically asking me to lecture on a literary topic. And there were those who spoke of my efforts on behalf of "my people," without ever mentioning the name of that people. "Palestine" was still a word to be avoided.

Even in the Arab world Palestine earned me a great deal of opprobrium. When the Jewish Defense League called me a Nazi in 1985, my office at the university was set fire to and my family and I received innumerable death threats, but when Anwar Sadat and Yasser Arafat appointed me Palestinian representative to the peace talks (without ever consulting me) and I found it impossible to step outside my apartment, so great was the media rush around me, I became the object of extreme left-wing nationalist hostility because I was considered too liberal on the question of Palestine and the idea of co-existence between Israeli Jews and Palestinian Arabs. I've been consistent in my belief that no military option exists for either side, that only a process of peaceful reconciliation, and justice for what the Palestinians have had to endure by way of dispossession and military occupation, would work. I was also very critical of the use of slogan-clichés like "armed struggle" and of the revolutionary adventurism that caused innocent deaths and did nothing to advance the Palestinian case politically. "The predicament of private life today is shown by its arena," Adorno wrote. "Dwelling, in the proper sense, is now impossible. The traditional residences we grew up in have grown intolerable: each trait of comfort in them is paid for with a betrayal of knowledge, each vestige of shelter with the musty pact of family interests." Even more unyieldingly, he continued:

The house is past . . . The best mode of conduct, in the face of
all this, still seems an uncommitted, suspended one: to lead a
private life, as far as the social order and one's own needs will
tolerate nothing else, but not to attach weight to it as something still socially substantial and individually appropriate. "It
is even part of my good fortune not to be a house-owner,"
Nietzsche already wrote in the *Gay Science*. Today we should
have to add: it is part of morality not to be at home in one's
home.

For myself, I have been unable to live an uncommitted or suspended
life: I have not hesitated to declare my affiliation with an extremely unpopular cause. On the other hand, I have always reserved the right to
be critical, even when criticism conflicted with solidarity or with what
others expected in the name of national loyalty. There is a definite, almost palpable discomfort to such a position, especially given the irreconcilability of the two constituencies, and the two lives they have
required.

The net result in terms of my writing has been to attempt a greater
transparency, to free myself from academic jargon, and not to hide behind euphemism and circumlocution where difficult issues have been
concerned. I have given the name "worldliness" to this voice, by which
I do not mean the jaded savoir-faire of the man about town, but rather
a knowing and unafraid attitude toward exploring the world we live in.
Cognate words, derived from Vico and Auerbach, have been "secular"
and "secularism" as applied to "earthly" matters; in these words, which
derive from the Italian materialist tradition that runs from Lucretius
through to Gramsci and Lampedusa, I have found an important corrective to the German Idealist tradition of synthesizing the antithetical, as we find it in Hegel, Marx, Lukács, and Habermas. For not only
did "earthly" connote this historical world made by men and women
rather than by God or "the nation's genius," as Herder termed it, but
it suggested a territorial grounding for my argument and language,
which proceeded from an attempt to understand the imaginative geographies fashioned and then imposed by power on distant lands and
people. In *Orientalism* and *Culture and Imperialism,* and then again in
the five or six explicitly political books concerning Palestine and the

Islamic world that I wrote around the same time, I felt that I had been fashioning a self who revealed for a Western audience things that had so far been either hidden or not discussed at all. Thus in talking about the Orient, hitherto believed to be a simple fact of nature, I tried to uncover the longstanding, very varied geographical obsession with a distant, often inaccessible world that helped Europe to define itself by being its opposite. Similarly, I believed that Palestine, a territory effaced in the process of building another society, could be restored as an act of political resistance to injustice and oblivion.

Occasionally, I'd notice that I had become a peculiar creature to many people, and even a few friends, who had assumed that being Palestinian was the equivalent of something mythological like a unicorn or a hopelessly odd variation of a human being. A Boston psychologist who specialized in conflict resolution, and whom I had met at several seminars involving Palestinians and Israelis, once rang me from Greenwich Village and asked if she could come uptown to pay me a visit. When she arrived, she walked in, looked incredulously at my piano—"Ah, you actually play the piano," she said, with a trace of disbelief in her voice—and then turned around and began to walk out. When I asked her whether she would have a cup of tea before leaving (after all, I said, you have come a long way for such a short visit), she said she didn't have time. "I only came to see how you lived," she said without a hint of irony. Another time a publisher in another city refused to sign my contract until I had lunch with him. When I asked his assistant what was so important about having a meal with me, I was told that the great man wanted to see how I handled myself at the table. Fortunately none of these experiences affected or detained me for very long: I was always in too much of a rush to meet a class or a deadline, and I quite deliberately avoided the self-questioning that would have landed me in a terminal depression. In any case the Palestinian intifada that erupted in December 1987 confirmed our peoplehood in as dramatic and compelling a way as anything I might have said. Before long, however, I found myself becoming a token figure, hauled in for a few hundred written words or a ten-second soundbite testifying to "what the Palestinians are saying," and determined to escape that role, especially given my disagreements with the PLO leadership from the late eighties.

I am not sure whether to call this perpetual self-invention or a constant restlessness. Either way, I've long learned to cherish it. Identity as such is about as boring a subject as one can imagine. Nothing seems less interesting than the narcissistic self-study that today passes in many places for identity politics, or ethnic studies, or affirmations of roots, cultural pride, drum-beating nationalism, and so on. We have to defend peoples and identities threatened with extinction or subordinated because they are considered inferior, but that is very different from aggrandizing a past invented for present reasons. Those of us who are American intellectuals owe it to our country to fight the coarse anti-intellectualism, bullying, injustice, and provincialism that disfigure its career as the last superpower. It is far more challenging to try to transform oneself into something different than it is to keep insisting on the virtues of being American in the ideological sense. Having myself lost a country with no immediate hope of regaining it, I don't find much comfort in cultivating a new garden, or looking for some other association to join. I learned from Adorno that reconciliation under duress is both cowardly and inauthentic: better a lost cause than a triumphant one, more satisfying a sense of the provisional and contingent—a rented house, for example—than the proprietary solidity of permanent ownership. This is why strolling dandies like Oscar Wilde or Baudelaire seem to me intrinsically more interesting than extollers of settled virtue like Wordsworth or Carlyle.

For the past five years I have been writing two columns a month for the Arabic press; and despite my extremely anti-religious politics I am often glowingly described in the Islamic world as a defender of Islam, and considered by some of the Islamic parties to be one of their supporters. Nothing could be further from the truth, any more than it is true that I have been an apologist for terrorism. The prismatic quality of one's writing when one isn't entirely of any camp, or a total partisan of any cause, is difficult to handle, but there, too, I have accepted the irreconcilability of the various conflicting, or at least incompletely harmonized, aspects of what, cumulatively, I appear to have stood for. A phrase by Günter Grass describes the predicament well: that of the "intellectual without mandate." A complicated situation arose in late 1993 when, after seeming to be the approved voice of the Palestinian struggle, I wrote increasingly sharply of my disagreements with Arafat

and his bunch. I was immediately branded "anti-peace" because I had
the lack of tact to describe the Oslo treaty as deeply flawed. Now that
everything has ground to a halt, I am regularly asked what it is like to
be proved right, but I was more surprised by that than anyone:
prophecy is not part of my arsenal.

For the past three or four years I have been trying to write a memoir
of my early—that is, pre-political—life, largely because I think it's a
story worthy of rescue and commemoration, given that the three
places I grew up in have ceased to exist. Palestine is now Israel,
Lebanon, after twenty years of civil war, is hardly the stiflingly boring
place it was when we spent our summers locked up in Dhour el Shweir,
and colonial, monarchical Egypt disappeared in 1952. My memories of
those days and places remain extremely vivid, full of little details that
I seem to have preserved as if between the covers of a book, full also of
unexpressed feelings generated out of situations and events that occurred decades ago but seem to have been waiting to be articulated
now. Conrad says in *Nostromo* that a desire lurks in every heart to write
down once and for all a true account of what happened, and this certainly is what moved me to write my memoir, just as I had found myself writing a letter to my dead mother out of a desire once again to
communicate something terribly important to a primordial presence
in my life. "In his text," Adorno says,

> the writer sets up house . . . For a man who no longer has a
> homeland, writing becomes a place to live . . . [Yet] the demand
> that one harden oneself against self-pity implies the technical
> necessity to counter any slackening of intellectual tension with
> the utmost alertness, and to eliminate anything that has begun
> to encrust the work or to drift along idly, which may at an ear-
> lier stage have served, as gossip, to generate the warm atmo-
> sphere conducive to growth, but is now left behind, flat and
> stale. In the end, the writer is not even allowed to live in his
> writing.

One achieves at most a provisional satisfaction, which is quickly am-
bushed by doubt, and a need to rewrite and redo that renders the text
uninhabitable. Better *that*, however, than the sleep of self-satisfaction
and the finality of death.

46

The Clash of Definitions

Samuel P. Huntington's essay "The Clash of Civilizations?" appeared in *Foreign Affairs* in the summer of 1993, announcing in its first sentence that "world politics is entering a new phase." By this he meant that whereas in the recent past world conflicts were between ideological factions grouping the first, second, and third worlds into warring camps, the new style of politics would entail conflicts between different, and presumably clashing, civilizations: "The great divisions among humankind and the dominating source of conflict will be cultural . . . The clash of civilizations will dominate global politics." Later Huntington explains that the principal clash will be between Western and non-Western civilizations, and indeed he spends most of his time in the article discussing the fundamental disagreements, potential or actual, between what he calls the West on the one hand and the Islamic and Confucian civilizations on the other. In terms of detail, a great deal more attention is paid to Islam than to any other civilization, including the West.

Much of the subsequent interest taken in Huntington's essay, as well as the ponderously ineffective book that followed it in 1995, I think, derives from its timing, rather than exclusively from what it actually says.

As Huntington himself notes, there have been several intellectual and political attempts since the end of the Cold War to map the emerging world situation; this included Francis Fukuyama's contention about the end of history and the thesis put about during the latter days of the Bush administration, the theory of the so-called New World Order. More recently Paul Kennedy, Conor Cruise O'Brien, and Eric Hobsbawm—all of whom have looked at the new millennium—have done so with considerable attention to the causes of future conflict, which has given them all reason for alarm. The core of Huntington's vision (not really original with him) is the idea of an unceasing clash, a concept of conflict which slides somewhat effortlessly into the political space vacated by the unremitting bipolar war of ideas and values embodied in the unregretted Cold War. I do not, therefore, think it is inaccurate to suggest that what Huntington is providing in this essay of his—especially since it is primarily addressed to Washington-based opinion and policy-makers who subscribe to *Foreign Affairs,* the leading U.S. journal of foreign policy discussion—is a recycled version of the Cold War thesis, that conflicts in today's and tomorrow's world will remain not economic or social in essence but ideological; and if that is so then one ideology, the West's, is the still point or locus around which for Huntington all others turn. In effect, then, the Cold War continues, but this time on many fronts, with many more serious and basic systems of values and ideas (like Islam and Confucianism) struggling for ascendancy and even dominance over the West. Not surprisingly, therefore, Huntington concludes his essay with a brief survey of what the West might do to remain strong and keep its putative opponents weak and divided (it must "exploit differences and conflicts among Confucian and Islamic states; . . . support in other civilizations groups sympathetic to Western values and interests; . . . strengthen international institutions that reflect and legitimate Western interests and values and . . . promote the involvement of non-Western states in those institutions," p. 49).

So strong and insistent is Huntington's notion that other civilizations necessarily clash with the West, and so relentlessly aggressive and chauvinistic is his prescription for what the West must do to continue winning, that we are forced to conclude that he is really most interested in continuing and expanding the Cold War by means other than advancing ideas about understanding the current world scene or trying to reconcile different cultures. Little in what he says expresses the slightest doubt or skepticism. Not only will conflict continue, he says on the first page, but "conflict between civilizations will be the latest phase in the evolution of conflict in the modern world." It is as a very brief and rather crudely articulated manual in the art of maintaining a wartime status in the minds of Americans and others that Huntington's essay has to be understood. I would go so far as to say that it argues from the standpoint of Pentagon planners and defense industry executives who may have temporarily lost their occupations after the end of the Cold War, but have now discovered a new vocation for themselves. Huntington at least has the merit of underlining the cultural component in relationships among different countries, traditions, and peoples.

The sad part is that "the clash of civilizations" is useful as a way of exaggerating and making intractable various political or economic problems. It is quite easy to see how, for instance, the practice of Japan-bashing in the West can be fueled by appeals to the menacing and sinister aspects of Japanese culture as employed by government spokespersons, or how the age-old appeal to the "yellow peril" might be mobilized for use in discussions of ongoing problems with Korea or China. The opposite is true in the practice throughout Asia and Africa of Occidentalism, turning "the West" into a monolithic category that is supposed to express hostility to non-White, non-European, and non-Christian civilizations.

Perhaps because he is more interested in policy prescription than in either history or the careful analysis of cultural formations, Huntington in my opinion is quite misleading in what he says and how he puts things. A great deal of his argument depends on second- and third-hand opinion that scants the enormous advances in our concrete and theoretical understanding of how cultures work, how they change, and how they can best be grasped or apprehended. A brief look at the people and opinions he quotes suggests that journalism and popular demagoguery rather than scholarship or theory are his main sources. For when you draw on tendentious publicists, scholars, and journalists like Charles Krauthammer, Sergei Stankevich, and Bernard Lewis you already prejudice the argument in favor of conflict

and polemic rather than true understanding and the kind of cooperation between peoples that our planet needs. Huntington's authorities
are not the cultures themselves but a small handful of authorities
picked by him because they emphasize the latent bellicosity in one or
another statement by one or another so-called spokesman for or about
that culture. The giveaway for me is the title of his essay—"The Clash
of Civilizations"—which is not his phrase but Bernard Lewis's. On the
last page of Lewis's essay "The Roots of Muslim Rage," which appeared
in the September 1990 issue of *The Atlantic Monthly,* a journal that has
on occasion run articles purporting to describe the dangerous sick-
ness, madness, and derangement of Arabs and Muslims, Lewis speaks
about the current problem with the Islamic world: "It should by now
be clear that we are facing a mood and a movement far transcending
the level of issues and policies and the governments that pursue them.
This is no less than a clash of civilizations—the perhaps irrational but
surely historic reactions of an ancient rival against our Judeo-
Christian heritage, our secular present, and the worldwide expansion
of both. It is crucially important that we on our side should not be
provoked into an equally historic but also equally irrational reaction
against that rival."

I do not want to spend much time discussing the lamentable features of Lewis's screed; elsewhere I have described his methods—the lazy
generalizations, the reckless distortions of history, the wholesale demo-
tion of civilizations into categories like irrational and enraged, and so
on. Few people today with any sense would want to volunteer such
sweeping characterizations as the ones advanced by Lewis about more
than a billion Muslims, scattered throughout at least five continents,
speaking dozens of differing languages, and possessing various traditions and histories. All he says about them is that they are all enraged
at Western modernity, as if a billion people were but one and Western
civilization were no more complicated a matter than a simple declarative sentence. But what I do want to stress is first of all how Huntington
has picked up from Lewis the notion that civilizations are monolithic
and homogenous, and second, how—again from Lewis—he assumes the
unchanging character of the duality between "us" and "them."

In other words, I think it is absolutely imperative to stress that like
Bernard Lewis, Samuel Huntington does not write a neutral, descrip-

tive, and objective prose, but is himself a polemicist whose rhetoric not only depends heavily on prior arguments about a war of all against all, but in effect perpetuates them. Far from being an arbiter between civilizations, therefore, Huntington is a partisan, an advocate of one so-called civilization over all others. Like Lewis, Huntington defines Islamic civilization reductively, as if what matters most about it is its supposed anti-Westernism. For his part Lewis tries to give a set of reasons for his definition—that Islam has never modernized, that it never separated between Church and State, that it has been incapable of understanding other civilizations—but Huntington does not bother with them. For him Islam, Confucianism, and the other five or six civilizations (Hindu, Japanese, Slavic-Orthodox, Latin American, and African) that still exist are separate from one another, and consequently potentially in a conflict which he wants to manage, not resolve. He writes as a crisis manager, not as a student of civilization, nor as a reconciler between them.

At the core of his essay, and this is what has made it strike so responsive a chord among post–Cold War policy-makers, is this sense of cutting through a lot of unnecessary detail, of masses of scholarship and huge amounts of experience, and boiling all of them down to a couple of catchy, easy-to-quote-and-remember ideas, which are then passed off as pragmatic, practical, sensible, and clear. But is this the best way to understand the world we live in? Is it wise as an intellectual and a scholarly expert to produce a simplified map of the world and then hand it to generals and civilian law-makers as a prescription for first comprehending and then acting in the world? Doesn't this method in effect prolong, exacerbate, and deepen conflict? What does it do to minimize civilizational conflict? Do we *want* the clash of civilizations? Doesn't it mobilize nationalist passions and therefore nationalist murderousness? Shouldn't we ask the question, Why is one doing this sort of thing: to understand or to act? to mitigate or to aggravate the likelihood of conflict?

I would begin to survey the world situation by commenting on how prevalent it has become for people to speak now in the name of large, and in my opinion undesirably vague and manipulable, abstractions like the West or Japanese or Slavic culture, Islam or Confucianism, labels that collapse religions, races, and ethnicities into ideologies that are considerably more unpleasant and provocative than those of Gobineau and Renan 150 years ago. Strange as it may seem, these examples of group psychology run rampant are not new, and they are certainly not edifying at all. They occur in times of deep insecurity, that is, when peoples seem particularly close to and thrust upon one another, as either the result of expansion, war, imperialism, and migration, or the effect of sudden, unprecedented change.

Let me give a couple of examples to illustrate. The language of group identity makes a particularly strident appearance from the middle to the end of the nineteenth century as the culmination of decades of international competition between the great European and American powers for territories in Africa and Asia. In the battle for the empty spaces of Africa—the dark continent—France and Britain as well as Germany and Belgium resort not only to force but to a whole slew of theories and rhetorics for justifying their plunder. Perhaps the most famous of such devices is the French concept of civilizing mission, *la mission civilisatrice*, an underlying notion of which is the idea that some races and cultures have a higher aim in life than others; this gives the more powerful, more developed, more civilized the right therefore to colonize others, not in the name of brute force or raw plunder, both of which are standard components of the exercise, but in the name of a noble ideal. Joseph Conrad's most famous story, *Heart of Darkness*, is an ironic, even terrifying enactment of this thesis, that—as his narrator Marlow puts it—"the conquest of the earth, which mostly means the taking it away from those who have a different complexion or slightly flatter noses than ourselves, is not a pretty thing when you look into it too much. What redeems it is the idea only. An idea at the back of it, not a sentimental pretence but an idea; and an unselfish belief in the idea—something you can set up, and bow down before, and offer a sacrifice to."

In response to this sort of logic, two things occur. One is that competing powers invent their own theory of cultural or civilizational destiny in order to justify their actions abroad. Britain had such a theory, Germany had one, Belgium had one, and of course in the concept of manifest destiny, the United States had one, too. These redeeming ideas dignify the practice of competition and clash, whose real purpose, as Conrad quite accurately saw, was self-aggrandizement, power, conquest, treasure, and unrestrained self-pride. I would go so far as to say that what we today call the rhetoric of identity, by which a member of one ethnic or religious or national or cultural group puts that group at the center of the world, derives from that period of imperial competition at the end of the nineteenth century. And this in turn provokes the concept of "worlds at war" that quite obviously is at the heart of Huntington's article. It received its most frightening futuristic application in H. G. Wells's fable *The War of the Worlds,* which, recall, expands the concept to include a battle between this world and a distant, interplanetary one. In the related fields of political economy, geography, anthropology, and historiography, the theory that each "world" is self-enclosed, has its own boundaries and special territory, is applied to the world map, to the structure of civilizations, to the notion that each race has a special destiny, psychology, ethos, and so on. All these ideas, almost without exception, are based not on the harmony but on the conflict, or clash, between worlds. It is evident in the works of Gustave LeBon (cf. *The World in Revolt*) and in such relatively forgotten works as F. S. Marvin's *Western Races and the World* (1922) and George Henry Lane-Fox Pitt Rivers's *The Clash of Culture and the Contact of Races* (1927).

The second thing that happens is that, as Huntington himself concedes, the lesser peoples, the objects of the imperial gaze, so to speak, respond by resisting their forcible manipulation and settlement. We now know that active primary resistance to the white man began the moment he set foot in places like Algeria, East Africa, India, and elsewhere. Later, primary resistance was succeeded by secondary resistance, the organization of political and cultural movements determined to achieve independence and liberation from imperial control. At precisely the moment in the nineteenth century that a rhetoric of civilizational self-justification begins to be widespread among the European and American powers, a responding rhetoric among the colonized peoples develops, one that speaks in terms of African or Asian or Arab unity, independence, self-determination. In India, for example, the Congress party was organized in 1880 and by the turn of the century had convinced the Indian elite that only by supporting *Indian* languages, industry, and commerce could political freedom come; these are ours and ours alone, runs the argument, and only by supporting our world against *theirs*—note the us-versus-them construction here—can we finally stand on our own. One finds a similar logic at work during the Meiji period in modern Japan. Something like this rhetoric of belonging is also lodged at the heart of each independence movement's nationalism, and shortly after World War Two it achieved the result not only of dismantling the classical empires, but of winning independence for dozens and dozens of countries thereafter. India, Indonesia, most of the Arab countries, Indochina, Algeria, Kenya, and so on: all these emerged onto the world scene sometimes peacefully, sometimes as the effect of internal developments (as in the Japanese instance), ugly colonial wars, or wars of national liberation.

In both the colonial and the post-colonial context, therefore, rhetorics of general cultural or civilizational specificity went in two potential directions, one a utopian line that insisted on an overall pattern of integration and harmony among all peoples, the other a line which suggested that all civilizations were so specific and jealous, monotheistic, in effect, as to reject and war against all others. Among instances of the first are the language and institutions of the United Nations, founded in the aftermath of World War Two, and the subsequent development out of the U.N. of various attempts at world government predicated on coexistence, voluntary limitations of sovereignty, and the harmonious integration of peoples and cultures. Among the second are the theory and practice of the Cold War and, more recently, the idea that the clash of civilizations is, if not a necessity for a world of so many different parts, then a certainty. According to this view, cultures and civilizations are basically *separated* from each other. I do not want to be invidious here. In the Islamic world there has been a resurgence of rhetorics and movements stressing the inimicability of Islam with the West, just as in Africa, Europe, Asia, and elsewhere, movements have appeared that stress the need for excluding designated others as undesirable. White apartheid in South Africa was such a movement, as is the current interest in Afrocentrism and a totally independent Western civilization to be found in Africa and the United States respectively.

The point of this short cultural history of the idea of the clash of civilizations is that people like Huntington are products of that history, and are shaped in their writing by it. Moreover, the language describing the clash is laced with considerations of power: the powerful use it to protect what they have and what they do, the powerless or less powerful use it to achieve parity, independence, or a comparative advantage with regard to the dominant power. Thus to build a conceptual framework around the notion of us-versus-them is in effect to pretend that the principal consideration is epistemological and natural—our civilization is known and accepted, theirs is different and strange—whereas in fact the framework separating us from them is belligerent, constructed, and situational. Within each civilizational camp, we will notice, there are official representatives of that culture or civilization who make themselves into its mouthpiece, who assign themselves the role of articulating "our" (or for that matter "their") essence. This always necessitates a fair amount of compression, reduction, and exaggeration. So on the first and most immediate level, then, statements about what "our" culture or civilization is, or ought to be, necessarily involve a contest over the definition. This is certainly true of Huntington, who writes his essay at a time in U.S. history when a great deal of turmoil has surrounded the very definition of Western civilization. Recall that in the United States many college campuses have been shaken during the past couple of decades over what the canon of Western civilization is, which books should be taught, which ones read or not read, included, or otherwise given attention. Places like Stanford and Columbia debated the issue not simply because it was a matter of habitual academic concern but because the definition of the West and consequently of America was at stake.

Anyone who has the slightest understanding of how cultures work knows that defining a culture, saying what it is for members of the culture, is always a major and, even in undemocratic societies, a democratic contest. There are canonical authorities to be selected and regularly revised, debated, re-selected, or dismissed. There are ideas of good and evil, belonging or not belonging (the same and the different), hierarchies of value to be specified, discussed, re-discussed, and settled or not, as the case may be. Moreover, each culture defines its enemies, what stands beyond it and threatens it. For the Greeks beginning with Herodotus, anyone who did not speak Greek was automatically a barbarian, an Other to be despised and fought against. An excellent recent book by the French classicist François Hartog, *The*

Mirror of Herodotus, shows how deliberately and painstakingly Herodotus sets about constructing an image of a barbarian Other in the case of the Scythians, more even than in the case of the Persians.

The official culture is that of priests, academies, and the state. It provides definitions of patriotism, loyalty, boundaries, and what I have called belonging. It is this official culture that speaks in the name of the whole, that tries to express the general will, the general ethos and idea which inclusively holds in the official past, the founding fathers and texts, the pantheon of heroes and villains, and so on, and excludes what is foreign or different or undesirable in the past. From it come the definitions of what may or may not be said, those prohibitions and proscriptions that are necessary to any culture if it is to have authority.

It is also true that in addition to the mainstream, official, or canonical culture there are dissenting or alternative unorthodox, heterodox cultures that contain many anti-authoritarian strains that compete with the official culture. These can be called the counter-culture, an ensemble of practices associated with various kinds of outsiders—the poor, the immigrants, artistic bohemians, workers, rebels, artists. From the counter-culture comes the critique of authority and attacks on what is official and orthodox. The great contemporary Arab poet Adonis has written a massive account of the relationship between orthodoxy and heterodoxy in Arabic culture and has shown the constant dialectic and tension between them. No culture is understandable without some sense of this ever-present source of creative provocation from the unofficial to the official; to disregard this sense of restlessness within each culture, and to assume that there is complete homogeneity between culture and identity, is to miss what is vital and fecund.

In the United States the debate about what is American has gone through a large number of transformations and sometimes dramatic shifts. When I was growing up, the Western film depicted Native Americans as evil devils to be destroyed or tamed; they were called Red Indians, and insofar as they had any function in the culture at large—this was as true of films as it was of the writing of academic history—it was to be a foil to the advancing course of white civilization. Today that has changed completely. Native Americans are seen as victims, not villains, of the country's Western progress. There has even been a change in the status of Columbus. There are even more dramatic reversals in the depictions of African Americans and women. Toni Morrison has noted that in classic American literature there is an obsession with whiteness, as Melville's Moby Dick and Poe's Arthur Gordon Pym so eloquently testify. Yet she says the major male and white writers of the nineteenth and twentieth centuries, men who shaped the canon of what we have known as American literature, created their works by using whiteness as a way of avoiding, curtaining off, and rendering invisible the African presence in the midst of our society. The very fact that Toni Morrison writes her novels and criticism with such success and brilliance now underscores the extent of the change from the world of Melville and Hemingway to that of Du Bois, Baldwin, Langston Hughes, and Toni Morrison. Which vision is the real America, and who can lay claim to represent and define it? The question is a complex and deeply interesting one, but it cannot be settled by reducing the whole matter to a few clichés.

A recent view of the difficulties involved in cultural contests whose object is the definition of a civilization can be found in Arthur Schlesinger's little book *The Disuniting of America*. As a mainstream historian Schlesinger is understandably troubled by the fact that emergent and immigrant groups in the United States have disputed the official, unitary fable of America as it used to be represented by the great classical historians of this country, men like Bancroft, Henry Adams, and more recently Richard Hofstadter. They want the writing of history to reflect, not only an America that was conceived of and ruled by patricians and landowners, but an America in which slaves, servants, laborers, and poor immigrants played an important but as yet unacknowledged role. The narratives of such people, silenced by the great discourses whose source was Washington, the investment banks of New York, the universities of New England, and the great industrial fortunes of the Middle West, have come to disrupt the slow progress and unruffled serenity of the official story. They ask questions, interject the experiences of social unfortunates, and make the claims of frankly lesser peoples—of women, Asian and African Americans, and various other minorities, sexual as well as ethnic. Whether or not one agrees with Schlesinger's *cri de coeur,* there is no disagreeing with his underlying thesis that the writing of history is the royal road to the definition of a country, that the identity of a society is in large part a function of historical interpretation, which is fraught with contested claims and counter-claims. The United States is in just such a fraught situation today.

There is a similar debate inside the Islamic world today which, in the often hysterical outcry about the threat of Islam, Islamic fundamentalism, and terrorism that one encounters so often in the Western media, is often lost sight of completely. Like any other major world culture, Islam contains within itself an astonishing variety of currents and counter-currents, most of them undiscerned by tendentious Orientalist scholars for whom Islam is an object of fear and hostility, or by journalists who do not know any of the languages or relevant histories and are content to rely on persistent stereotypes that have lingered in the West since the tenth century. Iran today—which has become the target of a politically opportunistic attack by the United States—is in the throes of a stunningly energetic debate about law, freedom, personal responsibility, and tradition that is simply not covered by Western reporters. Charismatic lecturers and intellectuals—clerical and non-clerical alike—carry on the tradition of Shariati, challenging centers of power and orthodoxy with impunity and, it would seem, great popular success. In Egypt two major civil cases involving intrusive religious interventions in the lives of an intellectual and a celebrated filmmaker respectively have resulted in the victory of both over orthodoxy (I refer here to the cases of Nasir Abu Zeid and Yousef Chahine). And I myself have argued in a recent book (*The Politics of Dispossession*, 1994) that far from there being a surge of Islamic fundamentalism as it is reductively described in the Western media, there is a great deal of secular opposition to it, in the form of various contests over the interpretation of *sunnah* in matters of law, personal conduct, political decision-making, and so on. Moreover, what is often forgotten is that movements like Hamas and Islamic Jihad are essentially protest movements that go against the capitulationist policies of the PLO and mobilize the will to resist Israeli occupation practices, expropriation of land, and the like.

I find it surprising and indeed disquieting that Huntington gives no indication anywhere in his essay that he is aware of these complex disputes, or that he realized that the nature and identity of a civilization are never taken as unquestioned axioms by every single member of that civilization. Far from the Cold War being the defining horizon of the past few decades, I would say that it is this extremely widespread attitude of questioning and skepticism toward age-old authority that characterizes the post-war world in both East and West. Nationalism and decolonization forced the issue by bringing whole populations to consider the question of nationality in the era after the white colonist had left. In Algeria, for example, today the site of a bloody contest between Islamists and an aging and discredited government, the debate has taken violent forms. But it is a real debate and a fierce contest nonetheless. Having defeated the French in 1962, the National Front for the Liberation of Algeria (FLN) declared itself to be the bearer of a newly liberated Algerian, Arab, and Muslim identity. For the first time in the modern history of the place, Arabic became the language of instruction, state socialism its political creed, non-alignment its foreign affairs posture. In the process of conducting itself as a one-party embodiment of all these things, the FLN grew into a massive, atrophied bureaucracy, its economy depleted, its leaders stagnating in the position of an unyielding oligarchy. Opposition arose not only from Muslim clerics and leaders but from the Berber minority, submerged in the all-purpose discourse of a supposedly single Algerian identity. The political crisis of the past few years, then, represents a several-sided contest for power, and for the right to decide the nature of Algerian identity: what is Islamic about it, and what kind of Islam, what is national, what Arab and Berber, and so on.

To Huntington, what he calls "civilization identity" is a stable and undisturbed thing, like a roomful of furniture in the back of your house. This is extremely far from the truth, not just in the Islamic world but throughout the entire surface of the globe. To emphasize the differences among cultures and civilizations—incidentally, I find his use of the words "culture" and "civilization" extremely sloppy, precisely because for him the two words represent fixed and reified objects, rather than the dynamic, ceaselessly turbulent things that they in fact are—is completely to ignore the literally unending debate or contest (to use the more active and energetic of the two words) about defining the culture or civilization within those civilizations, including various "Western" ones. These debates completely undermine any idea of a fixed identity, and hence of relationships between identities, what Huntington considers to be a sort of ontological fact of political existence, to wit the clash of civilizations. You don't have to be an expert on China, Japan, Korea, and India to know that. There is the American instance I mentioned earlier. Or there is the German case, in which a major debate has been taking place ever since the end of World War Two about the nature of German culture, as to whether Nazism derived logically from its core, or whether it was an aberration.

But there is more to the question of identity even than that. In the field of cultural and rhetorical studies, a series of recent discoveries/advances has given us a much clearer insight not only into the contested, dynamic nature of cultural identity, but into the extent to which the very idea of identity itself involves fantasy, manipulation, invention, construction. During the 1970s Hayden White published an extremely influential work called *Metahistory*. It is a study of several nineteenth-century historians—Marx, Michelet, and Nietzsche among them—and how their reliance upon one or a series of tropes (figures of speech) determines the nature of their vision of history. Thus Marx, for instance, is committed to a particular poetics in his writing which allows him to understand the nature of progress and alienation in history according to a particular narrative model, stressing the difference in society between form and substance. The point of White's extremely rigorous and quite brilliant analysis of Marx and the other historians is that he shows us how their histories are best understood, not according to criteria of "realness" but rather according to how their internal rhetorical and discursive strategies work: it is these, rather than facts, that make the visions of Tocqueville or Croce or Marx actually work as a system, not any external source in the so-called real world.

The effect of White's book, as much as the effect of Michel Foucault's studies, is to draw attention away from the existence of veridic confirmations for ideas that might be provided by the natural world, and focus it instead on the kind of language used, which is seen as shaping the components of a writer's vision. Rather than the idea of clash, for instance, deriving from a real clash in the world, we would come to see it as deriving instead from the strategies of Huntington's prose, which in turn relies on what I would call a managerial poetics, a strategy for assuming the existence of stable and metaphorically defined entities called civilizations which the writer proceeds quite emotively to manipulate, as in the phrase "the crescent-shaped Islamic bloc, from the bulge of Africa to central Asia, has bloody borders." I am not saying that Huntington's language is emotive and shouldn't be, but rather that quite revealingly it is, the way all language functions in the poetic way analyzed by Hayden White. What is evident from Huntington's language is the way he uses figurative language to accentuate the distance between "our" world—normal, acceptable, familiar, logical—and, as an especially striking example, the world of Islam, with its bloody borders, bulging contours, and so on. This suggests not so much analysis on Huntington's part but a series of determinations which, as I said earlier, creates the very clash he seems in his essay to be discovering and pointing to.

Too much attention paid to managing and clarifying the clash of cultures obliterates the fact of a great, often silent exchange and dialogue between them. What culture today—whether Japanese, Arab, European, Korean, Chinese, or Indian—has not had long, intimate, and extraordinarily rich contacts with other cultures? There is no exception to this exchange at all. One wishes that conflict managers would have paid attention to and understood the meaning of the mingling of different musics, for example, in the work of Olivier Messiaen or Toru Takemitsu. For all the power and influence of the various national schools, what is most arresting in contemporary music is that no one can draw a boundary around any of it; cultures are often most naturally themselves when they enter into partnerships with one another, as in music with its extraordinary receptivity to developments in the musics of other societies and continents. Much the same is true of literature, where readers of, for example, García Márquez, Mahfuz, and Oe exist far beyond the boundaries imposed by language and nation. In my own field of comparative literature there is an epistemological commitment to the relationships between literatures, to their reconciliation and harmony, despite the existence of powerful ideological and national barriers between them. And this sort of cooperative, collective enterprise is what one misses in the proclaimers of an undying clash between cultures: the lifelong dedication that has existed in all modern societies among scholars, artists, musicians, visionaries, and prophets to try to come to terms with the Other, with that other society or culture that seems so foreign and so distant. One thinks of

Joseph Needham and his lifelong study of China, or in France, of Louis Massignon, his pilgrimage within Islam. It seems to me that unless we emphasize and maximize the spirit of cooperation and humanistic exchange—and here I speak not simply of uninformed delight or of amateurish enthusiasm for the exotic, but rather of profound existential commitment and labor on behalf of the other—we are going to end up superficially and stridently banging the drum for "our" culture in opposition to all others.

Two other recent seminal works of cultural analysis are relevant here. In the compilation of essays entitled *The Invention of Tradition* and edited by Terence Ranger and Eric Hobsbawm, two of the most distinguished historians alive today, the authors argue that tradition, far from being the unshakable order of inherited wisdom and practice, is frequently a set of invented practices and beliefs used in mass societies to create a sense of identity at a time when organic solidarities—such as those of family, village, and clan—have broken down. Thus the emphasis on tradition in the nineteenth and twentieth centuries is a way that rulers can claim to have legitimacy, even though that legitimacy is more or less manufactured. In India, as a case in point, the British invented an impressive array of rituals to celebrate Queen Victoria's receipt of the title of Empress of India in 1872. By doing so, and by claiming that the durbars, or grand processions, commemorating the event had a long history in India, the British were able to give her rule a pedigree that it did not have in fact, but came to have in the form of invented traditions. In another context, sports rituals like the football game, a relatively recent practice, are regarded as the culmination of an age-old celebration of sporting activity, whereas in fact they are a recent way of diverting large numbers of people. The point of all this is that a great deal of what used to be thought of as settled fact, or tradition, is revealed to be a fabrication for mass consumption in the here and now.

To people who speak solely of the clash of civilizations, there exists no inkling of this possibility. For them cultures and civilizations may change, develop, regress, and disappear, but they remain mysteriously fixed in their identity, their essence graven in stone, so to speak, as if there were a universal consensus somewhere agreeing to the six civilizations Huntington posits at the beginning of his essay. My contention is that no such consensus exists, or if it does, it can hardly withstand the analytic scrutiny brought to bear by analyses of the kind provided by Hobsbawm and Ranger. So in reading about the clash of civilizations we are less likely to assent to analysis of the clash than we are to ask the question, Why do you pinion civilizations into so unyielding an embrace, and why then do you go on to describe their relationship as one of basic conflict, as if the borrowing and overlappings between them were not a much more interesting and significant feature?

Finally, my third example of cultural analysis tells us a great deal about the possibilities of actually creating a civilization retrospectively and making that creation into a frozen definition, in spite of the evidence of great hybridity and mixture. The book is *Black Athena,* the author, the Cornell political scientist Martin Bernal. The conception most of us have today about classical Greece, Bernal says, does not at all correspond with what Greek authors of that period say about it. Ever since the early nineteenth century, Europeans and Americans have grown up with an idealized picture of Attic harmony and grace, imagining Athens as a place where enlightened Western philosophers like Plato and Aristotle taught their wisdom, where democracy was born, and where, in every possible significant way, a Western mode of life completely different from that of Asia or Africa held sway. Yet to read a large number of ancient authors accurately is to note that many of them comment on the existence of Semitic and African elements in Attic life. Bernal takes the further step of demonstrating by the skillful use of a great many sources that Greece was originally a colony of Africa, more particularly of Egypt, and that Phoenician and Jewish traders, sailors, and teachers contributed most of what we know today as classical Greek culture, which he sees as an amalgam therefore of African, Semitic, and later northern influences.

In the most compelling part of *Black Athena,* Bernal goes on to show how with the growth of European, and in particular German, nationalism the original mixed portrait of Attic Greece that obtained into the eighteenth century was gradually expunged of all its non-Aryan elements, just as many years later the Nazis decided to burn all books and ban all authors considered non-German, non-Aryan. So from being the product of an invasion from the South—that is, Africa—as in reality it really was, classical Greece was progressively transformed into the product of an invasion from the Aryan north. Purged of its troublesome non-European elements, Greece thereafter has stood in the Western self-definition—an expedient one to be sure—as its fons et origo, its source of sweetness and light. The principle underlined by Bernal is the extent to which pedigrees, dynasties, lineages, and predecessors are changed to suit the political needs of a later time. Of the unfortunate results this produced in the case of a self-created white Aryan European civilization none of us need to be convinced.

What is even more troubling to me about proclaimers of the clash of civilizations is how oblivious they seem of all we now know as historians and as cultural analysts about the way definitions of these cultures themselves are so contentious. Rather than accepting the incredibly naive and deliberately reductive notion that civilizations are identical with themselves, and that is all, we must always ask which civilizations are intended, created, and defined by whom, and for what reason. Recent history is too full of instances in which the defense of Judeo-Christian values has been urged as a way of quelling dissent or unpopular opinions for us passively to assume that "everyone" knows what those values are, how they are meant to be interpreted, and how they may or may not be implemented in society.

Many Arabs would say that their civilization is really Islam, just as some Westerners—Australians and Canadians and some Americans—might not want to be included in so large and vaguely defined a category as Western. And when a man like Huntington speaks of the "common objective elements" that supposedly exist in every culture, he leaves the analytic and historical world altogether, preferring instead to find refuge inside large and ultimately meaningless categories.

As I have argued in several of my own books, in today's Europe and the United States what is described as "Islam" belongs to the discourse of Orientalism, a construction fabricated to whip up feelings of hostility and antipathy against a part of the world that happens to be of strategic importance for its oil, its threatening adjacence to the Christian world, and its formidable history of competitiveness with the West. Yet this is a very different thing from what, to Muslims who live within its domain, Islam really is. There is a world of difference between Islam in Indonesia and Islam in Egypt. By the same token, the volatility of today's struggle over the meaning of Islam is evident in Egypt, where the secular powers of society are in conflict with various Islamic protest movements and reformers over the nature of Islam. In such circumstances the easiest, and the least accurate, thing is to say: *that* is the world of Islam, and see how it is all terrorists and fundamentalists, and see also how different *they* are from us.

But the truly weakest part of the clash of civilizations thesis is the rigid separation assumed among civilizations, despite the overwhelming evidence that today's world is in fact a world of mixtures, of migrations, of crossings over. One of the major crises affecting countries like France, Britain, and the United States has been brought about by the realization now dawning everywhere that no culture or society is purely one thing. Sizeable minorities—North Africans in France, the African and Caribbean and Indian populations in Britain, Asian and African elements in the United States—dispute the idea that civilizations that prided themselves on being homogenous can continue to do so. There are no insulated cultures or civilizations. Any attempt made to separate them into the water-tight compartments alleged by Huntington does damage to their variety, their diversity, their sheer complexity of elements, their radical hybridity. The more insistent we are on the separation of cultures and civilizations, the more inaccurate we are about ourselves and others. The notion of an exclusionary civilization is, to my way of thinking, an impossible one. The real question, then, is whether in the end we want to work for civilizations that are separate or whether we should be taking the more integrative, but perhaps more difficult, path, which is to try to see them as making one vast whole whose exact contours are impossible for one person to grasp, but whose certain existence we can intuit and feel. In any case, a number of political scientists, economists, and cultural analysts have for some years been speaking of an integrative world system, largely economic, it is true, but nonetheless knitted together, overriding many of the clashes spoken of so hastily and imprudently by Huntington.

What Huntington quite astonishingly overlooks is the phenomenon referred to frequently in the literature as the globalization of capital. In 1980 Willy Brandt and some associates published *North-South: A Program for Survival*. In it the authors noted that the world was now divided into two vastly uneven regions: a small industrial North, comprising the major European, American, and Asian economic powers, and an enormous South, comprising the former Third World plus a large number of new, extremely impoverished nations. The political problem of the future would be how to imagine their relationships as the North would get richer, the South poorer, and the world more interdependent. Let me quote now from an essay by the Duke political scientist Arif Dirlik that goes over much of the ground covered by Huntington in a way that is more accurate and persuasive:

> The situation created by global capitalism helps explain certain phenomena that have become apparent over the last two or three decades, but especially since the eighties: global motions of peoples (and, therefore, cultures), the weakening of boundaries (among societies, as well as among social categories), the replications in societies internally of inequalities and discrepancies once associated with colonial differences, simultaneous homogenization and fragmentation within and across societies, the interpenetration of the global and the local, and the disorganization of a world conceived in terms of three worlds or nation-states. Some of these phenomena have also contributed to an appearance of equalization of differences within and across societies, as well as of democratization within and among societies. What is ironic is that the managers of this world situation themselves concede that they (or their organizations) now have the power to appropriate the local for the global, to admit different cultures into the realm of capital (only to break them down and remake them in accordance with the requirements of production and consumption), and even to reconstitute subjectivities across national boundaries to create producers and consumers more responsive to the operations of capital. Those who do not respond, or the "basket cases" that are not essential to those operations— four-fifths of the global population by the managers' count— need not be colonized; they are simply marginalized. What the new flexible production has made possible is that it is no longer necessary to utilize explicit coercion against labor at

home or in colonies abroad. Those peoples or places that are not responsive to the needs (or demands) of capital, or are too far gone to respond "efficiently," simply find themselves out of its pathways. And it is easier even than in the heyday of colonialism or modernization theory to say convincingly: It is their fault. (*Critical Inquiry*, Winter 1994, 351)

In view of these depressing and even alarming actualities, it does seem to me ostrich-like to suggest that we in Europe and the United States should maintain our civilization by holding all the others at bay, increasing the rifts between peoples in order to prolong our dominance. That is, in effect, what Huntington is arguing, and one can quite easily understand why it is that his essay was published in *Foreign Affairs*, and why so many policy-makers have drifted toward it as allowing the United States to extend the mind-set of the Cold War into a different time and for a new audience. Much more productive and useful is a new global mentality that sees the dangers we face from the standpoint of the whole human race. These dangers include the pauperization of most of the globe's population; the emergence of virulent local, national, ethnic, and religious sentiment, as in Bosnia, Rwanda, Lebanon, Chechnya, and elsewhere; the decline of literacy and the onset of a new illiteracy based on electronic modes of communication, television, and the new global information superhighway; the fragmentation and threatened disappearance of the grand narratives of emancipation and enlightenment. Our most precious asset in the face of such a dire transformation of tradition and of history is the emergence of a sense of community, understanding, sympathy, and hope which is the direct opposite of what in his essay Huntington has provoked. If I may quote some lines by the great Martiniqean poet Aimé Césaire that I used in my recent book *Culture and Imperialism*:

> but the work of man is only just beginning
> and it remains to man to conquer all
> the violence entrenched in the recesses of his passion
>
> And no race possesses the monopoly of beauty,
> of intelligence, of force, and there
> is a place for all at the rendez-vous of victory.

In what they imply, these sentiments prepare the way for a dissolution of cultural barriers as well as of the civilizational pride that prevents the kind of benign globalism already to be found, for instance, in the environmental movement, in scientific cooperation, in the universal concern for human rights, in concepts of global thought that stress community and sharing over racial, gender, or class dominance. It would seem to me, therefore, that efforts to return the community of civilizations to a primitive stage of narcissistic struggle must be understood not as descriptions about how in fact they behave but rather as incitements to wasteful conflict and unedifying chauvinism. And that seems to be exactly what we do not need.

NOTES

CREDITS

INDEX

NOTES

1. Labyrinth of Incarnations:
The Essays of Maurice Merleau-Ponty

1. Maurice Merleau-Ponty, *The Primacy of Perception and Other Essays*, ed. James M. Edie, trans. William Cobb (Evanston, Ill.: Northwestern University Press, 1964); Maurice Merleau-Ponty, *Sense and Non-Sense*, trans. Hubert L. Dreyfus and Patricia Allen Dreyfus (Evanston, Ill.: Northwestern University Press, 1964); Maurice Merleau-Ponty, *Signs*, trans. Richard C. McCleary (Evanston, Ill.: Northwestern University Press, 1964).

3. Amateur of the Insoluble

1. E. M. Cioran, *The Temptation to Exist*, trans. Richard Howard, intro. Susan Sontag (Chicago: Quadrangle Books, 1968).

4. A Standing Civil War

1. Phillip Knightley and Colin Simpson, *The Secret Lives of Lawrence of Arabia* (New York: McGraw-Hill, 1970).
2. André Malraux, "Lawrence and the Demon of the Absolute," *Hudson Review* 8:4 (Winter 1956).

5. Arabic Prose and Prose Fiction After 1948

1. For the broadest and most literate examination of the connection between the novel as an institution and society see Harry Levin, *The Gates*

of Horn (New York: Oxford University Press, 1963); on the general problem of literary form and social reality see Lucien Goldmann, *Le Dieu caché* (Paris: Gallimard, 1955), and his *Recherches dialectiques* (Paris: Gallimard, 1959).

2. Georg Lukács, *The Theory of the Novel,* trans. Anna Bostock (Cambridge, Mass.: MIT Press, 1971), p. 88.

3. "Molestation and Authority in Narrative Fiction," in *Aspects of Narrative,* ed. J. Hillis Miller (New York: Columbia University Press, 1971).

4. See also Le Gassick's articles: "A Malaise in Cairo: Three Contemporary Egyptian Authors," *Middle East Journal* 21:2 (Spring 1967); "Some Recent War-Related Arabic Fiction," *Middle East Journal* 25:4 (Autumn 1971); "The Literature of Modern Egypt," *Books Abroad* 46 (Spring 1972).

5. Constantine K. Zurayk, *The Meaning of the Disaster,* trans. R. Bayly Winder (Beirut: Khayat's College Book Cooperative, 1956).

6. See his introduction to the collection of essays in *Sociologie de l'impérialisme* (Paris: Editions Anthropos, 1971), pp. 15–63, and his interview with the Beirut quarterly *Al-Thaqafa al Arabiyah* (Spring 1973).

7. Ghali Shukri, *Thawrat al-fikr fi adabina al-hadith* (Cairo: Maktabat al-Anjlu al-Misriyah, 1965), p. 107.

8. Ghali Shukri, *Adab al muqawamah* (Cairo: Dar al-Maarif, 1970), p. 128.

9. Raja al-Naqqash, *Adab wa urubah wa hurriya* (Cairo: al-Dar al-Qawmiyah lil-Tibaah wa-al-Nashr, 1964), p. 100.

10. *Yawmiyyat na'ib fil aryaf* (reprinted Cairo, 1965), p. 96.

11. There is an even worse sort of analysis—the kind that purports to deliver the "content" of literature as evidence of political attitudes and (this is its real intent) of the so-called Arab "mind" or "character." There is a time-honored tradition of such analyses in the West, most of them deriving from the profession of "Orientalism." More recently, in Israel and the United States, cultivated racialism of this sort is to be found in many places, mostly academic and governmental. A typical and influential example is Gen. Yehoshafat Harkabi's *Arab Attitudes to Israel,* trans. Misha Louvish (New York: Halsted Press, 1972).

12. Ghassan Kanafani, *Rijal fil shams* (Beirut, 1963), pp. 7–8 (my translation).

13. Raja al-Naqqash, *Udaba' mu'asirun* (Cairo: Maktabat al-Anjlu al-Misriyah, 1968), p. 153.

14. Abdullah Laroui, "Pour une méthodologie des études islamiques: L'Islam au miroir, de G. von Grunehaum," *Diogène* 83 (July–Sept., 1973): 41.

15. This is especially true of two works produced shortly after the 1967 war: *Al naqd al thati ba'ad al hazima* (Beirut, 1969) and Sadiq Jalal al-Azm, *Naqd al fikr al dini* (Beirut: Dar al-Taliah, 1969).

16. Georg Lukács, *The Historical Novel*, trans. Hannah and Stanley Mitchell (London: Merlin Press, 1962), p. 24.

17. *Al adab fi alam mutaghayyir* (Cairo, 1971), pp. 147–148.

18. Peter Dodd and Halim Barakat, *River without Bridges: A Study of the Exodus of the 1967 Palestinian Arab Refugees* (Beirut: Institute for Palestine Studies, 1968).

19. See his recent study "Social and Political Integration in Lebanon: A Case of Social Mosaic," *Middle East Journal* 27:3 (Summer 1973).

7. Conrad and Nietzsche

1. Edward Garnett, *Letters from Joseph Conrad, 1895–1924* (Indianapolis: Bobbs-Merrill Company, 1928), pp. 157, 158.

2. *The Portable Nietzsche*, ed. and trans. Walter Kaufmann (New York: Viking Press, 1966), pp. 46–47. Wherever they are available I cite Kaufmann's excellent translations. On one occasion I cite another translation, but I have also used the German text edited by Schlechta.

3. Friedrich Nietzsche, *The Will to Power*, trans. Walter Kaufmann and R. J. Hollingdale (New York: Vintage Books, 1967), p. 327.

4. Friedrich Nietzsche, *The Gay Science, with a Prelude in Rhymes and an Appendix of Songs*, trans. Walter Kaufmann (New York: Vintage Books, 1974), p. 336.

5. Friedrich Nietzsche, *Beyond Good and Evil: Prelude to a Philosophy of the Future*, trans. Walter Kaufmann (New York: Vintage Books, 1966), p. 201.

6. Nietzsche, *Gay Science*, pp. 298–299.

7. Edward W. Said, "Conrad: The Presentation of Narrative," *Novel* 7:2 (Winter 1974): 116–132.

8. Friedrich Nietzsche, "We Philologists," trans. William Arrowsmith, *Arion*, New Series 1/2 (1973–1974): 299.

9. Friedrich Nietzsche, *Menschliches, Allzumenschliches*, in vol. 1 of *Werke*, ed. Karl Schlechta (Frankfurt: Ullstein, 1972), p. 464.

10. Nietzsche, *Gay Science*, p. 218. See also pp. 221–222.

11. Ibid., p. 343.

12. Nietzsche, *Will to Power*, p. 524.

13. Ibid., p. 428.

14. Joseph Conrad, *Heart of Darkness*, in *Youth and Two Other Stories*, vol. 16 of *Complete Works* (Garden City: Doubleday, Page and Company, 1925), p. 159.

15. Nietzsche, "We Philologists," p. 308.

16. Nietzsche, *Beyond Good and Evil*, p. 29.

17. Nietzsche, *Will to Power*, p. 13.

18. Ibid., p. 550.

19. Nietzsche, *Gay Science,* p. 168.
20. Nietzsche, *Will to Power,* p. 548.
21. Conrad, *Heart of Darkness,* p. 93.

8. Vico on the Discipline of Bodies and Texts

1. *The Autobiography of Giambattista Vico,* trans. Max H. Fisch and Thomas G. Bergin (Ithaca: Cornell University Press, 1963), p. 200.
2. Arabic numbers in parentheses refer to paragraphs in *The New Science of Giambattista Vico,* trans. Thomas G. Bergin and Max H. Fisch (Ithaca: Cornell University Press, 1968).
3. Ibid., pp. 112–113.
4. The term is to be found in Pierre Guiraud, "Etymologie et ethymologia (Motivation et rétromotivation)," *Poétique* 11 (1972): 407.
5. In a new appendix ("La Fole, l'absence d'oeuvre") to the republication (1972) of his *Histoire de la folie à l'âge classique* (Paris: Gallimard, 1961), Michel Foucault characterizes this *system* of ideas for dealing with texts as represented by Jacques Derrida:

   > Système dont Derrida est aujourd'hui le représentant le plus décisif, en son ultime éclat: réduction des pratiques discursives aux traces textuelles: élision des événements qui s'y produisent pour retenir que des marques pour une lecture; inventions de voix derrière les textes pour n'avoir pas à analyser les modes d'implication du sujet dans les discours; assignation de l'originaire comme dit et non dit dans le texte pour ne pas replacer les pratique discursives dans le champ des transformations où elles s'effectuent. . . .
   >   Je dirais que c'est [this system] une petite pédagogie historique-ment bien déterminée qui, de manière très visible, se manifeste. Pédagogie qui enseigne à l'élève qu'il n'y a rien hors du texte, mais qu'en lui, en ses interstices, dans ses blancs et ses non-dits, règne la réserve de l'origine; qu'il n'est donc point nécessaire d'aller chercher ailleurs, mais qu'ici même, ni point dans les mots certes, mais dans les mots comme natures, dans leur *grille,* se dit "le sens de l'être." Pédagogie qui inversement donne à la voix des maîtres cette sou-veraineté sans limite qui lui permet indéfiniment de redire le texte.
   >   (p. 602)

   See also Foucault, *Surveiller et punir: Naissance de la prison* (Paris: Gallimard, 1975), pp. 135–229 for a discussion of *discipline.*
6. There is a valuable demonstration of how Vico's making of meaning can be analyzed in Isaiah Berlin, "A Note on Vico's Concept of Knowledge," in *Giambattista Vico: An International Symposium,* ed. Giorgio Tagliacozzo and Hayden White (Baltimore: The Johns Hopkins University Press, 1969), pp. 371–377.

7. See Leon Pompa, *Vico: A Study of the "New Science"* (London: Cambridge University Press, 1975), p. 23.

8. The theories of Harold Bloom, who calls the textual community "misreaders," are relevant here. See his books *The Anxiety of Influence: A Theory of Poetry* (New York: Oxford University Press, 1973); *A Map of Misreading* (New York: Oxford University Press, 1975); and *Poetry and Repression: Revision from Blake to Stevens* (New Haven: Yale University Press, 1976). The importance of Vico to Bloom is especially striking, although unlike Vico, Bloom confines himself to the world of poetry, which is an intensification (and revisionist abstraction) of Vico's notion of the poetic world.

13. Opponents, Audiences, Constituencies, and Community

1. See Ronald Steel, *Walter Lippman and the American Century* (Boston: Little, Brown, 1980), pp. 180–185 and 212–216.

2. Antonio Gramsci to Tatiana Schucht, in Giuseppe Fiori, *Antonio Gramsci: Life of a Revolutionary,* trans. Tom Nairn (London: NLB, 1970), p. 74.

3. Antonio Gramsci to Tatiana Schucht, *Lettere dal Carcere* (Turin: Einaudi, 1975), p. 466; my translation.

4. Antonio Gramsci, *Selections from the Prison Notebooks,* trans. Quintin Hoare and Geoffrey Nowell Smith (New York: International Publishers, 1971), p. 171.

5. Fredric Jameson, *The Political Unconscious* (Ithaca: Cornell University Press, 1981), p. 10; all further references to this work will be included in the text. Perhaps not incidentally, what Jameson claims for Marxism here is the central feature of nineteenth-century British fiction according to Deirdre David, *Fictions of Resolution in Three Victorian Novels* (New York: Columbia University Press, 1980).

6. Terry Eagleton, "The Idealism of American Criticism," *New Left Review* 127 (May–June 1981): 59.

7. J. Hillis Miller, "The Function of Rhetorical Study at the Present Time," *ADE Bulletin* 62 (Sept. 1979): 12.

8. Robert Darnton, "A Journeyman's Life under the Old Regime: Work and Culture in an Eighteenth-Century Printing Shop," *Princeton Alumni Weekly,* Sept. 7, 1981, p. 12.

9. Michael Bakunin, *Selected Writings,* ed. and trans. Arthur Lehning (London: Cape, 1973), p. 160.

10. See Perry Anderson, "Components of the National Culture," in *Student Power,* ed. Alexander Cockburn and Robin Blackburn (Middlesex, England: Penguin Books, 1969).

11. David Dickson and David Noble, "By Force of Reason: The Politics of Science and Policy," in *The Hidden Election*, ed. Thomas Ferguson and Joel Rogers (New York: Pantheon Books, 1981), p. 267.

12. John Berger, "Another Way of Telling," *Journal of Social Reconstruction* 1 (Jan.–March 1980): 64.

22. Foucault and the Imagination of Power

1. "Question à Michel Foucault sur la géographie," *Hérodote*, no. 1 (Jan.–March 1976).

2. Peter Dews, "The *Nouvelle Philosophie* and Foucault," *Economy and Society* 8 (1979): 147.

3. C. Wright Mills, *The Power Elite* (New York: Oxford University Press, 1956), pp. 266–267.

4. Michel Foucault, *L'Ordre du discours* (Paris: Gallimard, 1971), p. 12.

5. Raymond Williams, *Politics and Letters: Interview with "New Left Review"* (London: New Left Books, 1979), p. 252.

23. The Horizon of R. P. Blackmur

1. T. S. Eliot, "Ulysses, Order and Myth," *The Dial* 75 (Nov. 1923): 480–483.

2. R. P. Blackmur, *Language as Gesture: Essays in Poetry* (London: George Allen and Unwin, 1954), p. 82.

3. R. P. Blackmur, *The Lion and the Honeycomb: Essays in Solitude and Critique* (New York: Harcourt, Brace and Company, 1955), p. 303.

4. Ibid., p. 282.

5. Ibid., p. 196.

6. R. P. Blackmur, *Eleven Essays in the European Novel* (New York: Harcourt, Brace and World, 1964), p. 4.

7. Blackmur, *The Lion and the Honeycomb*, p. 197.

8. Blackmur, *Language as Gesture*, p. 274.

9. Ibid., p. 173.

10. Robert Fitzgerald, *Enlarging the Change: The Princeton Seminars in Literary Criticism, 1949–1951* (Boston: Northeastern University Press, 1985), p. 38.

11. For example, in Blackmur, *The Lion and the Honeycomb*, pp. 222–223.

12. Fitzgerald, *Enlarging the Change*, p. 39.

13. Blackmur, *The Lion and the Honeycomb*, p. 41.

14. Ibid., p. 158.

15. Ibid., p. 187, footnote.

16. Ibid., p. 187.

17. Ibid., p. 241.

18. Ibid., p. 261.

19. Ibid., p. 272.

20. Ibid., p. 286–287.
21. Ibid., p. 178.
22. Ibid., p. 161.
23. R. P. Blackmur, *A Primer of Ignorance* (New York: Harcourt, Brace and World, 1967), p. 78.
24. Theodor Adorno, "The Essay as Form," trans. Bob Hullot-Kentor and Frederic Will, *New German Critique* 32 (Spring–Summer 1984): 166, 170.
25. Denis Donoghue, in the foreword to R. P. Blackmur, *Henry Adams,* ed. and with intro. by Veronica A. Makowsky (New York: Harcourt Brace Jovanovich, 1980), viii.
26. Blackmur, *The Lion and the Honeycomb,* p. 109.
27. See my "The Future of Criticism," Chapter 16 of this volume.

27. Representing the Colonized: Anthropology's Interlocutors

1. See Frantz Fanon, *The Wretched of the Earth,* trans. Constance Farrington (New York: Grove Press, 1966); and Albert Memmi, *The Colonizer and the Colonized,* trans. Howard Greenfield (New York: Orion Press, 1965).
2. See Carl E. Pletsch, "The Three Worlds, or the Division of Social Scientific Labor, circa 1950–1975," *Comparative Studies in Society and History* 23 (Oct. 1981): 565–590. See also Peter Worsley, *The Third World* (Chicago: University of Chicago Press, 1964).
3. See Fanon, *Wretched of the Earth,* p. 101.
4. See Eqbal Ahmad, "From Potato Sack to Potato Mash: The Contemporary Crisis of the Third World," *Arab Studies Quarterly* 2 (Summer 1980): 223–234; Eqbal Ahmad, "Post-Colonial Systems of Power," *Arab Studies Quarterly* 2 (Fall 1980): 350–363; Eqbal Ahmad, "The Neo-Fascist State: Notes on the Pathology of Power in the Third World," *Arab Studies Quarterly* 3 (Spring 1981): 170–180.
5. See *Anthropology as Cultural Critique: An Experimental Movement in the Human Sciences,* ed. George E. Marcus and Michael M. J. Fischer (Chicago: University of Chicago Press, 1986), and *Writing Culture: The Poetics and Politics of Ethnography,* ed. James Clifford and George E. Marcus (Berkeley: University of California Press, 1986).
6. Richard Fox, *Lions of the Punjab: Culture in the Making* (Berkeley: University of California Press, 1985), p. 186.
7. See, for example, Sherry B. Ortner, "Theory in Anthropology since the Sixties," *Comparative Studies in Society and History* 26 (Jan. 1984): 126–166.
8. See *Anthropology and the Colonial Encounter,* ed. Talal Asad (London: Ithaca Press, 1973); Gérard Leclerc, *Anthropologie et colonialisme: essai sur l'histoire de l'africanisme* (Paris: Fayard, 1972), and *L'Observation de l'homme:*

une histoire des enquêtes sociales (Paris: Seuil, 1979); Johannes Fabian, *Time and the Other: How Anthropology Makes Its Object* (New York: Columbia University Press, 1983).

9. See Ortner, "Theory in Anthropology," pp. 144-160.

10. In Marcus and Fischer, *Anthropology as Cultural Critique;* p. 9 and thereafter, the emphasis on epistemology is very prominent.

11. James Clifford, "On Ethnographic Authority," *Representations* 1 (Spring 1983): 142.

12. Jürgen Golte, "Latin America: The Anthropology of Conquest," in *Anthropology: Ancestors and Heirs,* ed. Stanley Diamond (The Hague: Mouton, 1980), p. 391.

13. Jonathan Friedman, "Beyond Otherness or: The Spectacularization of Anthropology," *Telos* 71 (1987): 161-170.

14. Defense Science Board, *Report of the Panel on Defense: Social and Behavioral Sciences* (Williamstown, Mass., 1967).

15. I have discussed this in my book *Covering Islam: How the Media and the Experts Determine How We See the Rest of the World* (New York: Pantheon Books, 1981). See also "The MESA Debate: The Scholars, the Media and the Middle East," *Journal of Palestine Studies* 16 (Winter 1987): 85-104.

16. See *Blaming the Victims: Spurious Scholarship and the Palestinian Question,* ed. Edward W. Said and Christopher Hitchens (London: Verso, 1988), pp. 97-158.

17. Richard Price, *First-Time: The Historical Vision of an Afro-American People* (Baltimore: Johns Hopkins University Press, 1983), pp. 6, 23.

18. James C. Scott, *Weapons of the Weak: Everyday Forms of Peasant Resistance* (New Haven, Conn.: Yale University Press, 1985), pp. 278-350. See also Fred R. Myers, "The Politics of Representation: Anthropological Discourse and Australian Aborigines," *American Ethnologist* 13 (Feb. 1986): 138-153.

19. See George W. Stocking, Jr., *Victorian Anthropology* (New York: Free Press, 1987); and Curtis M. Hinsley, Jr., *Savages and Scientists: The Smithsonian Institution and the Development of American Anthropology, 1846–1910* (Washington, D.C.: Smithsonian Institution Press, 1981).

20. See Edward Said, "Permission to Narrate," *London Review of Books* (Feb. 16-29, 1984): 13-17.

21. See Jean-François Lyotard, *The Postmodern Condition: A Report on Knowledge,* trans. Geoff Bennington and Brian Massumi, *Theory and History of Literature,* vol. 10 (Minneapolis: University of Minnesota Press, 1984), pp. 23-53.

22. See Irene L. Gendzier, *Managing Political Change: Social Scientists and the Third World* (Boulder, Colo.: Westview Press, 1985).

23. Georg Lukács, *History and Class Consciousness: Studies in Marxist Dialectics,* trans. Rodney Livingstone (Cambridge, Mass.: MIT Press, 1971), pp. 126–134.

24. The argument is made more fully in my book *Culture and Imperialism* (New York: Knopf, 1994).

25. Albert Camus, *Actuelles, III: Chronique algérienne, 1939–1958* (Paris: Gallimard, 1958), p. 202: "Si bien disposé qu'on soit envers la revendication arabe, on doit cependant reconnâitre qu'en ce qui concerne l'Algérie, l'indépendance nationale est une formule purement passionelle. Il n'y a jamais eu encore de nation algérienne. Les Juifs, les Turcs, les Grecs, les Italiens, les Berbères, auraient autant de droit à réclamer la direction de cette nation virtuelle."

26. Frantz Fanon, *Les Damnés de la terre* (Paris: F. Maspero, 1976), p. 62.

27. Aimé Césaire, *Cahier d'un retour au pays natal [Notebook of a Return to the Native Land]: The Collected Poetry,* trans. Clayton Eshleman and Annette Smith (Berkeley: University of California Press, 1983), pp. 76, 77.

28. Ibid.

29. See Raymond Williams, *Problems in Materialism and Culture: Selected Essays* (London: NLB, 1980), pp. 37–47.

28. After Mahfouz

1. Farouk Abdel Wahab's translation of *Zayni Barakat* was published by Viking (1988).

2. The translation, by Maia Tabet, is published by University of Minnesota Press.

36. Nationalism, Human Rights, and Interpretation

1. Samuel Johnson, *Rasselas: Poems and Selected Prose,* ed. Bertrand H. Bronson (New York: Holt, Rinehart and Winston, 1958), pp. 544–548.

2. Matthew Arnold, *Culture and Anarchy,* ed. J. Dover Wilson (Cambridge: Cambridge University Press, 1932), p. 203.

3. Ibid., pp. 203–211. See also Edward Said, *The World, the Text, and the Critic* (Cambridge, Mass.: Harvard University Press, 1983), pp. 9–11.

4. Tom Paulin, *Minotaur: Poetry and the Nation State* (London: Faber and Faber, 1992), p. 212.

5. Lionel Trilling, *Matthew Arnold* (New York: Meridian Books, 1949), p. 258.

6. Aimé Césaire, *Discourse on Colonialism,* trans. Joan Pinkham (New York: Monthly Review, 1972), p. 16 (emphasis added by Césaire).

7. Melvin Richter, "Tocqueville on Algeria," *Review of Politics* 25 (1963): 373–374.

8. Marwan R. Buheiry, *The Formation and Perception of the Modern Arab World,* ed. Lawrence I. Conrad (Princeton: Darwin Press, 1989), p. 63. See also Edward Said, *Culture and Imperialism* (New York: Alfred A. Knopf, 1994), chap. 2.

9. Richter, "Tocqueville on Algeria," pp. 384–385.

10. J. S. Mill, *Disquisitions and Discussions,* vol. 3 (London: Longmans, Green, Reader and Dyer, 1875), pp. 167–168.

11. See, for an example of his critical reinterpretations, Adonis, *An Introduction to Arab Poetics,* trans. Catherine Cobham (London: Saqi Books, 1990).

12. Ernest Gellner, *Nations and Nationalism* (Oxford: Basil Blackwell, 1983), p. 18.

13. Ibid., p. 57.

14. Ibid., p. 138.

15. Eric Hobsbawm, *Nations and Nationalism since 1870: Programme, Myth, Reality* (Cambridge: Cambridge University Press, 1990), p. 138.

16. Ibid., pp. 151–152 (emphasis added).

17. Gellner, *Nations and Nationalism,* p. 6.

18. Partha Chatterjee, *Nationalist Thought and the Colonial World: A Derivative Discourse?* (London: Zed Books, 1986), pp. 26–28.

19. Ibid., p. 170.

20. Christopher Sykes, *Crossroads to Israel, 1917–1948* (1965; reprint Bloomington, Ind.: Indiana University Press, 1973), p. 5.

37. Traveling Theory Reconsidered

1. Michael Löwy, *Georg Lukács: From Romanticism to Bolshevism,* trans. Patrick Camiller (London: NLB, 1979).

2. Georg Lukács, *Theory of the Novel,* trans. Anna Bostock (London: Merlin Press, 1971), p. 92.

3. Theodor Adorno, *Philosophy of Modern Music,* trans. Anne G. Mitchell and Wesley V. Blomster (New York: Seabury Press, 1973), p. 40. Quotations will hereafter be cited in parentheses in the text.

4. Georg Lukács, *History and Class Consciousness: Studies in Marxist Dialectics,* trans. Rodney Livingstone (London: Merlin Press, 1971), p. xlvi.

5. Frantz Fanon, *The Wretched of the Earth,* trans. Constance Farrington (New York: Grove Press, 1963), p. 44.

6. Frantz Fanon, *Black Skins, White Masks,* trans. Charles S. Markmann (New York: Grove, 1967), p. 220.

38. History, Literature, and Geography

1. Eric Auerbach, "Philology and *Weltliteratur*," trans. M. Said and E. Said, *Centennial Review* (Winter 1969): 4–5.

2. Georg Lukács, *Soul and Form,* trans. Anna Bostock (Cambridge, Mass.: MIT Press, 1972), p. 22.

3. Georg Lukács, *The Theory of the Novel,* trans. Anna Bostock (London: Merlin Press, 1971), pp. 84, 92–93.

4. Georg Lukács, *History and Class Consciousness,* trans. Rodney Livingston (London: Merlin Press, 1971), p. 186.

5. Antonio Gramsci, *The Prison Notebook Selections,* trans. Quintin Hoare and G. Nowell-Smith (New York: International Publishers, 1971), pp. 144, 157–158, 192 ff.

6. Raymond Williams, *The Country and the City* (New York: Oxford University Press, 1973), p. 210.

CREDITS

Chapter 35: Originally published in *Times Literary Supplement*, June 19, 1992.

Chapter 36: Originally published in *Freedom and Interpretation: The Oxford Amnesty Lectures in 1992*, ed. Barbara Johnson (New York: Basic Books, 1993).

Chapter 37: Originally published in *Critical Reconstructions: The Relationship of Fiction and Life*, ed. Robert M. Polhemus and Roger B. Henkle. Reprinted with the permission of the publishers, Stanford University Press. Copyright 1994 by the Board of Trustees of the Leland Stanford Junior University.

Chapter 38: Originally published in *History in Literature*, ed. Hoda Gindy (Cairo: University of Cairo, 1995).

Chapter 39: Originally published in *London Review of Books*, March 9, 1995.

Chapter 40: Originally published in *London Review of Books*, September 21, 1995.

Chapter 41: Originally published in *Times Literary Supplement*, August 9, 1996.

Chapter 42: Originally published in *Beyond the Academy: A Scholar's Obligations*, ACLS (American Council of Learned Societies) Occasional Paper, No. 31, Winter 1996.

Chapter 43: Originally published in *Raritan: A Quarterly Review*, Vol. 17, No. 2 (Summer 1997).

Chapter 44: Originally published in *The Tanner Lectures on Human Values*, Vol. 18, ed. Grethe B. Peterson (Salt Lake City: University of Utah Press, 1997).

Chapter 45: Originally published in *London Review of Books*, May 7, 1998.

Chapter 46: "The Clash of Definitions" has not been previously published.

INDEX

OTHER BOOKS IN THE
CONVERGENCES SERIES